The Standard Book of Jewish Verse

The

STANDARD BOOK
OF JEWISH VERSE

COMPILED BY
JOSEPH FRIEDLANDER

EDITED BY
GEORGE ALEXANDER KOHUT

NEW YORK
DODD, MEAD AND COMPANY
1917

EDITOR'S INTRODUCTION

A MELANCHOLY interest attaches to the publication of this work. Its compiler, after devoting many arduous years to its preparation, had read the last proofs, when death summoned him. Like the prophet Moses, who was permitted to get a glimpse of the Promised Land ere he was translated to Eternity, this modest, patient scholar, toiling with touching devotion and sublime unselfishness in the vineyard of the Lord, was destined only to vision the rich vintage he had sown, but not to taste of its fruits.

This Anthology will serve as a fitting memorial of the man, whose profound love for his people was the keynote of his life and whose keen appreciation of Hebrew melody make him a worthy critic and historian of the art of Jewish song.

It is with pleasure, not unmixed with some poignancy, that I recall the early days of our comradeship, when, as incumbents of almost adjacent pastorates, we were privileged, far away from the centres of culture and learning, to discuss matters that deeply interested us both. It was then that I learned how rich was his mind, how mature his judgment, and how ardent his faith in the future of his people, for whom he cherished such deep love and devotion. Isolated though he was in a small hamlet, with no

v

442173

congenial spirits to bear him company, he lived a
life full of idealism and noble activity, esteemed by
Jew and Gentile alike; cherished and revered no less
for his lofty character than for his charity and sweet
human nature. Though a staunch and uncompromis-
ing Jew, he did not exclude from the fellowship of
his heart men of all creeds, and among the host of
those who mourn for him today, will be found many
men, not of his own faith, who beheld in him an
"Israelite without guile." It may be truly said of
him that he was a man of God, possessed of rare
simplicity and a spiritual passion which more than
once sapped the well-springs of his vitality and hur-
ried him to an untimely grave.

Joseph Friedlander was born in 1859, at Edin-
burgh, Scotland. He received his early education at
New Castle on Tyne and at Middlesborough, graduat-
ing from Jews' College, London, England. His first
charge was at Victoria, Australia. Returning to Eng-
land, he became minister of the North West London
Synagogue. For four years he served as Secretary to
the Chief Rabbi of the British Empire and likewise as
Secretary to the English Zionist Federation. He came
to America in 1895, and for ten years occupied the
Rabbinate of Congregation Emanu-El, at Beaumont,
Texas. He also held pastorates at Waco, Texas;
Ontario, Hamilton (Canada); Greensborough, N. C.;
Orange and Plainfield, N. J., where he died, after
a brief illness, induced by overwork, incident to the
preparation of this Anthology. He was a frequent
contributor to the religious and secular press of Eng-
land and America, and, judging from his single ven-
ture in Jewish journalism, he was particularly well

qualified for literary work. Had he lived, he would undoubtedly have produced several books of lasting merit. From May, 1906, to September, 1907, during his incumbency at Waco, Texas, he issued a periodical which he entitled *The Jewish Hope*. It was published, at San Antonio, first as a monthly, then as a bi-monthly, and the twelve numbers it comprises give ample evidence of his intellectual fertility, poise, discrimination and scholarship. Only one complete file of this paper has been preserved. It is now a part of the Jewish collection at the New York Public Library.

This journal was his organ and oracle. Into it he poured all the wealth of his rich mind, and those who read its pages with discerning eyes may almost feel the beating of his heart. The earnestness and fervency of his appeals; the integrity of his convictions; the candor with which he met squarely every issue and problem which agitated American Jewry; his unflinching courage and uncompromising loyalty, are all elements which make the newspaper he created a distinctive human document, to which lovers of Zion will yet have to go for counsel and inspiration.

Being himself a man of exceptional poetic gifts, he had a fine appreciation of poetic values. Already in the "old Texas days," when we discussed books and bookmen, and occasionally scanned together a fine hymn of some mediæval Hebrew bard, he was full of enthusiasm over the plan of bringing together, in a compact and convenient form, poems that were the most typical of the varying moods of Jewish genius. The present collection, therefore, may be said

vii

to actually represent the concentrated thought of twenty years. A few weeks before his death, my lamented friend did me the honor of consulting me, at frequent intervals, regarding the plan and scope of the work, and while we did not agree on certain basic principles and some essential details, he was so modest and self-effacing, and deferred so gently and genially to the advice of others, that, in the end, his own view was subordinated, and what he accepted as superior judgment prevailed. In this, as in all his dealings with his fellow men, his sweet docility, amiability and chivalrous courtesy were the attributes which gave strength and power to his character and served to endear him to all with whom he came in contact.

Although the title, "The Standard Book of Jewish Verse," seems to imply that it is a collection which comprises poems of recognized merit that bear the stamp of general approval, it must be understood that, in no sense, has it been placed before a literary tribunal and that its value is yet to be appraised. The compiler was a man of catholic sympathies. He included in this Anthology almost every phase of the Jewish spirit. If by dint of rare diligence, acute discrimination, and by all the subtle processes of racial sympathy he has succeeded in producing a work which will be acclaimed as a classic, so that this volume may take a notable place among other similar collections, his arduous and devoted labor will yield rich recompense.

The compiler's untimely death, before the final revision of the book had been completed, necessitated a careful re-reading of the entire text. With the aid of another mutual friend, who prefers to remain nameless, this irksome and difficult task has been adequately accomplished. While it has not been possible, for obvious reasons, to verify, line by line, the accuracy of numerous fugitive pieces, by minor poets —scattered as they are in periodicals not readily accessible—it may safely be assumed that no errors of any consequence remain. The poems of classical authors have been scrupulously collated with, the editions generally accepted as definitive and standard.

The Introduction was pieced together from fragments of manuscript left by the author, and particular care has been taken to reproduce as much of the original phrasing as possible and to round out some paragraphs, here and there, in the same spirit in which they were conceived.

The Editor has also added a comprehensive Index, which will facilitate reference, and desires distinctly to state that he holds himself responsible only for this feature of the work, as well as the revision of the compiler's Introduction, but in no wise for the arrangement of the material, and the general character of the contents.

GEORGE ALEXANDER KOHUT.

NEW YORK, *August* 1, 1917.

INTRODUCTION

JEWISH poetry has its own place in the Song-History of the world. Dryden has significantly summarized the great poets of their representative countries:

"Three poets—three distinct ages born—
Greece, Italy and England did adorn.
The first in loftiness of thought surpassed;
The next in majesty; in both the last.
The force of nature could no further go.
To make a third, she join'd the former two."

But he said nothing of Hebrew poetry. Probably he had in mind that the sacred poetry of the Jews stood on a plane of its own—unapproachable, lofty, sublime—the poetry that lifted up to infinite heights of subliminal consciousness the peoples who absorbed it. It was the poetry whose marked influence on the destinies of the higher races of mankind moulded in no small degree the civilization we enjoy. Indeed, it might be said that it has revolutionized its intellectual and spiritual conceptions.

Certainly there is a marked difference between Greek and Jewish poetry. Let us understand by the former an inclusive term, embracing all profane and secular poetry of other lands and ages—Russian, Persian, Italian, German, English, Celtic, Spanish—for, in the last analysis, all poetry of whatever kind, lyrical, epical and dramatic, must be finally traced to the Greeks. Their culture and development conduced to the free practice of every kind of poetic art. Both in form and spirit, all later poetry was derived from

INTRODUCTION

the Attic poets, and, to this day, our best singers go
to them for inspiration and for imitation. Being
themselves possessed of a deathless afflatus, of a divine
form or a divine mould of beauty, their poetry,
whether dramatic or lyrical, remains the source from
which all nations have drunk.

In no less universal degree has Hebrew poetry fash-
ioned the modern soul to its finely-tempered edge. It
was essentially religious, flowing from an intense racial
consciousness and developing to an exalted spiritual
mood, under stress of mingled storm and sunshine of
national fortune. It was dominated by the personal
emotional note. The soul of the singer was linked
in all its moods to the relationship it bore to God.
The overshadowing presence of the Almighty in all
its varied and infinite manifestations was an ever con-
stant influence.

In the Psalms, Israel sang his hymn of spiritual
love to God. They were the outpourings of his daily
experience. The consciousness of God in all his
thoughts and actions, was the mainspring of all his
personal emotions. If he circumvented an enemy, or
defeated him by the prowess of his arms, the victory
was attributed to Elohim, to Jehovah, the special
guardian of Israel. If he enjoyed prosperity and
lived at ease under his fig and vine tree, it was as-
cribed to God. Whatever happiness came to him was
vouchsafed by his Adonai, Who had the power and
will to bring to him either joy or sorrow, fortune
or adversity, life or death. He acknowledged that in
all His dealings, God was just and merciful, Who
ordered all things for the best. And the Jew clung
to his God with every fibre of his being; loved Him
with all his strength, with all his heart and with all
his mind.

These two species of poetic art dominated the world.
Yet, although each had its own distinctive charm and
greatness, some affinity can be traced between them.
The deathless dramas of the Greek poets were per-

meated by a spiritual emotion. In Job, as in the Greek tragedies, especially by Euripides, there is a common meeting ground for the Jew and the Greek. As Achad Ha-am points out, in his essay on "Job and Prometheus," there is in every people something which transcends individual culture, and, while a national soul underlies its characteristics, in each one, human nature is common to all. The operation of physical and natural laws produces like results. In the Jew, however, the moral spirit was supreme, while, in the Greek, the passion for beauty was the governing impulse. The Hebrew spirit was a spirit of hope and faith; the Greek was one of blind fatalism and unrelieved pessimism where the future was concerned. What the gods willed was to be accepted with fortitude and resignation. In the Hebrew scheme of things, prayer, repentance and good conduct could avert the evil decree.

In the poetry of the Hebrews—and that is its distinctive note—there is an abiding and keen consciousness of its relationship to a personal God. In Greek poetry, it is a blind, inexorable destiny that rules, against which man and all his efforts are vain.

It will be easy to see why the genius of Hebrew poetry, as exemplified in the Psalter, should have immeasurably surpassed the Greek poetry as an influence on character. Human nature has always inclined to rest its hopes on a just Providence, on a Mightier Power than itself, Who, if He does not change the immutable laws of the world, yet rules it with intelligence and benevolent wisdom. Greek and Jewish poetry, the one by virtue of its classic grace of form, and the other by virtue of its abiding spiritual charm, constitute the two great divisions in which the art of song is resolved. All other subordinate schools of poetry are directly traceable to one or another of these primary sources. Greek and Jewish poetry constitute in their circumference the embracing and all-sufficient needs of the world for at-

tuning to the human harp the immortal themes of the
soul.

Jewish poetry was strongly imbued with its national
spirit. This is always its underlying *motif*. The
Jewish bard sang of God and His wonderful Provi-
dence. He sang, too, of his hopes and aspirations in
the future—a future which, however dark in the pres-
ent, had always a bright silver lining. He sang of a
restored nationality, of a spiritual kingdom, of a reign
of righteousness, of a reconciled world, where all the
children of men, however diverse their beliefs and
ideals, would at last unite with Israel in the worship
of one Supreme and Holy God.

This is still the dominant note of all Jewish poetry.
It is varied here and there by a bitter cry of despair
and suffering, by an appeal for heavenly vengeance
against the enemies of Israel, against those who
crushed Judah in the thraldom of oppression. The
main themes are the hope of the rehabilitation of the
nation's ancient glory and the immortalizing of the
great heroes of the race, with the recital of their
achievements and martyrdoms.

That the Jewish race, through exile and persecu-
tion, has not lost its national heritage of song is amply
proved in these pages. The Ghetto was not a favor-
able nursing-ground for the Muses, and the narrow,
confined life there was all but fatal to the cultivation
and development of the poetic temperament. Only in
times of great stress and suffering did the strong
natural impulse of the soul for expression yield to its
overwhelming need and desire. There were two main
streams of poetic activity in the Jews of post-exilic
times. The first was an ardent feeling to glorify
God in song, which contributed so largely to the en-
richment of the ritual. The *Piyutim* (hymnology)
were the principal media through which this feeling
found utterance. Very little of this rich psalmody
of Israel has found its way to the ear of the world.
Yet, in beauty and majesty of thought, as in fanciful

and sublime diction, few productions of the religious poetry of the world can compare with these matchless outpourings of the soul. They reach to the highest planes of spiritual thought and seraphic fire. It will be worth while to study the religious poems in the section of this book entitled "Liturgical and Mediæval Period," to estimate the wealth of Jewish hymnology it contains. Solomon ibn Gabirol, Jehudah Halevi, the Ibn Ezras, Israel Nagara and many more, were masters of this art, and their contributions constitute a mine of richest ore, not merely for the synagogue service, but for the spiritual elevation of Israel. No other factor in the life of this much-tried nation has so helped it to bear its burdens as the consolation afforded by these glorious hymns. It gave the Jew the courage and strength to undergo the long series of cruel martyrdoms which he endured through the Middle Ages. His sublime faith and his kinship with God were nourished on these *Piyutim*.

It is only within recent years that these liturgical poems have been made accessible to the English reading public, chiefly through a band of able and scholarly interpreters, whose poetic grace of style is not by any means inferior to their thorough knowledge and insight into the spirit of the composers. In particular, the translations of Alice Lucas, Mrs. Redcliffe Salomon (Nina Davis), Israel Zangwill, Israel Abrahams, Solomon Solis Cohen and Israel Cohen are splendid renditions of the originals.

It may not be out of place to contrast the striking difference between the manner in which the Jews of the Middle Ages met their fate and that in which the Jewish poets of our own times regarded the pogroms and persecutions in these latter days. Our forefathers were evidently of much more heroic mould. They sang their hymns of glory to God, as they mounted their funeral pyres, and expired with the ancient confession of the Unity upon their lips. They were animated by a sublime self-surrender to the will of God; a complete faith in His overshadowing Providence and in the ultimate adjustment of the apparent inequalities of reward and punishment, of unmerited suffering and undeserved prosperity and enjoyment.

In the series of poems in the Mediæval Section are to be found some of the most moving and tragic hymns in the whole range of human history. Especially is this the case in the Section headed "In the Crusades." In the lurid glare they cast upon the grim, dark horrors which the Jewish communities passed through in that age of ruthless fanaticism, there shines forth, in strong contrast, an unfaltering spirit of loyalty and devotion to faith, which caused them to welcome the most excruciating deaths with singular heroism. It was a triumph of sublime courage over the fears of bodily pain and suffering. God had decreed that the crown of martyrdom should be bestowed upon His chosen ones, and they submitted almost joyfully to the ordeal, voicing their invincible fealty in plaintive and heart-stirring song.

How different was the spirit in which modern poets, both Hebrew and secular, apostrophised the Russian pogroms! These latter upbraid God for permitting their enemies to massacre the Jews. They draw realistic pictures of the unspeakable outrages they endured, including all the hideous details, without that artistic touch with which the Greek dramatists and the Hebrew poets of old depicted tragedy. The difference is that of a soul still firmly anchored and clinging to its Maker and one overpowered by a crushing sense of dark despair and death, for whom there is no gleam of a brighter existence beyond the eternal stars.

That oppression and persecution were the prime causes why the Jewish muse did not flourish is sufficiently evident from the fact that, when this condition disappeared, even for a brief interval, it was immediately followed by a renaissance of surpassing poetic activity. When, under the Arabs, Spain enjoyed for a few centuries comparative peace and tranquillity, and inaugurated a new era of science and learning, the Jews of the country rivalled the scholars, poets and philosophers in their contributions in that field. From the twelfth to the fifteenth centuries a galaxy of brilliant poets and writers appeared, than whom no greater have yet been seen. Their works, for the most part written in Hebrew and Arabic, have not yet been fully revealed to the world.

In the Sections of this book entitled "The Mediæval Period," "The Jewish Year," and "Liturgical Poems," will be found a sufficient number of translations to convey some idea of the extent and variety of their poetic horoscope. They do not merely vie with Klopstock and Milton and other religious poets, but far surpass them in sublimity of thought, in range of philosophic intuition and in elevation of moral tone. Especially rich in these qualities are the liturgical poems embodied in the ritual. The religious psalmody of these writers is wonderfully touching and inspiring. We get from them something more than a glimpse of the inward nobility of their hearts, the purity of their souls and the godliness of their lives. In these impassioned synagogue melodies Israel sang his anthem of spiritual love to God.

Poetry may be said at least to have been the ground on which Jew and Gentile could make their common humanity felt, and it is not the least satisfaction to the compiler of this Anthology that here they stand side by side in a great cause, with one aim before them and united in its performance as never before. The history of Jewish Emancipation and the gradual dispulsion of prejudice and injustice may very well be traced through Byron and Lessing and Browning and Swinburne and many others, to these days of liberty and enlightenment, blazing the onward march of civilization through centuries of dark superstition and intolerance, teaching lessons of the highest import to the world of true brotherhood, wise reconciliation of dif-

ferent beliefs and a higher philosophy of life and con-
duct.

In these, most conspicuous are the poems of non-
Jewish poets, who have eagerly employed their gifts
to crush down prejudice and oppression. Byron and
Lessing were the first in this army of equally dis-
tinguished sons of the Muse: Longfellow, Browning,
Joaquin Miller, Wordsworth, Townsend and many
others. The most eloquent diatribes on the Dreyfus
Case were written by Swinburne, and the Russian
pogroms called forth a great number of stirring poems
by Christian writers.

A new era was ushered in when the flamboyant
genius of Byron burst upon the world, under the im-
pulse of a strong devotion to the cause of liberty,
ardent love for the ancient glory of Greece and a
growing sympathy with all oppressed and weak na-
tionalities. Byron conceived a generous emotion for
the downtrodden Hebrew race. The grandeur of
their ancient tradition and the dark tragedy of their
history in the Middle Ages, their outlawry from the
world, powerfully appealed to him, and he gave ex-
pression to his sympathies in a series of strikingly
beautiful poems. His "Hebrew Melodies" stand out
as the most efflorescent of his minor poems. They
are instinct with a wonderful understanding of the
Hebrew spirit. No one else has interpreted the soul
of the ancient Hebrew so truly as when he pictured
him overwhelmed in the final catastrophe that over-
took him when the Temple—the symbol of his na-
tionality and the visible embodiment of his eternal
faith—went up in flames to the sky at the hands of
the Romans. To the patriotic Hebrew, that was an
evidence that all for him was lost, that God had
withdrawn his protection and favor from his people,
and that henceforth the hand of Destiny would lay
heavily upon them.

The Jews of modern times have never done justice
to the great service rendered them by Byron, and it

xviii

INTRODUCTION

would only be fitting that a monument be raised in England to that great poet, commemorating his glorious aid in vindicating for the Jews their rightful place among the nations of the world. So, too, Lessing, in his drama "Nathan the Wise," and through his friendship with Moses Mendelssohn, brought about a powerful reaction in favor of the Jew. To these two gifted men, must be attributed the impetus that was given to both Jewish and non-Jewish poets to find in the Jew a fit subject for poetical illustration. Most of the distinguished poets of the past and present generation have added to the rich store of poetic lore some sterling work of Jewish interest. These comprise our greatest poets, among them Wordsworth, Browning, Scott, Longfellow, Tennyson, Swinburne, George Eliot, Thomas Bailey Aldrich and others too numerous to mention, but who should be remembered with honor and gratitude.

The Jews themselves, to whom poetry had almost become a forgotten art, awakened again to the fact that the strains of the harp of Judah still lingered in their souls. Some sang in Hebrew, like Luzzatto, Wessely, Salom Cohen, David Franco and a host of minor poets. All were outranked by Heinrich Heine, whom it would be superfluous to describe as one of the immortals in the Valhalla of Song. His "Jehuda ben Halevi" and "Prinzessin Sabbat" are but a few examples of his quaint, delicate and inimitable art. They are limned in eternal colors, like one of the great dramas of Shakespeare or Euripides, and, like ancient Grecian sculpture, they are things of beauty and a joy forever.

Without taking the form of an historical survey, these poems easily portray, if not exactly in chronological order, at least in panoramic sequence, the most striking events in Jewish history. They set forth the character of the nation's achievements, its heroes, its prophets, kings and statesmen and, above all, the eternal ideals of the race, the unquenchable fire of its

INTRODUCTION

faith, which has burned on, not fitfully, but steadily
and grandly through all the dark and moving cen-
turies.

Although here and there a false quantity may be
detected and imperfect technique may be apparent, yet
the poems on the whole are surprisingly good. It
would be unfair to compare them, in idiomatic dic-
tion and graceful execution, with poetry which flour-
ished in a national atmosphere—the outcome of con-
ditions altogether favorable for the production of
genuine lyrics. Many of them, however, are possessed
of the highest poetic qualities and are instinct with
rare spiritual fervor. Jessie E. Sampter's poem on
"Anemones" is a fine example of a true lyric, which
can vie with the best; and scattered through these
pages are many which will delight the reader with
their exquisite and perfect phrasing. A number of
these modern writers, too, are either alien born or
the offspring of foreign parents. They acquired a
wonderful mastery of the niceties and intricacies of
what is comparatively a new language. Poetry of a
decidedly high order may be ascribed to many of
the selections included from the pen of George A.
Kohut, Joseph Leiser, Alter Abelson, Harry Weiss,
Miriam del Banco, Penina Moïse, Rebecca Altman
and numerous others. Of those who have not writ-
ten in the vernacular, but either in Hebrew or Yid-
dish, translations of which will be found in this vol-
ume, may be mentioned Byalik, Frug, Morris Rosen-
feld, "Jehoash" and Raskin.

Many of the poems are notable for the beautiful
thoughts and sentiments they enshrine; fragrant and
delicate flowers of the spirit, enriching the intellectual
heritage of humanity.

If this Anthology serves no other purpose than to
impress the reader, both Jew and Gentile, with the
consciousness of the age-long idealism of the race,
from whose loins sprang that sweet singer of Israel
whose Psalmody is still the greatest spiritual inheritance

INTRODUCTION

of humanity, it will not have been compiled in vain.
May it be the will of Providence that our brethren
of the faith of Israel, who have so miraculously sur-
vived persecution and martyrdom through the cen-
turies, be at last admitted into the fellowship of na-
tions, with their national glory restored and
rehabilitated, and Palestine, the land of their fathers,
once again established as the cultural centre whence
all moral and spiritual forces are to emanate which
will enrich and ennoble the world.

JOSEPH FRIEDLANDER
(Edited by G. A. Kohut)

(June 25, 1917.)

ACKNOWLEDGMENTS

MY indebtedness extends to a long range of sources and authorities, which are in the main responsible for any merit this book may possess. To the following publishers, periodicals and newspapers, my acknowledgments are preeminently due:

The Macmillan Company, New York.
William Heineman, London, England.
George Routledge & Sons, London, England.
John Lane & Company, New York City.
Funk & Wagnalls Company, New York.
Houghton Mifflin Company, Boston.
The Jewish Publication Society of America.
Dr. Israel Abrahams, Cambridge, England.
Mrs. Alice Lucas, London, England.
Mrs. Redcliffe Salaman (Nina Davis), London, England.
Mr. Israel Zangwill, London, England.
Jewish Religious Educational Board, London, England.
Jewish Chronicle, London, England.
The Reform Advocate, Chicago, Ill.
The American Israelite, Cincinnati, Ohio.
The Jewish Exponent, Philadelphia, Pa.
The Jewish Comment, Baltimore, Md.
The American Hebrew, New York.
The Hebrew Standard, New York.
The Maccabœan, New York.
The Menorah Monthly, New York.
The Ark, Cincinnati, Ohio.

ACKNOWLEDGMENTS

I am also indebted to a number of periodicals and newspapers for poems—notably *The Jewish Quarterly Review, The Menorah Monthly* (formerly the official organ of the B'nai Berith), *The Jewish Hope, The Jewish Messenger,* and various scattered, short-lived, fugitive periodicals.

Various other Anthologies have also greatly helped me in my work—more particularly the excellent and exhaustive *Hebrew Anthology* of my friend, Dr. George Alexander Kohut, who has also permitted the use of a number of poems from his own pen, printed in an edition only privately circulated.

The indulgence of both publishers and authors is asked, if due acknowledgment is not herein made for the use of any copyright material which may be included in these pages.

[Owing to the untimely death of the compiler, it has not been possible to ascertain whether the above list of Acknowledgments is complete. As Dr. Friedlander was most scrupulous in his relations with others, it is safe to assume that he has not failed to record his indebtedness, so far as it lay in his power.]

TABLE OF CONTENTS

PAGE

Editor's Introduction v
Introduction xi
Acknowledgments xxiii

I. BIBLICAL AND POST-BIBLICAL

OK all real

The Bible—*Anonymous* 1
The Bible—*Richard Barton* 1
The Bible—*David Levi* 1
The Light and Glory of the World—*William Cowper* 3
The Bible—*Phoebe Palmer* 4
The Written Word—*Sir Robert Grant* 5
Book of God—*Horatius Bonar* 5
The Old Book—*Abram S. Isaacs* 7
Israel and His Book—*Felix N. Gerson* 7
The Ha' Bible—*Robert Nicoll* 8
Fullness of the Bible—*H. J. Betts* 9
Inspiration of the Bible—*John Dryden* 9
Contents of the Bible—*Peter Heylyn* 10
Esteeming the Bible—*Horatius Bonar* 11
Judah's Hallowed Bards—*Aubrey De Vere* 11
Poets of Old Israel—*John Vance Cheney* 12
On Translating the Psalms—*Sampson Guideon, Jr.* .. 12
To God—*Gregory Nanziansen (translated by Allen W. Chatfield)* 13
Thou Art of All Created Things—*Calderon* 14
The Seeing Eye—*Reginald Heber* 15
O Thou Eternal One—*Gabriel Romanovitch Derzhavin (translated by Sir John Bowring)* 15
The Infinity of God—*Emily Brontë* 15
Adoration—*Madame Guyon* 16
"Whither Shall I Go?"—*Eliza Scudder* 17
Creation's Psalm—*Swithin Saint Swithaine* 17
Making of Man—*Edwin Arnold* 18
Adam and Eve—*John Milton* 20
Adam to Eve—*John Milton* 20

TABLE OF CONTENTS

TABLE OF CONTENTS

TABLE OF CONTENTS

xxviii

TABLE OF CONTENTS

II. TALMUDICAL PERIOD

TABLE OF CONTENTS

III. MEDIAEVAL PERIOD

TABLE OF CONTENTS

xxxi

TABLE OF CONTENTS

TABLE OF CONTENTS

V. LITURGICAL ✓

Poems left out of "Liturgical" to page 456 (from p. 390)

left out more poems from (Liturgical) and part of Title (Book V) → (National) not listed of Book 6 not listed at all

after Adon Olam by Zangwill to end of Liturgical and Book Six title (Nat.) which is not shown at all

"Book Six From "Hatikvah" to "The Shoshana" which can be found on line by googling "Friedlander at Bartleby.com!!"

TABLE OF CONTENTS

xxxvi

TABLE OF CONTENTS

VII. THE MODERN PERIOD

TABLE OF CONTENTS

TABLE OF CONTENTS

xxxix

TABLE OF CONTENTS

xl

TABLE OF CONTENTS

TABLE OF CONTENTS

VIII. IN LIGHTER VEIN

TABLE OF CONTENTS

xliii

I
BIBLICAL AND POST-BIBLICAL

The Bible

THIS book—this holy book, on every line
    Marked with the seal of high divinity,
On every leaf bedew'd with drops of love
Divine; . . . this ray of sacred light,
This lamp from off the everlasting throne
Mercy took down, and in the night of Time
Stood . . . evermore beseeching men with tears
And earnest sighs, to read, believe and live.

                                        ANONYMOUS.

The Bible

LAMP of my feet, whereby we trace
    Our path, when wont to stray!
Stream from the fount of heavenly grace
    Brook by the traveller's way!

Bread of our souls, whereon we feed,
    True manna from on high!
Our guide and chart, wherein we read
    Of realms beyond the sky.

Pillar of fire through watches dark,
    Or radiant cloud by day!
When waves would whelm our tossing bark,
    Our anchor and our stay!

                                    RICHARD BARTON.

The Bible

AS to an ancient temple
    Whose vast proportions tower
With summit inaccessible
Among the stars of Heaven;
While the resistless Ocean
Of peoples and of cities
Breaks at its feet in foam,
Work that a hundred ages
Hallow; I bow to Thee.

From out thy mighty bosom
Rise hymns sublime, and melodies
Like to, the Heavens singing
Praises to their Creator;
While at the sound, an ecstasy,
A trance, fills all my being
With terror and with awe—
I feel my proud heart thrilling
With throbs of holy pride.

Oh! come, Thou high, beneficent
Heritage of my fathers,
Our country, altar, prophet!
Thou art our all, Thou only.
Through doubt, through pain, through outrage,
Through pangs of dissolution
Wringing our tortured hearts;
Come, open the rosy portals
Of hope to us once more!

In Thee, eternal, limitless,
The Earth is bound to Heaven;
The ages in immensity
Are one in Thine infinity;
Rapt by Thy power, the Spirit
Springs ever high and higher
Through care and grief and love,
Groans in mysterious ecstasy,
Exults in bitter pain.

Idylls of love and tenderness,
Home joys and pure affections,
Voices of Hope unconquered
By torture or by agony,
Austere and fruitful suffering,
Terror and doubt and faith,
Oh! for the whole Creation
A voice is found in Thee.

2

Like an inspired Sibyl
Thou thunderest in anger,
Tyre, Babylon, demolished,
Vanish with throne and altar;
Thou singest, Heaven lets open,
Mankind awakes to harmony
And holy truth and peace;
Like blessed springs descending,
Thou fillest all the world.

Ah me! what countless miseries,
What tears all unregarded
Hast Thou consoled and softened
With gentle voice and holy!
How many hearts that struggle
With doubt, remorse, anxiety,
With all the woes of ages,
Dost Thou, on ample pinions,
Lift purified to Heaven!

DAVID LEVI.

The Light and Glory of the World

THE Spirit breathes upon the word,
And brings the truth to sight;
Precepts and promises afford
A sanctifying light.

A glory gilds the sacred page,
Majestic like the sun;
It gives a light to every age,—
It gives, but borrows none.

The hand that gave it still supplies
The gracious light and heat;
His truths upon the nations rise,—
They rise, but never set.

3

Let everlasting thanks be thine,
For such a bright display,
As makes a world of darkness shine
With beams of heavenly day.

* * *

WILLIAM COWPER.

The Bible

BLESSED Bible! how I love it!
How it doth my bosom cheer!
What hath earth like this to covet?
O, what stores of wealth are here!
Man was lost and doomed to sorrow;
Not one ray of light or bliss
Could he from earth's treasures borrow,
'Till his way was cheered by this?

Yes, I'll to my bosom press thee,
Precious Word, I'll hide thee here;
Sure my very heart will bless thee,
For thou ever sayest "good cheer":
Speak, my heart, and tell thy ponderings,
Tell how far thy rovings led,
When This Book brought back thy wanderings,
Speaking life as from the dead.

Yes, sweet Bible! I will hide thee
Deep, yes, deeper in this heart;
Thou, through all my life will guide me,
And in death we will not part.
Part in death? No! never! never!
Through death's vale I'll lean on thee;
Then, in worlds above, for ever,
Sweeter still thy truths shall be!

PHOEBE PALMER.

The Written Word

THE starry firmament on high,
  And all the glories of the sky,
Yet shine not to Thy praise, O Lord,
So brightly as Thy written word.

The hopes that holy word supplies,
Its truths divine and precepts wise,
In each a heavenly beam I see,
And every beam conducts to Thee.

When, taught by painful proof to know
That all is vanity below,
The sinner roams from comfort far,
And looks in vain for sun or star;

Soft gleaming then those lights divine,
Through all the cheerless darkness shine,
And sweetly to the ravished eye
Disclose the dayspring from on high.

Almighty Lord, the sun shall fail,
The moon forget her nightly tale,
And deepest silence hush on high,
The radiant chorus of the sky;

But, fixed for everlasting years,
Unmoved amid the wreck of spheres,
Thy word shall shine in cloudless day,
When heaven and earth have passed away.

SIR ROBERT GRANT.

The Book of God

THY thoughts are here, my God,
  Expressed in words divine,
The utterance of heavenly lips
  In every sacred line.

Across the ages they
  Have reached us from afar,
Than the bright gold more golden they,
  Purer than purest star.

More durable they stand
  Than the eternal hills;
Far sweeter and more musical
  Than music of earth's rills.

Fairer in their fair hues,
  Than the fresh flowers of earth,
More fragrant than the fragrant climes
  Where odors have their birth.

Each word of thine a gem
  From the celestial mines,
A sunbeam from that holy heaven
  Where holy sunlight shines.

Thine, Thine, this book, though given
  In man's poor human speech,
Telling of things unseen, unheard,
  Beyond all human reach.

No strength it craves or needs,
  From this world's wisdom vain;
No filling up from human wells,
  Or sublunary rain.

No light from sons of time,
  Nor brilliance from its gold;
It sparkles with its own glad light,
  As in the ages old.

A thousand hammers keen,
  With fiery force and strain,
Brought down on it in rage and hate,
  Have struck this gem in vain.

Against this sea-swept rock,
  Ten thousand storms their will
Of foam and rage have wildly spent;
  It lifts its calm face still.

It standeth and will stand,
  Without or change or age,
The word of majesty and light,
  The church's heritage.

HORATIUS BONAR.

The Old Book

O BOOK of books, and friend of friends alone,
    How deep the debt of gratitude to thee!
For every human ill thou hast a charm,
With fragrance fresh as in Judæan days.
How clear the message that thy pages bring
To rich and poor, to old and young the same,
Forever sounding 'mid the centuries:—
That God's our father, tender, just and true,
And we His children all, both bond and free
Though clouds and darkness meet us on the way,
Thy radiant light is ever shining there.

ABRAM S. ISAACS.

Israel and His Book

AN age-worn wanderer, pale with thought and tears,
    With heart heroic and prophetic look,
  Comes clasping to his breast the Sacred Book—
The amulet of Israel through the years!
"Behold!" he says, "through ages dark with fears,
  Through travail and through miseries that shook
  The soul of Judah, this he ne'er forsook.
It is his Book!—Therein his God appears!"

7

His Book! more glorious with supernal light
  Than all the beacons reared by mortal hands
Since time first lisped its anguish in the night.
  His Book! That gave a God to all the lands;
Whose pages shall through us again reveal
The wondrous promise grief could not conceal!

FELIX N. GERSON.

The Ha' Bible

AH, I could worship thee!
  Thou art a gift a God of love might give;
For love and hope and joy
  In thy Almighty-written pages live;—
The slave who reads shall never crouch again;
For, mind-inspired by thee, he bursts his feeble chain!

God! unto thee I kneel,
  And thank thee! Thou unto my native land—
Yea, to the outspread earth—
  Hast stretched in love thy everlasting hand,
And thou hast given earth, and sea, and air—
Yea, all that heart can ask of good and pure and fair!

And, Father, thou hast spread
  Before men's eyes this charter of the free,
That all thy book might read,
  And justice, love, and truth, and liberty.
The gift was unto men,—the giver, God!
Thou slave! it stamps thee man,—go spurn thy weary
      load!

Thou doubly precious book!
  Unto thy light what does not Scotland owe:—
Thou teachest age to die,
  And youth in truth unsullied up to grow!
In lowly homes a comforter art thou,—
A sunbeam sent from God,—an everlasting bow!

ROBERT NICOLL.

8

Fullness of the Bible

THERE is a lamp whose steady light
    Guides the poor traveller in the night :—
'Tis God's own word! Its beaming ray
Can turn a midnight into day.

There is a storehouse of rich fare,
Supplied with plenty and to spare :—
'Tis God's own word! it spreads a feast
For every hungering, thirsting guest.

There is a chart whose tracings show
The onward course when tempests blow :—
'Tis God's own word! There, there is found
Direction for the homeward bound.

There is a tree whose leaves impart
Health to the burdened, contrite heart :—
'Tis God's own word! It cures of sin,
And makes the guilty conscience clean.

Give me this lamp to light my road;
This storehouse for my daily food;
Give me this chart for life's rough sea;
These healing leaves, this heavenly tree.

H. J BETTS.

Inspiration of the Bible

WHENCE, but from Heaven, could men unskill'd
    in arts,
In several ages born, in several parts,
Weave such agreeing truths? or how, or why,
Should all conspire to treat us with a lie?
Unask'd their pains, ungrateful their advice,
Starving their gain, and martyrdom their price.

If on the book itself we cast our view,
Concurrent heathens prove the story true:

The doctrine, miracles; which must convince,
For Heaven in them appeals to human sense;
And though they prove not they confirm the cause,
When what is taught agrees with nature's laws.

Therefore the style, majestic and divine,
It speaks no less than God in every line:
Commanding words; whose force is still the same
As the first fiat that produc'd our frame.
All faiths beside, or did by arms ascend;
Or sense indulg'd has made mankind their friend:

This only doctrine does our lusts oppose;
Unfed by nature's soil, in which it grows;
Cross to our interests, curbing sense and sin;
Oppress'd without, and undermin'd within,
It thrives through pain; its own tormentors tires,
And with a stubborn patience still aspires.

JOHN DRYDEN.

Contents of the Bible

IF thou art merry, here are airs;
    If melancholy, here are prayers;
If studious, here are those things writ
Which may deserve thy ablest wit;
If hungry, here is food divine;
If thirsty, nectar, heavenly wine.

Read, then; but, first, thyself prepare
To read with zeal and mark with care;
And when thou read'st what here is writ,
Let thy best practice second it;
So twice each precept read shall be—
First in the book, and next in thee.

PETER HEYLYN.

Esteeming the Bible

THIS holy book I'd rather own,
    Than all the gold and gems
That e'er in monarchs' coffers shone,
    Than all their diadems.

Nay, were the seas one chrysolite,
    The earth one golden ball,
And diadems all the stars of night,
    This book outweighs them all.

Ah, no, the soul ne'er found relief
    In glittering hoards of wealth;
Gems dazzle not the eye of grief,
    Gold cannot purchase health.

But here a blessed balm appears
    To heal the deepest woe,
And those who read this book in tears,
    Their tears shall cease to flow.
                    HORATIUS BONAR.

Judah's Hallowed Bards

LET those who will hang rapturously o'er
    The flowing eloquence of Plato's page;
Repeat, with flashing eyes, the sounds that pour
    From Homer's verse as with a torrent's rage;
Let those who list ask Tully to assuage
    Wild hearts with high-wrought periods, and restore
The reign of rhetoric; or maxims sage.
    Winnow from Seneca's contentious lore,
Not these, but Judah's hallowed bards, to me
Are dear: Isaiah's noble energy;
The temperate grief of Job; the artless strain
    Of Ruth and pastoral Amos; the high songs
    Of David; and the tale of Joseph's wrongs.
Simply, pathetic, eloquently plain.
                    AUBREY DE VERE.

11

The Poets of Old Israel

OLD Israel's readers of the stars,
I love them best. Musing, they read,
In embers of the heavenly hearth,
High truths were never learned below.
They asked not of the barren sands,
They questioned not that stretch of death;
But upward from the humble tent
They took the stairway of the hills;
Upward they climbed, bold in their trust,
To pluck the glory of the stars,
Faith falters, knowledge does not know,
Fast, one by one, the phantoms fade;
But that strange light, unwavering love,
Grasped from the lowered hand of God,
Abides, quenchless forevermore.

JOHN VANCE CHENEY.

One of the earliest specimens of English verse writ-
ten by an English-born Jew addressed to Daniel Israel
Lopez Laguna, who published in 1720 a metrical
translation of the Psalms in Spanish under the title
"Espejo fiet de Vidas."

On Trànslating the Psalms

HOW great thy Thoughts, how Glorious thy De-
signs,
How every Musick varies in thy Lines;
The Praise of God in every Verse is found,
Art strengthening Nature, Sense improv'd by Sound;
Your strains are Regularly Bold and Please,
With unforst Care and unaffected Ease:
Whene'er I look in thy Delightful Page,
The Godly Verse my busy Thoughts engage,
And David's Psalms so Perfect does appear
True to the Sense, Harmonious to the Ear.

12

Happy the Man who strings his tuneful Lyre,
That like King David's Harp, it do's Inspire:
Thrice Happy thee and Worthiest to Dwell,
Amongst those Precepts thou hast Sung so well;
Your Wondrous Song with Raptures I Rehearse,
Then ask who wrought this Miracle of Verse:
Triumph LAGUNA with Immortal Lays
'Tis you alone that do's Deserve this Praise:
'Tis you alone could chuse so great a Theme,
That all the world in Duty must Esteem.

SAMPSON GUIDEON, JR.

To God

O THOU, the One supreme o'er all!
    For by what other name
May we upon thy greatness call,
    Or celebrate thy fame?

Ineffable! to thee what speech
    Can hymns of honor raise?
Ineffable! what tongue can reach
    The measure of thy praise?

How, unapproached, shall mind of man
    Descry Thy dazzling throne,
And pierce and find thee out, and scan
    Where thou dost dwell alone?

Unuttered thou! all uttered things
    Have had their birth from thee;
The one unknown! from thee the springs
    Of all we know and see!

And all things, as they move along
    In order fixed by thee,
Thy watchword heed, in silent song
    Hymning thy majesty.

13

And lo! all things abide in thee,
   And through the complex whole,
Thou spread'st thine own divinity,
   Thyself of all the goal.

One being thou, all things, yet none,
   Nor one nor yet all things;
How call thee, O mysterious One?
   A worthy name, who brings?

All-named from attributes thine own,
   How call thee as we ought?
Thou art unlimited, alone,
   Beyond the range of thought.

GREGORY NANZIANZEN.
(Translated by Allen W. Chatfield).

Thou Art of All Created Things

THOU art of all created things,
   O Lord, the essence and the cause,
The source and centre of all bliss;
What are those veils of woven light
Where sun and moon and stars unite,
The purple morn, the spangled night;
But curtains which thy mercy draws
Between the heavenly world and this?
The terrors of the sea and land—
When all the elements conspire,
The earth and water, storm and fire—
Are but the sketches of thy hand;
Do they not all in countless ways—
The lightning's flash, the howling storm,
The dread volcano's awful blaze—
Proclaim Thy glory and Thy praise?

CALDERON.

14

The Seeing Eye

THERE is an eye that never sleeps
   Beneath the wing of night;
There is an ear that never shuts
   When sink the beams of sight;
There is an arm that never tires
   When human strength gives way;
There is a love that never fails
   When earthly loves decay.
That eye is fix'd on seraph throngs,
That ear is filled with angels' songs,
That arm upholds the worlds on high,
That Love is throned beyond the sky.

REGINALD HEBER.

O Thou Eternal One!

O THOU Eternal One! whose presence bright
   All space doth occupy, all motion guide:
Unchanged through time's all-devastating flight;
   Thou only God! There is no God beside!
Being above all beings! mighty One!
   Whom none can comprehend and none explore;
Who fill'st existence with Thyself alone:
   Embracing all, supporting, ruling o'er,—
Being whom we call God, and know no more!

GABRIEL ROMANOVITCH DERZHAVIN.
Translated by SIR JOHN BOWRING.

The Infinity of God

NO coward soul is mine,
   No trembler in the world's storm-troubled sphere:
I see Heaven's glories shine,
   And faith shines equal, arming me from fear.

O God within my breast,
  Almighty, ever-present Deity!
Life—that in me has rest,
  As I—undying Life—have power in Thee!

Vain are the thousand creeds
  That move men's hearts: unutterably vain;
Worthless as withered weeds,
  Or idle froth amid the boundless main.

To waken doubt in one
  Holding so fast by Thine infinity;
So surely anchored on
  The steadfast rock of immortality.

With wide-embracing love
  Thy spirit animates eternal years,
Pervades and broods above,
  Changes, sustains, dissolves, creates, and rears.

Though earth and man were gone,
  And suns and universes ceased to be,
And Thou were left alone,
  Every existence would exist in Thee.

There is not room for Death,
  Nor atom that his might could render void:
Thou—Thou art Being and Breath,
  And what Thou art may never be destroyed.

EMILY BRONTË.

Adoration

I LOVE my God, but with no love of mine,
    For I have none to give;
I love thee, Lord, but all the love is thine,
    For by thy life I live.
I am as nothing, and rejoice to be
    Emptied and lost and swallowed up in thee.

16

Thou, Lord, alone art all thy children need,
    And there is none beside;
From thee the streams of blessedness proceed;
    In thee the blest abide.
Fountain of life, and all-abounding grace,
Our source, our centre, and our dwelling-place!

MADAME GUYON.

"Whither Shall I Go?"

I CANNOT find thee! still on restless pinion
    My spirit beats the void where thou dost dwell;
I wander lost through all thy vast dominion,
    And shrink beneath thy light ineffable.

I cannot know thee! even when most adoring
    Before thy shrine I bend in lowliest prayer;
Beyond these bounds of thought, my thought upsoar-
    ing,
    From further quest comes back; thou art not there.

Yet high above the limits of my seeing
    And folded far within the inmost heart,
And deep below the deeps of conscience being,
    Thy splendor shineth; there, O God, thou art.

I cannot lose thee; still in thee abiding
    The end is clear, How wide so'er I roam;
The law that holds the worlds my steps is guiding.
    And I must rest at last in thee, my home.

ELIZA SCUDDER.

Creation's Psalm

A DEEP-BASSED thunder-rolling psalm
    Sweeps thro' the reeded throat of Time,
    And charms the ear of every clime
With music of the great "I Am."

17

It drags the planets in their orbs,
   And smites the sun, and shakes the stars,
   And strikes the rocky-bedded bars,
And beats about the aerial curbs!

Creation chants the nameless Name,
   The winging worlds in chorus ring;
   The great lands shout; the huge seas sing;
The thundering heavens roar, "I Am!"

SWITHIN SAINT SWITHAINE.

Making of Man

AL-MUZAWWIR! the "Fashioner!" say thus;
   Still lauding Him who hath compounded us:
When the Lord would fashion men,
   Spake He in the Angels' hearing,
"Lo! Our will is there shall be
   On the earth a creature bearing
Rule and royalty. Today
We will shape a man from clay."

Spake the Angels, "Wilt Thou make
   Man who must forget his Maker,
Working evil, shedding blood,
   Of Thy precepts the forsaker?
But Thou knowest all, and we
Celebrate Thy majesty."

Answered Allah, "Yea! I know
   What ye know not of this making;
   Gabriel! Michael! Israfel!
   Go down to the earth, and taking
Seven clods of colors seven,
Bring them unto Me in Heaven.

18

Then those holy Angels three,
  Spread their pinions and descended;
Seeking clods of diverse clay,
  That all colors might be blended;
Yellow, tawny, dun, black, brown,
White and red as men are known.

But the earth spake sore afraid,
  "Angels! of my substance take not,
Give me back my dust and pray
  That the dread Creator make not
Man, for he will sin and bring
Wrath on me and suffering."

Therefore, empty-handed came
  Gabriel, Michael, Israfel,
Saying, "Lord! Thy earth imploreth
  Man may never on her dwell;
He will sin and anger Thee,
Give me back my clay!" cried she.

Spake the Lord to Azrael,
  "Go thou, who of wing art surest,
Tell my earth this shall be well;
  Bring those clods, which thou procurest
From her bosom, unto Me;
Shape them as I order thee."

Thus 'tis written how the Lord
  Fashioned Adam for His glory,
Whom the Angels worshipped,
  All save Iblis; and this story
Teacheth wherefore Azrael saith
"Come thou!" at man's hour of death.

EDWIN ARNOLD.

Adam and Eve
(From "Paradise Lost")

TWO of far nobler shape, erect and tall,
  Godlike erect, with native honor clad,
In naked majesty seemed lords of all:
And worthy seemed; for in their looks divine
The image of their glorious Maker shone.
Truth, wisdom, sanctitude severe and pure,
(Severe, but in true filial freedom placed),
Whence true authority in men; though both
Not equal, as their sex not equal seemed;
For contemplation he and valor formed;
For softness she and sweet attractive grace;
He for God only, she for God in him.

JOHN MILTON.

Adam to Eve
(From "Paradise Lost")

O FAIREST of creation, last and best
  Of all God's works, creature in whom excelled
Whatever can to sight or thought be formed
Holy, divine, good, amiable, or sweet.

JOHN MILTON.

Eve

FOR the first time a lovely scene
  Earth saw and smiled,
A gentle form with pallid mien
Bending o'er a new-born child;
The pang, the anguish, and the woe
That speech hath never told,
Fled, as the sun with noontide glow
Dissolves the snow-wreath cold,
Leaving the bliss that none but mothers know;
While he, the partner of her heaven-taught joy
Knelt in adoring praise beside his beauteous boy.
She, first of all our mortal race,
Learn'd the ecstasy to trace

20

BIBLICAL AND POST-BIBLICAL

The expanding form of infant grace
From her own life-spring fed;
To mark each radiant hour,
Heaven's sculpture still more perfect growing,
More full of power;

The little foot's elastic tread,
The rounded cheek, like rose-bud glowing,
The fringéd eye with gladness flowing
As the pure, blue fountains roll;
And then those lisping sounds to hear,
Unfolding to her thrilling ear
The strange, mysterious, never-dying soul,
And with delight intense
To watch the angel-smile of sleeping innocence.

No more she mourned lost Eden's joy,
Or wept her cherish'd flowers,
In their primeval bowers
By wrecking tempests riven;
The thorn and thistle of the exile's lot
She heeded not.
So all-absorbing was her sweet employ
To rear the incipient man, the gift her God had
     given.

And when his boyhood bold
A richer beauty caught,
Her kindling glance of pleasure told
The incense of her idol-thought;
Not for the born of clay
Is pride's exulting thrill,
Dark herald of the downward way,
And ominous of ill.
Even his cradled brother's smile
The haughty first-born jealously survey'd
And envy marked the brow with hate and guile,
In God's own image made.

LYDIA HUNTLEY SIGOURNEY.

The Rainbow

BRIGHT pledge of peace and sunshine! the surety
　　Of thy Lord's hand, the object of His eye!
When I behold thee, though my light be dim,
Distant and low, I can in thine see Him
Who looks upon thee from His glorious throne,
And minds the Covenant 'twixt All and One.

　　　　　　　　　　　　　FELICIA HEMANS.

———

BOW of beauty, arching o'er us, tinted with un-
　　earthly dyes,
Stealing silently before us on the cloud of stormy skies;
In the beaming radiance seeming, like an angel-path
　　from heaven;
Or a vision to our dreaming, of some fairy fabric
　　given.

Thou art Mercy's emblem, brightly smiling through
　　an angry frown;
Fairer for the gloom, as nightly glow the gems in
　　Ether's crown.
And when wrath is darkest glooming on the coun-
　　tenance divine,
Love's and Mercy's light assuming, like the rainbow
　　it doth shine.

　　　　　　　　　　　　HENRY VAUGHAN.

Translation of the Patriarch
(Genesis v. 24.)

NO tombstone saw they there,
　　No sepulchre's pallid gleam;
But a quiver went through the blue bright air,
　　Like a thrill of a glorious dream.

22

And the stately palm trees bowed,
  By old Euphrates' tide;
And the deep sky glowed, like a burning cloud,
  Or a spirit glorified.
When the good old Patriarch's footsteps trod
  The sapphire pavements, that lead to God.
Where was he, when the gates
  Of Heaven were opened wide?
Praying alone, like one that waits,
  By Tigris' sacred tide.
Or by some lonely shore
  Where the hollow echo dwells,
And sounding sea beats evermore,
  'Mid rocks and strange bright shells?
Or chanting God's praises, with happy cheer,
  When the songs of the angels broke on his ear?
And the gray Chaldean plains
  With a golden radiance shone,
As Earth caught full the light that reigns
  Beside the Eternal Throne.
Far off, and low, she heard
  The flow of Life's bright stream,
And the music of strange sweet melodies
  That haunts her like a dream;
And only God's angels, with solemn eye,
  Saw the glorious pageant passing by.
And still the rocks frown high,
  Amid the shadows lone—
But their echoes nevermore reply,
  To the sweet angelic tone;
And an awful mystery fills
  That land of unknown graves,
And ever thrills the solemn hills
  That guard Euphrates' waves;
But the word of God through ages dim,
Reveals how Enoch went home to Him.

                       LUCY A. RANDALL.

Abraham and His Gods

BENEATH the full-eyed Syrian moon,
   The Patriarch, lost in reverence, raised
His consecrated head, and soon
   He knelt and worshipped while he gazed:
"Surely that glorious Orb on high
Must be the Lord of earth and sky."

Slowly towards its central throne
   The glory rose, yet paused not there
But seemed by influence not its own
   Drawn downwards through the western air
Until it wholly sunk away,
And the soft Stars had all the sway.

Then to the hierarchy of light.
   With face upturned the sage remained—
"At least Ye stand forever bright—
   Your power has never waxed or waned!"
Even while he spoke, their work was done
Drowned in the overflowing Sun.

Eastward he bent his eager eyes—
   "Creatures of Night! false gods and frail!
Take not the worship of the wise;
   There is the Deity we hail.
Fountain of light, and warmth, and love
He only bears our hearts above."

Yet was that One—that radiant One
   Who seemed so absolute a King,
Only ordained his round to run
   And pass like each created thing;
He rested not in noonday prime
But fell beneath the strength of time.

Then like one laboring without hope
   To bring his toil to fruitful end,
And powerless to discern the scope
   Whereto his aspirations tend,

24

Still Abraham prayed day and night
"God! Teach me to what God to pray."

Nor long in vain; an inward Light
  Arose to which the sun is pale.
The knowledge of the Infinite,
  The sense of Truth that must prevail:—
The presence of the only Lord
By angels and by men adored.

RICHARD MONCKTON MILNES
(Lord Houghton).

Abraham

I WILL sing a song of heroes,
  Crowned with manhood's diadem,
Men that lift us when we love them
  Into nobler life with them.

I will sing a song of heroes
  To their God-sent mission true,
From the ruin of the old time
  Grandly forth to shape the new:

Men that, like a strong-winged zephyr,
  Come with freshness and with power,
Bracing fearful hearts to grapple
  With the problem of the hour:

Men whose prophet-voice of warning
  Stirs the dull, and spurs the slow,
Till the big heart of a people
  Swells with hopeful overflow.

I will sing the song of Terah,
  Abraham in tented state,
With his sheep and goats and asses,
  Bearing high behests from Fate;

Journeying from beyond Euphrates,
  Where cool Orfa's bubbling well
Lured the Greek and lured the Roman,
  By its verdurous fringe to dwell.

When he left the flaming idols,
  Sun by day and Moon by night,
To believe in something deeper
  Than the shows that brush the sight,

And, as a traveller wisely trusteth
  To a practiced guide and true,
So he owned the Voice that called him
  From the faithless Heathen crew.

And he travelled from Damascus
  Southward where the torrent tide
Of the sons of Ammon mingles
  With the Jordan's swelling pride.

To the pleasant land of Schechem,
  To the flowered and fragrant ground
'Twixt Mount Ebal and Gerizim,
  Where the bubbling wells abound.

To the stony slopes of Bethel,
  And to Hebron's greening glade,
Where the grapes with weighty fruitage
  Droop beneath the leafy shade.

And he pitched his tent in Mamre,
  'Neath an oak-tree tall and broad
And with pious care an altar
  Built there to the one true God.

And the voice of God came near him,
  And the angels of the Lord
'Neath the broad and leafy oak-tree
  Knew his hospitable board;

BIBLICAL AND POST-BIBLICAL

And they hailed him with rare blessing
  For all peoples richly stored,
Father of the faithful, elect
  Friend of God, Almighty Lord.

And he sojourned 'mid the people
  With high heart and weighty arm,
Wise to rein their wandering worship,
  Strong to shield their homes from harm.

And fat Nile's proud Pharaohs owned him,
  As a strong, God-favored man,
Like Osiris casting broadly
  Largess to the human clan.

And he lived long years a witness
  To a pure high-thoughted creed,
That in ripeness of the ages
  Grew to serve our mortal need.

Not a priest and not a churchman
  From all proud pretentions free,
Shepherd chief and shepherd-warrior
  Human-faced like you and me:

Human-faced and human-hearted,
  To the pure religion true,
Purer than the gay and sensuous
  Grecian, wider than the Jew.

Common sire, whom Jew and Christian,
  Turk and Arab, name and praise;
Common as the sun that shines
  On East and West with brothered rays.

JOHN STUART BLACKIE.

The Tent of Abraham

THE shadows of an Eastern day
  Lengthened along the sandy way,
    When, toiling faint and lone,
An aged wanderer crossed the plain,
As if his every step were pain,
    His every breath a groan!
Till Abraham's tent appeared in view,
And slowly towards his rest he drew.

And Abraham met his wayworn look
With pity, for the old man shook
    With years at every tread;
For he the wrinkled impress bore
Of full one hundred years or more
    Upon his silver head;
Then Abraham washed his aching feet,
Assuaged their pain, and brought him meat.

You should have known the burning glare
Of soil and sun, and sultry air,
    To tell how sweet the draught
That blessed those lips so parched and old;
Oh! water—not a world of gold
    Could buy that joy he quaffed!
You should have toiled the burning waste,
To taste how sweetly food can taste!

But Abraham saw with deep amaze
The old man's strange and godless ways;
    For ere he bent to eat,
Nor praise nor thanks he uttered there,
Nor raised his grateful eyes in prayer
    To God who sent him meat;
Sudden he sat, in eager mood,
And called no blessing on the food!

"Ownest thou not the God of Heaven,
That unto thee these things hath given?"

Said Abraham in his ire;
He answered, "Five-score years I've trod,
Yet worshipped but one only God,—
  The eternal God of Fire!"
And Abraham, wroth, his anger spent,
And thrust him, storming, from his tent.

An Eastern night is dread to bear—
There's fever in the sickly air,
  And evils few can speak
Save those whose wandering lives have known
The perils 'mid the desert thrown,
  Or heard the tempest's shriek;
Yet pitiless, from out his sight,
Stern Abraham cast him to the night.

Then there was sudden awe on Night—
The pale West quivered with wild light—
  The stars apart were thrown;
And all the air around the sky
Seemed like a glory hung on high,—
  A gleam of worlds unknown;
And from that glory high installed,
A voice—God's voice—to Abraham called:

"Why went this stranger from thy board?"
And Abraham answered, "Know, O Lord,
  That he denied Thy name;
Neither would worship Thee, nor bless;
So forth, unto the wilderness,
  I drove him, in his shame!"
And God said, "If I still allow
Peace to his errors, couldst not thou?

"If I, these hundred years, have borne
The wanderer's sin, neglect, and scorn,
  Yet ne'er did vengeance seek,
How is't that thou, for one poor night,
Couldst bear him not within thy sight?
  Look up to Me, and speak!"

Then towards the Voice, with trembling steps he trod,
And Abraham stood rebuked before his God.
                                    CHARLES SWAIN.

The Ballade of Dead Cities

WHERE are the cities of the plain?
    And where the shrines of rapt Bethel?
And Calah built of Tubal-Cain?
    And Shinar whence King Amraphel
Came out in arms and fought, and fell,
    Decoyed into the pits of slime
By Siddim and sent sheer to hell;
    Where are the cities of old time?

Where now is Karnak, that great fane,
    With granite built, a miracle?
And Luxor smooth without a stain,
    Whose graven scripture still we spell?
The jackal and the owl may tell;
    Dark snakes around their ruins climb,
They fade like echo in a shell;
    Where are the cities of old time?

And where is white Shushan, again,
    Where Vashti's beauty bore the bell,
And all the Jewish oil and grain
    Were brought to Mithridath to sell,
Where Nehemiah would not dwell,
    Because another town sublime
Decoyed him with her oracle?
    Where are the cities of old time?

Envoi

Prince, with a dolorous, ceaseless knell,
    Above their wasted toil and crime
The waters of oblivion swell:
    Where are the cities of old time?
                                    EDMUND GOSSE.

30

Hagar

LONE in the wilderness, her child and she,
   Sits the dark beauty, and her fierce-eyed boy.
A heavy burden and no winsome toy
To such as she, a hanging babe must be.
A slave without a master—wild, nor free,
With anger in her heart! and in her face
Shame for foul wrong and undeserved disgrace,
Poor Hagar mourns her lost virginity!
Poor woman fear not—God is everywhere;
The silent tears, thy thirsty infant's moan,
Are known to Him whose never-absent care
Still wakes to make all hearts and souls his own;
He sends an angel from beneath his throne
To cheer the outcast in the desert bare.

HARTLEY COLERIDGE.

The Meeting of Isaac and Rebecca

WHO is this man that walketh in the field,
   O Eleazer, steward to my lord?
And Eleazer answered her and said,
Daughter of Bethuel, it is other none
But my lord Isaac, son unto my lord.
Who as his wont is, walketh in the field,
In the hour of evening meditating there.

Therefore Rebekah hasted where she sat,
And from her camel 'lighting to the earth,
Sought for a veil and put it on her face.

But Isaac also, walking in the field,
Saw from afar a company that came,
Camels, and a seat as where a woman sat;
Wherefore he came and met them on the way.
Whom, when Rebekah saw, she came before
Saying, Behold the handmaiden of my lord,
Who, for my lord's sake travel from my land.

But he said, O thou blessed of our God,
Come, for the tent is eager for thy face,
Shall not thy husband be unto thee more than
Hundreds of kinsmen living in thy land?

And Eleazer answered: Thus and thus,
Even according as thy father bade,
Did we; and thus and thus it came to pass:
Lo! is not this Rebekah, Bethuel's child?
And as he ended, Isaac spoke and said,
Surely my heart went with you on the way
When with the beasts ye came unto the place.

Truly, O child of Nahor, I was there
When to my mother and my mother's son
Thou madest answer, saying, I will go.
And Isaac brought her to her mother's tent.

ARTHUR HUGH CLOUGH.

Jacob's Dream
(Genesis xxviii, 10-12)

OH, pilgrim, halting on the rock-strewn sod
  To thee this Bethel vision still appears!
The golden ladder of the love of God
  Shines on the weary eyes, all wet with tears.

He leads thee on by ways thou hast not known,
  He bids thee rest in desert stillness deep,
He gives thee pillows of the barren stone;
  And lo! His angels dawn upon thy sleep.

He shows thee how Eternal Love unites
  Thy sin-marred earth with His own sphere of bliss
And sends His bright ones from their radiant heights,
  Laden with blessings from that world to this.

32

Thy solitude is no darkness unto Him,
The solitudes are peopled with His host
Close the dim eye, and rest the wayworn limb—
The Lord is near when thou dost need Him most.

S. D.

Pillow and Stone

UPON a stone in olden time
A wanderer sank to rest.
A wondrous vision soothed his heart
How strangely was he blessed!

The arched sky was his coverlet,
The night-wind cradle song;
A ladder mounted heavenward
Which bore an angel throng.

Ah, in these sober days of ours
When we soft close our eyes,
No lofty ladder climbs above,
No angel hosts arise.

And tho our bed be richly draped
And royal fares our own,
For oft we waken unrefreshed—
The pillow's changed to stone!

ABRAM S. ISAACS.

Beth-el

A RUGGED stone,
For centuries neglected and alone,—
Its destiny unknown.

The tide of light
Sped o'er it, and the breakers of the night,
In alternating flight.

33

And it was wet
With twilight dew, the sacramental sweat
    That mystic dreams beget.

There Jacob lay,
Dark struggling, till the wrestler, white as day
    Brake from his arms away.

Upon the sod
A pillow; then, by countless angels trod,
    A stepping stone to God.

                                JOHN B. TABB.

As Jacob Served for Rachel

'TWAS the love that lightened service!
    The old, old story sweet
That yearning lips and waiting hearts
    In melody repeat.
As Jacob served for Rachel
    Beneath the Syrian sky,
Like the golden sands that swiftly drop
    The toiling years went by.

Chill fell the dews upon him,
    Fierce smote the sultry sun;
But what were cold and heat to him,
    Till that dear wife was won!
The angels whispered in his ear
    "Be patient and be strong!"
And the thought of her he waited for
    Was ever like a song.

Sweet Rachel, with the secret
    To hold a brave man leal;
To keep him through the changeful years
    Her own in woe and weal;

So that in age and exile,
   The death damp on his face,
Her name to the dark valley lent
   Its own peculiar grace.

And "There I buried Rachel,"
   He said of that lone spot
In Ephrath, near to Bethlehem,
   Where the wife he loved was not;
For God has taken from him
   The brightness and the zest,
And the heaven above thenceforward kept
   In fee his very best.

Of the love that lightens service,
   Dear God, how much we see,
When the father toils the livelong day
   For the children at his knee;
When all night the mother wakes,
   Nor deem the vigil hard,
The rose of health on sick one's cheek,
   Her happy heart's reward.

The love that lightens service
   The fisherman can tell,
When he wrests the bread his dear ones eat
   Where the bitter surges swell;
And the farmer in the furrow,
   The merchant in the mart,
Count little worth their weary toil
   For the treasures of the heart.

   ·   ·   ·   ·   ·   ·

As Jacob served for Rachel
   Beneath the Syrian sky,
And the golden sands of toiling years
   Went swiftly slipping by,
The thought of her was music
   To cheer his weary feet,
'Twas love that lightened service,
   The old, old story sweet.   ANONYMOUS.

Mizpah

"The Lord watch between me and thee when we
are absent from each other."—Gen. xxxi. 49.

A BROAD gold band engraven
   With word of Holy Writ
A ring, the bond and token,
   Which love and prayer hath lit,
When absent from each other
   O'er mountain, vale and sea,
The Lord, who guarded Israel,
   Keeps watch 'tween me and thee,

Through days of light and gladness,
   Through days of love and life,
Through smiles, and joy, and sunshine,
   Through days with beauty rife;
When absent from each other,
   O'er mountain, vale, and sea,
The Lord of love and gladness,
   Keep watch 'tween me and thee.

Through days of doubt and darkness,
   In fear and trembling breath;
Through mists of sin and sorrow,
   In tears, and grief and death,
The Lord of life and glory,
   The King of earth and sea,
The Lord who guarded Israel,
   Keep watch 'tween me and thee.

                    ANONYMOUS.

Israel

WHEN by Jabbok the patriarch waited
   To learn on the morrow his doom
And his dubious spirit debated
In darkness and silence and gloom,

BIBLICAL AND POST-BIBLICAL

There descended a Being with whom
He wrestled in agony sore,
With striving of heart and of brawn,
And not for an instant forbore
Till the east gave a threat of the dawn;
And then, the Awful One blessed him;
To his lips and his spirit there came,
Compelled by the doubts that oppressed him,
The cry that through questioning ages
Has been rung from the hinds and the sages,
  "Tell me, I pray Thee, Thy name!"
Most fatal, most futile of questions!
Wherever the heart of man beats,
In the spirits' most sacred retreats,
It comes with its sombre suggestions
Unanswered forever and aye.
The blessing may come and may stay,
For the wrestler's heroic endeavor;
But the question, unheeded forever,
Dies out in the broadening day.

In the ages before our traditions,
By the altars of dark superstitions,
The imperious question has come;
When the death-stricken victim lay sobbing
At the feet of his slayer and priest,
And his heart was laid smoking and throbbing
To the sound of the cymbal and drum
On the steps of the high Teocallis;
When the delicate Greek at his feast
Poured forth the red wine from his chalice
With mocking and cynical prayer;
When by Nile Egypt worshipping lay,
And afar through the rosy, flushed air
The Memnon called out to the day;
Where the Muezzin's cry floats from his spire;
In the vaulted Cathedral's dim shades,
Where the crushed hearts of thousands aspire

Through art's highest miracle higher,
This question of questions invades
Each heart bowed in worship or shame;
In the air where the censers are swinging,
A voice, going up with the singing,
Cries, "Tell me I pray Thee Thy name."
No answer came back, not a word,
To the patriarch there by the ford;
No answer has come through the ages
To the poets, the seers and the sages
Who have sought in the secrets of science
The name or the nature of God,
Whether crushing in desperate defiance
Or kissing his absolute rod;
But the answer which was and shall be,
    "My name! Nay, what is it to thee?"
The search and the question are vain.
By use of the strength that is in you,
By wrestling of soul and of sinew
The blessing of God you may gain.
There are lights in the far-gleaming Heaven
That never shall shine on our eyes;
To mortals it may not be given
To range those inviolate skies.
The mind, whether praying or scorning,
That tempts those dread secrets shall fail;
But strive through the night till the morning,
    And mightily thou shalt prevail.

                                    JOHN HAY.

The Cry of Rachel

I STAND in the dark; I beat on the floor,
    Let me in, Death.
Through the storm am I come; I find you before:
            Let me in, Death.
For him that is sweet, and for him that is small,
I beat on the door, I cry, and I call:
            Let me in, Death.

38

For he was my bow of the almond-tree fair:
    Let me in, Death.
You brake it; it whitens no more by the stair:
    Let me in, Death.
For he was my lamp in the House of the Lord;
You quenched, and left me this dark and the sword:
    Let me in, Death.

I that was rich do ask you for alms:
    Let me in, Death.
I that was full, uplift your stripped palms:
    Let me in, Death.
Back to me now give the child that I had;
Cast into mine arms my little sweet lad:
    Let me in, Death.

Are you grown so deaf that you cannot hear?
    Let me in, Death.
Unclose the dim eye, and unstop the ear:
    Let me in, Death.
I will call so loud, I will cry so sore,
You must for shame's sake come open the door:
    Let me in, Death.

           LIZETTE WORDSWORTH REESE.

Dirge of Rachel

AND Rachel lies in Ephrath's land,
    Beneath her lonely oak of weeping;
With mouldering heart and withering hand,
    The sleep of death forever sleeping.

The spring comes smiling down the vale,
    The lilacs and the roses bringing;
But Rachel never more shall hail
    The flowers that in the world are springing.

The summer gives his radiant day,
   And Jewish dames the dance are treading;
But Rachel, on her couch of clay,
   Sleeps all unheeded and unheeding.

The autumn's ripening sunbeam shines,
   And reapers to the field is calling;
But Rachel's voice no longer joins
   The choral song at twilight's falling.

The winter sends his drenching shower,
   And sweeps his howling blast around her,
But earthly storms possess no power
   To break the slumber that hath bound her.

WILLIAM KNOX.

Moses

THRONES that stood and realms that flour-
      ished,
   Races that have ruled the world,—
They have fallen, they have perished,
   And new standards are unfurled.
Gods are banished at whose altars
   Nations have been wont to pray,
   And where Wisdom erst held sway
Ignorance supinely falters.

Deeds that once with blare and clangor
   Filled the earth, have ceased to be;
Even their renown no longer
   Lives in lays of minstrelsy.
Lo! the hero's might is broken
   And his sword is gone to rust;
   Lips are steeped in death and dust
That have sweetly sung and spoken.

40

But athwart the gulf of ages
  From whose all-devouring deep
Songs of bards and words of sages
  Mist like in tradition sweep,—
Radiant and serene reposes,
  Unattained by mist and gloom,
  Undiminished by the tomb;
A colossal image—Moses.

Though we wot not of his feature,
  Of such ken there is no need,
For his aspect is the creature
  Of his word and of his deed,—
Of the word that is engraven
  Even on the soul that's lost
  Of the deed that led his host
Toward freedom, truth and Heaven.

Thus we see him; Superhuman
  In his purpose and in might,
Tender is his love as woman,
  Fierce in the defense of right;
Meek and faltering, yet compliant,
  In the presence of the Lord,—
  In obedience of his word
Bold, unyielding and defiant.

Even as the luminary
  Of our days from fumous height—
Lifeless, barren, solitary—
  Beams with life diffusing light;
So he rises on our vision
  From the past which phantoms shroud,
  Life-impregnate, halo-browed,
In the garb of his tradition.

What he wrought and what he uttered,
  Where he trod and where he stood;
Where the flaming briar fluttered
  In the desert's solitude;

At the throne of him who trifled
  With the wrath revealed of God,
  And where with uplifted rod
The pursuing hosts he stifled;

On that pilgrimage unequaled
  When he smote the barren rock,
Or by marvel or decree quelled
  Ingrate murmurs of his flock;
When from Sinai, rent with thunder,
  He descended with the Law:—
  Thrills with reverential awe
And compels transcendent wonder.

As he lived so was his passing
  Self-obscuring, tranquil, grand,
As with eyes that death was glassing
  He beheld the promised land—
Did he ween as on that mountain
  He expired meek and brave,
That while man still man would be,
Far into eternity,
  He would look on Moses' grave
As his birthright's sacred fountain?

N. N.

Rescue of Moses

IN Judah's halls the harp is hushed,
  Her voice is but the voice of pain;
The heathen heel her helms has crushed,
  Her spirit wears the heathen chain.
From the dark prison-house she cried,
  "How long, O Lord, Thy sword has slept!
Oh, quell the oppressor in his pride!"
  Still Pharoah ruled, and Israel wept.

The morning breezes freshly blow,
  The waves in golden sunlight quiver;

42

BIBLICAL AND POST-BIBLICAL

The Hebrew's daughter wanders slow
  Beside the mighty idol river.
A babe within her bosom lay;
  And must she plunge him in the deep?
She raised her eyes to heaven to pray;
  She turned them down to earth to weep.

She knelt beside the rushing tide,
  Mid rushes dark and flow'rets wild;
Beneath the plane-tree's shadow wide,
  The weeping mother placed her child.
"Peace be around thee, though thy bed
  A mother's breast no more may be;
Yet He that shields the lily's head,
  Deserted babe, will watch o'er thee!"

She's gone! that mourning mother! gone.
  List to the sound of dancing feet,
And lightly bounding, one by one,
  A lovely train the timbrels beat.
'Tis she of Egypt: Pharoah's daughter,
  That with her maidens come to lave
Her form of beauty in the water,
  And light with beauty's glance the wave.

The monarch's daughter saw and wept;
  (How lovely falls compassion's tear!)
The babe that there in quiet slept,
  Blest in unconsciousness of fear.
'Twas hers to pity and to aid
  The infant chief, the infant sage;
Undying fame the deed repaid,
  Recorded upon heaven's own page.

Years pass away, the land is free!
  Daughter of Zion! mourn no more!
The oppressor's hand is weak on thee,
  Captivity's dark reign is o'er.

43

Thy chains are burst; thy bonds are riven;
  On! like a river strong and wide:
A captain is to Judah given—
  The babe that slept by Nile's broad tide.

ANONYMOUS.

The Young Moses

THE world was at his feet . . ,
  But overhead, the stars!
From Luxor's roof he saw their light on pillared
  Karnak fall,
And knew what gods and ghosts of monarchs
Alien to his blood
Kept guard among the shadows there . . . .
While far upon the breathing plain
Hushed Memnon brooded, holding at his heart
A golden cry that trembled for the dawn . . . .
Upon a temple's roof at Thebes the young Moses
  stood
In commune with his dreams . . .

A kingdom at his feet . . .
Fostered of Pharaoh's daughter,
And a Prince in Egypt:
In statecraft, priestcraft, lifecraft, skilled:
Wise in his youth, and strong, and conscious of his
  powers:
Dowered with the patience and the passion that are
  genius:
Ambitious, favored, subtle, sure and swift—
Already Prince in Egypt!
And later, anything he willed . . .
Fledged early, with a soaring instinct in his wings.

He mused, and for an infinite moment
All the world streamed by him in a mist . . .

44

BIBLICAL AND POST-BIBLICAL

Cities and ships and nations,
Temples and armies, melted to a mist; and swirling
    past beneath the stars:
And a faint tumult filled his ears of trumpets and
    the clash of brazen arms,

The wind and sound of empire,
And he felt the mighty pulse of his own thought and
    will transmuted to the tread of marching hosts
That shook the granite hills,
And saw chained kings cringe by his chariots, lion-
    drawn . . .
And felt himself on Seti's throne and crowned with
    Seti's crown,
And all earth's rhythms beating to his sense of law,
And half earth's purple blood, if so he would, poured
    out to dye his robes with deeper splendor . . .
And all the iron delight of power was his . . .
This Egypt was a weapon to his hand,
This life was buoyant air, and his the eagle's plume.
For one measureless moment this vision moved and
    glittered,
Rushing by . . .
Master of men he knew himself; he thrilled;
There an empire at his feet.

But overhead, a God . . .
Implacable divinity that, as he looked, was of a sud-
    den manifest
In all the burning stars . . .
Relentless, searching spirit,
Cruel holiness that smote him with the agony of love,
Stern sweetness piercing to the soul,
Silence articulate that turned the universe to one un-
    spoken word,
Violent serenity that plucked at his roots of being . . .
And a voice that answered him before he questioned
    it . . .

For one eternal instant Moses stood,
The cup of empire lifted to his lips,
And struggled with the God that is not if we are not
    He . . .

And then . . . descended from the temple's roof,
And cast his princely trappings off,
And took his slow way through the shadowed town
Unto the quarter where an outcast people and op-
    pressed
Labored beneath the lash
And put their lives and hopes into the bricks because
    there was no straw,
And cast his lot in with those sickly slaves,
To lead them, if he might, from bondage . . .

                     ANONYMOUS.

Moses

I WILL sing high-hearted Moses
    By the Nile's sweet-watered stream,
In the land of strange taskmasters,
    Brooding o'er the patriot theme.

Brooding o'er the bright green valleys
    Of his dear-loved Hebrew home,
Whence the eager pinch of Famine
    Forced the Patriarch to roam.

Brooding o'er his people's burdens,
    Lifting vengeful arm to smite,
When he saw the harsh Egyptian
    Stint the Hebrew of his right.

Brooding far in lonely places,
    Where on holy ground unshod,
He beheld the bush that burned
    With consuming flame from God.

46

Saw, and heard, and owned the mission
  With his outstretched prophet-rod,
To stir plagues upon the Pharoah,
  Scorner of the most high God.

God, who brought His folk triumphant
  From the strange taskmaster free,
And merged the Memphians, horse and rider,
  In the deep throat of the sea.

Then uprose the song of triumph,
  Harp and timbrel, song and dance,
And with firm set will the hero
  Led the perilous advance.

And he led them through the desert
  As a shepherd leads his flock,
Breaking spears with cursed Amalek,
  Striking water from the rock.

And he led them to Mount Sinai's
  High-embattled rock; and there,
'Mid thick clouds of smoke and thunder,
  Like trumpet clave the air.

To the topmost peak he mounted,
  And with reverent awe unshod,
As a man with men discourseth,
  So he there communed with God.

Not in wild ecstatic plunges,
  Not in visions of the night,
Not in flashes of quick fancy,
  Darkness sown with gleams of light.

But in calm untroubled survey,
  As a builder knows his plan,
Face to face he knew Jehovah
  And His wondrous ways, with man.

Ways of gentleness and mercy,
　　Ways of vengeance strong to smite,
Ways of large unchartered giving,
　　Ever tending to the right.

In the presence of the Glory
　　What no mortal sees he saw,
And from hand that no man touches
　　Brings the tables of the Law.

Law that bound them with observance
　　Lest untutored wit might stray,
Each man where his private fancy
　　Led him in a wanton way.

Law that from the life redeemed them
　　Of loose Arabs wandering wild,
And to fruitful acres brought them
　　Where ancestral virtue toiled.

Law that dowered the chosen people
　　With a creed divinely true,
Which the subtle Greek and lordly Roman
　　Stooped to borrow from the Jew.

John Stuart Blackie.

On the Picture of the Finding of Moses by Pharaoh's Daughter

THIS picture does the story express
　　Of Moses in the bulrushes,
How lively the painter's hand
By colors makes us understand.
Moses that little infant is,
This figure is his sister. This
Fine stately lady is no less
A personage than a princess,

Daughter of Pharaoh, Egypt's king
Whom Providence did hither bring
This little Hebrew child to save.
See how near the perilous wave
He lies exposèd in the ark,
His rushy cradle, his frail bark!
Pharaoh, King of Egypt land,
In his greatness gave command
To his slaves they should destroy
Every new-born Hebrew boy.
This Moses was a Hebrew's son;
When he was born, his birth to none
His mother told, to none revealed
But kept her goodly child concealed.
Three months she hid him; then she wrought
With bulrushes this ark, and brought
Him in it to this river's side,
Carefully looking far and wide
To see that no Egyptian eye
Her ark-hid treasure should espy.
Among the river-flags she lays
The child. Near him his sister stays.
We may imagine her affright
When the King's daughter is in sight.
Soon the princess will perceive
The ark among the flags and give
Command to her attendant maid
That its contents shall be displayed.
Within the ark the child is found,
And now he utters mournful sound.
Behold he weeps as if he were
Afraid of Egypt's cruel heir!
She speaks, she says, "This little one
I will protect though he the son
Be of an Hebrew." Every word
She speaks is by the sister heard.
And now observe, this is the part
The painter chose to show his art.
Look at the sister's eager eye,

As here she seems advancing nigh.
Lowly she bends, says "Shall I go
And call a nurse for thee? I know
A Hebrew woman liveth near.
Great lady, shall I bring her here?"
See! Pharaoh's daughter answers "Go."
No more the painter's art can show.
He cannot make his figures move.
On the light wings of swiftest love
The girl will fly to bring the mother
To be the nurse. She'll bring no other.
To her will Pharaoh's daughter say,
"Take this from me away,
For wages nurse him." To my home
At proper age this child may come.
When to our palace he is brought,
Wise masters shall for him be sought
To train him up befitting one,
I would protect as my own son.
And Moses be a name unto him,
Because I from the waters drew him.

CHARLES and MARY LAMB.

Moses in the Desert

GO where a foot hath never trod,
    Through unfrequented forests flee;
The wilderness is full of God,
    His presence dwells in every tree.

To Israel and to Egypt dead,
    Moses the fugitive appears,
Unknown he lived, till o'er his head
    Had fallen the snow of fourscore years.

But God the wandering found
    In his appointed time and place,
The desert sand grew holy ground,
    And Horeb's rock a throne of grace.

The lonely bush a tree became,
  A tree of beauty and of light,
Involved with unconsuming flame
  That made the moon around it night.

Then came the Eternal voice that spake
  Salvation to the chosen seed,
Thence went the Almighty arm that brake
  Proud Pharaoh's yoke, and Israel freed.

By Moses, old and slow of speech,
  These mighty miracles were shown;
Jehovah's messenger! to teach
  That power belongs to God alone.
                    JAMES MONTGOMERY.

The Destroying Angel

HE stopped at last
  And a mild look of sacred pity cast
Down on the sinful land where he was sent
To inflict the tardy punishment.
"Ah! yet," said he, "Yet, stubborn king, repent,
Whilst thus armed I stand
Ere the keen sword of God fill my commanded hand.
Suffer but thyself and thine to live
Who would alas! believe
That it for man," said he
"So hard to be forgiven should be,
And yet for God so easy to forgive!"

Through Egypt's wicked land his march he took,
And as he marched, the sacred first-born strook
Of every womb; none did he spare,
None, from the meanest beast to Pharaoh's purple heir.
Whilst health and strength and gladness doth possess
The festal Hebrew cottages;

The blest destroyer comes not there
To interrupt the sacred cheer:
Upon their doors he read and understood.
God's protection writ in blood;
Well was he skilled in the character divine,
And though he passed·by it in haste,
He bowed and worshipped as he passed
The mighty mystery through its humble sign.

ABRAHAM COWLEY.

The Passover

'TIS night, dark night! a solemn stillness reigns
    O'er Egypt's land; the midnight hour is come,
Whilst Pharaoh's disobedience still detains
    Against God's will his people; such a doom
Ne'er fell on land, and ne'er will fall again,
    These were the words divine, which Moses gave
To Egypt's king and court; but all in vain.
    His heart is hardened, nothing now can save
The land from desolation; for 'twas He,
    The Immutable, who gave this dread command,
Death in his stead shall reign; Eternity
    Shall swallow up the first-born of the land.
But hard and harder grew the tyrant's heart;
    No fear of God had ever entered there;
    With Israel's children; how could man so dare,
Not love but tyranny, forbade him part
Against high Heaven's designs, his own to place,
    In competition! (what, but want of fear
Of that high Power, could with unblushing face
    Have made him tempt Omnipotence, and rear
His haughty head? but God in wisdom knew,
    In wisdom infinite divinely planned;
Th' Eternal mind already had in mind
    Glorious redemption—infinitely planned
Oh great deliverance! what love too great,
    What gratitude of ours can e'er repay

BIBLICAL AND POST-BIBLICAL

The mercy which released us from that state
    Of servile bondage and tyrannic sway?
In every house is silence most profound,
    Th' Egyptians sleep—not so the chosen race
Who, all prepared, now wait without a sound,
    Whilst anxious hope is pictured on each face.
Now suddenly along the midnight air
    A low and piteous wailing first is borne,
Then loud and fearful shrieks of sad despair
    Echo from house to house, where death has gone.
Swiftly upon the sable wing of night,
    The angel has gone forth; upon his brow
No pity can be traced; for in his sight
    The prince and meanest slave are equalled now.
Then Pharaoh's voice amid the general cry,
    In grief and haste for Moses loudly called,
Moses and Aaron he implored to fly,
    For death surrounds him, he stands appalled.
Then did the Israelites come forth as one,
    Their wives, their children—cattle in arrear
In silence and in haste their flight began;
    They marched triumphant, for their God was near.
He was their only guide by night and day,
    A cloud by day—a pillar of fire by night
Thus gloriously He led them on their way.
    And thus He ever keeps us in His sight.
Now scarce encamped besides the sea, they view,
    With dread and horror Pharaoh and his host,
His chariots and his horsemen all pursue
    To overtake them ere they reach the coast.
But what are human plans if God oppose,
    "Fear not," then Moses said, "but wait and see
Salvation of the Lord; for these our foes
    Will never more on earth be seen by thee."
He scarce had said, when at the voice of God
    The sea divides—they walk upon dry land,
Then, at the voice Divine, he lifts his rod—
    Two upright walls of sea majestic stand.

'The cloud, which until now, had gone before,
  Suddenly changes its resplendent light,
The Israelites now crossed—the sea once more
  Resumes its place, but in the Egyptians' sight
The light is darkness now; for all is seen
  Dark on that side, where Pharaoh's horsemen dash
On with rapid speed; while still between
  That cloud remains. A loud and fearful crash,
Another and another quick succeed,
  'Tis God who fights against them; vain the thought
To flee from Israel's face; for whence proceeds
  Such wond'rous power, if not from God who fought
On Israel's side? who safe had reached the shore
  Ere morning's faintest blush began to spread,
They saw the Egyptians sink to rise no more,
  Not one that was not numbered with the dead.
Then all the multitude, with one accord
  Joined Moses in a loud and heartfelt cry
Of gratitude and praises to the Lord;
  "They sang to Him who triumphed gloriously."

R. E. S.

Out of Egypt

THE flaming sunset bathed the distant hills
  In gold, the air was chill, and darkness fell
Upon the silent land. Then through the night
A cry of pain rose like a wave, and fell,
Again and yet again it soared aloft,
But dying to be born anew; a wail
Of anguish wild, of hoarse and deep despair
From countless hearts, who called unto their gods
With tears and sobs, with broken prayers in vain!
For death attired in red, with scourge and flail
Had swept through Egypt at the voice of God.
And as he passed behold his steps were stained
With blood. All first-born children in the land
Were dead. The Pharaoh and the shepherd mourned

54

Alike, for blood red tracks were traced from door
To door; from palace garden to the home
Of those who lived in pinch of utter want.
Then God spake, and the voices of the crowds
Were stilled: "I am the Lord. I am the Lord,
My children you have treated like the dust,
My chosen people you have bound with shame.
You hold them, and you would not let them go,
So I the Lord their God have taken all
The first-born in your land . . .
But Israel's children have I spared to live,
And death into their house hath entered not.
Repent, repent, and pray you be stiff-necked
And proud no more." Then ceased the voice of God.
And mourning into hatred turned, the fumes
Of passion smote upon their souls—"Begone,
Begone accursed of our sight, arise
And flee, lest we be all dead men; take gold,
And silver, flocks and herds, and leave us peace."
So Israel fled out in the night, and came
Not to that land again. And now once more
A silence fell, and stars of heaven gazed
Upon the stricken homes, upon the palm
Trees listening to the whisper of the wind,
Upon the silent Nile, upon the land
Of sin.
DOROTHEA DE PASS.

Psalm CXIV

WHEN Israel from proud Egypt's yoke
    Of bondage first came forth,
And the house of Jacob from the land
    Of strange tongues, in the North.

Judah His Sanctuary stood,
    And Israel proud was His domain,
. The Sea beheld, and straightway fled,
    And Jordan backward, drove amain.

55

Like mountains, skipped the wethers, then,
Like playful lambs, the mighty hills;
Oh Sea! Why flee'st thou about?
And, Jordan, whence thy tiny rills?

Ye Mountains, that ye skip apace,
Ye mighty hills, like tiny sheep;
The earth in trembling fears the Lord,
For Jacob's God 'tis now ye weep.

Who turneth to a watery pool
The hard unstable rock,
The flint unto a living fount
Of waters, for His flock.

MYRTILLA E. MITCHELL.

The Passage of the Red Sea

'MID the light spray their snorting camels stood,
Nor bathed a fetlock in the nauseous flood—
He comes—their leader comes!—the man of God
O'er the wide waters lifts His mighty rod.
And onward treads—the circling waves retreat
In hoarse deep murmurs, from his holy feet;
And the chased surges, inly roaring, show
The hard wet sand and coral hills below.
With limbs that falter, and with hearts that swell,
Down, down they pass—a steep and slippery dell.
Around them rise, in pristine chaos hurled,
The ancient rocks, the secrets of the world;
The flowers that blush beneath the ocean green,
And caves, the sea-calves' low-roofed haunt, are seen.
Down, safely down the narrow pass they tread;
The beetling waters storm above their head:
While far behind retires the sinking day,
And fades on Edom's hills its latest ray.
Yet not from Israel fled the friendly light,
Or dark to them or cheerless came the night,

Still in their van, along the dreadful road,
Blazed broad and fierce the brandished torch of God.
Its meteor glare a tenfold lustre gave
On the long mirror of the rosy wave:
While its blest beams a sunlike heat supply,
Warm every cheek, and dance in every eye—
To them alone—for Mizraim's wizard train
Invoke for light their monster gods in vain;
Clouds heaped on clouds their struggling sight confine,
And tenfold darkness broods above their line.
Yet on they fare, by reckless vengeance led,
And range unconscious through the ocean's bed.
Till midway now—that strange and fiery form
Showed his dread visage lightning through the storm;
With withering splendor blasted all their might,
And brake their chariot wheels and marred their cour-
    ser's flight.
"Fly, Mizraim, fly!"—From Edom's coral strand
Again the prophet stretched his dreadful wand:—
With one wild crash the thundering waters sweep,
And all is waves—a dark and lonely deep.

REGINALD HEBER.

The Destruction of Pharaoh

MOURN, Mizraim, mourn! The weltering
      wave
Wails loudly o'er Egyptia's brave
  Where, lowly laid, they sleep;
The salt sea rusts the helmet's crest;
The warrior takes his ocean-rest,
   Full far below the deep.
   The deep, the deep, the weary deep!
  Wail, wail, Egyptia! mourn and weep!
For many a mighty legion fell
Before the God of Israel.

Wake, Israel, wake the harp. The roar
Of ocean's wave on Mizraim's shore

Rolls now o'er many a crest.
Where, now, the iron chariot's sweep?
Where Pharaoh's host? Beneath the deep
    His armies take their rest.
Shout, Israel! Let the joyful cry
Pour forth the notes of victory;
High let it swell across the sea,
For Jacob's weary tribes are free!

JOHN RUSKIN.

The Passage of the Red Sea

ON the sand and sea-weed lying,
    Israel poured her doleful sighing,
While before the deep sea flowed,
And behind fierce Egypt rode,
To their fathers' God they prayed,
To the Lord of Hosts for aid.

On the margin of the flood
With lifted rod the prophet stood;
And the summoned east wind blew,
And aside it sternly threw
The gathered waves that took their stand,
Like crystal rocks, on either hand,
Or walls of sea-green marble piled
Round some irregular city wild.

Then the light of morning lay
On the wonder-paved way,
Where the treasures of the deep
In their caves of coral sleep.
The profound abysses, where
Was never sound from upper air,
Rang with Israel's chanted words:
King of king and Lord of lords!

Then, with bow and banner glancing,
On exulting Egypt came,

58

With her chosen horsemen prancing,
And her cars on wheels of flame,
In a rich and boastful ring,
All around her furious king.

But the Lord from out his cloud —
The Lord looked down upon the proud,
As the host drave heavily
Down the deep bosom of the sea.
With a quick and sudden swell
Prone the liquid ramparts fell;
Over horse and over car,
Over every man of war,
Over Pharaoh's crown of gold,
The loud thundering billows rolled.
As the level water spread,
Down they sank, they sank like lead,
Down without a cry or groan.
And the 'morning sun that shone
On myriads of bright-armed men,
Its meridian radiance then
Cast on a wide sea, heaving as of yore
Against a silent, solitary shore.
Then did Israel's maidens sing,
Then did Israel's timbrels ring,
To Him, the King of kings that in the sea
The Lord of lords had triumphed gloriously!

HENRY HART MILMAN.

Passage of the Red Sea

IN doubt, in weariness, in woe,
    The host of Israel flee;
Behind them rode the raging foe,
    Before them was the sea.

The angry waters at their feet,
    All dark and dread, rolled on;
And where the sky and desert meet,
    Spears flashed against the sun.

59

But still along the eastern sky
　The fiery pillar shone,
And o'er the waves that rolled so high
　It bade them still come on.

Then Moses turned the sea toward,
　And raised his hand on high;
The angry waters know their lord:
　They know him, and they fly.

Where never gleamed the red sunlight,
　Where foot of man ne'er trod,
Down, down they go, and left and right
　The wall of waters stood.

Full soon along that vale of fear,
　With cymbals, horns, and drums,
With many a steed and many a spear
　The maddening monarch comes.

A moment—far as eye could reach,
　The thronging myriads tread;
The next—the waste and silent deep
　Was rolling o'er their head.

ANONYMOUS.

The Song of Miriam

"Sing ye to the Lord, for he hath triumphed gloriously; the horse and his rider hath he thrown into the sea."—Exod. xv. 21.

YE daughters and soldiers of Israel look back!
　Where—where are the thousands that shadowed
　　your track,
The chariots that took the deep earth as they rolled
The banners of silk and the helmets of gold?

60

Where are they—the vultures whose beaks would have
    fed
On the tide of your hearts ere the pulses had fled?
Give glory to God, who in mercy arose,
And strewed 'mid the waters the strength of our foes.

When we traveled the waste of the desert by day,
With his banner-cloud's motion he marshalled the way:
When we saw the tired sun in his glory expire
Before he walked, in a pillar of fire.

But this morn, and the Israelites' strength was a reed
That shook with the thunder of chariot and steed,
Where now are the swords and their far-flashing
    sweep?
Their lightnings are quenched in the depth of the deep.

O thou, that redeemest the weak one at length
And scourgest the strong in the pride of their strength,
Who holdest the earth and the sea in thine hand,
And rulest Eternity's shadowy land—

To thee let our thoughts and our offerings tend,
Of virtue the Hope, and of sorrow the Friend.
Let the incense of prayer still ascend to thy throne,
Omnipotent—glorious—eternal—alone.

ANONYMOUS.

Sound the Loud Timbrel

SOUND the loud timbrel o'er Egypt's dark sea!
    Jehovah hath triumphed—His people are free.
Sing—for the pride of the tyrant is broken,
    His chariots, his horsemen, all splendid and brave,
How vain was their boasting—the Lord hath but
    spoken,
    And chariots and horsemen are sunk in the wave.
Sound the loud timbrel o'er Egypt's dark sea!
Jehovah has triumphed—His people are free.

Praise to the Conqueror, praise to the Lord,
His word was our arrow, His breath was our sword!—
Who shall return to tell Egypt the story
  Of those she sent forth in the hour of her pride?
For the Lord hath looked out from His pillar of glory,
  And all her brave thousands are dashed in the tide.
Sound the loud timbrel o'er Egypt's dark sea!
Jehovah has triumphed—His people are free.

THOMAS MOORE.

Song at the Red Sea

Exodus xv. 1

SING to Jehovah, who gloriously triumphs,
  The God of our fathers, the God of the free!
For Jah is our strength, our song and salvation!
  The horse and his rider are drowned in the sea!

The Lord is a warrior, His name is Jehovah!
  Thy right hand, O Lord! is exalted in might!
Thou dashest in pieces the foes of Thy people!
  Thy wrath has consumed them and swept them to
    night!

The chariots of Pharaoh, his captains and princes,
  The hosts of oppression, the legions of wrong,
The blast of Thy nostrils with floods overwhelms them,
  And Israel shouts in her thunders of song!

What God of the nations is like to Jehovah?
  Glorious in holiness, fearful in praise!
All people shall fear Him, all ages adore Him!
  He reigns in His glory, through infinite days!

GEORGE LANSING TAYLOR.

The First Song of Moses

Exodus xv

I

NOW shall the praises of the Lord be sung;
　For he a most renowned Triumph won:
Both horse and men into the sea he flung,
　And them together there hath overthrown.
The Lord is he whose strength doth make me strong
And he is my salvation and my song:
My God, for whom I will a house prepare
My father's God whose praise I will declare.

II

Well knows the Lord to war what doth pertain,
　The Lord Almighty is his glorious name;
He Pharaoh's chariots, and his arméd train
　Amid the sea o'erwhelming, overcame;
Those of his army that are most renowned
He hath together in the Red Sea drown'd,
The deeps a covering over them were thrown,
And to the bottom sunk they like a stone.

III

Lord, by thy power thy right hand famous grows;
　Thy right hand, Lord, thy foe destroyéd hath;
Thy glory thy opposers overthrows,
　And stubble-like consumes them in thy wrath.
A blast but from thy nostrils forth did go
And up together did the waters flow;
Yea, rolled up on heaps the liquid flood
Amid the sea, as if congealéd, stood.

IV

I will pursue them (their pursuer cried),
　I will o'ertake them, and the spoil enjoy;
My lust upon them shall be satisfied;
　With sword unsheathed my hand shall them de-
　　stroy.

Then from thy breath a gale of wind was sent;
The billows of the sea quite o'er them went.
And they the mighty waters sunk into
E'en as a weighty piece of lead will do.

V

Lord, who like thee among the Gods is there!
  In holiness so glorious who may be!
Whose praises so exceeding dreadful are!
  In doing wonders, who can equal thee!
Thy glorious right hand thou on high didst rear,
And in the earth they quickly swallowed were,
But thou in mercy onward hast conveyed
Thy people, whose redemption thou hast paid.

VI

Them by thy strength thou hast been pleased to bear
  Unto a holy dwelling place of thine;
The nations at report thereof shall fear,
  And grieve shall they that dwell in Palestine.
On Edom's princes shall amazement fall;
The mighty men of Moab tremble shall
And such as in the land of Canaan dwell,
Shall pine away, of this when they hear tell.

VII

They shall be seized with a horrid fear.
  Stone-quiet thy right hand shall make them be,
Till passed over, Lord, thy people are;
  Till those pass over, that were brought by thee.
For thou shalt make them to thy hill repair,
And plant them there (O Lord) where thou art heir,
E'en there where thou thy dwelling hast prepared,
That holy place which thine own hands have reared.

VIII

The Lord shall ever and forever reign,
  His sovereignty shall never have an end:

For when as Pharaoh did into the main
  With chariots and with horsemen, down descend,
The Lord did back again the sea recall,
And with those waters overwhelm'd them all.
But through the very inmost of the same
The seed of Israel safe and dry-shod came.

              GEORGE WITHER.

Miriam

OH, for that day, that day of bliss entrancing
  When Israel stood, her night of bondage o'er.
And leaped in heart to see no more advancing
  Egypt's dark host along the desert shore;
For scarce a ripple now proclaimed where lay
The boasting Pharaoh and his fierce array.

Miriam! she silent stood, that sight beholding,
  And bowed with sacred awe her wondering head.
Till lo! No more their hideous spoils withholding
  The depths indignant, spurned their buried dead;
And all along that sad and vengeful coast
Pale corpses lay,—a monumental host.

Miriam! She saw; then all to life awaking,—
  "Sing to the Lord," with a great voice she cried;
"Sing to the Lord," their many timbrels shaking,
  Ten thousand ransomed hearts and tongues replied;
While, leading on the dance in triumph long
Thus the great Prophetess broke forth in song:

      "Oh, sing to the Lord,
        Sing his triumph right glorious;
      "O'er horse and rider
        Sing his right arm victorious;
      Pharaoh's horsemen and chariots
        And captains so brave,
      The Lord hath thrown down
        In the bottomless wave.

"Man of war is the Lord
  And Jehovah is His name;
We trusted his pillar
  Of cloud and of flame.
Proud boasters, ye followed
  But where have ye gone?
Down, down in the waters
  Ye sank like a stone.

"O Lord thou didst blow
  With thy nostrils a blast
And upheaved, the huge billows
  Like mountains stood fast!
Egypt shuddered with wonder
  That pathway to see,
Those depths all congealed
  In the heart of the sea.

" 'I, too, will march onward'
  (The enemy cried)
I shall soon overtake
  I, the spoil will divide
I will kill'—O my God!
  The depths fell at thy breath
And like lead they went down
  In those waters of death.

"But o'er us the soft wings
  Of thy mercy outspread,
To thine own chosen dwelling
  Our feet have been led.
Palistrina, affrighted,
  The tidings shall hear,
And your hearts, O ye nations,
  Shall wither with fear.

"Thus brought in with triumph
  Safe planted and blessed
On thy own holy mountain
  Thy people shall rest.

66

Shout! Pharaoh is fallen
  To rise again never.
Sing! The Lord he shall reign
  Forever and ever."

             E. DUDLEY JACKSON.

Exodus x: 21-23

WHEN Israel dwelt in Egypt's land,
  And groan'd beneath the tyrant's pow'r,
O Lord, 'twas Thine Almighty hand
  Sustain'd him thro' that dreary hour.
When all the air at noon of day
  Was filled with gloom "which might be felt,"
Thy smile was still a cheerful ray
  In every tent where Israel dwelt.

And thus, O Lord, the faithful heart
  Believes that it will ever be;
Thy love, we know, will ne'er depart
  From those who truly trust in Thee.
When all the world grows dark through sin,
With them Thy smile will still be found;
Diffusing joy and peace within,
  While all seems dark and cheerless round!

             J. W. BURGON.

Mount Sinai

FROM Sinai's top the lightnings flashed;
  The thunders rolled around—around—
As if the heavenly orbs had clashed
  Together with destructive bound,
And down their shattered fragments hurled
Upon a desolated world.

And on the mount there hung a cloud,
  Dark as the midnight's darkest gloom;
And blew a trumpet long and loud,
  Like that which shall wake the tomb.
And terror like a sudden frost
Fell on the Israelitish host.

In radiant fire the mighty God
  Descended from the heavenly throne;
And on the mountains where He trod,
  A pavement as of sapphire stone
Appeared like glittering stars of even
When storms have left the deep-blue heaven.

And as the wondering people turned
  To see the glory of the Lord,
The smoke—as if a furnace burned
  Within the mountain, swelled and roared,
And all its lofty summits shook
Like sedge leaves by the summer brook.

And Moses from the trembling crowd
  Went up to God's dark secret place
And heard from the surrounding cloud
  His message to the Hebrew race,
Who vowed with fervor and accord
To keep the covenant of the Lord.

For they had marked the trump that blew
  The fires that gleamed, the peals that roared—
In shadowed glory shine to view
  The presence of the eternal Lord,
Bright as His mercy chose to give,
For none can see His face and live.

                    HORATIUS BONAR.

At Sinai

DOWN from the mist-clad mountain Moses came,
  His face aglow with some strange inward flame—
Down the long slope with winged feet he trod,
And vision clear, for he had talked with God!

Before the mount he saw his people stand,
As he had bidden. Slow he raised his hand—
A solemn stillness bound them as they saw,
Their restive hearts athrill with reverent awe.

Deep was his voice and tender. E'en the birds
Poised on their moveless wings to hear his words.
From out the misty cloud that wraps the hill,
There came the voice of God, so small and still.

And thus it said: "These words to Israel bring:
As I have borne them forth on eagle's wing
From Egypt's bonds, so will I guard them still
If they obey my voice, and do my will.

"Yea, Israel shall a priestly people be,
A most peculiar treasure unto Me;
If they do heed the Law that I do give.
My people, say! Will ye obey and live?"

With hands uplifted stood the leader there,
His face ablaze! And on the desert air
There rose a murmur swelling loud and true,
"All that the Lord doth bid us, will we do!"

So went he once again within the mist
That hid the somber mountain, grey, cloud-kissed;
And as they watched, the waiting people saw
Him come again, and in his arms, the Law!

Thus came the Word—and thus the right to hear
The message, that the world might know and share.
Yea, theirs the gift! But theirs the promise, too.
Whate'er the Lord hath spoken, that we'll do.

Tho' there at Sinai's foot, in age long dead,
Our fathers hath the sacred covenant said,
Their blood 'is ours! and their promise true!
Whate'er the Lord hath bidden, shall we do!

ISABELLA R. HESS.

Divine Love

"And thou shalt love the Lord thy God with all
thine heart and with all thy soul, and with all thy
might."—Deut. vi, 5.

I KNOW not what this world would be
  (Not even by analogy)
If love were banished for a time
To other realm, or other clime;
But no, it is not bound by space,
But with illimitable grace
Glides through all worlds, and lives in all,
All hearts and souls it does enthral;
Some, where the spirit seldom dwelt
'Tis not quite banished or forgot;
It were indeed a dreary spot
Without one single ray of love,
That heavenly blessing from above,
For what were virtue, goodness, truth,
Without the light of love? in sooth
They would not be—they could not last
Without this heavenly antepast;
This foretaste of celestial love
Vicegerent here, but crowned above.
Oh! love, thou pure and holy thing,
What are the blessings thou dost bring?
Nay, rather, what is happiness
But love in some new guise or dress?
Even from birth 'tis love that fills
Each avenue of soul—instils

Its spiritual influence
And makes us all love excellence,
Whatever bears the noble stamp
Of great and good; 'tis this pure lamp
Which lights our path and gives us hope,
Extends our views to higher scope.
We love to read, to hear, to earn,
And why? because our spirits burn.

ANONYMOUS.

"Moses as Lamp-Bearer"

A CURIOUS fancy seized on Moses' soul,
  To know if God, the Lord, slept like a man:
So Allah sent an angel from on high,
Who to the Holy Prophet this wise spake—
"Take, Moses, in thy hands two burning lamps,
Then take thy stand and hold thyself upright,
With both arms stretched full length, and keep them
    so;
And watch then the whole night through and
    through."
Then Moses took the lamps and placed himself
And held them fast on high a long, long time.
But at the last such weariness came on him,
That the lamps fell to earth from out his hands.
"Thus," cried the angel, "thus, O simple man,
Thus would the sun and moon and starry host,
Thus would the joined fabric of the world
In waste and ruin fall, did Allah sleep!"

WILLIAM STIGAND.

Aaron's Breastplate

"Aaron shall bear their names before the Lord
upon his two shoulders for a memorial. . . . Aaron
shall bear the names of the children of Israel in the
breast-plate of judgment upon his heart, for a me-

71

morial before the Lord continually."—Exodus xxvii.
12, 29.

IN the wondrous breastplate golden,
　Safely on His bosom holden,
　　See the jewels from the mine!
Amethyst and onyx wearing
Mystic marks, and each one bearing
　　Traces of the hand divine.

Sapphires 'mid the gorgeous cluster
Sparkle with celestial luster,
　Like the crystal dome above;
Ruby rare and topaz blending
In that glory never-ending,
　Safe upon the breast of love.

Emerald and beryl throwing
Chastened hues, the fairer growing
　As the jasper blends the rays.
Chrysoprase, like kings' attire
Glowing like a star of fire,
　Or a soul that loves to praise.

Who the love and praise can measure
Ere revealed this hidden treasure
　One by one in dazzling light!
On his breast our High Priest wears them,
On his shoulder, see he bears them,
　Ever in our Father's sight.
　　　　　　　　　ANNA SHIPTON.

Lights in the Temple

"And Aaron shall burn thereon sweet incense every
morning; when he dresseth the lamps he shall burn
incense upon it. And when Aaron lighteth the lamps
at even, he shall burn incense upon it; a perpetual

incense before the Lord, throughout your genera-
tions."—Exod. xxx. 7, 8.

NOW the stars are lit in heaven,
    We must light our lamps on earth;
Every star a signal given
    From the God of our new birth:
Every lamp an answer faint,
Like the prayer of mortal Saint.

Mark the hour and turn this way,
    Sons of Israel, far and near!
Wearied with the world's dim day,
    Turn to Him whose eyes are here,
Open, watching day and night,
Beaming unapproachéd light!

With sweet oil-drops in His hour
    Feed the branch of many lights,
Token of protecting power,
    Pledg'd to faithful Israelites,
Emblem of the anointed Home,
When the glory deigns to come.

Watchers of the sacred flame,
    Sons of Aaron! serve in fear,—
Deadly is th' avenger's aim,
    Should th' unhallowed enter here;
Keen his fires, should recreants dare
Breathe the pure and fragrant air.

There is One will bless your toil—
    He who comes in Heaven's attire,
Morn by morn, with holy oil;
    Eve by eve, with holy fire!
Pray!—your prayer will be allowed,
Mingling with His incense cloud!

                JOHN KEBLE.

73

Bezalel

BEZALEL, filled with wisdom to design
   Stones, precious wood, rich-embroidered fabrics,
     gold,
Fed not the few with cunning manifold
Nor empty loveliness; his art divine
Set up a tabernacle as a sign
Of oneness for a rabble many-souled,
So that each span of desert should behold
A nomad people with a steadfast shrine.

But we, its sons, who wander in the dark,
   Footsore, far-scattered, growing less and less,
What whiteness glooms our brotherhood to mark,
   What promised land our journey's end to bless!
We are, unless we build some shrine or ark,
   A dying rabble in a wilderness.

ISRAEL ZANGWILL.

Moses and the Angel

*Praise Him, Al-Mutahali! Whose decree is wiser
than the wit of man can see*

'TIS written in the chapter of "the Cave,"
   An Angel of the Lord, a minister,
Had errands upon earth, and Moses said,
"Grant me to wend with thee, that I may learn
God's ways with men." The Angel answering, said:
"Thou canst not bear with me; thou wilt not have
Knowledge to judge; yet if thou followest me,
Question me not, whatever I shall do,
Until I tell thee."

               Then they found a ship
On the sea-shore, wherefrom the Angel struck
Her boards and brake them. Moses said, "Wilt drown

74

The mariners? This is a strange thing wrought!";
"Did I not say thou couldst not bear with me?"
The Angel answered—"Be thou silent now!"

Yet farther, and they met an Arab boy;
Upon his eyes with mouth invisible
The Angel breathed; and all his warm blood froze,
And, with a moan, he sank to earth and died.
Then Moses said, "Slayest thou the innocent
Who did no wrong? this is a hard thing seen!"
"Did I not tell thee," said the Minister,
"Thou wouldst not bear with me? Question me
    not!"

Then came they to a village, where there stood
A lowly hut; the garden-fence thereof
Toppled to fall; the Angel thrust it down.
A ruin of gray stones, and lime, and tiles,
Crushing the lentils, melons, saffron, beans,
The little harvest of the cottage folk.
"What hire," asked Moses, "hadst thou for this deed,
Seeming so evil?"

                                    Then the Angel said,
"This is the parting betwixt me and thee:
Yet will I first make manifest the things
Thou couldst not bear, not knowing, that my Lord—
'Exalted above all reproach'—be praised.

The ship I broke serveth poor fisherfolk
Whose livelihood was lost, because there came
A king that way seizing all boats found whole:
Now they have peace. Touching the Arab boy,
In two moons he had slain his mother's son,
Being perverse; but now his brother lives
Whose life unto his tribe was more, and he
Dieth blood-guiltless. For the garden wall,
Two goodly youths dwell there, offspring of one
That loved his Lord, and underneath the stones

The father hid the treasure, which is theirs.
This shall they find, building their ruin up,
And joy will come upon their house!
       But thou,
Journey no more with me, because I do,
Nought of myself, but all by Allah's will."
                    EDWIN ARNOLD.

Moses and the Dervish

GOD, that heaven's seven climates hath spread
    forth,
To every creature, even as is the worth,
The lot apportions, and the use of things.
If to the creeping cat were given wings
No sparrow's egg would ever be a bird.

Moses the Prophet, who with God conferred,
Beheld a Dervish, that, for dire distress
And lack of clothes to hide his nakedness
Buried his body in the desert sand.
This Dervish cried:
            "O Moses, whom the Hand
Of the Most High God favors! make thy prayer
That he may grant me food and clothes to wear
Who knows the misery of me and the need."

Then Moses prayed to God, that he would feed
And clothe that Dervish.
           Nine days after this,
Returning from Mount Sinai in bliss,
Having beheld God's face, the Prophet met
The Dervish in the hands of Justice, set
Between two officers; and all about
The rabble followed him with hoot and shout
And jeer.
The Prophet asked of those that cried,
"What hath befallen this man?"
           And they replied,

"He hath drunk wine, and having slain a man,
Is going to the death."

                        Moses began
To praise the Maker of the Universe,
Seeing that his prayer, though granted, proved per-
    verse,
Since God to every living soul sets forth
The circumstance according to the worth.
                        OWEN MEREDITH.

The "Moses" of Michael Angelo

AND who is He that sculptured in huge stone,
    Sitteth a giant, where no works arrive
Of straining Art, and hath so prompt and live
The lips, I hasten to their very tone?
Moses is He—Ay, that makes clearly known
    The chin's thick boast, and brow's prerogative
Of double ray; so did the mountain give
Back to the world that visage, God was grown
Great part of! Such was he when he suspended
    Round him the sounding and vast waters; such
When he shut sea on sea o'er Mizraim.
And ye, his hordes, a vile calf raised, and bended
    The knee? This Image had ye raised, not much
Had been your error in adoring Him.
                      ROBERT BROWNING.

Moses on Mount Nebo

I

HE stood on Nebo's lofty crest,
    Above him arched the azure sky,
Beneath the valley was at rest,
    A gem in Nature's pageantry;
Behind him lay the toil of years,
    And chains of bondage meekly borne,
And pathways moistened with his tears—
    A life of many a pleasure shorn.

77

II

No more for him the drowsy Nile,
  Where long had slaved God's chosen race,
No more the swarth Egyptian's guile,
  The trembling hand, the haggard face;
For he had led his brethren far
  Beyond the whip, beyond the chain,
And now beneath the brightest star
  Lay Canaan sweet with hill and plain.

III

He saw that land whose portals fair
  Would never open to his tread,
And Jordan old was flowing where
  He ne'er would rest his weary head;
And Amram's son from Nebo's crest
  Gazed long upon the matchless scene;
An untold longing filled his breast
  To reach the promised pastures green.

IV

He knew that on the mountain high,
  Far from the vale that slept below,
'Neath heaven's softest canopy
  The ceaseless years would o'er him go;
That Israel, anchored safe at last,
  Where Jordan singing, sought the sea.
With toil and danger ever past,
  Would, thro' God's watchful care, be free.

V

In sweet communion with his God
  Stood Israel's leader true and bold;
His grave was not to be the sod
  Where Canaan's rose its petals fold;
He bowed his head and looked no more,
  Perchance he for a moment wept;
He knew the pilgrimage was o'er.
  God touched him gently and he slept.

VI

No mortal eye hath found the place
  Where Moses laid his mantle down.
For high on Nebo's rugged face,
  His service done, he won the crown;
Jehovah made that lonely grave
  And left His servant old alone;
Afar from Jordan's sunlit wave
  He sleeps, his sepulchre unknown.

I. SOLOMON.

The Kiss of God

WHEN the great leader's task was done,
  He stood on Pisgah's height,
And saw, far off, the westering sun
  Drop down into the night;

Saw, too, the land in which, alas!
  He might not hope to dwell
Spread fairly out; and then—for so
  Talmudic legends tell—.

Jehovah touched him and he slept;
  And smooth the mountain sod
Was levelled o'er him and 'twas writ
  "Died by the kiss of God."

The kiss of God! We talk of death
  In many learned ways,—
We know so much,—which of them all
  So simple in its praise

As this which from the oldest days
  Has treasured been apart,
To comfort in this heel of time
The mourner's aching heart?

79

We walk our bright or desert road
　And, when we reach the end,
Bends o'er us with gentle face
　The Universal Friend.

Upon our lips his own are laid:
　We do not strive or cry.
The kiss of God! Upon that kiss
　It is not hard to die.
　　　　　　　　JOHN WHITE CHADWICK.

Weep, Children of Israel

WEEP, weep for him, the man of God,—
　In yonder vale he sunk to rest;
But none of earth can point the sod
　That flowers above his sacred breast.
Weep, children of Israel, weep!

His doctrine fell like heaven's rain,
　His words refreshed like heaven's dew—
Oh, ne'er shall Israel see again
　A chief, to God and her so true.
Weep, children of Israel, weep!

Remember ye his parting gaze,
　His farewell song by Jordan's tide,
When, full of glory and of days,
　He saw the promised land—and died.
Weep, children of Israel, weep!

Yet died he not as men who sink,
　Before our eyes to soulless clay;
But, changed to spirit, like a wink
　Of summer lightning pass'd away.
Weep, children of Israel, weep!
　　　　　　　　THOMAS MOORE.

"No Man Knoweth His Sepulchre"

WHEN he who, from the scourge of wrong,
    Aroused the Hebrew tribes to fly,
Saw the fair region promised long,
    And bowed him on the hills to die;

God made his grave, to men unknown,
    Where Moab's rocks a vale infold,
And laid the aged seer alone,
    To slumber while the world grows old.

Thus still, whene'er the good and just
    Close the dim eye on life and pain,
Heaven watches o'er their sleeping dust
    Till the pure spirit comes again.

Though nameless, trampled, and forgot,
    His servant's humble ashes lie,
Yet God has marked and scaled the spot,
    To call its inmate to the sky.

              WILLIAM CULLEN BRYANT.

Burial of Moses

"And he buried him in a valley in the land of Moab,
over against Beth-peor; but no man knoweth of his
sepulchre unto this day."

BY Nebo's lonely mountain,
    On this side Jordan's wave,
In a vale in the land of Moab,
    There lies a lonely grave;
But no man built that sepulchre,
    And no man saw it e'er;
For the angels of God upturned the sod,
    And laid the dead man there.

That was the grandest funeral
  That ever passed on earth;
Yet no man heard the trampling,
  Or saw the train go forth;
Noiselessly as the daylight
  Comes when the night is done,
And the crimson streak on ocean's cheek
  Grows into the great sun;

Noiselessly as the spring time
  Her crown of verdure weaves,
And all the trees on all the hills
  Unfold their thousand leaves:
So without sound of music
  Or voice of them that wept,
Silently down from the mountain's crown
  The great procession swept.

Perchance the bald old eagle
  On gray Beth-peor's height
Out of his rocky eyry
  Looked on the wondrous sight;
Perchance the lion stalking
  Still shuns that hallowed spot;
For beast and bird have seen and heard
  That which man knoweth not.

But, when the warrior dieth,
  His comrades of the war,
With arms reversed and muffled drums,
  Follow the funeral car:
They show the banners taken;
  They tell his battles won;
And after him lead his masterless steed,
  While peals the minute-gun.

Amid the noblest of the land
  Men lay the sage to rest,
And give the bard an honored place,
  With costly marbles drest,

In the great minster transept
  Where lights like glories fall,
And the sweet choir sings, and the organ rings
  Along the emblazoned hall.

This was the bravest warrior
  That ever buckled sword;
This the most gifted poet
  That ever breathed a word;
And never earth's philosopher
  Traced with his golden pen
On the deathless page truths half so sage
  As he wrote down for men.

And had he not high honor?—
  The hillside for a pall!
To lie in state while angels wait,
  With stars for tapers tall!
And the dark rock-pines, like tossing plumes,
  Over his bier to wave,
And God's own hand, in that lonely land,
  To lay him in his grave!—

In that strange grave without a name,
  Whence his uncoffined clay
Shall break again—O wondrous thought!—
  Before the judgment-day,
And stand, with glory wrapped around,
  On the hills he never trod,
And speak of the strife that won our life
  In the heavenly peace of God.

O lonely tomb in Moab's land!
  O dark Beth-peor's hill!
Speak to these curious hearts of ours,
  And teach them to be still:
God hath his mysteries of grace,
  Ways that we cannot tell,
He hides them deep, like the secret sleep
  Of him he loved so well.

CECIL FRANCES ALEXANDER.

83

Ode to the Statue of Moses

The Masterpiece of Michael Angelo

STATUE! whose giant limbs
      Old Buanorotti planned,
And Genius carved with meditative hand,
      Thy dazzling radiance dims
The best and brightest boast of sculpture's favorite
    land.
      What dignity adorns
      That beard's prodigious sweep!
That forehead, awful with mysterious horns
      And cogitation deep,
Of some uncommon mind the rapt beholder warns.

      In that proud semblance, well
      My soul can recognize
The prophet fresh from converse with the skies;
      Nor is it hard to tell
The liberator's name, the guide of Israel.

      Well might the deep respond
      Obedient to that voice,
When on the Red Sea shore he waved his wand
      And bade the tribes rejoice,
Saved from the yawning gulf and the Egyptian's
    bond!

      Fools! in the wilderness
      Ye raised a calf of gold,
Had ye then worshipped what I now behold
      Your crime had been far less—
For ye had bent the knee to one of godlike mould!

                  ANONYMOUS.

"Speak, Lord, for Thy Servant Heareth"

HUSH'D was the evening hymn,
  The temple courts were dark;
The lamp was burning dim
  Before the sacred ark:
When suddenly a voice Divine
Rang through the silence of the shrine.

The old man, meek and mild,
  The priest of Israel slept;
His watch, the temple child,
  The little Levite kept.
And what from Eli's sense was seal'd
The Lord to Hannah's son reveal'd.

Oh! give me Samuel's ear,
  The open ear, O Lord.
Alive and quick to hear
  Each whisper of Thy word;
Like him to answer at Thy call
And to obey Thee first of all.

Oh! give me Samuel's heart,
  A lovely heart that waits;
Where in thy house Thou art,
  Or watches at Thy gates.
By day and night, a heart that still
Moves at the breathing of Thy will.

Oh! give me Samuel's mind,
  A sweet unmurmuring faith,
Obedient and resign'd.
  To Thee in life and death.
That I may read with child-like eyes,
Truths that are hidden from the wise.

                    JAMES DRUMMOND BORTHWICK.

Jephthah's Daughter

SINCE our country, our God—oh, my sire!
Demand that thy daughter expire;
Since thy triumph was bought by thy vow—.
Strike the bosom that's bared for thee now!

And the voice of my mourning is o'er,
And the mountains behold me no more.
If the hand that I love lay me low
There cannot be pain in the blow!

And of this, O my father! be sure—
That the blood of thy child is as pure
As the blessing I beg ere it flow,
And the last thought that soothes me below.

Though the virgins of Salem lament,
Be the judge and the hero unbent!
I have won the great battle for thee,
And my father and country are free.

When this blood of thy giving hath gush'd,
When the voice that thou lovest is hush'd,
Let my memory still be thy pride;
And forget not I smiled as I died.

LORD BYRON.

Jephthah's Daughter

"And it became a custom in Israel that the daughters of Israel went from year to year to lament for the daughter of Jephthah, the Gileadite, four days in the year."—Judges xi.

THERE is a lonely mountain-top,
A curse upon it lies;
No blade of grass upon it grows,
No flowers greet the eyes.

86

But cold, bare cliffs of granite stand,
　Like sentinels of stone,
Year after year, through wind and snow,
　Around a craggy throne.

And on the topmost, coldest peak
　There is a spot of woe—
A little tomb, an old gray tomb,
　Raised centuries ago.

For there within her grave she lies
　Plucked in an evil hour—
The martyred daughter of her race,
　Israel's fairest flower!

There Jephthah's maid forever sleeps—
　The victim that he vowed—
But, four days in the dreary year,
　The loneliness is loud.

And Gilead's mourning daughters
　Up from the valley throng—
The mountain glens reverberate
　With sorrow and with song!

Oh, loud and long and wild they wail
　The light untimely spent,
And dance upon the mountain-top
　A choral of lament.

And as they dance they seem to see
　Another dancer, too,
And hear, amidst the measure rise,
　The voice of her they rue!

　　　　　　JEHOASH.
　　　　(Translated by Alter Brody.)

Samson

(From "Samson Agonistes")

O WHEREFORE was my birth from heaven fore-
    told
Twice by an angel, who at last, in sight
Of both my parents, all in flames ascended
From off the altar, where an offering burned,
As in a fiery column charioting
His godlike presence, and from some great act
Or benefit revealed to Abraham's race?
Why was my breeding ordered and prescribed
As of a person separate to God,
Destined for great exploits, if I must die
Betrayed, captive, and both my eyes put out,
Made of my enemies the scorn and gaze;
To grind in brazen fetters under task
With this Heaven-gifted strength? O glorious
    strength,
Put to the labor of a beast, debased
Lower than bond-slave! Promise was, that I
Should Israel from Philistian yoke deliver;
Ask for this great deliverer now, and find him
Eyeless in Gaza, at the mill with slaves,
Himself in bonds under Philistine yoke.

                JOHN MILTON.

Ruth

SHE stood breast-high amid the corn,
    Clasped by the golden light of morn,
Like the sweetheart of the sun,
Who many a glowing kiss had won.

On her cheek an autumn flush
Deeply ripened;—such a blush
In the midst of brown was born
Like red poppies grown with corn.

Round her eyes her tresses fell,—
Which were blackest none could tell;
But long lashes veiled a light
That had else been all too bright.

And her hat with shaded brim,
Made her tressy forehead dim—
Thus she stood among the stooks,
Praising God with sweetest looks.

Sure, I said, Heaven did not mean
Where I reap thou shouldst but glean;
Lay thy sheaf adown and come
Share my harvest and my home.

THOMAS HOOD.

Ruth and Naomi

FAREWELL? Oh, no! It may not be;
My firm resolve is heard on high!
I will not breathe farewell to thee,
Save only in my dying sigh.
I know not that I now could bear
Forever from thy side to part,
And live without a friend to share
The treasured sadness of my heart.

I will not boast the martyr's might
To leave my home without a sigh,—
The dwelling of my past delight,
The shelter where I hoped to die.
In such a duty, such an hour,
The weak are strong, the timid brave,
For love puts on an angel's power,
And faith grows mightier than the grave.

For rays of heaven serenely bright
Have gilt the caverns of the tomb;

And I can ponder with delight
 On all its gathering thoughts of gloom.
Then, mother, let us haste away
 To that blest land to Israel given,
Where faith unsaddened by decay
 Dwells nearest to its native heaven.

For where thou goest, I will go;
 With thine my earthly lot is cast.
In pain and pleasure, joy and woe,
 Will I attend thee to the last.
That hour shall find me by thy side,
 And where thy grave is, mine shall be;
Death can but for a time divide
 My firm and faithful heart from thee.
    WILLIAM OLIVER BOURN PEABODY.

Ruth

LEAVE thee alone in sorrow! Ask me not,
 Oh, mother of my dead love, I entreat;
Although I fain would linger near the spot
 Where rests one I on earth no more shall greet.

Should we who shared our pleasures side by side,
 Apart in sorrow and bereavement be?
No; I will cleave to thee, whate'er betide,
 Knowing no comfort, unless shared with thee.

Then seek not to divide my path from thine;
 Tread not alone thy journey, full of woe;
For his dear sake thy people shall be mine,
 And whither thou goest will I also go.
    H. HYMAN.

Ruth

THE plume-like swaying of the auburn corn
 By soft winds to a dreamy motion fann'd,
Still brings me back thine image—Oh! forlorn
 Yet not forsaken Ruth—I see thee stand

90

Lone 'midst the gladness of the harvest band——
    Lone as the wood-bird on the ocean's foam,
Fall'n in its weariness. Thy fatherland
    Smiles far away! yet to the sense of home,
That finest, purest, which can recognize
    Home in affection's glance, for ever true
Beats thy calm heart; and if thy gentle eye
    Gleam tremulous through tears, 'tis not to rue
Those words, immortal in their deep Love's tone,
    "Thy people and thy God shall be mine own."

                  FELICIA HEMANS.

The Moabitess

SWEET Moab gleaner on old Israel's plain,
    Thy simple story moveth like a power.
Thy pure, calm face looks from the ripened grain,
Wherein thou gleanest, on our toil and pain,
And in the light of thy soft eyes again
    Our dead lives bud and blossom into flower.
But lives like thine, sweet Ruth, are holy things,
    Rich, simple, earnest in their wealth of duty;—
God's love forever to their music sings,
His angels shield them with their sheltering wings,
His spirit truth and trust and comfort brings,
    And God Himself smiles on their godlike beauty.

                  PHILLIPS BROOKS.

Ruth and Naomi

A RABBI'S child and Puritan's once met;
    And, like those fabled mates, with each a
        wing,
That only soar when they together cling,
These comrades happy joined in mutual debt
For rich ancestral stores most alien. Yet
    As greatest pleasures know no lasting spring—
    Death came; but sunny Mem'ry comforting,
In tears with brightest rays her rainbow set;

Might Naomi not often glean with Ruth,
And thus give time a double joy and worth?
  It takes the each and all from every clime
To cull auspiciously the seeds of truth;
To win anew a Paradise for earth
  And reap in joy the harvest—truth sublime.
LOWELL COURIER.

Song of Saul Before His Last Battle

WARRIORS and chiefs! should the shaft or the
          sword
Pierce me in leading the host of the Lord,
Heed not the corpse, though a king's, in your path,
Bury your steel in the bosom of Gath!

Thou who art bearing my buckler and bow,
Should the soldiers of Saul look away from the foe,
Stretch me that moment in blood at thy feet!
Mine be the doom which they dared not to meet.

Farewell to others, but never we part,
Heir to my royalty, son of my heart!
Bright is the diadem, boundless the sway,
Or kingly the death, which awaits us to-day.
LORD BYRON.

The Field of Gilboa

THE sun of the morning looked forth from his
          throne
  And beamed on the face of the dead and the dying,
For the yell and the strife, like the thunder, had flown,
  And red on Gilboa the carnage was lying.

And there lay the husband that lately was prest
  To the beautiful cheek that was tearless and ruddy,
But the claws of the eagle were fixed in his breast
  And the beak of the vulture was busy and bloody.

92

And there lay the son of the widowed and sad,
- Who yesterday went from her dwelling forever,
Now the wolf of the hills a sweet carnival had
  On the delicate limbs that had ceased not to quiver.

And there came the daughter, a delicate child,
- To hold up the head that was breathless and hoary,
And there came the maiden, all frantic and wild
  To kiss the loved lips that were gasping and gory.

And there came the consort that struggled in vain
  To stem the red tide of a spouse that bereft her,
And there came a mother that sunk 'mid the slain
  To weep o'er the last human stay that was left her.

Oh! bloody Gilboa, a curse ever lie
  . Where the king and his people were slaughtered to-
        gether,
May the dew and the rain leave thy herbage to die,
  Thy flocks to decay and thy forests to wither.

WILLIAM KNOX.

Kynge David, Hys Lamente Over the Bodyes of Kynge Saul of Israel and His Sonne Jonathan

The beautye of the lande ys slayne,
How lowlye are the myghte layne!

I

NOW lette us shede the brinie teare,
  And lette us heave the pityinge moane!—
  But whyle we strowe the willowe biere
For Ysrael's pryde to lye upon;
  Oh! lette not Gath the tidynges heare
Oh, tell yt not yn Askalon,
Lest every wayling sounde of ours
Rayse triumpe-shoutes in heathen bowers!

II

May raine or dew droppe neuer lyghte
  Upon thy mountaynes, Gilboa!
May offerynge flame ne'er crowne thyne heighte
  In deepe of nyght or noon of daye!
Where worsted yn unholie fyghte
  The myghtie flung hys shielde away;
Cast meanlie on the fouled greene,
As he had ne'er anoynted beene!

III

From battel fyelde they turned them ne'er
  With bowe unstrunge, or blade untryede—
Pleasant They Were Yn Life, and Fayre
Nor Yette Did Deathe Theyre Loues Divide—
Theyre nervous armes mighte scathelesse dare
  To bearde the lyon yn hys pryde;
Yette theyre lyghte limbs made fleeter speede
Than eagles stoopynge o'er the meade.

IV

Ye daughteres of the lande, deplore,
  For Saule the bounteous and the bolde,
Whose kynglie hande hath founde you store
  Of crimson geare and clothe of golde.
Alack! that hande can giue noe more,
  That worthie harte ys stille and colde;
Unknown amongst the deade and dyinge,
The mightie with the mean are lying!—

V

Ah! Jonathan! my brother! lorne
  And friendless I must looke to be!—
That harte whose woe thou ofte hast borne
  Is sore and strickene nowe for thee.
Young brydegroome's loue on brydal morne,
Oh! yt was lyghte to thyne for me.

Thy tymelesse lotte I now must playne,
Even on thyne owne high places slayne!
How lowlie now the mightie are!
How still the weapons of the war. ·

SIR PHILIP SIDNEY.

David's Lament

LET the voice of the mourner be heard on the moun-
    tain,
  And woe breathe her sigh over Besor's blue wave;
Upon Gilboa's hill there is opened a fountain,
  And its fast-flowing stream is the blood of the
        brave!
Oh! dry be that hill from the rains of the morning,
  On its brow may no dew of the evening fall,
But the warriors of Israel, from conquest returning,
  View herbless and withered the death-place of Saul!
From the borders of Judah let gladness be banished,
  Ye maidens of Israel, be deep in your woe;
For the pride of the mighty in battle is vanished,
  The chief of the sword, and the lord of the bow.
And long shall the chieftains of Gilead deplore them,
  And mourn the dark fate of the high and the brave;
The song of the minstrel will oft be breathed o'er
    them,
  And holy the tear that shall fall on their grave.

ROBERT STEPHEN HAWKER.

David and Jonathan

ON the brow of Gilboa is war's bloody stain,
  The pride and the beauty of Israel is slain;
O publish it not in proud Askelon's street,
Nor tell it in Gath, lest in triumph they meet,
                For how are the mighty fallen!

95

O mount of Gilboa, no dew shalt thou see,
Save the blood of the Philistine fall upon thee;
For the strong-pinioned eagle of Israel is dead,
Thy brow is his pillow, thy bosom his bed!
                    O how are the mighty fallen!

Weep, daughters of Israel, weep o'er his grave!
What breast will now pity, what arm will now save?
O my brother! my brother! this heart bleeds for thee,
For thou wert a friend and a brother to me!
                    Ah, how are the mighty fallen!
                         LUCRETIA DAVIDSON.

The Lamentation of David Over Saul and Jonathan His Son

II. Sam. i: 17.

I

THY beauty, Israel, is gone
    Slain in the places high is he;
The mighty now are overthrown;
    O thus how cometh it to be!
Let not this news their streets throughout
    In Gath or Askalon be told;
For fear Philistia's daughters flout,
    Lest vaunt the uncircumcised should.

II

On you, hereafter, let no dew,
    You mountains of Gilboa, fall;
Let there be neither showers on you
    Nor fields that breed an offering shall.
For there with shame away was thrown
    The target of the strong (alas),
The shield of Saul, e'en as of one,
    That ne'er with oil anointed was.

96

III

Nor from their blood that slaughter'd lay,
  Nor from the fat of strong men slain,
Came Jonathan his bow away,
  Nor drew forth Saul his sword in vain.
In lifetime they were lovely fair,
  In death they undivided are.
More swift than eagles of the air
  And stronger they than lions were.

IV

Weep, Israel's daughters, weep for Saul,
  Who you with scarlet hath array'd;
Who clothed you with pleasures all
  And on your garments gold hath laid.
How comes it he, that mighty was
  The foil in battle doth sustain!
Thou, Jonathan, oh thou (alas)
  Upon thy places high wert slain.

V

And much distressèd is my heart,
  My brother Jonathan, for thee;
My very dear delight thou wert,
  And wonderous was thy love to me;
So wonderous, it surpassèd far
  The love of woman (every way).
Oh, how the mighty fallen are!
  How warlike instruments decay!

GEORGE WITHER.

Jehovah-Nissi. The Lord My Banner

BY whom was David taught
    To aim the deadly blow,
When he Goliath fought,
    And laid the Hittite low?
Nor sword nor spear the stripling took,
But chose a pebble from the brook.

97

'Twas Israel's God and King
　Who sent him to the fight;
Who gave him strength to sling,
　And skill to aim aright.
Ye feeble saints, your strength endures
Because young David's God is yours.

Who ordered Gideon forth,
　To storm the invaders' camp
With arms of little worth,
　A pitcher and a lamp?
The trumpets made his coming known
And all the host was overthrown.

Oh! I have seen the day
　When with a single word,
God helping me to say,
　"My trust is in the Lord,"
My soul hath quell'd a thousand foes,
Fearless of all that could oppose.

But unbelief, self-will,
　Self-righteousness and pride,
How often do they steal
　My weapon from my side!
Yet David's Lord, and Gideon's friend,
Will help his servant to the end.

WILLIAM COWPER.

The Song of David

HE sang of God, the mighty source
　Of all things,—that stupendous force,
Of which all strength depends;
From whose right arm, beneath whose eyes,
All period, power, and enterprise
　Commences, reigns and ends.

The world, the clustering spheres he made;
The glorious light, the soothing shade,
  Dale, champaign, grove and hill,
The multitudinous abyss
Where secrecy remains in bliss;
  And wisdom hides her skill.

Tell them I Am, Jehovah said
To Moses, while earth heard in dread
  And smitten to the heart.
At once, above, beneath, around,
All Nature without voice or sound,
  Replied, "O Lord Thou art."

CHRISTOPHER SHARP.

The Poet's Soul

WOULD you know the poet's soul,
  Why he doth wondrous sing?
Come, read the tale the Rabbis told
  Of Israel's poet king.

From the orb of day, a golden ray,
  From the moon its silvery beam,
From the twinkling star in heaven afar,
  He took its shimmering gleam.

From the azure sky and the clouds on high,
  He borrowed their mingled glow,
And the verdant green,—all the varying scene,
  Of beauteous world below.

And the grateful praise for joyous days,
  That comes from out the heart,
And the happy smile of romping child
  Yet free from guile and art.

99

From the murmuring brook, its plaint he took
  Whilst dreamily flowing by;
And the whispering breeze amidst the trees
  Lent its low and mournful sigh.

And the dulcet note from the warbling throat
  Of the lark as it soared on high,
And the linnet's song, as it sped along
  'Neath the dome of the summer sky.

And blending these beautiful things one with the other
  In one harmonious whole,
The Lord breathed it into the sovereign bard,—
  For such was King David's soul.

                    ANONYMOUS.

King David

OF Israel's sweetest singer now I sing,
  His holy style and happy victories;
Whose muse was dipt in that inspiring dew,
Archangels 'stilled from the breath of Jove,
Decking her temples with the glorious flowers
Heaven rained on tops of Sion and Mount Sinai.
Upon the bosom of his ivory lute
The cherubim and angels laid their breasts;
And when his consecrated fingers struck
The golden wires of his ravishing harp,
He gave alarum to the host of heaven
That, wing'd with lightning, brake the clouds, and cast
Their crystal armour at his conquering feet.
Of this sweet poet, Jove's musician,
And of his beauteous son, I press to sing:
That help, divine Adonai, to conduct
Upon the wings of my well-tempered verse
The hearers' minds above the towers of heaven
And guide them so in this thrice haughty flight,

Their mounting feathers scorch not with the fire,
That none can temper but thy holy hand;
To thee for succour flies my feeble muse,
And at thy feet her iron pen doth use.

GEORGE PEELE.

To David

O ISRAEL'S God-anointed warrior king,
    Who from the Lord of Hosts thy valor drew,
  And single-handed dread Goliath slew
(Though boasting he swift death should on thee
      bring):
Nor e'en yet feared when wrathful Saul did fling
  A furious javelin at thy head to do
  Thee harm, for Jesse's son that one well knew
Should one day after him be Israel's king;
'Tis not alone thy lion strength of heart,
  Nor yet thy triumphs nor thy hero's deeds
That lift my soul in boundless love to thee!
Ah, no! 'Tis this in but the lesser part,
  For more than all, my soul exultant feeds
On thine more precious gift of psaltery.

MIRIAM SUHLER.

David

DO you wonder why such longing
    Transport, pain and love impassioned
In the psalms are interwoven?
    Listen how God's bard was fashioned.

Murmurings of brooks and fountains,
    Passion of tempestuous seas,
Solemn sounds of winds and forests,
    The lorn nightingale's love-pleas.

And the pæans of men who triumphed
  Over grief and tempting glee—
All these divers notes God gathered
  From the fount of melody.

And He fused them in one anthem,
  Bade the music live, and lo!
David rose, he who to mankind
  How to speak with God did show.

Therefore lives there such a yearning,
  Such a rapture, exultation,
In the songs that David chanted
  For the heart of every nation.

ALTER ABELSON.

The Harp of Faith

AT midnight, so the rabbis tell,
    When David slept profound,
A harp suspended on his couch
  Gave forth a trembling sound.

Up sprang the royal bard inspired,
  His fingers touched the chord,
And with strange gladness in his soul,
  In psalms he praised the Lord.

At midnight, when the doubts assail,
  And anxious fears surround,
O Soul of mine, amid all gloom,
  Give forth a joyous sound.

O bid me seize the harp of faith,
  And sing a holy strain,
Until each day my life and thought
  Resound in glad refrain.

ABRAM S. ISAACS.

The Harp of David

WHEN the night her vision is weaving
   With moonlight and starlight for warp,
The King in his chamber arises
   And wakens the voice of his harp.

He sees not the hands of him playing,
   He hears but a melody sweet;
He hears but the heart of him beating
   With a musical, magical beat.

He gazes out through the window
   On the world in beauty bedight—
Forgotten the throne and the sceptre
   In a holier, higher delight!

He sees like a picture before him,
   The quiet, green fields where he spent
His youthful years as a shepherd,
   His only palace—a tent—

His sceptre—the flute of the shepherd,
   Carved of the cedar-wood hard;
His fortune and lonely treasure—
   The soulful pride of the bard.

Then pours he his soul on the harp-strings—
   Forgetful of sorrow and pain—
The old, gray monarch of Jndah
   Is a youthful Poet again!

                JEHOASH.
          (Translated by Alter Brody.)

Absalom

* * * * *

THE pall was settled. He who slept beneath
  Was straighten'd for the grave; and, as the folds
Sunk to the still proportions, they betray'd
The matchless symmetry of Absalom.
His hair was yet unshorn, and silken curls
Were floating round the tassels as they sway'd
To the admitted air, as glossy now
As when, in hours of gentle dalliance, bathing
The snowy fingers of Judea's daughters.
His helm was at his feet: his banner, soil'd
With trailing through Jerusalem, was laid,
Reversed, behind him: and the jewell'd hilt,
Whose diamonds lit the passage of his blade,
Rested, like mockery, on his cover'd brow.
The soldiers of the king trod to and fro,
Clad in the garb of battle; and their chief,
The mighty Joab, stood beside the bier,
And gazed upon the dark pall steadfastly,
As if he fear'd the slumberer might stir.
A slow step startled him. He grasp'd his blade
As if a trumpet rang; but the bent form
Of David enter'd, and he gave command,
In a low tone, to his few followers,
And left him with his dead. The king stood still
Till the last echo died; then, throwing off
The sackcloth from his brow, and laying back
The pall from the still features of his child,
He bow'd his head upon him, and broke forth
In the resistless eloquence of woe.

"Alas! my noble boy! that thou shouldst die!
  Thou, who wert made so beautifully fair!
That death should settle in thy glorious eye,
And leave his stillness in this clustering hair!
How could he mark thee for the silent tomb!
  My proud boy, Absalom!

BIBLICAL AND POST-BIBLICAL

"Cold is thy brow, my son! and I am chill,
 As to my bosom I have tried to press thee!
How was I wont to feel my pulses thrill,
 Like a rich harp-string, yearning to caress thee,
And hear thy sweet 'My Father' from these dumb
 And cold lips, Absalom!

"But death is on thee. I shall hear the gush
 Of music, and the voices of the young;
And life will pass me in the mantling blush,
 And the dark tresses to the soft winds flung;—
But thou no more, with thy sweet voice, shalt come
 To meet me, Absalom!

"And oh! when I am stricken, and my heart,
 Like a bruised reed, is waiting to be broken,
How will its love for thee, as I depart,
 Yearn for thine ear to drink its last deep token!
It were so sweet, amid death's gathering gloom,
 To see thee, Absalom!

"And now, farewell! 'Tis hard to give thee up,
 With death so like a gentle slumber on thee;—
And thy dark sin!—Oh! I could drink the cup,
 If from this woe its bitterness had won thee.
May God have call'd thee, like a wanderer, home,
 My lost boy, Absalom!"

He cover'd up his face, and bowed himself
A moment on his child: then, giving him
A look of melting tenderness, he clasp'd
His hands convulsively, as if in prayer;
And, as if strength were given him of God,
He rose up calmly, and composed the pall
Firmly and decently—and left him there—
As if his rest had been a breathing sleep.

NATHANIEL PARKER WILLIS.

In That Day

ABSALOM! Absalom!
  Put back thy fragrant hair!
Loud is the city's hum.
Why dost thy linger there
  To set soft hearts on fire?
That thou may'st reign and be
  What mainly men desire
What best it liketh thee?
  Hark to the City's hum,
  Absalom, Absalom!

Absalom, Absalom!
Canst thou not clearer see
  The thronging forms that came
Beneath the branching tree?
  The green ways of the wood,
And dropping from the dart
  The small dull pool of blood
That drains the traitorous heart?
  See the dim forms that come,
  Absalom, Absalom.

A. C. BENSON.

The Chamber Over the Gate

II. Sam. xviii: 33.

IS it so far from thee
  Thou canst no longer see,
In the Chamber over the Gate,
That old man desolate,
Weeping and wailing sore
For his son, who is no more?
O Absalom, my son!

Is it so long ago
That cry of human woe

106

From the walled city came,
Calling on his dear name,
That it has died away
In the distance of to-day?
O Absalom, my son!

There is no far or near,
There is neither there nor here,
There is neither soon nor late,
In that Chamber over the Gate,
Nor any long ago
To that cry of human woe,
O Absalom, my son!

From the ages that are past
The voice comes like a blast,
Over seas that wreck and drown,
Over tumult of traffic and town;
And from ages yet to be
Come the echoes back to me,
O Absalom, my son!

Somewhere at every hour,
The watchman from his tower,
Looks forth, and sees the fleet
Approach of the hurrying feet
Of messengers, that bear
The tidings of despair.
O Absalom, my son!

He goes forth from the door,
Who shall return no more.
With him our joy departs;
The light goes out in our hearts;
In the Chamber over the Gate
We sit disconsolate.
O Absalom, my son!

That 't is a common grief
Bringeth slight relief;

Ours is the bitterest loss,
Ours is the heaviest cross;
And forever the cry will be,
"Would God I had died for thee,
O Absalom, my son!"

HENRY WADSWORTH LONGFELLOW.

On Viewing a Statue of David

THIS was the shepherd boy who slung the stone
   And killed the giant; sunshine and the wind
Had given his harp so clear and strange a tone
   That all the world forgave him when he sinned.

The gently formed and stately Greek who stood
   On the Piazza, throned in classic pride,
Was not the boy who roamed through field and wood,
   Fighting and singing on the bright hillside.

Swift on the mountains, swift to save or slay;
   Eager and passionate and lithe of form;
Fighting and singing, pausing but to pray,
   Unto his God of music and of storm.

The bare hillside and sharp rocks castellate
   Rang with the clanging of his bow;
Where in the dawn of the world's love and hate,
   He found and would not slay his sleeping foe.

No sorrowful shades of the evil years
   Falls in the boy's face of the wood and wild;
Vanished are rags and lust and passionate tears;
   The King is dead, immortal stands the child.

EVA GORE-BOOTH.

Sleep

OF all the thoughts of God that are
    Borne inward unto soul afar
Along the Psalmist's music deep,
Now tell me if there any is
For gift or grace, surpassing this—
"He giveth his beloved sleep."

   *   *   *   *

     ELIZABETH BARRETT BROWNING.

Psalm VII

O LORD, my God, in Thee I put my trust,
    From them that persecute me save and guard;
Lest I be straight confounded in the dust,
    And they, like raving lions tearing hard,
Devour my captive soul in furious lust,
    By no deliverer in their conquest marred.
O Lord, my God, if I have done this wrong
Or if aught wicked be my deeds among;

If I have evil wrought unto my friend,
    If I have not preserved alive my foe,
Let then the enemy my body rend
    And o'er my spirit the proud victor go.
Let him my fame with base dishonor blend,
    And crush my life upon the earth below.
Stand up, O Lord, in anger at my foes,
Who in fierce indignation 'gainst me rose!

Arise, O Lord, and fight on my behalf,
    Give judgment for me as Thou hast ordained!
So shall with joy the congregation laugh,
    And flock around, in reverence constrained.
Then for this cause lift up Thy mighty staff,
    For those whose trust is on Thy power contained!
All men our God shall judge, help me, O Lord!
Heed Thou my righteousness and upright word!

May soon ungodly ways decay and cease,
  And Thy protection aid the humble just!
The hearts and inmost veins th' Almighty sees,
  For help from God appearing is my lust.
Unto the true of heart He giveth ease,
  Nor will permit them to lie in the dust.
A righteous Judge is God, patient and strong,
And each day angered by a sinning throng.

Will they not hear, th' avenging sword He whets,
  Doth bend His bow and towers aloft in ire;
The instruments of death to hand He sets,
  Against the persecutor's arrows dire.
All fruitless are the plots my foe begets;
  Sorrow doth he conceive, of ill the sire.
Graven hath he, and digged a noisome pit;
By him prepared, he falleth into it.

Upon his head shall his bad works return,
  His wickedness recoil upon his pate;
In self-inflicted torments shall he burn
  And pain of soul that none can satiate.
But I in grateful thanks to God will turn
  And all His righteousness will celebrate,
The name of God our Lord will I extol,
And to the heavens my tongue His fame shall roll.
         —ALFRED S. SCHILLER-SZINESSY.

My Times Are in Thy Hands!

"I trusted in thee, O Lord; I said, Thou art my
God. My times are in Thy hand!"—Ps. xxxi., 14, 15.

MY times are in Thy hand!
    I know not what a day
Or e'en an hour may bring to me,
But I am safe while trusting Thee,
    Though all things fade away.

All weakness, I
On Him rely
Who fixed the earth and spread the starry sky.

My times are in Thy hand!
Pale poverty or wealth,
Corroding care or calm repose,
Spring's balmy breath or winter's snows,
Sickness or buoyant health,—
Whate'er betide,
If God provide,
'Tis for the best; I wish no lot beside.

My times are in Thy hand!
Should friendship pure illume
And strew my path with fairest flowers,
Or should I spend life's dreary hours
In solitude's dark gloom,—
Thou art a friend,
Till time shall end
Unchangeably the same; in Thee all beauties blend.

My times are in Thy hand!
Many or few my days,
I leave with Thee,—this only pray,
That by Thy grace I, every day
Devoting to Thy praise,
May ready be
To welcome Thee
Whene'er Thou com'st to set my spirit free.
CHRISTOPHER NEWMAN HALL.

"The Lord Is My Shepherd, I Shall Not Want"

THE Lord my Shepherd is, no want I know,
He leadeth me where tranquil waters flow,
I lie in pastures green.
Yea, though I walk within the gloomy shade
Where Death doth lurk, I will not be afraid,
For on Thy staff I lean.

In vain mine enemies would me despoil,
My cup o'erfloweth still with wine and oil,
    My food Thou dost provide.
Thy mercy and Thy goodness both will last,
And when my days upon this earth are past,
    With Thee I yet shall bide.

                RE HENRY.

The Prayer of Solomon at the Consecration of the Temple

A GORGEOUS structure! rich with fretted gold
    And radiant with gems. A white robed choir,
Sackbut and psaltery, and the tuneful harp
Waft their sweet melody unto high Heaven.
A mighty monarch bows his head in prayer.
What boon has he to ask of pitying Heaven?
Seeks he for riches, or for pomp and power
Or asks he vengeance on unconquered foes?
Peace! peace! he breathes a lowly prayer to Heaven,
Even for others' sins as for his own,
            Asking forgiveness.

Father! when man forgetting Thy just decree,
  Shall wrong his brother, and by fraud or wile
Pervert the holy faith that leads to Thee
  And turn his heart to sinfulness and guile;
Yet when they both are brought before Thy face,
  And purer feelings in each bosom strive,
Hear Thou and judge in heaven Thy dwelling-place
  And when Thou hearest, have mercy and forgive.

When Thy frail children, for their many sins,
  Shall smart beneath the oppressor's iron rod,
And when the tortured conscience first begins
  To waken to the anger of its God;
Then when they come to Thee, that erring race,
  And pray that Thou the heavy load remove,
Hear Thou in heaven Thy holy dwelling-place,
  And when Thou hearest forgive, oh! God of love!

And when the heavens are shut, and the parched land
   Must bear the burden of their sinful way,
And Thou shalt teach them with Thy mighty hand,
   And bend their stubborn hearts to own Thy sway,—
And they repent and turn towards this place,
   Let not Thine ear be deaf unto their voice;
But hear Thou from Thy heavenly throne of grace,
   Hear and forgive the children of Thy choice.

And when the stranger, for Thy great name's sake
   Turneth toward this house, oh! mighty King,
Whatever supplication he may make,
   Whatever sin or sorrow he may bring;
Yet when he bendeth here to ask Thy grace,
   And prayeth Israel's God to heal his grief.
Hear Thou in Heaven, Thy dwelling-place,
   And when Thou hearest, forgive and grant relief.

If any sin (and what man sinneth not),
   And Thou art wroth and angered with their shame,
And the sad captive's lone and bitter lot
   Be theirs, until they call upon Thy name;
Yet when they turn repentant towards this place,
   And pray to Thee in supplicating tone,
Hear Thou in heaven Thy holy throne of grace,
   Forgive and have compassion on Thine own.

No gorgeous temple, rich with fretted gold
   And bright with flashing gems, now meets our eye;
No holy prophet king, like him of old,
   Now offers up our sacrifice on high;
Yet when we come with prayer to seek Thy face
   Each with sin's burning plague-spot in his breast,
Hear Thou, oh God! in heaven Thy dwelling-place
   And when Thou hearest, forgive, and grant us rest.

               REBEKAH HYNEMAN.

Solomon and the Bees

I

WHEN Solomon was reigning in his glory,
   Unto his throne the Queen of Sheba came;
(So in the Talmud you may read the story)
   Drawn by the magic of the monarch's fame,
To see the splendours of his court, and bring
Some fitting tribute to the mighty King.

II

Nor this alone: much had her highness heard
   What flowers of learning graced the royal speech;
What gems of wisdom dropped with every word;
   What wholesome lesson he was wont to teach
In pleasing proverbs; and she wished in sooth,
To know if rumor spake the simple truth.

III

Besides, the Queen had heard (which piqued her
   most)
   How through the deepest riddles he could spy;
How all the curious arts that women boast
   Were quite transparent to his piercing eye;
And so the Queen had come—a royal guest—
To put the Sage's cunning to the test.

IV

And straight she held before the monarch's view,
   In either hand a radiant wealth of flowers;
The one, bedeckt with every charming hue,
   Was newly culled from Nature's choicest bowers,
The other, no less fair in every part,
Was the rare product of divinest art.

V

"Which is the true, and which the false?" she said.
   Great Solomon was silent.   All amazed,

Each wondering courtier shook his puzzled head;
    While at the garlands long the Monarch gazed,
As one who sees a miracle, and fain,
For very rapture ne'er would speak again.

VI

"Which is the true?" Once more the woman asked,
    Pleased at the fond amazement of the king;
"So wise a head should not be hardly tasked
    Most learned Liege, with such a trivial thing!"
But still the sage was silent; it was plain
A deep'ning doubt perplexed his royal brain.

VII

While thus he pondered, presently he sees,
    Hard by the casement—so the story goes—
A little band of busy bustling bees,
    Hunting for honey in a withered rose.
The monarch smiled, and raised his royal head:
"Open the window!"—that was all he said.

VIII

The window opened at the King's command.
    Within the room the eager insects flew,
And sought the flowers in Sheba's dexter hand,
    And so the king and all the courtiers knew,
That wreath was Nature's—and the baffled Queen,
Returned to tell the wonders she had seen.

IX

My story teaches (every tale should bear
    A fitting moral) that the wise may find,
In trifles light as atoms of the air,
    Some useful lesson to enrich the mind—
Some truth designed to profit or to please—
As Israel's king learned wisdom from the bees.

                                JOHN GODFREY SAXE.

The Chief Among Ten Thousand

(Song of Solomon)

BEHOLD thou art all fair, my love;
  Thine eyes, thy locks, thy brow
All excellence and comeliness—
  How beautiful art thou!

Stately thy neck, like David's tower,
  With splendor overspread;
Whereon a thousand bucklers hang,
  Shields of the mighty dead.

Till the day break and shadows flee,
  Myself betake I will
To the spice-mountain's fragrant heights,
  And incense-breathing hill.

Thou art beautiful, my love,
  There is no spot in thee;
Come then, my bride, from Lebanon,
  From Lebanon with me!

Look from Amana's summit, look
  While I am by thy side;
Look from the top of Shinar, look
  From Hermon, look, my bride!

Love, sister, bride, thy beauty hath
  Ravished this heart of mine!
Won it thou hast, and now it is
  No longer mine, but thine!

Sister and spouse, how fair thy love,
  How better far than mine!
Thy fragrance steals my heart; it is
  No longer mine, but thine!

Thy lips are sweetness, and thy words
  Are pleasantness each one;
Thy very raiment breatheth forth
  The breath of Lebanon.

A garden is my sister-bride,
  A paradise shut in;
A guardian spring, a fountain sealed,
  With water pure within.

Thine are the pleasant fruits and flowers,
  Beneath, around, above;
Spikenard and balm, and myrrh and spice,
  A paradise of love.

Thine are the springs, which freshly o'er
  A thousand gardens run,
· The well of living waters Thou,
  And streams from Lebanon.

Awake, O north wind; come, thou south,
  Upon my garden blow!
So shall the happy fragrance out
  From all its spices flow.

Then forth through all His Paradise,
  Let my beloved rove,
To breathe the gladness of its air
  And eat His fruits of love.

HORATIUS BONAR.

Solomon's Song

"I sleep, but my heart waketh. . . ."

HAST thou heard the voice of my Belov'd?
  Alack! is he silent still?
Didst thou smell the perfume of his locks
  As he skipped upon the hill?

Did he say: "Go down and greet my Bride
  Amid the tents of Kedar?
In the house whose rafters are of fir,
  Whose casements are of cedar.

Is she dreaming at the pleasant feast
  All laved in spice and roses?
With cool ointment on her throat and hands
  From secret garden-closes.

O, why must I dwell far from her
  And from her running fountains?
I am lonely on the barren heights,
  Yet God calls from the mountains. . . ."

Behold! if ye hear my lover cry
  As Ammi-nadib's lances,
Then say: "She sleeps but her heart waketh,
  She neither sings nor dances."

As fish-pools of Heshbon weep her eyes,
  As willows trail her tresses,
Her neck is like a drooping tower,
  She yearns for thy caresses.

Come down from the hills and harp to her,
  Come down and stay her sorrow:
Is not the winter over and past
  And lilies bloom to-morrow?

   .   .   .   .

Yet she only saith: "He bideth long,
  Ah, when is he returning?"
                    REGINA MIRIAM BLOCH.

The Rose of Sharon

IN his chamber sat the Rabbi
  Poring o'er the book of learning,
When a knight with clanking armor
Sudden stood upon the threshold.

Gleamed the cross upon his shoulder,
And his countenance was warlike.
For the tall commanding figure
Was from Palestine returning.

As he gazed at the Crusader
Ceased the rabbi's heart its beating,
But—upon his lips warm praises
And a sturdy hand did clasp him.

Spoke the Knight, "We both are striving
Toward the same end, good and holy;
My strong arm I must confide in,
But thy help's thy stronger spirit.

"Seekers of the truth, O Rabbi,
Comrades are we with one purpose.
Pledge and promise your friendship,
Take this rose from soil of Zion."

Said the Rabbi: "Dost thou know not
Wondrous miracle that clusters
In the withered Rose of Sharon,
How it blossoms in the love-glance?

"Ah, how like the rose, my people!
Parched and drooping in its exile;
But when love-gleam rests upon it,
Dwelling safe in happy freedom,

"Swells its soul, then, in sweet rapture,
Fragrant too, its spirit blossoms
While it wakens to the new life
And forgets its olden sorrows."

ABRAM S. ISAACS.

Azrael

KING SOLOMON, before his palace gate
    At evening, on the pavement tessellate
Was walking with a stranger from the East,
Arrayed in rich attire as for a feast,
The mighty Runjeet-Sing, a learned man,
And Rajah of the realms of Hindostan.
And as they walked the guest became aware
Of a white figure in the twilight air,
Gazing intent, as one who with surprise
His form and features seemed to recognize;
And in a whisper to the King he said:
"What is yon shape, that, pallid as the dead,
Is watching me, as if he sought to trace
In the dim light the features of my face?"

The King looked, and replied: "I know him well;
It is the Angel men called Azrael.
'Tis the Death Angel; what hast thou to fear?"
And the guest answered: "Lest he should come near,
And speak to me, and take away my breath!
Save me from Azrael, save me from death!
O king, thou hast dominion o'er the wind,
Bid it arise and bear me hence to Ind."

The King gazed upward at the cloudless sky,
Whispered a word, and raised his hand on high,
And lo! the signet-ring of chrysoprase
On his uplifted finger seemed to blaze
With hidden fire, and rushing from the west
There came a mighty wind, and seized the guest
And lifted him from earth, and on they passed,
His shining garments streaming in the blast,
A silken banner o'er the walls upreared,
A purple cloud, that gleamed and disappeared.
Then said the Angel, smiling: "If this man
Be Rajah Runjeet-Sing of Hindostan,
Thou hast done well in listening to his prayer;
I was upon my way to seek him there."
HENRY WADSWORTH LONGFELLOW.

Wisdom

GOD got me ere His works began,
The first in all creation's plan.
From everlasting was my birth,
Yea, from the first, before the earth.
Ere there were deeps I was begot
When water-laden springs were not.
I was brought forth before, as yet
The hills and mountains had been set;
Ere He the land and wastes had made,
Ere He the world's first dust had laid.

When He prepared the heavens new,
And on the face a circle drew
Of the vast deep, there I was, too:
When skies above He firm did frame;
When the deep's fountains strong became;
When to the sea its bounds He set,
So that its borders ne'er should get
Beyond its borders, and when He
Marked out what should earth's bases be;

I as His foster-child did stay
With Him, delighting Him each day,
And in His presence e'er did play,
Exulting at His world in sight;
The sons of men were my delight.
Now children, hearken unto me;
Who keep my ways they blest shall be.
Instruction hear ye and be wise,
Yea, no instruction e'er despise.
Happy the man that heeds my say,
That watches at my gates each day,
That at my door-posts waits alway.

For he that findeth me finds Life;
He'll from the Lord get favour rife;

But he that misses me, the goal,
Does violence to his own soul;
Yea, Death is courted by all those
That hate me ever as my foes.

ISIDORE MYERS.

Habakkuk's Prayer

Habakkuk iii: 17-18.

YET though the fig-tree should no burden bear,
    Though vines delude the promise of the year;
Yet though the olive should not yield her oil,
Nor the parch'd glebe reward the peasant's toil;
Though the tired ox beneath his labors fall,
And herds in millions perish from the stall;
Yet shall my grateful strings
Forever praise Thy name;
Forever Thee proclaim
The everlasting God, the mighty King of kings.

WILLIAM BROOME.

Trust

Habakkuk, iii: 17-18.

THOUGH bare of bloom the broad-leafed fig
    And vines no luscious clusters show;
And toil that sinewed arms bestow
On olive erst with berries big
Shall fail, and fields shall yield no meat,
Nor herds more in the stables low,
Nor woolly flocks in fold shall bleat,
I yet with joy the Lord shall greet,
With song my Strength and Saviour praise,
Who renders like to hinds my feet
And doth me to high places raise.

M. M.

Trustfulness

Trust in the Lord with all thine heart and rely not
on thine own understanding.—Prov. iii: 5.

THOU, God, the only God,
    Father of all!
Thou gladly hearest us,
    If we but call.
When sin controls with power,
When fears our hopes devour,
In sorrow's chastening hour,
    Be Thou e'er nigh.

Oft we forget Thy love,
    O God most kind!
Oft we neglect Thy law,
    Light to the blind.
Our every joy is Thine,
Gift of Thy grace divine,
Long let Thy mercy shine
    On us below.

Thou Master of all worlds,
    Of all adored!
Aid us to do Thy will,
    Eternal Lord!
Let not Thy love depart,
Enter the prayerful heart,
With wrong we then shall part
    For evermore.

Where'er Thou leadest us,
    O Thou most High!
Humbly we follow Thee,
    To do or die.
Should'st Thou our path make bright,
Should'st Thou afflict with blight,
Yet both by day and night
    We trust in Thee.   J. LEONARD LEVY.

123

Watchman! What of the Night?

THE burden of Dumah. Silence. What of the
    night?
I hear the Watchman crying through the dark.
When to the golden cover of Thine Ark
Thy Mercy seat, wilt Thou, O God of Light
Return? How long wilt Thou Thy remnant smite,
    And thresh the scattered corn upon Thy floor,
    And winnow with Thy purging fan, before
That last least grain be garnered! Will Thy might
    Destroy, nor spare? Lo, as a tale that is told,
Our days pass quickly, nor as yet the thorn
    Yields to the fir. No more from us withhold
The Prince of Peace, that unto us is born:
    Our bones, O Lord, are vexed, our eyes wax old
With longing for that Messianic morn.

JAMES MEW.

Come Not, O Lord

COME not, O Lord, in the dread robe of splendor
    Thou worest on the Mount, in the day of Thine ire;
Come veiled in those shadows, deep, awful, but tender,
    Which Mercy flings over Thy features of fire.

Lord, Thou rememberest the night, when Thy nation
    Stood fronting her foe by the red-rolling stream;
On Egypt Thy pillar frowned dark desolation,
    While Israel basked all the night in its beam.

So, when the dread clouds of anger enfold Thee,
    From us, in Thy mercy, the dark side remove;
While shrouded in terror the guilty behold Thee,
    Oh, turn upon us the mild light of Thy love!

THOMAS MOORE.

Think on God

A Fragment

"Can a maid forget her ornaments or a bride her attire? Yet my people have forgotten me days without number."—Jeremiah ii, 32.

FORGET Thee, oh my God! and ca.1 this be?
   Earth with thy thousand voices answer me!
Ye midnight heavens gazing with eyes so bright
Upon the silent eloquence of night
Speak of thy Maker! Speak thou glorious sun
And thou enchanting moon! ethereal one
Tell me of Him.
            Oh! exquisite and clear
Were those soft words upon my listening ear;
Oh! eloquence divine of Nature's voice
Whose thrilling accents spoke:
             "Fond heart rejoice,
For we forget not God; there is no hour
When we could live without His love—His power."
"Each moment," sighed the pale and blushing rose,
"The wonders of my Maker I disclose;"
And every flower throughout the garden fair
Mingles its grateful perfume with the air,
Like incense, rising with a heavenly prayer,
Speaks each in varied tone its faithful love
Crowned with eternal beauty from above.
"Ah! not in thee forgetfulness," I said,
"Emblems of faithful love! I too would shed
My heart's best incense on that holy shrine
To burn forever." Then, with sound divine,
Teeming with melody the stately trees
And graceful wheat bowing to every breeze
In whispered chorus spoke His wonderous skill
And their obedience to His blessed will.
I gazed in rapture on those fields so sweet
Whose every blade bowed low as if to meet

125

The faintest breath of wind which seemed to bring
The thought of God upon its angel wing.
Oh! Nature, exquisitely calm and bright!
Your Maker is your life, your soul's delight.

R. E. S.

Job's Confession

THOU canst accomplish all things, Lord of might;
And every thought is named to Thy sight,
But O, Thy ways are wonderful, and lie
Beyond the deepest reach of mortal eye.
Oft have I heard of Thine Almighty power,
But never saw Thee till this dreadful hour,
O'erwhelmed with shame, the Lord of life I see,
Abhor myself, and give my soul in Thee.
Nor shall my weakness tempt Thine anger more;
Man is not made to question, but adore.

EDWARD YOUNG.

Dying—Shall Man Live Again?

IN dying, will the parting breath
Renew our life,—is there no death?
Go ask it of the winter's snow,
Or of the winds that fiercely blow.
Or ask it of the moaning seas,
Or of the naked, barren trees;
Or of dead leaves that withered lie,
Where autumn saw them fall and die.

Ask of the stars that nightly gleam—
Or ask it of the frozen stream
That in a shroud, all glorious, white,
Lies buried through the wintry night.

126

This question of another birth,
Go ask it of old mother earth;
Ask it of her when she receives,
The glory of the newer leaves.

Ask it of joyous birds that sing,
Or ask it of the new born spring;
Or of the mists in valleys low,
That sleep—where swollen rivers flow.
Or ask the thunder-toned roar
Of the old ocean breaking o'er
The barriers of some rock-bound shore—
This question of forevermore.

And yet the answer, strong, and sure,
That conquers every human fear,
And wipes away each bitter tear—
Is found in Him whose heart is pure;
This is the answer that He gives,
"Who dies to self, forever lives."

ALBERT FRANK HOFFMANN.

The Destruction of Sennacherib

THE Assyrian came down like the wolf on the fold,
And his cohorts were gleaming in purple and
gold;
And the sheen of their spears was like stars on the
sea,
When the blue wave rolls nightly on deep Galilee.

Like the leaves of the forest when Summer is green,
That host with their banners at sunset were seen;
Like the leaves of the forest when Autumn hath
blown,
That host on the morrow lay wither'd and strown.

127

For the Angel of Death spread his wings on the blast,
And breathed in the face of the foe as he pass'd;
And the eyes of the sleepers wax'd deadly and chill,
And their hearts but once heav'd, and forever grew
    still!

And there lay the steed with his nostril all wide,
But through it there roll'd not the breath of his
    pride.;
And the foam of his gasping lay white on the turf,
And cold as the spray of the rock-beating surf.

And there lay the rider distorted and pale,
With the dew on his brow, and the rust on his mail;
And the tents were all silent, the banners alone,
The lances unlifted, the trumpets unblown.

And the widows of Ashur are loud in their wail,
And the idols are broke in the temple of Baal;
And the might of the Gentile, unsmote by the sword,
Hath melted like snow in the glance of the Lord!

LORD BYRON.

Jeremiah, the Patriot

"Thou fallest away to the Chaldeans."—Jer.
xxxvii. 13

THEY say, "The man is false, and falls away":
    Yet sighs my.soul in secret for their pride;
Tears are mine hourly food, and night and day
    I plead for them, and may not be denied.

They say, "His words unnerve the warrior's hand,
    And dim the statesman's eye and disunite
The friends of Israel"; yet, in every land,
    My words, to Faith, are Peace, and Hope, and
    Might.

128

They say, "The frenzied one is fain to see
　Glooms of his own; and gathering storms afar;—
But dungeons deep, and fetters strong have we."
　Alas! Heaven's lightning would ye chain and bar?

Ye scorners of th' Eternal! wait one hour;
In His seer's weakness ye shall see His power.

JOHN KEBLE.

The Ruler of the Nations

"I have set thee this day over the nations, and over the
kingdoms."—Jer. i. 10

THE Lord hath set me o'er the kings of earth,
　To fasten and uproot, to build and mar;
　Not by mine own fond will: else never war
Had still'd in Anathoth the voice of mirth,
Nor from my native tribe swept bower and hearth;
　Ne'er had the light of Judah's royal star
　Fail'd in mid heaven, nor trampling steed and car
Ceas'd from the courts that saw Josiah's birth.
　" 'Tis not in me to give or take away,
But He who guides the thunder-peals on high,
　He tunes my voice, the tones of His deep sway
Faintly to echo in the nether sky.
　Therefore I bid earth's glories set or shine,
　And it is so; my words are sacraments divine."

JOHN KEBLE.

The Fall of Jerusalem

JERUSALEM! Jerusalem!
　Thou art low; thou mighty one,
How is the brilliance of thy diadem,
How is the lustre of thy throne
Rent from thee, and thy sun of fame
Darken'd by the shadowy pinion
Of the Roman bird, whose sway

129

All the tribes of earth obey,
Crouching 'neath his dread dominion,
And the terrors of his name!

How is thy royal seat—whereon
Sat in days of yore
Lowly Jesse's godlike son,
And the strength of Solomon,
In those rich and happy times
When the ships from Tarshish bore
Incense, and from Ophir's land,
With silken sail and cedar oar,
Wafting to Judea's strand
All the wealth of foreign climes—
How is thy royal seat o'erthrown!

Gone is all thy majesty;
Salem! Salem! City of kings,
Thou sittest desolate and lone,
Where once the glory of the Most High
Dwelt visibly enshrined between the wings
Of Cherubins, within whose bright embrace
The golden mercy-seat remain'd;
Land of Jehovah! view that sacred place
Abandon'd and profaned!

* * * * *

ALFRED TENNYSON.

Hebrew Melody
(Jeremiah x: 17)

FROM the hall of our fathers in anguish we fled,
Nor again will its marble re-echo our tread,
For the breath of the Siroc has blasted our name,
And the frown of Jehovah has crushed us in shame.

His robe was the whirlwind, his voice was the thunder,
And earth, at his footstep, was riven asunder;
The mantle of midnight had shrouded the sky,
For we knew, where He stood by the flash of His eye.

O Judah! how long must thy weary ones weep,
Far, far from the land where their forefathers sleep?
How long ere the glory that brightened the mountain
Will welcome the exile to Siloa's fountain?

MRS. JAMES GORDON BROOKS.

Lament for Jerusalem

JERUSALEM! on thy ruin'd walls
  The sun yet sheds its glittering rays,
And shines amid thy lonely halls
  As once it shone in happier days:
And Judea's clime is still as fair,
Though Judah's sons are outcasts there.

How long shall pagan foot profane
  Jehovah's hallowed shrine;
And memories alone remain
  Of all that once was thine?
How long shall we, thy children, roam
As exiles from our native home?

To weep o'er Salem's blighted fame,
  To gaze upon her strand,
Is all the heritage we claim
  Within our fatherland;
To mourn o'er our free parents' graves
That we, their children, are but slaves.

When will that glorious hour come?
  When shall we once more see
Thy temple rear its stately dome,
  Thy children with the free?
And thou, our fair, ill-fated land
Amongst the nations take thy stand?

MARION and CELIA MOSS.

Song of the Jewish Captives

WE sat us down by Babel's streams
    And dreamed soul-saddening memory's
      dreams;
And dark thoughts o'er our spirits crept
Of Sion—and we wept, we wept!
Our harps upon the willows hung
Silent, and tuneless, and unstrung;
For they who wrought our pains and wrongs,
Asked us for Sion's pleasant songs.

How can we sing Jehovah's praise
To those who Baal's altars raise?
How warble Judah's freeborn hymns,
With Babel's fetters on our limbs?
How chant thy lays, dear Fatherland,
To strangers on a foreign strand?
Ah no! we'll bear grief's keenest string,
But dare not Sion's anthems sing.

Place us where 'Sharon's roses blow;
Place us where Siloe's waters flow;
Place us on Lebanon, that waves
Its cedars o'er our fathers' graves:
Place us upon that holy mount,
Where stand the temple, gleams the fount;
And love and joy shall loose our tongues,
To warble Sion's pleasant songs.
                  HENRY NEILE.

The Jewish Captive's Song

GONE is thine hour of might,
    Zion, and fallen art thou;
Thy temple's sacred height
    Is desecrated now.
That I should live to see
    The ruins of that dome,
And Judah's children be,
    Bondsmen, and slaves to Rome.

When I saw heaven's wrath descending,
　Why 'scap'd I from the grave,
While thousands died defending
　The shrine they could not save;
But bless'd are those who sleep
　In their quiet resting place,
That they did not live to weep
　O'er the scattering of their race.

　　　　　MARION and CELIA MÓSS.

The Hebrew Minstrel's Lament

FROM the hills of the West, as the sun's setting
　　beam
Cast his last ray of glory o'er Jordan's lone stream,
While his fast-falling tears with its waters were blent,
Thus poured a poor minstrel his saddened lament:—

"Awake, harp of Judah, that slumbering hast hung
On the willows that weep where thy prophets have
　　sung;
Once more wake for Judah thy wild notes of woe,
Ere the hand that now strikes thee lies mouldering
　　and low.

"Ah, where are the choirs of the glad and the free
That woke the loud anthem responsive to thee,
When the daughters of Salem broke forth in the song,
While Tabor and Hermon its echoes prolong?

"And where are the mighty, who went forth in pride
To the slaughter of kings, with their ark at their side?
They sleep, lonely stream, with the sands of thy shore,
And the war-trumpet's blast shall awake them no more.

"O Judah,.a lone, scattered remnant remain,
To sigh for the graves of their fathers in vain,
And to turn toward thy land with a tear-brimming eye,
And a prayer that the advent of Shiloh be nigh.

133

"No beauty in Sharon, on Carmel no shade;
Our vineyards are wasted, our altars decayed;
And the heel of the heathen, insulting, has trod
On the bosoms that bled for their country and God."

ANONYMOUS.

Jewish Hymn in Babylon
(From "Belshazzar.")

GOD of thunder! from whose cloudy seat
    The fiery winds of Desolation flow;
Father of vengeance, that with purple feet
    Like a full wine-press tread'st the world below;
The embattled armies wait thy sign to slay,
Nor springs the beast of havoc on his prey,
Nor withering Famine walks his blasted way,
    Till thou hast marked the guilty land for woe.

God of the rainbow! at whose gracious sign
    The billows of the proud their rage suppress;
Father of mercies! at one word of thine
    An Eden blooms in the waste wilderness,
And fountains sparkle in the arid sands,
And timbrels ring in maidens' glancing hands,
And marble cities crown the laughing lands,
    And pillared temples rise thy name to bless.

O'er Judah's land thy thunders broke, O Lord!
    The chariots rattled o'er her sunken gate,
Her sons were wasted by the Assyrian's sword,
    Even her foes wept to see her fallen state;
And heaps her ivory palaces became,
Her princes wore the captive's garb of shame,
Her temples sank amid the smouldering flame,
    For thou didst ride the tempest cloud of fate.

O'er Judah's land thy rainbow, Lord, shall beam,
    And the sad City lift her crownless head,

And songs shall wake and dancing footsteps gleam
  In streets where broods the silence of the dead.
The sun shall shine on Salem's gilded towers,
On Carmel's side our maidens cull the flowers
To deck at blushing eve their bridal bowers,
  And angel feet the glittering Sion tread.

Thy vengeance gave us to the stranger's hand,
  And Abraham's children were led forth for slaves,
With fettered steps we left our pleasant land,
  Envying our fathers in their peaceful graves;
The stranger's bread with bitter tears we steep,
And when our weary eyes should sink to sleep,
In the mute midnight we steal forth to weep,
  Where the pale willows shade Euphrates' waves.

The horn in sorrow shall bring forth in joy;
  Thy mercy, Lord, shall lead thy children home;
He that went forth a tender prattling boy
  Yet ere he die, to Salem's streets shall come;
And Canaan's vines for us their fruit shall bear,
And Hermon's bees their honeyed stores prepare,
And we shall kneel again in thankful prayer,
  Where o'er the cherub-seated God full blazed the
          irradiate dome.
          HENRY HART MILMAN.

Oh! Weep for Those

OH! weep for those that wept by Babel's stream,
  Whose shrines are desolate, whose land a dream;
Weep for the harp of Judah's broken shell;
Mourn—where their God hath dwelt, the godless
    dwell!

And where shall Israel lave her bleeding feet?
And when shall Zion's songs again seem sweet?
And Judah's melody once more rejoice
The hearts that leap'd before its heavenly voice?

Tribes of the wandering foot and weary breast,
How shall ye flee away and be at rest?
The wild-dove hath her nest, the fox his cave,
Mankind their country—Israel but the grave!

LORD BYRON.

Na-Ha-Moo

"Comfort Ye—Comfort Ye, my people."—Isaiah,
xl. 1.

BY Babel's streams, thy children wept,
    And mute, O Israel, was thy choir,
While as thy weary exiles slept,
    And on the willow hung thy lyre,
A seraph's voice, soft as the dew,
Fell on their dreams with "Na-ha-moo."

No song made glad that mournful voice,
    No ease was for that bruised breast,
Till He who bade thee to rejoice
    Sent forth on Zion His behest—
Firm as thy faith in Him was true,
Like manna fell the "Na-ha-moo."

The stranger hath usurped the seat,
    Where, throned in glory, blazed the fane.
The hallowed walls, thy sacred feet,
    Still guard, O Zion, still remain,
To mark the ruin and renew
The memory of thy "Na-ha-moo."

God's mercy shines a lingering beam,
    The pilgrim on his path to light,
From Sinai's brow, from Jordan's stream,
    From offerings of the heart contrite—
His promises our hopes imbue,
With blessings of his "Na-ha-moo."

J. C. LEVY.

By the Rivers of Babylon We Sat Down and Wept

(Psalm cxxxvii.)

WE sat down and wept by the waters
   Of Babel, and thought of the day
When our foe, in the hue of his slaughters,
   Made Salem's high places his prey;
And ye, O her desolate daughters!
   Were scatter'd all weeping away.

While sadly we gazed on the river
   Which roll'd on in freedom below,
They demanded the song; but, oh, never
   That triumph the stranger shall know!
May this right hand be wither'd for ever,
   Ere it string our high harp for the foe!

On the willow that harp is suspended,
   O Salem! its sound should be free;
And the hour when thy glories were ended
   But left me that token of thee;
And ne'er shall its soft tones be blended
   With the voice of the spoiler by me!

                    LORD BYRON.

By Babel's Streams

(Paraphrase of Psalm 137)

I

BY Babel's streams we sat, we wept,
   Rememb'ring Zion's fallen state:
We hung the harp whose music slept
   On willows 'neath whose solemn shade
We talked of Zion's glory.

137

II

The captor cruel mocked the sigh
  And bade us sing of Zion's songs.
With breaking hearts we made reply
  "To Zion's land alone belongs
The sounds of Zion's glory."

III

How can we from the harp-string wake
  In stranger's land the sacred lay?
Each harp-string, aye, our hearts would break
  Before our fingers would obey,
For lost is Zion's glory.

IV

O Salem! If thy sacred land
  Forgotten be, if false we prove
May memory fail,—may palsied hand
  And dastard tongues refuse to move,
If we forget thy glory.

                              H. PEREIRA MENDES.

The Jewish Captive

(Psalm cxxxvii.)

OH Zion! if I cease for thee
  My earliest vows to pay—
If for thy sad and ruined walls
I ever cease to pray—
If I no more thy sacred courts
  With holy reverence prize,
Or Zion-ward shall cease to turn
  My ever-longing eyes—
Or if the splendor round me thrown
  Shall touch this Jewish heart,
And make me cease to prize thy joy
  Above all other art,—

138

Oh, may this hand no more with skill
　　E'er touch this sacred string,
And may this tongue grow cold in death,
　　Ere I shall cease to sing
And pray for Zion's holy courts,
　　Or dare to bow the knee
To these poor, blind and helpless gods,
　　Forgetful, Lord, of thee."

ELIZABETH OAKES (PRINCE) SMITH.

The Return From the Captivity

ARISE! Sons of Israel, arise!
　　The days of thy liberties dawn;
The Lord hath relented his wrath,
　　The night of thy slavery's gone.

Let the hills in thy gladness rejoice,
　　That freedom now smiles upon thee;
'Till the ocean's loud echoless voice,
　　Roars back to the valleys we're free.

They roar, and the mountain replies:
　　In your dwellings let joyfulness be;
Arise! Sons of Israel, arise!
　　Raise the hymn of thanksgiving,—thou'rt free.

MARION and CELIA MOSS.

The Wild Gazelle

THE wild gazelle on Judah's hills
　　Exulting yet may bound,
And drink from all the living rills
　　That gush on holy ground;
Its airy step and glorious eye
May glance in tameless transport by:—

139

A step as fleet, an eye more bright,
  Hath Judah witness'd there,
And o'er her scenes of lost delight
  Inhabitants more fair.
The cedars wave on Lebanon,
But Judah's statelier maids are gone!

More blest each palm that shades those plains
  Than Israel's scatter'd race;
For, taking root, it there remains
  In solitary grace;
It cannot quit its place of birth,
It will not live in other earth.

But we must wander witheringly,
  In other lands to die;
And where our fathers' ashes be,
  Our own may never lie:
Our temple hath not left a stone,
And Mockery sits on Salem's throne.

                                    LORD BYRON.

Nehemiah to Artaxerxes

(Nehemiah ii. 1-5.)

'TIS sorrow, O King! of the heart,
  Not anguish of body or limb,
That causes the hue from my cheek to depart,
  And mine eye to grow rayless and dim.

'Tis the mem'ry of Salem afar,
  Of Salem the city of God,
In darkness now wrapped like the moon and the star
  When the tempests of night are abroad.

The walls of the city are razed,
  The gates of the city are burned;
And the temple of God, where my fathers have praised,
  To the ashes of ruin are turned.

The palace of kings is consumed,
  Where the timbrels were wont to resound;
And the sepulchre domes, like the bones they entombed,
  Are mould'ring away in the ground.

And the fugitive remnant that breathe
  In the land that their fellows have trod,
Sit in sorrow and gloom; for a shadow like death
  O'erhangs every wretched abode.

I have wept, I have fasted, and prayed
  To the great and terrible God,
For this city of mine that in ruin is laid,
  And my brethren who smart by His rod.

And now I beseech thee, O King!
  If favor I find in thy sight,
That I may revisit my home, where the wing
  Of destruction is spread like the night.

And when I to Shushan return
  From rebuilding my forefathers' tomb,
No more shall the heart of thy cup-bearer burn
  With those sorrows that melt and consume.

                                WILLIAM KNOX.

Belshazzar

BELSHAZZAR is king! Belshazzar is Lord!
  And a thousand dark nobles all bend at his board;
Fruits glisten, flowers blossom, meats steam, and a flood
Of wine that man loveth runs redder than blood;
Wild dancers are there, and a riot of mirth,
And the beauty that maddens the passions of earth;
And the crowds all shout, till the vast roofs ring—
"All praise to Belshazzar, Belshazzar the king!"

141

"Bring forth," cries the monarch, "the vessels of gold,
Which my father tore down from the temples of old;
Bring forth!" and before him the vessels all shine,
And he bows unto Baal, and he drinks the dark wine,
While the trumpets bray and the cymbals ring,—
"Praise, praise to Belshazzar, Belshazzar the king!"

Now what cometh—look, look!—without menace or
    call?
Who writes with the lightning's bright hand on the
    wall?
What pierceth the king like the point of a dart?
What drives the bold blood from his cheek to his
    heart?
"Chaldeans! Magicians! the letters expound!"
They are read,—and Belshazzar is dead on the ground!
Hark!—The Persian is come on a conqueror's wing;
And a Mede's on the throne of Belshazzar the king.

BRYAN WALLER PROCTOR,
(Barry Cornwall).

Daniel

IMPERIAL Persia bowed to his wise sway—
    A hundred provinces his daily care;
    A queenly city with its gardens fair
Smiled round him—but his heart was far away,
Forsaking pomp and power "three times a day."
    For chamber lone, he seeks his solace there;
    Through windows opening westward floats his prayer
Towards the dear distance where Jerusalem lay,
So let me morn, noon, evening, steal aside
    And shutting my heart's door to earth's vain pleasure
And manifold solicitudes, find leisure
The windows of my soul to open wide
    Towards that blest city and that heavenly treasure
Which past these visible horizons hide.

RICHARD WILTON.

Vision of Belshazzar

THE King was on his throne,
  The Satraps throng'd the hall;
A thousand bright lamps shone
  O'er that high festival.
A thousand cups of gold,
  In Judah deem'd divine—
Jehovah's vessels hold
  The godless Heathen's wine.

In that same hour and hall
  The fingers of a hand
Came forth against the wall,
  And wrote as if on sand:
The fingers of a man;—
  A solitary hand
Along the letters ran,
  And traced them like a wand.

The monarch saw, and shook,
  And bade no more rejoice;
All bloodless wax'd his look,
  And tremulous his voice.
"Let the men of lore appear,
  The wisest of the earth,
And expound the words of fear,
  Which mar our royal mirth."

Chaldea's seers are good,
  But here they have no skill;
And the unknown letters stood
  Untold and awful still.
And Babel's men of age
  Are wise and deep in lore;
But now they were not sage;
  They saw—but knew no more.

143

A captive in the land,
  A stranger and a youth,
He heard the king's command,
  He saw that writing's truth.
The lamps around were bright,
  The prophecy in view;
He read it on that night—
  The morrow proved it true!

"Belshazzar's grave is made,
  His kingdom pass'd away,
He, in the balance weigh'd,
  Is light and worthless clay;
The shroud his robe of state,
  His canopy the stone;
The Mede is at his gate!
  The Persian on his throne!"

LORD BYRON.

Babylon

THOU glory of a thousand kings,
  Proud daughter of the East!
That dwellest as on sea-birds' wings,
  Upon Euphrates' breast;
As lofty as thy pride of old,
  So deep shall be thy doom;
Thy wealth is fled, thy days are told,
  Awake! thine end is come!

A sound of war is in the lands!
  A sword is on thy host!
Thy princes and their mighty bands—
  The Lord shall mock their boast!
His Hand has rein'd the rushing steed,
  And quell'd the rage of war;
Shall stay the flying lance's speed
  And burn the whirling car.

Set ye the standard in the lands;
    The Lord of Hosts hath said,
Bid trumpets rouse the distant bands
    Of Persia and the Mede;
The bucklers bring, make bright the dart,
    I lead thee forth to war,
To burst the gates of brass apart
    And break the iron bar!

The spoiler's hand is come upon
    Thy valiant men of might,
Their lion hearts, proud Babylon,
    Have failed thee in the fight;
Thy cities are all desolate,
    Thy lofty gates shall fall,
The hand that wrought Gomorrah's fate
    Shall crush thy mighty wall.

The shepherd shall not fold his flocks
    Upon the desert plain,
But, lurking in thy cavern'd rocks,
    The forest beast shall reign.
Fair Babylon, Lost Babylon!
    Sit in the dust and mourn,
Hurled headlong from thy lofty throne—
    Forgotten and forlorn!

                                    ANONYMOUS.

Herod's Lament for Mariamne

OH, Mariamne! now for thee,
    The heart for which thou bled'st is bleeding;
Revenge is lost in agony,
    And wild remorse to rage succeeding.
Oh! Mariamne! where art thou?
    Thou canst not hear my bitter pleading:
Ah! couldst thou—thou wouldst pardon now,
    Though Heaven were to my prayer unheeding.

And is she dead,—and did they dare
    Obey my frenzy's jealous raving?
My wrath but doom'd my own despair:
    The sword that smote her o'er me waving.
But thou art cold, my murder'd love!
    And this dark heart is vainly craving
For her who soars alone above,
    And leaves my soul unworthy saving.

She's gone, who shar'd my diadem;
    She sunk, with her my joys entombing;
I swept that flower from Judah's stem,
    Whose leaves for me alone were blooming;
And mine's the guilt, and mine the hell,
    This bosom's desolation dooming;
And I have earn'd those tortures well,
    Which unconsumed are still consuming!

LORD BYRON.

The Ark of the Covenant

THERE is a legend full of joy and pain,
    An old tradition told of former years,
When Israel built the Temple once again
    And stayed his tears.

'Twas in the chamber where the Wood Pile lay,
    The logs wherewith the altar's flame was fed;
There hope recalled the Light of vanished day,
    The Light long fled.

A priest moved slowly o'er the marble floor,
    Sorting the fuel in the chamber stored;
Frail was his form;—he ministered no more
    Before the Lord.

BIBLICAL AND POST-BIBLICAL

Wrapt in still thought, with sad and mournful mien,
  Pyking his axe with oft a troubled sigh,
He dreamed of glory which the House had seen
  In days gone by;

Mused of the time when in the Holy Place
  God's Presence dwelt between the Cherubim,
And of the day He turned away His face,
  And light grew dim;

When the Shechinah from that erring throng,
  Alas, withdrew, yet tarried in the track,
As one who lingereth on the threshold long
  And looketh back;

Then step by step in that reluctant flight
  Approached the shadow of the city wall,
And lingered yet upon the mountain height
  For hoped recall.

The Temple standing, pride of Israel's race,
  Hath resting there no sacred Ark of Gold;
God's Glory filleth not the Holy Place
  As once of old.

Surely the glory of the House is o'er;
  Gone is the Presence, silent is the Voice;—
They who remember that which is no more,
  Can they rejoice?

To him, so musing, sudden rapture came;
  The axe fell from his trembling hand's control;
A fire leapt upward, and a burning flame
  Woke in his soul.

His eyes had seen; his soul spoke; he had gazed
  Upon one stone of that smooth marble plain:—
Lo! from its place it surely had been raised,
  And set again.

Into his heart there flashed prophetic light;
   With sudden force the secret was revealed;
What but one treasure, sacred in his sight,
   Lay there concealed?

As one of Heaven bid who dare not wait,
   With step grown firm as with the strength of youth,
He hastened to his comrade to relate
   The wondrous truth.

With hand uplifted, and a light sublime
   In eyes that full of some new wonder shone,
He seemed a holy seer of olden time
   To look upon.

Yet from his parted lips no message came;
   In silence reached he his immortal goal;
And from its dwelling in the earthly frame
   Went forth his soul.

Soon o'er the house flew, murmuring, strange reports,
   And men and women trembled at the sound,
And priests came swiftly from the sacred courts,
   And thronged around.

And all these came from all their paths away,
   In hurried gathering which none gainsaid,
And stood in utter silence where he lay,
   The priestly dead.

Lo! in the hush the spirit, as it passed
   Beyond the still form and the peaceful brow,
Seemed to speak audibly: "O Lord, at last!
   I see Thee now.

"Mine eyes have seen this day my life's fair dream,
   In this my death have seen that dream fulfilled—
The longing of my heart, the wish supreme
   That grief instilled.

"I said, God's Ark is captive far away,
  So wept I, Ichabod, for glory fled,
And mourned because the brightness of the day
  Was quenched and dead.

"Yet, verily, if in a far-off land
  The Ark of God in exile dwelleth still,
Yea, even so 'tis with the pure of hand
  Who do His will.

"Know then, ye priests and Levites, Israel all,
  Hid in its place the Ark of God doth lie,
His presence hath not gone beyond recall,
  But bideth nigh.

"Haste, brethren, let the gates asunder burst;
  Regain the Ark, the Covenant hold fast;
And by the glorious Second House, the First
  Shall be surpassed!

"Behold, thou comest as the dawn of day!
  Shechinah! changeless, to illume the night!
O Thou, Who art a lamp upon the way,
  Who art the light!"

So sang his soul, with life's full radiance crowned;
  So dawned again the shining of God's face;
For each heart knew the Ark could yet be found
  Within its place.

                              NINA DAVIS.

Before the Ark

WHEN Solomon, great King of Israel,
    Builded the Temple of old,
He fashioned the "Ark of the Cov'nant"
  Within and without of gold.

He moulded two Cherubim splendid
  (At God, the Eternal's command)
Whose pinions the Holy of Holies
  Like a luminous symbol spanned.

The wings of these wonderful angels
  He welded together where
The Lord from His high seat of Mercy
  Re-echoed the voice divine.

And thus when the people lay prostrate
  Before the shimmering shrine,
From betwixt the horns of the Altar
  Re-echoed the voice divine.

We, also, dear children of Israel,
  Are bending before the Ark,
And our spirits' gold wings are shining
  Bright in the mystical dark.

As they touch, we whisper devoutly
  The great ineffable name,
And His voice, like music celestial,
  Chimes from the *Ner Tamid's* * flame.

The words we can clearly distinguish—
  Their meaning is solemn and grand;
"O, Children of Israel, remember!
  Know ye before Whom you stand!"

GEORGE ALEXANDER KOHUT.

---

* The "Perpetual Lamp," burning at the Altar.

BIBLICAL AND POST-BIBLICAL

Menorah

WE'VE read in legends of the books of old
  How deft Bezalel, wisest in his trade,
At the command of veiled Moses made
The seven-branched candlestick of beaten gold—
The base, the shaft, the cups, the knobs, the flowers,
Like almond blossoms—and the lamps were seven.

We know at least that on the templed rock
Of Zion hill, with earth's revolving hours
Under the changing centuries of heaven,
It stood upon the solemn altar block,
By every Gentile who had heard abhorred—
The holy light of Israel of the Lord;
Until that Titus and the legions came
And battered the walls with catapult and fire,
And bore the priest and candlestick away,
And, as memorial of fulfilled desire,
Bade carve upon the arch that bears his name
The stone procession ye may see today
Beyond the Forum on the Sacred Way,
Lifting the golden candlestick of fame.

The city fell, the temple was a heap;
And little children, who had else grown strong
And in their manhood venged the Roman wrong,
Strewed step and chamber, in eternal sleep.
But the great vision of the sevenfold flames
Outlasted the cups wherein at first it sprung.
The Greeks might teach the arts, the Romans law;
The heathen hordes might shout for bread and games;
Still Israel, exalted in the realms of awe,
Guarded the Light in many an alien air,
Along the borders of the midland sea
In hostile cities, spending praise and prayer
And pondering on the larger things that be—
Down through the ages, when the Cross uprose

On every tongue but one language,
    In every heart but one prayer?
Oh, all the world is my temple,
    I'm one of the worshipers there!

But evening came with the twilight,
    And lo! Now my Sun-God was gone;
And far the sun-worshipers scattered
    When the last glow of light was done.
Then all of them lit their own candles,
    Each followed a star of his own,
And there in his own light's glimmer
    He worshiped a God of his own!

And so I relit my Menorah,
    By its light my own God I extol;
And by the dim flaming Menorah
    I seek to discover my soul.
Its oil is a life-giving fountain,
    Its wick as our union appears,
And I see by its flame ascending
    The course of our future years!

HARRY WOLFSOHN.
(Translated by H. B. Ehrmann.)

The Holy Flame "Menorah"

THOU sacred flame, so mellow and subdued,
    Burning with tremulous, flickering beam
    In the holy place, before the all Supreme,
As though the very fire were all imbued

With that almighty prophet's humble soul,
    With Moses' sense of deep humility,
Whose height of feeling knew no humble goal,
    Whose aims bore naught of man's futility.

Thou, holy fire, whose light shall ever guide
The steps of wandering Israel, to the shrine
Of Him who was, who is, and ne'er will cease to be;
Whose luminous fire gleams down the tide
Of centuries, both of greatness and of woe,
When Israel's greatness bore a trace divine,
When Israel's fortune sank, far, far below
Even the lot of those poor Nubian slaves,
Who served our fathers in the promised land;
To thee, oh ancient light! whose very name
Is a memorial of God's earliest word,
We look to thee, and hail the conquering hand
Of wisdom's day, o'er spiritual night,
And breathe with God: "Let there be Light."

GEORGE JAY HOLLAND.

The Prayer of the High Priest

100 Years B. C. E.

THE High Priest at the altar lingering stood—
    The service o'er.
The worshippers with faces kind and good,
    Passed from the door.

The synagogue was empty; only one—
    A Child—remained;
With eager eyes as shining as the Sun
    He stood as chained.

"Kohen Gadol," said he, "When I grow
    To man's estate,
I hope that I shall know the things you know
    And be as great.

"And Oh, I wish such glorious robes to wear
    As these of yours,
Dear Master, intercede for me in prayer,
    For that secures

155

"What e'er you ask.   And here—behold I bring
  These beauteous flowers;
Upon the brink of Kedron they did cling
  These many hours.

"Accept them.   With the other blossoms—see?—
  Are here, so fair,
The Valley Lilies; these I give to thee,
  Now make thy prayer."

On that boy's head the High Priest—smiling—laid
  A kindly hand.
He said: "My child, these lilies here have prayed;
  They understand

"As well as I the mysteries of God.
  I ask for you
Such raiment as the flowers of the sod
  When fresh with dew.

"Abide thou in thine innocence, for lo!
  The Great High Priest
May even less of God—Jehovah—know
  Than thou, the Least."

MARIE HARROLD GARRISON.

The High Priest to Alexander

"Derrame en todo el orbe de la tierra
Las armas, el furor, y nueva guerra."
La Araucana, Canto xvi.

GO forth! thou man of force!
  The world is all thine own;
Before thy dreadful course
  Shall totter every throne.
Let India's jewels glow
  Upon thy diadem:
Go, forth to conquest go,
  But spare Jerusalem.

For the God of gods, which liveth
  Through all eternity,
'Tis He alone which giveth
  And taketh victory:
'Tis He the bow that blasteth,
  And breaketh the proud one's quiver;
And the Lord of armies resteth
  In His Holy of Holies for ever!

For God is Salem's spear,
  And God is Salem's sword;
What mortal man shall dare
  To combat with the Lord?
Every knee shall bow
  Before His awful sight;
Every thought sink low
  Before the Lord of might.
For the God of gods, which liveth
  Through all eternity,
'Tis He alone which giveth
  And taketh victory:
'Tis He the bow that blazeth,
  And breaketh the proud one's quiver;
And the Lord of armies resteth
  In His Holy of Holies for ever!

ALFRED TENNYSON.

On the Day of the Destruction of Jerusalem
by Titus

FROM the last hill that looks on the once holy
    dome,
I beheld thee, O Sion, when render'd to Rome;
'Twas thy last sun went down, and the flames of thy
    fall
Flash'd back on the last glance I gave to thy wall.

I look'd for thy temple, I look'd for my home,
And forgot for a moment my bondage to come;
I beheld but the death-fire that fed on thy fane,
And the fast-fetter'd hands that made vengeance in
    vain.

On many an eve, the high spot whence I gazed
Had reflected the last beam of day as it blazed;
While I stood on the height and beheld the decline
Of the rays from the mountains that shone on thy
    shrine.

And now on the mountain I stood on that day,
But I mark'd not the twilight beam melting away!
Oh! would that the lightning had glared in its stead,
And the thunderbolt burst on the conqueror's head!

But the gods of the Pagan shall never profane
The shrine where Jehovah disdain'd not to reign;
And scatter'd and scorn'd as thy people may be,
Our worship, O Father! is only for Thee.

LORD BYRON.

At Samaria

WE climbed the hill where from Samaria's crown
    In marble majesty once looked away
  Toward Hermon, white beneath the Syrian day;
And lo, no vestige of the old renown.

Save a long colonnade bescarred and brown,
  Remained to tell of Herod's regal sway,
  The gold, the gauds, the imperial display,
He heaped on Judah's erewhile princely town.

Ruin was riotous; decay was king;
  An olive -root engript the topmost stone
  As tho it clutched and crusht the thing called fame;

158

Seemed as a fragile wind-flower petal blown
  Into the void, the past's vain glorying,
  And Herod but the shadow of a name!

CLINTON SCOLLARD.

The Temple

GO forth, O people,
    Sacred to thought, to labour and to sorrow,
And through the centuries pursue thy way.
God of Infinity, He is thy God,
And measureless alike 'mid alien fanes,
Along the sea and lands that thou shalt tread,
Pilgrim of endless years, thy path shall be.
The road is dark, is long and full of pain;
Beside thee still shall go, at God's behest,
Like to the fiery column, quenchless Hope.
As winnowed grain is flung into the air,
So, 'midst all peoples God shall scatter thee,
And thou shalt bear, as well as thine own griefs,
The griefs and burdens of all other races.
Peoples shall rise, shall shine, shall pass away,
But thou, sacred to life, beside the graves
Of all shall pass immortal, vaster far than time
Or than this earth, no tomb can hold
Thy thoughts immeasurable.

       Sorrowful and grand,
Thou to the rush confused of years to come,
And in the wreck of peoples and of empires,
Thou in all ages, living, speaking witness,
Shalt say to all—"I am." And to the past
The future thou shalt bind, and race to race,
People to people, and the scattered limbs
Of Adam drawing into thine own self,
In thee, new Adam, one mankind shall grow
Like unto God, and holy on the earth.
Thou the reviving universe shalt fill
With truth and peace.

DAVID LEVI.

Ode to the Sacred Lamps

O FUGITIVES from black Oppression's bread,
  Scourged of your God, through flames and
    furies led
To Babel's streams, to Persia's milder shore,
  To Afric's marge, and isles of pensive Greece;—
'Twas not with magic, not with priestly lore,
  But with high wisdom, folded in a fleece,
You spread, broadcast, the seeds of Hebrew power!
Oppression's head was bruised in Israel's bower,
  By you, who steeped your souls' high-centered pride
  In day dreams of old Zion's new built State;
With cunning hands, you raised unto your bride,
  Temples and schools, defying death and fate;
In Yavneh and in Pumbadissa, Egypt, Spain and
    Rome,—
You toasted deep the Torah's health and dreamed of
    your "Old Home."

The Western surge keeps ringing in mine ears,
Music too sweet, to stir my breast with fears.
  Out there, fine vistas shaping life, I view,
    To mart and farm, and mansions by the sea,
On soils superb, divine as Hermon's dew;—
    Visions ecstatic, splendours new to me,
Wind round my heart, a fragrant benison:—
"Israel ne'er shall orphaned be again";
  Her Talmud schools, her Temples' gilded shrines,
    Imaged by men of high magnetic zeal,
  Floating the Stars and Stripes' triumphant signs,
    Shall build a race strong for the Commonweal;
Apt for affairs, keen in debate; with scholar strata-
    gem,
Enkindled by the sacred lamps of Old Jerusalem.
                    M. L. R. Breslar.

II

TALMUDICAL PERIOD

The Sea of the Talmud

THE moon is up, the stars shine bright,
  The milky way glows soft and white.
We've spread our sails to catch the breeze
That frets the vast rabbinic seas.

We've spread our sails to roam amain
That profits neither gold nor gain,
Whose shores are stretched along a land,
Unmapped by man's designing hand.

Beneath no lowering, storm-mad skies
We start on our strange enterprise—
Set outward bound, where signals gleam
Beyond the shadows of our dream,

To realms no feet of mortal man
Have trodden on or ever can,
And port at quays no ship-bound crew
Has sighted in the cosmic blue.

The ports there made are set afar
Like distant morn or evening star,
And golden as the halls of Ind
Where hush the sobbings of the wind.

Who rides this main, he travels wide
And sees the flood and ebbing tide
Run up and down a fabled shore
Outlined complete in cryptic lore.

Our rigging firm, our compass true
And manned with brave and seasoned crew
We sail at ease this unplumbed sea
Of knowledge and of mystery.

163

Enroute we pass odd crafts and barks
Whose pennants fly the signal marks
Of playful whims that, fancy free,
Glide o'er this vast rabbinic sea.

Then undulating like to grain
We rock, as out we head again
Our graceful sloop—or east or west—
It matters not which way the quest.

There flows in this rabbinic sea
The streams whose springs are poetry;
And rivulets from fancy's height
Drop down to add their welcome mite.

And islands, where the palm trees dim
The visions of the Anakim;
And animals as high as these
Play quoits with fishes in the seas.

Along this course there's ever found
Elijah on his daily round,
Who unafraid of good or ill,
Strives but to do another's will.

What pageantry of kings we pass
Resplendent as the royal glass
The sages quaff, when at their feast,
The banquet hall lights up the east.

And all the winds that make the round
Of heaven bring their freighted sound
From halls where grey-haired sages sit
And questions of their Torah knit.

Yet mists at times befog the way
Where fretful white caps madly play;
Then midst the storm the seraphim
Becalm the waves by praising Him.

TALMUDICAL PERIOD

No other sea full-ebbed as this,
Bequeathed its sailors so much bliss,
For old as are its thundering shores,
Were ne'er bestrewn with spoils of wars.

No craft that ever dents their waves
Discharged its freight in watery graves;
For he who sails this unique sea
Returns with his own argosy.

The moon is up. The stars shine bright;
This mystic sea is swathed in light,
And from its depths droll voices lure
The land beset forth on a tour.

Far from the teeming ports and quays,
Where men and women fret their days,
No cruise as this makes sport of time,
Or breed or border, land or clime.

And in its wake a thousand ships
In gathering darkness evening dips,
Yet happy is each crew, and free,
That sails this vast rabbinic sea.

JOSEPH LEISER.

The Talmud

ANCIENT pages of the Talmud,
  Legends, tales that there I view,
In my mournful life and dreary
  Oftentimes I turn to you.

When at night amid the darkness
  On mine eyes sleep will not rest,
And I sit alone, and wretched,
  With my head upon my breast,

165

In those hours, as a star shines
  In the azure summer night,
Memories amid my sadness
  Then begin to glimmer bright.

I recall my love, my childhood;
  Those sweet hours come back again
When I still was free from sorrow,
  Free from anger, free from pain.

I recall those times, long vanished,
  When I quaffed, without alloy,
Life's first, best and sweetest chalice,
  Freedom, mirthfulness and joy.

Those old years so sweet and precious
  Pass again before mine eyes,
And the pages of the Talmud
  In my memory arise.

Oh! the precious ancient pages!
  All the lights and stars I see
Burning, shining in those pages;
  They can ne'er extinguished be!

Myriad streams and myriad rivers
  Have flowed o'er them in the past;
Sand has covered them and hid them,
  Storms have rent them—still they last.

Yes, the ancient, ancient pages
  Still survive and perish not,
Although yellowed, torn and blackened,
  Here a hole and there a spot.

What of that? Indeed it truly
  Is a graveyard, old and hoar,
Where within the tomb lies buried
  All that we shall see no more.

S. Frug.

(Translated by Alice Stone Blackwell.)

TALMUDICAL PERIOD

Hillel and His Guest

A Talmudic Legend

Boast not thyself of to-morrow; for thou knowest not
what a day may bring forth.—Proverbs xxvii. 1.

HILLEL, the gentle, the beloved sage,
Expounded day by day the sacred page
To his disciple in the house of learning;
And day by day, when home at eve returning,
They lingered, clust'ring round him loth to part
From him whose gentle rule won every heart.
But evermore, when they were wont to plead
For longer converse, forth he went with speed,
Saying each day; "I go—the hour is late—
To tend the guest who doth my coming wait."
Until at last they said: "The Rabbi jests
When telling us thus daily of his guests
That wait for him." The Rabbi paused awhile,
And then made answer; "Think you I beguile
You with an idle tale? Not so, forsooth!
I have a guest, whom I must tend in truth.
Is not the soul of man indeed a guest,
Who in this body deigns a while to rest,
And dwells with me all peacefully to-day;
To-morrow—may it not have fled away?"

ALICE LUCAS.

Akiba

O HEART, who art a fable, new and true;
O soul, a legend strange and sweet as joy;
Lover, whose love has built, not razed a Troy;
Akiba, whom heaven and angels taught to woo.

Lover, and lawyer, all Israel's sceptred mind,
Who luminous mists hast orbed into a sun
Of Oral Law, and logic's praises won;
A shepherd's crook you left, a wand to find.

Our blameless Lancelot of lists of lore,
  Who made Romance a theme for cherubim;
    And love, God's Song of Songs, His heavenly
      hymn;
And law, a mine where mercy digs for ore.

God's patriot, who heaven with life hast sought,
  And Holylands in Holyland hast known;
    Thou art a part of heaven, thou hast shown,
Thou art a part of "Torah" thou hast taught.

What wonder you have traversed Paradise,
  It was your gentle spirit's element;
    What wealth to heaven, what penury hell, you
      sent;
Courage and wisdom hailed you brave and wise.

And virtue named you saint, and greatness, great;
  Patriotism, patriot; and knowledge, sage.
    And love, a lover; your heart, its golden page.
And holiness rejoiced to own you, mate.

What, though the foe your frame with fires shod?
  What, though he drained the wine-vats of your
    veins?
    He only precious made like gems, your pains;
Aye, kissed by God, your feet on crowns have trod.

ALTER ABELSON.

Sunshine After Storm

A Tale from the Talmud

THE rabbi viewed on Zion's hill
  A fox the holy ruins treading,
Expanding griefs their bosoms fill,
  Who suppliant hands to heaven are spreading.

TALMUDICAL PERIOD

With dancing eyes and ringing laugh,
  Akiba marks the fox descending;
Exulting, waves aloft his staff;
  His ill-timed mirth his friends offending.

How canst thou smile? See God's own house,
  His holy place wild beasts infesting.
Such would indignant pity rouse,
  If grace be still within thee resting.

Why weep? quoth he, when near fulfilled:
  Her doom of trouble we're beholding.
Join you with what another skilled
  In heavenly purpose, is unfolding.

Comes next, the later, happier seer
  Who Salem's glory sees in vision,
Of men and dames whose hundredth year
  Abounds in peace and rich provision.

Jeshurun toils through grief to joy.
  Whom God would choose, He first must chasten,
Let Israel faith and hope employ
  His higher destiny to hasten.

                    WILLIAM DEARNESS.

Who Serves Best

IN stern debate, all through the night they strove
  The sages of the Talmud, to record
What man deserved the favor of the Lord.
The ancient Rabbi Judah, he who throve
On fasting and on prayer, spake of one
Who lavished wealth, as worthy. "Nay," quoth Saul,
The scribe and scholar, looming gaunt and tall,
"None but the wise is fit to look upon!"

"Not so," exclaimed the zealot Zadok. "Place
Him first who best observes the Law!" Lo, then was
    heard
A child's sweet voice which thrilled the men who
    erred:—
"To him alone is vouchsafed God's good grace
Who renders loving service to his kind!"—
And ere they grasped the vision, it declined.
GEORGE ALEXANDER KOHUT.

Be Not Like Servants Basely Bred

ANTIGONUS of Socho said:
    Be not like servants basely bred,
Who to their master minister
In hope of gift he may confer.
But be you like those servants still,
Who strive to do their master's will
Without a thought of guerdon given,
And be on you the fear of Heaven.

And this did Rabbi Tarphon say:
The work is great and short the day,
Sluggish the labourers, their Lord
Urgent, but mighty the reward.
He also said: 'Tis not on thee
Incumbent, that thou shouldest end
The work, but neither art thou free
To cease from it. If thou dost spend
Much time in studying the divine
Torah, much guerdon shall be thine,
For faithful thine employer is
To pay thee for thy labour's sum,
And know thou that the righteous is
Rewarded in the time to come.

And Rabbi Jacob said of old:
Do thou this world of ours behold

170

TALMUDICAL PERIOD

As though a vestibule it were
Into the world to come. Prepare
Thyself the Vestibule within,
That thou the hall may'st enter in.
And further thus his saying reads:
One hour's repentance and good deeds
In this world better is than all
The world to come, but yet withal
In yonder world one hour of bliss
Is better than all life in this.

ALICE LUCAS.

The Commandment of Forgetfulness

RABBI BEN ZADOK, o'er the sacred law
Bending with reverent joy, with sacred awe
Read the commandment: "When thy harvest yields
Its fruit and thou when reaping in the fields,
Dost there forget a sheaf of golden grain,
Fetch it not in to thee! It shall remain—
The poor, the stranger and the widow's store
And the Lord God shall bless thee evermore."
Rabbi ben Zadok closed the well-loved book,
And, gazing upward with a troubled look,
He said: "With joy do I obey, O Lord,
Each hest and precept of Thy holy word,
For which Thy name at morn and eve I bless.
But this commandment of forgetfulness
I have not yet performed as Thou hast willed
Since to remember leaves unfilled."
So mused the Rabbi. But when autumn came,
And waves of corn glowed 'neath the sunset's flame,
It chanced at evening, that, his labors o'er,
He stood and gazed upon his garnered store,
And suddenly to him his little son
Came saying: "Father, see what thou hast done!

Three sheaves in yonder field I have espied
Forgotten!" "Oh!" the pious rabbi cried,
"Blessed art Thou, O Lord, whose gracious will
Enables me Thy bidding to fulfil,
Even through some oversight!" And with the day
Unto the house of God he took his way,
And offered of his flocks and herds the best,
For joy to have obeyed the Lord's behest.

Thus runs the Talmud tale! O God, may we
Thus evermore rejoice in serving Thee.

ALICE LUCAS.

Who Are the Wise?
From Ethics of the Fathers

THEY who have governed with a self control
  Each wild and baneful passion of the soul—
Curbed the strong impulse of all fierce desires,
But kept alive affection's purer fires;
Those who have passed the labyrinth of life
Without one hour of weakness or of strife;
Prepared each change of future to endure,
Humble tho' rich, and dignified tho' poor—
Skilled in the latest movements of the heart—
Learned in that lore which nature can impart;
Teaching that sweet philosophy aloud
Which sees the silver lining of the cloud;
Looking for good in all beneath the skies—
Those only can be numbered with the wise.

ANONYMOUS.

What Rabbi Jehosha Said

RABBI JEHOSHA used to say
  That God made angels every day,
Perfect as Michael and the rest
First brooded in creation's nest,

172

Whose only office was to cry
Hosanna! once and then to die;
Or rather, with Life's essence blent,
To be led home from banishment.

Rabbi Jehosha had the skill
To know that Heaven is in God's will;
And doing that, though for a space
One heart-beat long, may win a grace
As full of grandeur and of glow
As Princes of the Chariot know.

'T were glorious, no doubt, to be
One of the strong-winged Hierarchy,
To burn with Seraphs, or to shine
With Cherubs, deathlessly divine;
Yet I, perhaps, poor earthly clod,
Could I forget myself in God,
Could I but find my nature's clue
Simply as birds and blossoms do,
And but for one rapt moment know
'T is Heaven must come, not we must go;
Should win my place as near the throne
As the pearl-angel of its zone,
And God would listen mid the throng
For my one breath of perfect song,
That, in its simple human way,
Said all the Host of Heaven could say.

JAMES·RUSSELL LOWELL.

Brotherly Love

THE Rabbi Judah, so the scribes relate,
  Sat with his brethren once in a warm debate
About those things which each considered best
To bring to earth immunity and rest.
Then said the one requested to begin:
"Rest comes from wealth, if there be peace within."

The second said: "It springs from honest fame,
And having all men magnify your name."
The third said: "Rest is being truly great,
Coupled with power to rule some mighty state."
The fourth said: "Such a rest as we presage
Reach men in only the extremest age,
When wealth and power and fame unite to go
To children—and unto their children flow."

The fifth said: "All these various things are vain;
Rest comes to those who all the law maintain."
Then said the Rabbi Judah, grave and old,
The tallest of the group with him enrolled:
"You all speak wisely, but no rest is deep
To him who the traditions fails to keep."

Now spoke a fairhaired boy up from the grass—
A boy of twelve, who heard these words repass,
And dropped the lilies from his slender hands;
"Nay, father; none among you understands.
True rest he only finds who evermore
Looks not behind, but to the things before;
Who, scorning fame and power and home and pelf,
Loveth his brother as he loves himself."

ATTRIBUTED TO THOMAS BAILEY ALDRICH.

God's Messengers

Rabbon Gamaliel said: "Make His will thy will, . . .
subvert thy will to His will."—Aboth 2, 4

I ASKED the wind, "Where hast thou been
　Since last thy voice I heard,
Since last the quivering of thy wings
　The leafy branches stirred,
And freighted from its moss-clad home
　Each gentle nestling bird?

"Ah, wherefore didst thou swell the storm
  When good ships went to sea;
And why was bent the tall stout mast—
  The cordage rent by thee;
And why, when shattered bark went down,
  Thy shout of victory?"

"If o'er the ocean I have swept
  And lashed its waves to heaven,
While high before me on the surge
  The hapless bark was driven,
And loud and fearful rose the cry,
  Of men from warm life riven,

"I did His bidding who doth hold,
  In His all-powered hand,
The whirlwind that hath swept in might
  O'er ocean wave and land;
I questioned not why such things were—
  Can mortal understand?"

Do thou His bidding—question not
  Nor cower like frightened dove;
Thou art the messenger of God,
  Sent from the heights above:
Know thou art by the Father bid,
  Thy God—and God is Love.

MRS. A. R. LEVY.

Ben Karshook's Wisdom

I

"WOULD a man 'scape the rod?"
  Rabbi Ben Karshook saith,
"See that he turn to God
  The day before his death."

"Ay, could a man inquire
  When it shall come!" I say.
The Rabbi's eye shoots fire—
  "Then let him turn today!"

II

Quoth a young Sadducee;
  "Reader of many rolls,
Is it so certain we
  Have, as they tell us, souls?"

"Son, there is no reply!"
  The Rabbi bit his beard:
Certain, a soul have *I*—
  We may have none," he sneered.

Thus Karshook, the Hiram's-Hammer,
  The Right-hand Temple-column,
Taught babes in grace their grammar,
  And struck the simple, solemn.

ROBERT BROWNING.

The Vision of Huna

THE sun had set upon Jerusalem,
  And scattered rosy circles round the mount,
Whereon the ruins of the Temple lay.

Beneath the shadow of a crumbling wall
Stood Rabbi Huna. His mind was sad;
For on this spot, not many years before,
The holy Temple shone to all the earth,
And now was changed, alas! and desolate.

"Oh, how I love thee, my Jerusalem."
So sighed the rabbi, as he sank to rest,
"Oh, how I love thee, tho' upon thy neck
With crushing force the conqueror's foot is pressed.
The last rapt strains of the prophetic lyre

I seem to hear across thy sloping hills.
Bright visions of the glory thrill me yet,
When in thy prophet's words in bridal robe
Thou wast betrothed unto Israel's God;
And now——." The rabbi faltered as he thought,
Then sighing fell into a restless sleep.

Strange fancies came to Huna as he slept.
Again he trod the Temple's sacred courts,
But there no altar dripped with streaming gore;
No groans of sacrificial sheep were heard,
No swelling chant, no pomp of liturgy,
No loudly spoken prayer, no mumbling lips,
No smiting of the breast, no postures vain;
A reverent throng with every impulse bent
To worship God in simple brotherhood.
They had, indeed, their holy litanies,
Which not in book or scroll alone were writ;
An open hand, a humble heart and mind,
An overflowing fount of love and truth,
With aspirations for the beautiful,
The true, the good, the pure.

          The rabbi wakes.
Dead sounds of tumult rouse him from his sleep,
A sprawling band of Roman soldiery,
With cries of triumph, track him to the spot.
His helpless form the savage spears soon pierced,
And with "Shema Yisroel!" Huna dies.
Upon his face there rests a placid smile,
As if he trod the New Jerusalem.

ABRAM S. ISAACS.

Rabbi Ben Hissar

RABBI BEN HISSAR rode one day
    Beyond the city gates. His way
Lay toward a spot where his own hand
Had buried deep within the sand

A treasure vast of gems and gold
He dared not trust to man to hold.

But riding in the falling light,
A pallid figure met his sight—
An awful shape—he knew full well
'Twas the great Angel Azrael.
The dreadful presence froze his breath;
He waited tremblingly for death.

"Fear not," the Angel said, "I bear
A message. Rabbi Ben-Hissar,
One thing the Lord hath asked of thee
To prove thy love and loyalty.
Therefore now I am come to bring
Thy rarest jewel to thy King."

Rabbi Ben-Hissar bowed his head,
"All that I have is his!" he said.
The angel vanished. All that day
He rode upon his lonely way
Wondering much what precious stone
God would have chosen for his own.
But when he reached the spot he found
No other hand had touched the ground.

Rabbi Ben-Hissar looked and sighed
"It was a dream!" he sadly cried.
"I thought that God would deign to take
Of my poor store for his dear sake.
But 'twas a dream! My brightest gem
Would have no luster meet for him!"

Slowly he turned and took his way
Back to the vale where the city lay.
The path was long, but when he came
Unto the street which bore his name
He saw his house stand dark and drear,
No voice of welcome, none of cheer.

He entered and saw what the Lord had done.
Lo! Death had stricken his only son!
Clay he lay, in the darkened hall,
On the stolid bier, with the funeral pall.
The pale death-angel Azrael
Had chosen a jewel that pleased him well.
Rabbi Ben-Hissar bent his head.
"I thank thee, Lord," was all he said.

ANONYMOUS.

The Messenger

RABBI BEN JOSEF, old and blind,
Pressed by the crowd before, behind,
Passed through the market place one day,
Seeking with weary feet his way.
The city's traffic loud confused
His senses, to retirement used;
The voice of them that bought and sold,
With clink of silver piece and gold.

"Jehovah," cried he, jostled sore,
Fearing to fall and rise no more,
"Thine angel send to guide my feet,
And part the ways where danger meet."
Just then a beggar, as he passed,
A glance of pity on him cast,
And, seeing so his bitter need,
Stretched forth his hand his steps to lead.

"Not so," Ben Josef cried, "I wait
A guide sent from Jehovah's gate."
The beggar left, thus rudely spurned
Where gratitude he should have earned.
As day wore on the hubbub rose,
Louder and harsher to its close,
The old man, weary, sought in vain
An exit from the crowd to gain.

179

Jostled at every turn his feet
Stumbled upon the ill-paved street;
Once more he cried, "Jehovah, where
The answer to thy servant's prayer?
No angel, swift-winged, from thy throne,
Has hither for the helping flown."
Then came a whisper, clear and low,
"My messenger thou didst not know.

"For in a beggar's humble guise
His outstretched hand thou didst despise,
Nor cared beneath his rags to find
The heart that made his action kind.
See now that thou the lesson learn,
Lest he whose face thou canst not see
Should prove a messenger from Me."

O. B. MERRILL.

The Forgotten Rabbi

("His memory for a blessing!")

RABBI BEN SHALOM'S wisdom none but his
  scholars know,
(High let his spirit journey, e'en as his flesh lies
  low!)
He, ere he spake the "Shema," prayed that his fame
  might cease:—
"How shall I give you blessing if you begrudge me
  peace?"

Rabbi Ben Shalom's teaching clings to his scholars
  still,
Oft to his school came, fasting, those who had
  dreamed of ill:
God in such dreams had spoken—how could they an-
  swer best?
"Laugh at the fear," said Rabbi. "God has a right
  to jest!"

Rabbi Ben Shalom's kindred long in his ear deplored
Alms they had spent to nourish one with a secret
    hoard;
Who of their daily table—robber of God!—had taste:
"Have I not heard," said Rabbi, "God has enough to
    waste?"

Rabbi Ben Shalom, silent, sat with a dead man's son.
"I, at his grave, O Rabbi, knew what my sins had
    done!
Great but for me, how humbled. . . . Can I appease
    the dead?"
"Cherish his seed," said Rabbi, "Strive to be great in-
    stead!"

Rabbi Ben Shalom's coming mirth unto mirth could
    bring—
Fill him the cup, he'd drain it; strike on the harp,
    he'd sing!
Blind seemed his joy to many, when on his brows
    death sat—
Only the few knew better; knew he rejoiced—in that!

Thus have Ben Shalom's scholars dug him a lowly
    bed—
(How can the soul and body ever a like path tread?)
Thus when in Shool they slight him, say that "his
    fame should cease,"
Whoso gainsays their folly grudges his master peace!
                              G. M. H.

The Two Rabbins

THE Rabbi Nathan, twoscore years and ten,
   Walked blameless through the evil world, and
    then,
Just as the almond blossomed in his hair,
Met a temptation all too strong to bear,

And miserably sinned. So, adding not
Falsehood to guilt, he left his seat, and taught
No more among the elders, but went out
From the great congregation girt about
With sackcloth, and with ashes on his head,
Making his gray locks grayer. Long he prayed,
Smiting his breast; then, as the Book he laid
Open before him for the Bath-Col's choice,
Pausing to hear that Daughter of a Voice
Behold the royal preacher's words: "A friend
Loveth at all times, yea, unto the end;
And for the evil day thy brother lives."
Marvelling, he said: "It is the Lord who gives
Counsel in need. At Ecbatana dwells
Rabbi Ben Isaac, who all men excels
In righteousness and wisdom, as the trees
Of Lebanon the small weeds that the bees
Bow with their weight. I will arise and lay
My sins before him."

                      And he went his way
Barefooted, fasting long with many prayers;
But even as one who, followed unawares,
Suddenly in the darkness feels a hand
Thrill with its touch his own, and his cheek fanned
By odors subtly sweet, and whispers near
Of words he loathes, yet cannot choose but hear,
So, while the Rabbi journeyed, chanting low
The wail of David's penitential woe,
Before him still the old temptation came,
And mocked him with the motion and the shame
Of such desires that, shuddering, he abhorred
Himself; and, crying mightily to the Lord
To free his soul and cast the demon out,
Smote with his staff the blankness round about.

At length, in the low light of a spent day,
The towers of Ecbatana far away
Rose on the desert's rim; and Nathan, faint

And footsore, pausing where for some dead saint
The faith of Islam reared a domed tomb,
Saw some one kneeling in the shadow, whom
He greeted kindly: "May the Holy One
Answer thy prayers, O stranger!" Whereupon
The shape stood up with a loud cry, and then,
Clasped in each other's arms, the two gray men
Wept, praising Him whose gracious providence
Made their paths one. But straightway, as the sense
Of his transgression smote him, Nathan tore
Himself away: "O friend beloved, no more
Worthy am I to touch thee, for I came,
Foul from my sins, to tell thee all my shame.
Haply thy prayers, since nought availeth mine,
May purge my soul, and make it white like thine.
Pity me, O Ben Isaac, I have sinned!"

Awestruck Ben Isaac stood. The desert wind
Blew his long mantle backward laying bare
The mournful secret of his shirt of hair.
"I too, O friend, if not in act," he said,
"In thought have verily sinned. Hast thou not read
'Better the eye should see than that desire
Should wander'? Burning with a hidden fire
That tears and prayers quench not, I come to thee
For pity and for help, as thou to me.
Pray for me, O my friend!" But Nathan cried,
"Pray thou for me, Ben Isaac!"

                                    Side by side
In the low sunshine by the turban stone
They knelt; each made his brother's woe his own,
Forgetting, in the agony and stress
Of pitying love, his claim of selfishness;
Peace, for his friend besought, his own became;
His prayers were answered in another's name;
And, when at last they rose up to embrace,
Each saw God's pardon in his brother's face!

Long after, when his headstone gathered moss,
Traced on the targum-marge of Onkelos
In Rabbi Nathan's hand these words were read:
"Hope not the cure of sin till Self is dead;
Forget it in love's service, and the debt
Thou canst not pay the angels shall forget;
Heaven's gate is shut to him who comes alone;
Save thou a soul, and it shall save thy own!"

JOHN GREENLEAF WHITTIER.

The Two Rabbis

THERE stood upon Moriah's mount,
   Two aged men with hoary hair;
One glanced around with smiling brow,
   The other wept in deep despair.

"Jerusalem, Oh! Jerusalem!
   Land of my love," the weeper cried;
"Thy scattered sons in exile weep,
   And alien are thy state and pride.

"Fierce jackals 'mid thy ruins howl;
   The prowling lion seeks his prey
On the spot where once thy temple stood;
   And thy brave children,—Where are they?

"With weary feet, and aching heart,
   Scattered, despised, a fallen race,
They wander far in alien lands,
   And seek in vain a resting place.

"And then how canst thou smile, to see
   Our hopes, our glory perish all?
How canst thou gaze with joyous glance
   Upon our temple's ruined wall?"

"I smile," the other said, "because,
  In all the Eternal's power I see,
And hope springs up within my heart,
  Even from our depths of misery.

"For surely as the Almighty hand
  Destroyed our land for guilt and crime,
So surely will he raise us up
  To joy, at his appointed time.

"Hath he not said that Israel's sons
  Shall once again be free and great?
Hath he not said, in Zion's halls
  Shall once again be kingly state?

"A great and glorious destiny
  Will yet be ours in future years;
And thus my face with smiles is glad,
  While thine is dewed with bitter tears."

                              MRS. LEVITUS.

At Last

THE Rabbi Levi let his thoughts be cast
  Upon the current of remembered life,
And saw the faces of his child and wife,
So fair and mystical, it well might seem
As if he saw by moonlight in a dream
  What he had seen in sunlight in the past.

Yet at remembered sin he starts to see
Remorse, most dreaded angel of the Lord,
Flash back the sunshine from his awful sword.
His wan cheek flushes like a dying brand;
"Take back, O Angel, in thy strong right hand
  This sweet but cruel gift of memory."

"Not so," the angel answered; "thou shalt live,
Love and remember till thy work is done."
And thus the Rabbi toiled, and did not shun
To look upon what he himself had wrought.
For years he freely learned and freely taught
   The wisdom that his own mistakes could give.

The Rabbi Levi, when his head was white,
Heard a soft voice, "Henceforth no more for you
Shall memory come as flame, but cooling dew;
"Take thou the comfort of thy heart's release,
For with thine own life thou shalt be at peace."
   So, smiling, he passed out into the light.
ADELAIDE G. WATERS.

The Passing of Rabbi Assi

OUTWORN by studious toil and age,
   The Rabbi Assi, saintly sage,
Upon his humble pallet lay,
Awaiting death, at close of day.
Silent and sad amid the gloom
Of that poor, pathetic room,
Some fond disciple hovered near,
Intent his parting words to hear.
The mellow light of sunset spread
A glory round his snow-white head,
And as, amazed, they saw the trace
Of tears upon his pallid face,
One came and knelt beside the bed,
Caressed the thin, white hand, and said:
"Dear Rabbi, wherefore weepest thou?
Let no sad thoughts disquiet now
The peace of thy departure hence
To heavenly rest and recompense.
Thou hast been pure in heart and mind,
Meek, modest, patient, gentle, kind,
Recall with gratitude and joy
Thy consecrated life's employ.

186

Devoted to the sacred law,
Thou didst unselfishly withdraw
From all publicities; and when
With one accord thy fellow-men
Chose thee their judge, thou didst refuse
All worldly service, and didst choose
To live sequestered from all care,
For God, in study and in prayer."

"Cease," cried the Rabbi in distress,
"Make not my cup of bitterness
More bitter with the shame and pain
Of praise as ignorant as vain.
My soul is sorrowful, my son,
For public duties left undone.
I mourn the quest of truth pursued
In disregard of brotherhood;
The narrow, blind, scholastic zeal
That heeded not the common weal;
The subtle selfishness and pride
In which I put the world aside
And sought an individual good
In self-complacent solitude,
Withheld my aid and stayed my hand
From truth and justice in the land,
And weakly failed to exercise
The law in which I would be wise.

"Wherefore with tears, I plead with you,
Dear friends, a nobler course pursue,
Beware the self-indulgent mood
Of unconcern for public good.
Think not in cloistered, studious ease
Wisdom to win or God to please.
For wisdom moulders in the mind
That shuts itself from human kind,
And piety, with self-content,
Becomes a barren sentiment,
The bread of life is turned to stone
For him who hoards it as his own.

O see betimes—what late I saw—
That only love fulfills the law,
In loving kindness hear and heed
The plaintive cries of human need,
Protect the weak against the strong,
Uphold the right and right the wrong.
Assuage life's miseries and pains,
Console its sorrows, cleanse its stains;
Count worthy of all toil and strife
These common interests of life
More precious than the richest store
Of secular or sacred lore—
Your mission and ambition be
God's service in humanity."

He paused, and, rapt in silent prayer,
His spirit seemed awhile elsewhere,
And at his prayer the peace was given
For which his sorrowing soul had striven;
At eventide the light had come
To guide him through the darkness home,
Then with a smile of sweet surprise
He woke and lifted up his eyes
And praised the Lord with trembling voice,
He bade his weeping friends rejoice,
And said, "Beloved, let me hear
Once more the Shepherd-psalm of cheer.".
And they repeated, soft and low,
That sweetest song that mortals know;
And then in accents calm and grave
His benison to them he gave.

"May God who comforts my sad heart
And bids me now in peace depart,
Bless, guide and keep you evermore!
Abundantly on you outpour
The riches of his truth and grace,
Show you the favor of His face,
Your minds and hearts with ardor fill
To know and do His holy will.

With heavenly wisdom make you wise
In service and self-sacrifice,
Give you rich fruits of toil and tears,
And—after long and useful years—
The blessedness of those who come
With sheaves and songs, rejoicing, home."

The Rabbi's failing strength was spent.
In silent sorrow o'er him bent
With bated breath the faithful few,
And heard him faintly say, "Adieu!
The night grows dark! the hour is late!
We now, dear friends, must separate.
A thousand-fold may God requite
Your love and care. Good-by; Good-night!
And peaceful rest till break of day!"
So Rabbi Assi passed away.

———

Fact, legend, parable of old?
What matters—so the truth be told—
Historic or fictitious frame?
The Rabbi's likeness is the same.
And whosoever hath an ear
To hear his counsel, let him hear!

EDWIN POND PARKER.

The Lent Jewels

A Jewish Apologue

IN schools of wisdom all the day was spent;
His steps at eve the Rabbi homeward bent,
With homeward thoughts, which dwelt upon the wife
And two fair children who consoled his life.
She, meeting at the threshold, led him in
And with these words preventing, did begin:
"I, greeting ever your desired return,
Yet greet it most today; for since this morn

189

I have been much perplexed and sorely tried
Upon one point, which you shall now decide.
Some years ago, a friend unto my care
Some jewels gave—rich, precious gems they were;
But having given them in my charge, this friend
Did afterward not come for them, nor send.
But in my keeping suffered them so long,
That now it almost seems to me a wrong
That he should suddenly arrive today,
To take those jewels, which he left, away.
What think you? Shall I freely yield them back,
And with no murmuring? so henceforth to lack
Those gems myself, which I had learned to see
Almost as mine for ever, mine in feel"

"What question can be here? your own true heart
Must needs advise you of the only part;
That may be claimed again which was but lent,
And should be yielded with no discontent;
Nor surely can we find in this a wrong,
That it was left us to enjoy it long."
"Good is the word," she answered; "may we now
And evermore that it is good allow!"
And, rising, to an inner chamber led,
And there she showed him, stretched upon one bed,
Two children pale, and he the jewels knew,
Which God had lent him, and resumed anew.

RICHARD CHENEVIX TRENCH.

The Loan

(Midrash Yalkut, iii, p. 165)

THE Rabbi Meir,
    A black cap on his white hair,
And him before
Unfurled the great book of the Law,
Sat in the school and taught.

Many a winged thought
Flew from his lips, and brought
Fire and enlightenment
Unto the scholars bent
Diligently at their writing.
And all the while he was inditing,
His soul was near to God.
Above the dull earth that he trod.
And as the lark doth sing
High up and quivering"
In the blue, on heavenward wing,
But ever its breast
Keepeth above its nest,
And singing it doth not roam
Beyond hearing of its home,
So the Rabbi, however high he soared
In his teaching, or praying, sung
Close to the ear of his Lord,
Yet ever above his home, his wife and young.

Slowly there stole the gloom
Of evening into the room,
Then he rose and shut the book
And casting about a look,
Said, with a wave
Of the hand: "God gave
The light, and hath taken away,
With the Lord begun,
With the Lord run,
With the Lord done,
Is the day."
Then his way
Homeward cheerfully he took.
In the little house, sedate,
For her husband did await
Beruriah. And for her lord
She had laid the supper on the board.
And a lamp was lighted up,
By which he might sup.

He kissed her upon the brow,
And spake to her gently: "How
Are the lads today?
Tell me, Beruriah, pray."
There glittered on her cheek
Two jewels, ere she could speak
And answer, "They are well,
Sit you and eat your supper, whilst I tell
What to me befell;
And assure me in what way
You think it had been best
That I had acted." Thus addressed,
He sat him at his meal,
And began to eat: "Reveal
Thy case," he said. "Yet tell me, I pray,
First—where are my boys today?"
Then suddenly she said,
With an averted head:
"Many years are flown
Since one a precious loan
Entrusted to my care, until he came
That treasure to reclaim."
The Rabbi spoke: "Of old
Tobit confided his gold
To Raguel
At Ecbatane. Well,
What further?—But say,
Where are my lads, I pray?"

"For many years that store
I jealously watched o'er,
Do you think, my lord, that loan
In fourteen years would become my own?"
Then, with a glance of blame,
He answered, as he shook his head:
    "For shame.
Wife of my bosom! It were not thine
Should forty years upon thee shine,
And the owner not return

192

To demand it. Beruriah, learn
Not to covet."

Then he paused, and said,
Moving the lamp: "Thine eyes are red,
   Beruriah: wherefore?"

But she broke
In on his question, and thus spoke:
"To-day there came
To the door the same
One who had lent the treasure,
And he said, 'It is my pleasure
To have the loan restored.'
What do you think, my lord?
Should I have withheld it, Meir?"
At his wife with astonished stare
Looked the Rabbi. "O my wife!
Light of my eyes, and glory of my life!
  Why ask this question?"

    Then he said,
As his eyes wandered towards the bed:
"Why is the sheet,
Usually smooth and neat,
Lifted into many a fold and pleat?"
But she asked: "Should I repine
At surrendering what was not mine
To him who claimed it?"

    "It was a trust,
Wife of my bosom! What do you ask?—Repine
What! do you lust
To keep what is not thine?"
And once again:
"Where are my boys?"

  She took him by the hand,
Whilst o'er her features ran a thrill of pain,
And brought him to the bed, and bid him stand
There, as she touched the sheet, and said:

"The Lord who gave hath taken. They are dead."
Softly she raised
The sheet; and with awe
The Rabbi his children saw
In the soft twilight
Lying silent, and still and white;
And he said, "Praised
Be the Name of the Lord.
My wife and I are content
That the goodly loan to us lent
Should be restored."
                                    SABINE BARING-GOULD.

The Two Friends

A Rabbinical Tale

GOOD Rabbi Nathan had rejoiced to spend
     A social se'nnight with his ancient friend,
The Rabbi Isaac. In devout accord
They read the Sacred Books, and praised the Lord
For all His mercies unto them and theirs;
Until, one day, remembering some affairs
That asked his instant presence, Nathan said,
"Too long, my friend (so close my soul is wed
To thy soul), has the silent lapse of days
Kept me thy guest; although with prayer and praise
The hours were fragrant. Now the time has come
When, all-reluctant, I must hasten home,
To other duties than the dear delights
To which thy gracious friendship still invites."
"Well, be it so, if so it needs must be."
The host made answer; "be it far from me
To hinder thee in aught that Duty lays
Upon thy pious conscience. Go thy ways
And take my blessing!—but, O friend of mine,
In His name, whom thou servest, give me thine!"
"Already," Nathan answered, "had I sought
Some fitting words to bless thee; and I thought

About the palm-tree, giving fruit and shade;
And in my grateful heart, O friend, I prayed
That Heaven be pleased to make thee even so!
O idle benediction! Well I know
Thou lackest nothing of all perfect fruit
Of generous souls, or pious deeds that suit
With pious worship. Well I know thine alms
In hospitable shade exceed the palm's;
And, for rich fruitage, can that noble tree,
With all her opulence, compare with thee?
Since, then, O friend, I cannot wish thee more,
In thine own person, than thy present store
Of Heaven's best bounty, I will even pray
That, as the palm-tree, though it pass away,
By others, of its seed, is still replaced,
So thine own stock may evermore be graced
With happy sons and daughters, who shall be,
In wisdom, strength, and goodness, like to thee!"

JOHN GODFREY SAXE.

The Rabbi's Vision

BEN LEVI sat with his books alone
   At the midnight's solemn chime,
And the full-orb'd moon through his lattice shone
   In the power of autumn's prime;
It shone on the darkly learned page,
And the snowy locks of the lonely Sage—
But he sat and mark'd not its silvery light,
For his thoughts were on other themes that night.

Wide was the learn'd Ben Levi's fame
   As the wanderings of his race—
And many a seeker of wisdom came
   To his lonely dwelling place;
For he made the darkest symbols clear,
Of ancient doctor and early seer.

195.

Yet a question ask'd by a simple maid
He met that eve in the linden's shade,
Had puzzled his matchless wisdom more
Than all that ever it found before;
And this it was: "What path of crime
Is darkest traced ón the map of time?"

The Rabbi ponder'd the question o'er
    With a calm and thoughtful mind,
And search'd the depths of the Talmud's lore—
    But an answer he could not find;—
Yet a maiden's question might not foil
A Sage inured to Wisdom's toil—
And he leant on his hand his aged brow,
For the current of thought ran deeper now:

When, lo! by his side, Ben Levi heard
    A sound of rustling leaves—
But not like those of the forest stirr'd
    By the breath of summer eves,
That comes through the dim and dewy shades
As the golden glow of the sunset fades,
Bringing the odors of hidden flowers
That bloom in the greenwood's secret bowers—

But the leaves of a luckless volume turn'd
    By the swift impatient hand
Of student young, or of critics learn'd
    In the lore of the Muse's land.
The Rabbi raised his wondering eyes—
Well might he gaze in mute surprise—
For, open'd wide to the moon's cold ray,
A ponderous volume before him lay!

Old were the characters, and black
As the soil when sear'd by the lightning's track,
But broad and full that the dimmest sight
Might clearly read by the moon's pale light;

But, oh! 'twas a dark and fearful theme
  That fill'd each crowded page—
The gather'd records of human crime
  From every race and age.

All the blood that the Earth had seen
Since Abel's crimson'd her early green;
All the vice that had poison'd life
Since Lamech wedded his second wife;
All the pride that had mock'd the skies
  Since they built old Babel's wall;—
But the page of the broken promises
  Was the saddest page of all.

It seem'd a fearful mirror made
For friendship ruin'd and love betray'd,
For toil that had lost its fruitless pain,
And hope that had spent its strength in vain;
For all who sorrow'd o'er broken faith—
Whate'er their fortunes in life or death—
Were there in one ghastly pageant blent
With the broken reeds on which they leant.

And foul was many a noble crest
  By the Nations deem'd unstain'd—
And, deep on brows which the Church had bless'd,
  The traitor's brand remain'd.

For vows in that blacken'd page had place
  Which time had ne'er reveal'd
And many a faded and furrow'd face
  By death and dust conceal'd—
Eyes that had worn their light away
In weary watching from day to day,
And tuneful voices which Time had heard
Grow faint with the sickness of hope deferr'd.

The Rabbi read till his eye grew dim
  With the mist of gathering tears,
For it woke in his soul the frozen stream
  Which had slumber'd there for years

And he turn'd to clear his clouded sight,
From that blacken'd page to the sky so bright—
And joy'd that the folly, crime, and care
Of Earth could not cast one shadow there.

For the stars had still the same bright look
  That in Eden's youth they wore;—
And he turn'd again to the ponderous book—
  But the book he found no more;
Nothing was there but the moon's pale beam—
And whence that volume of wonder came,
Or how it pass'd from his troubled view,
The Sage might marvel, but never knew!

Long and well had Ben Levi preach'd
  Against the sins of men—
And many a sinner his sermon reach'd
  By the power of page and pen;
Childhood's folly, and manhood's vice,
And age with its boundless avarice,
All were rebuk'd, and little ruth
Had he for the venial sins of youth.

But never again to mortal ears
  Did the Rabbi preach of aught
But the mystery of trust and tears
  By that wondrous volume taught.
And if he met a youth and maid
  Beneath the linden boughs—
Oh, never a word Ben Levi said,
  But—"Beware of Broken Vows!"
                              FRANCES BROWNE.

The Emperor and the Rabbi

"OLD Rabbi, what tales dost thou pour in mine ear,
  What visions of glory, what phantoms of fear,
Of a God, all the gods of the Roman above,
A mightier than Mars, a more ancient than Jove?

TALMUDICAL PERIOD

"Let me see but His splendors, I then shall believe.
'Tis the senses alone that can never deceive.
But show me your Idol, if earth be His shrine,
And your Israelite God shall, old dreamer, be mine!"

It was Trajan that spoke, the stoical sneer
Still played on his features sublime and severe,
For, round the wild world that stooped to his throne,
He knew but one god, and himself was that one!

"The God of our forefathers," low bowed the Seer,
"Is unseen by the eye, is unheard by the ear;
He is Spirit and knows not the body's dark chain;
Immortal His nature, eternal His reign.

"He is seen in His power, when the storm is abroad;
In His justice, when guilt by His thunders is awed;
In His mercy, when mountain and valley and plain
Rejoice in His sunshine, and smile in His rain."

"Those are dreams," said the monarch, "wild fancies
      of old;
But what God can I worship, when one I behold?
Can I kneel to the lightning, or bow to the wind?
Can I worship the shape, that but lives in the mind?"

"I shall show thee the herald He sends from His
      throne."
Through the halls of the palace the Rabbi led on,
Till above them was spread but the sky's sapphire
      dome,
And, like surges of splendor, beneath them lay Rome.

And towering o'er all, in the glow of the hour,
The Capitol shone, earth's high centre of power;
A thousand years glorious, yet still in its prime;
A thousand years more, to be conquered of Time.

But the West was now purple, the eve was begun;
Like a monarch at rest, on the hills lay the sun;
Above him the clouds their rich canopy rolled,
With pillars of diamond, and curtains of gold.

The Rabbi's proud gesture was turned to the orb:
"O King! let that glory thy worship absorb!"
"What! worship that sun, and be blind by the gaze?"
No eye but the eagle's could look on that blaze."

"Ho! Emperor of earth, if it dazzles thine eye
To look on that orb, as it sinks from the sky,"
Cried the Rabbi, "what mortal could dare to see
The Sovereign of him, and the Sovereign of thee!"

GEORGE CROLY.

He of Prayer

HIDDEN in the ancient Talmud,
    Slumbereth this legend old,
By the stately Jewish Rabbis
    To the listening people told;
Jacob's ladder still is standing,
    And the angels o'er it go
Up and down from earth to heaven,
    Ever passing to and fro;
Messengers from great Jehovah
    Bringing mortals good or ill,
Just as we from laws unchanging,
    Good or evil shall distill.
He of Death, with brow majestic,
    Cometh wreathed with asphodel;
He of life, with smile seraphic,
    Softly saying, "All is well."
He of Pain, with purple pinions,
    He of Joy, all shining bright;
He of Hope, with wings cerulean;
    He of innocence, all white.

200

And the rustling of their pinions,
　　With the falling of their feet,
Turneth into notes of music,
　　Grand and solemn, soft and sweet.
One—and only one—stands ever
　　On the ladder's topmost round,
Just outside the gate celestial,
　　List'ning as to catch some sound;
But it is not angel music
　　Unto which he bends his ear,
'Tis the passing prayer of mortals
　　That he patient waits to hear.
By him messengers are flitting,
　　But he ever standeth there,
For he is the Great Sandalphon
　　Who is gathering every prayer.
In his hands they turn to garlands,
　　From whose flowers a fragrance floats
Through the open gates celestial,
　　Mingled with the angels' notes.
For outside the golden portal
　　Of that city of the skies
All the earthly dross and passion
　　Of the prayer of mortal dies.
'Tis the heavenly essence only
　　That can find an entrance there,
Turned into the scent of flowers
　　By Sandalphon—Him of Prayer.

　　　　　　　　　　　　　　　　J. F.

The Angel of Truth

Based upon a passage of the Midrash, Bereshit Rabba,
Chapter VIII.

ONCE th' omnipotent Maker of world without end
　　Bade the hosts of His angels in council attend;
And thus in His wisdom supernal He spake:
"In the confines of earth in our image we'll make

201

Man, whose spirit divine shall from Heav'n proclaim
    him,
Yet as human we Adam, the earth-born, will name
    him."
Then the band of bright beings, in potent dissent,
Into two hostile factions asunder were rent.

"Create him, I pray," cried the Angel of Love,
"He will strive to resemble Thy nature above;
I behold his employment—his labours how blest,
He 'mid hunger and sickness will aid the distressed;
With a tear in his eye, and compassion at heart,
He will freely sweet solace where need is impart.
Create man, I pray," cried the Angel of Love,
"He will strive to resemble Thy spirit above."

But the Angel of Faithfulness thereupon rose,
The creation of man might and main to oppose;
"He will break the most sacred of compacts, I weet,
And the words that he utters be fraught with deceit;
Nought but falsehood will issue from man's teeming
    brain,
Whilst hypocrisy ever forms part of his train."
Quoth the Angel of Faithfulness; "God, in Thy plan
Of creation include not a being like man."

Then the Angel of Justice cried: "Heaven! create him,
Love of Law and promotion of concord await him;
I behold him fence in the possession of right,
And all barbarous violence putting to flight;
With firmly fixed laws states and cities he'll bind,
Whilst with order cementing the bonds of mankind.
Let man be created, then," Justice implored,
"By whom harmony jarred shall at last be restored."

"O do not make man!" cried the Angel of Peace,
"For ere long, 'neath his sway law and order shall
    cease;

States and cities laid waste will attest where he's been,
With his sword steeped in blood of his brother, I
    ween:
Dread war and destruction will follow his path,
And the world be o'erspread with dire carnage and
    wrath.
Great spirit of Life! engender him not,
Who from records of earth law and order will blot."

Thus in hopeless divergence, in Heaven's bright bow-
    ers,
The spirits angelic were spending their powers,
Till the Angel of Truth, in God's glory effulgent,
Thus was summoned to plead in a tone more indulgent.
"Truth! lead by thy light to the bliss of salvation,
Free from errors and prejudice man's aberration,
That each neighbour beside him a brother may seem,
God above him the Father of all he shall deem,
Tho' for thousands of years his pure mind be o'er-
    cast,
With thine aid it shall shine all unclouded at last,
Truth shall still of the claims of strict justice remind
    him,
Till persistently seeking blest peace she shall find
    him,
Then Truth, Justice, and Peace shall, in process of
    time,
Loud proclaim upon earth Heaven's kingdom sub-
    lime."

So man was created—though earth clogged his soul—
May have wandered full oft from its heavenly goal
To make known the One Father, who wills that man-
    kind
Be by Faith and by Truth, Peace and Justice com-
    bined,
Until God shall be King on that glorious day,
And His sovereign Law all His creatures obey.

                       LEOPOLD STEIN.

The Faithful Bride

A Midrashic Parable

THERE is a legend (and 'tis quaintly sweet),
  Of man and maid, who loved, long, long, ago.
But fate was cruel,—they were forced to part,
  And she was left alone in grief and woe.

And she was left alone in grief and woe,
  Nor heeded she their taunts and scornful jeers;
But in the secret vigils of the night,
  His letters read again with many tears.

Sweet promises, writ to her long ago—
  They warmed her heart these words of living flame;
And much men marveled, for her trust proved true;
  With pomp and glory back her lover came. ·

"My own," he said, "Why didst thou trust in me,
  When men but mocked,—and I away so long?"
"Dear heart," she said, "I read thy loving words,
  Read and believed, and so my love grew strong."

Wouldst read the moral in my simple lines?
  The bride is Israel, her Beloved, He
Who ruleth heaven and earth, the Lord our God;
  And she who was so sad, shall happy be.

And He shall say, "O tender rose of mine,
  Which I have taken back beyond recall,
What kept alive thy simple faith in Me?"
  "Thy Law, O Lord, which was my joy, my all!"

                              ANONYMOUS.

The Tongue

SAID Rabbi Simon to his son;
"To market-place do quickly run
   Naphtali, my lusty lad,
   And buy the 'best' that can be had
Of things to eat. I say the 'best,'
Put thou thy intellect to test!"

"A hind-let-loose," was Naphtali,
   And quick to strike the bargain best.
"Think ye, I bring a spicy tart,
   Or sweet-meats for our worthy guest?"
The youth replied, "if so ye're wrong,
I've bought a well-preserved tongue."

"The tongue had neither fat nor bone,
   Is tender, sweet and toothsome;
This the food that not alone
   Humans eat, but also angels gladsome."
"Well done," the rabbi said. "Now go
My boy, and buy the 'worst' you know."

Again the lad went out, and back
   He came with his bargain gruesome.
A goodly tongue he showed, the same,
   He first did say was wholesome.
"How's that, my son," the father said,
"Can one thing be both good and bad?"

"Yes, father," said young Naphtali,
   "In Holy Writ, in Book of Scriptures,
Much wisdom and delight I've found,
Thus saith the word of inspired song;
   Both life and death are in the tongue!"

JOHN D. NUSSBAUM.

The Tongue

"THE boneless tongue, so small and weak,
   Can crush and kill," declared the Greek.

"The tongue destroys a greater horde,"
The Turk asserts, "than does the sword."

The Persian proverb wisely saith,
"A lengthy tongue—and early death."

Or sometimes take this form instead:
"Don't let your tongue cut off your head."

"The tongue can speak a word whose speed,"
Say the Chinese, "outstrips the steed."

While Arab sage doth this impart;
"The tongue's great storehouse is the heart."

From Hebrew wit the maxim sprung,
"Though feet should slip, ne'er let the tongue."

The sacred writer crowns the whole,
"Who keeps his tongue doth keep his soul."

ANONYMOUS.

The Universal Mother

(Pirke Rabbi Eliezar, ii)

WHEN by the hand of God man was created,
   He took the dust of the earth from every quarter—
From east and west, and from the north and south—
That wheresoever man might wander forth,
He should be still at home; and, when a-dying,
On some far distant western shore, and seeking
A shelter on the bosom of the Mother,
The earth might not refuse to clasp him saying,
"My offspring art thou not, O roving Eastern."

206

Wherever now the foot of Man shall bear him,
Wherever by the final call o'ertaken,
He is no stranger reckoned, or an outcast,
But hears exclaim the Universal Mother,
"Come, child of mine, and slumber in my bosom."

SABINE BARING-GOULD.

Sandalphon

HAVE you read in the Talmud of old,
  In the Legends the Rabbins have told
    Of the limitless realms of the air,
Have you read it,—the marvelous story
Of Sandalphon, the Angel of Glory,
    Sandalphon, the Angel of Prayer?

How, erect, at the outermost gates
Of the City Celestial he waits,
    With his feet on the ladder of light,
That, crowded with angels unnumbered,
By Jacob was seen, as he slumbered
    Alone in the desert at night?

The Angels of Wind and of Fire
Chant only one hymn, and expire
    With the song's irresistible stress;
Expire in their rapture and wonder,
As harp-strings are broken asunder
    By music they throb to express.

But serene in the rapturous throng,
Unmoved by the rush of the song,
    With eyes unimpassioned and slow;
Among the dead angels, the deathless
Sandalphon stands listening breathless
    To sounds that ascend from below;—

From the spirits on earth that adore,
From the souls that entreat and implore

In the fervor and passion of prayer;
From the hearts that are broken with losses,
And weary with dragging the crosses
  Too heavy for mortals to bear.

And he gathers the prayers as he stands,
And they change into flowers in his hands,
  Into garlands of purple and red;
And beneath the great arch of the portal,
Through the streets of the City Immortal
  Is wafted the fragrance they shed.

It is but a legend, I know—
A fable, a phantom, a show,
  Of the ancient Rabbinical lore;
Yet the old mediæval tradition,
The beautiful strange superstition,
  But haunts me and holds me the more.

When I look from my window at night,
And the welkin above is all white,
  All throbbing and panting with stars,
Among them majestic is standing
Sandalphon, the angel, expanding
  His pinions in nebulous bars.

And the legend, I feel, is a part
Of the hunger and thirst of the heart;
  The frenzy and fire of the brain,
That grasps at the fruitage forbidden,
The golden pomegranates of Eden,
  To quiet its fever and pain.

HENRY WADSWORTH LONGFELLOW.

Repent One Day Before Thy Death

HOLD thou thy friend's honor dear as is
    thine own,
Be not to hasty passion prone;
And since life 's but a fleeting breath,
Repent one day before thy death.

RABBI ELEAZAR.

Value of Repentance

THE Doctors in the Talmud say
    That in this world one only day
In true repentance spent will be
More worth than Heaven's Eternitie.

ROBERT HERRICK.

III
MEDIAEVAL PERIOD

Now Die Away, My Tuneful Song

NOW die away, my tuneful song,
  A mournful time veils ancient grief
In recent shrouds.   ANONYMOUS.

Martyrdom

I

WITHOUT, the lonely night is sweet with stars:
  But me an ancient grewsome tale has bound
Of them He chose and later cast aground
As on a raging sea to drift like spars.

Great God! Was it but mockery Thy choice?
  Is martyrdom the highest crown you give?
  And shall a People, maimed and fugitive,
Be bearer of the thunder of Thy Voice?

Burn low, my lamp, I cannot further read;
  The woes of countless thousands o'er me flood!
From out the shadows lurid shapes arise:
Of executioners who foam with greed,
  Of "holy" swords that drip with infants' blood,
    Of flames that roar and shapes that agonize!

II

Behold! What strange procession do I see?
  Before my vision dimmed with tears of rage,
  Emerging as from mists that mar the page,
In sadness stern they tread so solemnly.

The shadows grimly lie to left and right
  Like huge and moving forests o'er them bent:
  Up winds the road in tortuous ascent,
And far and faint a Peak in misty white.

213

And see! From out the lurking shadows leap
  Uncanny shapes of beasts with howl and shriek!
    White flash their fangs, like points of fire their
        eyes!
The victims fall and neither groan nor weep;
  Each lifts his eyes unto the gleaming Peak
    And cries: "The Lord our God is One!" and dies!

III

And yet the night is sweet with stars: away
  Then put the tale of martyrs red with blood,
  Of them He chose to prove in fire and flood,
Of saints defiled, and blazing auto-da-fé.

Come! Ope your lattice; why forever read?
  The million-jewelled heavens are awake
  As when to Abraham the Voice outspake:
"As numberless as Heaven's stars thy seed!"

Sweet, friendly stars! Your splendor calm
  Has not since then diminished by a gleam!
    Are ye not witness to the promise still?
Then, heir of sorrow, purge your heart of qualm!
  Shall bitterness of soul dislodge the dream?
    The Peak still glimmers: thrill, my spirit, thrill!

                              RUFUS LEARSI.

During the Crusades

THY faithful sons, whom Thou in love hast owned,
  Behold! are strangled, burnt and racked and
      stoned;
Are broken on the wheel; like felons hung;
Or, living, into noisome charnels flung.
I see them yonder, of their eyes bereft,
And there their mangled limbs in twain are cleft.
Beneath the wine-press are their bodies drawn,
Crushed, drowned, or with harsh saws asunder sawn.

                              ELEAZAR.

214

SWIFT as birds of prey, they darted
On our helpless men and women,
Making martyrs of our people.
But they slew the body only,
And the soul escaped uninjured.
They assailed us with false pretexts,
Yea, with wrongful accusations—
"For the festive season," said they,
"Ye have slain a Christian infant!"
Yet, withal, they promised pardon,
If our faith we would relinquish.
None of the believers faltered!
First was Samuel executed;
Next his wife, and then his daughter,
Son's wife, brothers, and their offspring.
Simchah bent his head in prayer;
Joseph and his race we honor,
For he went to death in triumph.
Moses stood in fire encircled,
Followed by his son and daughter;
Who, entwined, would join their father.
Israel's tears in streams were flowing;
Nor could tears the flames extinguish.
Also Shabtai and his consort,
Who would not their faith abandon,
Were consumed to dust and ashes.
Gracious Lord, behold these victims,
Who in death the truth attested,
"God is One, there is no other!"

MENAHEM BEN JACOB.

THOU, to whom my name bears witness,
Be not silent, I entreat Thee;
Leave not hid mine ebbing life's blood!
High above in heaven's regions,
Far and wide in halls of learning,
And where people meet together,
Be my sacrifices published!

How my tender infants perished;
How their tortures laid me prostrate,
Learn to know their deeds of horror!
We were crushed and rent asunder,
Until corpse by corpse lay buried.

*　　*　　*　　*　　*　　*

When suffering under tryant's torture,
Our wives would practise priestly functions,
And sacrifice their cherished offspring;
While on the mother's knee they nestled,
The woeful work was calmly finished;
As if they went to sleep in quiet.
No heed was given to the precept,
"Slay not the young one with its mother";
For now no sheep from folds were taken.
Tied down like lambs prepared for slaughter,
There perished fathers, sons, whole households;
And God was hallowed in his glory.
When they beheld the pictured idols,
They cried: Depart! let us be murdered!

DAVID BEN MESHULLAM.

———————

CRUEL foes with hate inflamed,
Aimed at us their fatal blow;
Guileless was the man they seized;
And when savagely they slew him,
Angels came and bade him welcome;
Took his soul in charge, and blessed it.
O'er him Zion's daughter weepeth,
Israel for Elijah mourneth,
With the Holy One communing.

"Throughout the kingdom of the nations,
Who can be equalled to Thy people?
They followed Thee through flame and flood
As none on earth have followed Thee."
Alas! our hearts within us melted,

216

And all our pride sank into ashes.
Elijah rose in fire to heaven,
And round the pile the congregation
Gazed with amazement at the hero.

The pride of Israel, precious gems,
Were given over to the brute,
As undefended by their chief,
Baptizing tyrants seized on those
Who were the noblest of my race.
It was the month when blossoms fresh
Are ripening into golden fruit:
My flowers had their perfume spread,
When wicked men with fiery rage
Did carry off the helpless prey.
They all, as one, resolved to die.
No ransom would the priest accept,
But harshly pressed them with his creed.
They all who pined in prison's night
Were vainly tortured all the day;
As once, at Sinai, one in mind,
They swore allegiance to their faith.
Well would they die, but not rebel;
They dreaded none, but Judah's God.
"To Him," said they, "our troth is pledged,
Away with gods, the works of stone!"
To test the fearless heroes' strength
There stood prepared the funeral pile;
And they with joy awaited death,
Like those whose bridal-day has dawned.

HILLEL BEN JACOB.

YES, they slay us and they smite,
    Vex our souls with sore affright;
All the closer cleave we, Lord,
To thine everlasting word.
Not a word of all their Mass
Shall our lips in homage pass;

Though they curse, and bind, and kill,
The living God is with us still.
Yes, they fain would make us now,
Baptized, at Baal's altar bow;
On their raiment, wrought with gold,
See the sign we hateful hold;
And, with words of foulest shame,
They outrage, Lord, the holiest name.
We still are thine, though limbs are torn;
Better death than life forsworn.

Noblest matrons seek for death,
Rob their children of their breath;
Fathers, in their fiery zeal,
Slay their sons with murderous steel;
And in heat of holiest strife,
For love of Thee, spare not their life.
The fair and young lie down to die
In witness of Thy Unity;
From dying lips the accents swell,
"Thy God is One, O Israel";
And bridegroom answers unto bride,
"The Lord is One, and none beside";
And, knit with bonds of holiest faith,
They pass to endless life through death.

E. H. PLUMPTRE.

BEHOLD, O Lord, Thy faithful people!
The father slays his child, the dear one;
The mother has her task accomplished,
And sends to Thee her hallowed offspring.
Across their knees the parents brandish
The keen-edged knives for work of slaughter;
The mother ties the child,
The father makes the gash;
They say a sacrificial blessing,
For they are met to die together,
And to make known Thy holy Oneness.

And one announces to the other,
"This day we keep a feast of union!"
Their children all they immolate,
As free-will gifts, as bonds of love.

ANONYMOUS.

———

THEY seized our holy congregations,
  And sent among them fire, murder!
The heroes all, Thy true adorers,
Together met in convocation.
They spared no more their offspring,
Thy faith alone they honored.
The great and small, together
With mothers' babes, were slaughtered
Like offerings at the festive season.
They shouted out, "Remove your horrors,
Not them, but death we freely follow!"
And from the homes resounded wailing;
And in the streets the sword made havoc.
"O give me death!" the son entreated;
This filled the father's heart with gladness,
As though he went to joyous nuptials.
The loving hand had hushed all sorrows,
And from distress it brought deliverance;
It led the friend to blissful slumber.

EZRA BEN TANHUM.

———

ALTHOUGH tormented and ill-treated,
  And dragged to die upon the scaffold,
We cling to Thee with growing fervor.
They strike and wound us sorely,
To turn our hearts from Him that liveth,
And to impress us with their worship.
They tempt us with enticements,
And would ensnare us with their cunning;
That we, deserting Thee, should barter
Our faith for faith in Baal's power.

Embroidered even on their vesture
Is shown to us the sign of terror.
With flattery, too, they would beguile us;
But we are Thine, though maimed and shattered!
The pious wives despatch the work
And offer up their guileless babes,
The fathers quickly slay their sons,
And wish not to survive their dead.
To render homage to Thy unity,
The young, the fair, prepare for death,
With "Hear O Israel!" on their lips.
The bride and bridegroom now breathe forth
The dying words, "The Lord is One!"
They who, in life were wedded,
Through hallowed death are reunited.

KALONYMUS BEN JUDAH.

Israél Mocked

"WHY so sad, thou princely child?"
Moloch's servants scornfully chide,
Times appear and pass away
Why does son of Jesse hide?
If your God in Heaven's height
Will bring you to His holy hill
Wherefore then we seek to know
Why His chariots linger still?

I hoped that all my foes
Would see my swift redemption;
But they mock and say: "Away as a cloud
It passeth; no hope is left for thee."
I hearken shame-filled, and my tears
Flow unresistingly.

ANONYMOUS.

The Massacre of the Jews at York
An Historical Poem

"And scattered and scorn'd as thy people may be,
"Our worship, O Father, is only for thee." BYRON.

THERE is an old and stately hall,
    Hung round with many a spear and shield,
And sword and buckler on the wall
  Won from the foe in tented field:
Yet there no warrior bands are seen,
With martial step and lofty mien;
But men with care, not age, grown white,
Meet in York Castle hall to-night,
And groups of maids and matrons too,
With hair and eyes, whose jetty hue
Belong to Judea's sunny land,
Are mingling with that sorrowing band:
What doth the Jew—the wandering race
Of Israel, in such dwelling place?
From persecution's deadly rage
A refuge in those walls they sought,
The zealots of a barb'rous age,
Ruin upon their tribes had brought.

      .   .   .   .   .

All was silent without, there was not a sound,
There was not a whisper, there was not a breath
To disturb the silence still and profound,
All was hush'd as the vale of the shadow of death:
Within was tumult—loud and wild debate
'Mongst those who at that midnight council sate;
Famine was on each check, and every eye
Told fearfully of its wild ministry.
Starvation and despair their councils urg'd,
And in those feelings every other merged:
Parents almost forgot their children's cry
In their own overwhelming misery;
As the rush of the waves when the winds are in
    motion,
And the storm-gods abroad on the dark heaving ocean,

Was the voice of the crowd 'til the Rabbi arose,
Then at once every sound was hush'd into repose.
Bent was his form, but more with care than age,
Sorrow had worn the furrows in his face;
Yet in the features of the revered sage
Somewhat of youthful ardour might you trace,
As the old oak that's hollow'd out by time
Seems to retain the vigour of its prime,
"Men of Israel," he said, with a proud flashing eye,
"This night doth Jehovah command us to die,
The death of the brave, for the laws that He gave,
Leave bondage and chains for the coward and slave!
What is our crime, O what is the deed,
For which so many are doom'd to bleed?
Strangers—alike through every clime we are hurl'd,
Through every land our seed is spread abroad—
Scorn'd and despised, the outcasts of the world,
Yet still the chosen people of our God!
We asked these Britons for a home,
A shelter from the inclement skies:
Have we despoiled a Christian dome,
Or sought a Christian sacrifice?
We did but ask a dwelling place,
And in return our wealth we gave;
They spurn'd us as an outcast race,
And brand us with the name of slave:
They hate us, for we seek to tread
The peaceful path our fathers trod;
They hate us, for we bow our heads
Before the shrine of Israel's God;
And now because we sought to bring
A tribute to their new crown'd king,
Like savage beasts they hunt us down,
Their streets with Jewish dead are strewn;
And they who can boast of mercy and love,
And picture their God in the form of a dove,
Are athirst for our blood, our possession they crave!
But the wealth we have toiled for, they never shall
    have

222

While there's fire on the hearthstone or sword in the
    hall,
By the hand of each other 'tis better to fall:
There have been times, and this is such a time,
When even suicide is not a crime:
Behold how your wives and your children are cling-
    ing
Around ye, and pray for a morsel of bread,
While the cold heartless wretches beneath have been
    flinging
Profusion away, and they carelessly tread
On the food that your wives and your children would
    save
From the pangs of starvation—the jaws of the grave!
Then shall such monsters triumph o'er us?
They think that yield to them we must,
Where'er we turn, there's death before us;
We cannot to their mercy trust,
We cannot on their faith rely,
Then let us see our dear ones die;
Thus, thus will we defy our foes,
By our own hands they all shall bleed,
Their blood be on the heads of those
Who goaded us to such a deed.
The husband turneth to his wife,
The lover to his lov'd doth cling—
To raise an arm against the life
Of woman, is a fearful thing!
Aye, so it is: but I have here
A stake that is to me as dear,
The solace of my widow'd years,
The object of my fondest cares."
He pointed where there stood apart
Watching the chosen one of her heart,
A maiden passing fair;
Her raven hair was backward flung,
And on her brow of snow there hung
A dark cloud of despair,
Ah! little did poor Rachel deem

223

When in her spirits first bright dream
With beaming eyes and flushing brow
She listened to Manasseh's vow,
That such a fearful hour as this
Would ever blight her dream of bliss.
She was Ben Israel's only child,
A child of one long passed away,
And he upon their loves had smil'd,
And gladly named the bridal day.
He glanc'd his eyes around, as he paused,
To mark the effect which his words had caused:
The men sat silent, and scarce drew breath,
As they heard the decree that doom'd them to death.
The mother convulsively press'd to her heart
The lov'd babe from whom she so soon was to part.
The matron seem'd bound by a holier tie
To the lord of her heart, with whom she must die.
None murmured a sound—save a few who sate
At the end of the hall, in deep debate;
The quivering limb and downcast eye
Told they were cowards who fear'd to die.
At length Ben Ephraim rose and spoke,
And at once the death-like silence broke:—
"Ben Israel," he said, " 'tis a dread decree,
For we might once again be free:
We might bribe the foemen our lives to save,
And snatch our little ones from the grave."
Ben Israel rose, and dash'd the trace
Of the tears from off his rugged face
(Which had gathered there, in spite of his pride)
Then turn'd to the coward and thus replied:—
"Seek ye for mercy? ask yon man of blood
(Who dares to call himself a priest of God),
For mercy! and ye will such mercy find
As the pursuing huntsman gives the hind;
Such mercy as the hapless bird may seek
When closely clutch'd within the vulture's beak!
In yonder blood-stained city did they spare
The brave, the ag'd, the youthful, or the fair?

No! babes from their mother's breasts were torn,
And their dying shrieks on the air were borne;
Nor did they heed the father's accents wild,
Entreating them to save his darling child;
But hew'd them down like cattle, where they stood,
And wash'd out their religion in their blood!
Women of Israel! would ye not rather
Fall by the hand of a husband or father,
Than brave the insults that await
Ye, when they force the castle gate?
When the Israelites echoed the Maccabees' cry
As they raised the Asmonean banner on high,
They stayed not to think upon danger or death,
But glorified God with their last fainting breath,
And left in their country's annals a name
That will ne'er be erased from the records of fame.
Then think on the glorious dead
Of ages long gone by;
Think on the cause for which they bled,
And like them dare to die;
For the laws which our God to his prophet reveal'd,
Yes! our faith in their truth, with our blood must be
    seal'd.
Depart! all ye who would be slaves,
Nor dare disturb our latest breath:
Depart! and leave the glorious graves
For those who prefer to apostacy—Death."
A few of the weaker and cowardly-hearted,
Rose from their seats at his words and departed.
All became silent then around;
The very children hush'd their crying;
In that vast hall there was not a sound,
As Ben Israel read the prayers for the dying.
He ceased:—Five hundred voices raise
To heaven's high throne the hymns of praise,
And ever as the echoes rung,
The self-devoted victims sung—Halleluyah!

MARION AND CELIA MOSS.

The Harvesting of the Roses

FROM his garden bed our Lòrd
　　Blossoms for his pleasure chose,
Who came to gather many a rose.
Nòbles waited for his word;
Amidst the rage of murderous blows
They were in death to him restored.

MENAHEM BEN JACOB.

A Martyr's Death

"WHERE is now Elijah's God?"
　　When will scoff and scorning end?
Has our God forsaken us?
Higher and higher,
Winged by fire,
Soared Elijah's sainted soul,
Bliss to earn in spheres of life.
He saw his brethren sorely tried,
And died for them a martyr's death.

MENAHEM BEN JACOB.

The Jewish Martyr

"BRING forth the Jew!" Ben Hassim said, "the
　　caitiff of his creed,
Who has reviled our holy faith, and triumphed in the
　　deed;
Blaspheming great Mahomet's name—by Allah! he
　　shall die;
Upon his own accursed head the blasphemy shall lie.
Woe unto thee, thou Jewish dog! if thou fail to clear
　　the guilt
That is preferred against thee—deny it, if thou wilt!
But decided proof of innocence must in clearest light
　　be shown
Or, by Medina's holy shrine, the flame shall have her
　　own.
How say you, son of Israel, to the charge that's now
　　preferr'd?

226

By Mecca! 'tis the gravest that was ever told or
    heard;
Be cautious, then, and have a mind you add not lie to
    lie,
If truth is not found uppermost the bowstring's
    strength we'll try."

"I am not guilty of the charge—'tis foul and falsely
    made;
'Tis jealousy and malice in dreadful form convey'd—
Convey'd to suit the purpose of those who bring me
    here;
They're fellow-merchants with myself—we've traded
    many a year.
I never even thought the words, the blasphemy, you
    name,
I swear by Heaven I'm innocent! I'll ever swear the
    same;
It is against our holy creed, which teaches us to love
Each and all our fellow men—'tis true, as God's
    above!—
And not revile, or lightly speak, whate'er their creed
    may be;
As this is taught, so have I learnt—the guilt is not
    with me."

"Upon the Koran's holy book the solemn truth is
    seal'd,
The accusation's verified—your guilt is now reveal'd!
Thy star has set, thy doom is fix'd; before the setting
    sun
Shall light the tops of yonder hills, know that thy
    course is run;
For death awaits, with greedy hand, so great a gain as
    thou,
And what avails thy holy soul in such a time as now?
That boasted zeal that warms your youth, that burns
    within your breast,
Mayhap we'll try; your courage, too, shall also feel the
    test.

A Mufti waits, in solemn guise, say, wilt thou join his
    band,
And with him swell the numbers that overrun the land,
Who believe in our holy Prophet—Mahomet, blest
    be he?
Wilt thou a Mussulman become? If so, thou shalt be
    free.
You'll not, and say, you'd rather die—by my faith, in-
    deed you're true;
First hear the roar and see the blaze—you know not
    what you do."

          *   *   *   *   *

The faggots flame in fiery wreath; behold a funeral
    pyre;
Before its glowing embers fierce shall blanch, shall
    wane, expire—
A sacrifice of human blood, of human flesh and bone,
Must, drop and crackle in that blaze—'tis there no
    mercy's shown.
Yet there he stands a martyr, unerring, true to God,
So earnest in his dire resolve—so firm he pac'd the sod;
Undaunted by the quiv'ring thought of the death that
    did await—
A death of bitter agony, of pain and anguish great.
With arms across his stricken breast, and eyes serenely
    set,
Calm was his gaze, so full of hope that speaking eye
    of jet;
Upon that brow all dignified, sat piety resigned—
A piety all hallow'd, with hope and trust combin'd.
His was the hope, the vital hope, the hope that never
    dies,
The light that even torture with its deadliest throes
    defies;
The solemn, grand, and heavenly thought, of devotion
    —constant, true,
That had mark'd his young and pious life, now gave
    him life anew;

And through the bitter vale of tears, the vale that leads
    to death,
The unity of Israel's God he prais'd with sacred breath;
"O Lord! receive my soul," he cried; "I am resign'd
    to die;
Blest be Thy name, the terror's past, the horror I defy.
The devouring flames may crackle, and sere the thews
    of youth,
But mine it is the triumph—I die for faith and truth."

                        MOSS MARKS.

A Song of Redemption

CAPTIVE of sorrow on a foreign shore,
    A handmaid as 'neath Egypt's slavery;
Through the dark day of her bereavement sore
        She looketh unto Thee.
Restore her sons, O Mighty One of old!
Her remnant tenth shall cause man's strife to cease.
O speed the message; swiftly be she told
Good tidings, which Elijah shall unfold:
Daughter of Zion, sing aloud! behold:
        Thy Prince of Peace!

Wherefore wilt Thou forget us, Lord, for aye?
        Mercy we crave!
O Lord, we hope in Thee alway,
        Our King will save!

Surely a limit boundeth every woe,
But mine enduring anguish hath no end;
My grievous years are spent in ceaseless flow,
      My wound hath no amend.
O'erwhelmed, my helm doth fail, no hand is strong
To steer the bark to port, her longed for aim.
How long, O Lord, wilt Thou my doom prolong?
When shall be heard the dove's sweet voice of song?
O leave us not to perish for our wrong,
    Who bear Thy Name!

Wherefore wilt Thou forget us, Lord, for aye?
    Mercy we crave!
O Lord, we hope in Thee alway,
    Our King will save!

Wounded and crushed, beneath my load I sigh,
Despised and abject, outcast, trampled low;
How long, O Lord, shall I of violence cry,
    My heart dissolve with woe?
How many years, without a gleam of light,
Has thraldom been our lot, our portion pain!
With Ishmael as a lion in his might,
And Persia as an owl of darksome night,
Beset on either side, behold our plight
    Betwixt the twain.

Wherefore wilt Thou forget us, Lord, for aye?
    Mercy we crave!
O Lord, we hope in Thee alway,
    Our King will save!

    Is this Thy voice?
The voice of captive Ariel's woe unhealed?
Virgin of Israel, arise, rejoice!
In Daniel's vision, lo, the end is sealed:
    When Michael on the height
    Shall stand aloft in strength,
    And shout aloud in might,
And a Redeemer come to Zion at length.
    Amen, amen, behold
    The Lord's decree foretold.
E'en as Thou hast our souls afflicted sore,
So wilt Thou make us glad for evermore!

Wherefore wilt Thou forget us, Lord, for aye?
    Mercy we crave!
O Lord, we hope in Thee alway,
    Our King will save!

          SOLOMON IBN GABIROL.
          (Translated by Nina Davis.)

Jehuda Ben Halevy

(Fragment)

I

"IF, Jerusalem, I ever
  Should forget thee, to the roof
Of my mouth then cleave my tongue,
May my right hand lose its cunning—"

In my head the words and music
Round and round keep humming, ringing,
And I seem to hear men's voices,
Men's deep voices singing psalms—

And of long and shadowy beards
I can also catch some glimpses—
Say, which phantom dream-begotten
Is Jehuda ben Halevy?

But they swiftly rustle past me,
For the ghosts avoid, with terror,
Rude and clumsy human converse;
Yet, in spite of all, I knew him.

Yes, I knew him by his forehead
Pale and proud with noble thought,
By the eyes of steadfast sweetness;
Keen and sad they gazed in mine.

But more specially I knew him
By the enigmatic smiling
Of the lovely lips and rhythmic
That belong to poets only.

Years they come, and years they vanish;
Seven hundred years and fifty
It is now since dawned the birthday
Of Jehuda ben Halevy.

At Toledo in Castile
First he saw the light of heaven,
And the golden Tagus lulled him
In his cradle with its music.

The unfolding of his powers
Intellectual was fostered
By his father strict, who taught him
First the book of God, the Thora.

With his son he read the volume
In the ancient text, whose fair,
Picturesque and hieroglyphic,
Old-Chaldean, square-writ letters

From the childhood of our world
Have been handed down, and therefore
Seem familiarly to smile on
All with naive, childlike natures.

And this ancient, uncorrupted
Text the boy recited also
In the Tropp—the sing-song measure,
From primeval times descended.

And the gutturals so oily,
And so fast he gurgled sweetly,
While he shook and trilled and quavered
The Schalscheleth like a bird,

And the boy was learned early
In the Targum Onkelos,
Which is written in low-Hebrew
In the Aramaean idiom,

Bearing somewhat the resemblance
To the language of the prophets
That the Swabian does to German—
In this curious bastard Hebrew,

As we said, the boy was versed,
And ere long he found such knowledge
Of most valuable service
In the study of the Talmud. . .

Yes, his father led him early
To the Talmud, and threw open
For his benefit that famous
School of fighting the Halacha.

Where the athletes dialectic,
Best in Babylon, and also
Those renowned in Pumbeditha
Did their intellectual tilting.

He had here the chance of learning
Every art and ruse polemic;
How he mastered them was proven
In the book Cosari, later.

But the lights are twain, and differ,
That are shed on earth by heaven;
There's the harsh and glaring sunlight,
And the mild and gentle moonlight.

With a double radiance also
Shines the Talmud; the Halacha
Is the one, and the Hagada
Is the other light. The former

I have called the school of fighting;
But the latter, the Hagada
I will call a curious garden,
Most fantastic, and resembling

Much another one that blossomed
Too in Babylon—the garden
Of Semiramis; 'mongst wonders
Of the world it was the eighth.

Queen Semiramis, whose childhood.
With the birds was spent, who reared her,
Many birdlike ways and habits
In her later life retained;

And, unwilling to go walking
On the flat and common earth,
Like us other common mortals,
Made a garden in the air—

High on pillars proud, colossal,
Shone the cypresses and palms,
Marble statues, beds of flowers,
Golden oranges and fountains;

All most cunningly and surely
Bound by countless hanging bridges,
That might well have passed as creepers,
And on which the birds kept swinging—

Birds of many colours, solemn,
Big, contemplative and songless,
While the tiny, happy finches,
Gaily warbling, fluttered round them—

All were breathing, blest and happy,
Breathing pure and balmy fragrance,
Unpolluted by the squalid,
Evil colour of the earth.

The Hagada is a garden,
Is just such another whimsy
Of a child of air, and often
Would the youthful Talmud scholar,

When his heart was dazed and dusty
With the strifes of the Halacha,
With disputes about the fatal
Egg the hen laid on a feast day,

Or concerning other problems
Of the same profound importance—
He would turn to seek refreshment
In the blossoming Hagada,

Where the beautiful old sagas,
Legends dim, and angel-fables,
Pious stories of the martyrs,
Festal hymns and proverbs wise,

And hyperboles the drollest,
But withal so strong and burning
With belief—where all, resplendent,
Welled and sprouted with luxuriance!

And the generous heart and noble
Of the boy was taken captive
By the wild romantic sweetness,
By the wondrous aching rapture,

By the weird and fabled terrors
Of that blissful secret world,
Of that mighty revelation
For which poetry our name is.

And the art that goes to make it,
Gracious power, happy knowledge,
Which we call the art poetic,
To his understanding opened.

And Jehuda ben Halevy
Was not only scribe and scholar,
But of poetry a master,
Was himself a famous poet;

Yes, a great and famous poet,
Star and torch to guide his time,
Light and beacon of his nation;
Was a wonderful and mighty

Fiery pillar of sweet song,
Moving on in front of Israel's
Caravans of woe and mourning
In the wilderness of exile.

True and pure and without blemish
Was his singing, like his soul—
The Creator having made it,
With His handiwork contented,

Kissed the lovely soul, and echoes
Of that kiss forever after
Thrilled through all the poet's numbers,
By that gracious deed inspired.

As in life, in song the highest
Good of all is simply grace,
And who hath it cannot sin in
Either poetry or prose.

And that man we call a genius,
By the grace of God a poet,
Monarch absolute, unquestioned,
In the realm of human thought:

None but God can call the poet
To account, the people never—
As in art, in life the people
Can but kill, they cannot judge us.

HEINRICH HEINE.
(Translated by Margaret Armour.)

To Judah Ha-Levi

IMPASSIONED hours, when Hebrew was the key
To sweetest rivalries 'twixt man and man.
And poets sat enthroned amidst a clan
Of choristers divine. How blithesomely

Those skylarks trilled, and flooded earth and sea
  With music, till the words enchanted fell
  In mute prostration 'neath the wizard's spell,
And master note in Hebrew minstrelsy.

At sunrise, or in watches of the night,
  When half a world is sunk in drowsiness,
Sing to me of Castilian skies, O Sprite!
  Where Lilith veils her luresome loveliness,
And I will stretch a tankard for the wine,
And froth it full of tears for Spain's decline.

M. L. R. BRESLAR.

How Long?

HOW long wilt thou in childhood's slumber lie?
  Know that youth flies like chaff the wind before.
Can spring forever last? Nay, soon draws nigh
Old age's messenger with tresses hoar.
Shake thyself free from sin, as ere they fly,
The birds shake of the night-dews' pearled store.
Cast off temptations that thy peace defy,
Like troubled waves upon a rocky shore,
And follow after that pure company
Of souls that seek God's goodness evermore

JUDAH HA-LEVI.

Back, My Soul

I

BACK, my soul, into thy nest;
  Earth is not for thee;
Still in heaven find thy nest;
  There thou canst be free.

Strive not for this world's command,
  Look to what thou hast,
Thou amidst the angels' band
  Shar'd the great repast.

Demean thee 'fore the majesty
  Of him who reigneth there,
And in a lordly company
  Be thou the courtier.

JUDAH HA-LEVI.
(Translated by M. Simon.)

Oh! City of the World

OH! city of world, most chastely fair;
  In the far west, behold I sigh for thee.
And in my yearning love I do bethink me
Of bygone ages; of thy ruined fane,
Thy vanished splendor of a vanished day.
Oh! had I eagles' wings I'd fly to thee,
And with my falling tears make moist thine earth;
I long for thee; what though indeed thy kings
Have passed forever; though where once uprose
Sweet balsam trees the serpent makes his nest.
Oh! that I might embrace thy dust, the sod;
Were sweet as honey to my fond desire.

JUDAH HA-LEVI.
(Translated by Kate Magnus.)

The Immortality of Israel

THE sun and moon unchanging do obey
  The laws that never cease or night or day.
Appointed signs are they to Jacob's seed
That life eternal hath been them decreed.

238

And though, O Lord, thy left hand dealeth pain,
Thy right shall lead them back to joy again.
Let not despair oppress their quailing heart,
Though radiant Fortune from their midst depart.
But let this constant faith their soul uphold,
That in the Book of Life their name's enrolled
For all eternity: nor shall they cease
While night and day do alternate in peace.

JUDAH HA-LEVI.
(Translated by Israel Cohen.)

The Pride of a Jew

WITH all my heart, in truth, and passion strong,
    I love Thee; both in solitude and throng
Thy name's with me, alone I shall not bide:
My friend art Thou, though others from me glide,
My lamp art too: my light shall never fade,
Nor shall my foot e'er slip, by Thee upstayed.
They little knew who have despised me so,
That shaming me doth cause my pride to glow.
O Fountain of my life, I'll bless Thee aye,
And sing Thy praises, O my song, alway!

JUDAH HA-LEVI.
(Translated by Israel Cohen.)

The Lord Is My Portion

SERVANTS of time, lo! these be slaves of slaves;
    But the Lord's servant hath his freedom whole,
Therefore, when every man his portion craves,
    "The Lord God is my portion," saith my soul.

JUDAH HA-LEVI.

239

My Heart Is in the East

MY heart is in the East, tho' in the West I live,
    The sweet of human life no happiness can give,
Religion's duties fail to lift my soul on high;
'Neath Edom Zion writhes, in Arab chains I lie!
No joy in sunny Spain mine eyes can ever see
For Zion, desolate, alone hath charms for me!

JUDAH HA-LEVI.
(Translated by H. Pereira Mendes.)

Separation

AND so we twain must part! Oh linger yet,
    And let me still feed my glance upon thine eyes.
Forget not, love, the days of our delight,
    And I our nights of bliss shall ever prize.
In dreams thy shadowy image I shall see,
    Oh, even in my dream be kind to me!

Though I were dead, I none the less would hear
    Thy step, thy garment rustling on the sand.
And if thou waft me greetings from the grave,
    I shall drink deep the breath of that cold land.
Take thou my days, command this life of mine,
    If it can lengthen out the space of thine.

No voice I hear from lips death-pale and chill,
    Yet deep within my heart it echoes still,
My frame remains—my soul to thee yearns forth.
    A shadow I must tarry still on earth.
Back to the body dwelling here in pain,
    Return, my soul, make haste and come again!

JUDAH HA-LEVI.

"From Thee to Thee"

WHEN all within is dark,
   And former friends misprise;
From them I turn to Thee,
   And find Love in Thine eyes.

When all within is dark,
   And I my soul despise;
From me I turn to Thee,
   And find Love in Thine eyes.

When all Thy face is dark,
   And Thy just angers rise;
From Thee I turn to Thee,
   And find Love in Thine eyes.

SOLOMON IBN GABIROL.
(Translated by I. A.)

The Cry of Israel

THOU knowest my tongue, O God,
   Fain would it bring
A precious gift—the songs
   Thou makest me sing!

Thou guidest my steps from eld;
   If boon too high
I ask—Thou gavest me speech,
   Spurn not my cry!

My thoughts hast Thou made pure
   As whitest fleece;
Thou wilt not that mine heart
   Shall ne'er have peace.

Oh, be my refuge now,
  Even as of yore.
My God, my Savior, Thou—
  Tarry no more!

                SOLOMON IBN GABIROL.
        (Translated by Solomon Solis Cohen.)

O Soul, with Storms Beset!

O SOUL, with storms beset,
      Thy griefs and cares forget!
  Why dread earth's transient woe,
When soon thy body in the grave unseen
      Shall be laid low,
And all will be forgotten then, as though
      It had not been?

      Wherefore, my soul, be still!
      Adore God's holy will,
    Fear death's supreme decree.
Thus mayst thou save thyself, and win high aid
      To profit thee,
When thou, returning to thy Lord, shalt see
      Thy deeds repaid.

      Why muse, O troubled soul,
      O'er life's poor earthly goal?
      When thou hast fled, the clay
Lies mute, nor bear'st thou aught of wealth, or might
      With thee that day,
But, like a bird, unto thy nest away,
      Thou wilt take flight.

      Why for a land lament
      In which a lifetime spent
      Is as a hurried breath?
Where splendour turns to gloom and honours show
      A faded wreath
Where health and healing soon must sink beneath
      The fatal bow.

MEDIAEVAL PERIOD

What seemeth good and fair
Is often falsehood there.
Gold melts like shifting sands,
Thy hoarded riches pass to other men,
And strangers' hands
And what will thy treasured wealth and lands
Avail thee then?

Life is a vine, whose crown
The reaper Death cuts down.
His ever-watchful eyes
Mark every step, until night's shadows fall,
And swiftly flies
The passing day, and ah! how distant lies
The goal of all.

Therefore, rebellious soul,
Thy base desire control;
With scantily given bread
Content thyself, nor let they memory stray
To splendours fled,
But call to mind affliction's weight and dread
The judgment day.

Prostrate and humbled go,
Like to the dove laid low.
Remember evermore
The peace of heaven, the Lord's eternal rest.
When burdened sore
With sorrow's load, at every step implore
His succour bless'd.

Before God's mercy-seat
His pardoning love entreat.
Make pure thy thoughts from sin,
And bring a contrite heart as sacrifice
His grace to win—
Then will His angels come and lead thee in
To Paradise.   SOLOMON IBN GABIROL.
                (Translated by Alice Lucas.)

Rabbi Don Santob, or Santo

THIS poet, a Jew by birth, flourished about 1360.
His name is not known, but he seems to have received the title of Santo by way of honor; "perhaps," says Sanchez, "for his moral virtues and his learning." He is supposed to have been either a native or a resident of Carrion.

THE DANCE OF DEATH

Here begins the general dance, in which it is shown how Death gives advice to all, that they should take due account of the brevity of life, and not to value it more highly than it deserves; and this he orders and requires, that they see and hear attentively what wise preachers tell them and warn them from day to day, giving them good and wholesome counsel that they labor in doing good works to obtain pardon for their sins.

Lo! I am Death! With aim as sure as steady,
  All beings that are and shall be I draw near me.
I call thee,—I require thee, man, be ready!
  Why build upon this fragile life?—Now hear me!
  Where is the power that does not own me, fear me?
Who can escape me, when I bend my bow?
I pull the string,—thou liest in dust below,
  Smitten by the barb my ministering angels bear me.

Come to the dance of Death! Come hither, even
  The last, the lowliest,—of all rank and station!
Who will not come shall be by scourges driven:
  I hold no parley with disinclination.
  List to yon friar who preaches of salvation,
And hie ye to your penitential post!
For who delays,—who lingers,—he is lost,
  And handed o'er to hopeless reprobation.

I to my dance—my mortal dance—have brought
  Two nymphs, all bright in beauty and in bloom.
They listened, fear-struck, to my songs, methought;
  And truly, songs like mine are tinged with gloom.
  But neither roseate hues nor flowers' perfume
Will now avail them,—not the thousand charms
Of worldly vanity;—they fill my arms,—
  They are my brides,—their bridal bed the tomb.

    •   •   •   •   •

And since 'tis certain, then, that we must die,—
  No hope, no chance, no prospect of redress,—
Be it our constant aim unswervingly
  To tread God's narrow path of holiness:
  For He is first, last, midst. O, let us press
Onwards! and when Death's monitory glance
Shall summon us to join his mortal dance,
  Even then shall hope and joy our footsteps bless.

Song of the Spanish Jews

"It was in Spain that the golden age of the Jews
shone with the brightest and most enduring splendour.
"In emulation of their Moslemite brethren, they
began to cultivate their long disused and neglected
poetry; the harp of Judah was heard to sound again,
though with something of a foreign tone."—*Milman's
History of the Jews.*

OH, dark is the spirit that loves not the land,
  Whose breezes his brow have in infancy fann'd;
That feels not his bosom responsively thrill
To the voice of her forest the gush of her rill.

Who hails not the flowers that bloom on his way,
As blessings there scattered his love to repay;
Who loves not to wander o'er mountain and vale,
Where echoes the voice of the loud rushing gale.

Who treads not with awe where his ancestors lie;
As their spirits around him are hovering nigh.
Who seek not to cherish the flowers that bloom,
Amid the fresh herbs that o'ershadow the tomb.

Oh, cold is such spirit; and yet colder still
The heart that for Spain does not gratefully thrill;
The land, which the foot of the weary had pressed,
Where the exile and wand'rer found blessing and rest.

On the face of the earth our doom was to roam,
To meet not a brother, to find not a home,
But Spain has the exile and homeless received,
And we feel not of country so darkly bereaved.

Home of the exile! oh ne'er will we leave thee,
As mother to orphan, fair land we now greet thee,
Sweet peace and rejoicing may dwell in thy bowers,
For even as Judah, fair land thou art ours.

Oh, dearest and brightest! the homeless do bless thee,
From ages to ages they yearn to possess thee,
In life and in death they cling to thy breast,
And seek not and wish not a lovelier rest.

GRACE AGUILAR.

I Will Not Have You Think Me Less

I WILL not have you think me less
　　Than others of my faith,
Who live on a generous king's largess,
　　Forsworn at every breath.

And if you deem my teachings true,
　　Reject them not with hate,
Because a minstrel sings to you
　　Who's not of knight's estate.

246

The fragrant, waving reed grows tall
  From feeble root and thin,
And uncouth worms that lowly crawl
  Most lustrous silk do spin.

Because beside a thorn it grows,
  The rose is not less fair;
Though vine from gnarled branches flows,
  'Tis sweet beyond compare.

The goshawk, know, can soar on high,
  Yet low he nests his brood,
A Jew true precepts doth apply,
  Are they therefore less good?

Some Jews there are with slavish mind
  Who fear, are mute, and meek.
My soul to truth is so inclined
  That all I feel I speak.

There often comes a meaning home
  Through simple verse and plain,
While in the heavy, bulky tome
  We find of truth no grain.

Full oft a man with furrowed front,
  Whom grief hath rendered grave,
Whose views of life are honest, blunt,
  Both fool is called and knave.

SANTOB DE CARRION.

Why Should I Wander Sadly?

WHY should I wander sadly,
  My harp within my hand,
O'er mountain, hill, and valley?
  What praise do I command?

Full well they know the singer
  Belongs to race accursed;
Sweet *Minne* doth no longer
  Reward me as at first.

Be silent, then, my lyre,
  We sing 'fore lords in vain,
I'll leave the minstrels' choir,
  And roam a Jew again.

My staff and hat I'll grasp, then,
  And on my breast full low,
By Jewish custom olden
  My grizzled beard shall grow.

My days I'll pass in quiet,—
  Those left to me on earth—
Nor sing for those who not yet
  Have learned a poet's worth.

SUSSKIND VON TRIMBERG.

Sonnet

MY sweet gazelle! From thy bewitching eyes
  A glance thrills all my soul with wild delight,
Unfathomed depths beam forth a world so bright—
With rays of sun its sparkling splendor vies—
One look within a mortal defies.
  Thy lips, the gates where through dawn wings its
    flight,
Adorn a face suffused with royal light,
Whose radiance puts to shame the vaulted skies.
Two brilliant stars are they from heaven sent—
  Their charm I cannot otherwise explain—.
By God but for a little instant lent,
  Who gracious doth their lustrous glory deign,
To teach those on pursuit of beauty bent,
  Beside those eyes all other beauty's vain.

IMMANUEL BEN SOLOMON OF ROME.

248

Sonnet

MY soul surcharged with grief now loud complains,
And fears upon my spirit heavily weigh,
"Thy poem we have heard," the people say,
"Who like to thee can sing melodious strains?"
"They're naught but sparks," outspeaks my soul in
      chains,
"Struck from my life by torture every day.
But now all perfume's fled—no more my lay
Shall rise; for, fear of shame my song restrains."
A woman's fancies lightly roam, and weave
Themselves into a fairy web. Should I
Refrain? Ah! soon enough this pleasure, too,
Will flee! Verily I cannot conceive
Why I'm extolled. For woman 'tis to ply
The spinning wheel—then to herself she's true.

RACHEL MORPURGO.

Sonnet

O LORD, Thou know'st my inmost hope and
      thought,
Thou know'st whene'er before Thy judgment throne
I shed salt tears, and uttered many a moan.
'Twas not for vanities that I besought.
O turn on me Thy look with mercy fraught,
And see how envious malice makes me groan!
The pall upon my heart by error thrown,
Remove; illume me with Thy radiant thought.
At truth let not the wicked scorner mock,
O Thou, that breath'dst in me a spark divine.
The lying tongue's deceit with silence blight,
Protect me from its venom, Thou, my Rock,
And show the spiteful sland'rer by this sign
That Thou dost shield me with Thy endless might.

SARA COPIA SULLAM.

Friendship

WHAT treasure greater than a friend
  Who close to us hath grown?
Blind fate no bitt'rer lot can send
  Than bid us walk alone.

For solitude doth cause a dearth
  Of fruitful, blessed thought,
The wise would pray to leave this earth,
  If none their friendship sought.

Yet sad though loneliness may be,
  That friendship surely shun
That feigns to love, and inwardly
  Betrays affections won.

SANTOB DE CARRION.

IV

THE JEWISH YEAR

The Spirit of the Sabbath

"Come my beloved to meet the bride, the presence
of the Sabbath let us receive."—JEWISH PRAYER
BOOK.

ON evening's bosom snowy cloudlets weave,
   Light fantasies the veil of night shall hide.
The wraiths of spectral cares that softly glide
In silentness, and plaintive sighs that heave
From those who have no strength to loudly grieve,
Are hushed; and in an ecstasy of pride,
The soul of rest and stillness glorified.
Welcome the beauty of the Sabbath Eve!
Peace folds the soul, as petals fold a flower,
Hushed in sweet slumbers with night's darkened spell,
The bride has entered in her lovely bower,
Where love entrenched in radiance doth dwell,
And decked in sweetness, purity and truth,
We greet her in her everlasting youth.

ISIDORE G. ASCHER.

Princess Sabbath

IN Arabia's book of fable
  We behold enchanted princes
Who at times their form recover,
Fair as first they were created.

The uncouth and shaggy monster
Has again a king for father;
Pipes his amorous ditties sweetly
On the flute in jewelled raiment.

Yet the respite from enchantment
Is but brief, and, without warning,
Lo! we see his Royal Highness
Shuffled back into a monster.

253

Of a prince by fate thus treated
Is my song. His name is Israel,
And a witch's spell has changed him
To the likeness of a dog.

As a dog, with dog's ideas,
All the week, a cur, he noses
Through life's filthy mire and sweepings,
Butt of mocking city Arabs;

But on every Friday evening,
On a sudden, in the twilight,
The enchantment weakens, ceases,
And the dog once more is human.

And his father's halls he enters
As a man, with man's emotions,
Head and heart alike uplifted,
Clad in pure and festal raiment.

"Be ye greeted, halls beloved,
Of my high and royal father!
Lo! I kiss your holy door-posts,
Tents of Jacob, with my mouth!"

Through the house there passes strangely
A mysterious stir and whisper;
And the hidden master's breathing
Shudders weirdly through the silence.

Silence! save for one, the steward
(Vulgo, synagogue attendant)
Springing up and down, and busy
With the lamps that he is lighting.

Golden lights of consolation,
How they sparkle, how they glimmer!
Proudly flame the candles also
On the rails of the Almemor.

By the shrine wherein the Thora
Is preserved, and which is curtained
By a costly silken hanging,
Whereon precious stones are gleaming.

There, beside the desk already
Stands the synagogue precentor,
Small and spruce, his mantle black
With an air coquettish shouldering;

And, to show how white his hand is,
At his neck he works—forefinger
Oddly pressed against his temple,
And the thumb against his throat.

To himself he trills and murmurs,
Till at last his voice he raises;
Till he sings with joy resounding,
"Lecho dodi likrath kallah!"

"Lecho dodi likrath kallah—
Come, beloved one, the bride
Waits already to uncover
To thine eyes her blushing face!"

The composer of this poem,
Of this pretty marriage song,
Is the famous minnesinger,
Don Jehudah ben Halevy.

It was writ by him in honour
Of the wedding of Prince Israel
And the gentle Princess Sabbath,
Whom they call the silent princess.

Pearl and flower of all beauty
Is the princess—not more lovely
Was the famous Queen of Sheba,
Bosom friend of Solomon,

Who, Bas Bleu of Ethiopia,
Sought by wit to shine and dazzle,
And became at length fatiguing
With her very clever riddles.

Princess Sabbath, rest incarnate,
Held in hearty detestation
Every form of witty warfare
And of intellectual combat.

She abhorred with equal loathing
Loud declamatory passion—
Pathos ranting round and storming
With dishevelled hair and streaming.

In her cap the silent princess
Hides her modest, braided tresses,
Like the meek gazelle she gazes,
Blooms as slender as the myrtle.

She denies her lover nothing
Save the smoking of tobacco;
"Dearest, smoking is forbidden,
For to-day it is the Sabbath.

"But at noon, as compensation,
There shall steam for thee a dish
That in very truth divine is—
Thou shalt eat to-day of schalet!

"Schalet, ray of light immortal!
Schalet, daughter of Elysium!"
So had Schiller's song resounded,
Had he ever tasted schalet,

For this schalet is the very
Food of heaven, which, on Sinai,
God Himself instructed Moses
In the secret of preparing,

At the time He also taught him
And revealed in flames of lightning
All the doctrines good and pious,
And the holy Ten Commandments.

Yes, this schalet's pure ambrosia
Of the true and only God:
Paradisal bread of rapture;
And, with such a food compared,

The ambrosia of the pagan,
False divinities of Greece,
Who were devils 'neath disguises,
Is the merest devils' offal.

When the prince enjoys the dainty,
Glow his eyes as if transfigured,
And his waistcoat he unbuttons;
Smiling blissfully he murmurs,

"Are not these the waves of Jordan
That I hear—the flowing fountains
In the palmy vale of Beth-el,
Where the camels lie at rest?

"Are not these the sheep-bells ringing
Of the fat and thriving wethers
That the shepherd drives at evening
Down Mount Gilead from the pastures?"

But the lovely day flits onward,
And with long, swift legs of shadow
Comes the evil hour of magic—
And the prince begins to sigh;

Seems to feel the icy fingers
Of a witch upon his heart;
Shudders, fearful of the canine
Metamorphosis that waits him.

Then the princess hands her golden
Box of spikenard to her lover,
Who inhales it, fain to revel
Once again in pleasant odours.

And the princess tastes and offers
Next the cup of parting also—
And he drinks in haste, till only
Drops a few are in the goblet.

These he sprinkles on the table,
Then he takes a little wax-light,
And he dips it in the moisture
Till it crackles and is quenched.

HEINRICH HEINE.
(Translated by Margaret Armour.)

The Sabbath Lamp

(Suggested by a picture painted by S. A. Hart, R.A.)

SHINE, Sabbath Lamp, oh shine with tender ray!
  Pierce the soft wavelets of the fading light;
Speed the faint footsteps of the waning day,
  And greet the shadows of the coming night.

Cast thy rays upward,—cleave the darkening air,
  And lift a stream of brilliant light on high;
Shine on the wings of Faith, and may they bear
  The wavering wandering heart from earth to sky!

Fling thy beams forward,—may their radiance meet
  The welcome presence of the heaven-sent guest;
Illume the path she treads with glistening feet;
  The Sabbath Bride of Israel's panting breast!

Cast thy gleams backward—Six days' toils are told;
  Soothe with thy smile the wearied breast and brain;
And may thy glittering lustre change to gold
  Each seventh link in life's dull iron chain.

258

THE JEWISH YEAR

Shed thy rays downward—may their sacred ray
  On life's rough road of earthly travel shine;
And strew the crags that fret the rugged way,
  With sparkling gems which breathe a light divine!

Cast thy beams inward—may they pierce the fold
  That each one gathers round his secret breast;
Shew forth the idol in its godless mould,
  That we may crush it in our bosom's nest!

Shed thy rays outward,—lest at last we grow,
  Centered in self—and life's best purpose mock;
And dwell, unmindful of a brother's woe,
  Like callous limpet on the weed-bound rock.

Cast thy beams homeward—may they sweetly bear
  The smiles of household peace where'er they shine;
Test of an earthly mother's tender care,
  Type of the heavenly Father's love divine.

Shine near and far—in every Jewish home—
  In every clime—on every distant shore,—
Where in the stranger land the loved ones roam:
  Oh! let us greet them in thy gleams once more!

Ah, shine afar! and may thy waves of light
  Bring near the absent dear ones far away,
Show us our loved ones in our dreams to-night,—
  Our dead who rest in Heaven's bright Sabbath day!

For Faith, like Light, sheds beams on every side;
  Faith shares with Light its radiating power,
Then shine, oh Lamp! and greet the Sabbath bride,
  And shine, oh Faith! and bless the Sabbath hour.

Shine on the Past—and, as the raindrops gleam
  With rainbow tints where'er the sunbeams rest,
So may our tears grow bright beneath thy beam,
  And every grief be sanctified and blest.

Shine on the Present—may thy beacon-light
   Beam on life's sea where mists and tempests reign;
And may its radiance guide our course aright,
   And fling its silvery track across the main.

Shine on the Future—lead these hearts of ours
   Far beyond home and clime and native strand;
Light up the East—gleam on yon ruined towers;
   And rend the gloom that veils our long-lost land.

Shine Sabbath Lamp, with ray of heavenly birth,
   Emblem of Faith and Hope in Mercy given;
Gleam on the rude, dark path we tread on earth,
   And light our souls to find the road to Heaven.

GRACE AGUILAR.

Blessing the Lights

SILVER candlesticks that beam,
   Holding candles ranged in line,
Stand on snowy tablecloth,
   Near the Sabbath bread and wine.

Lovingly my mother lights
   Six white candles, one for each
Dear and loving, living child,
   When the twilight hours reach

Bringing in the Sabbath bride;
   And in festive robes arrayed,
Spreads her palms before her eyes
   Moistened by the tears that strayed;

And, like beamings of Shekinah,
   Some ethereal beauty plays
Round her lips as, nodding, she
   In a plaintive murmur prays,

260

By the candle's light and flame;
  And her face begins to shine,
And her brow with grace is haloed
  And transfigured, calm, divine

Looks she, chanting soft and low;
  "Lord of life and joy and light,
Man whose flame of life is short
  Makes his light all clear and bright.

"May my children, plants of Zion,
  Love Thee, doing Thy behest,
Fed on manna of the Bible,
  Nourished by the Torah's breast.

"Make us, scions of the prophets,
  Happy in a life lived whole;
Lived in honor, labor, love,
  Lived in holiness of soul.

"I, Thy handmaid, what am I?
  But to all you deign your grace;
Make my children little lights,
  Lighting well their little place.

"Make us, seed of Abraham,
  Love-flames burning far and free;
Lights of love and lights of virtue,
  Shining, beaming, God, for Thee."

ALTER ABELSON.

Song for Friday Night

THOU beautiful Sabbath, thou sanctified day,
  That chasest our cares and our sorrows away,
O come with good fortune, with joy and with peace,
To the homes of thy pious, their bliss to increase!

In honour of thee are the tables decked white;
From the clear candelabra shines many a light;
All men in the finest of garments are dress'd,
As far as his purse, each hath got him the best.

For as soon as the Sabbath-hat 's put on the head,
New feelings are born and old feelings are dead;
Yes, suddenly vanish black care and grim sorrow,
None troubles concerning the things of tomorrow.

New heavenly powers are given to each;
Of everyday matters now hush'd is all speech;
At rest are all hands that have toil'd with much pain;
Now peace and tranquillity everywhere reign.

Not the choicest of wines at a banqueting board
Can ever such exquisite pleasure afford
As the Friday-night meal when prepared with due zeal
To honour thee, Sabbath, thou day of sweet rest!

With thy angels attending thee, one at each side,
Come on Friday betimes in pure homes to abide,
In the homes of the faithful that shine in their bliss,
Like souls from a world which is better than this!

One Angel, the good one, is at thy right hand,
At thy left doth the other, the bad Angel, stand;
Compell'd 'gainst his will to say "Amen," and bless
With the blessing he hears the good Angel express:

That when Sabbath, dear Sabbath, thou comest again,
We may lustily welcome thee, free from all pain,
In the fear of the Lord, and with joy in our heart,
And again keep thee holy till thou shalt depart!

Then come with good fortune, with joy and with
    peace,
To the homes of thy pious, their bliss to increase!
Already we've now been awaiting thee long,
All eager to greet thee with praise and with song,
ISIDORE MYERS.

The Hebrew's Friday Night

"COME, my beloved, to meet the Bride; the Face
    of the Sabbath let us welcome."

Sweet Sabbath-Bride, the Hebrew's theme of praise,
    Celestial maiden with the starry eyes,
Around thine head a sacred nimbus plays,
    Thy smile is soft as lucent summer skies,
    Before thy purity all evil dies,
In wedding-robe of stainless sunshine drest,
    Thou dawnest on Life's darkness and it dies;
Thy bridal-wreath is lilies Heaven-blest,
Thy dowry Peace and Love and Holiness and Rest.

For in thy Presence he forgets a while
    The gloom and discord of man's mortal years,
To seek the Light that streameth from thy Face,
    To list thy tender lullaby, which cheers
    His soul and lies like music on his ears.
His very sorrows with soft splendor shine,
    Transfigured by a mist of sacred tears;
He drinks thy gently offered Anodyne,
And feels himself absorbed into the Peace divine.

The Father from the Synagog returns
    (A singing-bird is nestling at his heart),
And from without the festive light discerns
    Which tells his faithful wife has done her part
    To welcome Sabbath with domestic art,
He enters and perceives the picture true,
    And tears unbidden from his eyelids start,
As Paradise thus opens on his view,
And then he smiles and thanks his God he is a Jew.

For "Friday-night" is written on his home
    In fair, white characters; his wife has spread
The snowy Sabbath-cloth; the Hebrew tome,
    The flask and cup are at the table's head,

263

There's Sabbath magic in the very bread,
And royal fare the humble dishes seem;
  A holy light the Sabbath candles shed,
Around his children's shining faces beam,
He feels the strife of every day a far-off dream.

His buxom wife he kisses, then he lays
  Upon each child's young head two loving hands
Of benediction, so in after-days,
  When they shall be afar in other lands,
  They shall be knit to God and home by bands
Of sacred memory. And then he makes
  The blessing o'er the wine, and while each stands,
The quaintly convoluted bread he breaks,
Which tastes to all to-night more sweet than honeyed
  cakes.

And now they eat the Sabbath meal with laugh
  And jest and gossip till all fun must cease,
While Father chants the Grace, all singing half,
  And then the Sabbath hymns of Love and Peace
  And Hope from alien lands to find release.
No evil can this night its head uprear,
  Earth's joys loom larger and its ills decrease;
To-night of ghosts the youngest has no fear—
Does not his guardian Sabbath-Angel hover near?

So in a thousand squalid Ghettoes penned,
  Engirt yet undismayed by perils vast,
The Jew in hymns that marked his faith would spend
  This night and dream of all his glorious Past
  And wait the splendors by his seers forecast.
And so while medieval creeds at strife
  With nature die, the Jew's ideals last,
The simple love of home and child and wife,
The sweet humanities which make our higher life.

                              ANONYMOUS.

Sabbath Hymn

COME forth, my friend, the bride to meet,
　Come, O my friend, the Sabbath greet.

"Observe ye" and "remember" still
The Sabbath—thus His holy will
God in one utterance did proclaim.
The Lord is One, and One His name
To Him renown and praise and fame.
　Come forth, my friend, the bride to meet,
　Come, O my friend, the Sabbath greet.

Greet we the Sabbath at our door,
Well-spring of blessing evermore
With everlasting gladness fraught,
Of old ordained, divinely taught,
Last in creation, first in thought.
　Come forth, my friend, the bride to meet,
　Come, O my friend, the Sabbath greet.

Arouse thyself, awake and shine,
For lo! it comes, the light divine;
Give forth a song and over thee
The glory of the Lord shall be
Revealed in beauty speedily.
　Come forth, my friend, the bride to meet,
　Come, O my friend, the Sabbath greet.

Crown of thy husband come in peace.
Come, bidding toil and trouble cease.
With joy and cheerfulness abide
Among thy people true and tried,
Thy faithful people—come O bride.
　Come forth, my friend, the bride to meet,
　Come, O my friend, the Sabbath greet.

SOLOMON ALKABIZ.

265

Come, My Beloved

COME, my beloved, to meet the Bride
  With joy, at Sabbath even-tide;
Her presence then will surely dower
Your home with peace at Sabbath hour.

To meet the Bride, beloved, come,
Greet her with welcome in your home,
The doors of Jewish faith ope wide,
And greet with love the Sabbath bride.

Come, my beloved, the Bride to meet—
Hasten thy steps, the Bride to greet;
But not to every passing show
To meet her, let thy footsteps go.

The presence of the Sabbath Bride
Seek thou, by happy fireside,
Where young and old their voices blend
And Sabbath songs from both ascend;

But, see, who comes with mien so sad?
The Sabbath Bride, in mourning clad!
The beloved fails the Bride to meet,
And Sabbath eve again to greet.

Sadly she goes from door to door—
To her they're shut forevermore!
For her no festal board is spread,
With Sabbath cup and blessing bread.

But, Bride, thou art not quite bereft—
Of those who loved thee, some are left
Who gladly give at eventide
A welcome to the Sabbath Bride.

Then thither let thy footsteps roam,
Your holy presence fill their home,
Where, all united, side by side,
With joy receive the Sabbath Bride.

M. M.

The Sabbath Eve

IN quaint old Talmud's pages,
Where speak the Jewish sages,
I found this pearl tonight:
Behold it, fair and white!

For, as the rabbins say,
Two angels guard the way
  Of him on Sabbath eve
Who turns his homeward feet
Off through the busy street,
  The synagogue to leave.
And if the lamps are lit,
If there the maidens sit
With the mother by their side;
If there the youths abide
At the quiet eventide—
Then speaks the spirit blest—
"Here let all blessing rest!
May every Sabbath be
Like this one unto thee;
Peace to this dwelling, peace!"
And he of little ease,
The restless demon, then,
Mutters a rough "Amen!"

But if the darkness there
Obscures the evening prayer;
If matron and if maid
Show worldliness displayed;
And if the youths have place
In regions low and base—
Then sneers the evil one:
"Be all thy blessings gone!
Make every Sabbath be
Like this one unto me!"

And, with his head bent low,
The other in his woe,
Must weep and utter then
His sorrowful, "Amen!"

SAMUEL AUGUSTUS WILLOUGHBY DUFFIELD.

Friday Night

FRIDAY NIGHT! come draw the curtain;
  I am weary with the week;
Sit before the grate-fire with me,
  And together let us speak;
Put aside your books and papers—
  It is neither night nor day,
And the Sabbath morn approaches;
  Put your endless toil away.

Watch the fire-light—how it flickers!
  See the light and shadow play;
From the fender to the carpet
  And across the curtain gay;
See its gentle fairy-fingers
  Touch the pictures on the wall,
Giving them a life-like beauty
  Lending grace to each and all.

Over yonder hangs a picture
  Sheltered from the dancing gleam;
See its dim, uncertain outlines,
  Like the mem'ry of a dream;
Watch the light dispel the shadows,
  And observe the lovely face;
See, it seems the Sabbath Spirit,
  Cloth'd with pure and tender grace;

Calling to your mind the missing
  Angels of our household band,
Who, on bygone Sabbath evenings,
  Sat beside us, hand in hand;

268

Bringing back our hopes and longings,
  Crowning them with light divine,
Showing us our vain endeavors,
  Softened by the glow of time;

Speaking of its own sweet image,
  As our fathers knew it best—
Beautiful in true thanksgiving
  For the day of peace and rest;
Teaching us to break the shadows
  Hovering o'er its lov'd face,
With the glowing light of fervor
  Kindled by our ancient race.

But I know I'm only dreaming,
  'Tis a picture—nothing more—
Image of some lovely maiden
  Famed in song or fairy lore;
Drop the curtain, watch the fire
  Till the shadows flee the light;
Rest awhile within its gleaming,
  On this peaceful Sabbath night.

MIRIAM DEL BANCO.

Friday Night

THE majesty of sunset in the west
    Has glorified the ebbing hours of day!
  The world is hushed as if its heart would pray!
In busy, Jewish homes there enters rest;
The weary soul no longer is depressed,
  A Sabbath calm has come, the children stray
  And prattle every sombre care away,
Our Friday night has made our portals blest!

The lamps are lit in solemn joy and prayer,
  And curtains folded close to hide the night,
  A glow of love in every Sabbath light!

Unspoken blessings fill the chastened air,
And happiness pursues time's gentle flight,
And over all God's blessings everywhere!

                              ISIDORE G. ASCHER.

Sabbath Hymn

DESCEND, descend, O Sabbath Princess,
      With rays of Shechinah in your eyes,
Descend and bring us peaceful tidings,
   From yonder gently dreaming skies!
Behold, in darkness, and in sadness
   We wander here, we climb, we grope,
Descend and give us Faith and Gladness,
   Descend and give us Light and Hope!

Descend, descend, O Sabbath Princess,
   For we are weary here and blind,
Descend and lighten all the burdens
   Of dreary souls and faithless mind.
The paths of life are rough and thorny,
   Our feet are bleeding, bleeding sore,
Descend and bring us Heaven's promise,
   And Sabbath peace for evermore.

                              AARON COHEN.

The Sabbath

NOT for us the Sabbath of the quiet streets,
   Sabbath peaceful o'er the world outspread,
Felt where every man his neighbor greets,
   Heard in hush of many a slowly passing tread.
Not the robe of silence for our holy day:—
   Noisy flock the worker and the player;
Toil and stir and laughter of the way
   Surge around the steps that seek a place of prayer.
Silent we while through the thronging street and mart
   Work-day clamor of the city rolls:—
Cloistered inly, from the world apart,
   Ours 'tis to bear the Sabbath in our souls.

                              NINA DAVIS.

270

Sabbath

THE Sabbath is here, and the heavens are beaming,
    The Shekinah within us is brooding and dreaming,
The soul found a form and a vestment of glory,
And lo, a new Eden and Genesis story.
Peace in an ecstasy came from the mountains,
And opened the heavens, and bliss flows in fountains;
The earth is a heaven, for man has ascended,
And the soul and Shekinah in rapture are blended.
The cherubim young-eyed around us are winging,
My soul is among them; to heaven 'tis clinging;
My soul is on wings now, a soul that is singing;
Holiness, poesy won their sceptre.
And man, man, himself, is a Biblical chapter.
Our souls, we discovered—to-day we have two,
The new life is old, and the old life is new;
O, see how the spirit is wooing God's beauty,
Rapt lovers are we.   Our love is a duty,
Songs of songs our souls are; the heart is a canticle,
In the sunshine of Sabbath, our joy is nigh frantical,
Our transport of peace, it is sweet without cloyance,
We are kings, we are queens, we are princes of joy-
        ance;
The swords are withdrawn and the goal is attained,
One is all mankind, the Eden regained,
The wine of the Kiddush pour forth to o'erflowing,
And sing hymeneals, sing "Zmiroth" all glowing,
For lo, it is Sabbath, the day of God's dreaming,
The day of the perfect—a day without scheming—
Our soul is in heaven, the Star of the Seven,
Then sing like an angel at the gateway of heaven!

                                    ALTER ABELSON.

The Day of Rest

COME, O Sabbath day, and bring
　　Peace and healing on thy wing,
And to every troubled breast
Speak of the divine behest:
　　Thou shalt rest!

Earthly longing bid retire,
Guard our passions' hurtful fire;
To the wayward, sin-oppressed,
Bring thou the divine behest;
　　Thou shalt rest.

Wipe from every cheek the tear:
Banish care, and silence fear;
All things working for the best,
Teach us the divine behest,
　　Thou shalt rest.

　　　　　　　　GUSTAV GOTTHEIL.

When Is the Jew in Paradise?

WHEN is the Jew in Paradise,
　　Unchained from want and care;
When joy wings word of happiness
　　And peace perfumes the air?
When is the hour his heart is light
　　And slow he is to grieve?
The Jew has but one Paradise,
　　And that is Friday eve.

A noble queen, she comes to bless
　　And bear his cares away.
To every home this Princess comes
　　And sanctifies the day.

272

The rich and poor, both old and young,
  With gratitude receive
The Sabbath Princess of the Jew,
  Their guest of Friday eve.

Who sees her face, Shekinah-like,
  He lives a hundred years;
His children's children bless her name
  And all that she endears;
Her sacred, silent footsteps pass
  Through every heart and leave
A thousand blessings for the joy
  She gives on Friday eve.
                              JOSEPH LEISER.

Sabbath Thoughts

I BLESS Thee, Father, for the grace
  Thou me this day hast given,
Strengthening my soul to seek Thy face,
  And list the theme of heaven.

I bless Thee that each work-day care
  Thy love hath lull'd to rest,
And every thought whose wing has prayer
  Thine answering word hath blest.

I bless Thee, Father! Those dark fears
  That linger'd round my heart,
That called for murmurs, doubts and tears,
  Thy mercy bade depart.

O Thou alone couldst send them hence
  On this blessed day of peace,
And with Thy spirit's pure incense
  Bid work-day turmoil cease.
                              GRACE AGUILAR.

God of the World

(A Sabbath Hymn)

GOD of the World, eternity's sole Lord!
  King over kings, be now thy Name adored!
Blessed are we to whom thou dost accord
  This gladsome time thy wondrous ways to scan!

God of the World, eternity's sole Lord!
Early and late to thee our praises ring,
Giver of life to every living thing!
Beasts of the field, and birds that heavenward wing,
  Angelic hosts and all sons of man!

God of the World, eternity's sole Lord!
Though we on earth a thousand years should dwell,
Too brief the space, thy marvels forth to tell.
Pride thou didst lower, all the weak who fell
  Thy hand raised up e'er since the world began!

God of the World, eternity's sole Lord!
Thine is the power, thine the glory be!
When lions rage, O deign thy flock to free!
Thine exiled sons O take once more to thee,
  Choose them again as in thine ancient plan!

God of the World, eternity's sole Lord!
Turn to thy city, Zion's sacred shrine!
On yon fair mount again let beauty shine!
There, happy throngs their voices shall combine,
  There, present joy all former ill shall ban!

God of the World, eternity's sole Lord!
King over kings, be now thy Name adored!

ISRAEL NAGARA.

(Translated by Israel Abrahams.)

A Sabbath of Rest

(A Sabbath Hymn)

THIS day is for Israel light and rejoicing,
  A Sabbath of rest.

Thou badest us standing assembled at Sinai
  That all the years through we should keep thy be-
    hest—
To set out a table full-laden, to honor
  The Sabbath of rest.
This day is for Israel light and rejoicing,
  A Sabbath of rest.

Treasure of heart for the broken people,
  Gift of new soul for the souls distrest,
Soother of sighs for the prisoned spirit—
  The Sabbath of rest.
This day is for Israel light and rejoicing,
  A Sabbath of rest.

When the work of the worlds in their wonder was
    finished,
  Thou madest this day to be holy and blest,
And those heavy-laden find safety and stillness,
  A Sabbath of rest.
This day is for Israel light and rejoicing,
  A Sabbath of rest.

If I keep Thy command I inherit a kingdom,
  If I treasure the Sabbath I bring Thee the best—
The noblest of offerings, the sweetest of incense—
  A Sabbath of rest.
This day is for Israel light and rejoicing,
  A Sabbath of rest.

Restore us our shrine—O remember our ruin
  And save now and comfort the sorely opprest

275

Now sitting at Sabbath, all singing and praising
  The Sabbath of rest.
This day is for Israel light and rejoicing,
  A Sabbath of rest.

                Attributed to ISAAC LURIA.
                (Translated by Nina Davis.)

Hymn for the Conclusion of the Sabbath

MAY He who sets the holy and profane
  Apart, blot out our sins before His sight,
And make our numbers as the sand again,
  And as the stars of night.

The day declineth like the palm-tree's shade,
  I call on God, who leadeth me aright,
The morning cometh—thus the watchman said—
  Although it now be night.

Thy righteousness is like Mount Tabor vast;
  O let my sins be wholly put to flight,
Be they as yesterday, forever past,
  And as a watch at night.

The peaceful season of my prayers is o'er,
  Would that again had rest my soul contrite,
Weary am I of groaning evermore,
  I melt in tears each night.

Hear Thou my voice: be it not vainly sped,
  Open to me the gates of lofty height;
For with the evening dew is filled my head,
  My locks with drops of night.

O grant me Thy redemption, while I pray,
  Be Thou entreated, Lord of power and might,
In twilight, in the evening of the day,
  Yea, in the gloom of night.

THE JEWISH YEAR

Save me O Lord, my God I call on Thee!
  Make me to know the path of life aright,
From sore and wasting sickness snatch Thou me,
  Lead me from day to night.

We are like clay within Thy hand, O Lord,
  Forgive us all our sins both grave and light,
And day shall unto day pour forth the word,
  And night declare to night.

May He who sets the holy and profane
  Apart blot out our sins before His sight,
And make our numbers as the sand again,
  And as the stars of night.

ALICE LUCAS.

The Twin Stars

UP above me star and star—
  Side by side like twins they are:
Like the eyes of God they seem,
  As in Heaven's height they gleam.

Like on Sabbath light and light,
By my mother twinkle bright.
Are there eyes that watch on high?
Are there Sabbaths in the sky?

If Almighty's eyes they be,
Do they fondly look at me?
But if lights for Sabbath-day—
Who'll the Blessing o'er them say?

JOEL BLAU.

(Translated by the author from his Hebrew original.)

277

The Twin Stars

TWO stars are shining in the skies,
  Like twins they are united;
They look like God's own beaming eyes
  In distant darkness lighted.

Like tapers on the Sabbath eve
  That mother kindles for us—
Are there then Sabbaths up on high
  And real eyes gleaming o'er us?

If God Almighty's eyes they are,
  Their soft glance is caressing;
But if they're only Sabbath lamps,
  Who will pronounce the blessing?

JOEL BLAU.

(Translated by George Alexander Kohut.)

The Sabbath Day—Kiddush and Habdalah

THOU sweet Sabbath of rest! Priceless gift from
    above!
Sacred symbol of faith! Fruitful token of Love!
Thrice welcome to him who hath cast off the coil
Of wearisome, worrying, work-a-day toil;
Then in spirit ecstatic that thrills the heart's chord
He exclaims: "Enter hither thou blest of the Lord."
For prepared is my home as a fit dwelling-place
For Heavenly Messengers, Angels of Grace,
Who bear on their wings a new spirit benign
That suffuses man's soul with afflatus divine;
Thus bestowing upon him, for one day in seven,
While a creature incarnate, a foretaste of Heaven.

ANONYMOUS.

278

The Outgoing of Sabbath

THE shadows have taken the place of the sun,
　The Sabbath is over, the glory is gone;
With the gold of the sunset the new soul has flown,
And God, He has shattered his heavenly throne
And closed the effulgent gold gates of the sky,
And the peace and the dream and the rapture all die;
And childhood, the cherub, behold; it takes wing—
A usurper has stolen the crown of the king!
The shew-bread is eaten, no dainties are left,
Of silver and china the table's bereft;
The cover of damask is folded away,
And the household is wrapped in dreariness gray,
The poesy paused, and the weekday's dull prose
Ascended the throne—the thorn for the rose!
No candles are lighted for mothers to bless,
The queen's jewels are hidden and changed is her
　　dress;
The Talith is folded, the incense suppressed,
The golden-clasped Bible is laid in the chest;
A fire is set to the drippings of wine,
The Habdalah light quenched in the smouldering
　　shine;
The last of the wine cup is drained by the young,
And Zemiroth, last strain of the Sabbath is sung;
Unaccountable sadness, some shadowy pain
On the mind and the memory lies like a stain;
The heart with the tumult of being is tossed,
The swords they are blazing, the Paradise 's lost!
The shadow—the shadow replaces the sun,
The last strain of Sabbath's Zemiroth is sung.

ALTER ABELSON.

The Last Sabbath Light

THE last lone Sabbath candle sheds
    Its light as pure as Torah;
Three other wicks as black as night
    Lie spent in the Menorah.

Without, the darkness gathers thick;
    The window panes are frozen—
"Oh, God, let not for my last breath
    A pall of gloom be chosen.

"On me a mother's tears were shed
    One evening of each seven;
So gather up my dying flame
    And build a star in heaven."

H. ROSENBLATT.
(Translated by Leah W. Leonard.)

Selichoth

WHEN the pride of the rose is the image of sor-
    row,
And the leaf that is yellow, steals joy from to-mor-
    row,
When the night is the darkest, and the stars are the
    brightest,
When sleep is the soundest, and dreams are the light-
    est,
When warm is the home, and the heavens are chilly,
And soft is the couch, and the rising is hilly,
When the nests and the flowers are dreaming and
    sleeping,
Who is it, with heaven is silently weeping
As he dashes a dream from his dim drowsy eye,
When searching for signs of the dawn in the sky?
Who is it in shadows, a lantern is lighting,
And fondles a hymnal, days darkened with blighting,

THE JEWISH YEAR

The covers all frayed, and the folios yellowed;
Ah, ages with ages of tear stains here followed;
Who is it with hymnal o'er mountains is running,
Through mists that are mazy, and ways that are cun-
ning,
O'er royalties fallen with manifold sighings,
Where the spirit of autumn is silently crying,
O'er Eden in ruins though dewdrops are falling,
Where things that are widowed and orphaned are
calling,
Through bowers where silent the birds are in dream-
ing
Of songs they will sing when the heavens are beam-
ing,
O'er gems that are sparkling on bluebells and grasses,
O'er flowers unseen, like a spirit who passes
With the dew on his brow, the malign mists defy-
ing?
'Tis the Jew, who to God from the shadow is flying,
And the night's shining soul with a star and a ray,
It brothers the palmer to pray for the Day—
The synagogue seeks he with lights all ashimmer,
And finds there the daylight ere morning stars glim-
mer;
Behold it is Selichoth—the storming of heaven
With prayers and tears till with woe it is riven;
And all the white hymns that are winged with white
fire,
And shod with the lightnings of souls that aspire,
Make way through the seraphs that stand by His
glory,
And tell the Almighty sad Israel's story.
O hearken how myriads of martyrs are crying,
And ages with ages in sorrows are vying!
"O God, who of mercy made sceptre and station,
Who keepeth His love to the thousandth generation,
Long suffering heaven, forgiving transgression
How long will we suffer? O, use your compassion,
And banish injustice, and stay the oppressor,

Redeemer of Israel, sole intercessor!
Make righteousness triumph, make love hold the scep-
    tre,
O write Thy humaner and heavenlier chapter,
Bring the Jew a new morn, bring the world a new
    morrow."
So prayeth the Jew with the Genius of Sorrow!

                    ALTER ABELSON.

The Turn of the Years

HOW may we know you, year of all?
    You come as others came,
Night-sandaled, and your flying feet
Set bells a-swing in every street—
    But you are dumb.

We run, unwearied travelers
    Still on the upward slope
Of life, to take your strong young hand,
To search, to dare, to understand—
    Pilgrims of hope.

You lead us on, you lead us up;
    We seek your avatar
By fords of faith, the pass of tears,
Peaks of delight—O rest of years,
    You take us far!

And then you go. We hear your voice,
    We know your name at last,
You were the Future that we sought,
And all the years may bring us naught
    But you, the Past.

              H. B. FRIEDLANDER.

Into the Tomb of Ages Past

INTO the tomb of ages past
  Another year hath now been cast;
Shall time, unheeded, take its flight,
Nor leave one ray of moral light,
That no man's pilgrimage may shine,
And lead his soul to spheres divine?

Ah, which of us, if self-reviewed,
Can boast unfailing rectitude?
Who can declare his wayward will
More prone to righteous deeds than ill?
Or, in his retrospect of life,
No traces find of passion's strife?

A "still small voice," as time departs,
Bids us inspect our secret hearts,
Whose hidden depths too oft contain
Some spot, which suffered to remain,
Will (slight at first) by sad neglect
The hue of vice at last reflect.

With firm resolve your bosoms nerve
The God of Truth alone to serve,
Speech, thought, and act to regulate,
By what His perfect laws dictate;
Nor from His sanctuary stray,
By worldly idols lured away.

Peace to the house of Israel!
May joy within it ever dwell!
May sorrow on the opening year,
Forgetting its accustomed tear,
With smiles again fond kindred meet,
With hopes revived the festal greet!

PENINA MOÏSE.

Rosh-Hashanah

I STOOD, to-day, in a temple,
  Like one of the olden time;
And I dreamt a dream recalling
  The scenes in an Orient clime;
And I felt, though somewhat strangely,
  An influence sublime!

And before me hung the tablets
  Of the old Mosaic law;
And the white-robed ancient Rabbis,
  Again, in that dream I saw;
And the Hebrew psalms are chanted,
  Those hymns of praise and awe.

And Israel's pristine splendor
  Arose, as in days of old,
When each prophet after prophet
  His tale of promise told;
And the shades of by-gone glories
  Before my vision rolled.

'Tis the New Year of the Hebrew;
  That ancient sacred day,
When the memories of the ages,
  Awake from time's decay,
And the hopes of future glories
  Are bright as the morning's ray!

I beheld the chosen children
  Of the Great Eternal God,
Still bend in mute submission
  To sorrow's painful rod;
Desirous still to follow
  The road by their fathers trod.

And I asked if a faith so lofty
  Could be but a passing show?

And the echoes of the by-gone
    Replied to my doubtings, "No."
And I felt in their constant waiting,
    Their strength must nobler grow!
              JOSEPH K. FORAN.

New Year

ACROSS the life-path of our destiny
        The tempests roll,
Chill mists of doubt, dread harbingers of ill
        Assail the soul.
Behind the veil that hides our future fate
        We stand in fear,
While yet the shaft of day illumes the dawn
        Of this New Year.
How far along the road of life shall be
        Our pilgrimage?
Or has the book of our day's journey reached
        Its farthest page?
Will star-crowned joy breathe in our ear sweet songs
        Of love and mirth,
Or will sad grief with tear-filled eyes bow down
        Our hearts to earth?

    .   .   .   .   .

Rest sure in Faith. Our times are in His hand,
        He guides our way,
And guards our feet thro' darkness and thro' storm
        To perfect day.
              FLORENCE WEISBERG.

5666—New Year—1905

FROM old to new, with broadening sweep,
    The stream of life moves on;
And still its changing currents keep
    A changeless undertone.

In prophet word and martyr faith,
　　Visions of saint and seer,
The poet's song, the hero's death—
　　That undertone we hear.

A sense we have of things unseen,
　　Transcending thing of time;
We catch earth's broken chords between
　　The everlasting chime.

And light breaks through the rifted haze
　　In shining vistas broad;
We stand amid the eternal ways,
　　Held by the hand of God.

JACOB KLEIN.

Shofar Echoes

I'M but a child, and childish toys
　Make up the sum of all my joys—
But hark! while I am playing here
A strange sound falls upon my ear,
A note of music weird and wild,
And lo, I am a changeling child—
Where I stand with my childish feet,
The centuries around me meet;
Though fresh the laughter in mine eyes,
And on my lips, yet full of sighs
The air about me, and I seem
To live and move as in a dream.
With that strange music rise and swell
Old memories of what befel
The children of my ancient race.
The Shofar brings me face to face
With all the martyrdoms of old
That are in song and story told;
And as its tones ring shrill and loud,
They make me feel both sad and proud

That I am heir to all this woe,
That all this glory I should know.
And though I see strange children play
With all the baubles of the day,
I know I have more precious things;
My gifts are from the King of kings,
Whose angels He before me sent,
And to them of His glory lent.
The Shofar, hark! it tells my soul
That as the ages onward roll,
I more and more shall feel and hear
The Spirit's speech around and near.
My feet shall forward, upward press,
Until a perfect wilderness
Of flowers springs where'er I tread,
And blessings rain down on my head.

So may the Shofar peal on peal,
The heart unto itself reveal;
'Till thou again, O Israel,
In "Jacob's goodly tents" shall dwell.

ANNETTE KOHN.

Kol Nidré

IN lonely hours of thought I long
  To hear again that sacred song,
So solemn, beautiful and soft,
Which years ago I heard so oft!

No song of war or jilted love,
Nor of the moon and stars above;
A wandering tribe without a goal
Asks pardon from its very soul.

Kol Nidré, masterpiece of art,
Thou outcry of a weary heart,
Sublime, seraphic, seems to me
The sweetness of thy melody.

No other song is half so rich,
And none may ever so bewitch
Like thee—For magic is thy spell
O hymn of Israel.

M. OSIAS.

Kol Nidré

LO! above the mournful chanting,
  Rise the fuller-sounded wailings
Of the soul's most solemn anthem.
Hark! the strains of deep Kol Nidré—
Saddest music ever mortal
Taught his lips to hymn or sound!

Not the heart of one lone mortal
Told his anguish in that strain;
All the sorrow, pain, and struggles
Of a people in despair,
Gathered from the vale of weeping,
Through the ages of distress.
'Tis a mighty cry of beings
Held in bondage and affliction;
All the wailing and lamenting
Of a homeless people, roaming
O'er the plains and scattered hamlets
Of a world without a refuge,
All the sorrows, trials, bereavements,—
Loss of country, home, and people,—
In one mighty strain uniting,
Chant for every age its wail;
Make the suffering years re-echo
With the wounds and pains of yore;
Give a voice to every martyr
Ever hushed to death by pain,
Every smothered shriek of laughter
Burned upon the fagot's bier;
Bring the wander-years and exile,

THE JEWISH YEAR

Persecution's harsh assailment,
Ghetto misery and hounding,
To the ears of men to-day;
Link the dark and dreary ages
With the brighter future's glow;
Weave the past and hopeful present;
Bind the living with the sleeping,
Dust unto the dust confessing,
Even with the dead uniting,
When the soul would join with God.

. . . . .

Slowly creep the muffled murmurs.
As the leaves and flowers conspiring,
Steal a breeze from summer's chamber,
Hum and mumble as they stroke it,
Smooth, caress, and gently coy it,
So this murmur spreads the voices
Of the praying synagogue,
As each lip repeats the sinning
Of his selfish, godless living,
By each mutter low recounting
Every single sin and crime—
How he falsified his neighbor,
Made a stumbling-block for blindness,
Cursed the deaf, unstaid the cripple,
Played his son and daughter wrong,
Tattled of his wife's behavior,
Made his father's age a load,
Spoke belittling of his mother,
Took advantage of the stupid,
Made the hungry buy their bread,
Turned the needy from his threshold,
Clothed the naked with his bareness,
Shut the stranger from his fold,
Never begged forgiveness, pardon,
For a wrong aimed at a foe,
Never weighed the love or mercy
Of the Father of the world.
Low the lips are now repenting;

Every mutter is a sob
Ebbing from the font of being;
Conscience speaks in lowest accents,
Lest the voice cry out to men.

Who has ever heard Kol Nidré
Gushing from the breast of man,
Rising, falling, as the ocean
Lifts the waves in joy or fear.
From Time's ocean has it risen;
Every age has lent a murmur,
Every cycle built a wall;
Every sorrow ever dwelling
In the tortured heart of man,
Tears and sighs together swelling,
Answer for the pangs of ages.
'Tis the voice of countless pilgrims,
Sons of Jacob, with a cry,
Moaning, sighing, grieving, wailing,
Answering in thousand voices
Fate and destiny of man,
Winning soul a consolation
For their sad allotment's creed;
Wander-song of homeless traveller,
Outcast from the ranks of men;
Echoes from the throes of mortals,
Questioning the ways of God;
Song hummed by the lonely desert,
Prompted by the heart of night,
Lisped across the sandy borders
By the desert's trailing wind;
Hymn of midnight and the silence,
Song the friendless stars intone,
Sung whene'er the tempest hurtles,
Bruits destruction to the world;
Song of every song of sorrow,
Wail for every grief and woe,
World affliction, world lamenting;
Sorrow of the lonely desert;

Sadness of a homeless people;
Anguish of a chided mortal,
Hounded, tracked, oppressed, and beaten,
Made the scourge of God on earth;
Outcry of a sinful bosom
Warring with his guilt and wrong.
'Tis a saintly aspiration
Of a holy soul in prayer;
'Tis the music hummed by mercy,
When the heart is touched by love,
'Tis the welding of all mercy,
Love, forgiveness, in a union,
Sweeping o'er the span of ages,
Flooding earth with one majestic,
Universal hymn of woe,
As if God had willed his children
Weep in but one human strain.

Who can hear this strange Kol Nidré
Without dropping in the spell?
Lift the vestige of the present,
Link the momentary fleeting
Of the evening with the past;
Dwell a spirit in the ages,
Living in the heart of time:
Lose the sense of outer worlds,
Soul alone in endless time,
Breathing but the breath of ages.

JOSEPH LEISER.

Kippur

OH, thou Eternal and Omnipotent!
    How shall thy erring children come to Thee
And ask for peace? Although the head be bent,
    Even as a bulrush, 'tis but a mockery
If the dark, sin-struck heart still cling to earth;
    Still make its idol of the world's frail clay,
And the pure and glorious forget its birth
    Before the glittering bubble of a day.

291

Or if a spark of hatred linger still
  Against a brother, sinful though he be,
Oh! Thou in Heaven, how shall we come to Thee?
  Vain are the words that spring with empty sound
While the insensate heart betrays no wound,
And we are slaves unto our stubborn will.

But if, oh, Thou eternal God of love,
  If we perchance, find favor in Thy sight,
  Guide us oh, Holy One! from this our night
And grant remission from thy courts above.
Low in the dust we mourn the fatal sin
  That hath beguiled our souls from the true path.
  Oh, deal not on our heads thy fearful wrath!
Forgive the past and grant us strength to win
  The glorious prize of immortality,
  The bliss to dwell forevermore with thee.
We are thy children—let our prayers arise
Like the sweet incense of a sacrifice,
And from this day henceforward let us be
Bound by love's holiest ties, our God, to Thee.

REBEKAH HYNEMAN.

Day of Atonement

THIS day sublime elect, my God, to Thee
    Is gift so grand
That on this morn of grace from sin set free,
    I pleading stand
Before Thy holy dwelling place
Where light and beauty interlace.
Oh, that the priceless power were mine
  To glorify Thy throne divine!

ANONYMOUS.

Yom Kippur

O LORD of Hosts, Thou Only One,
   Art radiant in star and sun,
"Thy Will be done!"

All life is Thine ere life's begun,
All life is Thine when life is run,
"Thy Will be done!"

The scarlet thread of sin is spun,
Forgive us, Gracious, Holy One,
"Thy Will be done!"
                    GEORGE ALEXANDER KOHUT.

Prayer for the Day of Atonement

(Yom Kippur, 5662.)

IF I have failed, my God, to see
   That Thy great Love was guiding me;
If I have missed the open path
Of Truth, which e'er Thy sanction hath;
If, busy with the passing hour,
I noted not Thy glorious Power;
And, 'mid the boast and pomp of things,
Restrained my spirit on its wings;
Then, Father, show me Grace I pray,
And lead me toward the righteous way;
Then, Lord of Hosts, compassion me,
And let Thy Love my shelter be!
                    GEORGE ALEXANDER KOHUT.

Yom Kippur

TO Thee we give ourselves today,
   Forgetful of the world outside;
We tarry in Thy House, O Lord,
   From eventide to eventide.

From Thy all-seeing, righteous eye
Our deepest heart can nothing hide;
It crieth up to Thee for peace
From eventide to eventide.

Who could endure, should'st Thou, O Lord,
As we deserve, forever chide?
We therefore seek Thy pardoning grace
From eventide to eventide.

O may we lay to heart how swift
The years of life do onward glide;
So learn to live that we may see
Thy light at our life's eventide.

GUSTAV GOTTHEIL.

The White and Scarlet Thread

The Message of the Atonement

TURN, O Israel, turn and live;
Thought to thread of warning give.
Lo! the solemn hour is here.
May the thread be white and clear
Though deep sin the conscience darken.
Sinner, pray and God will hearken.

ANONYMOUS.

After Yom Kippur

THE great white fast! the day that solemnly
Its clarion-call sent over land and sea,
In gracious summons of the Voice Divine;
That bade the soul before truth's inner shrine,
Clad in the whiteness of humility,
Itself disrobed of all externals be;—
What mandate gave the day to you and me?

THE JEWISH YEAR

It is the judgment day of all the year!
Unmasked, life's vices hideously appear,
As conscience struggles with its deadly fear;
With introspection's force by memory driven,
We find the flower-strewn path led far from heaven.
At cost of highest aims flung in the dust,
We have been faithless, merciless, unjust.

As by Thy shrines of prayer, devout we stood,
Throbbed heart with will-power's love of brotherhood?
With invocations to Thy holy name,
Looked we beyond reward of earthly fame?
Dared we Thy present inspiration seek,
With might of gold's oppression 'gainst the weak?

The glowing friendship, as a meteor's flight,
Lost in the storm depths of swift falling night;
O'er all the beautiful, cast worldly blight.
Shall the reverberating call in vain
Echo throughout the awaiting world's domain?
Nor summon Israel from lethargic sleep,
In broader fields, on grander heights to reap?

The Past is o'er; has justice entered in
The awakened conscience? and the worldly din
Died into silence 'neath the voice of God?
Know we the wherefore of the chastening rod?
That mercy's tenderness our hearts enshrine
Are we uplifted to the heights divine?
Cleansed from the idol worship of our pride,
White robed humility be teaching guide;
And Israel's heart of kinship link the hands,
Of the compassionate throughout all lands.
The righteousness of freedom, understood
Bind all of life in one vast brotherhood.

CORA WILBURN.

Palms and Myrtles

(Hymn for the First Day of Tabernacles)

THY praise, O Lord, will I proclaim
  In hymns unto Thy glorious name;
O Thou Redeemer, Lord and King,
Redemption to Thy faithful bring!
Before thine altar they rejoice
  With branch of palm and myrtle-stem,
To Thee they raise the prayerful voice—
  Have mercy, save and prosper them.

May'st Thou in mercy manifold,
Dear unto Thee Thy people hold,
When at Thy gate they bend the knee,
And worship and acknowledge Thee
Do thou their hearts' desire fulfil;
  Rejoice with them in love this day,
Forgive their sins, and thoughts of ill,
  And their transgressions cast away.

They overflow with prayer and praise
To Him, who knows the future days.
Have mercy Thou, and hear the prayer
Of those who palms and myrtles bear.
Thee day and night they sanctify
  And in perpetual song adore,
Like the heavenly host, they cry,
  "Blessed art Thou for evermore."

ELEAZAR KALIR.
(Translated by Alice Lucas.)

The Tabernacle

(Leviticus xxxiii., 33-43)

LET us build to the Lord of the earth in each place
  The Tent, which His glorious presence will grace.
'Twill be hallowed with light that descends from on
  high,

Where the prayers and the praises are heard thro' the
    sky.
'Tis the time when the beauty of earth is fulfilled,
And the stars all look down on the Tent that we build;
When the moon in her robing of silver attire,
Approaches in silence, the sun's crimson fire!
All the splendour of heaven, the beauties of earth,
Exult in the love that has given them birth!
The boughs of thick trees with their leaves all entwine,
Round the delicate stems of the Myrtle and Vine;
The Palm trees are clasping the Willows with joy,
A rapture that death cannot change or destroy;
Each tree that was bearing its fruit o'er the land,
Owes renewal of life, to the One mighty hand!
Its exquisite beauty enchanting our sight,
One thought has created, for taste and delight.
Choice flowers in manifold colours and scent,
Adorn the frail walls of the gorgeous built tent;
Where "showers of blessings" from promise divine,
Replete with His mandates, eternally shine!
Now twilight glides gently o'er trees, fruit and flower;
And fragrant the breath of the exquisite bower.
The lamps that were burning, are fast growing dim,
While angels have enter'd, and chant a soft hymn;
'Tis the music of heaven! their voices ascending,
In tones most celestial, with praises are blending.
The trees are all trembling with joy, and the Rose
Has awaken'd to see where the angels repose;
But they folded their wings all impervious thro' night,
And vanish'd ere dawn spread her roseate light!

ROSE EMMA COLLINS.

Succoth

WHAT offerings can we bring Thee, Lord?
    Thy ruined Temple stands forlorn;
Its stones are level with the sward
    Or alien altars now adorn.

And bitter desolation stills
   The lowings of the stately herds,
The bleatings on a hundred hills,
   The shepherds' songs of joyous words.
No fields of corn or luscious vines
   Thy people's toiling hands engage,
And from the Ghetto's dark confines
   They make no holy pilgrimage
To bring their offerings to Thy shrine
   With sound of tabret and of lute;
They pour a draught of bitter wine
   And lay before Thee Dead Sea fruit!
Oh, give us back our fathers' days,
   The land they trod in festive glee,
When harvestings were acts of praise
   And best ripe fruits were gifts to Thee!

M. M.

A Tabernacle Thought

LOVELY grapes and apples,
   And such pretty flowers,
Blooming in the Succah
   That in the backyard towers.

Green leaves for the ceiling
   Sift the sun and shade
To a pretty pattern
   As in forest glade.

Cool retreat and dainty
   For a little child,
Toddling in, by prospect
   Of its joys beguiled.

Round he casts his blue eyes,
   Stretches hand in haste;
Darling baby, all this
   Just is to his taste.

But soon his eyes brim over
  As with sudden tears,
Ah, he learns the lesson
  Of the coming years.

ISRAEL ZANGWILL.

A Succoth Hymn

FOR garnered fields and meadows cropped
  And orchards plucked of peach and pear—
Lord, what Thy hand has given us,
  For this we bring our grateful prayer.

To Thee we come with hearts made glad:
  For wheat that is our staff and stay;
For oats and rye that caught the glint
  Of sunset on a summer's day.

With face upturned in sun and rain,
  And stout resolves to do our task—
O Lord, who gives to each his due,
  Thy blessings for these do we ask:—

That never faltering, though our arms
  Were weary and and our spirits spent;
That bravely we endured the toil
  And anguish that the seasons sent;

We thank Thee, yea, for throbs of Love
  That glorify each earth-born soul,
And link all pulsing hearts to Thee
  In one vast, universal whole.

JOSEPH LEISER.

299

Simchas Torah

(The Rejoicing of the Law)

"SIMCHAS-TORAH! skip and hop
    On your feet till down you drop!
In your mouth a merry jest—
And a burden in your breast."
                                        (*Old Song.*)

So frisky and fit,
At table we sit,
We eat what we choose,
We drink and are gay.
Sing, brother Jews,
Be merry today!
Cup after cup—
Drink it all up
No need to fear.
Lift up your voice,
To-day we rejoice,
Sing brothers dear.

Alas, Jewish singing!
And alas! Jewish gladness,
What means it; O tell me,
And whence is the sadness
That weighs on my heart when I hear.
I hang down my head
Like a child that is chidden.
And oft, ere I know it,
Uncalled for, unbidden,
Falls bitter and burning,
A tear!

Not always with sorrow
Our hopes are requited;
And often the sunshine

Has brightened our way.
We once were a nation
Both strong and united,
And yet, O my brothers,
And yet, to this day
We keep not one feast day
But still doth remind us
Of swords that lie shivered
And broken behind us.
And old tattered banners,
Now useless and furled,
Of all our dead heroes,
Our great ones who perish,
The altars forgotten,
The ruins uncherished.
And scattered abroad o'er the world
No song but contains but
Two words of rejoicing,
In which we discern not
The jesting below,
An echo of laughter,
Of false bitter laughter,
A cry half-despairing
Of shame and of woe! . . .

O great and happy feast-day, Simchas-Torah!
  High above your head thy bright star flashes
To win such a feast-day, one such feast-day,
  Ten we spend fasting in sackcloth and ashes.

MORRIS ROSENFELD.

Simchas Torah

LECHAYIM, my brethren, Lechayim, I say!
  Health, peace and good fortune I wish you to-day.
To-day we have ended the Torah once more,
To-day we begin it anew as of yore.
Be thankful and glad and the Lord extol,
Who gave us the Law on its parchment scroll.

301

The Torah has been our consolation,
Our help in exile and sore privation.
Lost have we all we were wont to prize,
Our holy temple a ruin lies.
Laid waste is the land where our songs we sung;
Forgotten our language, our mother tongue;
Of kingdom and priesthood are we bereft,
Our faith is our only treasure left.
God in our hearts, the Law in our hands,
We have wandered sadly through many lands;
We have suffered much, yet behold we live
Through the comfort the Law alone can give.

Come, my dear brethren, come, let us look!
Quick let us ope an historical book!
See, all the tales and the chronicles old,
They tell but of robbers and bandits bold.
World-wide is the scene of our story, and still
'Tis traced with a sword-point instead of a quill;
The ink is of blood, mixed with tears of distress,
In exile, not Leipzig it passed through the press;
No gilding it shows, and in iron 'tis bound,
Where we met not with suffering and fierce oppression
For the sake of the Torah, our sole possession.

In the very beginning, a long time ago,
We held up our heads with the best, as you know;
When householders sitting at home we were,
Nor needed the strangers' meal to share.
May none have to bear at the hands of men
What we from our neighbors have borne since then.
How bitter alas! was the lot we knew
When our neighbours to our landlords grew.
And we were driven by fate unkind
Our lodgings beneath their roof to find.
How did we live then? How did we rest?
Ask not, I pray you, for silence is best;
Like cabbage heads, hither and thither that fall,
With the holy Law we traversed through all.

THE JEWISH YEAR

Two thousand years, a little thing when spoken,
Two thousand years, tormented, crushed and broken,
Seven and seventy dark generations;
Filled up with anguish and lamentations.
Their tale of sorrow did I unfold
No Simchas Torah today we'd hold.
And why should I tell it you all again?
In our bones 'tis branded with fire and pain.
We have sacrificed all. We have given our wealth,
Our homes, our honors, our land and our health.
Our lives—like Hannah her children seven—
For the sake of the Torah that came from Heaven.

And now what next? Will they let us be?
Have the nations then come at last to see
That we Jews are men like the rest, and no more
Need we wander homeless as hithertofore.
Abused and slandered wherever we go!
Ah! I cannot tell you, but this I know
That the same God still lives in heaven above,
And on earth the same Law, the same Faith, that we
    love.

Then fear not, and weep not, but hope in the Lord
And the sacred Torah, his holy word.
Lechayim, my brother, Lechayim, I say.
Health, peace and good fortune I wish you to-day,
To-day we have ended the Torah once more,
To-day we begin it again as of yore.
Be thankful and glad and the Lord extol,
Who gave us the Law on its parchment scroll.

J. L. GORDON.

Simchas Torah

FULL oft has the ark been opened
    And in the sad procession,
Our Fathers bore the sacred Law
    Their one most dear possession.

While unto the foe abandoned
  To ravish and to spoil,
They left their rich and plenteous store,
  The fruits of a life of toil.

And into the regions unfathomed
  They bore the precious scroll,
To shield it or to die for it,
  To pay the exile's toll.

Yet in to-day's pageant procession
  Of banner and scroll and light,
The Jew clasps tight the self-same Law
  He bore through oppression's night.

Rejoice then, O Israel! Thy praise
  Unto thy Maker give.
No more the Torah bids thee die;
  To-day it bids thee live!

To live for it, and to cherish
  Each sacred memory,
Which time has woven in a crown
  Of glory unto thee.

Let revelry hold its sway, then,
  And the hour be given to cheer;
For the cycle of reading is ended
  On the happiest day of the year.

And lest the mocker, derisive,
  Avow you delight to be through,
Lovingly wind it from end to start;
  Begin to read it anew.

                C. DAVID MATT.

THE JEWISH YEAR

Judas Maccabeus

VICTOR of God! O thou whose lamp of Fame
  Fed with the fire of immortality,
Doth swing, triumphant, 'cross the glooming sea
Of Time! Preserver of thy Country's name!
Judas, whose heart and arm were as a flame
  To burn and burst the chains of slavery,
  And rage about the witching upas-tree
Of Grecian glamour and of Grecian shame!
Soul of th' undying dead! Arise, and hear
  The troubled cry of Israel that comes,
  And quivers o'er his fathers' ancient tombs,
And perishes in night of Doubt and Fear;
While East and West voice self-shaped destinies,
Come, Great Deliverer, arise! arise!

HENRY SNOWMAN.

The Maccabean

WHETHER of Fate, or by the hand of man,
  His hallowed soul glows still the ages through;
  Their flux the body changes, hue on hue,
But, brooding Ivanese or quick American,
His heart must answer to the Yaweh-clan
  When thrills its call the earth or cracks the blue,
  His spirit leaps onto the fray anew,
As when he shamed Olympus with his ban.

Not his is it to lag in the world-war
  Nor to question whether he live or die,
And though his soul and sense red strife abhor,
  His task forever is to purify.
Behold the standard that of old he bore
  Flash like the sun into the clouded sky.

HORACE M. KALLEN.

The Maccabean Call

OUT of dense darkness, stress of the ages,
   Flashes a star, conquering night;
Visions of seers, path guide of sages,
   Portent of dawn's purpled glad light.

Names one all heroes men would remember
   Leaders of hosts, battling for right:—
Quenches their glory's flickering ember
   Glow of that star's intenser might.

Hammer of prophet, despot defying,
   Banner with God's lettered signs,
Priest and true soldier sends he aflying,
   Chaff like the king's cowardly lines.

Slingshot and bowstring, buckler and lances
   David of old wielded with skill—
Harpstring as sweetly toning glad dances
   Woke he to echo silv'ry rill.

Judah's last lion, David's sole better,
   Sword and the harp equally knew,
Psalming his faith's music and letter,
   Joying light's birth song, melody new.

Judah, thou hero, song still inspiring,
   Wilt thou not rout this weak day's doubt?
Israel, martyr, newly aspiring,
   Raise thou again Maccabee's shout.

What if barbed arrows black hatred hurling,
   Unsheaths the sword Syrians once drew,
Wave not the flag, God's sign unfurling,
   Judah the Hammer's purpose still true?

Choir not the ages, boldly defying
   Tyrants' and bigots' hoarse battle-cry,
Singing this one song, surely relying
   Mi Kamokha Baelim Adhonay?

Up Thou and shine forth, thy light unhidden
Must rally round thee, livers of right!
Cleanse thou thy temple, All men be bidden
Join thee, God's Priest, at thy altared light!

EMIL G. HIRSCH.

The Maccabees

WHEN you tell of Israel's heroes, those who lived
  in days of old,
Sing aloud the well-earned praises of the Maccabees
  so bold;
Men who never shrank from danger, fought right
  nobly for their God,
Though a handful 'gainst a myriad, though their life-
  blood stained the sod.

Though so great the odds against them, never feared
  they mortal foe,
Fiercely fighting and subduing those who worked their
  brethren woe;
Inspired with holy zeal were they, nought could quell
  their spirits brave,
No mercy e'er their foemen knew and no quarter Judas
  gave. .

Mayhap their war-cry—"Mi Kamocha Baelim
  Adonay"—
Excited all to courage great, animated them with joy;
"Who is like unto Thee, O Lord," they sang with
  reverent love;
With their lips attuned to praises for the God who
  dwells above.

Oh, heart-inspiring shibboleth, that nerved to deeds of
  glory
The tender youth, maturer men, as well as sages
  hoary!

307

No wonder heathen, senseless gods Israel's worship
    could not gain,
While they sang in joyful harmony that glorious
    refrain!

Not for love of savage-warfare fought brave Judas
    and his band—
But religion true and holy, those they loved, their
    homes, their land,
With that liberty of conscience man should ever yield
    to man—
These the Maccabees desired—these that placed them
    under ban.

Surely, hist'ry ne'er recorded, nor has poet ever sung,
More gallant deeds, I trow, than these, that have
    down the ages rung;
Not for self they fought so bravely, not for pelf or
    sordid gold,
But for love of God Almighty, was their banner e'er
    unrolled.

Of their battles and their vict'ries, it were bootless to
    relate—
All have heard their wondrous triumphs, of their
    great and glorious fate;
How they vanquished foes tyrannic, how they won
    their cause at length,
How they kept their war-cry ever as their watchword
    and their strength.

To that noble band all honor for their gallant acts of
    yore,
For their high-born, peerless courage, for the woes they
    bravely bore!
When you tell of Israel's heroes, those who lived in
    days of old,
Sing aloud the well-earned praises of the Maccabees
    so bold.   MIRIAM MYERS.

The Banner of the Jew

WAKE, Israel, wake! Recall today
   The glorious Maccabean rage,
The sire heroic, hoary-gray,
   His five-fold lion-lineage:
The Wise, the Elect, the Help-of-God,
The Burst-of-Spring, the Avenging Rod.

From Mizpeh's mountain-side they saw
   Jerusalem's empty streets, her shrine
Laid waste where Greeks profaned the Law,
   With idol and with pagan sign.
Mourners in tattered black were there,
With ashes sprinkled on their hair.

Then from the stony peak there rang
   A blast to ope the graves: down poured
The Maccabean clan, who sang
   Their battle-anthem to the Lord.
Five heroes lead, and following, see,
Ten thousand rush to victory!

Oh, for Jerusalem's trumpet now,
   To blow a blast of shattering power,
To wake the sleepers high and low,
   And rouse them to the urgent hour!
No band for vengeance—but to save,
A million naked swords should wave.

Oh, deem not dead that martial fire,
   Say not the mystic flame is spent!
With Moses' law and David's lyre,
   Your ancient strength remains unbent.
Let but an Ezra rise anew,
To lift the Banner of the Jew!

A rag, a mock at first—ere long,
   When men have bled and women wept,

To guard its precious folds from wrong,
  Even they who shrunk, even they who slept,
Shall leap to bless it and to save.
Strike! for the brave revere the brave!

EMMA LAZARUS.

The Jewish Mother and Her Sons Before Antiochus

THE sun shone bright upon a kingly throne
  Where, clad in state, there sat a mighty one,
Courtiers around him thronged—below, a mighty
    crowd
Of mingled heads, with voices low and loud,
Swayed, as do tresses in tempest weather-tossed,
By winds conflicting, or ships to safety lost,
Heaving on billowy seas, and rudely driven
Now here and there yet farther from a haven.

Thus swayed the crowd, gazing with awe-struck mien,
On royalty, clad in its glorious sheen,
While from his throne Antiochus grimly smiled,
Upon that sea of heads, as if beguiled,
To see so many slaves, with flattery meek
Waiting to know what his one will might seek.
"Bring of her seven sons," he fiercely cried,
And cruel shouts arose from every side.

She came, tho' deadly pale, yet calm her face,
And sternly graceful her majestic pace,
Supported by her first born warrior son,
Of all her braves, the bravest, noblest one.
The swaying crowd is hushed to murmurs low,
"Wilt thou worship the King's God?" "By my fore-
    fathers, no!"
Rose on the air; again the shouts rise,
Then low on earth the martyr'd soldier lies,

310

His blood flows o'er the mother's feet, she bends in
    prayer;
Then looks on her heroic band, ah! one is wanting
    there.

Again the summons came, two now before the king
In manhood's earliest glories stand in the fatal ring
Alike in lineaments, with arms entwined
They seem two forms, in but one soul combined.
"Wilt bow, stiff necks? bethink ye well, 'tis death
By one refusal." "Our God has given us breath,
We may not bow." "Ah, bind them on the wheel,"
The King cries fiercely, and with hearts of steel
His myrmidons obey—by her sons' side
The mother stands, hushing the anguish tide
Of woe too deep for tears, to comfort them,
And give to them their last prayers, her soft amen.
"Wilt now receive our God? methinks thou see'st
Thine in thine hour of danger flee."
But feebly with joined hands the upward sign,
The sufferers put back; and so they died.

Thus, one by one, three others rendered up
In torture drear, life's young hope-jeweled cup,
Rather than to profane God's jealous right
And be apostates in their mother's sight,
But one was left; a fair-haired, blue-eyed boy,
The household idol, and his mother's joy.
The lad's high bearing much the King admired,
And of this bloody sport e'en he had tired;
He told the child of death, its awful pangs,
Pictured the terror that around it hangs;
Then spoke of life, its joys, hopes, pleasures new,
Touching on things the brightest to the view,
But the mother's look pled with him as she wept,
And the brave child his God's commandment kept.

The King amazed to see such moral strength
In one so young would go to any length,

To save the boy. But crowds were standing 'round
The raised tribunal, watching without sound
This moral duel 'twixt the King and child
With admiration and excitement wild.
The royal word must not be humbled now
While gaping thousands watch to see him bow;
Some act of homage must the child perform
To blind the crowd, his friends or foes to warn
And show a will subdued. "Boy, I would save thy
    life
And shield thee from the torturer's cutting knife.
See! I but drop my ring; kneel, hand it to me
And this small act shall give life back to thee."
The child—boy paused—this act was but a right,
An homage due from all to royal might;
But looking 'round—his friends were too far now
To hear the King's last words; but they could see him
    bow.
Might not the King have given him the reprieve
To blind the many, his friends to deceive?
Might they not think he to the Idol bowed?
The boy turned thoughtful from th' admiring crowd
Towards the King,—firmly refused to kneel
For fortune or for any weal.

Where was the mother then? Torn from her boy
    away
She could but weep, and to the Almighty pray.
Oh! who could tell the fear and agony,
Lest he might kneel, and that she was not nigh
To warn him of the tempter's subtlety;
But when he turned, refusing to obey,
What pure meek triumph crown'd her queenly brow!
But see the King has from him sternly turned
With bitter hate, which for more bloodshed burned;
Now on they bear him to the fatal place,
While sadness troubled e'en the torturer's face,
To see him like a flower so rudely torn,
While her white face bent o'er him, thin and worn.

The mother knelt, clasping the little hand,
Kissing the lips that grew so cold and wan;
His curls dampened in death, he murmured low,
"Receive my soul! oh! God, I did not bow!"
Then bound they her upon that cruel place
Where smiling lay her martyred boy's dead face.
She prayed awhile, her eyes raised high above,
An eight-fold crown would there reward her love:
"I have surpass'd thee, Abraham," triumphantly she
    cried,
"Thou gavest One, I seven to God!" And so she
    died.
R. MANAHAN.

A Tale From the Talmud

IN Judah, in the days of story,
  When chronicles were gilt with glory,
Heroic dames and virgins then
The equal honors earned with men;
And God himself the prophet taught
To praise and bless them as he ought.

My heart exults to contemplate,
My rhyme runs eager to relate
Their courage firm, their high resolve,
Their faith that nothing could dissolve.
Oh, that enthusiasm strong
Would from the theme inspire the song;
That in this sad, degenerate time
I'd write in poetry sublime—
What might some grace of emulation
Raise in a faint and prostrate nation.

I leave to men of deeper knowing
The task of God's inerrant showing;
How nature's best and noblest sons
Are cursed and crushed by worthless ones;

313

But this I know, that virtues holy
Are brightened by contrasting folly,
And constant courage best was shown
When persecutors had the throne,
And columns high had ne'er been reared,
Had no invading foe appeared;
And when to desperate straits we're brought,
Then God's deliverance is wrought.

When Judah by the Gentile arms
Had seen th' extreme of war's alarms,
O'erthrown her temple and her city,
Her children slaughtered without pity;
The demon conqueror intended
Her name and fame should both be ended.
He thought one dreadful, dire example
Of horrid torture might be ample,
Now that Jehovah'd them forsaken
And from his folk his flight had taken.

One matron from the drove he chooses,
Her seven sons he also looses;
In public presence will them test,
To answer his supreme behest.

The eldest, he him sets before;
"Now, bending down, our gods adore."
"The Lord forbid," he reverent cries;
"His holy law such act denies.
I to no image—neither thee—
Shall kiss the hand nor bend the knee."

His life made forfeit then was taken—
His trust in Israel's God unshaken.

The next that sacred household cherished,
Who witnessed how his brother perished,
At once responded: "Shall I less
Than his my faith in God confess?

THE JEWISH YEAR

I love God's law—its second word
Is none but he is Israel's Lord."
And so he died for truth and faith.
The third, undaunted, also saith:
"None but Jehovah worship I"—
And likewise he was drawn to die.
The fourth the traitor's awful doom
Sets forth: "Who in Jehovah's room
Shall worship hero, god or demon"—
His young life, too, the sword makes claim on.

"Our God is one," the Scripture saith,
"And him alone I'll own in death."
So died the fifth; our watchword brave
Fresh courage to the next one gave:
"Jehovah—terrible is he
Who, Israel, dwells in midst of thee;
He may his awful plans conceal,
But in his time he'll them reveal."
So passed the youthful sixth, in dying,
"Jehovah, take me," meekly sighing.

Assuming now a tender mien
The tyrant pleads: "My boy, you've seen
How vain it is to trust in one
Who utmost unconcern has shown.
'Tis only to respect our law—
I'd put your countrymen in awe;
For Rome, supreme, must be obeyed—
Nor gods nor emperor gainsaid.
The test from thee's a simple thing—
In front of Jove I'll drop my ring,
Stoop down and pick it up; no thought
Of inferential change is wrought."

The bright-cheeked boy, his eyes upturned,
The tyrant's seeming mercy spurned;
His soul kept free from heathen stains
Breaks forth in rapt prophetic strains:

"Forever reigns our glorious Lord—
Performed shall be his faithful word;
His kingdom raised, while ruined thine
He'll to oblivion consign.
As chastened Israel suffers now,
So shall he purer offerings vow.
His faith in days that have gone by
Endear him to his God most high,
And future glories wait the day
When all mankind shall own his sway;

"But thou might'st save thy soul if He
Were but to show His power to thee."
He thus to Chaldea's king made known
His sovereign Lord and God alone.
The prostrate king the word obeyed
And favor found and humbly prayed.
To God's own folk he mercy showed
And so was blessed in his abode;
But thou, nor truth nor mercy giving,
Are but for greater vengeance living.

"To death!" the raging tyrant cries.
Prevention weak the mother tries,
With arms enfolding makes her plea:
"O let him not be torn from me—
My seventh, my last, my life, my all!
On me let first thy vengeance fall.
Sword, come on me, nor let me see
The death of one so dear to me!"

"Nay, nay," the scoffer made reply,
"Your law forbids that you should die;
'Ye dare not slay the dam that day
Ye take the offspring's life away.'"

"Thou scourge of man, thou hand of God!
Thy sins thy guilty soul shall load,
Till down to depths thou shalt be driven,
Transcending all that fell from heaven.

But go, my son, when Abra'm thou
In blissful peace shalt meet, avow
Superior reverence to me—
For I gave seven, but one gave he—
But tempted was his faith when tried,
See mine performed—my Isaacs died.

"What shall I add?" Her reason flown,
Why should she linger here alone—
Wandering unguarded, heedless, fell
She whom her Lord had honored well.

Has Judah now no valiant dame
That might such awful honors claim?
For answer: In my northern home
You'll see, ere wintry weather come,
The fields the cheery flowers adorn,
Bejeweled bright at early morn;
Then fierce the driving, biting storm
Will bare the meads of every form
That spring and summer spread around
So lavish on the fertile ground.
But brightly then the heather bell
Purple the hills I love so well.
When dangerous foxgloves, crimson clover
Lie hid till winter storms are over;
The bloom upon the Arcadian hills
Is blown by that which verdure kills.

If Judah's winter comes again,
Her hero dames shall bloom amain.

WILLIAM DEARNESS.

Song of Judas Maccabeus Before the Battle of Maspha

ON, warriors and chiefs! every step we have trod,
    Though blood-stained with carnage and heaped
            with the slain,
Bear witness we fight for the glory of God,
    Whose aid we have asked, nor entreated in vain.

317

Attest it your armies, whose glittering array
   At noonday outshown in his splendor the sun,
Attest it ye proud girded warriors, who lay
   Unhonored and cold when the battle was done.

They came to subdue us, Oh, God of the just!
   Thy arm was our shield, Thy protection our power,
Still aid and defend us, Oh, Thou whom we trust,
   In prosperity's pride and affliction's dark hour.

When we cease to remember the martyrs, whose blood
   They have poured out like water, may we be forgot;
When we cease to remember the fierce pangs they
     withstood,
   May our strength be derided, our memory a blot.

Oh, falter not when their fierce glittering host
   Comes spreading destruction and blight o'er the
     land;
Remember proud Syrian, how vain was his boast,
   And firm be your hearts like the rocks where you
     stand.

Then on! can ye waver when Heaven's pure light
   Smiles approvingly down on the path we have trod?
On! on! be it victory or death! ere the night
   We have conquered or died for the glory of God.
               REBEKAH HYNEMAN.

The Miraculous Oil

LITTLE cruet in the Temple
   That dost feed the sacrificial flame,
What a true expressive symbol
  Art thou of my race, of Israel's fame!
Thou for days the oil didst furnish
   To illume the Temple won from foe—
So for centuries in my people
  Spirit of resistance ne'er burnt low.

THE JEWISH YEAR

It was cast from home and country,
  Gloom and sorrow were its daily lot;
Yet the torch of faith gleamed steady,
  Courage, like thy oil, forsook it not.
Mocks and jeers were all its portion,
  Death assailed it in ten thousand forms—
Yet this people never faltered,
  Hope, its beacon, led it through all storms.
Poorer than dumb, driven cattle,
  It went forth enslaved from its estate,
All its footsore wand'rings lighted
  By its consciousness of worth innate.
Luckless fortunes could not bend it;
  Unjust laws increased its wondrous faith;
From its heart, exhaustless streaming,
  Freedom's light shone on its thorny path.
Oil that burnt in olden Temple,
  Eight days only didst thou give forth light!
Oil of faith sustained this people
  Through the centuries of darkest night!

CAROLINE DEUTSCH.

The Feast of Lights

KINDLE the taper like the steadfast star
  Ablaze on evening's forehead o'er the earth,
And add each night a lustre till afar
  An eightfold splendor shine above thy hearth.
Clash, Israel, the cymbals, touch the lyre,
  Blow the brass trumpet and the harsh-tongued horn;
Chant psalms of victory till the heart take fire,
  The Maccabean spirit leap new-born.

Remember how from wintry dawn till night,
  Such songs were sung in Zion, when again
On the high altar flamed the sacred light,
  And, purified from every Syrian stain,
The foam-white walls with golden shields were hung,
  With crowns and silken spoils, and at the shrine,

Stood, midst their conqueror-tribe, five chieftains
   sprung
From one heroic stock, one seed divine.

Five branches grown from Mattathias' stem,
   The Blessed John, the Keen-Eyed Jonathan,
Simon the fair, the Burst-of-Spring, the Gem,
   Eleazar, Help of God; o'er all his clan
Judas the Lion-Prince, the Avenging Rod,
   Towered in warrior-beauty, uncrowned king,
Armed with the breastplate and the sword of God,
   Whose praise is: "He received the perishing."

They who had camped within the mountain-pass,
   Couched on the rock, and tented 'neath the sky,
Who saw from Mizpah's height the tangled grass
   Choke the wide Temple-courts, the altar lie
Disfigured and polluted—who had flung
   Their faces on the stones, and mourned aloud
And rent their garments, wailing with one tongue,
   Crushed as a wind-swept bed of reeds is bowed,

Even they by one voice fired, one heart of flame,
   Though broken reeds, had risen, and were men,
They rushed upon the spoiler and o'ercame,
   Each arm for freedom had the strength of ten.
Now is their mourning into dancing turned,
   Their sackcloth doffed for garments of delight,
Week-long the festive torches shall be burned,
   Music and revelry wed day with night.

Still ours the dance, the feast, the glorious Psalm,
   The mystic lights of emblem and the Word.
Where is our Judas? Where are our five-branched
   palm?
Where are the lion-warriors of the Lord?
Clash, Israel, the cymbals, touch the lyre,
   Sound the brass trumpet and the harsh-tongued horn,
Chant hymns of victory till the heart take fire,
   The Maccabean spirit leap new-born!
                  EMMA LAZARUS.

Chanukah Hymn

LORD, the true that follow thee
   Beam in vict'ry's radiant light,
Fill'd their hearts with joyous glee,
   Even in the darkest night.

Roaring billows wild and fleet,
   Onward pressed the enemy's band;
Israel's remnant Jacob's seat,
   How wilt thou their might withstand?

Rise ye heroes, rise to fight
   For your standard, truth divine,
Not by numbers nor by might,
   By his spirit ye shall shine.

And inspired by such appeal
   Ev'ry man to hosts increased;
And they fought with holy zeal
   Till the tyrant-hold released.

Lord, thy truth, thy holy love,
   Is our cherish'd banner still;
And in faith for evermore,
   Thy command we follow will.

ADOLPH HUEBSCH.

Golden Lights for Chanukah

O GOLDEN lights, shine out anew,
   Shine out with radiance bright and true,
While gazing on your golden glow
You speak to me of long ago.
Of patriots who shed their blood
For Israel's cause, for faith, for God.
Did not they sacrifice their all
When clarion-like there came the call?
"Whose on the Lord's side, come to me,
Lord among the gods, who is like thee?"

JANIE JACOBSON.

At last, the wondrous lights are eight,
To six the little lamps have grown;
  In happy company they shed
Their brightness. None need stand alone
  Who by the light of God are led.
  Thus shall God's purpose reach its goal.

Anon, the lights have grown to seven,
  Behold, the night is as the day!
So can this earth grow like to Heaven,
  If men will walk in Heaven's way.
He lifts man from his low estate
  And breathes new hope into his soul.

M. M.

Chanukah Lights

YOU see these slender tapers standing there
  Like Lilliputians wrestling with the air,
In yellow garb, that strange suggestive hue
Of tragic reminiscence to the Jew?

These tiny lights have struggled thus for years;
Though often bathed in blood and drenched in tears,
They flicker still—It seems no mortal might
Can crush God's great miracle of light.

This little group of torches came to show
The hiding place of Heaven here below;
By lighting every corner of the earth,
They see and preach life's meaning and its worth.

Though weak and few they caused the very heart
Of all humanity to stir, and gave the start
To God's most sacred truths; Indeed proclaim
His Fatherhood, His purpose and His name.

THE JEWISH YEAR

Yea, Israel, it is Thy fate to fight
In darkened corners and to shed the light
Till all the world at last has learned to see
Its way to God and immortality.

HAROLD DEBREST.

Chanukah Lights

I KINDLED my eight little candles,
  My Chanukah-candles—and lo!
Fair visions and dreams half-forgotten
  To me came of years long ago.

I musingly gazed at my candles;
  Meseemed in their quivering flames
In golden, in fiery letters
  I read the old glorious names,

The names of our heroes immortal,
  The noble, the brave, and the true,
A battle-field saw I in vision
  Where many were conquered by few.

Where trampled in dust lay the mighty,
  Judea's proud Syrian foe;
And Judas, the brave Maccabæus,
  In front of his army I saw.

His eyes shone like bright stars of heaven,
  Like music rang out his strong voice:
"Brave comrades, we fought and we conquered,
  Now let us, in God's name, rejoice!

"We conquered—but know, O brave comrades,
  No triumph is due to the sword!
Remember our glorious watchword,
  'For People and Towns of the Lord!'"

He spoke, and from all the four corners
  An echo repeated each word;
The woods and the mountains re-echoed:
  "For People and Towns of the Lord!"

And swiftly the message spread, saying:
  "Judea, Judea is free,
Re-kindled the lamp in the Temple,
  Re-kindled each bosom with glee!"

    *   *   *   *   *

My Chanukah-candles soon flickered,
  Around me was darkness of night;
But deep in my soul I felt shining
  A heavenly-glorious light.

P. M. Raskin.

Legendary Lights

O, THE legendary light,
  Gleaming goldenly in night
Like the stars above,
Beautiful, like lights in dream,
Eight, the taper-flames that stream
  All one glory and one love.

In our Temple, magical—
Memories, now tragical—
Holy hero-hearts aflame
With a glory more than fame;
There where a shrine is every sod,
  Every grave, God's golden ore,
With a pæan whose rhyme to God,
  Lit these lamps of yore.

Lights, you are a living dream,
Faith and bravery you beam,
  Youth and dawn and May.
Would your beam were more than dream,
Would the light and love you stream,
  Stirred us, spurred us, aye!

326

THE JEWISH YEAR

Fabled memories of flame,
Till the beast in man we tame,
Tyrants bow to truth, amain,
Brands and bullets yield to brain,
Guns to God, and shells to soul,
Hounds to heart resign the rôle,
Pillared lights of liberty,
In your fairy flames, we'll see
Faith's and freedom's Phœnix-might,
The Omnipotence of Right.

ALTER ABELSON.

Chanukah

DOWN-TRODDEN 'neath the Syrian heel
Did Zion's sceptre lie;
Her shrine, where once God's glory flung
Its radiance, now wildly rung
With pagan revelry.

And in the Temple's secret place,
Where once the High Priest bowed
In homage to the King of kings,
The vilest of all earthly things
Was worshipped by the crowd.

And still the flaming altar smoked,
The priest was at his post,
Commanding Israel's sons to pray
To images of stone and clay,
Or swell the holocaust.

Seven glorious brethren there had stood,
Unflinching, side by side,
And, sooner than yield up their faith,
Had dared the faggot's burning breath,
And willing martyrs died.

327

Not unavenged and not in vain
  Fell that undaunted race;
For Judas, with his patriot band,
Drove the oppressors from the land,
  And cleansed the holy place.

Then the Menorah once again
  Illumed the holy shrine,
One little flask of sacred oil,
Saved unpolluted from the spoil
  Supplied the light divine.

Full twenty centuries have rolled
  The gulf of Time adown,
Since those heroic Maccabees,
The victims of Epiphanes,
  Assumed the martyr's crown.

And still the Festival of Lights
  Recalls those deeds of yore
That make our history's page sublime
And live for evermore.

MARION HARTOG.

Chanukah in Russia, 1905

SET high the light where all may see—
  The flame that since two thousand years
Has burned—now dim with misery.
  A light of mourning it appears;
Stand firm! still flows the cruse divine,
Our star with dazzling ray shall shine.

Raise up the flag! Our doubting hearts
  Too long have kept it closely furled;
Meekness and fear have played their parts,
  Valour alone can tame the world
And show, in might of unity,
That like our sires we shall be free.

E. L. LEVETUS.

Chanukah

LITTLE candles shed your light
And illuminate our night;
Tell your tale of conquests won,
Of Judea's warrior son;
Of the faith-born wondrous power,
Granted in our darkest hour;
Speak of him who made us free,
Israel's champion—Maccabee.

What is slav'ry's iron chain
To the thrall of heart and brain?
What's the tyrant's rage so blind,
To the listless human mind?
Or the champion's cunning skill,
To the independent will?
Which is worse—a cell's dim light,
Or the soul's perpetual night?

Wake, then, rouse then candles bright,
Sleeping Israel, with your light!
Tell them that our chains of old
Meant but passing pains untold.
But our fetters forged each day,
Are blots we must wipe away;
Had we courage to be free,
Would we need a Maccabee?

MARGARET FREEMAN.

Chanukah

THE hand of Time moves o'er the dial,
And guides the seasons through the year;
It drives the sorrow from our hearts—
Behold—the Feast of Lights is here!

329

The Feast of Lights—old mem'ries stir,
  And pride within our breast soars high,
We live again in ancient days,
  When Judah's glory was the cry.

We see the Maccabees of old
  Bow low within the house of God;
Where Syrian hands defiled the halls,
  Where Israel's patriarchs had trod.

Now light we tapers for their deeds;
  Awak'ning in each heart a prayer,
That we may like the Maccabees
  The glory and the valor share.

The Feast of Lights—a time when hope
  Throws off the yoke of sorrow's rod,
To wing its way above the flames
  That leap to glory and to God!
                    CECILIA G. GERSON.

Mo'oz Tsur Yeshu'osi
(A Chanukah Hymn)

MIGHTY, praised beyond compare,
      Rock of my salvation,
Build again my house of pray'r
      For Thy habitation!
Haste my restoration; let a ransomed nation
            Joyful sing
            To its King
      Psalms of dedication!

Woe was mine in Egypt-land
            (Tyrant kings enslaved me)
Till Thy mighty, outstretched Hand
            From oppression saved me.
Pharaoh, rash pursuing, vowed my swift undoing;
            Soon, his host
            That proud boast
      'Neath the waves was rueing!

330

THE JEWISH YEAR

To Thy Holy Hill, the way
      Mad'st Thou clear before me;
With false gods I went astray—
      Foes to exile bore me.
Torn from all I cherished, almost had I perished;
      Babylon fell,
      Zerubabel
    Bad'st Thou to restore me!

Then the vengeful Haman wrought
      Subtly to betray me;
In his snare himself he caught—
      He that plann'd to slay me.
(Haled from Esther's palace, hanged on his own
   gallows!)
      Seal and ring
      Persia's king
    Gave Thy servant zealous.

When the brave Asmonèans broke
      Javan's chain in sunder,
Through the holy oil, Thy folk
      Didst Thou show a wonder.
Ever full remain-ed the vessel unprofan-ed;
      These eight days,
      Lights and praise
    Therefore, were ordain-ed.

Lord, Thy Holy Arm make bare,
      Speed my restoration;
Be my martyr's blood Thy care—
      Judge each guilty nation.
Long is my probation; sore my tribulation;
      Bid, from Heaven,
      Thy shepherds seven,
    Haste to my salvation!

           Translated by Solomon Solis Cohen.

Chanukah

I

WE welcome thee joyfully, glorious night,
   We hail thee with pleasure, O Chanukah light!
Its lustre so brilliant, invites us to joy,
Invites us to praise Him, the great Adonoy.

He was our Redeemer in dark days of old,
When Syria's mad ruler, proud, cruel, and bold,
Proclaimed through Judea: "Your God I defy;
Bow down to my idols and worship—or die!"

Of brave, pious martyrs these bright candles tell,
Who yielded their soul, praying: "Hear, Israel!"
Of Hannah, the mother and seven sons so dear,
Who sealed with their life-blood their faith without
      fear.

But Israel's God never slumbers nor sleeps,
He ever is near him who mournfully weeps,
He saw our oppression, and, hearing our pleas,
Awakened, to save us the brave Maccabees.

Be welcome then, welcome, O glorious night,
We hail thee with pleasure, O Chanukah light!
Its lustre, so brilliant invites us to joy,
Invites us to praise Him the great Adonoy!

II

Let our grateful anthems ring,
   Joyous songs and gladsome lays,
To our God and Heavenly King,
   Sing His glory! Sound His praise!
      He who never sleepeth
      Israel safely keepeth,
Hears their cry, from on high,
      E'er when Judah weepeth.

332

THE JEWISH YEAR

Syria's mad and mighty host
    Fiercely down upon us swept.
To destroy us was their boast;
Israel trembled, Judah wept!
      But behold! salvation
      God wrought for our nation,
Sending light, clear and bright,
    'Midst our tribulation.

"Feast of Lights"—O glorious name!
    Cast thy rays o'er land and seas;
Kindle in all hearts the flame
    That inspired the Maccabees;
      Heroes to be ever,
      Cowards, traitors—never!
And to love God above,
    Right and truth forever.

                    LOUIS STERN.

Vashti

IN all great Shushan's palaces was there
    Not one, O Vashti, knowing thee so well,
    Poor uncrowned queen, that he the world could
      tell
How thou wert pure and loyal-souled as fair?
How it was love which made thee bold to dare
    Refuse the shame which madmen would compel?
    Not one, who saw the bitter tears that fell
And heard thy cry heart-rending on the air:

"Ah me! My Lord could not this thing have meant!
    He well might loathe me ever, if I go
    Before these drunken princes as a show.
I am his queen; I come of king's descent,
    I will not let him bring our crown so low;
He will but bless me when he doth repent!"

             HELEN HUNT JACKSON.

A Purim Poem

YOU know the tale of Queen Esther,
  The Queen so well named the "Star—"
And of Mordecai, humble and faithful,
  Who guided her life from afar;
Not alone with your lips, dear children,
  The beautiful story re-tell—
Let your hearts learn the lesson so noble,
  Till the story be yours as well.

Long, long ago lived Queen Esther!
  But you must be Esthers too,
You maidens with eyes so thoughtful,
  Who bear the proud name of Jew!
With a heart that is faithful and fearless,
  And a trust that is sacred and strong,
You must stand for the right, though you suffer—
  You must battle against the wrong.

And you boys with hearts a-flaming
  With the dawn of your manhood's might,
Remember how Mordecai humble
  Stood firm for his faith—and the right!
How, clad in sackcloth and ashes,
  As he sat in the dust by the gate,
Yet he pointed the way to Queen Esther
  To suffer, and dare, and be great.

You know how the old story ended—
  How Haman the dastard at last
Met the fate he had planned for another—
  And Israel's danger was past!
But Israel needs now, as ever,
  Strong hearts that are fearless and true—
And her honor that Mordecai guarded
  Is left now, dear children, with you.

334

Be fearless! Nay, why should you falter,
When God ever guardeth the right?
Be loyal! The faith of your fathers
Hath shown through dark years like a light!
And if ever you tire in the struggle,
And the right seems o'ercome and afar—
Then remember the old Purim story,
The story of Esther the "Star."

ISABELLA R. HESS.

Esther

SWEET Jewish maid, crown'd with a mon-
arch's love,
Thy gentle grace
Sought for no glory, for no sov'reign pow'r,
No pride of place.
"If thy handmaiden hath good favour found
In the king's eyes,
Grant but my people's lives (e'en tho' I be
The sacrifice);
For we are sold, my people and myself,
To cruel foe.
How can I bear to see my kindred's wrong,
My race's woe?"
So thou art honoured and thy name shall live
While Time shall be,.
O queenly heart! Our homage and our love
We bring to thee.

FLORENCE WEISBERG.

Maid of Persia

MAID of Persia, Myrtle named,
For thy graces rightly famed,
Esther, ours for evermore,
Queen to-day from oldest yore—
Ere we leave thee let thy grace
Linger with us for a space.

335

Israel's maidens be like thee,
Holding fast fidelity
To the cause of Israel,
That they yield not to the spell
Of the glitter and the gold
Shining in another fold.

Oh, our hearts are thine to-day
For the dread thou didst allay,
For the plot of Haman foiled
That our race was not despoiled,
For the worth of Mordecai
Who the plotters did defy.

Let thy spirit be our share
Through whatever lands we fare;
Mordecai and Esther be
Lord and queen eternally
In the heart of man and maid,
Making Israel unafraid.

Of "the foe that stalks by night,
Of the fowlers luring might,"
Of the envy and the hate
Which all centuries relate.
Maid of Juda, daughter dear,
Be thy spirit ever near.

HARRY WEISS.

Esther

A FACE more vivid than he dreamed who drew
Thy portrait in that thrilling tale of old!
Dead queen, we see thee still, thy beauty cold
As beautiful; thy dauntless heart which knew
No fear,—not even of a king who slew
At pleasure; maiden heart which was not sold,
Though all the maiden flesh the king's red gold
Did buy! The loyal daughter of the Jew,

No hour saw thee forget his misery;
Thou wert not queen until thy race went free;
Yet thoughtful hearts, that ponder slow and deep,
Find doubtful reverence at last for thee;
Thou heldest thy race too dear, thyself too cheap;
Honor no second place for truth can keep.

HELEN HUNT JACKSON.

Purim

QUEEN ESTHER—so the Scriptures say—
Fasted and prayed for many a day;
For Haman would her people slay,
On Purim.

Of her good deeds I need not tell,
Nor how she did the riots quell;
Suffice to know she felt quite well,
On Purim.

And Haman was straightway bereft
Of wealth acquired by fraud and theft;
In fact, he was quite badly left
On Purim.

This tale has run for quite a time,
And chestnut-cries may blast my rhyme,
Bad verse, howe'er, is not a crime,
On Purim.

And many things we never do,
And many sights we seldom view,
Are done and seen—enjoyed, too,
On Purim.

The ultra-rabbi, now the style,
And th' old-time rabbi without guile,
May greet each other with a smile,
On Purim.

337

The pious man, religion's prop,
Who lectures when and how to stop,
May take, himself, an extra drop,
      On Purim.

The youth who does for "Ethics" pine,
And of our Faith says: " 'Tis not mine,"
Is, strange enough, well up in line
      On Purim.

And editors, who never pray,
Who "squeech" each other every day,
Put hate and rancor far away,
      On Purim.

The rich relax, the poor receive,
The mourners smile and cease to grieve,
And all our misdeeds we retrieve (?)
      On Purim.

Long live Queen Esther's glorious fame;
For Jews in practice, Jews in name,
All seem to get there, just the same,
      On Purim.
                LABEL.

In Shushan

I

O'ER lordly Shushan's terrac'd walls
  The starry cloak of midnight falls,
And naught doth break the solemn spell
Save the soft note of Philomel,
Or some faint fountain's silvery tongue
Lulling the gardens with its song.
The yellow moon doth rule the sky
And gild the dark-blue dome on high,
And o'er the marble stairways cold
A robe of tissue, woof'd with gold,

338

Doth seem to cling, a garment rare
Enmantling shoulders lustrous fair!
The King doth wassail hold to-night—
For him the hours have pinions light;

II

The gladding bounty of the vine
He pledges in the ruddy wine,
And rears his dripping goblet high
To Love and Friendship's unity.
His arm encircling Haman's neck,
He views with many a nod and beck
O'er purple rugs the dancers fly
In mazy rounds of revelry.
Then sweetest minstrels tune their song,
    And the gold lamps with faltering ray
    In lovelier visions fade away,
As blessed legions float along
Of gods and heroes who began
    The wars of Darkness and of Light,
    Of dew-ey'd Morn and sullen Night,
Of Ormuzd fair and Ahriman.

III

A distant palace casement by
Queen Esther pauses wearily,
And gazes toward the shadowy fields
Of silent orbs, where clustering shields
Gleam faint—Heaven's warriors' loosen'd mail
By camp fires glinting far and pale.
Sweetly the rose-tint night-wind sues
To know her secret, as it woos
With kisses passion-warm and quick
The languish'd lilies of her cheek.
Ah, many fair flowers on earth there be,
But never a flower so fair as she!
And thus upon the midnight air
Wing'd skyward goes her hallow'd prayer;

339

"Sweet Lord of Heaven! who aye hast shown
Thy people grace, and from Thy throne,
Encircled with angelic throngs,
Hast heard their prayers and healed their wrongs,

IV

Great God of Israel's love and mine,
    When on the morrow 'fore the King,
    I dare my people's suit to bring
Touch thou my lips with power divine;
O make my presence balmy-sweet,
That from his purpl'd, royal seat,
The king shall smile and in his grace
Undo the sorrows of my race.
Grant, Lord! that like yon moon serene
    That sits enthron'd twixt earth and sky,
    And 'neath her sapphire canopy
Doth cheer the night, a blessed queen,
I, too, may be twixt those who haste
    To bring my people to the dust
    And Thee, sweet Heaven, with all thy host,
A Queen as bright and calm and chaste,
    As peerless, star-soul'd and as true,
As yon fair journeyer in the waste
    Of the deep-bosom'd, endless blue!"

E. YANCEY COHEN.

Purim

FROM Shushan's royal palace came the edict dread
        and dark;
"Exterminate God's chosen race, crush out life's vital
    spark."
This heard the youth and trembled, and the hoary
    head was bowed,
And in sackcloth and in ashes the faithful mourned
    aloud.

But lo! a maiden standeth now in royal garments
   dressed,
Though on her youthful brow a crown—'tis sadness,
   fills her breast;
The King upon his royal throne beholds that maiden
   fair,
The golden sceptre holdeth forth, and calls Queen
   Esther there.

"What wilt thou, Oh, Queen Esther? and what is
   thy behest?
Though e'en 'twere half my kingdom, it should be
   at thy request."
Then gently spake the maiden, as she stands in beauty
   there:
"Let the King and Haman come to-day to the banquet
   I prepare."

While thus with joy they feasted, and the wine cup
   held on high,
Again the King on Esther urged to tell her thoughts
   and why?
Upon her brow a shadow dark had cast its gloom this
   day,
But with a smile, then, Esther spake, and courage
   found to say:

"If I have pleased my lord the King and found grace
   in his eyes,
I beg that he will not refuse, or my request despise;
And that once more to-morrow, when a banquet I
   prepare,
The King and Haman shall again, with wine and song
   be there,
And then shall my petition before the King be laid,
And if 'tis granted, not in vain, hath Esther, fasting,
   prayed."

'Tis night! and though on royal couch Ahashverosh
    now lies,
He vainly woos the god of sleep to close his weary
    eyes.
"Bring in the chronicled events," the King now gives
    command,
"And thus amuse my waking thoughts with actions,
    as they stand."

Then heard the King how Mordecai his life from ruf-
    fian spared,
"What honor has been done for this?" "Yet nothing,"
    they declared.
Then asked the King of Haman, "What shall in re-
    ward be done
To him who hath my royal grace and honor justly
    won?"

And when the monarch heard, he cried, "Take Morde-
    cai the Jew,
And all the honors thou hast planned, make haste thee,
    quick to do."
Now at the second banquet, Queen Esther makes re-
    quest:
"I ask my life from out thy hand, My people at be-
    quest.

"For we are sold! both I and they; not for bondman
    o'er the land,
But utterly to be destroyed, cast out, and slain, 'tis
    planned."
Then rose the King in fury: "Whose bold plan this?"
    he cried,
"Behold him!" whispers Esther, "for 'tis Haman, at
    thy side."

"Appease mine anger, let him hang full fifty cubits
    high!"
'Tis done; and messengers off speed, the Jews' release
    is nigh.

Their sorrow now to joy is turned, and long shall
    Esther's name
Illumined shine in Israel's heart with faith's undying
    fame.

                 MYRTILLA E. MITCHELL.

Mordecai

Esther vii. 1-10; viii. 15

"NOW say, my queen," the monarch cries,
    "What boon dost thou demand?
Be it the half of my kingdom's worth,
    'Tis given to thy hand."

"O king, had all my race been sold
    To bondage and to shame,
No murmur from my lip had passed
    My sovereign's deed to blame;

"But sold to slaughter, doomed to death,
    I pour my humble prayer;
Oh, let thy royal clemency
    My guiltless kindred spare!"

"And who, my queen, hath dared the deed?"
    "Behold, our ruthless foe!
'Tis Haman whets the murd'rous steel
    And aims the fatal blow."

The king is wroth: the traitor shrinks;
    The stern command is given:
Bound and condemned they bear him forth
    To feed the fowls of heaven.

A gallows, by his impious hand
    For Mordecai designed,
Receives the tyrant's struggling form,
    And gives him to the wind.

Haman, thy wife hath well foretold
  The dark intent will fail;
Against Jehovah's chosen fold
  Thou never couldst prevail.

Who comes? His costly garments wave
  In many a purple fold,
Blest with the purest white; he wears
  A crown of burnished gold.

It is the Jew—'tis Mordecai,
  Type of his ransomed race;
For shame is double honor given,
  And glory for disgrace.

Such, Israel, is thy future lot,
  Purged in refining fires;
Queens shall thy nursing mothers be,
  And kings thy nursing sires.

And thou, in means and mercies rich,
  Loved Albion, happy land,
For Judah bend the suppliant knee,
  And work with willing hand.

Oh, help thine elder brother's need,
  Bid him thy blessings share,
Nor let him perish at thy gate
  While thou hast bread to spare!

                              ANONYMOUS.

Mordecai

MAKE friends with him! He is of royal line,
  Although he sits in rags. Not all of thine
Array of splendor, pomp of high estate,
Can buy him from his place within the gate,
The King's gate of thy happiness, where he,
Yes, even he, the Jew, remaineth free,

344

THE JEWISH YEAR

Never obeisance making, never scorn
Betraying of thy silver and new-born
Delight. Make friends with him, for unawares
The charmed secret of thy joys he bears;
Be glad, so long as his black sackcloth, late
And early, thwarts thy sun; for if in hate
Thou plottest for his blood, thy own death cry,
.Not his, comes from the gallows cubits high.

HELEN HUNT JACKSON.

Purim

COME, quaff the brimming festal glass!
  Bring forth the good old cheer!
For Esther's Feast has come at last,—
  Most gladsome in the year.

And now, when hearts beat glad and free,
  Come gather all about,
And tell once more how, long since, He
  Did put our foe to rout.

Full oft has beauty ruled a land
  And held its sceptred sway;
Full often foiled th' avenging hand,
  And bade oppression stay.

But ne'er did beauty so avail,
  As when fair Esther's charm
'Gainst vengeful Haman did prevail
  To 'fend the Jews from harm.

So all the dire impending woe
  That hovered o'er their head,
Did light upon their ruthless foe
  And ruined him, instead.

345

And thus, throughout the ages long,
  In every land and clime,
They chant an old thanksgiving song
  E'er mindful of that time.

Yea, Israel's Guardian never sleeps,—
  No slumber to His eye!—
But loving watch He ever keeps
  Upon his flock from high.

C. David Matt.

A Purim Retrospect

I

COME tell us the story again,
  You told us when we were young,
Of Esther, the great Jewish queen,
  And Haman—the one they hung;
And how the tables were turned,
  And Mordecai came to be great,
How he won the respect of the king,
  Though sprung from low estate.

II

We clustered around the broad table,
  On which all the dainties were spread,
And the rays seemed as soft as moonbeams,
  From the seven star lamp overhead;
And we seemed once more to be children,
  Aglowing with youthful glee,
The youngest—a baby of twenty,
Perched up on his mother's knee.

III

Well, father read out the Megillah,
  We knew it all, through and through,
Though it's wonderful, how in that small book,
  One always finds something that's new;

346

So we wept again where Esther
  Risked her own life to see the King,
And cried "Bravo" when Haman was ordered
  Upon his own gallows to swing.

IV

But when we came to the hero,
  (Who used to sit out by the gate,)
Led all over Shushan by Haman,—
  And robed in the king's own state,—
We clapped our hands for wonder,
  How strangely things came about,
And thought we could hear the thunder,
  That echoed the people's shout.

V

And then the ten sons of Haman,
  And those that rejoiced at the news—
That ranged on the side of the wicked,
  And perished instead of the Jews—
We thought how God in His wisdom
  His breath to each creature doth give,
And yet how he blots out millions,
  That millions of others may live.

VI

Our reading and feasting had ended,
  And father looked wisely at all,
And told us the lesson extended,
  That Esther's brave life did recall:—
"The path of the righteous is ever
  God's vigilant care and cause,
And honesty, virtue and justice,
  Are heaven's immutable laws.

VII

"The lowly shall rise from their thralldom,
  And sit on the kingly throne,

And God, in his infinite mercy,
  Will gather them for his own;
While those who sit in high places,
  And mingle not justice with power,
Shall merit the wrath of th' Almighty
  And perish from that dread hour.

VIII

"The outward has nothing to boast of,
  Nor figure, nor color of skin,
The image of God is implanted,
  Engraved on the heart within;
The gift to rule self is to each one,
  To rule over many, to few;
But a single brave heart may work wonders,
  If only that one heart be true."

W. S. HOWARD.

Purim, 1900

THOU poor wan phantom of a vanished joy,
  Pale wandered from the East! Upon thy brow
Hang once-fresh garlands, sadly withered now;
Time's hand hath marred what it might not destroy,
  Darkened thy fame, and made thee almost dumb
From cold neglect. Thy backward-gazing eyes
See visions of dead happy pasts arise
  To mock thee with sweet laughter. Children come
And wonderingly look on one they loved,
  Who brought them gifts and pleasure and a tale
  That even Repetition could not stale,—
Of Love triumphant, and of Hate removed,
  Now scatter ashes on thy reverend head,
  Israel forgets thee, Purim! thou art dead.

ALICE D. BRAHAM.

348

The Search for Leaven

LIKE a tender, loving maiden
　　Dusting her devoted room
When her sweetheart she awaiteth,
　　Often dreaming on her broom.

So when stars beglamour heaven,
　　And the vesper-prayer's said,
On the eve before the Seder,
　　Father takes some feathers, bread,

Rag, and wooden spoon, and taper;
　　And he breaks the bread in seven,
And like the child with playthings, playing,
　　He naïvely searches leaven.

First he hides in nook the bread-crumbs,
　　Then like Jason on the quest
For the glorified golden fleeces,
　　To the search for leaven, addrest,

By the lighted mystic taper,
　　He like one a-dreaming prays;
God be blest for sanctifying
　　Man with leaven-searching ways.

Then he locks the lips in silence,
　　Like a Bismarck guarding tongue,
Lest the deep-laid scheme of statecraft,
　　By an ill-timed word go wrong.

And with gravest mien and broodings,
　　Ferrets out each hiding hole,
Where he laid the treasured bread-crumbs,
　　Sweeps them to their burning goal,

In the spoon, with tuft and feathers;
　　Seals it with the rag, and lays
All away until the morrow,
　　When, ere burning it, he prays:

"All the leaven of my dwelling,
  All I saw or did not see,
All I did or didn't banish,
  Void, as dust of earth shall be."

Then he muses on the Seder,
  Like a maid who dusts her room
When her sweetheart she awaiteth,
  Often dreaming on the broom.

ALTER ABELSON.

The Moral of It

SO once more the ancient story lifts its voice un-
    dulled by age—
While the pyramids stand dimly strewn across the
    lettered page,
And we hear the slave gangs rattling loud their chains
    of vassalage—,

How the sea's avenging fury purged the immemorial
    wrong
How the fire cloud's angel pinions hovered o'er the
    nomad throng;
Till at last their wondering quavers struggled into
    paean song.

And the story has a sequel, and the sequel tears may
    tell,
How across the desert ages journeyed footsore Israel,
Ran the gauntlet of the nations, midst the scourgers'
    carrion-yell.

But the shrewd Ahasuerus* toughened with each
    strictest test,
Lingered round the Gentile's back-door, till the Gen-
    tile acquiesced
And from contraband intruder made him an unwel-
    come guest.

*The legendary name of the Wandering Jew.

For the world grew self-respecting, ordered things
    with light and law,
Gave the spoiler shorter tether, closer pared the vul-
    ture's claw,
And announced the grand commandment. Would'st
    thou bricks, then give the straw.

Has thy tree of life, emplanted decade-deep in sun-
    nier earth,—
Have thy virtue's olive branches, Judah, gained in
    girth and worth?
Is thy warrant of survival still the same that gave
    thee birth?

Walk we straighter-backed through Edom since the
    lightening of the yoke?
Lives the faith, the self-surrender that from stake and
    gibbet spoke?
Is the message of Jeshurun more than riddling equi-
    voque?

Faith and message waned to shadows, self-deceiving,
    self-belied,
Sapless mockery of substance, time's long-suffering
    petrified:
May the flesh not live for ever once the soul itself has
    died?

So we move, and move at random, know not when to
    leap or halt,
Pause and hear the by-word "sluggard," leap, and
    turn a somersault,
And we snarl, with pointing fingers: yours—and yours
    —and yours the fault.

Hence the heretic's revilings, rants of rabid tribalist,
Each would be the true adherent, each the only loyal-
    ist;
Matters it who makes the mischief, zealot or con-
    venticlist?

351

Zion listening 'midst her ruins lifts her haggard face
    and wan,
Queries: lives the recollection martyr-years have
    handed on?
Think they of the vows that echo from the brooks of
    Babylon?

Whose the shame, and whose the sorrow? Men and
    ages we condemn,
Cavil at the courtly cities, rail against the tents of
    Shem;
Whose the blame, if in our bosoms dwells a dead
    Jerusalem?   SAMUEL GORDON.

The Seder

RING in the glorious festal-tide
    That dawns o'er land and sea,
Proclaim the story far and wide
    That made a people free.

A wondrous tale and often told,
    Yet never dim it grows,
And now as in the days of old
    No fading light it knows.

But ever fresh and bright it comes
    Across the moving years,
And gayly in our festive homes
    Rings welcome in our ears.

A table set in spotless white
    With gladsome hearts around,
A hallowed scene of joy and light
    As nowhere else is found.

The symbols of our feast in line
    Before our view are spread,
The bitter herb and mystic wine,
    The Paschal meat and bread.

Then from the book of ancient lore
  The tale again is told,
With heightened tone and full rich store
  Of legend quaint and old.

How Israel came to Egypt's land
  And through long years did bide,
How on them Pharaoh laid his hand
  In all his godless pride.

Till God, He heard their bitter cry,
  And swift His vengeance wrought,
'Mid signs and wonders from on high
  The tyrant low was brought.

God led them on to victory:
  Freedom crowned their day,
They marched away a people free
  With banners high and gay.

And so with praise to God and song,
  Israel far and wide
Remembers through 'the ages long
  This happy festal-tide.

J. F.

Seder-Night

PROSAIC miles of streets stretch all round,
  Astir with restless, hurried life and spanned
By arches that with thund'rous trains resound,
  And throbbing wires that galvanize the land;
  Gin-palaces in tawdry splendor stand;
The newsboys shriek of mangled bodies found;
  The last burlesque is playing in the Strand—
In modern prose all poetry seems drowned.
Yet in ten thousand homes this April night
  An ancient People celebrates its birth

To Freedom, with a reverential mirth,
With customs quaint and many a hoary rite,
Waiting until, its tarnished glories bright,
Its God shall be the God of all the earth.

ISRAEL ZANGWILL.

Passover

FROM Egypt once, 'mid storm and flame,
Redeemed the hosts of Judah came.

What hymns triumphant did they raise
The God of freedom high to praise.

As 'mid the parting waters' flow
In terror sank the wily foe!

We break the bread, we drink the wine,
In memory of that olden time.

We sing the festal melodies
That swell along the centuries.

The snow-white cloth, the lights are here,
All peace and joy—love's atmosphere.

O Judah, cherish long the thought
That not for feasting was this wrought;

But ever struggling to be free,
In Pesach's fragrant text for thee!

Be free, no spirit bondage more!
Be free—and burst the prison door!

Be free—no hypocrite lies!
Be free—no empty mockeries.

Dost hear again the word divine?
"Set free the spirit—it is Mine."

ABRAM S. ISAACS.

A Passover Hymn from the Haggada

(El Beneh)

O! speed'ly build Thy temple shrine,
    Thy holy House restore,
And send again Thy light divine,
    As in the days of yore.
O Thou! whose special care we are
    Where'er our lot be cast
Become again our guiding star
    As in the distant past.

O! build again a firmer throne
    For Judah's royal race,
And give his sceptre rule alone
    And pour on him Thy grace,
His sons ingather to their fold,
    Far scattered and away,
And in his realm let Justice hold
    Her firm triumphant sway!

But more than Temple, shrine, or dome,
    Within our hearts build sure
For Thee, O Lord, a dwelling home
    Predestined to endure.
And vouchsafe, Lord, the world all o'er,
    A brighter day to shine,
And in one bond, forever more
    All humankind entwine.

J. F.

Passover

The First Declaration of Independence

THE sullen ice has crept from sunny fields,
    The conflict of the elements is passed!
Again the spring its wealth of verdure yields,
    The probing sun has conquered frost at last!

355

'Tis the Passover of reviving earth,
  The longed for resurrection of its charms,
Each peeping bud a type of Freedom's birth,—
  A conquest each o'er winter's dread alarms.

All, all the sunny joys till now concealed,
  Are prototypes of Liberty's blest morn
When Israel's rescue first that truth revealed,—
  "To free and equal rights all men are born!"

Infallible as Nature in her round
  Emancipates herself from winter's reign,
So shall the clarion note of Freedom sound
  And all the world the burden proud sustain.

Oh mankind hear!—and to all those proclaim
  Who languish for the light of Freedom's sun,—
Let all the Nations join the glad acclaim,—
  "Our God is One—Humanity is One!"

DEBORAH KLEINERT JANOWITZ.

By the Red Sea

(Hymn for the Seventh Day of Passover)

WHEN as a wall the sea
      In heaps uplifted lay,
A new song unto Thee
      Sang the redeemed that day.

Thou didst in his deceit,
Overwhelm the Egyptian's feet,
While Israel's footsteps fleet
      How beautiful were they.

Jeshurun! All who see
Thy glory cry to Thee:
"Who like thy God can be?"
      Thus even our foes did say.

THE JEWISH YEAR

O let Thy banner soar
The scattered remnants o'er,
And gather them once more,
  Like ours on harvest-day.

Who bear through all their line
Thy covenant's holy sign,
And in Thy name divine
  Are sanctified alway.

Let all the world behold
Their token prized of old,
Who on their garment's fold
  The thread of blue display.

Be then the truth made known
From whom, and whom alone,
The twisted fringe is shown,
  The covenant kept this day.

O let them, sanctified,
Once more with Thee abide,
Their sunshine far and wide
  And chase the clouds away.

The well-beloved declare
Thy praise in song and prayer;
"Who can with Thee compare,
  O Lord of Hosts?" they say.

When as a wall the sea
  In heaps uplifted lay,
A new song unto Thee,
  Sang the redeemed that day.

JUDAH HA-LEVI.
(Translated by Alice Lucas.)

The All Father's Word

WHEN ransomed Israel saw the returning sea
    O'erwhelm the vast array of Pharaoh's pride,
And raised exultant hymn above the tide:—
"Lord God eternal who is like to Thee,
Awful in praises, working wondrously!".
    God silent bode; but when His angels vied
    With men in choir antiphonal, and cried:—
"His outstretched arm hath set His children free!"
And heaven like earth rocked with tumultuous song,
    God spake rebuking; and the shamed, mute throng,
Awe-swept and trembling, glimpsed a vision new
    Of Love and Pity Infinite, as they heard
    The fathomless sorrow of the All Father's word:
"Peace. They that perish are My children too."
                EMILY SOLIS-COHEN, JR.

The Feast of Freedom

I REMEMBER in my childhood
    From my grandfather I heard
Charming tales of gone-by ages
    That my soul so deeply stirred.

Charming tales of ancient sages
    That I felt, I knew were true;
Stories of the hoary ages
    That remain forever new. . . .

Of the Pesach-days he told me,
    Days that joy and sunshine bring;
Of the Festival of Freedom,
    Of Revival and of Spring. . . .

Of the slave-people in Egypt,
    Whose hot blood so rashly spilt,
Soaked into cold bricks and mortar
    Of the fortresses they built.

How on them, the God-forsaken,
　After gloomy wintry days,
Shone at last the rays of freedom,
　Heaven's bright and cheerful rays.

How among them rose a leader,
　Star-like in a gloomy night,
And he pleaded for their freedom,
　And he crushed a tyrant's might.

How he taught the fettered people
　Not in vain their blood to spill,
Turning bondmen into freemen,
　Men of honor and of will.

How the people's march to Freedom
　Could no despot's might restrain,
Till before their will resistless
　Stormy ocean oped in twain. . . .

"Then it was our people's Spring-time,
　After which a Summer came,
Followed by a golden harvest,
　Free from yoke and free from shame."

"Grand-sire, dear," I asked enraptured,
　"How long did that Summer last?"
But he sadly gazed and pondered,
　And he answered me at last.

"Child, it was a long, bright Summer,
　But a winter came again,
Came with cold, and snow, and showers,
　With its gales of grief and pain.

"Frost and tempest-strife, contention—
　Raged once more in every part,
Stealing into souls and freezing
　Will and hope in every heart.

359

"Furious storm once more dispersed us;
  Israel rendered free and great,
Into lands of cruel despots
  Went to face a bondman's fate. . . ."

"Grand-sire, dear, why does this Winter
  Seem so endless, then?"—I sighed—
And two crystal tears were trembling
  In his eyes, when he replied.

"Yes, my boy, it seems so endless,
  But it cannot, will not be;
Israel will not slave for ever,
  One day, child, he will be free.

"In his soul will re-awaken
  Courage, will, and pride, and might;
Freedom's sunrise must needs follow
  Israel's starless exile night.

"But till then, ere Spring's arrival—
  For the winter's steps are slow—
Pesach is a sweet remembrance
  Of a spring of long ago. . . ."

P. M. RASKIN.

Pesach Le' Osid

(The Passover of the Future)

ISRAEL in fetters still! The prophet's wand
  Shall stretch across the tyrant's hapless land,
And prison doors shall straightway open wide,
And barring waters shall like walls divide,
To let the Lord's redeemed pass dry-shod o'er
And reach a brighter, freer, friendlier shore.
The angel that unseen spreads seeds of death
And on each house corrupt pours poisoned breath

360

Shall pass the homes of God's appointed by
And none that mark their lintel-posts shall die.
Hope paints this vision thus in golden hue
And, deathless as Hope, doth Faith bespeak it' true,
Affliction's bread shall yield to plenty's leaven,
The clouds shall pass and earth shall grow like heaven.

ANONYMOUS.

The Omer

SO, Lord, teach us to number our days,
    That our hearts in the process grow wise.
But what is there for man to appraise?—
        A measure of grain
        And a measure of pain.
And the end? The dead chaff from the sheaf?
So this trouble leaps forth to the skies;
When Death holds us in wintry embrace,
Shall we gaze, O our God, on Thy face?
Lo, the Spring to our craving replies,
        And the bud and the leaf
        Are the ground of belief
That the soul, spite of dying, ne'er dies,
Takes new life in God's springtime again.

M. M.

Sfere *

I ASKED my Muse had she any objection
    To laughing with me,—not a word for reply!
You see, it is Sfere, our time for dejection
    And can a Jew laugh when the rule is to cry?

You laughed then you say? 'tis a sound to affright one
    In Jewish delight, what is worthy the name?
The laugh of a Jew it is never a right one,
    For laughing and groaning with him are the same.

* Sephira, a period of mourning commemorating the disasters to Israel
during the Crusades.

You thought there was zest in the Jewish existence?
  You deemed that the star of a Jew could be kind?
The spring calls and beckons with gracious insistence,
  Jew,—sit down in sackcloth and weep yourself blind!

The garden is green and the woodland rejoices;
  How cool are the breezes, with fragrance how blent;
But Spring calls not you with her thousand sweet
    voices;
  With you it is Sfere,—sit still and lament.

The beautiful summer, this life's consolation,
  In moaning and sighing glides quickly away,
What hope can it offer to one of my nation?
  What joy can he find in the splendors of May?

                                   MORRIS ROSENFELD.

The Covenant of Sinai

LO, this is the law that I gave you,
    Who called you to honor My name:
(From the sweltering Nile did I bring you
    And lead you by cloud and by rain,
Even here unto this lonely Horeb,
    Where I, all enthroned do abide)
That you might be known as my people,
    Espoused unto me as a bride.

O'er shimmering plains have I led you
    As caravans pilgriming south,
'Mid swirling simoons and sand-storms
    To languish and thirst in the drought.
I led your host steadily onward—
    And the walls of the Red Sea I clove
Lest ye halt a day in your journey,
    Fear-stricken as sheep in a drove.

And here have I brought you to Sinai
    Where the silence and awe of the hills

Descends as the night with its terror,
  And the void with its grim darkness fills—
That here all alone and a-trembling
  You may list to the words that I speak:
Though My words ride the wind and the thunder
  Yet the contrite of heart do I seek.

And ye have I raised as an emblem
  And made you My sign to the world;
Wherever ye dwell, do I sojourn,
  And there is My purpose unfurled:
For you are My law to the peoples;
  Your ways are the paths I have trod—
In you is revealed My own being
  And through you Man knows I am God.

My glory is hung on these mountains,
  That 'neath them, encamped you may see
The luminous tables I've graven
  With truth that will make all men free.
For you I turned flint into fountains
  Whose waters o'er thirsty fields rolled—
You are Mine, e'en though you belie Me;
  You are Mine whom I summoned of old.

You are Mine, though I load you with burdens
  And lash you with woe and with pain.
I will send you from hence to all peoples,
  To hunger and want to be slain.
I charge you to go among nations
  And teach both the high and the meek,
That I am the I am Eternal
  And those who seek Me do I seek.

I gave you these tables of granite
  And the letters of each are writ large;
And you are to bear them and do them,
  Forever to keep them in charge;
To die for them, yea, if it must be,

363

But never to sell them for pelf—
But the law that is largest among them
    Is that law which each makes for himself.

Oh, hear as this old mountain rumbles
    As if it were shivering with dread.
To the living I call as my servants,
    Who bury their past and their dead:
Who serves each one in his fashion,
    In justice and love, I decree
Is living My law among peoples
    And harkened forever to Me.

JOSEPH LEISER.

What Praise Is on Our Lips?

WHAT praise is on our lips, what cheer
    To Him, who sitteth on His throne?
Firm master of the changing year,
    Who leads us on from zone to zone,
He gave to us His sacred cause—
The practice of His ancient laws.

From lands far off our fathers came,
    Lone pilgrims of a thousand years,
To bear the burden of a name
    Amid new ways and unlaid fears—
Still rings His message and His cause:
To teach all men His sacred laws.

No warring hosts our grand-sires marched,
    Sword-bound and panting for the spoil,
Long suffering from want, and parched,
    They mixed their heart throbs with the soil
That here, beneath these skies, His cause
Might live in men and be their laws.

364

The law of love was in their heart,
  Made warm through grief, grown strong through
          pain,
They mingled at the wharf and mart
  Unweaponing the strife of gain—
To make all men uphold His cause
And write upon their hearts His laws.

Long years are done. And we this day
  Praise Him who prospered land and men;
Our star of glory fades away
  To spaces hidden from our ken,
Unless each one espouse His cause,
Whose love gave us the Book of Laws.

O Lord, who guided Israel's host
  Across strange seas, to shores unknown,
Without Thee all our hope is lost
  And seaward all our pomp is blown:—
Still stands the edict of His cause
Proclaimed of old in Sinai's laws.

JOSEPH LEISER.

The Heavenly Light
Shevuoth

WHEN Israel in the wilderness
      Had fled from Pharaoh's cruel might,
The Eternal sent, to lead them on,
  A cloud by day, a fire by night.

And, guided by that heavenly flame,
  The beacon from Jehovah's hand,
The chosen people safely reached
  Their destined goal, the promised land.

Yet not alone in days of yore
  Has God his wondrous mercies shown,
For still He grants to all mankind
  A glorious light to lead them on.

A lamp of radiant, glowing hue,
  By Israel borne in every clime,
Through fire and flood, through tears and blood.
  With courage grand and faith sublime.

When all the world was steeped in sin,
  The Hebrews braved the nations' wrath
And nobly followed still the guide
  That led them on in virtue's path.

That beacon is the Decalogue,
  Proclaimed from Sinai's flaming height,
And burning, as each age rolls by,
  With purer, grander, holier light.

Oh glorious flame! Thy sparkling beams
  With radiant splendour shine to-day;
Nor time, nor change, nor tyrant's power
  Can quench or dim one holy ray.

Oh, heavenly lamp! Thy light shall shine
  Till sin and hate from earth depart;
Till wrong shall fail and right prevail,
  And justice rule the human heart.

May that bright beacon guide us still,
  E'en like God's own untiring hand,
That we, when this life's storms are o'er,
  May reach with joy the heavenly land.

                    MAX MEYERHARDT.

Pentecost

DOWN by the shining sea,
  Its swelling waves in sight—
A bare unvarnished hall,
Without, the working world
Its daily tasks did fill;

366

I stood within, and heard
And watched the passing scene.
It was that day of days,
The birthday of the Law.

An altar, rude of wood,
Stood plainly fashioned forth,
But pious hands had placed
A silken curtain there,
And 'neath its heavy folds
In 'broidered velvet wound,
And hung with silver chains,
There stood the sacred Law,
The parchment scroll of old,
With its strange Hebrew script.
The sunlight clear and strong.
That through the window shone,
Like the Shekinah old,
Looked just a sacred fire
That burned about the ark,
And seemed to write God's name.
A man of humble mien,
And humbler still in garb,
Stood forth and said the prayers,
And read the scrolled Law;
Tho poor and mean he was,
Yet great and grand he seemed,
All garmented and robed
In a strange majesty;
The ancient praying-shawl
About his shoulders wrapt,
And on his brow that look
Of very priest of God—
And presently there rose
The people reverently,
And stood with heads all bowed,
While in a tone of awe,
And in its ancient tongue,
The Decalogue was read.

367

Then solemnly "Amen"
Was said, as said of old,
While candles slim and white
Burned bright on either side,
And two most reverent men
A guard of honor stood.
The mean hall fell away—
The people disappeared—
The sounds all hushed and died;
But round about me closed
The sunlight shining full
Like spirit of the Lord.
I saw the lightning's flash,
I heard the thunder roll;
The strange, lone mountain peak
In Eastern desert sand
Rose plain before my eyes;
I felt the heaving earth
About Mount Sinai's feet,
While trembling slaves made free
Stood ready to be men,
And vowed their sacred oath
To take the righteous Law;
To teach it to all men,
Through ages that might roll.

And so this poor mean room
That held me in a spell,
Swelled to a grandeur vast,
A temple great and rich,
With altar of pure gold,
That held a jewel rare
And single in its worth.
The men before me seemed
To grow in statured height,
To put an air and mien
Of greatness and of power,
Attendants on a Lord,
Who owned the Jewel there—

Who felt and knew that they
Were guardians safe and true,
With privilege to bear
The Treasure of the Lord.

ANNETTE KOHN.

The Fast of Tebeth

LO! I recall the siege which fell on me:
  Within this month He struck me; He destroyed
  With three blows;—cut me down and left·me
      void;—
Now He hath made me weary utterly.

He silenced on the eighth day all my throng;
  (Have I not for three things a fast proclaimed?)
  The King bade; write the law in Greek; they
      maimed,
They ploughed on me; they made their furrows long.

Upon the ninth day—wrath, disgrace, and shame!
  Stripped off was my fair robe in honor worn;
  For he who gave sweet words was surely torn:
Ezra the scribe—yea, he of blessed name.

The tenth day; then the seer was bidden: "Yea
  Write thee within the book of vision; write
  This for remembrance; now shalt thou indite
For them despised and crushed this self-same day."

Counting the months, within the tenth the woe
  And wail he wakened; but the sorrow's smart—
  Its onward way was branded on my heart
When one came saying: "The city is struck low."

For these things I have scattered o'er me dust;
  O that a shaft had pierced mine heart that day!
  For such woe I would dig my grave;—but nay,
I wrought rebelliously: the Lord is just.

369

I call Thee, Thou Who hast repentance nigh
  For mine affliction; lo! my praying heed;
  Hear my beseeching; my salvation speed;
Hide Thee not at my sighing, at my cry.

O moon of Tebeth! exceeding is my sum
  Of pain therein, when His face changed for me.
  Yet, though I sinned, His goodness I shall see,
Who saith: "Ye waves, but so far shall ye come."
          JOSEPH BAR SAMUEL TOB ELEM.
           (Translated by Nina Davis.)

Lines for the Ninth of Ab

SHALL I sorrow, oh desolate city,
  For thy beauty and glory o'erthrown;
Shall I sing the dread day of destruction,
  When thy sins thou didst dearly atone—
When the Lord, from the place He had chosen,
  Withdrew the strong shield of His Name,
And its treasures were spoiled by the stranger,
  Its holiness given to shame—
When the shrieks of the daughters of Zion
  Sad echo'd the shouts of the foe,
And thy streets, ravished City, ran crimson
  With the blood of thy sons, lying low—
When the scepter departed from Judah,
  From Levi his birthright was riven,
And the people of God were led captive,
  Forsaken of earth and of Heaven!

Or shall I rejoice in the beauty
  And glory again to be thine,
When thy youth's loving Bridegroom shall ran-
    som
  His promise of comfort, divine—
In the courts of God's temple rebuilded,
  Thy priests, morn and eve, shall proclaim
"He is One!"—and the sons of the stranger
  Shall answer: "And One is His Name!"

With chorus of praise shall thy daughters
  Reëcho the Levites' glad song,
And thy gates night and day shall stand open
  For the pilgrims that thitherward throng.
For the scepter returneth to David,
  The miter to Aaron's proud line;
And neighbour shall welcome his neighbour
  To the shadow of fig-tree and vine.

Like Akiba, who laughed when the foxes
  Ran out from the Holiest place,
Saying: "True were the warnings of evil
  And true is the promise of grace,"
My thoughts, on this day of sad memories,
  Turn not back to the past in despair,
But forward in hope to the future
  Where visions of glory shine fair!
When I read in the book of the prophet
  Who voiced fallen Zion's distress,
I seek not alone words of grieving,
  But these rarer, that comfort and bless:
"Hear the word of the Lord, O ye nations,
  In the isles afar off be it told;
Who dispersed, will again gather Israel,
  And keep—as a shepherd his fold!"

SOLOMON SOLIS COHEN.

Ode to Zion

(Hymn for the Fast of Ab)

ART thou not, Zion, fain
    To send forth greetings from thy sacred rock
Unto thy captive train,
  Who greet thee as the remnants of thy flock?
Take thou on every side,
East, west, and south and north, their greetings multi-
      plied.

Sadly he greets thee still,
  The prisoner of hope who, day and night,
Sheds ceaseless tears, like dew on Hermon's hill.
  Would that they fell upon thy mountain's height!

Harsh is my voice, when I bewail thy woes.
  But when in fancy's dream
I see thy freedom, forth its cadence flows,
  Sweet as the harps, that hung by Babel's stream.
My heart is sore distressed
For Bethel ever blessed,
For Peniel and each ancient, sacred place.
  The holy presence there
  To me is present, where
Thy Maker opes thy gates, the gates of heaven to face.

The glory of the Lord will ever be
  Thy sole and perfect light;
No need hast thou then, to illumine thee,
  Of sun by day, or moon and stars by night.
I would that, where God's spirit was of yore
  Poured out upon thy holy ones, I might
There, too, my soul outpour.
  The house of kings and throne of God wert thou,
  How comes it then that now
Slaves fill the throne where sat thy kings before?

Oh, who will lead me on
  To seek the spots where, in far distant years,
The angels in their glory dawned upon
  Thy messengers and seers?
Oh, who will give me wings
  That I may fly away,
And there, at rest from all my wanderings,
  The ruins of my heart among thy ruins lay?

I'll bend my face unto thy soil, and hold
Thy stones as precious gold.
  And when in Hebron I have stood beside

My father's tombs, then will I pass in turn
  Thy plains and forest wide;
Until I stand on Gilead and discern
    Mount Hor and Mount Abarim 'neath whose crest
    Thy luminaries twain, thy guides and beacons rest.

Thy air is life unto my soul, thy grains
    Of dust are myrrh, thy streams with honey flow;
Naked and barefoot, to thy ruined fanes
    How gladly would I go
To where the ark was treasured, and in dim
Recesses dwelt the holy cherubim.

I rend the beauty of my locks, and cry
    In bitter wrath against cruel fate
That bids thy holy Nazirites to lie
    In earth contaminate.
How can I make of meat or drink my care?
    How can mine eyes enjoy
The light of day, when I see ravens tear
    Thy eagle's flesh, and dogs thy lion's whelps destroy?
Away, thou cup of sorrow's poisoned gall!
    Scarce can my soul thy bitterness sustain,
When I Aholah unto mind recall.

I taste the venom; and when once again
Upon Aholibah I muse, thy dregs I drain.

Perfect in beauty, Zion, how in thee
    Do love and grace unite!
The souls of thy companions tenderly
    Turn unto thee; thy joy was their delight,
And weeping they lament thy ruin now.
    In distant exile, for thy sacred height
They long, and towards thy gates in prayer they bow.
    Thy flocks are scattered o'er the barren waste,
Yet do they not forget thy sheltering fold,
    Unto thy garments' fringe they cling, and haste
The branches of the palms to seize and hold.

373

Shinar and Pathros! come they near to thee?
  Naught are they by thy light and right divine.
To what can be compared the majesty
  Of thy anointed line?
To what the singers, seers, and the Levites thine?
  The rule of idols fails and is cast down;
  Thy power eternal is, from age to age Thy crown.

The Lord desires thee for His dwelling-place
  Eternally, and bless'd
Is he whom God has chosen for the grace
  Within thy courts to rest.
Happy is he that watches, drawing near,
  Until he sees thy glorious lights arise,
And over whom thy dawn breaks full and clear
  Set in the orient skies.
But happiest he who, with exultant eyes,
  The bliss of thy redeemed ones shall behold,
  And see thy youth renewed as in days of old.

                    JUDAH HA-LEVI.
            (Translated by Alice Lucas.)

Ode to Zion

O ZION! of thine exiles' peace take thought,
  The remnant of thy flock, who thine have sought!
From west, from east, from north and south resounds,
Afar and now anear, from all thy bounds,
            And no surcease,
            "With thee be peace!"

In longing's fetters chained I greet thee, too,
My tears fast welling forth like Hermon's dew—
O bliss could they but drop on holy hills!
A croaking bird I turn, when through me thrills
Thy desolate state; but when I dream anon,
The Lord brings back thy ev'ry captive son—
            A harp straightway
            To sing thy lay.

THE JEWISH YEAR

In heart I dwell where once thy purest son
At Bethel and Peniel, triumphs won;
God's awesome presence there was close to thee,
Whose doors thy Maker, by divine decree,
      Opposed as mates
      To heaven's gates.

Nor sun, nor moon, nor stars had need to be;
God's countenance alone illumined thee
On whose elect He poured His spirit out.
In thee would I my soul pour forth devout!
Thou wert the kingdom's seat, of God the throne,
And now there dwells a slave race, not thine own,
      In royal state,
      Where reigned thy great.

O would that I could roam o'er ev'ry place
Where God to missioned prophets showed His grace!
And who will give me wings? An off'ring meet,
I'd haste to lay upon thy shattered seat,
      Thy counterpart—
      My bruised heart.

Upon thy precious ground I'd fall prostrate,
Thy stones caress, the dust within thy gate,
And happiness it were in awe to stand
At Hebron's graves, the treasures of thy land,
And greet thy woods, thy vine-clad slopes, thy vales,
Greet Abarim and Hor, whose light ne'er pales,
      A radiant crown,
      Thy priests' renown.

Thy air is balm for souls; like myrrh thy sand;
With honey run the rivers of thy land.
Though bare my feet, my heart's delight I'd count
To tread my way all o'er thy desert mount,
      Where once rose tall
      Thy holy hall.

Where stood thy treasure-ark, in recess dim,
Close-curtained, guarded o'er by cherubim,
My Naz'rite's crown would I pluck off, and cast
It gladly forth. With curses would I blast
The impious time thy people, diadem-crowned,
Thy Nazirites, did pass, by en'mies bound
          With hatred's bands,
          Through unclean lands.

By dogs thy lusty lions are brutal torn
And dragged; thy strong, young eaglets, heav'nward
      borne,
By foul-mouthed ravens snatched, and all undone.
Can food still tempt my taste? Can light of sun
          Seem fair to shine
          To eyes like mine?

Soft, soft! Leave off a while, O cup of pain!
My loins are weighted down, my heart and brain,
With bitterness from thee. Whene'er I think
Of Aholah, proud northern queen, I drink
Thy wrath, and when my Aholibah forlorn
Comes back to mind—'tis then I quaff thy scorn,
          Then, draught of pain,
          Thy lees I drain.

O Zion! Crown of grace! Thy comeliness
Hath ever favor won and fond caress.
Thy faithful lovers' lives are bound in thine;
They joy in thy security, but pine
          And weep in gloom
          O'er thy sad doom.

From out the prisoner's cell they sigh for thee,
And each in prayer, wherever he may be,
Towards thy demolished portals turns. Exiled,
Dispersed from mount to hill, thy flock defiled
Hath not forgot thy sheltering fold. They grasp
Thy garment's hem, and trustful, eager, clasp
          With outstretched arms,
          Thy branching palms.

Shinar, Pathros—can they in majesty
With thee compare? Or their idolatry
With thy Urim and thy Thummim august?
Who can surpass thy priests, thy saintly just,
   Thy prophets bold,
   And bards of old?

The heathen kingdoms change and wholly cease—
Thy might alone stands firm without decrease,
Thy Nazarites from age to age abide,
Thy God in thee desireth to reside.
Then happy he who maketh choice of thee
To dwell within thy courts, and waits to see,
   And toils to make,
   Thy light awake.

On him shall as the morning break thy light,
The bliss of thy elect shall glad his sight,
In thy felicities shall he rejoice,
In triumph sweet exult, with jubilant voice,
   O'er thee, adored,
   To youth restored.

      JUDAH HA-LEVI.
    (Translated by Nina Davis.)

In Memoriam, Ninth of Ab

AND all is lost! Thy valiant sons are dead
 Or slaves! The crown from off thy queenly brow
 Is plucked! Thy glory in the dust doth bowl.
Thine ancient splendours are for ever fled!
I see it all—thine altars gory red:—
 Around, Death lays the mighty heroes low,
 Awhile, revengeful and relentless glow
The fiendish flames, and from the foot to head
 Consume the Sanctuary! O woeful day!
 When Temple, Country, Freedom, all in one,

Most dire destruction, fell! Then to the skies
  Uprose the bitter cry of dark dismay,
  Oh, God, Almighty Lord, forgive, condone,
And in Thy glory, make our glory rise!

BEN AVROM.

A Thought for the Ninth of Ab

SWINGING low by a garden wall
    A flower bent its head,
Only a few its beauty knew,
  And the fragrance sweet it shed.

But a wind blew rough on the blossom rare,
  And its seeds were scattered wide,
Now one finds its bloom, where'er there's room
  On the great green countryside!

So stood the shrine on Zion's hill,
  For Truth's Temple fair,
'But all too few its beauty knew—
  Men knew not Truth dwelt there.

But came the foe like shattering storm,
  And Temple walls laid low,
'Neath weeping skies the ruin lies
  'Mid wails of mortal woe.

But like windblown blossom then
  The precious seeds were blown,
And Truth spread wide on every side
  Where'er the seeds were sown!

HADASSAH.

V

LITURGICAL

Hymn of Unity

WHO shall narrate Thy wonders wrought of old?
  The utterance of the lips Thou didst create,
But all Thy majesty and power untold,
  Who shall narrate?

Thy ways on earth in song we celebrate,
Though none may Thy similitude behold,
Yet know we by Thy works that Thou art great.

Thousands of angels, by Thy word controll'd
To do thy bidding, Thy commands await:
Yet of them all, Thy wonders manifold
  Who shall narrate?

SAMUEL BEN KALONYMUS.
(Translated by Alice Lucas.)

The Hymn of Glory

I

SWEET hymns shall be my chant and woven songs,
  For Thou art all for which my spirit longs—

To be within the shadow of Thy hand
And all Thy mystery to understand.

The while Thy glory is upon my tongue,
My inmost heart what love of Thee is wrung.

So though Thy mighty marvels I proclaim,
'Tis songs of love wherewith I greet Thy name.

II

I have not seen Thee, yet I tell Thy praise,
Nor known Thee, yet I image forth Thy ways.

For by Thy seers' and servants' mystic speech
Thou didst Thy sov'ran splendor darkly teach.

And from the grandeur of Thy work they drew
The measure of Thy inner greatness too.

They told of Thee, but not as Thou must be,
Since from Thy work they tried to body Thee.

To countless visions did their pictures run,
Behold through all the visions Thou art one.

III

In Thee old age and youth at once were drawn,
The grey of eld, the flowing locks of dawn,

The ancient Judge, the youthful Warrior,
The Man of Battles, terrible in war,

The helmet of salvation on His head,
And by His hand and arm the triumph led.

His head all shining with the dew of light,
His locks of dripping with the drops of night.

IV

I glorify Him, for He joys in me,
My crown of beauty He shall ever be!

His head is like pure gold; His forehead's flame
Is graven glory of His holy name.

And with that lovely diadem 'tis graced,
The coronal His people there have placed.

His hair as on the head of youth is twined,
In wealth of raven curls it flows behind.

His circlet is the home of righteousness;
Ah, may He love His highest rapture less!

And be His treasured people in His hand
A diadem His kingly brow to band.

By Him they were uplifted, carried, crowned,
Thus honored inasmuch as precious found.

His glory is on me, and mine on Him,
And when I call He is not far or dim.

Ruddy in red apparel, bright He glows
When He from treading Edom's wine-press goes.

Phylacteried the vision Moses viewed
The day he gazed on God's similitude.

He loves His folk; the meek will glorify,
And, shrined in prayer, draw their rapt reply.

V

Truth is Thy primal word; at Thy behest
The generations pass—O and our quest

For Thee, and set my host of songs on high,
And let my psalmody come very nigh.

My praises as a coronal account,
And let my prayer as Thine incense mount.

Deem precious unto Thee the poor man's song,
As those that to Thine altar did belong.

Rise, O my blessing, to the Lord of birth,
The breeding, quickening, righteous force of earth.

Do Thou receive it with acceptant nod,
My choicest incense offered to my God.

And let my meditation grateful be,
For all my being is athirst for Thee.

                                        JUDAH HE-HASID.
                    (Translated by Israel Zangwill.)

The Hymn of Glory

SWEET hymns I chant, and weave melodious
    songs
My God, to Thee, for whom my being longs.
O let my soul beneath Thy sheltr'ing hand
Enshaded, all Thy secrets understand.
Whene'er in words Thy glory I would prove,
My panting heart yearns ever for Thy love.
So when in glorious praise of Thee I sing,
With loving cadences my voice shall ring.

I tell Thy glory, God unknown by me,
   In metaphors by prophet lips expressed,
   Drawing from out Thine actions manifest,
A likeness of Thy power not of Thee.

They imaged Thee in visions manifold,
   Though Thou art One beneath all images;
   They saw Thee both in Age and Youthfulness,
Black-haired in youth or grey as one grown old.

Aged as Judge, and Young when war's alarm
   To manful striving calls. Then on Thy brow
   A helm of triumph binding, forth goest Thou
Victorious through Thy right and holy arm.

With dews of light His head is crowned, His hair
   Heavy with night-drops glistens; He shall be
   By me adorned for He delights in me,
My garland He, the beauteous crown I wear.

Like purest gold His lustrous head does shine,
   Graven in words, His holy name outstands,
   Its radiance brightened, by His people's hands,
Who bind a crown unto His crown divine.

384

LITURGICAL

And poets pictured His young loveliness,
  His black locks flowing in their curled array,
  Thus saw they Him. Yet knew His fairest trait,
His beauty's chosen Home, was righteousness.

His treasured people were His royal crown,
  He bore them, they were precious in His eyes;
  His glory on me rests, mine on Him lies,
He honours me when others cast me down.

In ruddy robe, as one whose red feet fall
  On Edom's vines, comes He a God of Woe!
  The God of Grace who did to Moses show
The symbol of His love embracing all.

His wrath the proud, His love the humble find,
  His heart delights to glorify the meek;
  His seekers He, with answering search, does seek;
Thus runs His truth, revealed to all mankind.

Then let my songs, my joyous ecstasies,
  Unto Thy diadem a gem confer;
  Or as the scented cassia and myrrh,
In fragrant incense unto Thee arise.

Do Thou as precious hold the poor man's cry
  As psalmody anigh Thine altar sung;
  And may my gift, those blessed gifts among,
Find gracious way to Thee enthroned on high.

And when I praise Thee, bounteous Lord, in song
  O deem my offering the choicest spice;
  And let my thoughts be a sweet sacrifice,
To lift my heart to Thee, for whom I long.

                  (Translated by I. A.)

Hymn of Glory

SWEET hymns and songs will I indite
  To sing of Thee by day and night,
Of Thee, who art my soul's delight.

How doth my soul within me yearn
Beneath Thy shadow to return,
Thy sacred mysteries to learn.

And even while yet Thy glory fires
My words, and hymns of praise inspires,
Thy love it is my heart desires.

Therefore will I of Thee relate
All glorious things, and celebrate
In songs of love Thy name most great.

Thy glory shall my discourse be,
In images I picture Thee,
Although Thyself I cannot see.

In mystic utterances alone
By prophet and by seer made known,
Hast Thy radiant glory shown.

Thy might and greatness they portrayed
According to the power displayed,
In all the works Thy hand has made.

In images of Thee they told
Of Thy great wonders wrought of old,
Thy essence could they not behold.

In signs and visions seen of yore
They pictured Thee in ancient lore,
But Thou art One for evermore.

386

They saw in Thee both youth and age,
The man of war, the hoary sage,
But ever Israel's heritage.

O Thou whose word is truth alway,
Thy people seek Thy face this day,
O be Thou near them when they pray.

May these, my songs and musings, be
Acceptable, O Lord, to Thee
And do Thou hear them graciously.

O let my praises heavenward sped,
Be as a crown unto Thy head,
My prayer as incense offered!

O may my words of blessings rise
To Thee, who throned above the skies,
Art just and mighty, great and wise!

And when Thy glory I declare
Do Thou incline Thee to my prayer,
As though sweet spice my offering were.

My meditation day and night
May it be pleasant in Thy sight,
For Thou art all my soul's delight.

       (Translated by Alice Lucas.)

The Kaddish

ACCORDING to His righteous will,
  Be magnify'd and hallow'd still,
Throughout the world; His glorious name—
The world which at His summons came.
And let Him suddenly and soon,
In glory, like the sun at noon,

On earth establish, to His praise,
His kingdom in your lives and days,
And in the lives of all the race
Of Israel, and fulfil his grace,
  O house of Israel, fear the Lord,
And say, Amen, with one accord.
Amen! His glorious name be blest
For evermore, through east and west.

  Still blessed, prais'd, with glory crowned,
Exalted, magnified around,
Rever'd, extoll'd, and lauded be
His holy name, for bless'd is He
'Bove blessings all, or hymns sublime,
Or praises in the tents of time,
Or blessednesses said or sung
By mortal or immortal tongue.
  O house of Israel, fear the Lord;
And say, Amen, with one accord.

  Let all the race of Israel's pray'rs
And supplications, in their cares,
Be grateful in their Father's sight,
Who's high in heaven, enthron'd in light.
  O house of Israel, fear the Lord;
And say, Amen, with one accord.

  Let peace, and joy, and bliss from heav'n,
From day to day be freely giv'n;
With life to us and ours in store,
And each of Israel, evermore,
  O house of Israel, fear the Lord;
And say, Amen, with one accord.

  Let Him, whose blessings never cease,
Who through his lofty heav'ns makes peace,
Make ever peace with us to dwell,
And all the race of Israel.
  O house of Israel, fear the Lord;
And say, Amen, with one accord.   W. W.

LITURGICAL

Ode on Chazanuth

ARISE and sing, thou deathless melody—
   Life's blended song—
Bearing on wings of sound aloft with thee
   A mortal throng.

Lo, living yet, beloved, lingering strain,
   My harp of old,
Voice of a patience that hath borne the pain
   Of years untold!

Each olden chord awaketh, every tone,
   Soaring at length,
Mingling a mighty gladness with a groan
   Of fallen strength.

Angels be gathering Earth's ascending prayer,
   That, heavenward bound,
Shall deck the Throne with wreathed garlands fair
   Of wafted sound.

Song of the ages, lo! the fettered soul
   Shall break its bond,
And, wrapt in thee, look forth upon the whole
   Of Heaven beyond.

Sing on, sweet minstrel, thine immortal song—
   My harp for aye,
Vision of hope to men that live and long
   And pass away.

NINA DAVIS.

Adon Olam

L ORD over all! whose power the sceptre swayed,
  Ere first Creation's wondrous form was framed,
When by His will divine all things were made;
  Then King Almighty was His name proclaimed.

When all shall cease—the universe be o'er,
  In awful greatness He alone will reign,
Who was, who is, and who will evermore
  In glory most refulgent still remain.

Sole God! unequalled, and beyond compare,
  Without division or associate;
Without commencing date or final year,
  Ominpotent He reigns in awful state.

To Him, no like, no equal e'er can be;
  He, without change or substitute remains,
Without divisibleness or adjunct, He
  In highest might and power supremely reigns.

He is my God! my living Savior He!
  My sheltering Rock in sad misfortune's hour!
My standard, refuge, portion, still shall be,
  My lot's Disposer when I seek His power.

Into His hands my spirit I consign
  Whilst wrapped in sleep, that I again may wake:
And with my soul, my body I resign;
  The Lord with me,—no fears my soul can shake.

D. A. DE SOLA.

Adon Olam

L ORD of the world, He reigned alone
  While yet the universe was naught,
When by His will all things were wrought,
Then first His sovran name was known.

390

And when the All shall cease to be,
　In dread lone splendor He shall reign.
　He was, He is, He shall remain
In glorious eternity.

For He is one, no second shares
　His nature or His loneliness;
　Unending and beginningless,
All strength is His, all sway He bears.

He is the living God to save,
　My Rock while sorrow's toils endure,
　My banner and my stronghold sure,
The cup of life whene'er I crave.

I place my soul within His palm
　Before I sleep as when I wake,
　And though my body I forsake,
Rest in the Lord in fearless calm.

ISRAEL ZANGWILL.

Adon Olam

REIGNED the universe's Master, ere were earthly
　　things begun;
When his mandate all created Ruler was the name
　　He won;
And alone He'll rule tremendous when all things are
　　past and gone.
He no equal has, nor consort, He, the singular and
　　lone,
Has no end and no beginning; His the sceptre, might,
　　and throne,
He's my God and living Saviour, rock to whom in
　　need I run;
He's my banner and my refuge, fount of weal when
　　called upon;
In His hand I place my spirit, at night-fall and rise
　　of sun,
And therewith my body also; God's my God—I fear
　　no one. 　　　　　　　　　　　GEORGE BORROW.

Paraphrase of Adon Olam

BEFORE the glorious orbs of light,
  Had shed one blissful ray,
In awful power, the Lord of might
  Reign'd in eternal day.

At His creative, holy word
  The voice of nature spoke,
Unnumber'd worlds with one accord,
  To living joys awoke.

Then was proclaim'd the mighty King,
  In majesty on high!
Then did the holy creatures sing
  His praises through the sky.

All merciful in strength he reigns
  Immutable! supreme!
His hand the universe sustains,
  He only can redeem.

He is the mighty God alone!
  His presence fills the world;
He will forever reign the one,
  Eternal, only Lord!

Almighty, powerful and just!
  Thou art my God, my friend,
My rock, my refuge and my trust,
  On Thee my hopes depend.

O! be my guardian whilst I sleep,
  For Thou didst lend me breath:
And when I wake, my spirit keep,
  And save my soul in death.

                    DAVID NUNES CARVALHO.

LITURGICAL

Adon Olam

BEFORE Thy heavenly word revealed the wonders
    of Thy will;
Before the earth and heaven came forth from chaos
    deep and still;
E'en then thou reignedest Lord supreme as Thou wilt
    ever reign,
And moved Thy holy spirit o'er the dark unfathomed
    main.

But when through all the empty space Thy mighty
    voice was heard,
Then darkness fled and heavenly light came beaming
    at Thy word;
All Nature then proclaimed Thee King most blessed
    and adored,
The great Creator, God alone, the Universal Lord!

And when this vast created world returns to endless
    night,
When heaven and earth shall fade away at Thy dread
    word of Might,
Still Thou in majesty will rule, Almighty One, alone,
Great God, with mercy infinite, on Thy exalted
    throne.

Immortal Power! Eternal One! with Thee what can
    compare?
Thy glory shines in heaven and earth, and fills the
    ambient air;
All time, all space, by Thee illumed, grows bright and
    brighter still,
Obedient to Thy high behest, and to Thy heavenly
    will.

To Thee dominion sole belongs and 'tis to Thee alone,
My Father, Saviour, Living God, I make my sor-
    rows known.

Thy love, celestial and divine, descends upon my
    heart,
Inspiring courage, hope and joy, and bidding grief de-
    part.

Protected by Thy boundless love, my body sinks to
    rest;
My soul within Thy Heavenly arm, reposes calm and
    blest.
Lord of my life! in darkened night I sleep and have
    no fear,
And in early dawn I wake and find Thee ever near.
ANONYMOUS.

Adon Olam

THE everlasting Lord who reigned
    Ere yet was formed or shape or thing,
When all was made as he decreed
    Was even then acknowledged King.

And after all that is shall end,
    Alone shall reign the feared one—He
In his resplendence glorious
    Who was, who is, and who will be.

And He is one and there is none,
    No second to compare or share—
Without beginning, without end—
    In his dominion everywhere.

He is my God—my helper lives—
    My rock when grievous times befall,
My banner He, my refuge He,
    And my cup's portion, when I call.
Within His hand I trust my soul
    In sleep and waking—He is near—
And with my soul, my body, too;
    The Lord's with me; I have no fear.
JESSIE E. SAMPTER.

Adon Olam

(A paraphrase for children.)

ETERNAL Lord, His praise I sing,
   Who reigned before the world was wrought;
Creation's voice acclaimed Him King,
   Whose Word created all from nought.

And when all things shall pass away,
   He will not pass, He still will reign,
Alone, unchang'd, of sov'reign sway,
   He was, He is, He will remain.

Yea, He is One, no second dares
   Compare with Him in wondrous might;
None owns His strength; His throne none shares;
   Without beginning, infinite.

My God, my living Saviour He;
   My Rock of Hope in sorrow's hour;
I thirst—my cup He fills for me;
   He is my Beacon and my Tower.

Whene'er I sleep, whene'er I wake,
   With Him I leave my soul so dear:
His care may He my body make!
   God guarding me, I have no fear.

ISRAEL GOLLANCZ.

Our Creed

"THERE is one only God
   Through nature's vast domains
A God of Righteousness,
   Whose love fore'er remains,

None can compare to Him,
　Eternal is His name,
He was of old, He is,
　And will be e'er the same.

He is the First and Last,
　And absolutely One,
Without divided parts,
　And equal has He none.
Unchanging is His law,
　Immutable His will,
And though we often err,
　His mercy guards us still.

Our inmost secret thought
　Before Him open lies,
Our deeds are all observed
　By His all-seeing eyes.
All goodness He rewards,
　On sin He sends a blight,
The clean and pure of heart
　Are His supreme delight.

This uncreated God,
　O man, is Father, Friend;
The heavens, earth and seas
　He made from end to end.
He is the King of kings,
　Of lords the highest Lord,
By all that has life's breath
　He is to be adored.

To love Him we must do
　True service for mankind,
For thus, a paradise
　On earth we all shall find.
In His most loving hands
　Our souls in faith we place,
In life and death we trust
　His justice and His grace.

J. Leonard Levy.

396

Yigdal

THE living God, O magnify and bless,
    Transcending Time and here eternally.
One Being, yet unique in unity;
A mystery of Oneness measureless.

Lo! form or body He has none, and man
No semblance of His holiness can frame.
Before Creation's dawn He was the same;
The first to be, though never He began.

He is the world's and every creature's Lord;
His rule and majesty are manifest,
And through His chosen, glorious sons exprest
In prophecies that through their lips are poured.

Yet never like to Moses rose a seer,
Permitted glimpse behind the veil divine.
This faithful prince of God's prophetic line
Received the Law of Truth for Israel's ear.

The Law God gave He never will amend,
Nor ever by another Law replace.
Our secret things are spread before His face;
In all beginnings He beholds the end.

The saint's reward He measures to his meed;
The sinner reaps the harvest of his ways.
Messiah He will send at end of days,
And all the faithful to salvation lead.

God will the dead again to life restore
In His abundance of almighty love.
Then blessed be His Name, all names above,
And let His praise resound for evermore.

ISRAEL ZANGWILL.

Yigdal

EXTOLLED be the living God and lauded be His
name;
He doth exist and will thro' endless æons be the same.

Our God is Unity, and Unity like His there's none;
Ah! inconceivable is He, and thro' all times is one.

He doth no form nor shape nor yet our mortal fashion
bear;
In heav'n, on earth, can naught like to His holiness
compare.

Prior to each created thing, of wondrous shape and
grace,
He was the first, and, ere He was, can none com-
mencement trace.

Behold! He rules the Universe, His creatures teach-
eth He
The greatness of His awful might, His glorious
sovereignty.

The spirit of His prophecy hath He bestowed on those
Whom, for the glory of His name, our Heav'nly
Father chose.

Though great the fame of Israel's sons, meek Moses
none excelled;
Alone, among her seers, he God's similitude beheld.

A law of truth and life He gave, our everlasting Rock,
By him who was the faithful guide and teacher of his
flock.

This law sublime and beautiful, for any new or
strange,
Our Shield, thro' all eternities, will nevermore ex-
change.

The secret courses of our thoughts doth th' Allwis.
    watch and know;
And clear to Him, all hidden ends their own com-
    mencements show,

His loving kindness blesseth those who well their task
    fulfil,
A chast'ning hand falls heavy on transgressors of His
    will.

His messenger He'll surely send upon the final day,
Redeeming those, who, strong in faith, for His salva-
    tion stay.

In love He will the dead revive that sleep beneath the
    ground,
For ever blessed be His name, His praise fore'er re-
    sound.

FLORENCE AHRONSBERG.

Yigdal

EXTOL we now the living God,
    His praises loud relate,
Who is—and whose existence is
    Not bound by time or date.

Who, One and only One, alone
    Invisible doth dwell;
And peerless in His unity,
    His limit who shall tell?

Material form, similitude,
    Or likeness, none hath He;
Nor can there to His holiness
    Comparison e'er be.

Ere glad Creation, at His word,
   To life and light outburst;
Of primal date—Eternal He—
   Without beginning—First!

In all the world—the wide expanse,
   Its dwellers all around,
Proclaim His might, His majesty,
   Which everywhere abound.

Prophetic powers he deigned below,
   Blest words of revelation,
To them, His treasured men of worth,
   In glorious inspiration.

But like to Moses none arose,
   'Mid Israel's chosen few,
Who face to face with God did speak,
   And did His semblance view.

And when in mercy, laws of truth,
   God for His people penn'd,
He by that faithful Prophet pleased
   His holy law to send.

Nor ever will our gracious Lord
   Another code bestow;
For, all complete, His perfect law
   No altering change can know.

Our hidden thoughts, our ev'ry act,
   From Him are ne'er conceal'd;
Yea! ere commenced, of all, the end
   To Him at once reveal'd.

Rewarding kindness, as his meed,
   The good man's just return;
But to the wicked, punishment
   His own misdoings earn.

Who at His time—in length of days—
　　Will our Messiah send,
Redeeming those who, anxious, wait
　　Salvation as their end.

In wondrous mercy, then the dead
　　Revive at God's behest;
Then be His praises ever sung,
　　His name be ever blest.

PHILIP ABRAHAM.

Yigdal

THE living God we praise, exalt, adore!
He was, He is, He will be evermore.

No unity like unto His can be,
Eternal, inconceivable is He.

No form or shape has th' incorporeal One,
Most holy beyond all comparison.

He was, ere aught was made in heaven or earth,
But His existence has no date or birth.

Lord of the Universe is He proclaimed,
Teaching His power to all His hand has framed.

He gave His gift of prophecy to those
In whom He gloried, whom He loved and chose.

No prophet ever yet has filled the place
Of Moses, who beheld God face to face.

Through Him (the faithful in His house) the Lord
The law of truth to Israel did accord.

This law God will not alter, will not change
For any other through time's utmost range.

He knows and heeds the secret thoughts of man:
He saw the end of all ere aught began.

With love and grace doth He the righteous bless,
He metes out evil unto wickedness.

He at the last will His anointed send,
Those to redeem, who hope, and wait the end.

God will the dead to life again restore,
Praised be His glorious name for evermore.

ALICE LUCAS.

The Mezuzah

THE Cerberus breakers that brawl and that cry,
  The sun and the sky with their Raphael eye,
The skylarks that soar and the serpents that creep,
The lilies that love and the willows that weep,
The grandeurs of heaven, the glamours of earth,
In Thy outdoors, O God, they are singing Thy worth.
And love and its wonder, the mother and child,
The lullabies sweet, and the elegies wild,
The sanctuary, Home, the spirit-realm's pole,
The Eden unlost, and the shrine of the soul,
In Thy indoors, O God, in the hearth we revere,
In its tears, in its triumphs, Thy splendors appear.
But leaving to heaven, the sun and the star,
When we grope on the threshold and wait for the bar
To slip, and the door of the home to unfold,
And see not the rising or sunsetting gold,
While we grope on the threshold expectant and tense,
All silent with fearful and hopeful suspense,
Dumb lintel above us, blind doorstep, before,
The heart, it is neither on ocean or shore,
What hint to the soul of the Master, what gleam,
What clue to His labyrinth's coil of dream?
It is the Mezuzah, the doorpost uplifts,

Enwrit with Thy statutes, Thy name and Thy gifts;
Coat of Arms of the knighthood of God, like a spell,
The Mezuzah holds sentry where Israelites dwell.
What heavenly romance, its blazonings seal,
What lists, and what Galahads that harm not but heal.
What Unity linking the shadow and sun,
Till shadow and sunshine one glory have spun;
And it isn't the parchment, the scroll or the case,
It's the charm of the Shaddai it bears on its face,
And the mystical Shema inscribed in the scroll,
We caress and we kiss. We are kissing its soul
In crossing the threshold; O hearken, we pray,
"Heaven keep our going and coming each day."
And they tell, Belial, the demon of vice,
In touching the threshold, must cease to entice.
For the doorstep's enchanted, the Mezuzah has charm
To keep from the threshold the harpies that harm.
The Mezuzah's the soul of the threshold, behold,
It touched with enchantment and mystical gold,
The portal: The threshold with witchcraft is shod,
On the threshold and doorpost, we also see God!

ALTER ABELSON.

Tephillin

ERECT he stands, in fervent prayer,
   His body cloaked in silken Tallis;
He seems a king, so free from care,
   His wife a queen, his home a palace,
His arm and head, his brawn and brain,
   He dedicates to God in Heaven;
For Him he suffers toil and pain,
   Endures whatever lot he's given.

Around his arm seven times is wrapped
   A wide phylactery, glistening thong;
His shaggy, curly hair is capped
   By still another, tough and strong.

403

These bands he wears while soft he prays,
　Devoting strength and mind to God;
His body slowly, gently sways,—
　He walks the ground his fathers trod.

This daily commune with the Master
　Lifts him above mere common clay;
The Jewish heart, like alabaster,
　Grows pure and purer every day,
For he who loves a Higher Being
　Must love all creatures here below;
And he who knows there's one All-Seeing,
　Knows all he can and e'er will know.

AARON SCHAFFER.

Morning Song

(The hymn beginning with these words is among
the most beautiful and heart-reaching preserved in our
liturgy, though evidently intended for private devo-
tion. Its author is R. Solomon Ibn Gabirol, one of
Israel's most tuneful and gifted poets.)

　　A T early morn, Thee will I seek
　　　In pray'r, O Rock of my defence!
　　'Fore Thy greatness stand I in awe,
　　　Abash'd at Thy omnipotence.

　　O, what avails the power of man!
　　　Thy hand its limits doth control;
　　O, where the beauty of the form
　　　That clothes in clay the god-like soul?

　　All these are naught; whate'er we are,
　　　Whate'er we have, Thy goodness gives;
　　Then let our praise to Thee ascend,
　　　Whilst yet in us the spirit lives.

HENRY S. JACOBS.

LITURGICAL

Morning Song

AT the dawn, I seek Thee,
  Refuge and rock sublime,—
Set my prayer before Thee in the morning,
  And my prayer at eventime.
I before Thy greatness
  Stand, and am afraid:—
All my secret thoughts Thine eye beholdeth
  Deep within my bosom laid.
And withal what is it
  Heart and tongue can do?
What is this my strength, and what is even
  This the spirit in me too?
But verily man's singing
  May seem good to Thee;
So will I thank Thee, praising, while there dwelleth
  Yet the breath of God in me.

SOLOMON IBN GABIROL.
(Translated by Alice Lucas.)

Song of Israel to God

MY Love! hast Thou forgotten
    Thy rest
      Upon my breast?
And wherefore hast Thou sold me
To be enslaved for aye?
Have I not followed Thee upon the way
Of olden time within a land not sown?
Lo! Seir and Mount Paran—nor these alone—
    Sinai and Sin—yea, these
      Be all my witnesses.
For Thee my love was ever,
    And mine
      Thy grace divine;
And how hast Thou apportioned
My glory away from me?

Thrust unto Seir, pursued, sent forth to flee
Unto Kedar, nor suffered to abide;
Within the Grecian fiery furnace tried;
      Afflicted, weighed with care,
      With Media's yoke to bear;—
And is there any to redeem but Thee?
Or other captive with such hope above?
Thy strength, O Lord; grant of Thy strength to me!
    For I give Thee my love.

JUDAH HA-LEVI.
(Translated by Alice Lucas.)

Morning Invocation

AT morn I ask Thee, lend Thy shelt'ring aid!
  My hopes and fears before Thy Throne are laid.
Like one abashed I stand, prostrate before Thy might,
My new-awakened heart hides nothing from Thy sight!

    My heart, my tongue, too, fails
    To utter what avails!
My skill, my strength, are naught!
    But Thou, of grace, dost take
    The prayers which mortals make,
The prayers Thy love has taught.
    So shall my voice ascend,
    Until my life shall end;
The while, within my body's shrine,
Dwelleth my soul, Thy gift divine!

SOLOMON IBN GABIROL.

The Night Prayer

THE bands of sleep fall on mine eyes,
  My lids in slumber close.
O Lord our God! I pray to Thee
  To guard me in repose.

406

LITURGICAL

O grant that I may lay me down
   In peace at fall of night,
And that in peace I may rise up
   To greet the rising light.

Let not my thoughts or evil dreams
   Or fancies trouble me,
Safe in Thy ever-watchful care
   My rest will perfect be.

Enlighten Thou mine eyes, O God!
   Lest I sleep the sleep of death;
O Thou, who givest life to all,
   From Thee we draw each breath.

FLORENCE WEISBERG.

BLESS'D art Thou, O Lord of all,
   Who mak'st the bands of sleep to fall
Upon mine eyes, and slumber press
Mine eyelids down with heaviness.

God of my fathers, may it be
Thy will, this night to suffer me
To lay me down in peace and rise
In peace, when morning gilds the skies.

From thoughts of ill my slumber keep
And, lest the sleep of death I sleep,
O lighten Thou mine eyes, for Thou,
Lord, dost with light the eye endow.

Bless'd art Thou, O Lord most high,
Who in Thy glorious majesty
And in Thy gracious love hast given
Light upon earth and light in heaven.

ALICE LUCAS.

CAUSE us, our Father, to lie down in peace,
  And raise us up, our King, to life again;
Direct us on our way
With Thy good counsel's stay
And let us 'neath Thy tent of peace remain.

O save us for the sake of Thy great name,
Be unto us a shield, Thou King of kings.
Remove from out our life
Sickness and care and strife;
Shelter us in the shadow of Thy wings.

Our guardian and deliverer Thou art,
Merciful King, whom heaven and earth adore!
Guard Thou from harm and sin
Our goings out and in,
With life and peace henceforth and evermore.

ALICE LUCAS.

Nishmas

THE breath of ev'ry living thing,
  O Lord, shall bless Thy Name;
The spirit of all flesh on earth
  Thy glory shall proclaim.

For Thou art God for evermore,
  Beside Thee we have none;
No king, nor saviour who redeems,
  Save Thou! Almighty One!

Thou settest free, and bring'st us aid
  In times of grief or woe;
With mercies great and manifold;
  No King but Thee we know!

FLORENCE WEISBERG.

LITURGICAL

Nishmas

ALL living souls shall bless Thy name,
   O just and gracious God!
All flesh Thy providence proclaim,
   Thy holy works applaud.

From age to age will we relate
   The wonders Thou hast wrought,
Delighting to expatiate
   On all which Thou hast taught.

Young men and maidens lift the voice,
   Thy wisdom to extol,
And children in Thy praise rejoice,
   Father and Friend of all!

But though our hands should be outspread,
   As are the eagle's wings,
To thank Thee for the daily bread,
   That from Thy bounty springs.

Though song, like sounding billows, too,
   Should from our lips proceed,
How large a debt would yet be due
   To Thee, from Jacob's seed!

Thrice holy, Lord of hosts! art Thou,
   Ineffable and pure!
Before Thy Majesty we bow,
   Great King, whom we adore.

PENINA MOÏSE.

Adoration

TO Israel the charge belongs
Their grateful hearts to raise;
To speak, in glad, triumphant songs,
The Lord Almighty's praise.

His hand the universe hath wrought,
The starry heavens o'erhead;
From darkness He His people brought
The light of truth to spread.

We bow the head, we bend the knee,
And worship Him alone;
The King of Kings whose majesty
And sovereign power we own.

He is our God, the only Lord,
Our King is truth indeed;
His sovereign power His laws record
As taught to Israel's seed.

Grant Thou our hope, Almighty King,
That promised day to see,
When nations shall Thy praises sing,
And bend the knee to Thee.

The reign of truth and peace begun,
Our sin and error flee;
Thou art alone, proclaimed the One,
And One Thy Name shall be.

DAVID LEVY.

The Benediction

THERE'S a memory that sweetens
My father's last adieu,
There's a solemn thought that deepens
When I think of him anew.

'Tis the blessing that he uttered
  When I took his last farewell,
The priestly threefold blessing
  Our people know so well.

Ah, bless thee, Lord, and keep thee,
  His countenance e'er shine,
And gracious be He to thee,
  And give thee peace and thine.
His hands were spread in blessing
  Above my bowing head,
His blessing lives within me,
  His spirit is not fled.

The dear old Jewish custom
  Made many a stout heart;
I always felt the better
  When thus I used to part.
And though he is gone forever,
  To sleep beneath the sod,
I still can hear him lifting
  The self-same prayer to God.

Ah, bless thee, Lord, and keep thee,
  His countenance e'er shine,
And gracious be He to thee,
  And give thee peace and thine.
His countenance be lifted,
  And may He grant thee peace,
The goal of earthly living,
  And Heaven's own surcease.

HARRY WEISS.

Grace After Meals

OUR Rock with loving care,
  According to His word,
Bids all His bounty share;
Then let us bless the Lord.

His flock our Shepherd feeds
With graciousness divine;
He satisfies our needs
With gifts of bread and wine.
Therefore with one accord
We will His name adore,
Proclaiming evermore
Holy, holy is the Lord.
     Our Rock, etc.

The land desired so long,
Our fathers' heritage,
Inspires our prayer and song
To God from age to age.
His bounteous gifts afford
Our sustenance each day,
His mercy is our stay,
Yea, faithful in the Lord.
     Our Rock, etc.

O be Thy mercy moved,
Our Rock, to dwell with us,
With Zion, Thy beloved,
Our temple glorious
May we redeemed, restored,
Be led there every one
By David's holy son,
The Anointed of the Lord.
     Our Rock, etc.

Thy city built once more,
Thy temple walls uprising,
There will we adore
With joyful songs of praise
Thee, merciful, adored,
We bless and sanctify
With wine-cups filled up high,
By blessing of the Lord.
     Our Rock, etc.   ANONYMOUS.
     (Translated by Alice Lucas.)

LITURGICAL

Man, the Image of God

EXULT, my soul, in consciousness proud,
  That I in God's image was made:
That 'mid nature's irrational crowd,
Moral light to me was conveyed;
When dust, by His pure breath refined,
In flesh the "vital spark" enshrined.

Oh! how shall I deserve the station
Omnipotence assigns to me;
Whose spiritual elevation
Is next to angels in degree?
How Mercy's likeness manifest,
Reflected in each mortal breast?

Perilous pre-eminence! to hold
Perfection's model in the mind;
Yet feel how the inferior mould
In which its essence is confined,
May all its majesty efface,
And leave of stamp divine no trace.

Immortal reason! hast thou no beam
Of bright intelligence to prove
Thy semblance to that Sire supreme,
Whose breath is life, whose blessing love?
Triumph! though passions dim thy ray,
In thee God's image we survey.

Justice, by thee e'er directed,
His strongest feature typifies;
In truth (through reason best reflected)
His spirit's light I recognize;
And in beneficence e'er trace
His brightest trait; celestial grace!

How glorious this filiation
Between the Lord of worlds and me!

413

Oh! how shall I deserve the station,
Next to the angels in degree?
Like these, by walking in His ways;
Like these, by singing e'er His praise.

PENINA MOÏSE.

Grace for the Sabbath

TO Israel this day is joy ever bless'd,
    Is light and is gladness, a Sabbath of rest.
Thou Sabbath of rest,
To a people distress'd,
To sorrowful souls,
A strong soul hast given.
From souls tempest-driven
Thou takest their sighing,
Thou takest their sighing,
Thou Sabbath of rest.

This Sabbath of rest,
O God, thou hast bless'd
And hallowed above
All the days of creation,
The care-laden nation
To peace and hope wakens,
To peace and hope wakens,
This Sabbath of rest.

To slaves giveth rest
The Sabbath behest,
We are free while we keep
Its statutes appointed.
A gift well anointed,
We bring thee, O loved One,
We bring thee, O loved One,
The Sabbath of rest.

O gladden our rest,
And our sanctuary bless'd
Restore thou, O Lord,
And grant Thy salvation
To Israel Thy nation,

LITURGICAL

Extolling and praising
Extolling and praising
The Sabbath of rest.
To Israel this day is joy ever bless'd
Is light and is gladness, a Sabbath of rest.

ALICE LUCAS.

Faith

And the Lord, He it is that doth go before thee; He
will be with thee, He will not fail thee, neither forsake
thee; fear not, neither be dismayed.—Deuteronomy,
xxxi, 8.
My presence shall go with thee, and I will give
thee rest.—Exodus, xxxiii, 14.

O F all Thy gifts the best.
On us Thy needy people, sore distress'd,
Sore travel worn, and stained with sin and woe,
Of all Thy gifts the best.

Then shall we find, amid life's toilsome quest,
The peace of God, from which all blessings flow.
Then shall no evil fears our souls molest.

Faith, faith in Thee, faith that, where'er we go,
Thy presence goes with us, and gives us rest
That is in heaven above, on earth below,
Of all Thy gifts the best!

ALICE LUCAS.

Rude Are the Tabernacles Now

R UDE are the tabernacles now,
Of Israel's scattered band;
Still to the East the faithful bow,
And bless their fatherland.
Oh! save us, we beseech Thee, Lord!
Through every chance and change adored.

Oh, when we think of Palestine,
Whose consecrated dust
Once bore the hallowed ark and shrine
Of Judah's only trust;
We mourn to mark the stranger there,
Who only mocks the Hebrew's prayer.

Wake ye, who in the deadly sleep,
Of self-delusion lie!
Arise! or ye may live to weep
The time now passing by.
Save us, O Everlasting Lord!
Thy aid against remorse afford!

Let us re-open mercy's law,
And in our bosoms lock
Precepts, that humble hearts shall draw
Towards salvation's rock;
Praises to Heaven's Supreme Lord,
Who did this sovereign gift accord!

ANONYMOUS.

From the Hymn Book of Congregation Beth Elohim. Charleston,
S. C., 5616.

God Is Nigh to Contrite Hearts

LORD of the world, we seek Thy face,
With contrite hearts implore Thy grace,
Not on our merits we depend,
To us Thy favor Thou wilt send;
But trusting in Thy mercy great,
That Thou wilt hear us supplicate.

For what are we, our life or deed?
Some broken staff; some bruised reed,
What are the virtues that we boast?
Of small account and vain at most.
What is our strength and what our power
That fails us in each tempting hour?

LITURGICAL

What can we urge our cause to plead,
  Our fathers' God, to intercede?
For what to Thee are men of power
  Who fade at last like grass or flower?
What are the wise, the most august?
  Thou art to them as star to dust.

The greatest of our works are vain,
  For life is fraught with sin and pain.
And how alike are beast and man,
  Whose longest years are but a span,
Save in that pure, immortal soul
  Which yearns for its celestial goal.

There at Thy throne in future time,—
  Though most momentous and sublime,—
The soul shall render its report
  At Mercy's just and last high court;
And there the favor of the Lord
  Shall be its true and blest reward.

DAVID LEVY.

A Prayer

Imitation of the Persian

LORD! who art merciful as well as just,
  Incline Thine ear to me, a child of dust,
  Not what I would, O Lord! I offer Thee,
Alas! but what I cán,
Father Almighty, who hast made me man
And bade me look to heaven, for Thou art there,
Accept my sacrifice and humble prayer.
  Four things which are not in Thy treasury,
I lay before Thee, Lord! with this petition;—
  My nothingness, my wants,
My sins and my contrition.

ALICE LUCAS.

417

A Prayer

LEAVE not a veil before my eyes,
Tear from my mind the shield of lies,
And from my soul the web of sophistries;
Yea, though I stricken, shirk and flee,
God, give me eyes to see.

Send me no song so honey-sweet
That I forget the harsher beat
Of life, the pulsing discords of the street,
Smite me with sorrow as a spear—
But give me ears to hear.

Grant me the will to pay for light,
For vision overtopping sight,
And dreams that are not of the passing night;
Yield, at what price Thou shalt demand,
A heart to understand.

V. H. FRIEDLANDER.

Sacred Lyric

WHEN Sorrow, blinded with her tears,
Upon my life in darkness stole
And quenched my hopes and roused my fears,
And smote and pierced my weary soul,
O, then, I turned my heart to Thee,
O Lord of Hosts, to comfort me.

When, like rough winds in stormy skies,
Fears lashed my heart and seared my brain,
Until before my aching eyes
Life's joys were pitilessly slain,
Alone, I turned, O God, to Thee,
To solace and to comfort me.

418

For cares may blind and gloom may shroud,
And desolation chill the heart,
But Thou canst rend the blackest cloud,
And heal life's anguish and its smart;
As humbly I may turn to Thee.
O Lord of Hosts! to comfort me.

ISIDORE G. ASCHER.

The Voice of God

I HEARD His voice in song of wren
  Beneath the hedge at daybreak, when
The dew like diamonds gleams.
I heard His voice in bubbling rills
That tumbled down the verdant hills,
  To swell the sea-ward streams.
I heard His voice in whisp'ring breeze,
That gleaned the secret of the trees
  And conned the flowers' dreams.
I heard His voice when squirrels woke
And dropped an acorn from the oak
  And whisked their bushy tails.
I heard His voice when Curly Locks
Drove forth to bathe her feathered flocks,
  And Meg cleaned out the pails.
I heard His voice when belfry tower
In lazy notes struck noonday hour
  And cattle shirked the sun.
I heard His voice when nine was tolled
And all the sheep had gone to fold,
  And bleated day was done.
I heard His voice as midnight crept
With murky steps o'er men that slept—
  Some pillowed 'neath the sod.
Yes, even in that silent hour
I heard in full majestic power
  The mighty voice of God.

M. M.

Prayer

UNTO thy Rock, O my soul, uplift thy gaze,
  His loving-kindness day and night implore.
Remember thy Creator in the days
Of youth, in song His glorious name adore.
He is thy portion through earth's troubled maze,
Thy shelter, when life's pilgrimage is o'er.
Thou knowest that there waits for thee always
A peaceful resting-place His throne before.
Therefore the Lord my God I bless and praise,
Even as all creatures bless Him evermore.

SOLOMON IBN GABIROL.

Hope for the Salvation of the Lord

HOPE for the salvation of the Lord,
  In Him I trust, when fears my being thrill;
Come life, come death, according to his word,
  He is my portion still.

  .   .   .   .

Him will I serve, His am I as of old;
  I ask not to be free.

  .   .   .   .

Sweet is ev'n sorrow coming in His name,
  Nor will I seek its purpose to explore;
His praise will I continually proclaim,
  And bless Him evermore.

ABRAHAM IBN EZRA.

God Everywhere

WHERESOE'ER I turn mine eyes
  Around on Earth or toward the skies,
I see thee in the starry field,
I see thee in the harvest's yield,
In every breath, in every sound,
An echo of Thy name is found.

420

The blade of grass, the simple flower,
Bear witness to Thy matchless pow'r.
My every thought, Eternal God of Heaven,
Ascends to thee, to whom all praise be given.

ABRAHAM IBN EZRA.
(Translated by D. E. de L.)

The Living God

I THIRST for God, to Him my soul aspires,
The living God it is my heart's desires.

The living God created me
To life. Yea, as I live, spake He,
No living man my face shall see,
Shall see my face and live.

He fashioned all with counsel wise
And purpose wonderful that lies
For ever hidden from our eyes,
The eyes of all who live.

Supreme o'er all His glory reigns,
Extolled on earth in holy strains,
Blessed is He whose hand maintains
The soul of all who live.

He separated Israel's seed
To teach them statutes, which indeed
If that a man do hear and heed,
His soul by them shall live.

Can pure and just themselves declare
They who of dust created were?
Lo, in Thy sight, O Lord, we dare
Call no man just who lives.

Like serpent's poison venomous,
The sinful passion dwells in us,
Can then from evil cankerous
Be any free that live?

But they the cords of sin who break
May yet the evil path forsake,
Ere in that house their rest they take,
That waits for all who live.

Call us in mercy unto Thee
Again Thy witnesses to be,
O Thou, who openest graciously
Thy hand to all that live.

ABRAHAM IBN EZRA.
(Translated by Alice Lucas.)

A Song of Life

FOR God, the living Lord, my soul's athirst
My heart and soul in joyous praise outburst.

A living God—He gives
    To me creation's call,
    But warneth mortals all;
    No man sees God and lives.

Behold His wisdom's might,
    Creating all in light,
    All to Him is clear and bright
    Howso hid from mortal sight.

Regal in His glory
    In all mouths its story,
    Blessed! in whose hand
    Our souls sustained stand.

422

LITURGICAL

Abraham's sons He set apart,
    His laws to them He did impart;
    Wise laws which to the World they give,
    For mortals to obey and live.

Man cannot do the right:
    Dust is he to Godlike sight:
    For who in Heaven's eye
    His way can justify?

Base the longing of our heart,
    Envenom'd as the scorpion's dart.
    How can our flesh in life abide
    When sin has seared and mortified?

Needs must we sinners then
    Repeat our evil courses. . . . When?
    Before we reach the end, the goal,
    Of all that boasts a living soul.

Enthralled by Thy love,
    We hail Thee, God above!
    That from Thine open hand
    Feedest our living band.

Sleeping children, Lord! awake:
    Pity for their fathers' sake:
    The promised days to hasten deign
    When Jesse's son once more will reign.

Regard the mother's truth when tested.
    How shrill the handmaid * hath protested:
    "The dead religion—it is thine,
    The living one is mine, is mine."

Awestruck I bow the head,
    In prayer my hands I spread,
    God's due from man my lips confess,
    Each soul of life his God must bless.

ABRAHAM IBN EZRA.
(Translated by E. N. A.)

* Hagar to Sarah, i. e., Mahomet to Israel.

God, Whom Shall I Compare to Thee?

GOD, whom shall I compare to Thee,
When Thou to none canst likened be?
Under what image shall I dare
To picture Thee, when everywhere
All Nature's forms Thine impress bear?

Greater, O Lord, Thy glories are
Than all the heavenly chariots far.
Whose mind can grasp Thy world's design?
Whose word can fitly Thee define?
Whose tongue set forth Thy powers divine?

Can heart approach, can eye behold
Thee in Thy righteousness untold?
Whom did'st Thou to Thy counsel call,
When there was none to speak withal
Since Thou was first and Lord of all?

Thy world eternal witness bears
That none its Maker's glory shares.
Thy wisdom is made manifest
In all things formed by Thy behest,
All with Thy seal's clear mark impress'd,

Before the pillars of the sky
Were raised, before the mountains high
Were wrought, ere hills and dales were known,
Thou in Thy majesty alone
Did'st sit, O God, upon Thy throne!

Hearts, seeking Thee, from search refrain,
And weary tongues their praise restrain.
Thyself unbound by time and place,
Thou dost pervade, support, embrace
The world and all created space.

The sages' mind bewildered grow,
The lightning speed of thought is slow.
"Awful in praises" art Thy name;
Thou fillest, strong in strength proclaimed,
This universe Thy hand has framed.

Deep, deep beyond all fathoming,
Far, far beyond all measuring
We can but seek Thy deeds alone;
When bow Thy saints before Thy throne,
Then is Thy faithfulness made known.

Thy righteousness we can discern,
Thy holy law proclaim and learn.
Is not Thy presence near alway
To them who penitently pray,
But far from those who sinning stray?

Pure souls behold Thee, and no need
Have they of light; they hear and heed
Thee with the mind's keen ear, although
The ear of flesh be dull and slow.
Their voices answer to and fro.

Thy holiness for ever they proclaim;
The Lord of Hosts! thrice holy is His name!

JUDAH HA-LEVI.
(Translated by Alice Lucas.)

O Lord, I Call on Thee

O LORD, I call on Thee when sore dismayed,
Thou wilt hear my voice and lend me aid,
Nor shall I be of myriads afraid,
For Thou wilt ever be
The portion of my lot—Thou savest me.

In troubled times Thy mercy's plenteous store
Is full to overflowing evermore,
And when in straitness I my plaint outpour
With words entreating Thee,
Then with enlargement Thou dost answer me.

Make known Thy love to those who trust and pray,
To those who hold Thy name their help and stay,
Waiting for Thy salvation day by day,
Yea, who, O Lord, but Thee
Shall make me glad, who else deliver me?

Do Thou from heavenly heights my pain behold,
And lead me back unto Thy sheltering fold,
That I may answer scorners as of old;
Yea, though my dwelling be ·
In darkest night, God is a light to me.

ABRAHAM IBN EZRA.

Lord, Thou Great Jehovah

CREATOR, Author of all things!
 Thou who didst give to me
My being, hear me while I pray:
 From evil set me free—
Give, O give me peace within,
Tho' unworthy I have been;
Help me conquer death and sin—
 Lord, Thou great Jehovah.

Thy name is love, I know that Thou
 Wilt leave none in despair
Who seek Thy face; I know that Thou
 Wilt hear the sinner's prayer—
Let me clasp Thy hand in mine,
Let me know Thy peace divine,
Let my will be lost in Thine—
 Lord, Thou great Jehovah.

426

Help me to bear the burden, Lord,
  With patience run the race;
And when the storms of life are past
  Grant I may see Thy face—
When earth's night has passed away,
In bright realms of endless day
May I dwell with Thee for aye—
  Lord, Thou great Jehovah.

ALBERT FRANK HOFFMANN.

Lord, Do Thou Guide Me

When thou passest through the waters, I will be with thee; and through the rivers, they shall not overflow thee; when thou walkest through the fire, thou shall not be burned; neither shall the flame kindle upon thee.—Isaiah xliii. 2.

LORD, do Thou guide me on my pilgrim way,
  Then shall I be at peace, whate'er betide me;
Then morn is dark, the clouds hang low and gray,
  Lord, do Thou guide me.

Let not the mists of sin from Thee divide me,
But pierce their gloom with mercy's golden ray,
Then shall I know that Thou in love hast tried me.
  Lord, do Thou guide me.

O'er rugged paths be Thou my staff and stay,
Beneath Thy wings from storm and tempest hide me,
Through life to death, through death to heavenly day.
  Lord, do Thou guide me.

ALICE LUCAS.

Song of the Dew

Pizmon from the Prayer for Dew of the Musaph
Service for the First Day of the Passover.—Sephardic
Liturgy.

O RAIN, depart with blessings,
　　With blessings come, O dew;
For Mighty to Deliver,
　Is He that sends the dew.

With psalm and song I'll praise Him,
　In rhythms like the dew;
My Rock, my Strong Deliv'rer,
　He is, that sends the dew.

His Name with glory covers
　His folk, as earth the dew;
A Prince to their deliv'rance
　He sends, that sends the dew.

Hasten, O God, Thy promise—
　"I will be Israel's dew"—
And Mighty to Deliver,
　Let fall this day Thy dew!

(Translated by Solomon Solis Cohen.)

And the Heavens Shall Yield Their Dew

O THOU, that art the Trust, the Strength,
　　The Shield of all that live,
Who givest food to man and beast,
　Our year's perfection give—
The crowning cloud of summer rain
　Or, from night's cloudless blue,
The gentle drops whereof Thou saidst,
"And the heavens shall yield their dew!"

428

LITURGICAL

On waving grain, on mead and wood,
　Let drops of blessing fall,
That all Thy children may have bread,
　And healing be for all;
But them that study in Thy Law,
　And to Thy Charge are true,
Exalt in splendor like the stars,
Whilst the heavens shall yield their dew!

Make green the pastures of the wild,
　Girdle the hills with mirth;
With bright-hued zone of budding flowers
　Cincture the gladsome earth.
All they together shall rejoice,
　And sing His praise anew,
Whose loving bounty shall not fail;
Whose heavens shall yield their dew!

To clothe with leaf and deck with bud
　The naked, tender vine,
That weary souls may be refreshed
　With heartening draughts of wine;
And hungry souls be filled with good,
　And toil its strength renew
Through luscious feast of ripened fruit—
Bid Thy heavens to yield their dew!

The trees of God are full of sap,
　In valley and on hill;
The threshing floors piled high with corn;
　Wine, oil, the vats o'erfill;
Where ruin was, a ransomed folk
　Upbuilds its homes anew,
And all the land resounds with song—
"And the heavens shall yield their dew!"

Solomon Ibn Gabirol.
(Translated by Solomon Solis Cohen.)

The Burning of the Law

A SK, is it well, O thou consumed of fire,
   With those that mourn for thee,
That yearn to tread thy courts, that sore desire
   Thy sanctuary;

That, panting for thy land's sweet dust, are grieved,
   And sorrow in their souls,
And by the flames of wasting fire bereaved,
   Mourn for thy scrolls;

That grope in shadow of unbroken night,
   Waiting the day to see
Which o'er them yet shall cast a radiance bright,
   And over thee?

Ask of the welfare of the man of woe,
   With breaking heart, in vain
Lamenting ever for thine overthrow,
   And for thy pain;

Of him that crieth as the jackals cry,
   As owls their moaning make,
Proclaiming bitter wailing far and nigh;
   Yea, for Thy sake.

And thou revealed amid a heavenly fire,
   By earthly fire consumed,
Say how the foe unscorched escaped the pyre
   Thy flames illumed!

How long shalt thou that art at ease abide
   In peace, unknown to woe,
While o'er my flowers, humbled from their pride,
   Thy nettles grow?

Thou sittest high exalted, lofty foe!
   To judge the sons of God;
And with thy judgments stern dost bring them low
   Beneath thy rod.

LITURGICAL

Yea, more, to burn the Law thou durst decree—
    God's word to banish hence;
Then blest be he who shall award to thee
    Thy recompense!

Was it for this, thou Law, my Rock of old
    Gave thee with flames begirt,
That in thine after-days should fire seize hold
    Upon thy skirt?

O Sinai! was it then for this God chose
    Thy mount of modest height,
Rejecting statelier, while on thee arose
    His glorious light?

Wast thou an omen that from noble state
    The Law should lowly be?
And lo! a parable will I relate
    Befitting thee.

'Tis of a king I tell, who sat before
    The banquet of his son
And wept: for 'mid the mirth he death foresaw;
    So thou hast done.

Cast off thy robe; in sackcloth folds of night,
    O Sinai! cover thee;
Don widow's garb, discard thy raiment bright
    Of royalty.

Lo, I will weep for thee until my tears
    Swell as a stream and flow
Unto the graves where Thy two princely seers
    Sleep calm below:

Moses and Aaron in the Mountain Hor;
    I will of them inquire:
Is there another to replace this Law
    Devoured of fire?

431

O thou third month most sacred! woe is me
　　For treason of the fourth,
Which dimmed the sacred light that shone from thee
　　And kindled wrath;

And break the tablets, yea, and still did rage:
　　And lo! the Law is burnt!
Ye sinful! is not this the twofold wage
　　Which ye have earnt?

Dismal hath seized upon my soul; how, then,
　　Can food be sweet to me,
When, O thou Law, I have beheld base men
　　Destroying thee?

They cast thee out as one despised, and burn
　　The wealth of God Most High;
They whom from thine assembly thou wouldst spurn
　　From drawing nigh.

I cannot pass along the highway more,
　　Nor seek thy ways forlorn;
How do thy paths their loneliness deplore!
　　Lo! how they mourn!

The mingled cup shall taste as honey sweet
　　Where tears o'erbrim the wine;
Yea, and thy chains upon my shackled feet
　　Are joy divine.

Sweet would it be unto mine eyes alway
　　A rain of tears to pour,
To sob and drench thy sacred robes, till they
　　Could hold no more.

But lo! my tears are dried, when, fast outpoured,
　　They down my cheeks are shed;
Scorched by the fire within: because thy Lord
　　Hath turned and fled.

LITURGICAL

Taking His holy treasure, He hath made
  His journey far away;
And with Him hath not thy protecting shade
  Vanished for aye?

And I am desolate and sore bereft,
  Lo! a forsaken one:
Like a sole beacon on a mountain left,
  A tower alone.

I hear the voice of singers now no more,
  Silence their song hath bound;
The strings are broken which on harps of yore
  Breathed forth sweet sound.

In sackcloth I will clothe and sable band,
  For well-beloved by me
Were they whose lives were many as the sand—
  The slain of thee.

I am astonished that the day's fair light
  Yet shineth brilliantly
On all things:—it is ever dark as night
  To me and thee.

Send with a bitter cry to God above
  Thine anguish, nor withhold:
Ah! that He would remember yet His love,
  His troth of old!

Gird on the sackcloth of thy misery
  For that devouring fire,
Which burst forth ravenous on thine and thee
  With wasting dire.

E'en as thy Rock hath sore afflicted thee,
  He will assuage thy woe,
Will turn again the tribes' captivity,
  And raise the low.

Yet shalt thou wear thy scarlet raiment choice,
    And sound the timbrels high,
And yet amid the dancers shalt rejoice
    With gladdened cry.

My heart shall be uplifted on the day
    The Rock shall be thy light,
When He shall make thy gloom to pass away,
    Thy darkness bright.

MEIR OF ROTHENBERG.

(Translated by Nina Davis.)

The Royal Crown

MY God, I know that those who plead
    To thee for grace and mercy need
All their good works should go before
And wait for them at heaven's high door.
But no good deed have I to bring,
No righteousness for offering,
No service for my Lord and King.

Yet hide not thou thy face from me,
Nor cast me out afar from thee;
But when thou bidd'st my life to cease,
O mayst thou lead me forth in peace
Unto the world to come, to dwell
Among the pious ones, who tell
Thy glories inexhaustible.

There let my portion be with those
Who to Eternal life arose;
There purify my heart aright,
In thy light to behold the light.
Raise me from deepest depths to share
Heaven's endless joys of praise and prayer,
That I may evermore declare.
Though thou wast angered, Lord, I will give thanks
    to thee,
For past is now thy wrath, and thou dost comfort me.

ISRAEL ABRAHAMS.

434

LITURGICAL

New Year Hymn

GONE another year—
  Gone beyond recall;
Gone its smile and tear,
  Gone its joy and thrall.
Vain is now lament,
  Naught canst thou efface;
Though thou now repent
  Naught canst thou erase.

Dawns another year—
  Open it aright;
Thou shalt have no fear
  In its fading light.
Live that not a stain,
  Live that not a deed
May awaken pain,
  May erasure need.

JOSEPH KRAUSKOPF.

The Royal Crown

HOW shall I stand before Thee, Lord, and I am
  bowed with shame?
For e'en as I am poor and humble, exalted is Thy
  name!
E'en as my mortal might is weak and limited, Thy
  power is eternal, infinite,
Sorely wanting as I am, Almighty! Thou art perfect
  and complete!
For Thou art One, the only living God, who dost
  exist for aye.
Thou art wise and Thy might and majesty endure
  alway,

435

And I am wrought of dust and for the earth destined,
Full of error, helpless as a stone upon the way and
    blind—
A flitting shadow, a wind that passeth and returneth
    not—
Wrathful as a serpent, of stony heart and harboring
    all evil thought!
Yea, of proud and boastful mien, of unclean lips, a
    mortal vain
Who followeth his heart's desire, and counsel doth
    despise, and thought disdain.
For what I am and what is even this my life and
    power?
What fruit may bear my righteousness through life's
    e'er-changeful hour?
I know not whence I come, nor whither I am bound!
Before Thy might in awe I stand, bowed low unto
    the ground!   SOLOMON IBN GABIROL.
        (Translated by Rebecca A. Altman.)

Servant of God
(*Hymn for the Day of Atonement*)

O WOULD that I might be
    A servant unto Thee,
Thou God of all adored!
Then, though by friends outcast,
Thy hand would hold me fast,
And draw me near to Thee, my King and Lord.
Spirit and flesh are Thine,
O Heavenly Shepherd mine;
My hopes, my thoughts, my fears, Thou seest all,
Thou measurest my path, my steps dost know
When Thou upholdest, who can make me fall?
When Thou restrainest, who can bid me go?
O would that I might be
A servant unto Thee,
Thou God by all adored.
Then, though by friends outcast,

LITURGICAL

Thy hand would hold me fast,
And draw me near to Thee, my King and Lord.

Fain would my heart come nigh
To Thee, O God on high,
But evil thoughts have led me far astray
From the pure path of righteous government.
Guide Thou me back into Thy holy way,
And count me as one impenitent.
O would that I might be
A servant unto Thee,
Thou God, by all adored!
Then, though by friends outcast,
Thy hand would hold me fast,
And draw me near to Thee, my King and Lord.

If in my youth I still
Fail to perform Thy will,
What can I hope when age shall chill my breast?
Heal me, O Lord; with Thee is healing found.
Cast me not off, by weight of years oppress'd,
Forsake me not when age my strength has bound.
O would that I might be
A servant unto Thee,
Thou God, by all adored!
Then, though by friends outcast,
Thy hand would hold me fast,
And draw me near to Thee, my King and Lord.

Contrite and full of dread,
I mourn each moment fled,
'Mid idle follies roaming desolate,
I sink beneath transgressions manifold
That from Thy presence keep me separate,
Nor can sin darkened eyes Thy light behold.
O would that I might be
A servant unto Thee,
Thou God by all adored!
Then, though by friends outcast,
Thy hand would hold me fast,
And draw me near to Thee, my King and Lord.

So lead me that I may
Thy sovereign will obey;
Make pure my heart to seek Thy truth divine,
When burns my wound, be Thou with healing
    near!
Answer me, Lord! for sore distress is mine, .
And say unto Thy servant, I am here.
O would that I might be
A servant unto Thee,
Thou God, by all adored!
Then, though by friends outcast,
Thy hand would hold me fast,
And draw me near to Thee, my King and Lord.

JUDAH HA-LEVI.
(Translated by Israel Zangwill.)

Yea, More Than They

YEA, more than they, who through the gloomy night,
   Through sleepless hours that loiter on their way,
Watch for the dawn above the eastern height;
   Yea, more than they.

Watching and waiting for return of day
   My soul waits for the Lord, the Lord of might,
With whom forgiveness is, my hope and stay.

And when His mercy thrills my soul contrite,
   My soul rejoices in His pardoning ray,
More than they joy to see the morning light.
   Yea, more than they.

ALICE LUCAS.

Adonai Melech

A Yom Kippur Hymn (Sephardic Liturgy)

ERE space exists, or earth or sky,
   The Lord is King!
Ere sun or star shone forth on high,
   The Lord was King!

438

LITURGICAL

When earth shall be a robe outworn,
And sky shall fade like mists of morn,
  Still shall the Lord fore'er be King!
The Lord is King! The Lord was King! Forever
shall the Lord be King!

When earth He flings mid star-filled space,
  . The Lord is King!
When living creatures there found place,
  The Lord was King!
When homeward from earth's corners four,
He calls the scattered folk once more,
  Then shall the Lord fore'er be King!
The Lord is King! The Lord was King! Forever
shall the Lord be King!

   (Translated by Solomon Solis Cohen.)

Thee I Will Seek

THEE I will seek, to Thee unveil my breast,
 O great in Judah and in Israel blest,
For He who searches mortals understands
How truly my transgressions are confest.

Ah, verily, not one of us is just!
Thy myriad mercies save us from the dust;
 Lo, unto Thee we stretch our guilty hands,
And in Thy holy Name we put our trust.

We put our trust, for 'tis our soul's delight
To seek in humbleness Thy shield of might;
 Thy strength is all the refuge of the poor,
And lowly souls Thou placest on the height.

The haughtiness of upstarts I have borne,
Unsated and unceasing is their scorn;
 Lo! we are wasted of the tyrant boor
Who left the helpless utterly forlorn.

Before Thy mercy-seat the beggars pray,
Their sins confest, abandoned in dismay;
   Lo, pardon them and be no longer vext,
For is it not the dread Atonement Day?

O Thou in majesty and glory girt,
Be pitiful and trample sin to dirt;
   Lo! sweet as honey tastes the holy text, .
"For He is one who healeth those He hurt."

Yea! He will heal and all shall bless His name,
He will remove the burden of our blame;
   Before His face His people shall avow
The sins presumption added to their shame.

Both these, and those from ignorance that mount,
O cease, according to their plea, to count;
   Lo, life eternal set upon their brow,
For, Lord, in Thee is life's eternal fount.

To all who worship Thee grant life and grace,
Their heart's perversity from them erase;
   Let sprinkled water purify each soul,
And let the dew revive each stony place.

With dew, O lave Thy lambs from stain and flake,
It is the hour, forgiveness is awake.
   Lo! cleanse them as 'tis written in the Scroll,
"For on this day he shall Atonement make."

And this Atonement shall not be less good,
Than when the altar in the Temple stood.
   Lo! known to Him each sinew of my breast,
My reins are fashioned by His fatherhood.

My inward parts I'll fit for serving Thee,
So due acceptance greet Thy servant's plea,
   For whoso honors Thee Thou honorest,
Thou sole-exalted in sublimity.

LITURGICAL

On Thee alone must rest the hope of man,
Iniquities Thou wilt not strictly scan;
   Lo! God the righteous loves not punishment,
His ways transcend the little human plan.

'Tis of the deed itself I am afraid,
Lest by my sin I shall be duly paid;
   Yet Him I trust, and wait in dumb assent;
Repentance ever brought consoling aid.

From soul-affliction did I comfort win,
Confessing every public, private sin;
   Lo! this is the appointed Judgment Day,
A covenant eternal set within.

The day of pardon set to wean from vice,
Remorse replacing ancient sacrifice.
   Ah, could I but beneath His shadow stay.
He knows the weakness of my own device.

The wonders of Thy grace let me explore,
When Thou Thy sheep and lambs art counting o'er;
   Lo! this Thy flock is shepherded of Thee,
Nor e'er forgets the wonders wrought of yore.

Renew Thy deeds to save Thy faithful flock,
The fear of Thee is all their treasure-stock;
   Ah, let the foes who judge us learn to see
How little is their rock beside our Rock.

When "Israel's Holy Rock" the heathen cry,
God in their eyes Himself shall sanctify.
   Thus righteousness in these He brings to bud,
Down-looking from His holy place on high.

He will restore the Temple and its laws,
The glory of His presence there shall pause;
   Lo! men shall tremble when the Judge of blood
Arises to espouse His people's cause.

Ah, side with us, make hostile clamor cease,
Thy people from accusing tongues release,
   So Thy beloved shall rechant Thy praise;
For happiness awaits the sons of peace.

Then let Thy peace irradiate all things,
Account our orisons as offerings;
   Ah, flood us with Thy Presence as with rays,
From Zion goes the Law, the prophet sings;

That Law the faithful heard at Sinai,
To which they brought attentive ear and eye,
   Lo! God this day His faithful nation thanks,
He is a God who softens at our cry.

The Lord shall lead us even after death,
He saves from wrath and pain our mortal breath;
   Lo! arrogance as ignorance He ranks,
"It is My people's ignorance," He saith.

SIMEON BEN ISAAC BEN ABUN.
(Translated by Israel Zangwill.)

Even as the Daily Offering

Wherewith shall I come before the Lord, and bow
myself before the high God? Shall I come before him
with burnt offerings, with calves of a year old? . . .
He hath shewed thee O man, what is good; and what
doth the Lord require of thee, but to do justly, and
to love mercy and to walk humbly with thy God?—
Mich. vi, 6 and 8.

JUDGE of the earth who wilt arraign
   The nations at Thy judgment seat,
With life and favour bless again
   Thy prostrate people at Thy feet.
And mayest Thou our morning prayer
Receive, O Lord, as though it were
The offering that was wont to be
Brought day by day continually.

Thou who art clothed with righteousness,
  Supreme exalted over all,
How oftsoever we transgress,
  Do Thou with pardoning love recall
Those who in Hebron sleep; and let
Their memory live before Thee yet,
Even as the offering unto Thee
Offered of old continually.

Trust in God's strength and be ye strong,
  My people and His laws obey,
Then will He pardon sin and wrong,
  Then mercy will His wrath outweigh.
Seek ye His presence and implore
His countenance forevermore,
Then shall your prayers accepted be
As offerings brought continually.

SOLOMON BEN ABUN.
(Translated by Alice Lucas.)

Supplication

(Paraphrased from the Hebrew of R. Jose ben Jose.)

OUR sins are many, and we sigh
    For that we hearkened not to Thee
When all the time we knew Thee nigh,
    But proud in our prosperity
We went our ways with head on high.

Now wasted is our strength, and we
  Are like an armless soldier grown;
All that our fathers wrought for Thee
  Is nought, and now we stand alone
In shame and dire infirmity.

443

We are like stubble on the plain
That no one seeks to gather in
Or load upon the harvest wain—
Consuming fire will purge our sin
And lead us pure to Thee again.

O Lord, Thy seal accounts us Thine;
Of yore when in our dire distress
We craved Thy charity divine,
Thou didst us with Thy mercy bless;
O be Thou in this hour benign!

The driven leaf let healing cure,
Repent Thee for this human dust.
O cleanse us that we may be pure,
Let all our sins from Thee be thrust—
Thy mercy is for ever sure!

JOSÉ BEN JOSE.

Lo! As the Potter Mouldeth

LO! as the potter mouldeth plastic clay
To forms his varying fancy doth display;
So in Thy hand, O God of love, are we:
Thy bond regard, let sin be veil'd from Thee.

Lo! as the mason's hand the block doth hew
To shapes sublime, or into fragments strew;
So in Thy hand, O God of life, are we:
Thy bond regard, let sin be veil'd from Thee.

Lo! as the smith the rigid steel hath bent,
Soften'd with fire and wrought with strength unspent;
So in Thy hand, O God of might, are we:
Thy bond regard, let sin be veil'd from Thee.

Lo! as the seaman's hand doth cast or weigh
The pond'rous anchor in the foaming spray;
So in Thy hand, O God of pardon, we:
Thy bond regard, let sin be veil'd from Thee.

444

LITURGICAL

Lo! as the worker melteth vitreous flow,
And shapeth vessels from the crystal blow;
So in Thy hand, O God of grace, are we:
Thy bond regard, let sin be veil'd from Thee.

Lo! as th' embroid'rer's hand the robe hath made,
At will in lines of beauty, light and shade;
So in Thy hand, O God of fear, are we:
Thy bond regard, let sin be veil'd from Thee.

Lo! as the smelter fuseth silv'ry vein,
Removing dross, that naught impure remain;
So in Thy hand, O God of healing, we:
Thy bond regard, let sin be veil'd from Thee.

Lo! as the potter mouldeth plastic clay
To forms his varying fancy doth display;
So in Thy hand, O God of love, are we:
Thy bond regard, let sin be veil'd from Thee.

ELSIE DAVIS.

Happy He Who Saw of Old

HAPPY he who saw of old
The high priest, with gems and gold
All adorned from crown to hem,
Tread thy courts, Jerusalem,
Till he reached the sacred place
Where the Lord's especial grace
Ever dwelt, the centre of the whole.
Happy he whose eyes
Saw at last the cloud of glory rise,
But to hear of it afflicts our soul.

Happy he that day who saw
How, with reverence and awe
And with sanctity of mien,
Spoke the priest: "Ye shall be clean

445

From your sins before the Lord."
Echoed long the holy word,
While around the fragrant incense stole.
Happy he whose eyes
Saw at last the cloud of glory rise,
But to hear of it afflicts our soul.

Happy he who saw the crowd,
That in adoration bowed,
As they heard the priest proclaim:
"One, Ineffable, the Name,"
And they answered, "Blessed be
God the Lord eternally,
He whom all created worlds extol."
Happy he whose eyes
Saw at last the cloud of glory rise,
But to hear of it afflicts our soul.

Happy he who saw the priest
Turning toward the shining East,
And, with solemn gladness thrilled,
Read the doctrine that distilled
As the dew upon the plain,
As the showers of gentle rain,
While he raised on high the sacred scroll.
Happy he whose eyes
Saw at last the cloud of glory rise,
But to hear of it afflicts our soul.

Happy he who saw the walls
Of the temple's radiant halls,
Where the golden cherubim
Hide the ark's recesses dim,
Heard the singer's choral song,
Saw the Levites' moving throng,
Saw the golden censer and the bowl.
Happy he whose eyes
Saw at last the cloud of glory rise,
But to hear of it afflicts our soul.

Ever thus the burden rang
Of the pious songs they sang.
All the glories past and gone
Israel once did gaze upon,
Glories of the sacred fane,
Which they mourned and mourned again,
With a bitterness beyond control.
Happy he whose eyes
Saw (they said) the cloud of glory rise,
But to hear of it afflicts our soul.

SOLOMON IBN GABIROL.
(Translated by Alice Lucas.)

The Lifting of Mine Hands

THE lifting of mine hands accept of me
  As though it were pure evening sacrifice,
And let my prayer be incense of sweet spice
Accounted right and perfect unto Thee.
And when I call Thee, hear; for day once more
Sinks to the hour when Israel brought of yore
      The evening sacrifice.

My words before Thee shall be savours sweet,
  O everlasting Rock; and all the waste
  Of strength and body spent in this my fast
Shall seem to Thee a sacrifice complete.
Take mine heart's prayer, which, these ten days within,
I have prepared like offerings for sin
      And evening sacrifice.

Seek them this day that seek Thee; let them find
  Thy mercy, sought from Thee by their lips' fruit,
  Look at their throng assembled destitute;
Cleanse them like silver seven times refined.
Accept their prayer like one lamb, where there stand
Two hundred sheep from Israel's pasture-land
      For evening sacrifice.

447

Count it a whole burnt offering when I call;
  Prevail with him that is my wrongful foe.
  O make my righteousness like light to glow
Before the sun shall set and evening fall.
Each man pours out his heart in this his word,
And brings his gift to offer to the Lord
      An evening sacrifice.

Jeshurun, thy people, of Thy mercy sing,
  Holding a goodly doctrine; bend Thine ear,
  Open Thine eyes on them, and see, and hear
How good it is to stand thus tarrying
At portals of Thy pity, till Thou lift
Out of the hand of him that brings his gift
      An evening sacrifice.

In Thy great mercy hear and understand
  My words, my meditation; if I hold
  Grace in Thy sight, O God, Who from of old
Hast been a dwelling-place, then from mine hand
Take Thou the gift I bring Thee, pleading here
With supplication when the hour draws near
      For evening sacrifice.

God whom we have not found, whose might is whole
  For them, Thou madest Thine in ages gone,
  If man give much or little 'tis all one—
When he returns Thou wilt accept his soul—
If but his heart be true when he shall draw
Night with his offering: this is all the law
      Of evening sacrifice.

When sanctuary and altar stood of old
  Within their border on the ancient spot,
  They made atonement, choosing forth by lot
He-goats for offering; now, if God should hold
That our trangression should our death demand,
He would not take burnt offering from our hand
      Nor evening sacrifice.

But supplications do Thy people speak,
  Seeking forgiveness with a bitter heart;
  Behold them standing at the siege apart,
Watching, entreating Thee whose face they seek,
Hoping Thou wilt give respite for their debt
At even—saying "I shall appease him yet
        With evening sacrifice."

Jerusalem Thy city build again,
   And all her cities strengthen round about,
  And her oppressed prisoners bring out
To freedom, loosened from the binding chain,
Sweet be their offering as in days of yore,
And Thou wilt turn, Thou wilt accept once more
        Their evening sacrifice.

All Israel's outcasts, Judah's scattered ones
  Shall yet again be gathered to Thine hand,
  And fed as by a shepherd in good land;
And God shall sit refining Israel's sons
Like gold until their cleansing shall be wrought
And they shall be to Him as though they brought
        An evening sacrifice.

                MORDECAI BEN SHABBETHAI.
                (Translated by Nina Davis.)

Since We Be Standing

SINCE we be standing even yet, to be
   As ministers before Thee in Thy Name,
And spread our hands out, having naught for Thee
  Of that oblation wherewith once we came—
Hear now, O Lord, Thy people's voice and hold
Their crying for their sacrifice of old.

That He maintain the cause of His servant and the
  cause of His people Israel, as every day shall
           require.

All those who watched Thy doors have passed away,
  Who guarded for Thy treasury its due;
There is no off'ring and no gift this day,
  And still can justice pierce a mountain through,
Yet so shall Jacob's sin be purged at last,
And his atonement made in this his fast.

See, for the coin for off'ring faileth now,
  The silver of the ransom for my soul;
But wherefore, O my soul, art stricken low?
  Nay, bless the Lord and verily extol.
For He will soon repent Him for His own
Judging His people from the eternal throne.

A day of pardon is appointed us
  To make repentance for our souls therein;
Yea, though Thine altar still be empty thus,
  Our soul's affliction pleadeth for our sin.
Of old our fathers trusted in Thy Name,
They trusted, and from Thee redemption came.

Because the hand was once sent forth to lay
  Their dwelling-places low, their cities fair,
No off'ring hath been brought Thee since the day
  The sanctuary was wasted and laid bare.
Yet vengeance on His foemen He will take,
And make atonement for His people's sake.

For incense brought to Thee, which is no more,
  Mine orison shall drop as fragrant spice;
The prayer of the afflicted, burdened sore,
  Shall be a handful sweet for sacrifice;
So that he may not perish in the pit,
Nor want for bread nor go forth lacking.

Keep Thou the portal of my lips, accept
  Their gift as that brought once in priestly hand;
Let those who call on stocks or trees be swept
  From where my fathers prayed on hallowed land.
Yet, let the Lord to jealousy be moved
For His own land, and pity those He loved.

Since we be standing even yet, to be
  As ministers before Thee in Thy Name,
And spread our hands out, having naught for Thee
  Of that oblation wherewith once we came—
Hear now, O Lord, Thy people's voice, and hold
Their crying for their sacrifice of old.

That He maintain the cause of His servant and the
  cause of His people Israel, as every day shall
      require.

EPHRAIM BEN ISAAC.
(Translated by Nina Davis.)

I Am the Suppliant

I AM the suppliant for my people here,
  Yea, for the House of Israel, I am he;
I seek my God's benign and heedful ear,
  For words that rise from me.

Amid the walls of hearts that stand around,
  My bitter sighs surge up to mount the sky;
Ah! how my heart doth part with ceaseless bound
  For God, my Rock on high.

With mighty works and wondrous He hath wrought,
  Lord of my strength, my God.   When me He bade
To make a sanctuary for Him, I sought,
  I labored, and 'twas made.

The Lord my God, He hath fulfilled His word—
  He ruleth as an all-consuming fire—
I came with sacrifice, my prayer He heard,
  He granted my desire.

My sprinkling He accepted at the dawn
  Of this, the holiest day, the chosen one,
When with the daily offering of the morn
  The High Priest had begun.

And when the services thereafter came
 In glorious order, each a sacred rite,
I, bending low, and calling on the Name,
 Confessed before His sight.

The holy Priests, the ardent, for their sin
 Upon this day made their atonement then,
With blood of bullocks and of goats, within
 The city full of men.

The Priest with glowing censer seemed as one
 Preparing for the pure a way by fire.
I brought two rams and entered as a son
 That cometh to his sire.

The bathings and ablutions, as 'twas meet,
 Were all performed according to their way;
Then passed before the throne of God complete
 The service of the day.

And when sweet strains of praise to glorify
 Burst forth in psalmody and songs of love,
Yea, when I heard the voice uplifted high,
 I raised mine hand above.

The rising clouds of incense mantled o'er
 The mercy-seat within its sacred space:
Then glory filled me and my soul would soar
 To yon exalted place.

Of ancient times I dream, of vanished days;
 Now wild disquiet rageth unrestrained;
Scorned and reproached by all from godly ways
 Have I, alas, refrained.

Afar mine eyes have strayed and I have erred,
 Even the hearing of mine ears I quelled;
And righteous is the Lord, for at His word
 I sorely have rebelled.

LITURGICAL

Perverseness have I loved, and wrongful thought,
  And hating good, strove righteousness to shun,
And in mine actions foolishness have wrought;
  Great evil have I done.

Pardon I pray Thee, our iniquity,
  O God, from Thine high dwelling, and behold
The souls that in affliction weep to Thee—
  For lo! I have grown old.

Work for me, I beseech Thee, marvels now,
  O Lord of Hosts! in mercy lull our fears;
Answer with potent signs and be not Thou
  Silent to all my tears.

Open Thine hand exalted, nor revile
  The hearts not comforted, but pierced with care,
Praying with fervent lips, that know not guile,
  O hearken to my prayer!

BARUCH BEN SAMUEL.
(Translated by Nina Davis.)

All the World Shall Come to Serve Thee

ALL the world shall come to serve Thee
    And bless Thy glorious Name,
And Thy righteousness triumphant
    The islands shall acclaim.
And the peoples shall go seeking
    Who knew Thee not before,
And the ends of earth shall praise Thee,
    And tell Thy greatness o'er.

They shall build for Thee their altars,
    Their idols overthrown,
And their graven gods shall shame them,
    As they turn to Thee alone.

453

They shall worship Thee at sunrise,
    And feel Thy Kingdom's might,
And impart their understanding
    To those astray in night.

They shall testify Thy greatness,
    And of Thy power speak,
And extol Thee, shrined, uplifted
    Beyond man's highest peak.
And with reverential homage,
    Of love and wonder born,
With the ruler's crown of beauty
    Thy head they shall adorn.

With the coming of Thy Kingdom
    The hills shall break into song,
And the islands laugh exultant
    That they to God belong.
And all their congregations
    So loud Thy praise shall sing,
That the uttermost peoples hearing,
    Shall hail Thee crownéd King.

                    (Translated by Israel Zangwill.)

In the Height and Depth of His Burning

IN the height and depth of His burning,
    Where mighty He sits on the throne,
His light He unveils and His yearning
    To all who revere Him alone.
His promises never are broken,
    His greatness all measure exceeds;
Then exalt Him who gives you for token
    His marvellous deeds.

He marshals the planets unbounded,
    He numbers the infinite years;
The seat of His empire is founded
    More deep than the nethermost spheres;

454

LITURGICAL

He looks on the lands from His splendor;
   They tremble and quiver like reeds;
Then exalt ye in lowly surrender
   His marvellous deeds.

The worlds He upholds in their flying,
   His feet on the footstool of earth;
His word hath established undying
   Whatever His word brought to birth.
The ruler of hosts is His title;
   Then exalt Him in worshipful creeds,
Declaring in solemn recital
   His marvellous deeds.

He is master of all He created,
   Sublime in His circle of light;
His strength with His glory is mated,
   His greatness at one with His might.
So that Seraphim over Him winging,
   Obeying an angel that leads,
Unite in the rapture of singing
   His marvellous deeds.

His renown fills the heavenly spaces:
   The world He beholds to its ends:
His foes, who are mine, too, He chases;
   I count all who love Him my friends.
Exalted be therefore His glory,
   His praises be scattered as seeds,
Till all the world learns the great story,
   His marvellous deeds.

But of man—ah! the tale is another,
   His counsels are evil and vain:
He dwells with deceit as a brother,
   And the worm is the close of his reign.
Into earth he is carted and shovelled,
   And who shall recount or who heeds,
When above earth he strutted or grovelled,
   His marvellous deeds?

Not so God!—earth on nothing He founded,
    And on emptiness stretched out the sky;
With land the great waters He bounded,
    And bade all their breeds multiply.
In light He is clad as a raiment:
    His greatness no eulogy needs;
Yet exalt, 'tis your only repayment,
    His marvellous deeds.

                        MESHULLAM BEN KALONYMUS.
                    (Translated by Israel Zangwill.)

Lord, I Remember

LORD, I remember, and am sore amazed
    To see each city standing in her state,
And God's own city to the low grave razed:
    Yet in all time we look to Thee and wait.

Send us Thy mercy, O Redeemer! Make,
    O Thou my soul, to Him thy mournful plaint;
And crave compassion for my people's sake:
    Each head is weary and each heart is faint.

I rest on pillars, on God's holy parts,
    On tears that flow with never-ceasing might;
I pour out prayer to Him who searcheth hearts:
    Herein I trust, and in the Father's right.

O Thou who hearest weeping, healest woe,
    Our tears within Thy vase of crystal store;
Save us, and all Thy dread decrees forego,
    For unto Thee our eyes turn evermore.

                        MORDECAI BEN SHABBETHAI.
                    (Translated by Nina Davis.)

IV U I

NATIONAL

NATIONAL

Hatikvah—A Song of Hope

O WHILE within a Jewish breast
    Beats true a Jewish heart,
And Jewish glances turning East
    To Zion fondly dart,—

CHORUS

O then our Hope—it is not dead,
    Our ancient Hope and true,
Again the sacred soil to tread
    Where David's banners flew!

O while the tears flow down apace,
    And fall like bounteous rain,
And to the Fathers' resting-place
    Sweeps on the mournful train,—

And while upon our eager eye
    Flashes the City's wall,
And for the wasted Sanctuary
    The tear-drops trembling fall,—

O while the Jordan's pent-up tide
    Leaps downward rapidly,
And while its gleaming waters glide
    Through Galilee's blue sea,—

And while upon the Highway there
    Lowers the stricken Gate,
And from the Ruins Zion's prayer
    Upriseth passionate,—

O while the pure floods of her eyes
    Flow for her People's plight,
And Zion's Daughter doth arise
    And weep the long, long night!—

O while through vein in ceaseless stream
  The bright blood pulses yet,
And on our Fathers' tombs doth gleam
  The dew when sun is set!—

Hear, Brothers mine, where e'er ye be,
  This Truth by Prophet won;
" 'Tis then our Hope shall cease to be
  With Israel's last son!"—

NAPHTALI HERZ IMBER.
(Translated by Henry Snowman.)

Zionist Marching Song

I

LIKE the crash of the thunder
    Which splitteth asunder
  The flame of the cloud,
On our ears ever falling,
A voice is heard calling
  From Zion aloud:
"Let your spirits' desires
For the land of your sires
  Eternally burn.
From the foe to deliver
Our own holy river,
  To Jordan return."
Where the soft, flowing stream
Murmurs low as in dream,
  There set we our watch.
Our watchword "The sword
Of our land and our Lord—"
  By Jordan there set we our watch.

II

Rest in peace, loved land,
For we rest not, but stand,

NATIONAL

Off shaken our sloth.
When the bolts of war rattle
To shirk not the battle,
  We make thee our oath,
As we hope for a Heaven,
Thy chains shall be riven,
  Thine ensign unfurled.
And in pride of our race
We will fearlessly face
  The might of the world.
When our trumpet is blown
And our standard is flown,
  Then set we our watch.
Our watchword, "The sword
Of our land and our Lord—"
  By Jordan then set we our watch.

III

Yea, as long as there be
Birds in air, fish in sea,
  And blood in our veins;
And the lions in might,
Leaping down from the height,
  Shake, roaring, their manes;
And the dew nightly laves
The forgotten old graves
  Where Judah's sires sleep,
We swear, who are living,
To rest not in striving,
  To pause not to weep;
Let the trumpet be blown,
Let the standard be flown,
  Now set we our watch.
Our watchword, "The sword
Of our land and our Lord—"
  In Jordan now set we our watch.

NAPHTALI HERZ IMBER.

(Translated by Israel Zangwill.)

Onward

I

WHERE are you going, soldiers,
        With banners and drawn sword?
We're marching East to Palestine
    To battle for the Lord!
What captain leads your bands
    Along the sandy coasts?
The Mighty One of Israel,
    His name is Lord of Hosts!
To Palestine, to Palestine,
    The Lord will lead us through—
To blow before the heathen walls
    The trumpets of the Jew.

II

What flag is this you carry,
    In this your Holy War?
The same our grandsires raised aloft,
    The same our fathers bore.
On many a battlefield, intact,
    It caught the crimson rain,
For what was woven in God's loom,
    No man can rend in twain.
To Palestine, to Palestine
    The Lord will lead us through,
To plant upon its mountain-heights
    The standard of the Jew.

III

What song is this you're singing?
    The same that Israel sang
When Moses led the mighty choir,
    And Miriam's timbrel rang.
"To Palestine, to Palestine!"
    Both young and old have cried;
"To Palestine, to Palestine"—
    The people's voice replied.

To Palestine, to Palestine,
  The Lord will lead us through
To thunder in the usurper's ear
  The anthem of the Jew.

IV

When Salem's foes are scattered
  And all the path lies free,
What follows next in order?
  Our God to that will see.
He'll break the tyrant's sceptre,
  He'll build the people's throne—
When half the world is Freedom's,
  Then all the world's our own.
To Palestine, to Palestine,
  The Lord will lead us through.

J. M. MANICOFF.

On!

WHEN Israel marched from Egypt land,
  And broke her yoke of slavery,
And standing by the Red Sea strand,
  Drank her first draught of Liberty,
And torrid Afric's horrid hordes came on with new-
  linked chains, once more
    Her limbs to bind;
And trembling Israel cried to Heaven when she beheld
  the sea before,
    The foe behind;
'Then burst a voice from high;
Why do the children cry—
Why do the children cry to me?
Why do they not go on?

And Israel found her promised home—
  And lost it; and her Destiny
Has forced her, ever since, to roam
  In search of it o'er land and sea.

And blood-soaked foot-prints mark her path, through
    briers, and beasts, and storms, and stress,
         —Her life one dirge;
Yet some of Israel's sons, from out the black medi-
    æval wilderness,
         Did at last emerge.
And now, from a foreign strand,
We long for our native land;
And again the command in our ears, as we stand:
Why do they not go on!

Yes! We are through—we favored few;
    And some of us would rest content,
If only our poor brother Jew
    Would not scream so when being rent.
We're tired of wandering through the world, but,
    brothers, we can have no rest
         Here on the strand;
Behind come foes more cruel far than the seas of hard-
    ship we must breast
         For our Fatherland.
—Now, brothers, which is it to be:
The foe, or the God-governed sea?
Come, make your choice with me, for the sea!
And let us on, on, on!   GEORGE BENEDICT.

To the Glory of Jerusalem

BEAUTIFUL height! O joy! the whole world's
         gladness!
  O great King's city, mountain blest!
My soul is yearning unto thee—is yearning
  From limits of the west.

The torrents heave from depths of mine heart's passion,
  At memory of thine olden state:
The glory of thee which was born to exile,
  Thy dwelling desolate.

464

And who shall grant me but to rise and reach thee,
  Flying on eagle's pinions fleet,
That I may shed upon thy dust, beloved,
  Tears, till thy dust grow sweet?

I seek thee, though thy King be no more in thee,
  Though where the balm hath been of old—
Thy Gilead's balm—be poisonous adders lurking,
  Winged scorpions manifold.

Is it not to thy stones I shall be tender?
  Shall I not kiss them verily?
Shall not the earth taste on my lips be sweeter
  Than honey—the earth of thee?

JUDAH HA-LEVI.

Jerusalem

JERUS'LEM! Jerus'lem! thy glories have fled,
  Thy Kings wander crownless, pale ghosts of the
      past;
Thy beauty, thy valor, thy might, are all dead;
  But Hope is still left thee—'tis all that thou hast!

Though the sword of the warrior's tarnished with rust,
  And the war-steed lies bleeding along the red earth;
Though thy towers have crumbled long since into dust,
  And the songs of the Priests but in sorrow have
      birth;

Yet the Great God of Heaven will brighten the stain,
  And breathe in the war-horse, strength, power, and
      might;
Thy ramparts, Oh Salem! shall tower again,
  And the Priests' Holy Temple arise in thy sight.

Then, Queen of the East! let thy tears cease to flow—
  Thy God liveth ever; He is mighty to save;
The diadem yet shall encircle thy brow,
  When those who now rule, shall have passed in the
      grave.

For the Future hath gladness for thee in its womb,
   And the harp will again sound thy triumph and
      praise;
Nor sorrow, nor blight, will e'er shadow with gloom,
   The Sun of thy Glory, the Light of thy Days.

And nations will bow, as they did once before,
   And quake in thy presence with dread and alarm;
For strong are the people, who rest them secure
   In the Faith of His word, and the Might of His
      arm.

P. C. L.

Zion

ON lovely dwellings fall the fervid rays,
   The naked rocks lift high their heads in air,
   Dust-covered stones fling back the noon-day's glare
And strange old ruins tell of ancient days.
A motley throng creeps through the narrow ways,
   Pilgrims from far off lands whose faces bear
   The look that tells of by-gone toil and care,
Of weary journeys and of long delays.
What magic is there in this torrid clime?
   What fascination in these hoary walls?
   What charm dwells here that sovereignly calls
To hearts of men throughout the reach of time,
   Heedless of earthly gain, yet draws the soul
   Through want and hardship, to what mighty goal?

This was the ancient home of Israel;
   Here lived our fathers fearless and free;
   Here lives a glory and a memory;
And we His chosen ones, once more shall dwell,
Majestic, jubilant, invincible,
   In this, our heritage; our eyes shall see
   The long-ago that is again to be;
The peace that has no ending shall dispel

The dreaming and the doubt, the hopes, the fears.
  With love and longing we await that day
Whose dawn beholds the yearning of the years
  Fulfilled at last, and, while we waiting, pray,
A newer life in Mount Moriah wakes,
All over Olivet the morning breaks.

Louis Federleicht.

A Song of Zion

I

JERUSALEM, my boast and pride,
  My heart, it yearns for thee,
The land where peace and joy abide,
  Thy shores when shall I see?

II

O perfect, pure and pleasant soil,
  Far-famed as Israel's race,
I love thy fields, thy fruits, thy toil,
  Thy trees of stately grace.

III

'Neath thy blue skies no mist is seen,
  No drear nor darksome night;
Thy very hills of splend'rous sheen,
  For God has made thee right.

IV

Of precious stones thy walls are made,
  Thy ramparts, jewels rare,
Thy gates of oriental jade,
  That spread a radiant glare.

467

V

Of ivory hue thy homes are built,
　　Thy windows, crystal clear;
And every soul is free from guilt,
　　For God hath sent His cheer.

VI

Jerusalem! my people's home,
　　Would God, I were in thee;
No more the Exile's aimless roam,
　　My paradise across the sea.

VII

Where shepherds and their flocks abound,
　　Where birds prolong their lay,
Where flowers bloom the whole year round,
　　And all the earth seems gay.

VIII

Thy mountains stand, as heroes bold,
　　Thy rivers softly pass;
Thy pastures oft in psalms extolled,
　　Of nectar, breathes thy grass.

IX

No thing that is not passing clean
　　Can come within thy gates;
On every side a smile is seen,
　　And joy e'en permeates.

X

There hate and envy cannot dwell,
　　There lucre holds no sway,
There malice died, and Sh'kina's spell,
　　Makes heavy hearts feel gay.

XI

Rememb'rest thou the ancient days,
  When prophets crowned thy streets,
When Levites with their chants of praise
  Recalled thy wond'rous feats?

XII

In foreign lands thy sons abide,
  We see thee but in dreams;
We sob, we sigh, our tears are dried
  And Hope, it becks and beams.

XIII

"Another year," we softly pray
  "O, Lord," Thy children cry;
"O, take us back to Yesterday,
  To Israel's cherished destiny."

XIV

Each day we pray, in accents low
  Would God I were with thee;
Our Faith is strong, our hopes they grow
  Our Fatherland to see.

                WALTER VERNON-EPSTEIN.

The Shoshanah

1

A LILY lies broken and bare on a highway—
  Broken and bare and maimed;
And people from many a neighboring byway
  Carelessly pass her, shamed.
Come carelessly passing her, lying there broken,
  Lying mud-spattered and torn;
Of once glorious beauty now scarcely a token,
  She seems man and God-forlorn.

In hope, though desponding,
She lies unresponding
To insults, to jibes, and to jeers;
Herself bruised and battered,
Her children wind-scattered—
A mother bemoaning in tears.

II

Lightly the all-crushing Time-wheel rolls o'er her,
Leans lightly, and then rolls on;
Softly the all-burning sunbeams do lower
Their fiercest rays for her, so wan;
Time lends his all-sheltering hand to her—bleeding—
And soon does the sun heal each cut.
But men—Ah! the passing men—push her unheeding,
From out of the refuge rut,
"What dost thou, poor lily,
On highways so hilly,
So far from the land of thy birth?
Thy hopes lead thee whither?
How camest thou hither—
This hard-hearted, rock-bestrewn earth?"

III

"I once was the fairest and happiest flower,
Proudest and haughtiest dame;
By the King's own hands tended, in his royal bower—
The Lily of Sharon, my name,
But the weeds they rose up in their envy to choke me,
And brought me very low;
And cast on this highway, the passersby broke me,
And filled my cup with woe.
My house, it is Zion;
My hope, Judah's Lion;
For a while he has left me in pain,
Not for e'er to debase me,
But soon to replace me
In Zion to flourish again."

GEORGE E. CHODOWSKY.

470

The Return

THE PEOPLE

WIDE open, ye doors, and raise up high, O gate,
  We are coming again, who have waited so long—
With shouts and rejoicing, with music and song;
Then haste ye, companions, nor linger nor wait.

ZION

O not as a beggar that seeketh for alms,
  As conquering host ye are coming to me,
  From valley and mountain, from land and from sea
With thunder of trumpets and waving of palms.

THE PEOPLE

Our flag shall be planted on Zion's fair side,
  We shall rest in its shade, who have wandered so
    long,
  Our tears turned to laughter, our sighs into song,
Rejoicing as Bridegroom that greeteth his Bride.

R. E. I.

On to the Promised Land

I

A DAWNING sun breaks through the sable cloud!
  Oh, see the East ablaze in crimson hue!
There peals a mighty blast triumphant, loud,
  A call to rouse the ever-striving Jew!

CHORUS

Arise my people grand in story,
Thy little ones and patriarchs hoary,
Illumined by thy pristine glory,
  And form one mighty band!
And let thy shout ascend to heaven,
For lo! the clouds thy dawn hast riven,
Behold fulfilled the promise given,
  On to the promised land!

II

Now beam the rosy rays throughout the lands,
    And eyes with sorrow dim light up anew!
In every clime the call is joining bands
    Who swing aloft the standard of the Jew!

III

Oh! let the mountain land beloved of God,
    Where heroes bled and prophets falsehood slew!
No longer mourning-wrapt, the sacred sod
    Blooms forth to greet the home-returning Jew!

IV

The torrent sweeps and melts the crags away,
    A nation's cherished dream at last comes true!
For now indeed has come the promised day
    Of freedom for the never-conquered Jew!

                        RUFUS LEARSI.

To Zion

O PEOPLE long oppressed and stricken sore,
    Condemned as wanderers on the earth to mourn
Across the age-long darkness of thy fate,
    There breaks at length the radiance of the dawn.
Behold a land, thy birthright and thy home,
    On thee by Heaven bestowed, by Heaven with-
        drawn,
Yet promised to thy seed forevermore;
    Yea, He, the Mighty One, Himself hath sworn.
Behold its plains unsown, its rock-strewn slopes,
    Whereon no more the vine and almond grows.

Those barren hills again shall cedars crown,
    The land for thee shall blossom as the rose.
Return to thy rest, at last return;
    Cry to the South "Give back! Give back O
        North!"

Those mountains summon and those valleys cry,
 By twos and threes, by tens, in troops go forth
Though yet afar the Peace of Zion waits,
  Perchance through flames and blood thy pathway
      lies,
Fear not—Be strong—Thy heritage regain
  O Judah, tarry not! Israel arise. M. B. S.

Zionism

I AM come with the dawn on the swift wings of light,
   Through the gloom of long ages of strife,
And will bear you away from these regions of night
   Far from the dull-plodding toil to new life.
Yet I come not in rage and my nets are not spread:
   Nor come I to inspire you to wrath.
But I come with the dawn—and by it you'll be led
   From the land of the shadow of death.

Lo! I find you in bondage, in hunger, and sorrow,
   Bending low 'neath the chains of the slave;
But with life in its wake will I bring you the morrow—
   To a life yond the gloom of this grave!
And filled with the spirit of joy I shall lead you
   To the land where you'll breathe freedom's breath;
From the scorn of your brothers to joy I will speed you
   From the land of the shadow of death!

                           SAMUEL ROTH.

Wandering

LITTLE man of sorrows, whither would you wander?
Whither from this sunny isle with step so firm and
      bold?
   "I am going to the City to hear the Word of God,
   My glory is to tread the soil on which my Fathers
      trod;
I am going to the City to hear the Word of God."

473

Little man of sorrows, whither would you wander?
Is thy quest a fairer heaven or a flower of brighter
    hue?
  "I am going to the City wherein my people strive,
  To share their wounds and slay their foes, encourage
    and revive;
I am going to the City wherein my people strive."

Little man of sorrows, whither would you wander,
When the Sun is in thy zenith here, and Hope so
    golden too?
  "I am going to the City to share my People's pain,
  To prove with deeds of daring that their struggle is
    not vain;
I am going to the City to share my People's pain."

Little man of sorrows, whither would you wander?
Whither from this sunny isle with step so firm and
    bold?
  "I am going to the country where my Fathers ruled
    of old,
  My quest is not a fairer sky, nor a sun of white and
    gold;
I am going to the country where my Fathers ruled of
    old."
                      SAMUEL ROTH.

The Promised Land

O LITTLE Land of lapping seas,
    Of vineyards, vales and hills;
Of tender rains and rainbow plains,
    Of deserts and of rills;
O little Land of mounting crags,
    Of lonely height and deep;
A world away thy children stray
    And long and wait and weep.

NATIONAL

From Egypt's flesh-pots, Lord of wrath,
  With mighty outstretched hand,
Through seas and mountains cleave our path;
  Oh! Lord, redeem our land!

I know the golden oranges
  Englobed beneath the moon,
The sky that spills 'twixt seas and hills
  Its shining draught of noon;
The vines that bind our holy hills
  With grapes like jewels set;
The silver green of olive sheen
  Oh, can my soul forget?

O little Land of holy men
  Of fearless dream and deed;
From clime to clime the storms of time
  Have strewn thy hardy seed,
And fearless still and holy still,
  We sang through hate and shame;
With faith we fought, with deed and thought
  And God's enduring name.

My heart is singing like a bird
  Of home that still may be,
And joys I dared to leave, and spared,
  Hold out their arms to me.
We cannot sleep in cushioned ease
  Nor yield to martial will,
But we must hear God's trumpet clear
  Sound peace upon His Hill.

                    JESSIE E. SAMPTER.

Jerusalem

I

THE ancient of cities!—the lady of nations!
　The home where the cherubims hovered in light!
Where the breeze has a voice like those old "lamenta-
　　　tions"
That saddened thy day with their omens of night,
And the river's low song seems to echo the strain
Which the prophet poured out to thy spirit—in vain!

II

Bright land of the promise!—whose vision of glory
　Had dazzled thy sense, till 't was feeble to see!
O, chosen for others to keep the high story
　Whose record was vain for thy children and thee!
Lone Esau of nations, that weepest alway,
While the gentile is rich in thy birthright today!

III

Lost land of the minstrel!—whose harp, in its sadness,
　Brought music from heaven, to play to thy heart,—
Whose spell of a moment came down on thy madness,
　And bade, for an hour, thy dark angel depart,—
Till the power of its warning expired with its strain,
And the spirit of evil came o'er thee again!

IV

And O, for the outcast who drank of thy glory,—
　The lost one of Judah,—the chosen of yore,—
The priest of thy temple,—the heir of thy story,—
　Who dwelt in thy vineyards, that blossom no more!
Afar, 'mid the heathen, he sitteth forlorn,—
And thy fruit is the bramble, thy greenness the thorn!

V

It was not for Edom that Zion was braided
　With crowns of the sunshine and garlands of bloom,
Where the wild Arab wanders the cedar hath faded,

The bird of the wild keepeth watch on the tomb;—
And the soil of the simoon awaits the far day,
When the rain shall return to the wilderness gray.

VI

Pale daughter of Zion!—all wasted with weeping,
  Thy footstool the desert,—its dust on thy head;
Thy long weary watch o'er the wilderness keeping,
  And sitting in darkness, like them that be dead;—
A veil like the widow's hath shadowed thy pride,
And a sorrow is thine like no sorrow beside!

VII

And sadly thy son by each far-foreign river
  Sits, as he sat in the Babel of old,—
Lone 'mid the nations,—all homeless forever,
  'Mid homes full of children,—and poor 'mid his
      gold;—
With a mark on his brow of the brand in his brain,
Like the record God wrote on the forehead of Cain!

VIII

Weary with wandering and wasted with sadness,
  And walking by lights that are all from the past,—
Wishes, scarce hopes, waken smiles without gladness,
  As backward his thoughts, like the mourner's, are
      cast;
For the tale of the Hebrew who wanders alway
Is the fable and type of his people today!

IX

A proverb to most, and a moral to all,
  And a lamp unto others, though sitting in gloom,—
He seems like a mute in a festival hall;
  And is still looking forward for that which hath
      come;—
Like the children of Eblis, he hideth his smart,
And walks through the world with his hand on his
      heart!

X

All lands are as Moab—all countries are Edom,
  To the Hebrew, who sits in his sackcloth of sin,—
Till the trumpets of God calling others to freedom,
  The Jews to that banner at length shall come in;—
And Salem must sit in her desert alone,
  Till the seed of the Lord by all rivers be sown.

XI

Then, daughter of Judah! look up from thy slumber!
  And lo! a bright vision of turrets and spires!
A hymn o'er the desert, from harps without number!
  Thy children at rest by the shrine of their sires!
The song-bird on Carmel,—the rose in the plain,—
And the streams flowing backward to Zion again!

JOHN KEBBLE HERVEY.

The Wailing Place in Jerusalem

WITH heads bowed down, they stand with stream-
        ing eyes,
  Before the ruined wall, whose grimy stones
Are crumbling with the weight of centuries,
  And read their Mincha-prayer in mournful tones

That spring from hearts that grieve for Judah's fate,
  For Jacob's seed whose loving memories dwell
On splendors past, and, kneeling, supplicate
  That mercy may be shown to Israel.

Their garb proclaims them men of many lands.
  Those dwell amid the northern snows, and these
Have wandered far from Yemen's burning sands,
  Or sought their way across the western seas.

Not here alone do wailing figures stand!
  Not here alone do tears of sorrow flow!
In every clime they beat, with clenched hand,
  Against the stones of Israel's wall of woe.

478

In every land there rises, stern and great,
This self-same wail of torment and of fears,
Its courses laid with stones of scorn and hate,
And bonded with cement of blood and tears.

But Judah should behold that brighter day,
For which these kneeling pilgrims humbly plead,
And like a star, on Zion's bosom lay
Her beautiful and shining golden head.

Her tattered robes shall turn to silken sheen,
Her shackles shall give way to golden chains,
As from her temple-heights she views, serene,
The flowers of peace that bloom in her domains.

Where Hermon's snows shine down on Lebanon,
Where Judah breaks the Dead Sea's sullen peace,
Where rise the ruined towers of Ascalon,
Or Carmel's vines look on the midland seas.

LOUIS FEDERLEICHT.

Lament of the Daughters of Zion

AWAY from our land,
　　Away from our home,
A sad captive band,
　　'Mong strangers we roam.

Away from our hills,
　　We are sundered apart,
And the clear crystal rills
　　Enshrined in our heart.

And Lebanon's palm trees
　　'Neath the purple domed skies,
And the sweet scented breeze
　　That wafted our sighs!

479

Away from the dew
On the hill terraced lines,
Where the pale olive grew
And the purple clad vines.

For past is that grandeur,
The glory and fame;
And faded the splendour
Of Judah's great name.

Dark was the hour,
And fierce was the blow,
That shattered our power
In a whirlwind of woe.

The days that are born
In sorrow, we pine;
In sadness we mourn,
For Salem's fair shrine.

But the Lord will again
Gather us round;
And Judah will reign
With vict'ry crowned.

On the wings of the breeze,
O'er mountain and mead,
Far o'er the seas,
The tidings will speed.

And from the ends of the world
The lowly and proud,
With their banners unfurled,
The nations will crowd.

In Glory revealed,
This song they'll raise;
The Lord is our shield,
The Lord is our Praise.　　　J. F.

Longing for Jerusalem

O CITY of the world, with sacred splendor blest,
  My spirit yearns to thee from out the far-off
    West,
A stream of love wells forth when I recall thy day,
Now is thy temple waste, thy glory passed away.
Had I an eagle's wings, straight would I fly to thee,
Moisten thy holy dust with wet cheeks streaming free.
Oh, how I long for thee! albeit thy King has gone,
Albeit where balm once flowed, the serpent dwells
    alone.
Could I but kiss thy dust, so would I fain expire,
As sweet as honey then, my passion, my desire!

                                  JUDAH HA-LEVI.
               (Translated by Emma Lazarus.)

Awakening

WHERE wait the soldiers of the Lord
    That smote in olden days?
Where stands in song his shining horde
    That chant and shout his praise?
They long are laid with flame and sword,
    Their corpses strew the ways.

A hundred gods of brass and gold
    Sit high with icy hands,
And those that praised his name of old
    Lie slain in many lands!
Their bones arise and join: Behold,
    The host of Israel stands!

Does Israel's heart such silence keep,
    It seems a stony crust,
And covered with the dust?
    No, 'tis a dragon fast asleep,
An ancient sword to flash and leap
    From scabbard's rust!   JESSIE E. SAMPTER.

481

Daughter of Zion

DAUGHTER of Zion! Awake from thy sadness:
　　Awake, for thy foes shall oppress thee no more;
Bright o'er thy hills dawns the day-star of gladness,
　　Arise! for the night of thy sorrow is o'er.
Strong were thy foes, but the arm that subdued them
　　And scattered their legions was mightier far.
They fled, like the chaff from the scourge that pur-
　　　　sued them;
For vain were their steed and their chariots of war!

Daughter of Zion that Power that hath saved thee,
Extolled with the harp and the timbrel should be;
Shout! for the foe is destroyed that enslaved thee.
The oppressor is vanquished and Zion is free!

　　　　　　　　　　　　　　ANONYMOUS.

But Who Shall See?

BUT who shall see the glorious day
　　When, throned on Zion's brow,
The Lord shall rend that veil away
　　Which hides the nations now?
When earth no more beneath the fear
　　Of His rebuke shall lie;
When pain shall cease, and every tear
　　Be wiped from every eye.

Then, Judah, thou no more shalt mourn
　　Beneath the heathen's chain;
Thy days of splendour shall return,
　　And all be new again.
The Fount of Life shall then be quaffed
　　In peace by all who come!
And every wind that blows shall waft
　　Some long-lost exile home.

　　　　　　　　　　　　　　THOMAS MOORE.

The Latter Day

HAIL, to the brightness of Zion's glad morn-
    ing:
  Joy to the lands that in darkness have lain;
Hushed to the accents of sorrow and mourning;
  Zion in triumph begins her mild reign!

Hail to the brightness of Zion's glad morning,
  Long by the prophets of Israel foretold;
Hail to the millions from bondage returning;
  Gentiles and Jews the blest vision behold!

Lo, in the desert rich flowers are springing;
  Streams ever copious are gliding along!
Loud from the mountain-tops echoes are ringing;
  Wastes rise in verdure, and mingle in song.

See, from all lands, from the isles of the ocean,
  Praise to Jehovah ascending on high;
Fallen are the engines of war and commotion;
  Shouts of salvation are rending the sky!

                                    THOMAS HASTINGS.

"And Zion Be the Glory Yet"

O TRIBE of ancestry, be dumb, thy parchment roll
    review!
What is thy line of ancestors to that which boasts the
    Jew?
The ancient Briton, where is he? The Saxons, who
    are they?
The Roman is a fleeting shade—a thing of yesterday.
But he may boldly lift his eyes and spread his hands
    abroad,
And say, "Four thousand years ago my sires on Canaan
    stood."

O, who shall dare despise the Jew, whom God hath
    not despised,
Nor yet forsaken in His wrath, though long and sore
    chastised?
From many a distant land the Lord shall bring His
    people forth,
And Zion be the glory yet and wonder of the earth.

ANONYMOUS.

The Harp of Zion

THE harp of Zion sleepeth
    In the shadow of the hill;
The child of promise weepeth
    His weary exile still;
The ages of his sorrow
    Flow on like Jordan's stream;
He looketh for the morrow,
    But cannot see its beam.

No beam of heaven discloseth
    His father's land of birth;
His footstep ne'er reposeth
    In the nations of the earth;
To them he blindly holdeth
    The lamp he cannot see;
While darkness deep enfoldeth
    The homes of Galilee!

Yet not, O God, for ever
    Thou'lt judge him in thy wrath;
But bid the darkness sever
    Above his destined path;
In thy dread book is written
    The period of his doom;
And the vale thy curse has smitten,
    As a garden yet shall bloom.

484

Even now the destined ages
  Are closing o'er the land;
And every sign presages
  The morn again at hand;
The darkness swiftly weareth,
  Light trembles from the shore;
Each wind of heaven prepareth
  The wanderer to restore!

JAMES WILLIS.

The Restoration of Israel

DAUGHTER of Zion, from the dust,
  Exalt thy fallen head;
Again in thy Redeemer trust,
  He calls thee from the dead.

Awake, awake, put on thy strength,
  Thy beautiful array;
The day of freedom dawns at length,
  The Lord's appointed day.

Rebuild thy walls, thy bounds enlarge,
  And send thy heralds forth;
Say to the South,—"Give up thy charge,
  And keep not back, O North!"

They come, they come;—thine exiled bands,
  Where'er they rest or roam,
Have heard thy voice in distant lands,
  And hasten to their home.

Thus, though the universe shall burn,
  And God his works destroy,
With songs the ransomed shall return,
  And everlasting joy.

JAMES MONTGOMERY.

Israel's God

NO longer the children of Zion need weep;
　　From Judea's fair mountains, from over the deep,
From hill top and valley the pæans are sung
In every known language, our own holy tongue;
Our cause is triumphant, our freedom is won,
"The God of our People, Our Lord, He is One."

United the sound of Israel's great host,
Descendants of Judah now their proud boast;
Ascending each hour in psalm and in praise,
Their voices together in harmony raise.
The cry of our faith from out the dim past,
From ages unknown, till mortal shall last,
From birth, until Death says our course has been run,
We continue to sing "Our God He is One."

Oh! land of our fathers; in God's chosen time,
May we speedily pray at thy sacred shrine,
And upward to Heav'n, as on wings of a dove,
Our reliance on Thee, Thy care, and Thy love,
To gather Thy children, as sheep in a fold,
To worship together in praise, as of old;
"Hear, O Israel," we'll sing then, as one mighty word,
"He is One, is our God; He is One, is our Lord."

LAWRENCE COHEN.

He Watcheth Over Israel

THOUGH our harps hang on the willows,
　　Near to Babylon's turgid stream;
Though our ancient glory mock us,
　　Like a half-remembered dream;
Still His word runs with the ages—
　　Still His Covenant He keeps—
Yea, He watcheth over Israel
　　And He slumbers not, nor sleeps.

486

Though we dwell in alien countries,
  Bound by, yet without, their law;
Though they spoil us, in their despite
  Of the source from whence we draw
That which ever cleaves us from them;
  He will heed when Jacob weeps—
Yea, he watcheth over Israel
  And He slumbers not, nor sleeps.

Though our sword arm be sore stricken,
  Although mute be David's lyre;
Though our lips be locked and silent—
  Lips once touched by living fire—
Still, the Temple Lamps are burning
  In His own mysterious deeps—
Yea, he watcheth over Israel
  And He slumbers not, nor sleeps.

Yea, His word is constant, constant,
  As the singing of the sea;
And the High Priest of the nations
  Yet shall stand unshackled, free!
And the First-born of the Promise
  Sow no more where despite reaps—
Yea, He watcheth over Israel
  And He slumbers not, nor sleeps.
                    SOLOMON L. LONG.

'Tis to the East

'T IS to the East the Hebrew bends
      When morn unveils its brow;
And while the dawning light ascends
    The East receives his vow.
And Hope still wings his thoughts afar,
  It tells to those that roam,
That He who rode the cloudy car
  Will guide His people home.
                    ANONYMOUS.

Ee-Chovoud

HOW long, O Lord! how long,
  Lonely and sad 'mid the world's great throng,
Shall we of the waters of bitterness drink?
Our cup is filled with gall to the brink;
Our shoulders are bent and our foreheads bowed,
Ine covoud lonoo, ee-chovoud.

Ee-chovoud, Lord, ee-chovoud!
Thy beautiful world is to us as a shroud;
For our feet no earth, for our breath no air,
Wrong and contumely our daily fare,
Thou Raiser of lowly, Righter of wrong,
How long, O Lord, oh! how long?

How long? Lord, how long
Shall the weak lie under the wheel of the strong?
God of justice, and love and grace
Find for Thy homeless a resting-place.
Black waters surround us, our sky is in cloud,
Ine covoud lonoo, ee-chovoud.

Ee-chovoud, Father, ee-chovoud!
In that word all our wrongs and our sufferings crowd,
Thou hast promised the clouds shall rend and lift,
Make, God of the mighty and helpless, a rift!
Keep our souls from fainting, our faith hold strong,
For 'tis long, O Father; oh, how long!

S. R. HIRSCH.

The Dawn of Hope

SEE how the people of Israel come trooping,
  Waving like victors their banners on high;
Joy has uplifted the hearts that were drooping,
  Promise enkindled the light in the eye.

Waking at length from the slumbers of ages,
  Eager they turn to welcome the light,
Making the dreams of their poets and sages
  Gloriously true with their zeal and their might.

Straight grow the backs that with stooping were dou-
    bled,
  Noble and straight as the cedar and pine;
Cleared are the brows which affliction sore troubled,
  Glad as the viners, who taste the new wine.

Hope has welled up in their hearts like a fountain,
  Bursting with power its way to the sun;
Freedom has come like bright dawn on the mountain,
  Flushed with the glow of its triumphs begun.

David, behold, to thy stronghold on Zion,
  Speed they like runners who make for their goal,
Bearing the flag of the Judean lion,
  Bearing a spirit as bold in the soul.

As to thy temple, O Israel, returning,
  Leave they the shores which as aliens they trod,
Ecstasy thrills them, all eager, all burning,
  Filled with the love of their land and their God.

Give to thy people the shield of salvation,
  Favor, O Lord, thy anointed of old;
Bring them together once more as a nation,
  Gather again in thy sheltering fold.
                                    C. PESSELS.

The Jews Weeping in Jerusalem

WHY, trembling and sad, dost thou stand there
    and mourn,
Son of Israel, the days that can never return?
And why do those tear-drops of misery fall
On the mouldering ruin, the perishing wall?

Was yon city, in robes of the heathen now clad,
Once the flourishing Zion, where Judah was glad?
And those walls, that disjointed and scattered now lie,
Were they once vowed to Heaven and hallowed on
   high?

Yet why dost thou mourn? Oh, to gladness awaken!
Though Jehovah this city of God has forsaken,
He preserves for His people a city more fair;
Which a ruthless invader no longer shall share.

No longer the tear for your city shall flow;
No longer thy bosom the sad sigh bestow;
But night shall be followed by glorious day,
And sorrow and sighing shall vanish away.

JAMES WALLIS EASTBURN.

Dying in Jerusalem

JERUSALEM! Jerusalem!
  Thou city of the blest,
I come, beneath thy hallowed soil
  To lay my bones to rest.

It is not mine to see thee rise
  In glory from the dust;
But God, the God of Abraham,
  Is kind as well as just.
And, happy but to die in thee,
  I hail the sacred ground
Where rest from all their wanderings
  The sons of Jacob found.

Jerusalem! Jerusalem!
  Thy towers shall rise again
When comes the Lord's anointed One
  In majesty to reign.
My sun will shortly set, but thou
  In glory shall appear;

Thy King, The God of all the earth;
  Thy name, "The Lord is here."
And Gentiles who have spurned thee long
  Shall make the glory known;
While all conspire to honor thee,
  My father's land! my own!

THOMAS RAGG.

When I Think of Thee, O Zion

WHEN I think of thee, O Zion,
    Glory of the Holy Land,
Recollecting thee as city,
    Chartered by Jehovah's hand;
Thy gates of pearl, thy walls of gold,
By sage and prophet long foretold,
I do wonder—I know not why
How camest thou so low to lie?

When I think of thee, O Zion,
    Of thy renown, of thy great fame;
When my lips the word doth whisper
    Mentioning thy Holy Name,
Name pronounced by many a tongue
In reverent accents often sung;
Name so cherished, tell me why
Recalling thee, my heart doth sigh.

"What if strangers do me honor,
    Carry my banner and call me free;
What if Gentiles 'Allelujah,'
    'Amen' shout and swear by me?
When those children I call mine
List not, and 'bide across the line?
This the reason I bitterly cry."
Thus sadly Zion doth reply.

491

"Can a mother forget her own,
  Her only son, her bosom child?
Will other children satisfy
  The craving for the first that smiled?
Will ever multitude replace
The laugh that lit the cradled face?
Never, never will Zion rest ·
Until her own are in her nest."

JOHN D. NUSSBAUM.

Redemption

AWAKE, oh Israel! and hear
  That thy Redemption draweth near;
Arise ye mourners! God hath sent
Fulfilment of His covenant!

It cometh not by war's decrees
And blood of martyrs broad as seas;
The deeper purposes of God
We learn in kindness, not by rod.

Within yourself, O Israel!
Deliverance cometh—heed this wail!
Then cease thy groans; Be men! Be men!
And God will send Redemption then.

What slave was freed, who loved his yoke?
Thou canst not rise with spirits broke.
God's beloved art thou still,
O Israel, obey his will.

And even now His chosen seed
Shall reap those blessings long decreed.
Be worthy then—your God shall see
And His Redemption send to thee.

Honor the God thy fathers loved
And love the God thy fathers praised;
Then Israel, thou'lt rise again
A people honored by all men. ANONYMOUS.

Good Tidings to Zion
(Isa. lii. 7)

ON the mountain's top appearing,
　Lo, the sacred herald stands,
Welcome news to Zion bearing,
　Zion long in hostile lands:
Mourning captive,
　God himself will loose thy hands.

Has thy night been long and mournful?
　Have thy friends unfaithful proved?
Have thy foes been proud and scornful,
　By thy sighs and tears unmoved?
Cease thy mourning;
　Zion still is well beloved.

God, thy God, will now restore thee;
　He himself appears thy Friend;
All thy foes shall flee before thee;
　Here their boasts and triumphs end:
Great deliverance
　Zion's King vouchsafes to send.

Enemies no more shall trouble;
　All thy wrongs shall be redressed;
For thy shame thou shalt have double,
　In thy Maker's favor blest;
All thy conflicts
　End in everlasting rest.
　　　　　　　　Thomas Kelly.

A Cry for Zion

"BEHOLD, as I sit here, alone and forlorn,
　Very often I wish I had never been born,
For of all of my travail, my sorrow and pain,
Oh, can ye, O nations, discover my gain?

493

Ye tread on my beard and ye spit in my face,
And ye clothe me in chains and the badge of disgrace.
And ye come and advise me to lose myself quite,
And assimilate with the dark shadows of night.
As well to exhort the Gulf Stream to be mixed
With the cold, icy ocean wherein it is fixed;
Or advise in the heavens the great Milky Way
To be lost in the stars that most everywhere lay.

"Oh, no! If true justice still lingers on earth
You will give me the home that was mine from my
 birth.
Return me the land where I battled and fought,
The land every inch of which dearly I bought,
Very dearly I bought with the blood of my veins,
Where I struggled for freedom and shatter'd my
 chains;
Where I strove with and conquer'd wild races of men,
Gog-Magog, the giants, I drove from their den;
Where I worshipped my God and expounded His law,
And where first the great light of His Wisdom I
 saw.

"In that land were my fathers for ages interred,
And the prophets and sages who lived by the Word,
There the graves of my martyrs abound on the plains,
And the roads are yet strewn with my children's
 remains!
Every stone in that land is a tear from my eye,
In its mountains still lingers the breath of my sigh.
In its forests my wailing can yet be discerned,—
Lives a soul who would say thus: 'I am not con-
 cerned?'
Then return me my country! If justice yet dwell
Here on earth, O return me, return my Beth-el!"

L. Smirnow.

A Song of Zion

(Dedicated to the Zionist Society of Montreal)

WE are coming, coming, coming. Fling our banner
    to the breeze.
In thousands we are coming from beyond remotest
    seas.
We are coming after centuries of sorrow and of toil,
To make our home in Palestine and tread its holy soil.

O, let the song of gladness rise; let all the nations
    hear
The anthem of a mighty host of Zion drawing near,
Across the mountains, through the vales, and o'er the
    ocean's foam,
Behold the hosts of Israel are coming, coming home!

'Twas said of old by one whose lips were touched by
    Heaven's fire,
That God's own house would be built up, than hills
    and mountains higher;
That from its portals would go forth to all the world
    the word,
That may we learn His ways, and walk in truth be-
    fore the Lord;

That Sword and Spear would broken be, and turned
    to arts of peace;
That all the panoply of war and strife forever cease;
That nation shall not lift up sword against nation, as
    of yore,
But listen to the voice of God and learn of war no
    more.

O, Children of the Covenant, perhaps the day is
    near,—
E'en now, if you will listen, you may hear the accents
    clear

Of One who calls the scattered brood—come to Me!
    children, Come!
My hills are vacant. Here I am. I bid you welcome
    home!

Then answer—we are coming! Fling our banner to
    the breeze!
In thousands we are coming from beyond remotest
    seas.
We are coming after centuries of sorrow and of toil
To make our home in Palestine and tread its holy
    soil.

O, let the songs of gladness rise, let all the nations
    hear
The anthem of the mighty host of Israel drawing near;
Across the mountains, through the vales, and o'er the
    ocean's foam,
Behold the hosts of Israel are coming, coming home!
CARROLL RYAN.

Zionism

O Star of Hope! O Blessed Star!
    That riseth in the East afar,
Thou shed'st a wondrous, holy light,
A pillar of fire art thou by night.

Shine forth, thou great and lovely Star!
That riseth in the East afar,
A beacon-light of faith and cheer,
Be thou to Israel far and near.
MIRIAM BLAUSTEIN.

Zionism

THE story that Herzl told was true—
    Too bitter true for tears;
The blood-marked trail of the homeless Jew
    Winds back two thousand years.

496

Walled out by hate from the Gentile's heart,
  And lashed by senseless lies,
The Jew has walked in the nigh-apart,
  And shunned his brother's eyes.

But now—at last—he stands erect,
  Nor fears to be alone;
No Czar—no king—no church—no sect,
  Can keep him from his own.

His flag shall fly where his fathers fought—
  In the homeland of the Jew;
One race! One flag! One nation! Why not?
  For the dream of the strong comes true.

HERBERT N. CARSON.

Rallying Song

MY people, my people! Arise, O bleeding East,
  Arise in the Westlands, you fools that blindly
    feast!
The nations call again
For faith, for deeds, for men,
Yet we that rise
When Israel cries
Are less than one in ten.

My brothers, my brothers! O wand'ring aimless
    horde,
A clarion from Zion is speaking for the Lord!
The thund'ring heavens command:
"Arise a mighty band;
With heart and voice
Make now the choice,
And straightly seek your land."

My heroes, my heroes, whose hearts and lives are free,
Arise and be counted that all the world may see!
Those ancient fields reclaim
Whence Israel's splendor came,

497

And win and hold
Our land of old
To consecrate her name.

JESSIE E. SAMPTER.

In the Land of Our Fathers

BLUE are the skies in the land of our fathers—
  A blue of the beauteous sheen;
Through the clear of the air on the farthest horizon
  The mountains of Judah are seen.

Broad are the dales in the land of our fathers,
  Sweet with the fragrance of flowers;
Fair-smelling groves where the almond-trees mur-
    mur—
  Vistas of grape-girded bowers.

High are the hills in the land of our fathers
  To reach to the vaulting sky;
Israelites, sturdily tilling and reaping,
  Are chanting their carols nearby.

Bright gleams the moon in the land of our fathers,
  Aglint on the evening-dew,—
Through myriad stars the queen of the even
  Sails on the sea of blue.

Fair are the babes in the land of our fathers,
  Comely and gladsome and gay;—
Godly the words of the songs they are singing—
  Sailing the ocean of blue.   K. L. SILLMAN.

On to the East

YOUR loins let girt be,
  Your staff in hand hold;
Upon your shoulders now fling ye
  Your treasures and gold.

498

In the Lord hope, and pleading
    His counsel implore,
Your band He'll be leading,
    To Canaan's green shore!

There in the land of our sires
    We never shall fear
The lash which hatred inspires
    In evil men here.
We, too, will the sword don,
    And the foe bravely breast,
Up, brethren! and lead on
    To our land in the East!

With joy we'll our land till,
    Her clods melt with caresses,
With plenty our stores fill,
    With old wine our presses.
We'll be gleeful and care-free,
    Our souls within will rejoice,
Up, brethren! why pause ye?
    On to Jerusalem, our choice!

On Moriah's high mountain,
    We'll our banner outspread,
We'll drink from God's fountain,
    Our ranks He will head!
From the City's high tower
    The Lord's standard will wave,
Brethren, up! summon power,
    March to Zion! Ye brave!

NAPHTALI HERZ IMBER.
(Translated by Rebecca A. Altman.)

The Cedars of Lebanon

BUT the waves of the fury of nations
    Swept down on the trees of the vale,
Like rolling and wild inundations
    Lashed on by the blasts of the gale.

And the strength of the cedars was shattered,
  Their frames into shreds were cleft,
And their limbs on the billows were scattered,—
  Yet the roots in the mountain were left.

And the seeds of the trees were taken
  And lodged in the land of their foes,
And there untended, forsaken,
  New cedars arose.

And the foe his proud branches entwining
  Above them, shut off from their view
The sun that upon them was shining,
  And robbed them of rain and of dew.

And mocked were the once mighty cedars,
  Their name a disgrace was become,
For they had not, they had not the leaders
  To bring them home.

HENRY SCHNITTKIND.

O Sweet Anemones!

O SWEET anemones on Sharon's plain,
  Light dancing seraphim of sun and rain,
Was he not one of us, was he not ours?
And yet he saved not us, O crimson flowers!

As stars that bloom in heaven, full-bloom and still,
As native stags that leap from hill to hill,
As you, dear blossom-stars, on native plains,
So planted here, with God, our home remains.

I, too, would perish here, where he has died,
But felled by horse and spear, not crucified;
I, man of peace, would pour, O Rock of God,
My freedom or my blood on Zion's sod.

500

When pagans sweep thy fields with withering blast,
My heart is sanctified to death at last;
Its taste is honey-sweet within my mouth,
For we that drink with God can dread no drouth.

O sweet anemones on Sharon's plain,
A spring shall come for us, to bloom again,—
To God a day, to us a thousand years,—
Who still remembers, lives, refreshed with tears.

JESSIE E. SAMPTER.

Zion

LAND of the cedar and palm,
   Land of the olive and myrtle,
Breathing of Gilead's balm
   Over fragrant fields and fertile,
From the sunset shore of the sea
Greeting of peace to thee!

Though the din of strange cities resound
   In our ears, forget we can never
Those piercing, lingering sounds
   Or David's lyre, that ever
To Zion's Redeemer upraise
Their pæan of deathless praise.

And we that long for that sunny field,
   The abode of our youth, where God's spirit
First to mortals revealed
   Those truths that we still inherit,
Field fertile with fruitage of glory
And haunted by memories hoary.

Happy are they that sow
   Thy seed and reap of their sowing!
Happy! they never shall know
   The exile's sorrow, not knowing
The infinite heart-ache and pain
Of the toilers that toil in vain.

From the land of our sojourning
  Zion, to thee, nor burn
With a fever or fretful yearning
  In the patience of hope we toil
  Again to possess thy soil.

Land of the cedar and palm,
  Land of the olive and myrtle,
Breathing Gilead's balm
  Over fragrant fields and fertile,
From the sunset shore of the sea
In God's time we shall come to thee.

EUGENE KOHN.

The Awakening of Israel

MUST the sea plead in vain that the river
  May return to its mother for rest
And the earth beg the rain-clouds to give her
  Of dews she has drawn from her breast?

Swing inward, Oh! gates of the future,
  Swing outward, ye doors of the past,
For the soul of Israel is waking
  And rising from slumber at last.

The black clouds of night are retreating,
  The white peaks have signaled the day;
And freedom her long roll is beating
  And calling her sons to the fray.

From the dust where his proud tyrants found him
  Unhonored, and scorned and betrayed,
He shall rise with the sunlight around him
  And rule in the realm he has made.

ANONYMOUS.

Sing Unto God a New Song

SING unto God a new song, sing no more
　　These melodies of melancholic strain
That mourn the vanished glory that did reign
O'er Zion in the golden days of yore.
Wherefore forever weep, fore'er deplore
　　Our loss? Vain are our tears, our prayer is vain
　　Would we our ancient heritage regain,
Then must our song on faith's own pinions soar.
　　Sing then to God a joyous song,
Yea, sing Redemption's sun new-risen in the East,
　　A song of triumph till the echoes ring
Back from the ample heaven's azure dome;
　　For yet shall we, from evil's chains released,
Zion, to thee return, our hallowed home.

EUGENE KOHN.

In Exile

GO, with the wand'rer's staff in hand,
　　Without a home, without a land,
Without to-morrow, or to-day,
Ne'er tolerated, e'er in flight
Not found by day where lodged by night.
Forever woe, woe, woe,
Forever go, go, go,
Forever drive, drive, drive,
The time we barely keep alive.

Our greatness lieth in the dust;
Our holy life—a life unjust;
Our glorious name—a danger great;
Our proud descent—a cause for hate;
Our genius—nothing but a crime;
Our culture—scoffed at all the time.

E'er troubles grave, grave, grave,
Forever slave, slave, slave,
E'er seek to know, know, know,
Joys in the curses of the foe.

And thus year after year, alas,
Yea, thus age after age doth pass
Without a hope, without a goal,
While dread and terror fill our soul,
As wildly wandering we go,
From pain to pain, from woe to woe,
E'er on the way, way, way,
Forever sigh, sigh, sigh,
And luckless e'en when we die.

But from our ancient city thus
Beckons our ancient God to us,
Whose voice conveys this message blest,
"Come here, at last you'll find your rest!
Yea, here, at last upon your desolate hill
The son of Judah dreameth still."
Then hear Him call, call, call,
Go, seek the Temple's ancient wall,
Yea, trust in God, God, God,
Lo, there will cease the tyrant's rod.

MORRIS ROSENFELD.
(Translated by Isidore Myers.)

Psalm CXXVI

WHEN Zion's dire captivity
  The Lord had turned once more,
And we, like those who dream amazed
  Could scarce believe it o'er,
Then was our mouth with laughter filled
  Our tongue with song too, fraught;
Then said the heathen Lo! the Lord
  For them great things hath wrought!

The Lord hath done great things for us,
  At which we are elate.
Turn, as the southern streams, again,
  O Lord! our captive state.
Who sow in tears, shall reap in joy,
  And he that wand'ring grieves,
Yet bearing precious seeds, ere long,
· Shall with the joyous voice of song,
  Come laden with his sheaves.   I. R. B.

Zionism

THE dreamers are not dead in Israel.
    To-day the young dream dreams, and with
  the old
Live visions of a deathless past. They dwell
  In every land, yet hills of Zion hold
More glory than the fame of kings can bring;
  More hope than ages have preserved.
The voices of a golden morning ring
  With victories, extolling gifts reserved
For those who 'neath the vine and fig tree sit,
  And people realms bereft of ancient charms.
The souls of prophets with their souls are knit,
  And martyred heroes call again to arms
The sons of Judah. Stars of morning shine,
And dawn breaks o'er an orphaned Palestine.

                          JOSEPH LEISER.

Theodore Herzl

SUCH men are rare—they tow'r above mankind
  Like Himalayan peaks that touch the skies,—
  Missioned for a majestic enterprise,
They sway not in the fury of the wind;
And on the scroll of life their names are signed
  In characters of flame. The great and wise
  Know them afar, and at their bidding rise
To nobler conquests of the heart and mind.

545

Thou, too, hast dreamed a world compelling dream—
  With glance prophetic and unfalt'ring soul
Thy Israel thou strovest to redeem,
  And lead the sorrowing to a longed-for goal.
If thou wert dreaming, Herzl, sleep content—
A dream like Thy God unto Moses sent.

FELIX N. GERSON.

To Theodore Herzl

WHO called thee to such holy high estate?
    Who taught thy lips the all-redeeming Word,
Which touched us to emotions as we heard
And soars aloft to Him, that guides our fate?
Who kindled Ardor's undiminished flame;
To make thee bold and eager to attain,
Despite all that gives thee deepest pain,
The highest good, not evanescent fame;
Who doth sustain the skyward lifted hand,
The hopeful sign and symbol of our zeal,
Upraised high our shattered nerves to steel
As if in warning that we dauntless stand?—
It is the God within the nation's soul
That spurs him on to dare to do the right.
He guides his steps and steadieth his sight
That he may strive unswerving towards the goal;
Like all true servants of the living God,
Thou gavest heed to that Celestial Voice
And didst assume our burdens, of Thy Choice.
Thy heart inspired, thy spirit overawed,
Remain our true exemplar in the strife,
Though good reward or evil be thy share
We follow thee, for Zion everywhere
To struggle for the newly dawning life.

GUSTAV GOTTHEIL.
(Translated by George Alexander Kohut.)

NATIONAL

Theodore Herzl

FAREWELL, O Prince, farewell, O sorely tried!
　You dreamed a dream and you have paid the cost:
To save a people leaders must be lost;
　By foes and followers be crucified,
　Yet 'tis your body only that has died.
The noblest soul in Judah is not dust
But fire that works in every vein and must
　Reshape our life, rekindling Israel's pride.

So we behold the captain of our strife
　Triumphant in this moment of eclipse;
Death has but fixed him to immortal life,
　His flag upheld, the trumpet at his lips.
And while we, weeping rend our garment's hem,
"Next year," we cry, "next year, Jerusalem."

ISRAEL ZANGWILL.

Theodore Herzl

PEACE! no tear for him who sleepeth near.
　　No mourning word,
Splendid pæan rather and ringing cheer
　　Be heard!
Let his white bones know,
Let his soul discover
Its loving overflow
Of him his people's lover
In our voices thunder,
In our labor's glory!
Find in each tone asunder
His triumphant story—
Of his hope grown free,
Of his battles won,
Of Lion's victory,

507

And Judah's noonday sun.
Hosannah! thou that sleepest here,
Hosannah! thou that sleepest here!
Hosannah, leader 'gainst all fear!
Israel lives anew!

HARRY MYERS.

The Poet's Spirit

To the Memory of Naphtali Herz Imber

NO dirge or solemn bell
    We toll for thee, oh Voice,
Stilled by the sudden knell
    That ends all mortal choice;
Thy tuneful spirit free of earth
    Must ever more rejoice.

Like gull or petrel free
    That soars o'er billows, brave,
Thy soul shall spring in glee
    Above the narrow grave;
Thy hymns shall live while Zion lives,
    While Israel's banners wave.

As perched on mountain crags
    The eagle finds a nest,
Free from earth's binding rags
    Wandering Soul take rest,
Till the full message of thy song
    Thy brothers here attest.

Singers like thee on earth
    Tuning the immortal lyre,
Old Nations give re-birth,
    Hopes shattered, new desire;
Beacons that prove for doubting sons
    Jehovah's living fire.

JOSEPH FITZPATRICK.

508

A Hymn of Zion

ZION, we love thee well,
  Fair land of Israel,
    For thee we long!
Thou art our heart's desire,
  Our altar's holy fire,
The breath that stirs our lyre,
    To Freedom's song!

Land which the Jordan laves,
Land of the sacred graves,
    For thee we weep!
Land where the Prophets trod,
Where Truth erst swayed the rod,
Where Psalmists sang of God,
    Thy faith we keep!

Thy dawn now fills our eyes,
Thy hope now tints our skies—
    Our soul's athrill!
A shoot from Jesse's stem,
Shall rule Jerusalem,
Bright be his diadem,
    O'er Zion's hill!

JOEL BLAU.

VII

THE MODERN PERIOD

Bar Kochba

WEEP, Israel! your tardy meed outpour
    Of grateful homage on his fallen head,
That never coronal of triumph wore,
    Untombed, dishonored, and unchapleted.
If Victory makes the hero, raw Success
    The stamp of virtue, unremembered
Be then the desperate strife, the storm and stress
    Of the last Warrior Jew. But if the man
Who dies for freedom, loving all things less,
    Against world-legions, mustering his poor clan;
The weak, the wronged, the miserable, to send
    Their death-cry's protest through the ages' span—
If such an one be worthy, ye shall lend
    Eternal thanks to him, eternal praise,
Nobler the conquered than the conqueror's end!

EMMA LAZARUS.

The Jewish Exile

    After the suppression of Bar Kochba's revolt, the
Jews were debarred by Hadrian from entering Jeru-
salem. They obtained the privilege, however, of as-
sembling once a year, upon the Mount of Olives, on
the anniversary of the burning of the Temple; and
from that eminence the patriots took a distant look
at the beloved city.

WHEREFORE weep our brethren yonder,
    Gathered from afar and near;
Wherefore, father, tell me, wherefore
    Are these weary pilgrims here?

Ah, my child, a day of mourning
    Brings together Israel's fold;
Many of these weary pilgrims
    Once were warriors, strong and bold.

See, my child, the city yonder,
  That was once thy father's home;
Now dishonored and forsaken,
  'Tis the seat of hated Rome.

For we rose in strong rebellion,
  I, my child, and all my kin,
And Judea's long lost freedom
  Once again we sought to win.

But the great decree of Heaven
  Was against our glorious band;
And at Bethar's bloody battle
  Died the noblest of the land.

Yet the fierce and vengeful Roman,
  Not content with such a prize,
Heeded not our women's mourning,
  Heeded not our children's cries.

But he cast them from their country,
  From their own and native soil;
Sold them into dreadful bondage,
  To a life of hated toil.

Then defiled the sacred places
  With a ruthless hand and bold;
And the heathen dwells unpunished
  Where the priesthood dwelt of old.

They have changed the walks of Zion,
  Even changed her sacred name;
They have reared a heathen temple
  On the ruins of our fame.

And to fill the cup of sorrow,
  And to fill it to the brim,
Hadrian hurled his mighty fiat
  With a purpose stern and grim,

That within yon sacred portals
  Israel's foot may never tread,
Though beneath that soil lie buried
  All the dearest of our dead.

Bitter, child, are all the tortures
  Of a cruel, heartless foe;
Yet a life of hopeless exile
  Is by far the greatest woe.

Here upon the Mount of Olives,
  Once a year, we still may meet,
Where the city of our fathers
  May our tearful vision greet.

So we gather from the mountains
  And we gather from the plain;
Here, amid her desolation,
  We behold her once again.

Till the sturdy sons of Judah
  Break the Roman's haughty pride,
Never shall I cease my mourning
  Never shall my tears be dried.

For I trust, the Lord in heaven,
  Mindful of his chosen gem,
Will some day restore to glory
  Israel and Jerusalem.   Leon Hühner.

The Jewish Pilgrim

ARE these the ancient holy hills
  Where angels walked of old?
Is this the land our story fills
  With glory not yet cold?
For I have passed by many a shrine
  O'er many a land and sea;
But still, oh! promised Palestine,
  My dreams have been of thee.

I see thy mountain cedar green,
　Thy valleys fresh and. fair,
With summers bright as they have been
　When Israel's home was there.
Tho' o'er thee sword and time have passed,
　And cross and crescent shone,
And heavily the chain has pressed
　Oh! they are still our own.

Thine are the wandering race that go
　Unblest through every land,
Whose blood hath stained the polar snow,
　And quench'd the desert sand.
And thine the home of hearts that turn
　From all earth's shrines to thee
With their lone faith for ages born
　In sleepless memory.

For throngs have fallen, nations gone
　Before the march of time,
And where the ocean rolled alone
　Are forests in their prime.
Since gentile ploughshares marr'd the brow
　Of Zion's holy hill
Where are the Roman eagles now?
　Yet Judah wanders still.

And hath she wandered thus in vain
　A pilgrim of the past?
No! long deferred her hope hath been
　But it shall come at last.
For in her wastes a voice I hear,
　As from a prophet's urn,
It bids the nations build not there
　For Jacob shall return.

Oh! lost and loved Jerusalem
　Thy pilgrim may not stay
To see the glad earth's harvest home
　In thy redeeming day.

But now resigned in faith and trust
  I seek a nameless tomb;
At least beneath thy hallowed dust
  Oh! give the wanderer room.

FRANCES BROWNE.

The Arch of Titus

CRUMBLING, age-worn, in Rome the eternal,
  Stands the arch of Titus' triumph,
With its carven Jewish captives
Shouldering the holy Menorah.
  And each nightfall, when the turmoil
  Of the Petrine clangor ceaseth,
  Seven flames the arch illumine,
  Mystic glowings, burning strangely.
Then cast off their graven shackles,
  Judah's sons of marble graven,
Living step they from the ruin,
Living stride they from the Jordan.
  They are healed in its waters,
  Till the freshness of each dawning,
  Then resume their ancient labor,
  Perfect marble, whole and holy.
Dust of dust the wheeling seasons
Grind that mighty arched splendor,
Rase the Gaul and rase the Roman,
Grind away their fame and glory,
  The shackled Jews alone withstand them,
  Shouldering their holy Menorah.

HARRY WOLFSOHN.

(Trans. from the Hebrew by Horace M. Kallen.)

Tourist and Cicerone

"GOOD sir, thou didst me order
  To lead thee through this border,
  To view this very place;
But through this archway Roman

517

With free will passeth no man
  Of all my suffering race.

"See! with its decoration,
This arch derides my nation,
  By Titus scourged and slain!
It pictures his achievements,
And all of our bereavements;
  Its sight fills me with pain.

"Then, sir, do not command me,
Indeed, I would withstand thee,
  The custom I'll not break!
Alone go through the gateway,
While I around and straightway
  Will meet thee," thus he spake.

"My faithful guide, know thy way
Is parallel with my way,"
  I forthwith made remark;
"I hate the chariots gory,
But love Judea's glory—
  The Candlestick and Ark."

Whereat he gazed in wonder
Upon my face,—and under
  His eyelids teardrops stole;
He touched my hand then quickly,
Half doubtfully, half meekly,
  And said, "Sh'ma Yisroel!"

Of course, my tears descended,
While I the greeting ended,
  "Adonoi Echod!"
Around the archway turning,
The past within us burning—
  "Jehovah is our God."

LUDWIG AUGUST FRANKL.
(Translated by Henry Cohen.)

Judea

I SAW in rift of cloud a beaming light
  That spread soft radiance over Judea's plain,
Where mother of a race watched sunny rain
Before red flashes told of stormy night.
She looked afar, through misty ages vast,
And saw her progeny the scorn of men,
Far scattered, trod to earth to rise again,
And hold distinction, though the world should last
Till sun and planets fell in void of time
And light was scant as when the world was born.
She saw her sons surmount the stings of scorn
With sad eyes and with brow of care; sublime
In aspect her breast throbbing with new life;
Beheld universal motherhood's young
Cease their dire bickerings, she stood among
The children of the earth unstirred by strife;
Saw creeds lose force in the long ages' span,
One God, one hope, and peace o'erspread the earth,
Regenerative man's new heart at bright,
The soul's broad scope, and brotherhood of man.

CHARLES M. WALLINGTON.

The Tombs of the Fathers

IN Babylon they sat and wept
  Down by the river's willowy side;
And when the breeze their harp-strings swept,
  The strings of breaking hearts replied:
  A deeper sorrow now they hide;
No Cyrus comes to set them free
From ages of captivity.

All lands are Babylons to them,
  Exiles and fugitives they roam:
What is their own Jerusalem?
  The place where they are least at home!

519

Yet hither from all climes they come,
And pay their gold for leave to shed
Tears o'er the generations fled.

Around, the eternal mountains stand,
  With Hinnom's darkling vale between;
Old Jordan wanders through the land,
  Blue Carmel's seaward crest is seen;
  And Lebanon, yet sternly green,
Throws, when the evening sun declines,
Its cedar shades in lengthening lines.

But, ah! forever vanished hence
  The Temple of the living God,
Once Zion's glory and defence—
  Now mourn beneath the oppressor's rod
  The fields where faithful Abraham trod;
Where Isaac walked by twilight gleam,
And heaven came down on Jacob's dream.

Forever mingled with this soil
  Those armies of the Lord of Hosts,
That conquer'd Canaan, shared the spoil,
  Quelled Moab's pride, stormed Midian's posts,
  Spread paleness through Philistia's coasts,
And taught the foes, whose idols fell,
"There is a God in Israel."

Now David's tabernacle gone,
  What mighty builder shall restore?
The golden throne of Solomon,
  And ivory palace, are no more:
  The Psalmist's song, the Preacher's lore,
Of all they did, alone remain
Unperished trophies of their reign.

Holy and beautiful, of old
  Was Zion 'midst her princely bowers;
Besiegers trembled to behold

Bulwarks that set at nought their powers;
Swept from the earth are all her towers;
Nor is there—so is she bereft—
One stone upon another left.

The very site whereon she stood,
In vain the foot, the eye would trace;
Vengeance, for saints' and martyrs' blood,
Her wails did utterly efface;
Dungeons and dens usurp their place;
The Cross and Crescent shine afar,
But where is Jacob's natal star?

Still inexterminable—still
Devoted to their mother-land,
Her offspring haunt the temple hill,
Amidst her desecration stand,
And bite the lip, and clench the hand;
Today in that lorn vale they weep,
Where patriarchs, kings, and prophets sleep.

* * * * *

And by the Gentiles in their pride
Jerusalem is trodden down;
"How long? forever wilt thou hide,
Thy face, O Lord! forever frown?
Israel was once thy glorious crown,
In sight of all the heathen worn;
Now from thy brow indignant torn,

"Zion, forsaken and forgot,
Hath felt thy stroke, and owns it just;
O God, our God! reject her not,
Whose sons take pleasure in her dust;
How is the fine gold dimmed with rust!
The city, throned in gorgeous state,
How doth she now sit desolate!"

JAMES MONTGOMERY.

521

The Wandering Jew

SEEK not what I am to know,
  What my name is, never crave,
God records it, Earth and Woe,
  It may radiate the grave,
If at last my tears' long flow
  Should melt the stones to hear.

Wandering ever—I, forlorn,
  Refuge seek for this poor frame.
Thinking, suffering;—Man, base-born,
  Spurns my right, ignores my claim—
I pass his tortures, scorn
  His piety and his jeers.

Wandering ever—storms and ire
  Burst with fury on my brow,
Adam's curse I bore entire,
  Wretched, yet too proud to bow;
Victim ever, on the pyre
  I laved in grief each sin.

Midst the whirlwind raging round,
  Vanished lands, seas disappeared,
Crumbled all, mere dust I found,
  Empires, temples, shrines revered;
But immortal lived Thought bound
  My heart's sad depths within.

From life's dawn that thought upgrew,
  Ever present to my mind,
Vast, sublime, it shone and grew,
  All to it,—a setless sun.
Glory o'er the Past it threw
  And o'er the Future—Light.

522

Longing for the Infinite
  Moved me ever, spurs me now,
But the end has not dawned yet,
  Hope unripe hangs on the bough,
Ages do I wait and fret
  For that which comes not nigh.

Years to me are moments brief,
  Small the Universe appears,
Deep in thought, immersed in grief,
  Weighing tyrants with men's fears,
Sweep I Hope's harp for relief
  And raise wild terror's cry.

Every suffering has been mine—
  Outrage, insult, struggle, pain,
Strong in sovereign thought divine,
  All I challenge, all disdain.
Foes will fail—not my faith's shrine,
  No time has that uptorn.

Seek not what I am to know,
  What my name is rests in gloom,
God records it, Earth and Woe,
  But 'tis hidden from the Tomb;
Torture me, contempt I show
  For pity as for scorn.   DAVID LEVI.

The Sentinel of the Ages

UNDER shining, under shadow,
  At the gates of every land,
All adown the lengthening ages,
  Men have seen a Sentry stand;
Looming grandly on the beauty
  Of the blue day's crystal light,
Then anon, in darkness blending
  With mystery of night;

While his meditations linger
  Over glories that are past,
And his keen prophetic vision
  Sees the good to come, at last.

At the portals of some nations,
  We beheld him, as he stands
Pale and haggard, weak and weary,
  With his grey head in his hands,
Bowed in retrospective sorrow,
  For the infamy and scorn,
For the ages of oppression
  By his people meekly borne;
Till his features are transfigured
  In a blaze of wrath divine,
And his glassy eyes brim over
  With their bitter burning wine.

At another gate we see him,
  In the vigor of full prime
Mounted on a stalwart courser,
  For some charge or quest sublime;
Be it to go forth to battle,
  In a cause of righteous strife,
Winning liberty, or glory,
  With the purchase of his life.
Or, at least, to gain his guerdon,
  And be named among the great,
By the aid of wealth's distinction,
  Or some service to the State.

Otherwhere, we see him, seated
  Underneath the arches vast
Of some old arcade, surrounded
  With the records of the past.
Over ancient tomes he ponders,
  Filled with figures rude and strange,
Yet their contents he deciphers
  Through Time's labyrinthine range;

Then to poesy he turneth
  And in numbers sweet recites:
Or he wakes the soul of music
  In the harp whose chords he smites.

Once again we see him, crouching
  On a devastated strand,
Silent as the Sphinx of Egypt
  Billowed in the surging sand,
For the lash of persecution,
  Heedless of all human right
Fell upon him, watching, waiting,
  Till he sank beneath its might.
And he lies there, bruised and bleeding
  But a brave old hero still,
Hoping for his destined future,
  When his Fate has wrought its will.

Nations, do you know this Sentry,
  Keeping guard, for ages long,
Over learning, arts, religion,
  Through all cruelty and wrong?
Patient under dire oppression,
  While the iron pierced his soul;
With no armor for protection;
  With no weapon but a Scroll—
His one treasure; hear him crying,
  "Though I die, let this be trued"
Is not his the voice of Jacob?
  Yes! it is—it is—the Jew.

Say you that his crime demanded
  Punishment from God and men?
Nay! With God alone be vengeance;
  He is merciful. But when
Man metes out his ruthless judgments,
  With a mad presumption blind,
He wreaks cruelties of demons
  On the weaker of his kind.

It is not for his defection
  That the Jew has met the sword:
Christians slay their fellow-Christians,
  In the name of their own Lord.

Has he sinned—this Jew immortal?
  Ay; but he is not alone;
Christ is crucified forever
  In the House He calls His own.
Multitudes bow down before Him
  And profess to own his sway,
While their hearts are filled with idols,
  And they, Judas-like, betray
Him who comes, as their Messiah,
  And their fealty would claim;
But they pierce His soul with sorrows,
  Shouting praises to His name.

Sinned the Jew? Well; he has suffered.
  When he saw his judgment come
He bowed meekly to his sentence;
  Like the shorn lamb, he was dumb:
Bearing shame, contempt, revilings,
  Grief and anguish, pain and death;
Only saying: "God is holy;
  He is One," with latest breath.
Like to Christ, in his submission
  He has met a martyr's fate.
But his resurrection cometh;
  Though it tarry, he can wait.

Yes! Already we perceive him,
  Rising up on every hand;
Gliding into power and station,
  With the world's wealth at command.
In the forum, in the senate,
  Lo! he wins immortal fame,
Halls of learning, marts of commerce,
  Ring with echoes of his name,

On each plane of high endeavor
　He is foremost in the strife
Culling everlasting laurels
　From the battlefields of Life.

So God's ancient, chosen people
　As His Sentinel still stands
With the standard of Jehovah
　In the strong, uplifted hands;
With his jewelled breastplate gleaming
　On his proudly heaving chest;
And a lamp forever burning,
　On his helmet's lofty crest;
While he welcomes the down-trodden
　To his hospitable shores,
And in streams of richest bounty
　Blessings on his brethren pours.

Standing thus, as great exemplar
　To the world, the Jew appears;
Bringing hope, as well as warning,
　To Humanity's late years,
Showing how, as King, God ruleth,
　When mankind would test His sway,
Yet is tender as a Father
　When, as children, they obey.
Prophet, statesman, warrior, scholar,
　Israel's glories shall increase,
When he claims his royal birthright;
　Brother to the Prince of Peace.

　　　　　　　　IBBIE McColm Wilson.

Before Battle

WE have toiled, O Lord, with our blood and might
    And have offered a hymn to Thee;
And in pain and rage we have spent our light,
    And our nights in misery;
We have dug the trench and built the site,
    That we might be near to Thee;
O Lord our God, we have spent our light
    In search of Thee.

Garish culture we spurned as we spurned all things
    That were not in the grace of Thee;
And we bowed our heads and our hearts to kings
    Who wore crowns by their claims in Thee;
In the deep of night we have sung Thy praise,
    Unperishing songs of Thee;
O Lord our God, we have spent our days
    In praise of Thee.

We've preserved our flesh from the joys of lust
    That we might be clean with Thee;
We have fed our souls on the dryest dust,
    That we might keep true to Thee;
We have fought, and many the odds have stood,
    We have conquered the world for Thee;
O Lord our God, we have spilled our blood
    For love of Thee.

We have toiled, O Lord, with our blood and might,
    And have offered a hymn to Thee;
Yet our days You've cursed with the gloom of night,
    And our nights with misery;
We have kept our faith through the bitterest strife,
    Through the bitterest strife for Thee;
O Lord our God, take of our dust,
    Our faith in Thee.

                        SAMUEL ROTH.

The Jew

(Dedicated to Benjamin F. Peixotto)

HIS dark face kindled in the East,
  He walks our Europe like a dream,
And in his great beard gravely seem
To meet the poet and the priest;
His nation spent, his temple sacked,
  A haughty exile under ban,
From pole to pole he holds intact
  The ancient grandeur of the man.

Vain burnt the fires his frame to melt,
  His tough will turned the rack to straw;
  The granite tablets were his law,
And to the one high God he knelt!
Before his zeal fell hate and spite;
  Wide grew the narrowness of marts,
Immortal, sole cosmopolite,
  He gave for freedom all the arts!

Always the ages' argonaut,
  The foremost sails he followed still,
  Gave to the Christian thrift and skill,
And peace and trade to heathens taught.
If ran to greed his heart sometimes,
  By reverend robbers wrung to pelf,
A child of genius in all climes,
  He drew the muses to himself.

Of God's august historian heir,
  Who made creation eloquent,
  To themes occult and grand he bent
The realms of letters everywhere;
His pencil spurned, his marble crushed
  When art to monks its lease resigned,
The splendor of his numbers hushed.
  The rude music of mankind.

529

Oh! human faith in God's good grace,
  Wait boldly and ye shall not fail,
  The patient ages must avail—
If freedom knows no waiting place,
The Zion holy to our hosts,
  This reverend world—made ruin by
The curse of shrines, and thrones, and ghosts—
  Art, toil, and hope shall purify.

GEORGE ALFRED TOWNSEND.

The Everlasting Jew

LIFT up thy head, O Israel, gird thine armor on
    anew,
There's a rainbow in the heavens, there is work for
    thee to do.
Hear not the jibing stranger, heed not the envious
    crew,
The only real aristocrat is the everlasting Jew!

Thou hast pride of ancient lineage, canst boast of
    blood that's blue,
Thine ancestors were princes, e'en when this old world
    was new—
Ere Greece and Tyre and Babylon had disappeared
    from view—
Thou wast still the sole aristocrat, the everlasting Jew!

Although a scattered people, e'en though thy numbers
    few,
Thy star is still ascending to rejuvenate anew
Thy ancient place and heritage to prove the mission
    true
That the only real aristocrat is the everlasting Jew!

HENRY B. SOMMER.

530

THE MODERN PERIOD

Israel

SHE stands among the nations of the earth,
　　Unique, a figure of pathetic grace;
　God's chosen daughter of the human race,
Destined to woe and grandeur from her birth.
She sees her children scattered, doomed to dearth,
　And in her dusky eyes there shines the trace
　Of tears, that wet her pale prophetic face,
Knowing her people's pristine power and worth.
　Oh, stricken Mother, unto whom we owe
The life and light that spring from one pure fount,
　Whence all our laws and inspirations flow;
　　Not vainly have ye shed your blood and tears,
　　Withstanding scorn and hatred all these years—
He guards thee still, Who spoke from Sinai's Mount!
　　　　　　　　IDA GOLDSMITH MORRIS.

Israel Forsaken

('Azubah)

I

AH! ingrate people whom I sought to please!
　　Ah! cruel people, scornful, careless men,
And dark, sly women, dreaming of new ease—
　Abandon me! Scowl calmly on me when
You do behold me! You who brought me wine
　To drink, fierce spiced, and pomegranates to eat,
And fat, black grapes, red apricots and fine
　Wheat cakes and glossy olives sweet:
Who gave me smoothly flowing, oily phrase
And guerdon brought me of ecstatic praise:
Lo! now because I sit alone forlorn,
Throw me your bitter herbs and crumbs of scorn.

531

II

I danced before you in the Satrap's hall;
  For you I trained my small elastic feet.
I wore your garlands, bowed and carried all
  Your flowery offerings. Freely did I eat
Of your rich banquet, cruel people, cold
  And scornful people!. Gifts ye cast me now,
Because I sit alone and have grown old
  Of sick'ning lees of wine, no wreaths for brow
Not ambergris nor cassia do ye bring,
Nor frankincense, nor any precious thing!
You only laugh and thrust your stinging words
At 'Azubah, stabbing her heart like swords.

III

Ye fondled once my black, smooth hair, and said,
  "See how her tresses glisten in the light!"
Ashes are now strewn upon my faded head,
  No longer lives in eyes of mine the sprite
Of joyance. All my face is worn and wan,
  My gold-embroidered raiment is threadbare;
The sea-shell color from my cheek hath gone,
  I sit and wrap myself in sack-cloth wear.
"Who cares for 'Azubah?" I say and sigh.
Forsake me cruel people; pass me by;
No pleasance grant me, sing me no joy-song,
Too old I am and weak, erst fair and strong.

IV

Ah! surely God shall cause to flow for me
  Some rills of comfort through the wilderness
And cause to grow some balm-exhaling tree
  On the wide desert of my loneliness!
I must not sit in hopeless solitude
  List'ning to the merry voices in the street,
Nursing my horrid pain to quietude,
  Envious of sunny faces I may meet.

'Azubah, once all joyless, joys shall glean,
The desert shall be fruitful and grow green;—
God whispers me! So feed me with your scorn,
Oh! ingrate people, while I sit forlorn!

CHARLES LEON GUMPERT.

Puissance of the Jew

FOR, if we be not of the lost Ten Tribes,
    At least we have procured them harbourage—
A shelter from the flouts, the sneers, the gibes
    Of malice that befits not this fair age!—
    Turn where you will, each blood-stained, guilty page,
The foreign hatred ever doth abide,
The Jew is menaced still from every side.

Are there not signs that still God loveth them?—
    Whate'er they touch turns golden in their hands,
And stone by stone the new Jerusalem
    Is rising 'mid the waste of other lands,
    For as their Wealth, so too their Power expands—
From East to West the sky is all aflame
With dawning greatness of the Jewish name!

C. W. WYNNE.

Honor of the Jews

THRICE happy nation! Favorite of heaven!
    Selected from the kingdoms of the earth,
To be His chosen race, ordained to spread
His glory through remotest realms, and teach
The Gentile world Jehovah's awful name.

WILLIAM HODSON.

Mock on! Mock on!

MOCK on, mock on, Voltaire, Rousseau,
　　Mock on, mock on, 'tis all in vain;
You throw the sand against the wind
　And the wind blows it back again.

And every sand becomes a gem
　Reflected in the beams divine,
Blown back they blind the mocking eye
　But still in Israel's paths they shine.
　　　　　　　　　　WILLIAM BLAKE.

"His People"

HE set us free—
　　To bear the yoke—
"Let them serve Me,"
　　'Twas thus He spoke.

He called us "Mine,"
　　Not for desire,
To be call'd Thine
　　Meant sword and fire,

And anguish sharp—
　In ev'ry land
The exile's harp
　Forgot his hand.

They reap'd their own;
　God's Acre ours!
On graves alone,
　Might we grow flowers.

But oh! worth while,
　Strong love divine
Outcast, or vile—
　To be call'd Thine.

To feel Thy love
  Like shepherding—
Like brooding dove,
  Like eagle's wing!

As mothers speak
  To sons distrest,
The sore and weak
  Thou comfortest.

Oh! worth the cost,
  And welcome pain!
World's love well lost
  Thy love to gain.

We will serve Thee,
  As Jacob swore,
"This God shall be
  Mine evermore!"

His oath we swear,
  His blessing take;
Thy yoke we bear
  For Thy name's sake!

ANONYMOUS.

The Jew is True

GO forth among this homeless race,
  This landless race that knows no place
Or name or nation quite its own,
And see their happy babes at play.
Palace or Ghetto, rich or poor,
As thick as birds about your door
At morn some sunny Vermont May,
Then think of Christ and these alone.
Yet we deride, we jeer, we gibe
To see their plenteous babes; we say
"Behold the Jew and all his tribe."
Yet Solomon upon his throne
Was not more kingly crowned,

535

More surely born to lord, to lead,
To sow the land with Abram's seed,
. Because their babes are healthful born
And welcomed as the welcome morn.
Hear me this prophecy and heed,
Except we cleanse us kirk and creed,
Except we wash us word and deed,
The Jew shall rule us—reign the Jew.
And just because the Jew is true,
Is true to nature, true to truth;
Is clean, is chaste, as trustful Ruth,
Who bore us David, Solomon—
The Babe that far, first Christmas dawn.

     *   *   *   *   *

The nation, aye, the Christian race,
Here fronts its Sybil, face to face,
And I must say, say now to you,
Whate'er the cost, of fortune, fame,
The Christian is a thing of shame—
Must say because I know it true,
The better Christian is the Jew.

JOAQUIN MILLER.

O Israel

O ISRAEL, thy glory gleamed
   Through long ages long ago;
O Israel, a David dreamed
   Within thy tents of snow;
Thy warriors wise, and brave, and good,
Thy women queens of womanhood,
A pillared cloud, and manna food,
   O Israel, sweet Israel.

.O Israel, again I see
   Thy chariot in the sky!
The seed of Abraham shall be
   Through all eternity;

THE MODERN PERIOD

Our fathers' faith, our fathers' God,
The paths of peace wherein they trod,
With love, with truth, thy soul be shod,
    O Israel, sweet Israel.

ROBERT LOVEMAN.

The Everlasting Jew
(From "Hellas")

THE Jew of whom I spake is old, so old
   He seems to have outlived a world's decay;
The hoary mountains and the wrinkled ocean
Seem younger still than he; his hair and beard
Are whiter than the tempest-sifted snow;
His cold pale limbs and pulseless arteries
Are like the fibres of a cloud instinct
With light, and to the soul that quickens them
Are as the atoms of the mountain-drift
To the winter wind; but from his eye looks forth
A life of unconsumèd thought which pierces
The present, and the past, and the to-come.

    *   *   *   *   *

    Thou art an adept in the difficult lore
Of Greek and Frank philosophy; thou numberest
The flowers, and thou measurest the stars;
Thou severest element from element;
Thy spirit is present in the past, and sees
The birth of this old world through all its cycles
Of desolation and loveliness,
And when man was not, and how man became
The monarch and the slave of this low sphere,
And all its narrow circles—it is much.
I honor thee, and would be what thou art
Were I not what I am; but the unborn hour,
Cradled in fear and hope, conflicting storms,
Who shall unveil? Nor thou, nor I, nor any
Mighty or wise. I apprehended not
What thou hast taught me, but I now perceive
That thou art no interpreter of dreams;

537

Thou dost not own that art, device, or God,
Can make the future present—let it come!
Moreover thou disdainest us and ours!
Thou art as God, whom thou contemplatest.

PERCY BYSSHE SHELLEY.

Jews

PRIDE and humiliation hand in hand
  Walked with them through the world where'er
    they went,
Trampled and beaten were as the sand,
  And yet as unshaken as the continent.

For in the background, figures vague and vast,
  Of patriarchs and of prophets rose sublime,
And all the great traditions of the past
  They saw reflected in the coming time.

ANONYMOUS.

Israel's Spiritual Lamp
(From "The Spanish Gypsy")

I ABIDE
  By that wise spirit of listening reverence
Which marks the boldest doctors of our race.
For Truth, to us, is like a living child
Born of two parents: if the parents part
And will divide the child, how shall it live?
Or, I will rather say: Two angels guide
The paths of man, both aged and yet young,
As angels are, ripening through endless years.
On one he leans: some call her Memory,
And some Tradition; and her voice is sweet,
With deep mysterious accords: the other,
Floating above, holds down a lamp which streams
A light divine and searching on the earth,
Compelling eyes and footsteps. Memory yields

538

Yet clings with loving cheek, and shines anew,
Reflecting all the rays of that bright lamp
Our angel Reason holds. We had not walked,
But for Tradition; we walk evermore
To higher paths, by brightening Reason's lamp.

GEORGE ELIOT.

The Spirit of Hebraism

THEY tell me my spirit's departed,
    That my body of soul is bereft;
And that barren 'midst strangers I wander
    And that no inspiration is left
But my vanishing fires ancestral
    Where the last faint flashes are seen,
And that like to the poor and the stranger,
    What is left by the world I glean.

They tell me, not knowing my Spirit
    Like an ember that never grows cold,
Tho' smouldering in its own ashes
    Yet murmurs and grows as of old.
Oh, my Spirit awaits but my seeking
    To burst like a spring from the soil,
And if once it be free from confinement
    It will vest in all fruit of my toil.

It will live in the colors on canvas,
    And survive in the hewn marble plan,
And in song and in music and story
    To the last generation of man.
It will speak from the lips of new Prophets,
    And their truth from the heights will be hurled,
From a model city of Justice
    Where its flag will blazon unfurled.

From the Hebrew of HARRY WOLFSOHN.
(Translated by H. B. Ehrmann.)

539

Zion's Universal Temple

UNDER the Orient skies of sapphire where the sun
 is all aglow,
With a radiance far surpassing all the western climes
 can know,
There's a pathos haunting ever in the sunlight's splen-
 dor there—
For old Zion's temple mould'ring, for old Zion once
 so fair.
  For old Zion once so fair,
  But now wrapt in deep despair;
   Fled the glory
   Of its story,
  Once of majesty so rare.

But away with all this moaning that is playing fast
 and loose
With the sentiments sure tending now to break a
 people's truce;
For affection once divided, try it may, can never stand
As the symbol of the union that shall mark Messiah's
 land—
  Vision-traced Messiah's land,
  Where true love shall sway its wand.
   Love the token
   Of unbroken
  Peace, that lords at God's command.

Liquid gold of sun's own moulding bent to make a
 world-wide dome,
Shall in future roof the temple marking every nation's
 home:
Paved by earth and sea together, shall its tesselated
 floor
On its huge mosaic gather all the nations that adore—
  Nations that shall soon adore
  Zion's God of cherished yore,
   With the pæans
   That the æons
  Echo shall forevermore.   HARRY WEISS.

A Song of Israel

O ISRAEL! wanderer through the weary years
      Of wild unrest;
A world-wide pilgrimage of hopes and fears,
Sometimes in joy, but oft'ner far in tears,
      As God knows best.

Since Jacob laid him down that night to sleep
      On Bethel's stone,
And saw the angel legions downward sweep,
Their watch around the fugitive to keep—
      Never alone.

Beside the majestic Nile, on Egypt's sand,
      He pitched his tent;
There on the desert saw the uplifted hand,
In cloud and fire still pointing to the land
      Of sweet content.

Beside the Euphrates, where Babylon's wall
      So proudly stood
He saw the giant empires rise and fall,
A captive exile, yet unharmed through all,
      Beside that flood.

And when in wrath the Roman eagles came
      To Zion's Hill,
And drove him out in thunder and in flame,
A stranger in the earth—Jehovah's name
      Upheld him still.

See yonder, on the snow-clad Russian plain,
      His children driven,
Beset and hunted by the imperial train
Like sheep by wolves. But surely not in vain
      They cry to Heaven.

541

Far brighter than the Northern-lights that gleam
       Upon the air,
The signals of the great Shekinah stream
And, like the memories of a blessed dream,
       Bid him good cheer!

Good cheer, O Jacob! though a wanderer still
       In all the earth.
Thy foes will but the promises fulfill
And drive the exile home to Zion's Hill,
       That gave him birth.

A nation scattered through the earth, yet one
       In every land;
As the blue waters of the Gulf-stream run
Through the high seas, yet mingling still with none,
       Behold God's hand!

God speed the day when Jew and Gentiles all
       Shall meet as one
At the glad welcome of their Father's call
In the dear home where shadows never fall,
       Their warfare done.
           J. H. CUTHBERT.

The Fated Race

WHAT! still reject the fated race
      Thus long denied repose,
What! madly striving to efface
      The rights that Heaven bestows!

Say, flows not in each Jewish vein,
      Unchecked, without control,
A tide as pure, as free from stain,
      As warms the Christian soul?

Do ye not yet the times discern
      That these shall cease to roam;
That Shiloh pledged for their return
      Will bring his ransomed home?

Be error quick to darkness hurl'd!
No more with hate pursue,
For He who died to save a world—
Immanuel—was a Jew. ANONYMOUS.

People of Zion

FROM far-off ages hath this people sprung,
   To Yahweh clinging still, as they have clung
The centuries through. Tenacity of mind
In every generation—well defined—
And purposes unshaken, are the fruit
Of worship such as theirs. They pay no suit
To king or prince for favors. Like a rock
That's beaten by the waves they stand the shock
Of prejudice, that, never ceasing, rolls
And rushes all around them. And their souls
Within their temples cluster, drawing near
The altar that has ever been so dear
To Israel; and Israel's mighty God
Seems here to speak the plainer. From the rod
Of gentile hatred here they turn to pray,
For this to them seems the most righteous way.
While we, whose minds in every season turn
To seek or find some "New Religion," learn
To look upon the Israelitish men
With reverence for their steadfast worship. When
The "candles" we have lighted waver so
That we are lost in "ists" and "isms," lo!
We see their great lamp burning still and bright;
A long white pathway shining on the night!
                    MARIE HARROLD GARRISON.

Israel's Mission

I HAD a mighty vision from the skies,
   A glorious vision of the years to come;
I saw a noble brotherhood arise
   And life was love, and every heart was one.

543

Bound by the golden chains that none can 'break
  Each unto each,
The morning stars together sang "awake!"
  And God did teach.

Ay e'en the God that Israel loved so well,
  Who taught of old upon the holy mount,
Whose glowing words made Moses' bosom swell,
  E'en as the waters of a living fount.

And then I cried: The prophet's words were true.
  Time's deathless page
Hath seen at last the promise old yet new:
  The Golden Age!

A great light like a blessing o'er them fell,
  A song of triumph burst upon the air,
The prophet's words were far too weak to tell
  Half of the glory that was pictured there.

All to the living God of Jacob bowed
  At set of sun,
A million voices chanted clear and loud—
  "His name is One!"

But ah! the vision was too pure and bright
  To linger on this fleeting earth of ours,
It faded like the glittering stars of night,
  Or like the fragrance of the summer flowers.

And yet a meaning mystically deep,
  Strange and intense,
Thrilled through that vision with a wildly sweet
  Prophetic sense!

O Israel from thy sleep arise, and dare
  To take the part God gave His chosen few!
Then rise! oh, nobly rise! all ye who bear
  The sacred though oft-hated name of Jew!

Thine is the work! then falter not—press on!·
  With heart and soul,
Press onward with a purpose true and strong
  To reach the goal!

Thy task once done, no more the Earth shall weep,
  But wear in peace, Love's sacred starry crown;
The nations shall their swords to ploughshares beat,
  And the fierce lion with the lamb lie down.

While God shall smile on those who dared to lead
  The sons of men,
And they who scorned thee in thy time of need,
  Shall bless thee then!

                              EVE DAVIESON.

To Young Israel

HOW cloudy is the sky!—
    And thou, thou askest me
If there's in Heav'n a God,
  A God of Liberty.
Oh, child, oh, ask me not!
                  I couldn't lie.

How cloudy is the sky,
  How gloomy is the world
But thou, thou art the same
  From land to land though twirled
Thy lips yet spell the name;
              "Help, Adonai!"

Don't listen to thy foes!
  My child, thy aim is near:
Thou willst not be their prey
  Thy deeds are good and clear
They are the thistles, they—
            Thou art the rose.

545

Don't listen to thy foes!
　Their Saviour was, too
A son of thine by birth:
　Tell them that He—a Jew—
Brought them redemption on earth;
　　　　　To heaven he rose.

Don't be afraid of them,
　They tell the same old lie—
Thou need'st their children's blood—
　But, child, they vainly try
To stamp thee in the mud
　　　　　'Tis but a flam!

Don't be afraid of them,
　Jehovah is thy guide;
Thou, tribe of worthy men,
　Thou'llst be the nation's pride,
　　　　　"The world's gem."

　　　　　　　　M. Osias.

The Mystic Tie

THERE is a mystic tie that joins
　　The children of the Hebrew race
In bonds of sympathy and love,
　Which time and change cannot efface.

When, 'mid the world's abuse and scorn,
　The sons of Israel bravely stood,
That bond was holier, stronger still—
　Cemented by their martyr's blood.

And though to-day the Hebrew dwells
　In every clime and every land,
Yet, joined to that immortal tie,
　A holy brotherhood they stand.

546

Go to the North where Polar stars
  Look down on fields of ice and snow;
Go where, in sunny tropic climes,
  The gentle breezes softly blow.

Go to the countries of the East—
  Arabia and the Hindoo land;
Go where the calm Pacific sweeps
  'Gainst California's golden strand;—

And there, in reverent tones, is heard
  The sacred cry, always the same,
"O Israel, hear! Our God is one,
  Blest be for aye His holy name!"

This is the mystic tie that joins
  The children of the Hebrew race;
This is the grand and holy bond
  Which time and change cannot efface.

MAX MEYERHARDT.

My Heritage

A GLORIOUS heritage is mine,
    Attained through blood and tears,
Enhaloed of Light Divine,
  My mission's truth appears;
The olden benedictions crown
  The strife of exiled years.

The noblest heritage is mine,
  That valiant heart may know,
For annals of my Past enshrine
  Life's boundless depths of woe;
While Memory's body watchword kept
  Great Freedom's light aglow!

547

E'en from the Ghetto's drear abode
  Hope's world-wide message sped,
'Neath cruel Persecution's load,
  Though brave hearts truly bled!
And tyrant scorn in bitter tears,
  Steeped Israel's daily bread.

The suffering of long ages borne
  With trust of faith sublime,
Now hail the radiance of the morn,
  As joy-bells sweetly chime;
Grant Israel's heritage of Peace,
  Lord! over Space and Time.

To all who guard the ancient fane,
  The purpose high and true,
The inspiration's holiest aim
  Endow with strength anew!
Keep from the worldliness of strife
  The heart-life of the Jew!

The glorious heritage is mine!
  The honored name I bear,
Refulgent with the Light Divine,
  Empowers to Do and Dare!
To conquer Prejudice and Wrong—
  In victory o'er despair!
          CORA WILBURN.

Shema-Yisroel-Adonai-Elohenu Adonai-Echod

O GOD of Israel, Lord on high,
  Hear, O hear, thy children cry.
Like the wave in stormy gale,
It rises with its mournful wail,
O'er the land in accents drear,
It sounds, and murmurs far and near.

The Russian with his tyrant hand,
Augments it in his cruel land.
His lash and scourge thy chosen race,
Doth scourge and lash with torments base.
He hears their hunger's fierce desire,
With mocking curses and with ire.
Unclothed and starving they may pine,
His heart is deaf to race of thine.
Therefore we pray thee, Israel's God,
Free thine own, and with thy rod,
Chastise the tyrant. Let him see,
That still thy race are one with thee;
That still thou art our Adonoy,
And that we worship thee with joy.

NATHAN BERNSTEIN.

Judaeis Vita Aeterna

NOT for our sake, O Lord!
 But for the glory of Thy name,
The splendor of Thine ancient word,
 The honor of Thy people's fame,
The promise of the truths that last
 From time unknown in Israel's heart,
We hold our ancient customs fast—
 We are for aye a folk apart!
Not for our sake, O Lord!
 But that the world shall see again
How Judah in her soul can hoard
 The faith that yet shall save all men—
The faith that in the olden days,
 Beneath the blue Judæan sky,
Sang loud as now its love and praise
 Unto our God, the Lord Most High!

CHARLES N. LURIE.

549

"The Children of the Pale"

WHENCE comes this motley, dark-eyed, swarthy
    crowd,
Of alien children in a London street,
With laughter and with chatter shrill and loud,
    And hurrying feet?

From that far land they come whose eagles look
    O'er east and west. Their fathers crossed the waves
Because they would no longer tamely brook
    The lot of slaves.

For generations in the gloom they dwelt
    Dark as the sombre forests of the North,
Till suddenly within their hearts they felt
    The call, "Come forth!"

The moss-grown walls of hoary synagogue
    And school, the field of Death than Life more kind,
The jewelled tables of the Decalogue,
    They left behind.

But in their hearts, as in the Holiest Place,
    They bore the ark, its manna and its rod,
The lust of knowledge and the pride of race,
    The awe of God.

And on their children's faces I behold
    Flashes and gleams, as from some inner shrine,
Recalling ancient stories proudly told
    Of Israel's line.

ANONYMOUS.

Judah

WHILE the tribes of earth yet in the dark-
　　ness groped,
　Ere iron savagery set free,
O Judah! had'st thou with science coped
　In law and poesy.

God's chosen people, thy songs are sung
　In the great world to-day;
In every clime, in every tongue,
　Thy name shall last for aye!

Since time began, yea, when the earth
　We're told was very young,
Fair Judah flourished and gave birth
　To wise men who have sung—

Psalms wherein human longings bring
　Home to each heart to-day
The unspoken hope, the desire to cling
　To a Higher Power alway.

Strong nations rise at last to fall
　Beneath the strokes of Fate;
But Judah rises like a wall—
　Invincible 'gainst hate.

Two thousand years have not sufficed,
　Tho' of Fatherland despoiled,
To destroy the race by all despised,
　Or tarnish a name unsoiled.

GEORGE R. DU BOIS.

551

The Chosen Ones of Israel

THE chosen ones of Israel are scatter'd far and
    wide;
Where flows the lordly Tiber, where rolls the Atlan-
    tic tide—
By Danube's winding waters, by Hudson's crystal
    springs,
Dwell the myriad descendants of the Prophets and the
    Kings,
Abroad along the valleys are their habitations found—
They are hunters in the forest, and tillers of the
    ground—
The rising sun beholds them in torrid realms afar
And on their broken legions looks down the northern
    star.
In the old world's crowded cities, in the prairies of
    the new,
Unchanged amid all changes, to their faith forever
    true—
Alike by Niger's fountains and by Niagara's flood
Still flow, unmix'd, the currents of the grand, heroic
    blood.
Ye mourn your lasting exile, your temple strewn in
    dust,
Yet forget not ye the promise of the righteous and
    the just—
Ye know ye shall be gathered, from every clime and
    shore,
And be again the chosen of Jehovah evermore,
From Assyria, Egypt, Elam—from Patmos, Cush,
    Shinar—
From Hamath, and the islands of foreign seats afar—
From all the earth's four corners, where Israel's chil-
    dren roam,
Shall the dispers'd of Judah throng to their long
    promis'd home,
And again like some high mountain whose tops are
    crown'd with snow,

Shall the Temple's thousand turrets in the golden
    sunset glow—   ·
And again before their altars shall the congregations
    stand,
On thy plains, O lov'd Jerusalem! the happy, holy
    land!
And it shall come to pass that the remnant in that day,
Upon the Lord of Hosts above, the great I Am, shall
    stay;
And the escap'd of Jacob, from the paths which they
    have trod,
Shall return to Him that smote them—your fathers'
    mighty God!   PARK BENJAMIN.

The Star of Discontent

O THOU, sweet friend, would I might soothe thy
    fear!
Our night is dark—the little vessel drifts
Unpiloted, and heedless of its rifts
The shipmen prank themselves in festal gear.
And shout that all is well, afar and near,
What need have ocean-drifters of God's gifts
Of chart and compass? Lo, as each wind shifts,
The wandering vessel reels; its plight how drear!
Brave hearts, despair not; all is not yet lost—
All is not lost beneath black Northern skies;
The slumberer awakens, tempest-tost,
And all his soul in anguish heavenward cries;
And Hope shines forth in Jewry's firmament—
One ray of hope—The Star of Disconent.
                                X.

They Call Us Jews

THEY call us Jews. Those men whose family tree
    Springs from a line of noble ancestry,
Who trace their title to the little band
That in the Mayflower came to freedom's land;

Or those within whose veins doth proudly run
The blood of men who fought with Washington.
How weak their proud pretensions are to ours
Whose pedigree with undiminished powers
We trace to him who first the truth made known;—
"The Lord is One.   He rules the world alone."

Yes, we are Jews;—proud scions of the race
That first enjoyed Jehovah's special grace;
To whom was given in Sinai's synagogue,
By hand Divine, the glorious decalogue;
Whose leader, Moses, formed the wondrous laws
Which still best serve Humanity's great cause;
Whose leader, Moses, formed the thoughts and deeds
That inspiration give to modern creeds;
Whose people still proclaim through every zone;—
"The Lord is One.   He rules the world alone."

Yes, we are Jews.   Scourged by relentless hate,
Our fathers wandered on from state to state;
Were forced to dwell in narrow Ghetto lanes,
Were fleeced by torture of their honest gains.
And though of every privilege deprived,
The persecuted people grew and thrived.
The nations might degrade them, might annoy,
But God-anointed man could not destroy.
And with our race the shibboleth has grown;
"The Lord is One.   He rules the world alone."

Yes, we are Jews.   The People of the Book,
Our duty 'tis to search out every nook
Where evil lurks, where ignorance and shame
Cast undeserved reproach on Israel's name.
On this Association falls the task
With pen and precept error to unmask.
To teach the Gentile world for what we stand,
To teach the Jew his passions to command.
To penetrate the homes and spread the light,
To preach the doctrine of Eternal Right.

Throughout the hostile world let Israel be
A synonym of stern morality.
Then will our prayer ascend to Heaven's throne;
"The Lord is One. He rules the world alone."

MILTON GOLDSMITH,

The Jew's Appeal to the Christian

CEASE, Christian, cease the word of scorn,
　　On Israel's name, on Judah's race;
Though lowly, humbled and forlorn,
　　He hath no home, no resting place;
Deem not the Hebrew's soul so dead,
　　So abject, that he cannot know,
Musing o'er Salem's glory fled,
　　The tear of shame, the pang of woe.

When by the streams of Babylon
　　Our captive exiled fathers sate,
On high their tuneless harps were hung,
　　They could not sing—disconsolate
They mourned their lost Jerusalem,
　　Her hallowed scenes of loveliness;
Their children too can weep with them—
　　They cannot sing for heaviness.

O! think upon the severed wave,
　　Obedient to the Prophet's word;
On that dread law Jehovah gave,
　　When Sinai trembled with the Lord.
Forget not those, our favored sires,
　　Led through the desert, bondage free,
By noonday cloud, and midnight fires,
　　Their guardian guide the Deity.

Boast ye of power, of glory won
　　By England's warrior chivalry?
Think, think, of what our sires have done,
　　Of Gideon, David, Maccabee,

555

When Judah trod his lofty way,
　Proud, fierce, and free; who then might dare,
Low crouching on his prostrate prey,
　Rouse the young lion from his lair?

Vaunt ye of Britain rich and great?
　Her beauties do ye fondly tell?
Such once was Zion's palmy state,
　Fair were thy tents, O Israel!
Her merchants were the chiefs of earth,
　Their vessels thronged the Eastern sea;
And Salem gloried in the worth
　Of Ophir, Indus, Araby.

Though changed, alas! not hers the doom,
　Thus ever hopelessly to pine;
Our father's pitying God shall come,
　And rear his loved, though wasted, vine,—
Were this a fond and idle dream,
　Our Prophet's sacred word were vain,
Jerusalem! Jerusalem!
　The Beautiful, shall rise again.

Virgin of Israel! yet once more
　Encircled by the choral throng,
Thou shalt lead forth the dance, and pour
　To tabret note the merry song:—
Once more, once more, exultingly,
　From holy Ephraim's mountainward,
Shall Jacob hear the watchman's cry,
　"Arise, and let us-seek the lord!"

Daughter of Zion! raise the voice!
　Clap the glad hand! beloved, forgiven,
The fainting spirit shall rejoice,
　Refreshed, once more, by dews from heaven.
The land that held the iron rod
　Shall wield the shepherd's crook, and prove
(Hear it, ye Isles)—that Israel's God
　Hath loved her with a father's love!

Cease, Christian, cease the word of shame
On Judah's race—on Israel's name.
J. W. BLENCOWE, JR.

The Jew to Jesus

O MAN of my own people, I alone
    Among these alien ones can know thy face,
I who have felt the kinship of our race
Burn in me as I sit where they intone
Thy praises,—those who, striving to make known
A God for sacrifice, have missed the grace
Of thy sweet human meaning in its place,
Thou who art of our blood-bond and our own.

Are we not sharers of thy Passion? Yea,
In spirit-anguish closely by thy side
We have drained the bitter cup, and, tortured, felt
With thee the bruising of each heavy welt.
In every land is our Gethsemane.
A thousand times have we been crucified.
FLORENCE KIPER FRANK.

Moses and Jesus

METHOUGHT on two Jews meeting I did
    chance—
One old, stern-eyed, deep-browed; yet garlanded
With living light of love around his head;
The other young, with sweet, seraphic glance.
Round them went on the Town's Satanic dance,
Hunger a-piping while at heart he bled.
Salom Aleikem mournfully each said,
Nor eyed the other straight, but looked askance.

Sudden from Church outrolled an organ hymn,
From Synagog a loudly chanted air,
Each with its prophet's high acclaim instinct,
Then for the first time met their eyes swift-linked
In one strange, silent, piteous gaze, and dim
With bitter tears of agonized despair.
ISRAEL ZANGWILL.

557

Lines to an Anti-Semite

STAND! as God saw thee of old time
　　We see and know thee now;
The brand of unforgotten crime
　　Still black upon thy brow,
That mark, Eternal Justice traced,
　　Thou coverest in vain;
Its blighting stigma uneffaced;
　　Where is thy brother, Cain?

Aye, hypocrite, and if thou wilt,
　　White hands, in protest, spread!
The blood by coarser murderers spilt
　　Was at thy bidding shed.
Thy speech inflamed each ignorant soul
　　With thine own maddening wine;
And when their fury burst control,
　　Their brutal acts were thine.

For thee the crowded Plaza seethed
　　Round Seville's high-built pyre;
And shrinking forms of women wreathed
　　With boiling snakes of fire.
Thy servants fanned their ardent breath
　　Into a fiercer flame;
And watched, well-pleased, the dallying death,
　　That lingered ere it came.

But thou hast darker secrets yet,
　　And deeds more dear to hell.
The sightless, sounding oubliette
　　Hath kept thy counsel well,
The silent hours that crush the heart,
　　The soul-destroying gloom;
Thine, devil, was the fiendish art
　　Devised that living tomb.

Woe, woe on the unhappy state
  That learns thy bloody creed,
And makes her mansion desolate
  Thy cruel lust to feed.
Before one dread, impartial Bar
  Her sons, shall find ere long,
How terrible the helpless are,
  The feeble ones how strong!

Lo! where the dotard Empress, Spain,
  With loosened necklace stands,
While those fair jewels, grain by grain,
  Slip from her nerveless hands!
Unmoved she sees her pearls depart
  And smiles with alien eyes;
For heavy on her palsied heart
  The curse of Israel lies.

Foul shark, whose malice never sleeps,
  On noblest victims fed;
What swimmer bold shall cleave the deeps
  Thy rivings left so red;
And when thy bulk sways up to breathe
  On that encrimsoned tide,
With one unerring home-thrust sheathe
  His dagger in thy side?

              EDWARD SYDNEY TYBEE.

I Would Reply

IF one should say, "Thou art a Jew,
  Of race for centuries downtrod!"
I would reply: "So was he, too,
  Whom you've exalted to your God!
Is it a stigma kin to be
With him who preached in Galilee?"

If one should say, "What are the deeds
  The Jew has done!" I would reply:—
"The corner-stone of modern creeds
  Was laid by him in years gone by.
He broke the gyves of tyranny
And taught the world humanity!"

If one should say, "Thy cult is old!"
  I would reply: "Why, so is Truth!
But like the brilliancy of gold
  It still shines with untarnished youth.
Whatever truths your church may show,
The Jew professed them long ago."

             MILTON GOLDSMITH.

"Only a Jew"

PATIENT in sorrow, and never repining,
  Bending submissively low to the blast;
Conscious that Heaven is never designing
  That sickness or sorrow forever should last,
Striving mid poverty, earnest and active,
  Nerving his efforts, industrious and true,
Spurning all wrong, howsoever attractive,
  Humble and pious, though "Only a Jew."

Prosperity crowning his efforts and striving,
  See, Fortune, propitious, his industry bless;
To comfort and competence, haply arriving,
  Still earnest and active, his energies press.
Gladly relieving all sorrow and anguish,
  While tears sympathetic his features bedew,
Where sad ones in poverty and wretchedness languish,
  God's angel on earth—though "Only a Jew."

Affectionate heart, throbs his bosom, e'er swelling
  For dear ones, who claim his attachment and love;
An earthly Elysium, his Eden-like dwelling
  (A foretaste on earth of bright heaven above.)

Obedient his child life, now his children adore him;
  His wife, with affection, does life's joys renew,
The bright rays of happiness ever shine o'er him,
  As father, as husband, though "Only a Jew."

Progressive in Science, in Art and in Learning;
  Dispensing their benefits, near and afar—
Till grateful, his worth now his country discerning
  He graces in honor the Senate—the Bar—
Pleading in eloquence 'gainst every oppression;
  He strives for the "Right," and does baseness pursue,
Yet "damned with faint praise," he hears envy's ex-
    pression,
  After all, you must own, that he's "Only a Jew."

His tongue free from evil, his lips from deceiving,
  E'en to those who may spurn him his heart remains
    dumb;
While sadly their bootless malignity grieving,
  . He knows that a time of Redemption will come.
When shining again in Empyrean splendor,
  The glories of Israel will beam forth anew,
Thus blessing in Life, does his blessed death render
  A pure soul to God, though he's "Only a Jew."

                                P. H.

Thou Art a Jew

THOU art a Jew, and all is said
  That need be said, fore'er to bar the way,
  To where doth linger the exclusive ray
Of social sunshine; here the dead
And foolish issues of the past
  Are born again, and bigotry appears
  And dares to sit in judgment on his peers,
A race immortal, ancient, vast.

Thou art a Jew, and by that name
  Alone, thou'rt judged; thy virtues play no part;
  Thy graces, strength of mind, or depth of heart,
All lost in the consuming flame
Of ignorance. Through eyes of love
  They look not at thee, fearing they may find
  Some merit, toward which they were ever blind;
Some soul, some grandeur from above.

Though here and there, a hollow tree
  Doth stand among the mighty tow'ring pines,
  Still is the forest beautiful. And mines
Of dazzling riches we could see
If we but delved beneath the clay.
  Below the surface we must seek to find
  True worth, true greatness, and the master mind;
Beyond the darkness, lingers day.

The social barrier that stands
  Grim sentinel between the faiths to-day,
  Is prejudice; it knoweth but the way
Its father, ignorance, demands
To judge the many by the few.
  Amid the weeds the dainty wild flower grows,
  Great good 'mid evil often may repose;
But as for thee, thou art a Jew.

Thou art a Jew; then let thy ways
  Not dim the lustre of thy fathers' creed.
  Let honor be thy star; thy every deed
Reflect its brightness on thy days.
Be faithful, patient, noble, true;
  Kindness and justice in thy heart abide;
  Live thus and thou wilt feel a worthy pride
When it is said, thou art a Jew.

                              I. N. L.

Israel

HEAR, O Israel, Jehovah, the Lord our God is one,
But we, Jehovah, His people, are dual and so
undone.

Slaves in eternal Egypts, baking their strawless bricks,
At ease in successive Zions, prating their politics.

Rotting in sunlit Rumania, pigging in Russian pale,
Driving in Park, Bois, and Prater, clinging to Fash-
ion's tail;

Reeling before every rowdy, sore with a hundred stings,
Clothed in fine linen and purple, loved at the courts of
Kings;

Faithful friends to our foemen, slaves to a scornful
clique,
The only Christians in Europe, turning the other cheek;

Priests of the household altar, blessing the bread and
wine,
Lords of the hells of Gomorrah, licensed keepers of
swine;

Coughing o'er clattering treadles, saintly and under-
paid,
Ousting the rough from Whitechapel—by learning the
hooligan's trade;

Pious, fanatical zealots throttled in Talmud-coil,
Impious, lecherous skeptics, cynical stalkers of spoil;

Wedded 'neath Hebrew awning, buried 'neath Hebrew
sod,
Between not a dream of duty, never a glimpse of God;

563

Risking our lives for our countries, loving our nations'
    flags,
Hounded therefrom in repayment, hugging our bloody
    rags;

Blarneying, shivering, crawling, taking all colors and
    none,
Lying a fox in the covert, leaping an ape in the sun.

Tantalus-Proteus of Peoples, security comes from with-
    in;
Where is the lion of Judah? Wearing an ass's skin!

Hear, O Israel, Jehovah, the Lord our God is One,
But we, Jehovah His people, are dual and so undone.
              ISRAEL ZANGWILL.

Israel

HOW great, O Israel, have thy sufferings been
    Since doomed in every land and clime to roam,
An exile and a wanderer on the earth,
    Without a country and without a home!

Throughout the world men scorned the Hebrew's
        faith—
    That holy creed of origin divine;
They stamped as crime his sacred, pure belief,
    And mocked his worship at Jehovah's shrine.

And Israel, once a nation proud and great,
    From whom sprang sages, kings and prophets grand,
Earth's mightiest race, the chosen of the Lord,
    Was mocked and scorned and jeered in every land!

In sunny Spain, the Inquisition dread
    Cast him in dungeons terrible and dire,
And with a thousand tortures racked his form,
    Then led him forth unto the death of fire.

THE MODERN PERIOD

Where'er the Hebrew roamed, on land or sea,
  Did persecution follow in his path,
And furious mobs deemed it a noble act
  To vent on him their hatred and their wrath.

Ten thousand martyrs died for Israel's cause,
  With fortitude sublime, 'mid smoke and flame;
And while their cruel foes stood mocking 'round,
  They called on God and blessed His sacred name!

Through all the horrors of that fearful time,
  Through gloom and death, the Hebrew saw afar,
With faith's unfailing and undying eye,
  Beyond the clouds, hope's bright and glorious star.

He knew that God would rise 'gainst Israel's foes
  As, long ago, upon the Red Sea coast,
With miracles He saved His chosen race,
  And in the sea 'whelmed Pharaoh's mighty host.

And gloriously was that bright trust fulfilled,
  For Israel triumphed over every foe,
And marching on with undiminished zeal,
  Emerged in triumph from the night of woe.

Yes, Judah proudly stands, 'midst all mankind,
  Once more as beautiful, sublime, and grand
As when, in blessèd days of old, she stood
  A mighty nation in the Holy Land.

Weep not, O Israel, for thy martyred ones,
  For though no monuments rise o'er their tombs,
Yet fame upon the sacred spot shall shed
  Her fairest garlands and her brightest blooms.

Their names are grav'n on honor's deathless page,
  And on the scroll of glory written high:
And though earth's proudest monuments decay,
  Their deeds sublime will never, never die!

Mourn not, O Israel, for the glorious past;
  The future holds a destiny more grand;
For 'tis thy mission great to teach God's laws
  To the inhabitants of every land,

And cause the nations of the world to know
  That unto Him alone shall prayers ascend,
And that before His great majestic throne
  All men in reverent suppliance shall bend.

Ah! may the time soon come when o'er the earth
  In thunder tones the glad acclaim will ring,
And nations, taking up the shout, shall cry,
  "The God of Judah is our Lord and King!"

MAX MEYERHARDT.

The Jews of England (1290-1902)

AN Edward's England spat us out—a band
    Foredoomed to redden Vistula or Rhine,
  And leaf-like toss with every wind malign,
All mocked the faith they could not understand.
Six centuries have passed. The yellow brand
  On shoulder nor on soul has left a sign
  And on our brows must Edward's England twine
Her civic laurels with an equal hand.

Thick-clustered stars of fierce supremacy
  Upon the martial breast of England glance!
She seems of War the very Deity.
  Could aught remain her glory to enhance?
Yea, for I count her noblest victory
  Her triumph o'er her own intolerance.

ISRAEL ZANGWILL.

The Right of Asylum

EASY the cry while vengeance now is wrought
  And from his lair the Anarchist is burned.
"Shut be our harbors, closed be every port
  And from our shore be every alien turned."
Yet while the clamor and the pursuit is hot
  And public anger public madness breeds,
Be it not soon nor easily forgot
  That England thus an ancient title cedes.
For centuries a pillow hath she spread.
  For all that widowed goes and wandering
And in her lap hath laid the unhappy head
  Or broken Statesman and of outcast King.
Shall she alarmed by that small horde deny
  This old sea-haven to world-misery?

STEPHEN PHILLIPS.

The Jewish Soldier

MOTHER England, Mother England, 'mid the
      thousands
Far beyond the sea to-day,
Doing battle for thy honour, for thy glory,
Is there place for us, a little band of brothers,
      England say?

Dost thou ask our name and nation, Mother England?
We have come from many lands,
Where the rod of the oppressor bowed and bent us,
Bade us stand with bated breath and humble gesture,
      Suppliant hands.

Long ago and far away, O Mother England,
We were warriors brave and bold,
But a hundred nations rose in arms against us,
And the shadow of exile closed o'er those heroes
      Days of old.

567

Thou hast given us home and freedom, Mother Eng-
    land,
Thou hast let us live again
Free and fearless midst thy free and fearless children,
Sharing with them, as one people, grief and gladness,
        Joy and pain.

Now we Jews, we English Jews, O Mother England,
Ask another boon of thee!
Let us share with them the danger and the glory,
Where thy best and bravest lead, there let us follow
        O'er the sea!

For the Jew has heart and hand, Mother England,
And they both are thine to-day—
Thine for life and thine for death, yea, thine forever!
Wilt thou take them as we give them, freely, gladly,
        England say!
                            ALICE LUCAS.

Israel and Columbia

O GLORY of an elder age!
    O wonder of time's later days!
Foremost for aye as priest and sage,
    Ne'er absent from broad history's ways,
Let us not fail on thee to place
    Some share of our Columbian crown,
For one of all thy favored race
    Sailed with that fleet from Palos town.

Prophetic dreams of worlds behind
    The secret of the sundown seas,
Slept deep in science heart-confined
    From Maneth on to Genoese.
Well said Isaiah, seer sublime,
    "Surely the isles shall wait for thee,
And ships of Tarshish bide the time
    When Hebrews face the western sea."

568

THE MODERN PERIOD

The gates of unknown worlds were sealed
  While progress waits the Jewish hand,
And David's earth possessing shield,
  To lead her to the Promised Land.
Herculean Pillars vainly rear
  Their frowning ne-plus-ultra bound
In paths where fiery pillars steer
  The conquest of the planet round.

Spain drove thee forth from mart and school,
  Princes of commerce, thought, and verse,
Thine angel led to broader rule
  In lands which laugh at Europe's curse.
We hear Jah's voice through all thy course,
  "More yet beyond, for thou art mine,"
And with thee dwells the secret force
  That makes the march of man divine.

For thou art Hebrew—Abram's seed—
  The child of him God called His friend,
And son of Whom the nations read,
  "Thy kingdom hath not bound nor end."
Yes, Hebrew, man from realms beyond,
  Upreared to lead hope's splendid quest,
Instinct with powers by ages crowned,
  Restless, thou guidest man to rest.

So Israel's world-wide moving sons,
  We hail you at each opening gate,
Through which your flaming promise runs,
  While Jacob's star leads on our fate.
And more than admiral or crew,
  Whose memory nations now adorn,
We hail that nameless sailor Jew
  As herald of the New World's morn.

                          JOHN J. McCABE.

The Jew in America

WING thee, my song, and in majestic flight
  Grace with fair melody the words I write;
That they, in some not too unworthy strain,
With pride and plaint, of glory tell and pain;
Say in what early dawn of history
High fate enmeshed our footsteps—made us be
The burdened bearers of a word sublime—
The portent and the amulet of time.

For that far vale, the cradle and the grave,—
Where we behold God and the world He gave,—
We have come hither for that high word's sake,
Bound each to each with bonds that naught could
    break.

The golden thread along the paths we trod
Gleamed bright from daily contact with our God,—
Through labyrinthine gloom of age on age
We knew its radiance as our heritage,—
And though in strange, far lands enforced to roam,
The broad earth held for us no alien home.

Spain saw us—Holland—and th' intrepid crew
Of the famed caravel whose captain knew
Where sky and ocean melted in the west
A new world waited for his wondrous quest.

A new world—with great portals far outflung—
Holding a hope more sweet than time had sung,
To which the Jew, of life's high quest a part,
A pilgrim came, the Torah in his heart.
Of his endeavor, how he thrived and came
To give new glory to his ancient name
And wore as diadem the thread of gold,
On many a page the chronicler has told.

THE MODERN PERIOD

A land of promise, and fulfilment too;
Where on a sudden olden dreams came true.
Man was man's equal—unto every race
The path was levelled to the highest place.
Here grew we part of an ennobled state,
Gave and won honor, sat among the great,
And saw unfolding to our 'raptured view
The day long prayed for by the patient Jew.

．　　．　　．　　．　　．　　．　　．

Pause thou, my song, that soarest proud and high,
Pause thou awhile, lest some far-echoed cry
Reverberating through the caves of time
Destroy the structure of thy vaulting rhyme.
A pale cadaver with lack-lustre eyes,
Touches the harp and stills its melodies.

Russia, thy name embitters history,
And in the ages that are yet to be,
A symbol thou for all the world holds worst—
Abhorred of heaven, by mankind accursed.
Prophetic made by frenzy of our grief,
By miseries that mount beyond belief,
We thee consign to be the scorn of time,
Shackled forever to earth's blackest crime.
The long forefinger of the future years
Shall point thee out the fountain-head of tears;
Nor ocean's waters may efface the stain
Branded in blood on thee—the brand of Cain!

Fain turns my song unto some fairer note—
We guard a promise voiced in days remote,
The words of prophets, and our deathless hope,
That in dark hours when we despairing grope
In ever clearer accents shall be heard:
No tyrant's perfidy may kill God's word.

Still trembling, in the valley, in the gloom,
About us frowning rocks strange shapes assume;
But unto faith that fears nor wreck nor storm
There dawns a golden day that shall transform

These spectres of a long and cruel night
To ministering friends in new-born light,
When tried by travail and by fire and rod
We shall emerge, unchanged, to face our God.

FELIX N. GERSON.

The Ghetto-Jew

I MARKED in the midst of the glittering throng
A figure all bent and retreating;
His raiment was shabby, and bearded his face,
His gaze was bewildering and fleeting;
And those whose drossiness glared through the gilt
Guffawed a contemptuous greeting.

Intently I peered in his time lined face
And read there his marvellous story;
His brows were large with the wisdom of pain,
His locks by affliction made hoary;
A memory lurked in the depth of his eyes,
A prayer and a vision of glory.

A mem'ry aglow with the splendors of old,
A prayer of patience and yearning,
And a vision of Home that gleamed in the dark,
Through ages of weary sojourning;
Yet they of the gilded and glittering throng
Had naught but derision and spurning.

He folded a dream to his quivering heart
And nursed it through vigils of ages;
He gave it the blood of his life to absorb
Yet mockery now is his wages.
Shall this be the word his story to close,
A jeer be the last of its pages?

RUFUS LEARSI.

The Melting Pot

BEARDED old patriarchs, flippant young men,
  Faces from synagogue, tenement, den,
Native and foreign and Gentile and Jew—
Faces of every contour and hue—
Bad faces, good faces, carved-out-of-wood faces,
Scarred faces, marred faces, tender and hard faces.
Clusters and bevies of trim little Jewesses,
Telling what "Abie" or "Ikey" or "Louie" says,
Beauties from Italy, Russia and France,
Clad in their gayest of clothes for a dance;
Hawksters and womenfolk bargaining, bickering,
Polyglot, clamoring, bartering, dickering
Under the lights that are flaring and flickering;
Lovers and criminals, preachers and panderers,
Lawyers and pawnbrokers, flashy philanderers.
Every conceivable garb for the viewing—
Rags that are fluttering, silks all frou-frouing;
Here shivers misery, near by we have a new
Modiste's creation as "swell as the Avenue";
Hats up to date and of hoariest lineage!
Simpering girls at the utterly ninny age,
Babies in arms and young boys at the skinny age
Mix in with fat men and beggars a-muttering,
Where from the pushcarts the peddlers are sputtering
Praises unending for wares they are vending;
Furniture, notions and kitchen utensils,
Suits, furs and underwear, pictures and pencils:
Stores all ablaze 'mid a babble that's furious—
Rich people, poor people, quaint folks and curious,
Painted dames, queens of a doubtful society,
Folks and more folks in an endless variety,
Scions of different nations and races
Coming and going from thousands of places!
Color and movement and bustle and noise,
Mothers and fathers and maidens and boys,
Glad folks and sorrowful, dreary or cheery,
Beautiful, horrible, lively or weary,

Loving and hateful and sober and bleary,
Glitter and grayness and laughter and pain,
Passing, repassing and passing again.
Life!—that is all, with its mirth and its toiling,
Life—like a kettle that's bubbling and boiling,
Under the glare of the merciless light—
Heart of the Ghetto on Saturday night!

BERTON BRALEY.

A Call to the Builders

I

YE may not rear it now,—though some aver
    The eye of man shall see it where it stood,—
The glittering House of God, with cedar-wood
Well builded, and with olive and with fir,
    Cunningly carved with wide-winged cherubim,
    And flowers full-blown, and palm-trees fair and slim.
    The ancient, unforgetting Eastern sky—
Blue as the sapphire in the breast-plate set,
That, watching waits, may not behold it yet;
    Though there be breasts where longing will not
        die;
Though still Jerusalem's holy earth be shed,
Dear symbol, o'er the unalienated dead!

II

Yet unto you, O sons of Israel!
    This year, this day, this hour, and in this land,
    'Tis given to lend with joy the helping hand.
To rear a mighty Temple builded well,
    Its blocks young souls, unhewn yet by the keen
    Steel of the desecrating world, and clean.
Bring, bring, bright gold, and melt it in the fire.
    So shall that faithful offering overspread
A spiritual altar, be ye sure;
So to the strength of Israel shall aspire
    From lamps of many branches flamelets pure,
    The light of lives with oil of knowledge fed!

HELEN GRAY CONE.

574

O Long the Way

O LONG the way and short the day,
   No light in tower or town,
The waters roar and far the shore,
   My ship, my ship goes down.

'Tis all in vain to strive again,
   My cry the billows drown,
The fight is done, the wind has won—
   My ship, my ship goes down.

Bid sun adieu! Thou'lt shine anew,
   When skies no longer frown,
But I—the deafening billows crash—
   My ship, my ship goes down.

                MORRIS ROSENFELD.

The Candle Seller

IN Hester Street, hard by a telegraph post
   There sits a poor woman as wan as a ghost.
Her pale face is shrunk, like the face of the dead
And yet you can tell that her cheeks once were red.
But love, ease and friendship and glory, I ween,
May hardly the cause of their fading have been.
Poor soul, she has wept so, she scarcely can see,
A skeleton infant she holds on her knee.
It tugs at her breast, and it whimpers and sleeps,
But soon at her cry it awakens and weeps:
"Two cents my good woman, three candles will buy,
As bright as their flame be my star in the sky!"
Tho' few are her wares, and her basket is small
She earns her own living by these, when at all,
She's there with her baby in wind and in rain,
In frost and in snow-fall, in weakness and pain;
She trades and she trades, through the good times and
   slack,

No home and no food, and no cloak to her back;
She's kirthless and kinless—one friend at the most
And that one is silent: the telegraph post!
She asks for no alms, the poor Jewess, but still
Altho' she is wretched, forsaken and ill
She cries Sabbath candles to those who come nigh
And all that she pleads is, that people will buy.
To honor the sweet Sabbath, each one
With joy in his heart to the market has gone
To shops and to pushcarts they hurriedly go
But who for the poor wretched woman will care?
A few of her candles you think they will take.
They seek the meat patties, the fish and the cake.
She holds forth a hand with a pitiful cry;
"Two cents, my good woman, three candles will buy!"
But no one has listened, and no one has heard;
Her voice is so weak, that it fails at each word.
Perchance the poor mite in her lap understood,
She hears mother's crying—but where is the good?

I pray you, how long will she sit there and cry
Her candles so feebly to all that pass by?
How long will it be, do you think, ere her breath
Gives out in the horrible struggle with Death?
How long will this frail one in mother-love strong
Give suck to the babe at her breast? Oh, how long?
The child mother's tears used to swallow before,
But mother's eyes, nowadays, shed them no more.
Oh, dry are the eyes now, and empty the brain,
The heart well-nigh broken, the breath drawn with
       pain.
Yet ever, tho' faintly, she calls out anew;
"Oh buy but two candles, good woman but two!"

In Hester Street stands on the pavement of stone,
A small orphaned basket, forsaken, alone.
Besides it is sitting a corpse, cold and stark,
The seller of candles—will nobody mark?
No, none of the passers have noticed her yet,

The rich ones on feasting are busily set,
And such as are pious, you well may believe
Have no time to spare on the gay Sabbath eve.
So no one had noticed and no one has seen,
And now comes the night-fall and with it serene,
The Princess, the Sabbath, from Heaven descends,
And all the gay throng to the synagogue wends.
Within where they pray, all is cleanly and bright;
The cantor sings sweetly, they list with delight.
But why in a dream stands the tall chandelier,
As dim as the candles that gleam round a bier?
The candles belonged to the woman you know
Who died in the street but a short time ago.
The rich and the pious have brought them tonight
For mother and child they have set them alight.
The rich and the pious their duty have done,
Her tapers are lighted who died all alone.
The rich and the pious are nobly behaved:
A body—what matters? But souls must be saved!

O synagogue lights, be ye witnesses bold,
That mother and child died of hunger and cold
Where millions are squandered in idle display;
That men all unheeded, must starve by the way.
Then hold back your flame, blessed lights hold it fast!
The great day of judgment will come at last.
Before the white throne, where imposture is vain,
Ye lights for the soul, ye'll be lighted again!
And upward your flame there shall mount as on wings,
And damn the existing false order of things.

MORRIS ROSENFELD.

The Jewish May

MAY has come from out the showers,
    Sun and splendor in her train.
All the grasses and the flowers
    Waken up to life again.

Once again the leaves do show
And the meadow's blossoms blow,
Once again through hills and dales
Rise the songs of nightingales.

Wheresoe'er on field and hillside,
   With her paint-brush Spring is seen
In the valley, by the rillside,
   All the earth is decked with green.
Once again the sun' beguiles—
Moves the drowsy world to smiles.
See! the sun with mother-kiss
Wakes her child to joy and bliss.

Now each human feeling presses
   Flower like, upward to the sun,
Softly through the heart's recesses
   Steal sweet fancies one by one.
Golden dreams their wings outshaking
Now are making
Realms celestial
   All of azure
New life waking
   Bringing treasure
   Out of measure
   For the soul's delight and pleasure.
Who then, tell me, old and sad,
   Nears us with a heavy tread
On the sward in verdure clad,
Lonely is the strange newcomer;
   Wearily he walks and slow,
His sweet springtime and his summer
   Faded long and long ago.

Say, who is it yonder walks
   Past the hedgerows decked anew,
While a fearful spectre stalks
   By his side thy woodland through—
'Tis our ancient friend the Jew!

No sweet fancies hover round him,
Naught but terror and distress;
　Wounds unhealed
　Where lie revealed
Ghosts of former recollections,
Corpses, corpses, old affections,
Buried youth and happiness.

Bier and blossom bow to meet him
　In derision round his path;
Gloomily the hemlocks greet him
　And the crow screams out in wrath.
Strange the birds and strange the flowers,
　Strange the sunshine seems and dim,
Folk on earth and heavenly powers!—
　Lo, the May is strange to him.

Little flowers, it were meeter,
　If ye made not quite so bold;
Sweet ye are, but oh, far sweeter
　Knew he in the days of old.
Oranges by thousands blowing
　Filled his groves on either hand,
All the plants were God's own sowing
　In his far-off happy land.

Ask the cedars on the mountain,
　Ask them for they know him well!
Myrtles green by Sharon's fountain
　In whose shade he loved to dwell.
Ask the Mount of Olives beauteous,—
　Ev'ry tree by ev'ry stream,
One and all will answer duteous
　For the fair and ancient dream.

O'er the desert and the pleasance
　Gales of Eden softly blew,
And the Lord His loving Presence
　Evermore declared anew.

Angel children at their leisure,
　　Played in thousands round His tent
Countless thoughts of joy and pleasure
　　Go to His beloved sent.

There in bygone days and olden
From a wonderous harp and golden
Charmed he music spirit-haunting,
Holy, chaste and soul-enchanting;
Never with the ancient sweetness,
Never in its old completeness
Shall it sound; his dream is ended
On a willow bough suspended.

Gone that dream so fair and fleeting!
　　Yet behold; thou dreamst anew;
Hark a new May gives thee greeting
　　From afar.　Dost hear it Jew?
Weep no more, although with sorrows
　　Bow'd e'en to the grave; I see
Happier years and brighter morrows
　　Dawning, Israel, for thee!
Hear'st thou not the promise ring
Where, like doves on silvery wing,
Thronging cherubs sweetly sing,
New made songs of what shall be?

Hark! your olives shall be shaken
　　And your citrons and your limes
Filled with fragrance. · God shall waken,
　　Lead you as in olden times;
In the pastures by the river
　　Ye once more your flocks shall tend,
Ye shall live and live forever
　　Happy lives that know no end.
No more wandering, no more sadness;
　　Peace shall be your lot and still;
Hero hearts shall throb with gladness
　　'Neath Moriah's silent hill.

Nevermore of dread affliction
  Or oppression need ye tell,
Filled with joy and benediction
  In the old home ye shall dwell.
To the fatherland returning
  Following the homeward path,
Ye shall find the embers burning
  Still upon the ruined hearth!

MORRIS ROSENFELD.

"The Light in the Eyes" ✓

The light of the eyes rejoiceth the heart—Proverbs xv, 30.
  And mine heart walked after mine eyes—Job xxxi, 7.

AS down the age he shambles, gaunt and gray,
  With sorry gait, nor one to bid him stay,
We mark what man to brother man may do.
The shrivelled skin, the Ghetto-gotten hue,
Time's Tragedy writ large upon his face
The old, world-weary epic of his race;
—Yet see, he lifts his head and we surprise
Some strange swift light of laughter in his eyes.

On shoulders still the burden and the smart,
While Hope fights hard to live in Jewish heart,
Yet not for him the Bitterness and Gall
Though Grief stalk with him to the Wailing Wall,
Give him a crumb of joy, and, boyish-wise,
There leaps the light of laughter to his eyes.

The crying of wild voices in the night,
The curses and the struggle and the flight,
The Bloody Hand of Spain, the Cossack's breath,
The Sacrifice at York, the Dance to Death;
As fiend hath done so fiend will still devise,
—Through all persists brave laughter—light in eyes.

His mirth, sometimes, hath ghastly hollow ring,
Elijah-like its grim, ironic fling,
The hate-engendered jest betrays its heat
Nor can the pulse forever calmly beat;
But ling'ring 'neath the fire we may surmise
Warm light of loving laughter in his eyes.

Come to the pious purlieus of his home,
Here Love hath wed with Laughter, door to dome,
The troubles that beset the tiny brood
Respective, vanish 'fore that bantering mood.
What of travail, what of self-sacrifice
If Laughter-light live long in little eyes?

From Hebron's rill the music long hath ceased,
The Temple moulders in the solemn East,
Yet from Siloa's depth men still may drink
Two draughts Israel of old quaffed from its brink—
The heart-young love of life that never dies,
The limpid light of laughter in the eyes!

As down the age he shambles, grimed and gray,
With falt'ring gait, and few to bid him stay,
We mark what man hath done to man, the Jew,
The shrunken shape, the dark-begotten hue;
The burden of his snatch of sorry song,
"How long, O Lord,"—the plaint—"O Lord, how
    long?"
Yet wait!—nor woe nor wail shall e'er disguise
Some sure, soft light of laughter in his eyes.

OSCAR LOEB.

"Yes, He's a Jew"

"YES, he's a Jew"—and then you shook your head
    As though the worst of all had just been said;
As though that word expressed the height of crime,
The depth of shame, the lowest moral slime.

Yet, when you use that term reproach to cast
You show your ignorance of what the past
To student eyes reveals; how Moses led
In safety through the desert them that fled
From Egypt's bondage; how he planned the laws
That after ages hailed with loud applause
To guide the race in whom no power subdued
Their loyalty to God; aye, from that brood—
That storm-tossed people, oft enslaved in chains,
Have sprung a line of men, in arms and brains
The peers of any—white, or black, or brown;
Whose deeds in camp or court e'er won renown.
When Celt, or Gaul, and Saxon chased the deer,
And slew their prey with simple bow and spear,
And dwelt in holes in hillsides, like the lairs
Of prowling beasts, and naught of fame was theirs,
The Jew in Orient lands had read the stars,
Had loved with Venus, and had fought with Mars;
Had won with voice and sword the crown of fame,
In field and forum earned an honored name.
And when the Celt and Saxon ruled the world,
And the blue smoke from peaceful chimneys curled,
Beside the generation that was new
There walked the scion of the ancient Jew.
When foes harassed and threatened Britain Great
A Jew's hand 'twas that steered the ship of State,
And when the bugle sounded war's alarm
And myriad men from factory and farm
Took up the sword to keep this Nation whole,
The names of loyal Jews were on the roll.
"Yes; he's a Jew," O pigmy of a clan
What say you when 'tis said "Yes, he's a Man"?
Does not that statement cover all the test
That can of any mortal be expressed?
Hark you—you simple-headed bigot hear
A whispered caution in your dullard ear:
Do you know that Christ, of whom you sue
Forgiveness, was a persecuted Jew?

JOHN PAUL COSGRAVE.

583

The Jew to the Gentile

THE priest bent angry gaze upon the Jew,
   "What base ingratitude. Shame, shame that you
Who love the Father, should deny His Son.
Christ, Jesus, is Divine, with God is one.
His coming was foretold. . His glorious birth,
A miracle, His gentle life on earth.

An inspiration and His body bled
For us, that through His death our souls be led
To God. He died for us. Oh, stiff-necked race,
Forever shall the glory of God's face .
Be turned from you. Christ is the Lord. Take heed.
Confess Him and from all your sins be freed."

     .   .   .   .

And swift the Jew replied: " 'Christ is the Lord!'
You forced upon the world with rack and sword.
Your sins are legion. Oh, the awful moan
Of babes and mothers, maids and men and youth
Who died because they dared refuse the truth
You claimed. For these things how can you atone,
How ease your burdened conscience, how forget
The needless misery you caused?

     .   .   .   .

                                   "And yet
Although you maimed us with the scourge and flame
And tortured and reviled us 'in His name';
We reach our arms in friendliness to you
And plead for peace. We are God's children, too,
Have known the love and mercy in the Face
He turned to us, His priests and chosen race,
'Acknowledge Christ,' you say, 'and save your soul.
Confess our creed. This is the only toll
Required to enter heaven and from sin
Be freed.' 'Serve thou no other God but Me
And love your fellowmen.' This is our key
To life. We love the Father, He is One.'
We need no mediator. 'Christ, the Son,'

Was but God's child like all of us.   His kin,
The atheist, agnostic, Jew and Turk
And Christian.   And his equal, all who shirk
No sacrifice for fellowmen.   Some may
Not hold like creed with you.   For one will say
He worships Reason.   One doubts Christ is King.
One calls God, allah.   Does that matter?   Fling
Afar your doctrine.   Cast aside your fears,
Seek out the weeping ones and dry their tears.
The sick, the halt, the sinner and the blind,
Oh, pity them and love them and be kind.
For, after all, the helpful human deed
By Christian, Turk or Jew to one in need
Can bring more souls to God than all man's creed."

SARA MESSING STERN.

The Yellow Badge

HUNDREDS of years agone, my brothers,
   And yet not so long ago,
They bound on our arms a yellow shame
The seal of their scorn for us of the Name,
   And laughed at our deep-sunk woe.

Hundreds of years are past my brothers,
   And the world sweeps on to its goal;
We walk the streets with a master's tread
And the fear we lived in is long since dead,
   But the badge we wear in our soul.

Aye, the centuries long of cringing, brothers,
   Lest worse than the fear might fall,
Have broken the back of our freeman's pride
And the terror of those who were cursed, and died
   Lives on in us one and all.

What could they do of old, my brothers?
   They killed us like sheep and then?

We waited for death in an ecstasy,
As the unfelt pang that should set us free,
   And give us our life again.

Ah! We live easily now, my brothers,
   A snug, complacent crew
With wealth and culture at our command
And the friendly glance and the outstretched hand
   Of those who mocked us and slew.

And we walk warily now, my brothers,
   With an eye cast round to view
Lest the Past that is in us may lift its head,
Betray to the world we love and dread,
   "Behold! This is a Jew."

We must love with the times, we say, my brothers,
   And the times are broad and free,
We too belong to the Brotherhood
We shout, lest it be not understood:
   "Liberal Jews" are we.

Liberal minds, indeed, my brothers,
   Hating with petty hate
Each other, our past, and the names we bear,
Quarreling meanly to snatch our share
   Of the gold that we think makes great.

O God, the yellow badge, my brothers,
   Is graven on Israel's heart;
And we render our language, our symbols, our songs,
Our honor, our martyrs, aye, even our wrongs
   For a smile on our neighbour's part.

In our Father's name arise, my brothers,
   Let us tear the shame from our souls,
We shall rend ourselves and the wounds will bleed
But the hurt and blood are our right and meed;
   They will heal us and make us whole.

THE MODERN PERIOD

Let us turn our eyes to the East, my brothers,
    Where under the sunshine lies
The land that is ours in every sod,
The gift of the King, our fathers' God,
    To His children and allies.

Then will we live and work, my brothers,
    And cleanse away our stain,
The ignoble and base forgot
With the daily frettings of scheme and plot,
    We shall stand upright again.

Come, ere it be too late, my brothers,
    And our just doom strikes us down,
And naught remain but a pinch of dust,
A flash of gold and a sword a-rust,
    Of the people God called His Crown.

                RUTH SCHECHTER ALEXANDER.

A Tribute to the Jews

SINCE Terah's son from Chaldea went,
    On Manfred's plains to spread his tent,
The Jewish race in every age
Illumines the historic page.

In ages dim, long past and gone,
The Hebrew warrior victories won,
Ere Priam's son in battle stood,
Or Roman soldier shed his blood.

The ancient Seer, in dreamy trance,
The past had seen in mystic glance,
And in the flaming bush had heard
The voice of God—Almighty's word.
On Sinai's mount, 'mid thunders loud,
From cavern dark, and curtaining cloud

587

Mysterious voices to him came
In which he heard Jehovah's name;
And in the clefted rock he saw
The Spirit of Eternal Law.

The history of this people old,
By poet writ and prophet told,
Gives pictures grand of highest thought,
From realms of inspiration caught;
Whether writ with pen of living fire,
Or told in words of burning ire;
Whether an Isaiah sternly warns,
Or Jeremiah weeping mourns;

Whether Daniel warning gives to kings
Or the lone captive sadly sings
Beneath the willow trees upon
The streams that flow by Babylon;
Whether David sings a hymn of praise,
Or Job laments his darkened days;
They all, in lofty numbers tell
Of thoughts sublime, that only dwell
In minds inspired by living beams
That wake to life the poet's dreams.

Dark was the day, and sad the hour,
When Judea passed to Roman power!
Her old men sighed, her maidens wept,
When havoc o'er Jerusalem swept;
And smouldering ruins, stained with blood,
Told where her sacred Temple stood.

And darker still, in after time,
When scattered far, in every clime,
Against her wandering children rose
The persecuting hand of foes,
Inspired by blind, malignant hate,
Which centuries long did not abate,
Which still in this enlightened day,
Has not entirely passed away;

THE MODERN PERIOD

And, yet for all, though scattered wide
On every shore where rolls the tide,
Her children e'er preserved the name
That told from whence their fathers came;
And worshipped still the Great Unknown,
As to the ancient Patriarch shown.

The gloomy ages testify
To what they did in times gone by,
In learned science, and the part
They acted in the realms of art,
While wandering o'er the face of earth,
Far from the land that gave them birth.

The student of historic lore,
As slow he turns the pages o'er,
Upon its musty leaves will see
Semitic names of high degree;
In many a dim and blotted line,
The Maccabæan warriors shine,
And bright and lustrous, too, he sees
The name of famed Maimonides.

And modern times bear witness, too,
To what the sons of Israel do—
Disraeli fills a shining place
In the history of the Saxon race;
And Benjamin high honors won
In the Senate Halls of Washington;
Montefiore long will stand
An honored name in every land;
The Baron Hirsch long, long will be
Remembered by humanity;
While now, to-day, the Bernhardt's name
Is clothed in histrionic fame!

While, though the Jews no country claim,
And, as a nation, have no name,
They still retain, where'er they be,
Their ancient skill and energy;

And whereso'er on earth they live
Obedience to the laws they give,
And merit well an honored place
'Mong children of a foreign race.

The Christ, who gave the Christians name,
And a redeeming Saviour came
To the transgressing sons of earth,
Was of an humble Jewish birth;
And, furthermore, the sacred book,
From which their creeds the Christians took,
And on whose truths their faith they base,
Sprang from the ancient Jewish race.

Then honored be that glorious race,
Whose genius still on earth finds place,
While classic Greece has passed away,
And Rome has lost her ancient sway;
And shame on him who would withhold
The credit due this people old,
Whoe'er have played such active part
In science, literature and art.

RUFUS C. HOPKINS.

At Ellis Island

ACROSS the land their long lines pass;
    More souls come to us sun by sun—
Each ship a city as she rides,—
    Than manned the march of Washington.

From ancient States where burdens lie
    Extortionate upon the poor,
Men rise like flocks from leafless woods,
    Their flight a shadow at our door.

A shadow passing life by life,
    Into the morrow of our race;
What know we of the unseen minds?
    These hands are riches, we embrace.

590

What common thought so many moves!
Our laws with Liberty are brave;
Beneath them men will take content
A wage, a lodging, and a grave.

Strange to each other as to us,
The races of the world are ours;
No sleepless frontiers here impede
A secret ballot's sacred powers.

Ye patient aliens! Sifting in
Where trades a fateful welcome burn
Bequeath your children what you find—
A land to which all peoples turn.

MARGARET CHANLER ALDRICH.

Ellis Island

THREE thousand miles of Atlantic seas and a throb
that cuts the top,
The rushed four-funneled fleeting ship, that, without
curb or stop,
Hurls on, while Earth ten times rolls round till, under
morning stars,
She breasts the mist of a continent and slows at the
groaning bars!

And lo, three-layered Humanity in her steerage bunks
asleep,
Rising at dawn and crowding aft, and in the infinite
sweep
Of gray—the sea, the sky,—see dim, dream greatened
and gigantic,
America, America, uprisen from the Atlantic!

Swift on dead centuries of faces a sun flames, ere the
Sun
Blows the blue bubble of the heavens vast—yea, flam-
ing one by one,

591

These faces are a psalm to God—a morning hymn—the
    sea,
The sky, the land are a living Temple with a thousand
    Souls set free.

Swing them the uplifted, crowded people in transport
    to our Isle—
Morning with strong sun and sweet gales and the Bay's
    yeasty mile,
Like hands holds forth a glorious City—her smoke's
    sky-swimming shoals,
Her flight of cliffs, her range of peaks all honey-
    combed with Souls!

O, come through the Ellis Island Gates—O rush the
    sweet routine,
Sweep to new birth on a planet new—for lo, at the
    wire screen
Of the waiting cage, the American clutch—yea, as
    starved people stare,
Watching your alien faces pass to see if one be there.

Yonder old trembling man three hours has stood!
    Through the shuffling crowd
A pink-shawled withered old woman shambles over
    her baggage bowed;
He pales; he cries her name; she bursts into his arms;
    the years
Melt back into the glory of youth, still seen through
    blinding tears.

Old Woman—strong girls, swart men, soft babes—
    you hordes across seas hurled,
O pioneers, as one dares Death, you dare a great new
    World!
You bring strong blood, and Faith, and Love, stout
    hearts and homely traits—
What shall our country do with you—deal out what
    Dooms, what Fates?

Shall we judge by your alien ways, and lose the gifts
  that are all our own?
Or shall we rise to grander heights than Earth has
  ever known?
Yea, shall we seize on you with love, far-building on
  our trust?
Are we great enough to swing to God what Europe
  trailed in dust?

O our America, O Mother, great have you been, our
  hearts
Are yours, our faith and love are yours—great are
  your trades and arts,
Your Men—fail not! Earth looks to you, her vast
  Experiment Station,
To test if souls may be borne to God in the arms of a
  Mother-Nation!

Shun not the Mission! Fearless, fearless mother,
  Earth's mightiest race—
Yea, seize your flashing stars and stripes and stamp
  across the face
That word, the strongest in our tongue, that sums the
  skies deep-starred,
The grain of sand, the Earth, the Soul, our country—
  the word "God!"

JAMES OPPENHEIM.

At the Gate

THEY drive me out of my country,
  They thrust me out of my land,
They call me an alien—I
  Who had fought in the foreign band.

On the ice of the Amur River,
  I and the starving few,
And my country paid me with curses
  And called me an alien Jew.

593

They worship the Jew in the churches,
  They murder the Jew in the street;
He taught them to love and to pity,
  His kindred, they murder and beat.

His name they honor and glory,
  His teachings they rarely do;
He cometh! · The Russian will mock Him—
  He, too, was an alien Jew.

How long! Oh, how long! is the wailing
  Till Russia is judged at Thy bar—
With Egypt and Spain and with Asshur
  Till Russia shall stand where they are?

See, the finger of God is writing,
  Blasting the murdering crew;
See, the Pole and the Finn and the Cossack
  And the God of the alien Jew.

They drive me out of my country,
  To a foreign land I go;
They trained me to be a soldier,
  They teach me to be their foe.

Their training will go with their teaching—
  This tongue of mine speaks true;
When the foes are crowding upon her
  They'll be led by the alien Jew.

NATHAN F. SPIELVOGEL.

The Magic Words

THE scene of conflict was a level plain
  That lay among the stretching hills of Spain,
And on the sand that glistened in the sun,
Ten thousand lay, whose hours of life had run.

'Till noonday's heat, from earliest sign of dawn,
The battling forces were in combat drawn,
And ere the sun sank in the silent West,
A host of men had found eternal rest.

Behind the battle-field, beneath a tent,
A soldier lay, on death his vision bent,
A kindly Priest, that spoke of God, was near,
A Doctor, he was there, but full of fear.

Each was a Jew, had each a Hebrew's zeal,
But neither dared his name or race reveal.
But death had robbed them of their mortal fears,
Here in his shadow they could spend their tears.

"Shemang Yisrael," the dying soldier breathed,
His face, in death, with smiles all wreathed.
"Adonai Elohenoo," said piously the man of God;
The Doctor murmured, "Adonai Echod."

The Priest reached out, and grasped the Doctor's hand,
These magic words had forged a mighty band,
And then upon the Doctor's bosom lay his head,
And wept.   The soldier now, alas! was dead.

MELVIN G. WINSTOCK.

Shema Yisrael Adonay-Elohainu
Adonay-Echod

"SHEMA YISRAEL," is the lesson we learn
In the earliest days of our youth.
"Adonay Elohainu," the Lord is our God,
How precious and blessed this truth!
"It never can fail;
Shema Yisrael!"

"Adonay Elohainu," this is our God
And ours forever shall be.
Through life he will bless us, in death be our guide
Till "Shalom"—"Peace eternal"—we see.
Through Him we prevail;
"Shema Yisrael!"

"Shema Yisrael," 'tis our mission alone,
"Adonay Echod" to proclaim
The Lord everlasting shall reign o'er the earth
And "One" be forever His name.
The future we hail;
"Shema Yisrael!"

IBBIE McCOLM WILSON.

Be Thou a Jew

BE thou a Jew! Let oppressors scoff
And jeer who will. But be thou steadfast,
And thy firm faith shall be to thee a shield,
Impenetrable and invincible,
Against thine enemies.
Be thou a Jew!
Thy people are the Chosen Ones, for God
Will ever champion the cause of Right;
And though storms of adversity compel
Thy faith to waver, hold thy grasp—
For brighter, better days are yet to come.

SAMUEL E. LOVEMAN.

The Chosen

CHOSEN of old, the guardians of the Law
(God's word to mortals, cleaving right from
wrong);
Destined to serve the world; its priestly race
Kept for that service strong.

596

THE MODERN PERIOD

Guarded of God through war and wilderness;
   Holding the truth no other people saw;
First of the nations to declare Him One;
   First to revere His Law!

Down from the ages of triumphant rule,
   Through the lost glory of a line of kings,
Bruised and lamenting in their brokenness—
   God heard their murmurings.

Scoffed at, they held their peace and overcame,
   Crowded by hate into the Ghetto's pale,
Sounded to Heaven their deathless harmony,
   Born of a people's wail.

Wide through the world that grief-born music rang,
   Hailed with a reverence to themselves denied;
Caged in the wall by tyrants built, they sang,
   Flinging their genius wide.

Out of the prisons of the Middle Age,
   Out of the reeking slums, they gave the light;
Thinkers of lofty thought, ordained of God,
   Prophets to point the right.

By their unfetterable dreams of youth,
   Joined to the genius that their race imbues,
Chains have been sundered till to-day remain
   Few barriers round the Jews.

History emblazons them in bondage great,
   Splendid in art, philosophy and song,
Now in awed wonder does the world await
   The freedom of the strong.

Elizabeth McMurtrie Dinwiddie.

God's Chosen People

IN the sadness of your eyes
  I see the grief of ages;
    Your voices throb
    With the sob
Of hearts forever still.
Yet yours the soul of sages—
    You are alive,
    Tho' nations strive
  Your cup of pain to fill:

Yet you call yourselves God's Chosen People,
  Yet you humbly bow to God's Great Will.

In your tills you hoard your gold,
In dread of gloomy morrow;
    In fear of fire,
    Tyrant's ire,
And sword of those who spill
Your blood, and bring you sorrow!
    A hunted race,
    Fell fate you face, .
When foes are out to kill:

Yet you call yourselves God's Chosen People,
  Yet you humbly bow to God's Great Will.

On this soil of Man's free rights,
I would not have your riches!
    Your pomp and pride,
    None can bide.
Your wives in flounce and frill,.
Their Eastern charm bewitches . . .
    And yet my breast,
    Remains at rest,
Nor does with envy thrill:

But oh! teach me your faith, you strange people,
  Teach me to humbly bow to God's Great Will.

Adapted by Joel Blau.

Our Password

NO hate can stifle our religion's birth,
　　This gift eternal, like the stars that shine
Point heavenwards, yet light each clod of earth,
　　Our footsteps press, when care and sorrow line
The groping paths of life; our souls shall knead
　　The visions of the past, the day's desire,
And all that beautifies our simple creed
　　In one eternal, and ethereal fire!
The flame that vivifies the Jewish race,
　　That consecrates the joys of common life,
Which time's corrosive touch can ne'er efface,
　　The boon in toil, the sweetness in the strife,
The truth that animates like Heaven's sun,
　　Our prayer in life and death that God is One.

　　　　　　　　　　　ISIDORE G. ASCHER.

Only a Jew

NOBODY cares, for he's only a Jew,
　　Crush him with vengeance in sight of the cross!
All of his allies are feeble and few,
　　Vice is his jewel and virtue his dross.

Only a Jew, like the prophets of yore,
　　Bearing with patience his burdens and wrongs;
Leader of liberty, maker of law,
　　Singing with David the sweetest of songs.

Only a Jew, with his epics and art,
　　Charming the ages with music divine;
Ravage his fireside and shiver his heart,
　　'Till he partakes of the bread and the wine.

Only a Jew—like the loved Nazarene,
　　Full of forgiveness and pity for all;
Giving them alms with a hand that's unseen,
　　Lifting the weak when they totter and fall.

599

Only a Jew in the reign of thought,
  Winning his way in the ranks of the great;
Marvels of beauty his genius has wrought,
  Cannot be blighted by passion or hate.

DAVID BANKS SICKLES.

"Jew"

SILENT and wise and changeless,
  Stamped with the Orient still;
In many a country nameless—
  In every land a Will.

Master of two things is he,
  Self, and the Power of Gold.
He thinks—the World is busy;
  They bargain—he has sold!

Lord of the Marts of Nations
  Where the World's wide commerce plies—
Master of infinite Patience,
  Slandered by infinite Lies!

Towering, fair-haired Norseman,
  Tartar at Novgorod,
Black-eyed Arab horseman
  Zulu chief unshod—

All borrow for War or trading
  And promise with oaths not new;
All turn, with the danger fading,
  And sneer at the lender—"Jew!"

GEORGE VAUX BACON.

Recognition

SO—you have "recognized" the Jew?
  Then—just perchance—you may have noticed, too,
And "recognized" the hills that pierce the sky
And hold their heads in pure, star-studded blue,
Whose heights command your plains which dully lie,
And dare not dream. You "recognized," perhaps,
The dark, thick shade of forests, æons old;
The mellow splendor of the moon that wraps
The night in glory, and the ruddy gold
That lies deep hidden in the pregnant earth
Perhaps you "recognize." The liquid mirth
And tender passion of a mountain stream
You "recognize"; the potence of a dream
May still be "recognized"—who knows?—by you,
Since, wisely, now you "recognize" the Jew.

MIRIAM TEICHNER.

Is It True?

SAID the child of the bright yellow hair
  To the child of the coal black curls;
"I do not think it is fair
  For we little Christian girls
To play with the girls like you;
  For our Sunday-school teacher—See?
Says your father is only a Jew;

  An' the Jews nailed Christ on the tree."
The great black eyes filled with tears
  As the child with the dark, dark hair
Said: "But that was hundreds of years
  Ago; an' I don't think it is fair
To blame us girls with the pain
  That was given to Jesus by men
That we didn't know. And it's vain—
  So my mamma says, to preten'
That any one church is the best.

601

We're as nicely behaved as you,
An' our dollies as prettily dressed;
 An' my mamma always says true."

So they quarreled and parted with eyes
 Flashing anger and tears. In the heart
Of the yellow-haired child would rise
 Unbidden—a pain like a dart.

That night she knelt by her bed—
 As she did every night—to pray,
She threw back her wee bright head
 And her eyes looked up and away—
Oh far, far away at the sky
 Through the unshaded window glass;
And she said: "Dear Lord, if I die
 In my sleep may my spirit pass
To you like an angel; and wear
 A little gold crown of my own;
And—my dear doll—I want her there,
 'Cause I hate to be there all alone."

Then she paused a little and said:
 "Lord—if Elsie was only like me,
A Christian, too, when she's dead
 I think I would like to see
Her also; but she cannot go
 'Cause her fore-fathers—teacher said—
Were nothing but Jews and so
 That settles it." Then on the bed
The bright little one sank to sleep,
 But a wee small voice in her breast
Seemed ever to rouse her and keep
 Her feverish pulses from rest.

She dreamed that out of the skies
 A great, white cross rose to view;
And Jesus looked at her with eyes
 Like Elsie's—and said: "I'm a Jew."

MARIE HARROLD GARRISON.

In the Hour of Need

D'YE see that shop at the corner, with the three balls
    over the door?
A pawnshop? Yes, it is, my lad—just that, and noth-
    ing more,
Nothing remarkable in that? You see 'em every day?
No doubt you do. But wait a bit, and let me say
    my say.

Four months ago my little wife was ill as she could
    be;
I thought I should have lost her, but you see 'she is
    still with me:
I owe her life to him, my lad! To who d'ye ask?—
    to who?
To the old man at that popshop there!—and mark
    me, he's a Jew!

That staggers you, I thought it would. But bear
    with me a bit;
It won't take long to let you have the sense and soul
    of it;
Fanny was ill, and times were bad, and I'd no work
    to do;
Fanny got worse, and then I took to visiting the Jew.

Fanny got worse, and worse, and worse,—my God;
    she was so ill;
And the times that were so tight before, my lad, got
    tighter still;
I pawned my things—such as they were—and I
    pawned my wife's things too,
Till nothing was left to pawn—and still I had no
    work to do!

I was starving—downright starving!—and Fanny was
    almost dead,
One night as I sat, with tight-clasped hands, beside
    my poor girl's bed;

I closed my eyes in a dreamy way—didn't sleep you
    understand;—
When I opened 'em I saw the Jew, with a basket in
    his hand!

He was only a hook-nosed, crook-back Jew, but he
    seemed an angel then,
For he brought new life to my dying wife, and made
    her strong again!
If Heaven is full when he dies, I know they'll make
    room for the Jew! . . .
There! that's the short of it, my lad,—and every word
    is true!

LETO.

(In the Graphic.)

The Little Jew

(A True Story)

WE were at school together,
  The little Jew and I,
  He had black eyes, the biggest nose,
  The very smallest fist for blows,
Yet nothing made him cry.

We mocked him often and often,
Called him all names we knew,—
  "Young Lazarus," "Father Abraham,"
  "Moses,"—for he was meek as a lamb,
The gentle little Jew.

But not a word he answered;
Sat in his corner still,
  And worked his sums, and counted his task;
  Would never any favor ask,
Did us nor good nor ill.

604

Though sometimes he would lift up
Those great dark Eastern eyes,
   Appealing, when we wronged him much,
   For pity? No! but full of such
A questioning surprise.

Just like a beast of the forest
Caught in the garden's bound,—
   Hemmed in by cruel creatures tame
   That seem akin, almost the same,
Yet how unlike are found!

He did his boyish duty
In play-ground as in school;
   A little put upon, and meek,
   Though no one ever called him "sneak"
Or "coward," still less "fool."

But yet I never knew him,—
Not rightly, I may say,—
   Till one day, sauntering round our square,
   I saw the little Jew boy there,
Slow lingering after play.

He looked so tired and hungry,
So dull and weary both,
   "Hollo!" cried I, "you ate no lunch.
   Come, here's an apple; have a munch!
Hey, take it! don't be loath."

He gazed upon the apple,
So large and round and red,
   Then glanced up towards the western sky,
   The sun was setting gloriously,—
But not a word he said.

He gazed upon the apple,
Eager as Mother Eve;
   Half held his hand out, drew it back;
   Dim drew his eyes, so big and black;
His breast began to heave.

"I am so very hungry!
And yet—No, thank you. No.
  "Good-by." "You little dolt," said I,
  "Just take your apple. There, don't cry!
Home with you! Off you go!"

But still the poor lad lingered,
And pointed to the sky;
  "The sunset is not very late;
  I'm not so hungry—I can wait.
Thank you. Good-by,—good-by!"

And then I caught and held him
Against the palisade;
  Pinched him and pommelled him right well,
  And forced him all the truth to tell,
Exactly as I bade.

It was their solemn fast-day,
When every honest Jew
  From sunset unto sunset kept
  The fast. I mocked; he only wept:
"What father does, I do."

I taunted him and jeered him,—
The more brute I, I feel.
  I held the apple to his nose;
  He gave me neither words nor blows,—
Firm, silent, true as steel.

I threw the apple at him;
He stood one minute there,
  Then, swift as hunted deer at bay,
  He left the apple where it lay,
And vanished round the square.

I went and told my father,—
A minister, you see;
  I thought that he would laugh outright,
  At the poor silly Israelite;
But very grave looked he.

Then said, "My bold young Christian,
Of Christian parents born,
   Would God that you may ever be
   As faithful unto Him—and me—
As he you hold in scorn!"

I felt my face burn hotly,
My stupid laughter ceased;
   For father·is a right good man,
   And still I please him all' I can,
As parent and as priest.

Next day, when school was over,
I put my nonsense by;
   Begged the lad's pardon, stopped all strife,
   And—well, we have been friends for life,
The little Jew and I.

DINAH MARIA MULOCK CRAIK.

Only a Jew

IN the land of Brittany, and long ago,
   Lived one of those
Despised and desolate, whose records show
     Insults and blows,
Their old inheritance of wrong, who were
Free once as the eyelids of the morn; nor care
     Knew, nor annoy,
     In that city of joy.
Heaven-chosen child, whom none to harm might dare;

Lived one who did as if his God stood near·
     Watching his deed,
Slow to give answer, ever swift to hear;
     Whose brain would breed,
Walking alone or watching through the night,
No idle thought; but he with ill would fight
     And day by day
     Would wax alway
Wiser and better and nearer to the light.

And in this land a mother lost her child,
        And charged the Jew
With crucifying him, who calmly smiled
        Denial. "You
Have slain," quoth she, "to keep your Passover
My son with sorceries." He answered her,
        "Your wit must fail;
        An idle tale
Is this; what proof thereof can you prefer?"

But she went from him raging. Then he fled
        Out of that land;
And those there set a price on his gray head,
        Who with skilled hand
Of craft had fed one daughter fair as day,
Now destitute. Soon gold before her lay
        The bait of shame;
        But she, aflame
With honor, flung such happiness away.

And writing, told her father, who came back
        By night, and bade
Her claim his life's reward. "Rather the rack
        Rend me," she said;
"And shall I give him death who life gave me?
Sell him and feed on him? Far sooner we
        Both died! Somewhere
        Beyond earth's care
Hereafter we shall meet it well may be

Somewhere hereafter." "Nay, you still shall live,"
        He murmured; then,
Went out into the market, crying, "Give
        This price, ye men,
For me to her, my daughter." But these laid
False hands on both, nor other duty paid
        Than death; for they,
        Gold hair and gray,
Were slain hard by in the holy minster's shade.

After, in no long time, the little child
                    Returned, a stray
Fresh from the sea: it by a ship beguiled,
                    In the hold at play,
Had sailed unseen till the land a small speck grew,
But still the people prayed in the porch, in view
                    Of the blood-splashed stone,
                    And made no moan;
" 'Twas only a Jew," the folk said, "only a Jew!"

ANONYMOUS.

Holy Cross Day

ON WHICH THE JEWS WERE FORCED TO ATTEND AN ANNUAL CHRISTIAN SERMON IN ROME

("Now was come about Holy-Cross Day, and now must my lord preach his first sermon to the Jews; as it was of old cared for in the merciful bowels of the Church, that, so to speak, a crumb at least from her conspicuous table here in Rome should be, though but once yearly, cast to the famishing dogs, under-trampled and bespitten upon beneath the feet of the guests. And a moving sight in truth, this, of so many of the besotted blind restif and ready-to-perish Hebrews! Now maternally brought—nay, (for He saith, 'Compel them to come in') haled, as it were, by the head and hair, and against their obstinate hearts, to partake of the heavenly grace. What awakening, what striving with tears, what working of a yeasty conscience! Nor was my lord wanting to himself on so apt an occasion; witness the abundance of conversions which did incontinently reward him: though not to my lord be altogether the glory."—Diary by the Bishop's Secretary, 1600.)

What the Jews really said, on thus being driven to church, was rather to this effect:—

609

I

FEE, faw, fum! bubble and squeak!
   Blessedest Thursday's the fat of the week.
Rumble and tumble, sleek and rough,
Stinking and savory, smug and gruff,
Take the church-road, for the bell's due chime
Give us the summons—'t is sermon-time!

II

Bob, here's Barnabas! Job, that's you?
Up stumps Solomon—bustling too?
Shame, man! greedy beyond your years
To handsel the bishop's shaving-shears?
Fair play's a jewel! Leave friends in the lurch?
Stand on a line ere you start for the church!

III

Higgledy piggledy, packed we lie,
Rats in a hamper, swine in a sty,
Wasps in a bottle, frogs in a sieve,
Worms in a carcass, fleas in a sleeve,
Hist! square shoulders, settle your thumbs
And buzz for the bishop—here he comes.

IV

Bow, wow, wow—a bone for the dog!
I liken his Grace to an acorned hog.
What, a boy at his side, with a bloom of a lass,
To help and handle my lord's hour-glass!
Didst ever behold so lithe a chine?
His cheek hath laps like a fresh-singed swine.

V

Aaron's asleep—shove hip to haunch,
Or somebody deal him a dig in the paunch!
Look at the purse with the tassel and knob,
And the gown with the angel and thingumbob!
What's he at, quotha? reading his text!
Now you've his curtsey—and what comes next?

610

VI

See to our converts—you doomed black dozen—
No stealing away—nor cog nor cozen!
You five, that were thieves, deserve it fairly;
You seven, that were beggars, will live less sparely;
You took your turn and dipped in the hat,
Got fortune—and fortune gets you, mind that!

VII

Give your first groan—compunction's at work;
And soft! from a Jew you mount to a Turk,
Lo, Micah,—the selfsame beard on chin
He was four times already converted in!
Here's a knife, clip quick—it's a sign of grace—
Or he ruins us all with his hanging face.

VIII

Whom now is the bishop a-leering at?
I know a point where his text falls pat.
I'll tell him to-morrow, a word just now
Went to my heart and made me vow
I meddle no more with the worst of trades—
Let somebody else pay his serenades!

IX

Groan altogether now, whee-hee-hee!
It's a-work, it's a-work, ah, woe is me!
It began, when a herd of us, picked and placed,
Were spurred thro' the Corso, stripped to the waist;
Jew brutes, with sweat and blood well spent
To usher in worthily Christian Lent.

X

It grew, when the hangman entered our bounds,
Yelled, pricked us out to his church like hounds;
It got to a pitch, when the hand indeed
Which gutted my purse, would throttle my creed:
And it overflows, when, to even the odd,
Men I helped to their sins help me to their God.

XI

But now, while the scapegoats leave our flock
And the rest sit silent and count the clock,
Since forced to muse the appointed time
On these precious facts and truths sublime,—
Let us fitly employ it, under our breath,
In saying Ben Ezra's Song of Death.

XII

For Rabbi Ben Ezra, the night he died,
Called sons and sons' sons to his side,
And spoke, "This world has been harsh and strange;
Something is wrong: there needeth a change.
But what, or where? at the last or first?
In one point only we sin, at worst.

XIII

"The Lord will have mercy on Jacob yet,
And again in his border see Israel set.
When Judah beholds Jerusalem,
The stranger-seed shall be joined to them:
To Jacob's House shall the Gentiles cleave.
So the Prophet saith and his sons believe.

XIV

"Ay, the children of the chosen race
Shall carry and bring them to their place:
In the land of the Lord shall lead the same,
Bondsmen and handmaids. Who shall blame,
When the slaves enslave, the oppressed ones o'er
The oppressor triumph for evermore?

XV

"God spoke, and gave us the word to keep:
Bade never fold the hands nor sleep
'Mid a faithless world,—at watch and ward,
Till Christ at the end relieve our guard.
By his servant Moses the watch was set:
Tho' near upon cock-crow, we keep it yet.

XVI

"Thou! if thou wast he, who at mid-watch came,
By the starlight, naming a dubious name!
And if, too heavy with sleep—too rash
With fear—O thou, if that martyr-gash
Fell on thee coming to take thine own,
And we gave the Cross, when we owed the Throne—

XVII

"Thou art the Judge. We are bruised thus.
But, the Judgment over, join sides with us!
Thine, too, is the cause! and not more thine
Than ours, is the work of these dogs and swine,
Whose life laughs through and spits at their creed!
Who maintain thee in word, and defy thee in deed!

XVIII

"We withstood Christ then? Be mindful how
At least we withstand Barabbas now!
Was our outrage sore? But the worst we spared,
To have called these—Christians, had we dared!
Let defiance to them pay mistrust of thee,
And Rome make amends for Calvary!

XIX

"By the torture, prolonged from age to age,
By the infamy, Israel's heritage,
By the Ghetto's plague, by the garb's disgrace,
By the badge of shame, by the felon's place,
By the branding-tool, the bloody whip,
And the summons to Christian fellowship,—

XX

"We boast our proof that at least the Jew
Would wrest Christ's name from the Devil's crew.
Thy face took never so deep a shade
But we fought them in it, God our aid!

A trophy to bear, as we march, thy band,
South, East, and on to the Pleasant Land!"

ROBERT BROWNING.

(Pope Gregory XVI abolished this bad business of
the Sermon.—R. B.)

The Guardian of the Red Disk

(Spoken by a citizen of Malta—1300)

A CURIOUS title held in high repute,
  One among many honors, thickly strewn
On my Lord Bishop's head, his grace of Malta.
Nobly he bears them all,—with tact, skill, zeal,
Fulfils each special office, vast or slight,
Nor slurs the least minutia,—therewithal
Wears such a stately aspect of command,
Broad-cheeked, broad-chested, reverend, sanctified,
Haloed with white about the tonsure's rim,
With dropped lids o'er the piercing Spanish eyes
(Lynx-keen, I warrant, to spy out heresy);
Tall, massive form, o'ertowering all in presence,
Or ere they kneel to kiss the large white hand.
His looks sustain his deeds,—the perfect prelate,
Whose void chair shall be taken, but not filled.

You know not, who are foreign to the isle,
Haply, what this Red Disk may be, he guards.
'Tis the bright blotch, big as the Royal seal,
Branded beneath the beard of every Jew.
These vermin so infest the isle, so slide
Into all byways, highways that may lead
Direct or roundabout to wealth or power,
Some plain, plump mark was needed, to protect
From degrading contact Christian folk.

The evil had grown monstrous: certain Jews
Wore such a haughty air, had so refined,
With super-subtile arts, strict, monkish lives,
And studious habit, the coarse Hebrew type,

614

One might have elbowed in the public mart
Iscariot,—nor suspected one's soul-peril.
Christ's blood! it sets my flesh a-creep to think!
We may breathe freely now, not fearing taint,
Praised be our good Lord Bishop! He keeps count
Of every Jew, and prints on cheek or chin
The scarlet stamp of separateness, of shame.

No beard, blue-black, grizzled or Judas-colored,
May hide that damning little wafer-flame.
· When one appears therewith, the urchins know
Good sport's at hand; they fling their stones and mud,
Sure of their game. But most the wisdom shows
Upon the unbelievers' selves; they learn
Their proper rank; crouch, cringe, and hide,—lay by
Their insolence of self-esteem; no more
Flaunt forth in rich attire, but in dull weeds,
Slovenly donned, would slink past unobserved;
Bow servile necks and crook obsequious knees,
Chin sunk in hollow chest, eyes fixed on earth
Or blinking sidewise, but to apprehend
Whether or not the hated spot be spied.
I warrant my Lord Bishop has full hands,
Guarding the Red Disk—lest one rogue escape!

EMMA LAZARUS.

Rabbi Ben Ezra

GROW old along with me!
   The best is yet to be,
   The last of life, for which the first was made:
Our times are in His hand
Who saith: "A whole I planned,
   Youth shows but half; trust God: see all, nor be
   afraid!"

*   *   *   *   *   *   *   *

Look not thou down but up!
To uses of a cup,
   The festal board, lamp's flash and trumpet's peal,

The new wine's foaming flow,
The Master's lips aglow!
  Thou, heaven's consummate cup, what needst thou
    with earth's wheel?

But I need, now as then,
Thee, God, who mouldest men;
  And since, not even while the whirl was worst,
Did I—to the wheel of life
With shapes and colors rife,
  . Bound dizzily—mistake my end, to slake Thy thirst.

So, take and use Thy work:
Amend what flaws may lurk,
  What strain o' the stuff, what warpings past the
    aim!
My times be in Thy hand!
Perfect the cup as planned!
  Let age approve of youth, and death complete the
    same!   ROBERT BROWNING.

The Angel

I DREAMT I saw an angel in the sky,
Her face was calm and fair up there on high;
She smiled at me—a strange and lovely smile
That had in it no thought of earthly guile.
She looked so fair, so strange and wondrous pure,
That 'twas an angel, I was passing sure;
She spoke—her voice was music in the air;
So sweet it was, it matched her person fair.
She asked me, "Is there aught that I can do?"
I humbly answered, "Make me fair as you."
She smiled again, that strange unearthly smile,
That made all mundane things seem crude and vile—
"Thou art not ready yet," she seemed to say
And with a sigh, she floated far away.
                 DOROTHY S. SILVERMAN.

616

A Legend

TO the home of the rabbi a Lord in his splendor,
  Comes riding at dead of night;
His glittering helmet with feathers is garnished,
  With stains his breast is bedight.

In a room where the flame of a lamplet is glowing,
  So wan and so lonely and dim;
The Lord of the Manor in quest of his learning,
  Attentively listens to him.

And yet ere the church bells at dawn o' the morning
  Their summons to prayer intone,
The Lord of the Manor rides forth from the Ghetto;
  To no one his secret is known.

By daylight the sage in his cloistered seclusion
  Sees never the Lord of the night;
But the dreams and the deeds of the noble disciple,
  Are fruit of the tree of his might.

And so through the squalor and dirt of the Ghetto,
  The Lord with his retinue rides,
And gazes with pensive and yearning attention,
  At the home where his teacher abides.

JEHOASH.
(Translated by Elias Lieberman.)

The Rabbi's Song

IF thought ever reach to Heaven,
  On Heaven let it dwell.
For fear that Thought be given
  Like Power to reach to Hell;
For fear that Desolation
  And darkness on thy mind
Perplex the habitation
  Which thou hast left behind.

617

Our lives, our tears as water
    Are poured upon the ground;
God giveth no man quarter,
    Yet God a means hath found,
Tho' faith and hope have vanished
    And even love grows dim,
A means whereby his banished
    Be not expelled from Him.

RUDYARD KIPLING.

A Sonnet

To the Beloved Memory of Robert Browning

SERENE, translucent as yon Maytime star
    In sanctuary of its bliss superb,
Accept, O Bard! a sprig of Israel's herb,
In bitterness no less familiar
To you, than is the knell of surging bar,
    When night-winds raving, dreamer's peace perturb,
    With blood and fire, and hell-groans from the curb,
Shrined in the tales you wrote in days afar,
Brave sharer in our nether fates, you bore
    Israel's death-crown, voiced his feeble rights,
Stood weeping by his side, and mourning wore,
    In those black days, whose memory still frights,
Still casts its spectral hue athwart the brain,
And feeds the heart with hopeless endless pain.

M. L. R. BRESLAR.

The Hebrew Mind

GIFTS, as romantic as the cruse of oil,
    Found in the days of mad Antiochus,
    Were brewed by Hadrian from henbane; spruce
For Israel's quaffing; potions, framed to foil
A nation's growth, they met with swift recoil!

Tempt never genius, with devil's juice!
  Vain arts, O Hadrian, and vain the ruse,—
When balked by birds, who garnered all the spoil.
For Hadrian, as for Vespasian,
  History sheds a tear of wonder blind;
    Mere vessels those, Balaam's sent to bless,
They scourged with fire and sword, till the dread ban
  Flowered, like Aaron's rod of loveliness,
And forged that wondrous thing, the Hebrew mind.

M. L. R. Breslar.

Who Gives in Love

NAUGHT is there in life worth living,
  Save it flavored be by love;
Naught is there in life worth giving,
  Save it sanctioned be above.
Who in evil mood bestoweth,
In his heart the canker groweth;
He who gives in truth and love
Shall a thousand pleasures prove.

Isidor Wise.

An Invocation

OH, harp of Judah! wake again!
  Can no one deftly touch thy strings
To scatter far the sacred strain
  Which from divinest patience springs!
Have all the strife-sown troublous years
  No joys for happy song to cast?
Can love distil no hope from tears,
  Or steal no beauty from the past?

Has music lost its spell and power
  To summon hopes that only rest?
Endowed with truths, our lasting dower,
  That mock the ages' wear and test;

619

Can no heart-stirring melody
  Imbued with light and touched with fire,
Flow from a nation proud and free
  Whose past must urge them to aspire?

Reproach, an ignominious sea,
  Can follow in our wake no more;
The poisoned waves of calumny
  Are washed away from Freedom's shore.
The justice of a nobler age
  Has reached and raised our scattered race;
Our history shows a fairer page,
  Our future wears a brighter face.

The rooted weeds of narrow thought
  Which closely cling, or idly spread,
Which ignorance has sown and wrought,
  Are crushed and buried with the dead.
A loftier sense of heavenly things,
  A wider view of human life
Have fashioned tolerance: which brings
  Its own repose to cast off strife.

Beyond man's vain imaginings,
  Is Israel's faith that never dies,
The boon of slaves—the pride of Kings—
  Its meanings make the nations wise,
And thro' the mists of ages gone,
  Its God-stamped visions still appear
As in the Bible's earliest dawn,
  Supremely true, divinely clear!

And who asserts that Judah's claim
  To any chosen land is o'er?
When all the earth contains her fame
  That spreads and widens evermore;
The truths that sanctify her creed
  Shall scatter hopes where'er they shine,
Until all men shall feel the need
  Of her own unity divine.

So wake, my harp, my fingers press
   Thy rust-worn strings, while fancy longs
To dower with melodiousness,
   The burden of unuttered songs;
My faltering touch may reach in vain
   The music of my sacred themes,
Still Truth may charm the feeble strain
   And lend its sweetness to my dreams!

ISIDORE G. ASCHER.

Adas Israel

O ISRAEL! in the morn's returning light,
   Thy temple stands, all crowned with splendor bright,
And there, high Salem's courts again shall tell
Jehovah's praise, and faith of Israel.

The watchman on thy long benighted walls
Hath marked the night's departing gloom, and calls;
Up, Israel! now thy darkness flies away,
And light is breaking into glorious day.

The dawn of freedom on a darkened earth,
Thy faith awakens to a brighter birth.
Thy promised king—awaited long in vain,
Now comes at last, in light and truth, to reign.

Through long oppression, God hath guided thee,
From darker Egypt, through a bloodless sea;
And by the chastening of his hand, hath strove
To make thee still more faithful to his love.

And now, no more thy race oppressed shall be,
But all thy foes shall strive to honor thee,
And nations at thy temple-altars bring
Their richest offerings to thy sovereign King—

O Israel! wandering in all lands afar,
Thy faith of old—be still thy guiding star,
And thy bright temple shall show forth again—
The shining glories of thine ancient reign.

M. BEYER.

Poetry

GOD made the world with rhythm and rime—
   The sun's refrain he made the moon;
He swung the stars to beat in time
   And set the universe in tune.
He gave the seas their mighty tongue,
   He gave his winds their lyric wings,
And thus the very soul of Song
   Was woven in the scheme of things.

To-day this wonder was revealed
   Upon a twilight colored plain;
I saw it in the town and field,
   I heard it in the singing rain.
The bows and birds repeated it,
   The streams intoned it as they ran,
And then I saw how closely knit
   Were God and Poetry with man.

A rift of sky—a group of trees,
   A ripple and a swallow's dart,
The cadence of a dying breeze,
   Like sudden music, swept my heart;
A laughing child looked up and sprang
   To greet me at the homeward climb—
And all about me surged and sang
   The world God made with rhythm and rime.

LOUIS UNTERMEYER.

THE MODERN PERIOD

Our Heritage

WE own no kingdom and we flaunt no king,
  No crown is ours to mock at or obey,
No superficial homage do we bring
  To any dastard tyranny to-day;
Our realms have broadened to the mighty world,
  The boundaries of our rule stretch far and wide,
Our racial flag is evermore unfurled,
  Where Jewish souls in freedom's air abide,
Our citadel is truth; our empty home,
  Our ramparts are the laws to make us wise,
Eternal as the azure-vaulted dome,
  Our heritage from Heaven never dies;
And from the nations' flux and change and strife,
  The Jews draw strenuous force and vigorous life.

ISIDORE G. ASCHER.

Israel's Heritage

HOW shall we spend, O Lord,
  Our priceless heritage;
The wealth of Holy Writ (Thy Word),
  Bequeathed from age to age.
How shall we use the garnered store
Of Israel's ancient song and lore?

Shall we, like misers, hoard
  The jewels in our care;
The gems, by Seer and Prophet stored,
  That all mankind might share;
The law from Sinai's summit hurled
To speak in thunder to the world.

Shall we not spread broadcast
  This wealth that shall endure?
These seeds of Faith, that in the past
  Burst into blossoms pure:
Whose roots were nourished through the years
By martyred Israel's blood and tears.

623

Heirs ot thy Love are we,
  The First-born, chosen race;
Holding in trust the legacy
  No tyrant can·efface!
Life of our life, breath of our breath,
Outliving scorn, and hate and death!

O let our Fathers preach
  Thy glory and Thy fame!
O let our tender mothers teach
  Their babes to lisp thy name;
That Israel in each coming age
May claim its precious heritage!

IDA GOLDSMITH MORRIS.

Fin de Siècle

WHAT! do I hear the nations boast
    Of what the century's shown,
The while on Córfu's distant coast
    The persecuted groan?
The while in Russia's spreading space
    No smallest place is found
Whereon a guiltless hunted race
    May find a resting ground?
The while e'en noblest charity
    But little can avail,
And bitter, widespread misery
    Relates a woful tale?
    The while some starve and have no bed
While others roll in gold,
    And socialism's spirit dread
The problem would unfold?
    The while in Europe's cultured lands
Vast armies still maintain,
    And men must learn from skilled commands
How men may best be slain?
    And to achieve this worldly lore
Must work more worthy cease,
    Constrained to practice art of war

624

In time of doubtful peace?
  The while so many a labor-strike
Speaks of injustice rife,
  On man and master's side alike,
And leads to endless strife?
  The while so many wretched cry
In vain for Work? Oh, say!
  Is aught herein to glorify?
Or reason for dismay!   ANONYMOUS.

Hope and Faith

HOPE! Not distant is the Springtime,
  Butterflies will soon be winging—
In new nests the merry songsters
  Their new songs will soon be singing.

Know! The night itself will vanish,
  Cloudlands drift and melt away—
Once again will skies shine azure,
  Stars by night and suns by day.

New the roses, new the flowers,
  Spring's new odors flow in waves,
Brilliant colors, scents and singing
  Will arise above our graves.

ISAAC LEIB PEREZ.
(Translated by Henry Goodman.)

Not by Power

"Not by might, nor by power, but by My spirit,
saith the lord of hosts."—Zachariah iv., 6.

NOT by power
  Blooms the flower
Of a growth unseen;
  Ye shall find it,
Ye shall bind it
  On your brows serene.

Not by might
  Darkest night
Yields at dawn this prize;
  Springing surely,
Slowly, purely,
  It shall humbly rise.

Faith is mine,
  Love Divine
Is its scented breath;
  Faith that brightens,
Cheers, enlightens,
  It shall conquer death!

MARY M. COHEN.

Lines

Written on hearing a learned Lawyer say in Court,
that "the Jews were hated alike by God and man."

SAY not that we are cut off by Thee, Guardian of
        Israel's race;
Despite of all our waywardness, in Thy love we hold
    a place;
And in our dark and bitter hours, we still can turn to
    Thee
For guidance or for comfort, when earthly pleasures
    flee.

Not utterly abhorred by Thee!—man cannot trace Thy
    ways
Nor reach into Thy hidden path, O Thou of ancient
    days.
And must we still be taunted and told we are forgot.
Condemned alike by Thee and man, our destiny a blot.

Believe it not, believe it not! we are God's chosen still
To whom He hath in mercy given the records of His
    will!

626

To whom He hath in kindness said, "Fear not, for
    thou art Mine,
I have called thee by My holy name, and glory shall
    be thine."

ALICE RHINE.

The Glory of God

On seeing the sun suddenly break forth and illumine
the Sepher while it was being carried to the Hechal.

WAS it thus, stricken remnant, the glory of God
    Burst forth on the fathers, and showered its
      light
Across the rude path that those weary ones trod,—
    A cloud-pillar by day, a flame-witness by night?

As it guided the sire, it now gleams on the son;
    As it shone in the wilderness lonely and drear,
So it burst to assure thee, O desolate one,
    That in sorrow and exile His presence is here.

Then say not the day of thy triumph has fled,
    Say not that the star of thy glory has set,
While the same holy blessing still rests on thy head,
    And the same "fire from heaven" illumines thee yet.

REBEKAH HYNEMAN.

Lessons of the Past

FROM mem'ry's lofty vantage ground
    Our mental gaze we shift around
O'er stretches of the past.
We see dim realms of fading glory
The trysting place of figures hoary,
Whose plaintive accents sound one story:
    God's world alone doth last.

627

We see the trophies won in strife
That graced the triumphs of our life
  Lie strewn in sad array.
Each mould'ring relic wails a strain,
The warning dirge of myriads slain
Whose echoes roll an old refrain:
  All earthly must decay.

But in this threnody that saddens
A message rings that ever gladdens,
  Ne'er perish soul and name,
Though strongest hopes be broken,
Yet every good word spoken
Remains sweet mem'ry's token
  Of amaranthine fame.

HARRY WEISS.

Rodef Shalom

WHEN ancient nations bowed the knee
    To idols made of wood and stone,
The Hebrew nation claimed to be
  The worshippers of God alone.

For this they suffer'd, bled, and died,
  A chosen people strong and free;
Strong in the faith that should abide
  Of God's own matchless majesty.

Chosen the heralds of a light,
  The blinded nations could not see,
Chosen to banish moral right
  And rescue from Idolatry.

Still strong in faith of God alone,
  They rear this Temple to His name,
Jehovah's power and love to own,
  His tender mercies to proclaim.

Hail! Holy One enthron'd above,
  The God and Father of us all,
The Triumphs of Fraternal Love
  Shall prove we heed Thy loving call.

Nor shall our labors e'er be done
  Till God is honor'd and ador'd
By every nation 'neath the sun,
  The one Jehovah, sovereign Lord.

W. G. Skillman.

The New Temple

A NEW shrine stands in beauty reared,
    Where scions of a faith revered
Renew their vows to God—
To Him this house they dedicate,
To Him their hearts they consecrate,
    Upon this sacred sod.

Here shall the words of praise be sung,
From days, when yet the world was young,
    Of Psalmist and of Seer;
Like torrent shall the chorus run,
"The Lord our God, the Lord is One,
    Hear thou, O Israel, hear!"

Hence shall ascend the fervent prayers
Of thanks for joys, for strength, when cares
    And sorrows the soul rack;
Here shall the breast where sin has surged,
By the atonement's fires be purged,
    To holiness led back.

On this new altar there shall blaze
Refulgently the Bible's rays,
    Of Righteousness and Truth;
Here shall the wond'rous tale be told
The miracle of Israel old,
    And its undying youth.

May justice ever here prevail,
May love of all Mankind ne'er fail,
  And Charity ne'er cease;
May God's Shekinah calmly rest,
And they who gather here be blessed
  With Concord and with Peace.

LOUIS MARSHALL.*

*Composed on the occasion of the dedication of the New Temple of
the "Society of Concord," Syracuse, New York.

Consecration Hymn

FATHER of Life and Light and Power,
  To Thee we consecrate this hour!
With earnest hope, with purpose pure,
Oh, make this happy promise sure.

Except Thou build, we work in vain,
With holy zeal dost Thou sustain.
Bind all our hearts in rich increase
Of helpful deeds that ne'er shall cease.

Help us to lay foundations strong
Of love for right, of grief for wrong,
And brotherhood with every race
That seeks or needs the Father's grace.

Help us to grow in pure desires,
Kindle our souls with heavenly fires,
That higher levels may be won,
And step by step Thy will be done.

Build in us all Thy spirit's shrine:
Then shall we beam with light divine,
"And work with heart and soul and might
For Truth and Freedom, God and Right."

R. WAGNER.

The Kingdom of God

THERE is no unbelief;
  Whoever plants a seed beneath the sod
And waits to see it push away the clod,
He trusts in God.

Whoever says when clouds are in the sky,
"Be patient, heart; light breaketh by-and-by,"
  Trusts the Most High.

Whoever sees, 'neath winter's field of snow,
The silent harvest of the future grow,
  God's power must know.

Whoever lies down on his couch to sleep,
Content to lock each sense in slumber deep,
  Knows God will keep.

                    EDWARD BULWER LYTTON.

Rebecca's Hymn

(From "Ivanhoe")

WHEN Israel, of the Lord beloved,
    Out of the land of bondage came,
Her fathers' God before her moved,
  An awful guide, in smoke and flame.
By day, along the astonish'd lands
  The cloudy pillar glided slow;
By night, Arabia's crimson'd sands
  Return'd the fiery column's glow.

There rose the choral hymn of praise,
  And trump and timbrel answer'd keen,
And Zion's daughters pour'd their lays,
  With priest's and warrior's voice between.

No portents now our foes amaze,
  Forsaken Israel wanders lone;
Our fathers would not know Thy ways,
  And Thou hast left them to their own.

But present still, though now unseen,
  When brightly shines the prosperous day
Be thoughts of Thee a cloudy screen
  To temper the deceitful ray.
And oh, when stoops on Judah's path
  In shade and storm the frequent night,
Be Thou, long-suffering, slow to wrath,
  A burning and a shining light!

Our harps we left by Babel's streams,
  The tyrant's jest, the Gentile's scorn;
No censer round our altar beams,
  And mute are timbrel, harp and horn,
But Thou hast said, the blood of goat,
  The flesh of rams, I will not prize;
A contrite heart, a humble thought,
  Are Mine accepted sacrifice.

Sir Walter Scott.

A Jewish Family

GENIUS of Raphael! if thy wings
    Might bear thee to this glen,
With faithful memory left of things
  To pencil dear and pen,
Thou wouldst forego the neighboring Rhine,
  And all his majesty—
A studious forehead to incline
  O'er this poor family.

The Mother—her thou must have seen,
  In spirit, ere she came
To dwell these rifted rocks between,
  Or found on earth a name;

An image, too, of that sweet Boy,
  Thy inspirations give—
Of playfulness, and love, and joy,
  Predestined here to live.

Downcast, or shooting glances far,
  How beautiful his eyes,
That blend the nature of the star
  With that of summer skies!
I speak as if of sense beguiled;
  Uncounted months are gone,
Yet am I with the Jewish Child,
  That exquisite Saint John.

I see the dark brown curls, the brow,
  The smooth, transparent skin,
Refined, as with intent to show
  The holiness within;
The grace of parting Infancy
  By blushes yet untamed;
Age faithful to the mother's knee,
  Nor of her arms ashamed.

Two lovely Sisters, still and sweet
  As flowers, stand side by side;
Their soul-subduing looks might cheat
  The Christian of his pride:
Such beauty hath the Eternal poured
  Upon them not forlorn,
Though of a lineage once abhorred,
  Nor yet redeemed from scorn.

Mysterious safeguard, that, in spite
  Of poverty and wrong,
Doth here preserve a living light,
  From Hebrew fountains sprung;
That gives the ragged group to cast
  Around the dell a gleam
Of Palestine, of glory past,
  And proud Jerusalem!

WILLIAM WORDSWORTH.

Rebecca, the Jewess

CLOSED are the tear-gates of Paradise now,
  And the shadows of death lie cold on the brow
    Of Rebecca, the Jewess so fair;
And her dark eyes that sparkled than diamonds more
    bright,
Have paled the soft rays of their pure, living light,
And vacant they gaze as a lone star of night,
    When darkness is filling the air,—
    The balmy, the soft summer air.

Weep, daughters of Zion! Weep, chosen of God!
For the morrow shall moulder, beneath the cold clod,
    The form of the spirit that's fled!
Wreathe the dark hair of the maiden laid low,
Spread violets over her bosom of snow,
And lay her down peacefully, calmly, below
    The green winding-sheet of the dead,
    The flower-decked robe of the dead.

There let her sleep, till the last trump shall sound
The call of the dead, that slumber around
    Earth's green hills, and by its streams;
Waked by the voice of the Angel of Doom,
Then may she burst in the dark gates of the tomb,
Arrayed in white robes, and radiant with bloom
    To sing in the Land of Dreams,—
    The beautiful Land of Dreams.
                    CLARK B. COCHRANE.

The American Jewess

O YOUNGEST daughter of thy ancient race,
  In thy behalf great progress has been wrought;
Thou hast advanced unto a higher place
  In this free land of stirring act and thought;
Unhampered child of liberty art thou,
  Upon whom smiles each science and each art;

634

The fetters of the past are rent and now
  Thou canst go freely forth and do thy part.
But more than this the present means to thee:
  Thou art the sponsor of thy people's weal,
And thine the sacred privilege to be
  The guardian spirit of its high ideal—
To seek the right, uphold the just, the true,
And make of each a better man, a worthier Jew.

ALBERT ULMANN.

Jewess

MY dark-browed daughter of the Sun,
  Dear Bedouin of the desert sands,
  Sad daughter of the ravished lands,
Of savage Sinai, Babylon—
O, Egypt-eyed, thou art to me
A God-encompassed mystery.

I see sad Hagar in thy eyes,
  The obelisks, the pyramids,
  Lie hid beneath thy drooping lids,
The tawny Nile of Moses lies
Portrayed in thy strange people's force,
And solemn mystery of source.

The black abundance of thy hair
  Falls like some sad twilight of June
  Above the dying afternoon,
And mourns thy people's mute despair.
The large solemnity of night,
O Israel, is in thy sight.

Then come where stars of freedom spill
  Their splendor, Jewess. In this land,
  The same broad hollow of God's hand
That held you ever, outholds still.
And whether you be right or nay,
'Tis God's, not Russia's, here to say.

JOAQUIN MILLER.

The Jewess

HER hair is winged with summer nights,
　　Her brow is like thé dawn,
Her voice is like an olden song.
　　That memory lingers on,
And all her movements are as soft
　　And gentle as a fawn.

A lovely, mild, and winsome girl
　　Of strange and Eastern grace—
I thought, "How happy art thou, child
　　In whom all gifts find place,"
Till deep within her eyes I saw
　　The story of her race.

ALLAN DAVIS.

Orientale

SHE'S an enchanting little Israelite,
　　A world of hidden dimples!—Dusky-eyed,
A starry-glancing daughter of the Bride—
With hair escaped from some Arabian Night;
Her lip is red, her cheek is golden-white,
　　Her nose a scimitar; and, set aside
The bamboo hat she cocks with so much pride,
Her dress a dream of daintiness and delight.

And when she passes with the dreadful boys
　　And romping girls, the cockneys loud and crude,
My thought to the Minories tied, but moved to range
　　The Land o' the Sun, commingles with the noise
　　Of magian drums and scents of sandal-wood,
A touch Sidonian, modern, taking, strange.

WILLIAM HENLEY.

An Oriental Maiden

THOU fairest one of Judah's daughters,
  I would thy lover be;
Oh, may thy heart be free from others,
  And treasured but for me.
I fain would see thy brown eyes brighten,
  Which all their love disclose;
To see thy cheeks, their colors brighten,
  Like tintings on the rose.

Thou maiden rare, of ancient nation,
  Thy soul is dear to me;
And does my heart, with each pulsation,
  Beat every stroke for thee.
Then grant the boon, I ask thy favor,
  And give thy word to-day,
Oh, let me come, thy truest lover,
  And bid me not away.   J. O. JENKYNS.

The Maid of the Ghetto

SAD eyes and dark she bends upon the throng,
  Man's exile and Earth's alien in all lands!
Her ears drink up the street's tempestuous song,
  And all its currents lave her where she stands.
Not Time nor Place shall rob her of her dower
  For rooted in her long remembrance dwell
The days of glory and the realms of power,
  The temples and the tribes of Israel.

Not this crushed, driven multitude she sees,
  But priests and patriarchs that chant their psalms;
Not these stark walls of brick, but, all at ease,
  Her white-robed sisters by the springs and palms.
And phantoms out of ancient days returning,
  Light up the amber vastness of her land;
Oblivious to this stygian asphalt burning,
  Her feet are cool on Jordan's silver sand.

637

Disparted long and reft from Palestine,
  Lorn maiden of Judaea, dost thou wait .
By these strange walls of ages reared between '
  Thee and some lover sealed and consecrate?
Dost thou seek here his face amidst these faces,
  His form from out this hurrying, sullen press,
Or is thy mystic longing but thy race's—
  Thou living statue of its mute distress?

Thou dusk-eyed daughter of Eternity,
  Thou standest in the Visible and Now;
The Past hath locked its mystery in thee,
  And Orient suns have rolled athwart thy brow.
Thy face foreshadows fruitful generations,
  O nymph of Jewry from the iron lands!—
Art thou some Esther in the house of nations,—
  Some Judith with a falchion in her hands?

ANONYMOUS.

The Jewish Mother

A STAR of guidance o'er Life's troubled ocean,
  A sunbeam flashing tempest-clouds in twain,
The wafted fragrance deepening, soul-emotion
  The benediction won from heights of pain.

A voice familiar with melodious calling;
  A solemn adjuration from on High;
A veiled and tender glory, earthward falling
  From unseen altars, 'neath eternal sky.

Pathetic memories of a father's blessing,
  When thornless roses crowned the lifted head;
The gentle touch of mother-hands caressing,
  Ere cypress paths to desert-wanderings led.

All-conquering joy of new-found inspiration,
  That healing balm pours on the longing breast;
The life ennobles that in consecration
  Keeps evermore the day of holy rest.

A DAUGHTER OF JUDAH.

638

Like unto Sharon's Roses

MY darling, your grace
     And the bloom of your face
  Are sweet as of Sharon the roses, . . .
And a radiance rare
Illumines your hair
  As verdure where moonlight reposes;
And your cadence is low
As Jordan's still flow
  When twilight day's revelry closes,

  My darling, your blush
Is like morning's full flush
  When over Mount Hermon he's scaling,
And the dream in your eye
Is like Galilee's sky
  When only one cloudlet is sailing,
And the lure of your smile
My sadness beguile
  And raise me from doubting and failing.

                              RUFUS LEARSI,

I saw a Maiden Sweet and Fair

I SAW a maiden sweet and fair
     Of an ancient wand'ring nation,
Her simple garb the signs did bear
  Of poor and humble station.

Knew she some other clime but late,
  This meek and gentle maiden?
Methought I marked her people's fate,
  On her black tresses laden.

I looked into her great dark eyes,
  Demure and sparkling tender;
They gazed serene as May-day skies,
  In calm and cloudless splendor.

639

Yet oft some inner mood would cast
    A sadness o'er her glances,
As flits a swallow's shadow past
    A brook where sunlight dances.

                    RUFUS LEARSI.

Lines to a Jewish Child

IN the dark depths of those great soulful eyes,
    My little Hebrew lad, I fain would read
The marvelous history of thy marvelous race;
The patience, silent suffering, cruel wrongs,
The courage shrinking not from tortuous death;
The constancy that wavers not or turns,
The faith and trust of deep devotion born,
The hope that triumphs over every woe,
The love of kindred, reverence for age,
The virtues manifold that make thy race.

Truly, God's chosen people these must be,
Else long since had they perished from the earth.
When blushing I recall the insults foul
That we have heaped on them in Christ's dear name,
And think how meekly they that own not Christ
Have suffered all and struggled bravely on,
Through sorrow, persecution, torture, death—
I can conceive, my little Hebrew lad,
What pride a Jew must feel to be a Jew!

                    C. D.

Rachel

I

IN Paris all look'd hot and like to fade.
    Sere, in the garden of the Tuileries,
    Sere, with September, droop'd the chestnut-trees.
'Twas dawn; a brougham roll'd through the streets
        and made

Halt at the white and silent colonnade
  Of the French Theatre. Worn with disease,
  Rachel, with eyes no gazing can appease,
Sate in the brougham and those blank walls survey'd.

She follows the gay world, whose swarms have fled
To Switzerland, to Baden, to the Rhine;
Why stops she by this empty play-house drear?

Ah, where the spirit its highest life hath led,
All spots, match'd with that spot, are less divine;
And Rachel's Switzerland her Rhine is here!

II

Unto a lovely villa, in a dell
  Above the fragrant warm Provençal shore,
  The dying Rachel in a chair they bore
Up the steep pine-plumed paths of the Estrelle,

And laid her in a stately room, where fell
  The shadow of a marble Muse of yore,
  The rose-crown'd queen of legendary lore,
Polymnia, full on her death-bed.—'Twas well!

The fret and misery of our northern towns,
  In this her life's last day, our poor, our pain,
Our jangle of false wits, our climate's frowns,

Do for this radiant Greek-soul'd artist cease;
  Sole object of her dying eyes remain
The beauty and the glorious art of Greece.

III

Sprung from the blood of Israel's scatter'd race,
  At a mean inn in German Aarau born,
  To forms from antique Greece and Rome uptorn,
Trick'd out with a Parisian speech and face,

Imparting life renew'd, old classic grace;
  Then, soothing with thy Christian strain forlorn,
  A-Kempis! her departing soul outworn,
While by her bedside Hebrew rites have place—

Ah, not the radiant spirit of Greece alone.
She had—one power, which made her breast its home!
  In her, like us, there clash'd, contending powers,

Germany, France, Christ, Moses, Athens, Rome.
  The strife, the mixture in her soul, are ours;
Her genius and her glory are her own.

MATTHEW ARNOLD.

Rachel

WHEN Memnon's sculptured form the god of day
      Touched from the orient gate with glance of
        fire,
As from the golden harps that seraphs play—
  Burst heavenly music from that silent lyre.
Thus caught the chiselled grace of ancient art
  Life from your touch, and beauty breathing soul;
Thus woke to startled life the panting heart
  That ne'er before knew passion's wild control,
Woke to the light of grace and love and power
  That ever holds enshrined your honored name.
What garland, woven in the Muses' bower,
  Can match the meed of such a glorious fame?
Queen of the realm of passion and of thought,
  What victor monarch's crown is with such gems
    enwrought.

ANONYMOUS.

Kalich, Inheritor of Tragedy

KALICH, thou of the dark and brooding face,
Born unto Tragedy by birthright of race,
The sorrows of uncounted years arise
And plead for utterance in thy mournful eyes,
And on thy lips, so poignant sweet with pain,
God's stamp of suffering marks thy calling plain.

So stood Rachel, of thy blood, in her day,
So Bernhardt, of that blood, holds now her sway.
And thou, full sister of these mighty two,
The same blood-heritage claimeth as thy due.

Valid thy claim. The centuries' seal is set
Upon its warrant. Tears and blood have wet
Its ancient and its modern countersigns.
Sorrow unspeakable breathes between its lines,
Where, down to Kishinev's cruel days, is told
A nation's woe that dates from Egypt old.

To thee descended—Lo, how dread the cry
That rises from thy throat! How tense and high
With strain of agony! Not alone the part
That now thou playest thus doth wring thy heart,
But all thy people's grief, accumulate,
Sounds in thy voice, till, with race anguish great,
Thou speakest not even one little, broken word,
But Tragedy's supremest note is heard.

This, then, the price of glory to thy name—
How dire the cost, how bitter high the game,
O, Kalich, on whose soul the forfeit lies
Of genius born from world-old sacrifice!
We yield us to the magic of thy spell,
With our applause the playhouse echoes swell,
We sound the praises of thy tragic power—
Yet still how bare, how empty, thy full hour!

What wonder, then that even at Fame's full flood,
Thy eyes still bear mute witness to thy blood,
Sombre with persecution—its wan sign
Still resting on those piteous lips of thine,
O, Kalich, thou in whom all Israel's woe,
Concentrate, makes the Genius-Gift we know!

RIPLEY D. SAUNDERS.

To the Memory of Grace Aguilar

Author of "Woman's Friendship," "Vale of Cedars,"
etc., etc.

AND thou art gone, Grace Aguilar,
  The "Darling" of the race;
Child of the "hated," thou wert one
  E'en any sphere to grace;
And O, like her, proud Hebrew maid,
  Thou didst awake a cry,
Pure as the northern peasant was,
  Is chronicled on high.

For though destruction's bosom swept
  Thy children o'er the earth,
They yet shall worship in the land
  Which gave their fathers birth;
And Zion's song shall yet be deemed
  Acceptable to God,
And Zion's maidens sweetly dance
  On Jordan's hallow'd sod.

And, lovely one, like Wilberforce,
  Thou scarce didst live to see
Thy prayer fulfill'd, the fact'ry child
  From slavery set free.
Like "Darling" thou didst raise the cry,
  The helpless heard thy voice,
And hoping still, thou help'dst them on,
  And bade their souls rejoice.

I mourn for thee, my sister friend,
    As kindred in that art
Which is Divine—a holy tie
    No human pow'r can part.
When first my muse essay'd to sing,
    'Neath Wilson's fostering care,
Thou, too didst grace the glowing page,
    And Youatt's name was there.

We knew no creed, save that which bound
    Our souls in ties as strong
As revelation e'er proclaimed
    Or grac'd the Psalmist's song;
Onward we went, one hope in view,
    Both pilgrims on the road,
Towards the "everlasting towers,"
    "The city of our God."

Peace to thine ashes! May there rise
    From out thine ashes now,
A genius of thy race, as bright,
    As purely bright as thou.
And when our earthly race is o'er,
    O may we meet above,
And join the bright-robed heav'nly throng
    Who sing that "God is Love."

                                    ANONYMOUS.

Moses Mendelssohn

ONCE, through a night of darkness and of shadow,
    A brilliant star swept softly into sight;
It scattered out its beams like silv'ry lances,
    And, in its pathway, left a streak of light.
But, when the rosy blushes of the morning
    Broke over earth, the star had passed away;
And yet its light still travels down to mankind
    Through endless dawnings of the golden day.

645

Once, through an age of mental gloom and shadow,
  When ignorance and superstition reigned,
When only those upon the heights of fortune
  A glimpse of light—of grace and culture gained,
There dawned for Israel a star of glory
  Whose friendly beam through doubt and darkness
    shone,
And led the gaze of mankind to the hill-tops;—
  This star of light was Moses Mendelssohn.

Poor Israel was then despised—rejected!
  For prejudice had built a boundless wall
O'er which no tendril of a common feeling
  Could twine itself,—no ray of sunlight fall;
Cut from the world,—its gladness and its sorrow—
  Poor patient souls, unconscious of their plight,
Submissive with the patience of the sightless,
  Whose eyes have ne'er beheld the blessed light.

And then came Mendelssohn; O God, and Father,
  We thank thee for this blessing to our race,
We, who to-day, in every art and science
  Hold an exalted and an honored place!
For only progress brought to us our freedom,
  And only Culture, as she scanned the Jew,
Could see and recognize the kindred spirit
  That loves the good, the beautiful, the true.

And Mendelssohn it was who broke the fetters
  That tyranny had strengthened year by year;
'Twas he who smote upon the rock of knowledge
  And freed for us its water, sweet and clear;
And lifting up our thoughts to vaster issues,
  Our fair ideals to heights before unknown,
Stood by our side, a Jew compelling nations
  To honor all the race he called his own.

O, when can Germany e'er cease to cherish
  The "Nathan Wise" its Lessing's graphic pen

Has drawn in glowing and immortal colors,
　And held before the wond'ring eyes of men!
The gentle sage, the friend of prince and poet,
　Whose every word ennobled and refined,
Who seemed to stand upon some mental summit
　And smile upon the factions of mankind.

Unsightly and deformed the suff'ring body,
　But, from the thoughtful eyes and noble face
The glory of the soul shone out in splendor,—
　A glowing gem in its translucent case!
And all the earth appeared to him in beauty,
　For o'er his heart-strings trembled, even then,
The heav'ly melody with which his offspring
　Soothed and enslaved the ardent hearts of men.

O, monarch in the realm of thought and reason!
　O, high-priest in the temple of the soul!
Thy hymn of progress, tolerance and freedom,—
　Through endless ages shall its echoes roll!
Thou couldst not prove to us that mental culture
　And Judaism never are at strife,
Nor show us immortality more clearly
　Than by the beauty of thy glorious life!

A century has passed on restless pinions
　Since death removed thine image from the earth;
An era of enlightenment and progress
　Has taught us to appreciate thy worth;
Look down and guide us from thy home in heaven
　To nobler deeds than we have ever known;
The purest thought—the broader field of action
　Should mark thy people, Moses Mendelssohn!

MIRIAM DEL BANCO.

Heine

GOD said: "I will make a poet,"
  And a soul was sent below
With the singer's wings of rapture,
  With the sufferer's weight of woe.

God laid on the eyes the poet's
  Awful gift of second sight,
On the restless, questioning spirit,
  All the blackness of the night.

On the body, pangs of torture,
  Hell's own pains and love's sharp sting;
Doubt you woe must dow'r the poet?
  Hush, draw close and hear him sing!

A. R. ALDRICH.

Heine

NOR life nor death had any peace for thee,
  Seeing thy mother cast thee forth, a prey
To wind and water, till we bade thee stay
And rest, a pilgrim weary of the sea.
But now it seems that on thine effigy
  Thy very host an impious hand would lay:
  Go then and wander, praising on thy way
The proud Republic's hospitality!

Yet oft with us wreathed brow must suffer wrong,
  The sad Enchanter of the land of Weir
  Is still uncrowned, unreverenced, and we fear
The Lords of Gold above the Lords of Song,
Were it not strange, then, should we honor more
The sweet-mouthed singer of a foreign shore?

GEORGE SYLVESTER VIERECK.

THE MODERN PERIOD

Heinrich Heine

I

SON of a mystic race, he came
　　When Europe faltered at one name,
And, to his youthful eyes, the sun
Darkened before Napoleon.
France brought his freedom, but it brought
To Germany the years that wrought
Her shame, her bondage, her despair—
Thus in the quiet Rhineland air
A deep division drew apart
The fighter's and the poet's heart.

II

The poet heard the linden croon
Tragic old ditties to the moon,
And sang with clear authentic voice
The music of his country's choice.
He knew the forest of romance,
The haunting wail, the elfin dance,
The wounded heart, the magic lance,
And first on German Islands he
Heard echoes of the Odyssey
Sonorous in the Northern Sea.

III

Then, as he dreamed, the loud world's brood
Cried out, the visionary mood
Broke, and the poet in his fear
Bade poisoned arrows sing and sear.
God touched him.　From his couch of pain
He sang, he fought, and in his strain
Thunder of olden battles stirred
By prophets in Judea heard.
.God touched him, but his long repose
Is broken still by clamorous foes.

IV

Yet battle dies, and song alone
With the Eternal is at one—
Great verse that is the warder of
Justice and wisdom, truth and love,
And of that beauty in all lands,
Not seen of eyes, not made with hands,
Whose harmony can so control
The sanctuary of the soul,
That we must know its prophets still
The child of a diviner will.

LUDWIG LEWISOHN.

To Heinrich Heine

AWAKE to lyric rapture once again,
    Great German bard! Not in resurgent
    France
Shall thy proud spirit rally from its trance
But in the Rhineland where the sabres glance;
Where spring to arms, each day, a myriad men.—
There now they need thy patriotic pen:
Its caustic wit, so dagger-keen and bold
That erstwhile smote with such relentless zeal
Yet had the art of tenderness to heal.
Once more thy sweet-voiced Lorelei shall steal
Into the nation's heart, whose tales were told
By thee, dear Troubador, in rhymes of gold—
And then thy matchless minstrelsy shall bring
The Fatherland swift healing on its wing.

GEORGE ALEXANDER KOHUT.

Ernest Renan

"TRUTH is an idol," spake the Christian age.
    "Thou shalt not worship Truth divorced from
    Love.
Truth is but God's reflection: Look above!"
So Pascal wrote, and still we trace the page.

650

"Truth is divine," said Plato, "but on high
  She dwells, and few may be her ministers,
  For truth is sad and lonely and diverse;
Heal thou the weakling with a generous lie!"

But thou in Truth delightedst! Thou of soul
  As subtle-shimmering as the rainbow mist,
  And still in all her service didst persist.
For me One truth thou livedst, but the Whole.
                    MARY DARMESTETER.

The Jews' Cemetery on the Lido

A TRACT of land swept by the salt seafoam,
    Fringed with acacia flowers and billowy deep,
In meadow-grasses, where tall poppies sleep,
And bees athirst for wilding honey roam,
How many a bleeding heart hath found its home,
  Under these hillocks which the seamews sweep!
  Here knelt an outcast race to curse and weep,
Age after age, 'neath heaven's unanswering dome.

Sad is the place and solemn. Grave by grave,
  Lost in the dunes, with rank weeds overgrown,
  Pines in abandonment; as though unknown,
Uncared for, lay the dead, whose records pave
  This path neglected; each forgotten stone
Wept by no mourner but the moaning wave.
            JOHN ADDINGTON SYMONDS.

The Jewish Cemetery at Newport

HOW strange it seems! These Hebrews in their
      graves,
  Close by the street of this fair seaport town,
Silent beside the never-silent waves,
  At rest in all this moving up and down!

651

The trees are white with dust, that o'er their sleep
  Wave their broad curtains in the south-wind's
    breath,
While underneath such leafy tents they keep
  The long, mysterious Exodus of Death.

And these sepulchral stones, so old and brown,
  That pave with level flags their burial-place,
Seem like the tablets of the Law, thrown-down
  And broken by Moses at the mountain's base.

The very names recorded here are strange,
  Of foreign accent, and of different climes;
Alvares and Rivera interchange
  With Abraham and Jacob of old times.

"Blessed be God! for he created death!"
  The mourners said, "and Death is rest and peace";
Then added, in the certainty of faith,
  "And giveth Life that nevermore shall cease."

Closed are the portals of their Synagogue,
  No Psalms of David now the silence break,
No Rabbi reads the ancient Decalogue
  In the grand dialect the Prophets spake.

Gone are the living, but the dead remain,
  And not neglected; for a hand unseen,
Scattering its bounty, like a summer rain,
  Still keeps their graves and their remembrance green.

How came they here? What burst of Christian hate,
  What persecution, merciless and blind,
Drove o'er the sea—that desert desolate—
  These Ishmaels and Hagars of mankind?

They lived in narrow streets and lanes obscure,
  Ghetto and Judenstrass, in mirk and mire;
Taught in the school of patience to endure
  The life of anguish and the death of fire.

All their lives long, with the unleavened bread
  And bitter herbs of exile and its fears,
The wasting famine of the heart they fed,
  And slaked its thirst with marah of their tears.

Anathema maranatha! was the cry
  That rang from town to town, from street to street;
At every gate the accursed Mordecai
  Was mocked and jeered, and spurned by Christian
    feet.

Pride and humiliation hand in hand
  Walked with them through the world where'er they
    went;
Trampled and beaten were they as the sand,
  And yet unshaken as the continent.

For in the background figures vague and vast
  Of patriarchs and of prophets rose sublime,
And all the great traditions of the Past
  They saw reflected in the coming time.

And thus forever with reverted look
  The mystic volume of the world they read,
Spelling it backward, like a Hebrew book,
  Till life became a Legend of the Dead.

But ah! what once has been shall be no more!
  The groaning earth in travail and in pain
Brings forth its races, but does not restore,
  And the dead nations never rise again.

            HENRY WADSWORTH LONGFELLOW.

France's Shame

TALK not of Christian France, lest mantling shame
  Glow in its fiery blush to burning flame,
And on the altar of the wide world's ire
Doom French injustice to eternal fire.

With public scorn we loath the vengeful lust
In which French soldiers have betrayed their trust,
And bide the time when in the coming years
Her infamy is purged with bloody tears.
All nations call for justice to the Jew,
Condemn the false, and magnify the true.
'Tis Israel's triumph, never more complete;
"Conviction" has brought victory, to France, defeat.
The world judges, France now bears the shame
And Dreyfus glories in unsullied name.
Let God avenge and man restrain his hate,
Jehovah's justice is immaculate;
Abide in faith and in the end we must
See France degraded, humbled in the dust.

                                        B. B. USHER.

To Dreyfus Vindicated

SOLDIER of Justice—fighting with her sword
    Since thine was broken! Who need now despair
To lead a hope forlorn against the throng?
For what did David dare
Before Goliath worthy this compare—
Thou in the darkness fronting leagued wrong?
What true and fainting cause shall not be heir
Of all thy courage—more than miser's hoard?

In times remote, when some preposterous ill
Man has not yet imagined, shall be King,
    While comfortable Freedom nods—
And Three shall meet to slay the usurping thing,
Thy name recalled shall clinch their potent will,
And as they cry, "He won—what greater odds!"
    They shall become as gods.

          *   *   *   *   *

Ours, too, thy champions! Who shall dare to say
The sordid time doth lack of chivalry.
When men thus all renounce, all cast away,

                        654

To walk with martyrs through a flaming sea!
Picquart!—how jealously will Life patrol
The paths of peril whither he is sent.
  Zola!—too early gone!
Whose taking even Death might well repent,
  Though 'twas to enrich that greater Pantheon
Where dwell the spirits of the brave of soul.

* * * * *

ENVOI

Oh! tremble, all oppressors, where ye be—
Throne, Senate, mansion, mart, or factory;
One against many, many against few!
Ye poor, once crushed, that crush your own anew;
Ye vulgar rich, now risen from the mud,
Despoilers of the flower in the bud:
For justice is the orbit of God's day,
And He hath promised that He will repay.

ROBERT UNDERWOOD JOHNSON.

Dreyfus

I

A MAN stood stained! France was one Alp of hate,
  Pressing upon him with its iron weight.
In all the circle of the ancient sun,
There was no voice to speak for him—not one.
In all the world of men there was no sound
But of a sword flung broken to the ground.
"'Tis done!" they said, "unless a felon soul
Can tear the leaves out of the Judgment Scroll."

Hell laughed a little season, then behold
How one by one the gates of God unfold!
Swiftly a sword by Unseen Forces hurled,
And then a man rising against the world!

II

Oh, import deep as life is, deep as time!
There is a Something sacred and sublime,
Moving behind the worlds, beyond our ken,
Weighing the stars, weighing the deeds of men.

Take heart, O world of sorrow, and be strong:
There is One greater than the whole world's wrong,
Be hushed before the high, benignant Power
That goes untarrying to the reckoning hour.

O men that forge the fetter, it is vain;
There is a Still Hand stronger than your chain,
'Tis no avail to bargain, sneer, and nod,
And shrug the shoulder for reply to God.

EDWIN MARKHAM.

Dreyfus

FRANCE has no dungeons in her island tomb
  So deep that she may hide her injustice there;
  The cry of innocence, despite her care,
Despite her roll of drums, her cannon's boom,
Is heard wherever human hearts have room
  For sympathy; a sob upon the air,
  Echoed and re-echoed everywhere,

It swells and swells, a prophecy of doom,
  Thou latest victim of an ancient hate!
In agony so awfully alone,
The world forgets thee not, nor can forget.
Such martyrdoms she feels to be her own,
And sees involved in thine her larger fate;
    She questions, and thy foes shall answer yet.

FLORENCE EARLE COATES.

THE MODERN PERIOD

Let Us Forget

THE shore once won, who counts the waves?
  Each hand, each oar, each spar that saves,
Record in heart—enshrine in song;
But all the weary, witless wrong,
      Let us forget.

Father forgive them! Thus prayed He,
Who drained the cup of Calvary,
The prisoner of Devil's Isle
May happy ask—erect the while —
      Let us forget.

We "witnesses" to "shew His praise"
Must shew it forth in divers ways,
By light of fame, or light of fires,—
All lower aims—all low desires,
      Let us forget.

The France of Picquart, Labori
And Zola. That is the France we see;
The foolish few who basely chose
In honor's name, dishonor—those
      Let us forget.   K. M.

The God of Israel

THE God of Israel sate on high,
  And methought He mocked the dead;
The twisted limbs of agony,
  The staring eyes of dread,
The lips that froze on a dying prayer
  And blessed Him as they bled.

The God of Israel sate on high,
  And He mocked His people's trust;
He heard the tyrant's blasphemy,
  He saw the Injustice just;
He saw the valley strewn with death
  And the wind that blew its dust.

657

I raised my voice and cried aloud
  (He smiled as if He heard):
"Behold, dishonour is their shroud
  For that they keep Thy Word:
They strangle them with thongs of shame
  Or hew them with the sword.

"With stripes and steel and bitter scorn
  They trample down their pride;
The silent souls of the yet unborn
  Lie maimed in the soul of the bride;
In bitterness their hearts awake,
  In bitterness abide.

"In bitterness, in bitterness
  They gaze upon the past,
Nor worship they Thy Word the less,
  Nor scorn Thy Word at last,
Who, free within Thy bounteous air,
  In bonds of hate are cast.

"For bonds that cleave the flesh are ill,
  But other bonds are base
That cleave the heart's benignant will,
  Or darken for a space
The eyes of reason and of right."
  Yea, thus I cried apace.

The God of Israel smiled on high
  As on a babbling child;
But I saw the bays of victory,
  And Justice undefiled,
And Mind and Honour hand in hand,
  And Envy reconciled.

The Past had doffed its robe of pain,
  Flung off its mourning-hood,
When Joy upraised her veil again
  And found the Future good;
She raised the folds of her lustrous cloak
  There—clear-eyed Duty stood.

                  C. M. KOHAN.

THE MODERN PERIOD

The Jews in Russia

FROM town and village to a wood, stript bare,
　　As they of their possessions, see them throng,
　Above them grows a cloud; it moves along,
As flee they from the circling wolf pack's glare.
Is it their Broken-Shadow of despair,
　The looming of their life of cruel wrong
　For countless ages? No; their faith is strong
In their Jehovah; that huge cloud is prayer.

A flash of light, and black the despot lies,
　What thunder round the world!
　　　　　'Tis transport's strain
　Proclaiming loud: "No righteous prayer is vain.
No God-imploring tears are lost; they rise
　Into a cloud, and in the sky remain,
Till they draw lightning from Jehovah's eyes."

EDWARD DOYLE.

On the Russian Persecution of the Jews

O SON of man, by lying tongues adored,
　By slaughterous hands of slaves with feet red-shod
　In carnage deep as Christian ever trod
Profaned with prayer and sacrifice abhorred
And incense from the trembling tyrant's horde,
　Brute worshippers or wielders of the rod,
　Most murderous even of all that call thee God,
Most treacherous even that ever called thee Lord;
Face loved of little children long ago,
Head hated of the priests and rulers then,
　If thou see this, or hear these hounds of thine
　Run ravening as the Gadarean swine,
Say, was not this thy Passion, to foreknow
　In death's worst hour the works of Christian men?

ALGERNON CHARLES SWINBURNE.

Russia and the Jews

O MUSCOVITE, blind is your wrath, with
   Your heel on the Israelite's neck,
And your hand on that baleful old blade,
   Persecution, 'twere wisdom to reck.
The Pharaoh's calm warning, Beware!
   Lo, the Pyramids pierce that grey gloom
Of a desert that is but a waste, by a river
   That is but a tomb,
Yet the Hebrew abides and is strong.

PUNCH.

The Kishineff Massacre

O LORD, Thy righteous wrath and vengeance pour
   Upon the bloody horde, who in Thy name,
The sacred name, hath stained with crimson gore
   The Russian land and filled Thy earth with shame.
   Let fall upon their heads the bolts of flame
To teach the vile oppressor, yet once more
A living God doth rule the nations o'er—
   A God of strength and might whose hand can tame
Their hireling hearts and teach their hate restraint.
Avenge Thy slaughtered sons, O Lord supreme!
   Their blood doth cry from rock and vale and height;
And Thou, to whom the sparrow's piping plaint
Is poignant as the eagle's piercing scream,
   Will not be deaf, but with Thy thunder smite.

ROSE STRAUSS.

On the Massacre

YE heavens, pray for mercy on my head!
   If God abides in you, and if a way
To Him exists, which yet I have not found,
   Do you my prayers unto His ear convey!

660

For me, my heart is dead, and no more prayers
  Are on my lips, for refuge against wrong.
My strength is gone, and there is no more hope.
  How long must we endure, how long, how long?

Headsman, here is an axe, arise and slay!
  Behead me like a dog; so let it be!
You have an arm, an instrument of death,
  And all the world a scaffold is to me.

Then let red blood, the blood of old and young,
  Besprinkle your red coat with ruddy gore,
So that the savage and ensanguined stain
  Shall not be wiped from it forevermore.

Cursed be he who for revenge cries out!
  For slaying guileless babes a vengeance meet
Satan himself has never yet devised.
  Then let our blood, poured out beneath your feet,

Sink penetrating to earth's lowest depths;
  Let blood of those who perished without blame
Sap and destroy the earth's foundations old—
  The bases deep of wickedness and shame.

CHAYIM NACHMAN BYALIK.

God and His Martyrs

FOR I have hither come, O ye dead bones,
  To beg of you, forgive me!
Forgive your God, you that are shamed forever!
For all your dark and bitter lives forgive me,
And for your ten times dark and bitter death!
For when you stand to-morrow at my threshold,
When you remind me, when you ask for payment,
I shall but answer you: "Come, see, I've nothing!"
It cries to heaven, I hear it, but I've nothing.
For I am poor myself, I'm beggared also.

661

And woe and woe and woe is all my worlds!
Let all the seven heavens moan for pity.
To bring such sacrifices all for nothing,
To live such lives and die such deaths for nothing,
Not knowing to what end, for what, for what!
Her head enwrapped in clouds, my old Shekinah;
Shall sit for evermore and weep for shame;
And night by night I too will lean from heaven,
And mourn myself upon your graves.

CHAYIM NACHMAN BYALIK.

The Jewish Martyrs

FROM far Siberia's frozen plains,
    They cry to heaven, they cry to us!
We hear the clanking of their chains
    And turn away! Not thus, not thus,
Our fathers, were your hearts made cold
By lust of power, by greed of gold!

They have not feared the scaffold rope,
    Nor cringed for whip or knotted cord;
They give up all and keep their hope;
    They die and call no despot lord;
Before the heaven that made men free,
They testify for liberty.

Who gave their tyrants leave to smite
    Truth's witnesses with knout or rod?
Who says such wrongs are in heaven's right,
    He lives before the throne of God,
And all the blood by despots shed,
Shall be a curse upon his head!

If to our altar one should come,
    With the czar's hounds upon his track,
Could e'en our buried dead be dumb
    Were we so base to drive him back;
Were we such craven, venal slaves,
Among our myriad hero-graves?   W. V. B.

662

The Persecuted Jew

WHEN strife is rampant in the world,
　　And men and devils loudly cheer;
The hearts of men have turned to stone,
　And cruel monsters, laugh and sneer.

In sorrow and the darkest gloom,
　Our brother Jew has suffered long;
The God of Israel knows His own,
　He their King is great and strong.

Defend the people, God of hosts,
　Thou God of Israel, grand and great;
Look down and bless that noble race,
　And lead them to the golden gate.
　　　　　　　STEPHEN TAYLOR DEKINS.

In the Name of Jesus of Nazareth

(Christmas, 1890)

GLOWS once more in the Russian sky, the blood-
　red dawn of a day of hate—
Shrills at the Throne of God, the cry of a people that
　　faints 'neath its cross's weight,
　Of a people hounded and done to death
　In the name of Jesus of Nazareth.

Bells are ringing and organs peal; a thousand choirs
　　their hymns upraise;
Peasant and pope at the altar kneel, and lone, in his
　　guarded palace, prays
　The fear-torn despot; and thus he saith:
　In the name of Jesus of Nazareth:

"Father in Heaven, thy reign of love come, and Thy
　　will on this earth be done,
Even as it is in Thy courts above. Forgive us, as we
　　forgive everyone;
　And tempt us never, but keep from scath
　In the name of Jesus of Nazareth."

Up to God's throne with the organ's voice and the
 chime of bells, goes the mob's fierce shout:
Drowned are the hymns by the horrid noise of curses
 and groans and the thud of knout;
  For the tyrant's prayer is a liar's breath—
  In the name of Jesus of Nazareth.

Christians, say, shall a savage Tsar blaspheme unchid-
 den the name of Christ?
Yours, not mine, is this holy war, by your faith in him
 that was sacrificed—
  By your faith that your souls may be saved from
  death
  In the Name of Jesus of Nazareth!

One is the Father—his sons all men. These brothers
 of mine are your brothers, too;
Save our brothers, I charge you, then, in their brother's
 name whom the Romans slew—
  In his name, who forgave with his dying breath—
  My brother, Jesus of Nazareth.
ANONYMOUS.

How Long?

HOW long, O Lord, shall sobs and sighs
 Re-echo in our ears?
How long, O Lord, shall groans and cries
 Compel our flowing tears?

How long, O Lord, shall blood be shed
 Of innocent and pure?
How long, O Lord, shall deathly dread
 O'er Israel endure?

How long, O Lord, shall darkness reign,
 And murder rage unchecked?
How long, O Lord, by crimson stain
 Our fateful page be flecked?

664

How long, O Lord, shall justice sleep
  And Truth her head abase?
How long, O Lord, into the deep
  Shall sink thy chosen race?

How long, O Lord, in exile yet,
  Thy people, must they pine?
How long, O Lord, wilt Thou forget
  The mercy that is Thine?

How long, O Lord, until the morn
  Of peace and bliss supreme,
When Thy own glory shall adorn
  The Zion of our dream?

ISRAEL COHEN.

Israel in Russia

THOU art but One! O God to Whom we bow
      In adoration;
E'en as in Egypt, Thou wilt hear us now—
    Thy Chosen Nation.

Much have we sinned; far from Thy face have fled,
    By passion driven.
Deep our repentance; Thou myself hast said
    We are forgiven.

Empires of old upon us heaped their chains,
    Burthens and lashes;
Thy thunders rolled—and of their might remains
    Stubble and ashes!

Still those we taught to hold Thy Name in awe
    Smite and berate us;
We are the leash that binds them to Thy Law—
    Wherefore they hate us!

Vengeance is Thine! yet Thine is mercy, too.
"Shield us, but grieve them
Not!" be our prayer: "They know not what they do.
Father! forgive them!"

ARTHUR GUITERMAN.

The Massacre of the Jews

A WAIL comes o'er the swelling seas
   From a far land, 'neath eastern skies,
And on the night wind's solemn dirge,
   We shuddering hear the shrieks, the cries,
Of that devoted band, who fell
   To glut the Moslem's savage hate,
That remnant of Judah's tribes,
   The victims of remorseless fate!

What was their crime? Had they rebelled
   Against the Sultan's despot power?
Had they with murder in their hearts
   Nursed into bloom the Blood-Red Flower
Of war? Say, was it theirs to throw
   The olive branch of Peace aside,
And see all sweet affections drift
   To death on the ensanguined tide?

They 'neath their vines and fig-trees dwelt,
   Pursuing each his peaceful trade,
Chanting at eve their psalms of praise,
   Molesting none, of none afraid!
And while the cheerful home fires blazed
   At eve, some Patriarch's voice was heard,
While little children gathered round
   To list with awe the sacred word!

But hark! what 'larum fills the air!
   A mighty roar as tho' the sea
Had burst its bound engulfing earth,
   And holding fierce, wild revelry!

666

Wake, Israel! Rouse! Your hour is come!
    The crazed fanatics thirst for blood;
A flash!—A glare!—Now ruins mark
    Where late your peaceful dwellings stood!
Demoniac yells! fierce glittering steel!
    The green turf red with many a stain,
The maddened populace rushing on,
    ' Trampling like beasts o'er heaps of slain.

Ah, face the tiger in his lair
    When thirsting-mad for human prey,
But not these zealots in their rage,
    He is more pitiful than they.
Their furiest passions all ablaze
    These blood-hounds lust for human game,
Seeming like devils loosed on earth,
    For they are men only in name.

No mercy in that zeal-crazed throng;
    The infant from its mother's breast
Is torn with blood-stained hands and slain,
    Her shrieks enjoyed with fiendish zest,
And from the mother's faithful heart,
    That would have died her child to save,
The life-blood flows, a sabre thrust,
    Yet she could bless the hand that gave.

Better to die than thus to live!
    With bleeding heart and maddened brain,
She sees her husband fall; her sire,
    His gray hairs dashed with crimson stain,
Nor age, nor sex were spared. O! God,
    Can such fiends curse thy beauteous earth?
And what their victim's high offense?
    The only crime of Jewish birth!

The crime of following in the path
    Their pious fathers early trod,
Marked by One, who on Sinai's heights,
    Revealed Himself a living God;

True, they knelt not to greet the sun,
  Nor made the Moslem's creed their own,
Nor forced they their belief on man,
  But asked the privilege alone

Of serving their Jehovah—God,
  As Abraham and Moses taught.
Their simple worship injured none,
  And they no controversy sought;
O! Israel! People of my God,
  When will thy weary wanderings cease,
O! when by Jordan's quiet wave,
  Thy scattered remnant dwell in peace?

When will base calumny and wrong
  Cease Judah to oppress thee more,
When will the wilderness bloom again
  On Palestina's sea-girt shore,
When will our Hebrew maids once more
  Chant Miriam's glad triumphant song?
The winds and waves swell with the cry,
  "How long, our Father, O! how long!"

                                  R. A. LEVY.

How Long, O Lord?

IN the weary night they come to me,
    The tears that I left unshed,
When I trudged the thorny wilderness
    With the sun-flame overhead.
I lie awake in the friendly night,
  My soul too numb to pray,
Enjoying the cool of its velvet black
    In the dread of the coming day.

For the day must come and the sting of it,
  As I bend to the endless road,
The light must come and the pain of it—
  The bite of the lashing goad.

668

But this I know as I reel along
 To the nations' hue and cry,
A burning truth in the hand of God;
 I know that I must not die.

They say my soul is twisted and warped,
 My ways are cringing and mean,
That I worship the bulk of the calf of gold,
 That my hands are not white and clean;
They say—but a thousand reasons hold
 To stalk the quarry then
When the lust for blood is hunger-felt
 By the beast that dwells in men.

When Kindness is taught at the end of a rope,
 And Love to the music of groans;
When Charity masks in a cloak of flame,
 And Mercy in falling stones—
What wonder the balm for the spirit fails
 When the wounds are kept so fresh
Through countless years of active hate
 In the rack of the tortured flesh?

I have ceased to long for the clasp of Love,
 To dream of the smile of a friend,
I grip my trusty wander-staff
 In a journey without an end.
My faith is strong as the primal rocks,
 And deep as my tearless woes;
I am Job of the nations—heir of wrongs,
 But why—Jehovah knows.

                    ELIAS LIEBERMAN.

In Exile

TWILIGHT is here, soft breezes bow the grass,
 Day's sounds of various toil break slowly off,
The yoke-freed oxen low, the patient ass
 Dips his dry nostril in the cool, deep trough.

Up from the prairie the tanned herdsmen pass
  With frothy pails, guiding with voices rough
Their udder-lightened kine. Fresh smells of earth,
The rich, black furrows of the globe send forth.

After the Southern day of heavy toil,
  How good to lie, with limbs relaxed, brows bare
To evening's fan, and watch the smoke-wreaths coil
  Up from one's pipe-stem through the rayless air.
So deem these unused tillers of the soil,
  Who stretched beneath the shadowing oak-tree, stare
Peacefully on the star-unfolding skies,
And name their life unbroken paradise.

The hounded stag that has escaped the pack,
  And pants at ease within a thick-leaved dell;
The unimprisoned bird that finds the track
  Through sun-bathed space, to where his fellows
     dwell;
The martyr, granted respite from the rack,
  The death-doomed victim pardoned from his cell,—
Such only know the joy these exiles gain,—
Life's sharpest rapture is surcease of pain.

Strange faces theirs, where through the Orient sun
  Gleams from the eyes and glows athwart the skin.
Grave lines of studious thought and purpose run
  From curl-crowned forehead to dark-bearded chin.
And over all the seal is stamped thereon
  Of anguish branded by a world of sin,
In fire and blood through ages on their name,
Their seal of glory and the Gentiles' shame.

Freedom to love the law that Moses brought,
  To sing the songs of David, and to think
The thoughts Gabirol to Spinoza taught,
  Freedom to dig the common earth, to drink
The universal air—for this they sought
  Refuge o'er wave and continent, to link
Egypt with Texas in their mystic chain;
And truth's perpetual lamp forbid to wane.

Hark! through the quiet evening air, their song
   Floats forth with wild sweet rhythm and glad re-
     frain.
They sing the conquest of the spirit strong,
   The soul that wrests the victory from pain;
The noble joys of manhood that belong
   To comrades and to brothers. In their strain
Rustle of palms and Eastern streams one hears,
And the broad prairie melts in mist of tears.

EMMA LAZARUS.

A Cry from Russia

BROTHERS, my brothers—you that are free
   In the golden lands, beyond the sea,
Are you blind that you do not heed the scars
Of my futile hands as they beat the bars?
Are you deaf that you do not heed the cry
Of the Little People who will not die?
Who will not die though with fear
Without their Ghetto walls. Ah, hear
The anguished cry of the mother of sons
Who are spat on thus by the lordly ones:
   "Ye may not labor. Ye have no goal.
Back to your hovels! Herd as the swine!
Be eaten with fear to your very soul!"
This is the birth of the coward's whine.
Brothers, my brothers, the days are long
For the wretched one who does no wrong,
But to live through beggary, misery—aye
Worse than these—a Jew till he die.
For he sucked, with the milk at his mother's breast,
Patient for scorn and patient for jest,
Wounds of the body and wounds of the soul
Till a day when the Lord God made him whole
The shining day he will bless the pain
That has brought the Jew to his own again.
He will bless the pain. But brothers mine
Easy for you not to herd as swine;

Prosperous, florishing—kith and kin,
Easy for you to stay clean within.
But, O my Brothers beyond the sea,
The days are long and bitter for me.

HERMINE SCHWED.

To Russia

WHO tamed your lawless Tartar blood?
    What David bearded in her den
The Russian bear in ages when
    You strode your black, unbridled stud,
A skin-clad savage of your steppes?
Why, one who now sits low and weeps,
Why, one who now wails out to you,—
The Jew, the Jew, the homeless Jew.

    Who girt the thews of your young prime
And bound your fierce divided force?
Why, who but Moses shaped your course
    United down the grooves of time?
Your mighty millions all today
The hated, homeless Jew obey.
Who taught all poetry to you?
The Jew, the Jew, the hated Jew.

    Who taught you tender Bible tales
Of honey-lands of milk and wine?
Of happy, peaceful Palestine?
    Of Jordan's holy harvest vales?
Who gave the patient Christ? I say
Who gave the Christian creed? Yea, yea,
Who gave your very God to you?
Your Jew! Your Jew! Your hated Jew!

JOAQUIN MILLER.

The Slaughter of the Jews

FOOLS who kill for the lust of blood, fiends of the
    slaughter pen,
Who wreak red malice on women and babes and gray
    and defenceless men;
Murderers, thugs, assassins, who, e'en in religion's
    name,
Dare the work of the ghouls to do, and crawl in your
    bestial shame—
This in the name of religion. Why, fools who are less
    than clod,
From the Jew you borrowed your altar, from the Jew
    you filched your God.
His was the great Jehovah whom your churchly rites
    attest,
And his was the wondrous Bible that shone on your
    darkened West.
      His David still is singing,
        Your souls oppressed to thrill,
      And Sinai's voice is ringing:
        "Thou shalt not, shalt not kill!"
Murderers! thugs! assassins! sodden and ingrate crew!
Most of the best ye now disdain was learned of the
    hated Jew!

In temples of desecration his psalms ye have mouthed
    today;
Then turned from the hollow praises to slaughter and
    kill and slay;
Ye have mourned with his Jeremiah, as great was your
    need to do,
But if mourning fostered brute alone, small was the
    gain to you.
"Why should ye be stricken any more?" Isaiah moan-
    eth still,
But all that ye learn from the broken words is kill—
    and kill—and kill!

673

And Rachel still is mourning that her children are no
    more,
While your hearts are mad with malice and your hands
    are red with gore.
        Still rolls the awful thunder
          O'er Sinai's darkened hill,
        While still—oh, deed of wonder!—
          Ye kill—and kill—and kill!
Fools who are less than brutish, tyranny's pestilent
    crew,
A beast may spring on his master—and ye do murder
    the Jew.

When your forbears sat in their frozen dens and mum-
    bled their rotten bones
From Palestine echoed northward the great Jehovah's
    tones.
The God of the Jew had spoken, and your ancestor
    heard and knew,
And his first dim knowledge of truth and right he
    learned of the hated Jew.
Aye, more! From Nazareth came one day the Man
    who is thine and mine,
And he set in the soul of the brutish man the germ
    of a thought divine,
And the germ took root in the soul of man, and ever
    it bloomed and grew,
And the Christ whom your crimsoned hands do flout
    was a Jew and the son of a Jew,
        His heart for the sad world bleeding,
          He loved and forgave us still;
        And yet, that lesson unheeding,
          Ye kill—and kill—and kill!
Fools who are less than brutish, tyranny's pestilent
    crew,
All that the world holds dearest is slaughtered in him
    —the Jew.
                A. J. WATERHOUSE.

The Crowing of the Red Cock

ACROSS the Eastern sky has glowed ·
    The flicker of a blood-red dawn,
Once more the clarion cock has crowed,
    Once more the sword of Christ is drawn.
A million burning rooftrees light
The world-wide path of Israel's flight.

Where is the Hebrew's fatherland?
    The folk of Christ is sore bestead;
The Son of Man is bruised and banned,
    Nor finds whereon to lay his head.
His cup is gall, his meat is tears,
His passion lasts a thousand years.

Each crime that wakes in man the beast,
    Is visited upon his kind.
The lust of mobs, the greed of priest,
    The tyranny of kings, combined
To root his seed from earth again,
His record is one cry of pain.

When the long roll of Christian guilt
    Against his sires and kin is known,
The flood of tears, the life-blood spilt,
    The agony of ages shown,
What oceans can the stain remove,
From Christian law and Christian love?

Nay, close the book; not now, not here,
    The hideous tale of sin narrate,
Reëchoing in the martyr's ear,
    Even he might nurse revengeful hate,
Even he might turn in wrath sublime,
With blood for blood and crime for crime.

Coward? Not he, who faces death,
　Who singly against worlds has fought,
For what? A name he may not breathe,
　For liberty of prayer and thought.
The angry sword he will not whet;
His nobler task is—to forget.

EMMA LAZARUS.

A Hymn for the Relief of Israel

WHEN Israel's sons in Egypt groaned,
　Beneath the proud oppressor's yoke,
The God of Love his children owned,
　The Lord of Might their bondage broke.

With mighty arm and outstretched hand,
　By signs and wonders great and sore,
He led them forth from Egypt's land,
　He gave them rest on Caanan's shore.

Now spread through far and distant lands,
　Yet never lost—enchained, yet free—
To Thee they lift their suppliant hands,
　And raise them with their hearts to Thee.

Thy word still lives—that word which taught
　The mouth that cursed Thy flock to bless;
That word which their salvation wrought,
　That faith which still their lips confess.

O! turn the hearts of those who still
　Tread down Thy living sanctuary,
Send forth the mandate of Thy will,
　And set Thy chosen people free!

CANON JENKINS.

THE MODERN PERIOD

To the Czar—a Prophecy

HOW canst thou face thy Maker, how canst thou
    ever dare
With all the guilt upon thy head to turn to Him in
    prayer?
Thou rearest thy religion to cloak thy evil deeds;
The torture thou inflicted on those of other creeds,
The exilings, the pogroms, the persecutions all,
Thou plannest with thy minions, within thy palace
    wall.

To thy corrupt officialdom thou givest a free rein
To murder, pillage, harass thy subjects for its gain.
With olden-time barbarity, with cruelty unsurpassed,
Thou rulest o'er an Empire, so wonderful, so vast,
Whose boundless wealth lies buried for ages, 'neath the
    soil,
Whose undeveloped resources wait but for honest toil,
While sore distress and famine go stalking in the land,
All enterprise, initiative stayed by a tyrant's hand.

Bright shines the torch of progress in every land but
    thine,
Illumining every pathway that leads to Freedom's
    shrine;
In thy realm superstition and ignorance hold sway,
Grim allies of oppression that darken every way;
That foster crime and vices of all the vilest sort
And make of human beings a beastly dangerous horde.
Thou art a shame, a byword among the nations all,
Thy subjects' execrations hang o'er thee like a pall!

*   *   *   *   *

How long wilt thou, O Russia, thy cruel burdens bear?
How long wilt thou meekly succumb to dull despair?
Rise up, throw off thy shackles, strike for the right
    to live!
For freedom, justice, tolerance, thy people's wrongs
    retrieve!

677

And thou wilt surely triumph, for tyrants cowards
    are,
They shrink beneath the radiance of Liberty's bright
    star.
For thee will dawn an era of brighter, happier days,
And all thy lamentations will change to songs of
    praise;

The present chaos, misrule, which now so hopeless
    seem,
Will then be but a memory, a nightmare in a dream,
Once more among the nations thou wilt then take thy
    place,
And with their march toward progress and culture
    keep apace.
Thy people will be blessed o'er all thy broad domain,
When Law and Order shall prevail, and Peace su-
    preme shall reign!

IDA (MRS. ISIDOR) STRAUS.

To Forgive is Divine

FATHER of Mercies, and all Human Love,
    Who peereth far beyond our sullen skies,
  Remember all the smile-borne agonies,
And stubborn scars of saintly men who strove
With glaives of griefless Faith, in dyke and grove,
  And byre and barn, 'gainst the barbarities
  Of priest and mob, and the atrocities
By traitors wreaked in passion for their dove.
Remember not those loathsome deeds, O Lord!
  But spread the light of Wisdom in the hearts
  Of Rulers, and of Nations in those parts,
Where ripens knowledge of Thine Holy Word,
  That in our day, Israel may once more
  Have Peace, and Sunshine, as in days of yore.

M. L. R. BRESLAR.

678

"Blood" v. "Bullion"

WELL then, it now appears you need my help,
  Go to then: you come to me, and you say,
  'Shylock, we would have moneys'—you say so;
  You that did void your rheum upon my beard,
  And foot me, as you spurn a stranger cur
  Over your threshold: moneys is your suit.
  What should I say to you? Should I not say
  'Hath a dog money?'"

> "Merchant of Venice," Act I, Scene 3.

"With bated breath and whispering humbleness?"
Not so! There comes a season when the stress
Of insolent and exacting tyranny
Makes the most patient turn.
                                    Autocracy,
Without the despot's vaunted virtue, pride,
Shows small indeed. Can Power lay aside
Its swaggering part, and low petition make
(Driven by those Treasury thirsts which never slake)
For help from those it harries? Pharaoh's scourge
Was the taskmaster's weapon used to urge
The Hebrew bondsmen to their tale of toil,
But they round whom the Russian's knouts' thongs coil
Are of the breed of the Russian palm
Can make petition to. Could triumphs balm
The wounds of ages, here were babes indeed;
But blood revolts.
                        Race of the changeless creed,
And ever-shifting sojourn, Shakespeare's type
Deep meaning hides, which, when the world is ripe
For wider wisdom, when the palsying curse
Of prejudice, the canker of the purse,
And blind blood-hatred, shall a little lift,
Will clearlier shine, like sunburst through a rift
In congregated cloud-wracks. Shylock stands
Badged with black shame in all the baser lands.
Use him, and—spit on him! That's Gentile wont;
Make him gold-conduit, and befoul the font,—

That's the true despot-plan through all the days,
And cackling Gratianos chorus praise.
"The Jew shall have all justice." Shall he so?
The tyrant drains his gold, then bids him—"Go!"
Shylock? The name bears insult in its sound;
But he was nobler than the curs who hound
The patient Hebrew from his home and drive
Deathward the stronger souls they dread alive.
Shylock? So brand him, boors and babbling wags,
Who scorn him, yet would share his money-bags;
Who hate him, yet can stoop to such appeal!
Beneath his meekness there's a soul of steel.
High-featured, amply-bearded, see he stands
Facing the Autocat; those sinewy hands
Shaped but for clutching—so his slanderers say—
The huckster bait can coldly put away
"Blood against bullion." The Jew-baiting band
Howl frantic execration o'er the land;
Malign and menace, pillage, persecute;
Though the heart's hot, the mouth must fain be mute.
The edict fulminates, the goad pursues;
Proscription, deprivation,—aye, they use
All the old tortures, nor are then content,
But crown the work with ruthless banishment.
And then—then the proud Muscovite seeks grace,
And gold, from kinsmen of the harried race!
"He would have moneys" from the Hebrew hoard,
To swell his state, or whet his warlike sword;
Perchance buy heavier scourges for the backs
Of lesser Hebrews, whom his wolfish packs
Of salaried minions hunt.
              Take back thine hand,
Imperious Autocrat, and understand
Gold buys not, rules not, serves not, salves not all,
Blood speaks—in favour of the helpless thrall
Of tyranny. Here's no tame Shylock: he
Shall not bend low, and in a bondsman's key,
Make o'er his money-bags with unctuous grace
To an enthroned enslaver of his race,

"Well then, it now appears you need my help"
(You—whose trained curs at my poor kinsmen yelp!)
"What should I say to you? Should I not say,
'Hath a dog money?'" Blood's response is—"Nay!"
PUNCH.

The Jews of Bucharest

"TAKE heed; the stairs are worn and damp!"
  My soft-tongued southern guardian said,
And held more low his twinkling lamp
  To light my cautious, downward tread.
Where that uncertain radiance fell
  The bat in startled circles flew;
Sole tenant of the sunless cell
  Our fathers fashioned for the Jew.

Yet, painted on the aching gloom,
  I saw a hundred dreadful eyes,
As out of their forgotten tomb
  Its pallid victims seemed to rise.
With fluttered heart and crisping hair,
  I stood those crowding ghosts amid,
And thought what raptures of despair
  The soundless granite walls had hid.

I saw their arsenal of crime:
  The rack, the scourge, the gradual fire,
Where priestly hangmen of old time
  Watched their long-tortured prey expire,
Then by dim warders darkling led
  Through many a rocky corridor,
Like one that rises from the dead,
  I passed into the light once more.

And does a careless brother say
  We stir this ancient dust in vain,
When palaced Bucharest to-day
  Sees the same devil loose again?

Again her busy highways wake
  To the old persecuting cry
Of men who for their Master's sake
  His chosen kindred crucify.

There oft the midnight hours are loud
  With echoes of pursuing feet;
As fired with bright zeal the crowd
  Goes raving down the Ghetto's street;
The broken shutter's rending crash
  That lets the sudden riot in,
And shows by those red torches' flash,
  The shrinking fugitive within.

But here are tales of deeper shame!
  Of law insulted and defied.
While Force, usurping Justice's name,
  Takes boldly the oppressor's side.
The bread whose bitterness so long,
  These sons of hated race have known;
Familiar, oft-repeated wrong
  That turns the living heart to stone.

Still Zion City lies forlorn:
  And still the Stranger in our gates,
A servant to the younger born,
  For his long-promised kingdom waits.
O, Brethren of the outer court,
  Entreat him well and speak him fair;
The form that makes your thoughtless sport
  Our coming Lord hath deigned to wear.
                    EDWARD SYDNEY TYBEE.

To Carmen Sylva (Queen of Roumania)

OH, that the golden lyre divine
    Whence David smote flame-tones were mine!
  Oh, that the silent harp which hung
        Untuned, unstrung,

682

Upon the willows by the river,
Would throb beneath my touch and quiver
With the old song-enchanted spell
        Of Israel!

Oh, that the large prophetic Voice
Would make my reed-piped throat its choice!
All ears should prick, all hearts should spring
        To hear me sing
The burden of the isles, the word
Assyria knew, Damascus heard,
When, like the wind, while cedars shake,
        Isaiah spake.

For I would frame a song to-day
Winged like a bird to cleave its way
O'er land and sea that spread between,
        To where a Queen
Sits with a triple coronet.
Genius and Sorrow both have set
Their diadems above the gold—
        A Queen three-fold!

To her the forest lent its lyre,
Hers are the sylvan dews, the fire
Of Orient suns, the mist-wreathed gleams
        Of mountain streams.
She, the imperial Rhine's own child,
Takes to her heart the wood-nymph wild,
The gipsy Pelech, and the wide
        White Danube's tide.

She who beside an infant's bier
Long since resigned all hope to hear,
The sacred name of "Mother" bless
        Her childlessness,

Now from a people's sole acclaim
Receives the heart-vibrating name,
And "Mother, Mother, Mother!" fills
      The echoing hills.

Yet who is he who pines apart,
Estranged from that maternal heart,
Ungraced, unfriended, and forlorn,
      The butt of scorn?
An alien in his land of birth,
An outcast from his brethren's earth,
Albeit with theirs his blood mixed well
      When Plevna fell?

When all Roumania's chains were riven,
When unto all his sons was given
The hero's glorious reward,
      Reaped by the sword,—
Wherefore was this poor thrall, whose chains
Hung heaviest, within whose veins
The oldest blood of freedom streamed,
      Still unredeemed?
      * * * *

              EMMA LAZARUS.

Lines on Carmen Sylva

TREMBLING old men are stamm'ring
    Scarce can their anguish tell—
Whisp'ring the ancient Hebrew,
The "Hear, O Israel!"
Some little Jew is falling,
    Clubbed in his narrow pale—
The Queen is singing sweetly
    Songs of the Nightingale.

Watchmen are growing fretful,
　Why should they longer wait?
Hurry the homeless wanderers
　Through the next dark suffering-gate.
What though anchors are lifted,
　What though poor exiles flee—
Carmen Sylva is warbling
　An Ode to Humanity.

EMMA LAZARUS.

The Russian Jewish Rabbi

I

OLD and gray, his shoulders bent,
　Tall and meagre like a cane,
To my door came up a man,
　When the day began to wane.
In one hand he held a staff,
　While the other wiped a tear,
Like the leaves on swinging boughs
　He had shrunk from cold and fear.
"Peace to you," he quietly said,
　And a tear had filled his eye;
On his face I noticed grief,
　From his heart I heard a sigh.
"Can you take me 'neath your roof?
　I am tired, and weak and old;
Just like death, severe and sharp,
　Crude and merciless the cold,
I am hungry, bare and poor,
　Orphan-like I am on soil
For I cannot tug for life
　By my hands, or mental toil.
I had been a teacher once
　And our children I had taught;
God's my witness,—I had e'er
　Perfectly my duties wrought.
Now my children have grown up,

Like grand flowers they still grow,
And I drink the bitter cup,
  Suffering in tears and woe."
Silent then became the man.
  And the tears have rolled and rolled.
On his sad and wrinkled face
  A reproach I could behold,
This was meant for him, whose heart
  In the careless body sleeps,
Who is merciless, unmoved,
  When a struggler sighs and weeps.

II

When in slumber earth was hushed,
  My fatigued and suff'ring guest
Finally in pleasant sleep
  Found forgetfulness and rest.
The night's queen, the wingy dream,
  Looked at him and sweetly smiled;
Carried him at once away,
  Where he lived while yet a child.
Here's his father's little house,
  Where he passed his childhood days;
Where his heart had freely breathed
  'Mong his friends, and mates at plays.
Here's the temple, where he oft
  With his father ran to pray,
"Tell me, dearest, why we haste,"
  To his 'pa, he used to say.
"Child, the Sabbath-hour is near,
  And the temple's open wide,—
There our souls will find repose,
  Far from care's and struggling's tide."
In the dismal synagog
  Darkness, gloom reigns over all.
Down the rigid sexton goes
  To the corner . . . By the wall
Stands a candle on a shelf;
  Fast to it he makes his way,

686

Then, by turn, he lights each lamp,
  And, when done, he walks away.
Thus the gloomy synagog
  Soon assumed an aspect bright;
And the boy with eager eyes
  Follows ev'ry trembling light.
"Where's the candle and the shaft,
  That, like in a fairy land,
Instantly created light?
Told in darkness, 'Be there light?'
  By the customary hand,
By the hand that used the light
It was slip-shod cast aside!"

III

Jewish, tired and suff'ring Rabbi,
  Such, poor teacher, is your fate!
Keeper of the Lord's commandments,
  Was your toil not holy, great?
Have you not with holy blazes
  Lit our children's heart and soul?
Have you not, inspired like prophets,
  Taught them life's true end and goal?
Rabbi, did you not instruct them
  To believe, to love and wait,
To be honest, true and faithful,
  "With a heart for any fate?"
Well, and now? . . . . With mute affliction
  You are wandering alone,
O'er your head a fearful darkness,
  In your heart a deathly moan.

     Translated by HERMAN BERNSTEIN.

"Mai-Ko-Mashma-Lon"
Cui Bono?
(Monologue of a Talmudical student.)

What's the meaning of the rainstorm?
    What's the story that it tells me?
On the window panes the rain-drops
Roll, a turbid stream of tears.
And the boots are worn and tearing,
And without 'tis muddy, stormy;
Winter, too, will soon be coming
And I have no wrap to warm me.

What's the meaning of the taper?
What's the story that it tells me?
The tallow downward drips and trickles,
Faintly flaring, dying slowly.
Like a taper weak and weary,
'Lone within this hut I wither,
Till some day in sullen quiet,
Dying they will bear me thither.

What's the meaning of the old clock?
What's the story that it tells me?
Its dial quaint and faded yellow,
Each weird stroke resounding heavy.
'Tis a lifeless, soulless object,
Merely striking at each hour,
Lacking spirit, lacking feeling,
Slave to another's will and power.

What's the meaning of my being?
What's the story that it tells me?
Days of youth are vegetating
Waxing old so prematurely.
Days of fast and tears a'plenty,
Bony knuckles for a pillow,
Sacrificing all life's pleasures
For a life that is to follow.

ABRAHAM RAISIN.
(Translated by Henry Greenfield.)

The Jewish Soldier

HARD by the walls of Plevna, not fifty yards away,
   There lies a grave forsaken, scarce visible to-day;
Forsaken and neglected, uncared for and unknown,
No wreath is there to mark it, no monument of stone.
No grass, no flowers, grow there beneath those sullen
      skies;
'Tis there a sleeping hero, a Jewish soldier lies—
A Jewish soldier fallen in Plevna's bloody fight,
When Russia, all victorious, put forth her conquering
      might.

The world is hushed to slumber and silence reigns
      around,
A silence all unbroken, no voice, no breath, no sound;
But when the chimes of midnight ring from the ancient
      tower,
Out of the east awakens a storm wind, strong in power.
Across the land it rushes, and, stronger and more
      strong,
It roars and howls and thunders in tumult wild and
      long,
Until the earth it cleaveth as with the trump of doom,
And, sword in hand, the soldier arises from his tomb.

Upon the wall he standeth, as in the dauntless past,
And from his heart sore-wounded, the blood flows free
      and fast.
His soldier's blood flows freely, his heart is wounded
      deep,
And in a voice of thunder he calls the dead from sleep.
"Awake my warrior comrades, awake and judge aright;
Say, did I not stand bravely beside you in the fight?
Like you, did I not perish on Plevna's battle plain
For Russia's greater glory, for Russia's greater gain?"

And as his words fall silent, there wakes to life once
more
A mighty host, unnumbered as sand upon the shore;
A mighty armed multitude arises at his hest,
From far and near they gather, they come from east
and west;
With marching and with clanging, with heavy, echo-
ing tread,
Until they stand before him, an army of the dead;
And ev'ry soldier answers, with high uplifted hand,
And swears: "Yea, thou hast fallen for Czar and fa-
therland."

And all again is silent, no voice, no breath, no sound,
The mighty host has vanished and stillness reigns
around;
But still the Jewish soldier stands on the fortress wall,
And soon his words, resounding, like fiery missiles fall,
"O! Russia, for thy honor did I lay down my life!
O! Russia thou hast torn me from children and from
wife!
Why dost thou now condemn them to exile and de-
spair?
My curse, my heavy curses, to thee the winds shall
bear."

And scarcely has he uttered these curses, fraught with
pain,
When swift the storm-wind carries him to his grave
again.
And at the self-same hour, and at the self-same place,
The self-same actors nightly that gloomy scene retrace.
The soldier's bitter curses grow deeper night by night,
They deepen and they gather until they rise in might,
Borne on the tempest's pinions, far o'er the land they
fly,
And on Gatschina's palace forevermore they lie.

ALICE LUCAS.

B'nai B'rith

ADOWN the vista of the long ago,
　　Like crimson flowers anod on slender stems,
Or like the gleam of iridescent gems
That half-concealed along the wayside glow,
　　Good deeds and great, and impulses divine
　　Mark man's endeavor on the paths of time.

Whene'er a noble deed is sung by Fame,
　　A flush of joy enkindles east and west;
　　Yea, half-unconsciously, all earth is blessed,
Since each life hath on every heart a claim.
　　Doth not the rose await the butterfly,
　　The brook assume the blue of summer sky?

Thus on the path of time a glowing light,
　　That gave its aid to weary, struggling men,
　　Reflected was again and yet again,
E'en a lamp between two mirrors bright;
　　And clearly burned that beacon-light wherewith
　　Men learned thy life, thy love, B'nai B'rith.

For to the lonely widow's bare abode
　　Thou bringest comfort, thou the tear dost dry
　　On pallid orphan cheek; the sufferer's cry
Has touched thy tender heart as with a goad;
　　The darkened chamber where the sick repose,
　　Thy helpful hand, thy cheering presence, knows.

And e'en to realms far, far across the seas,
　　Where Hunger toils, yet cannot ease its want,
　　Where chatt'ring Cold is clad in garments scant,
And dark Oppression reigns,—for even these
　　Thy strong right hand has snapped the iron rod,
　　And 'mid fierce conflict claimed a truce of God.

691

Here did thy foot, on Freedom's daisied turf,
  For far Roumania's child a refuge seek
  From fire, from sword, from crimes we dare not
    speak;
Here manhood crowned the erstwhile cowering serf.
  And thou didst teach him glorious liberty:
  Hark! the refrain, "My country, 'tis of thee!"

Ne'er has that country summoned thee in vain;
  Thy soul rose ever, ready at her call,
  Poor wind-swept Galveston, 'neath ruined wall,
Found swift relief from hunger, want and pain.
  No tardy charity thy offering mars—
  Brothers are all beneath the Stripes and Stars.

And now the pearl of fifty-seven years
  Glides on the slender golden thread of time;
  The while lost voices through our converse chime,
We see loved faces through a mist of tears—
  The friends who worked beside us long ago,
  Who slumber where the waning grasses grow.

Their hearts conceived a glorious brotherhood
  Of friendship and of love—a power that glides
  From man to man, and yet fore'er abides,
The pioneers of progress they, who stood
  Upon the starry mountain peaks of time,
  And saw the future in a light sublime.

Their task is done; they gave our outstretched hands
  The silken banner and the silvery horn,
  On! upward, then! A golden age is born!
A century its magic flower expands!
  On life's great summits seek ye out its birth,
  And with its bloom and fragrance fill the earth.
                   MIRIAM DEL BANCO.

B'nai Brith

PAUSE, O ye winds of Heaven, pause in your
    winged flight
To catch on your spreading bosom, on your circling
    pinions bright,
The voices of Heavenly joyance, the pæans of gladsome
    praise
That float from yon mansion of splendor, lit by eternal
    rays.

That float yon palace of beauty, that rears to a tower-
    ing height
In proud built, massive grandeur, its gleaming walls
    of light,
Yea, count ye, the many stories, and mark ye the noble
    air
'Tis the Order B'nai B'rith—a castle wondrous fair!

Then pause, O ye fleeting winds, and hark to the puls-
    ing swells,
The anthems of glorious hope, the peal of the Jubilee
    bells!
As they mount to the crystal skies, and gladden the
    welkin above
With their silvery voices of love, born of a golden love.

A myriad host of voices, that flood the night with glee
And grow from a muffled murmur to an outcry wild
    and free
As we climb from the level upward, in the wondrous
    palace of light,
And the bells increase in beauty, and the walls increase
    in might.

The sun-kissed heights at last; in pride subdued we turn
To cast a backward glance, and our souls within us
    burn,

Yea friends, a noble structure, framed from our hearts'
    best love
With willing hands well-wrought, and blessed by
    Heaven above.

See from the thousand windows, the streaming rays of
    light
Dispelling with warmth and splendor the darkness of
    the night,
And guiding the weary ones, lost in the blackness with-
    out,
Straight to the Beacon of hope, away from the laby-
    rinth of doubt.

The twilight of ignorance changing to the glorious
    noonday bright,
A lamp of life to the struggling, a torch to the blinded
    sight,
Enlightenment, fair motto engraved on our walls and
    souls;
Light! Light! for the night-wrapt world—yea, spread
    it to the poles.   ROSA STRAUSS.

On Attempting to Convert the Jews to Christianity

WHEN thou canst wash the Ethiopian white,
    Govern the winds or give the sun more light,
Cause by thy words the mountain to remove,
Control the seas or hurl the bolt of Jove,
Then hope—but not till then—to turn the Jews,
To Christian doctrines, and to Christian views;
For Christian faith, say conscience, is thy guide,
The Jews, for conscience sake 'gainst it decide.
One God thou callest three, and three but one,
The Jews acknowledge God as one alone,
To whom all honour, praise, and glory due,
From Christian, Pagan, Mussulman and Jew.

694

Were not the Jews from Abraham decreed
To be the holy and the chosen seed,
Appointed to receive and to record
The sacred scriptures of the Almighty's word,
While every prophet's tongue, and angels' voice
Proclaimed that people God's peculiar choice?
Then why should humanity presume
To question God's decree and assume
Wisdom, beyond the reach of mortal ken,
Unknown to angels, unconceived by men?

To Abraham, Isaac, and to Jacob too
God did sacred promises renew;
Told them, their seed, conducted by his hand
Should surely see and gain the promised land.
What though proud Pharaoh long in bondage kept
The sons of Jacob, while they mourned and wept?
Yet, in due time, the promises prevailed,
And God's beloved their great deliverer hailed.

Moses the holy prophet of the Lord,
With inspiration blessed, proclaimed the word;
Gave comfort when his brethren most despaired,
And all the mercies of their God declared;
By miracles and wonders set them free
From Pharaoh's proud and ruthless tyranny.
Led them triumphant from the fatal shore,
From which their enemies returned no more;
Who madly rash, and impiously brave,
All found in Israel's path a watery grave.
Thus Pharaoh and the host of Egypt failed—
Israel was saved—the Lord of Hosts prevailed.

Did not such wonders and such judgments prove
The Jews to be the object of God's love?
Then what art thou who darest dispute their claim
To blessings promised in the Eternal name?
Oppressed, distressed, and wandering o'er the world,
The ensign of their glory still unfurled?

695

What now supports them? What does joy afford?
Hope in the promises—faith in God the Lord.

Canst thou from hope and faith their tribes seduce
By specious arguments, howe'er profuse?
No, conversion must from conviction flow—
The mind to mere assertions cannot bow;
Man must believe what nature's reasons cite,
Until illumed by some superior light,
Canst thou communicate those rays divine?
Presumptuous man! let humbler thoughts be thine.

Serve thou thy God with all thy heart and soul,
Seek not thy neighbour's conscience to control;
But humbly hope that all who are sincere
In goodness, will eternal mercy share;
That every honest charitable heart
Will of celestial bliss enjoy its part;
When God shall summon all before his throne
Each one to answer for himself alone.

ANONYMOUS.

Autumn Songs

THE Jews, my brothers, will they understand me?
  And all that stirs within a poet's heart?
Will they believe how deep can be his sadness,
  How burning and incurable the smart?

A Jew has learned to think of other matters
  Since first from out the mud he raised
And stood upon his feet, and managed shortly
  To look like other people, God be praised!

For all eternity he had a teacher,
  On Sabbath days the Scripture to explain
And as he listened, full of deep contrition
  He sighed and sobbed; his tears fell down like rain.

696

And then, he had a crazy thing, a jester
  A man of brains, a youth sharp-witted, quick,
And in his verse he would find refreshment,
  And with his tongue would click.

And then sometimes, he brought him of a pedlar
  Or else at fairs, a tale,—upon my word,
It is the very drollest thing that ever
  Was seen or heard.

One reads and laughs and then a little farther
  One reads and laughs till one is like to split.
One laughs, because to that intent and purpose
  The thing was writ.

What then? Is Jewish life so cheerful?
  Contains it then so much at which to smile?
Are there so many things away from sadness
  The stricken heart one moment to beguile?

And do we then lament so very seldom?
  Let's reckon now and see if we can tell:
We weep throughout the fast-day of Atonement,
  The rich and poor, the young and old as well.

We weep o'er Lamentations and Confession,
  We weep the daylight and the darkness through,
And are we not to laugh a little ever?
  Go, let us be! why that would never do!

They've laughed in years gone by, and in the future
  To laugh they will continue, just so long
As there shall live a Jew—then hush, be silent
  My song, my melancholy song.

                S. FRUG.

(Translated by Alice Stone Blackwell.)

Feldmesten or Measuring the Graves

ON hill and glade, the flowers fade,
    The bleaching grass is all a-cold;
The leaves all frayed, in dust are laid,
    The shrewd and churlish winds grow bold.

Like jealous thieves, they tear the leaves
    That shiver, clinging to the tree,
The Eden leaves—the heart, it grieves,
    The chilly air's a prophecy.

The signs of loss and wreckage float;
    A tear is trembling in the sky;
The bird, a lump is in her throat,
    For song and summer that must die.

Granny, these Ellul penance days,
    Days, purgatorial, sad and sere,
Like pilgrim plods her dolorous ways
    To burial grounds to drop her tear.

With prophesying heart and look,
    The yarn in use for shrouds she buys,
And lays it in her prayer-book,
    And wipes, and wipes again her eyes.

And hobbling hies her to the graves;
    Her heart, a nest of gnawing fears;
And there unwinds, unwinds and laves
    The thread with tears—they weep, her years.

She sobs and sighs some sacred word,
    With pain as if the grave did yawn
Within her heart; as if she heard
    The whirr of worms in coffins spawn.

She bows her head, and lays the thread,
    And metes and measures every mound;
Each peaceful dwelling of the dead,
    Each holy home in silence bound.

Her tears, they well, her tears, they roll,
  As on the grave she lays the line;
And something sobs within her soul,
  "You, too, one day will have this shrine.

"Your sacred mound, some hands will mete;
  Who knows if not your fingers now
Have measured here your life's retreat,
  The grave which time for you will plow?"

She wipes a tear, winds up again
  The hallowed, dusty tear-touched thread,
She takes it home, and weaves amain
  A wick by which the Torah's read.

A wick, a lamp for Judah's camp,
  That keeps the Torah's law of life—
And then she sighs—"No more they tramp
  The dead, the dead are free from strife.

"O Lord, of love and living years,
  We lit Thy Torah's lamp so long,
With threads of graves, with threads of tears,
  When will we weave it threads of song?"

                                    ALTER ABELSON.

Nature and the Poet

MY Rabbi was Nature—she set me to learn,
  She taught me to sing and she taught me to play,
She taught me to think and to feel, day by day,
And all that is beautiful, swift to discern,
The heart must be fresh, and the brain clear and steady,
The scales and the measure be waiting and ready,
And I, after all, have become—why you know it;
A poet, my brothers, a poor Jewish poet.

                                    S. Frug.

On the Grave of Michael Gordon

ONE more gravestone—one more heart
  Cold and still has found relief,
From the joy and bitter smart,
  From the wrath of other's grief.

Where the ash is strewn about
  Lies the dear old fiddle lone
And the crazy song rang out
  With a sudden sound of moan.

Strong and earnest, unafraid
  Rose the song clear and high.
Ring the bell—the piece is played!
  Hushed the laughter, hushed the cry.

In the land where, free from pain,
  Thou, dear soul, art gone to live,
One assurance still retain
  All the comfort we can give.

This, while yet there lives a Jew,
  Through the many coming years
Shall thy songs be sung anew
  Some with laughter, some with tears.

Sleep thou spirit sweet and rare,
  Where the leaves of life are shed!
Thine own songs shall be the Pray'r
  Spoke in blessing o'er the dead.

                                    S. FRUG.

Sand and Stars

SHINES the moon, the stars are glowing,
  The night sweeps on o'er hill and plain;
In the tattered book before me
  I read, and read them once again.

Ancient words of promise holy,
  And loud at last they speak to me
"As the stars of heaven—my people
  And as the sand beside the sea."

Lord Almighty Thou hast spoken,
  Unchanging is Thy holy will,
Ev'rything at Thy commandment
  His own appointed place shall fill.

Yes, dear Lord, we're sand and pebbles,
  We're scattered, underfoot and trod,
But the stars, the bright and sparkling,
  The stars, the stars,—where are they, God?

S. Frug.

The False Hope

"Zionism's only Hope is in the Jews of America."—
Nordau.

METHOUGHT I saw the heavy eyelids rise,
  The Midased face shine clear of its gilt dream
The lightning gaze that should beseem
The answerer; the flash shall fire the skies
With beauty of a mighty heart that flies
  Strong with its hope and in its strength supreme
  With its own life a people's life redeem,
Ordained and sealed unto this enterprise.

This great thing was: dear God! what doth enhance
  The swinish sleep, the dream, the easihead!
What turns him from the master—Circumstance
  To slumber and a trough of unearned bread!
O sluggard, spendthrift of the fateful Chance!
  O shameless shame of our heroic dead.

Horace M. Kallen.

Out of the Depths

OUT of the depths of despair
　　There cometh a plaint and a prayer;
Give ear to this cry, O my brothers,
　　From lips that have pleaded for others!

"Must I die in the land of the living
　　A terrible two-fold death,
Or come ye with mercy, life-giving,
　　Ere the angel shall stifle my breath?

"I found a world of oppression,
　　Of merciless hatred and greed;
God's wrath—I gave it expression,
　　And the world it could not but heed.

"I heard how my people were groaning
　　'Neath tyranny's pitiless yoke,
And I uttered their muffled moaning
　　Till men turned pale as I spoke.

"And all the reward that I sought for
　　Was to share in the ending of wrong;
But I fell in the cause that I fought for,
　　Too weak for even a song.

"I am still in the land of the living
　　Where greed and oppression abound;
Yet spite of my saddest misgiving,
　　My voice can not utter a sound.

"Will you praise me and call me a prophet
　　When my bones lie under the sod?—
If I heed it at all, I shall scoff it
　　And call you to 'count before God.

"A crust of bread for each flower
　　You are saving to lay on my tomb,
Mayhap would yield me the power
　　The song of my youth to resume.

" 'Tis no marble pillar I task for
   But for Truth and Right alone;
Then stint not the pity I ask for,
   To pay me for bread, with a stone."

Out of the depths of despair
O hearken a plaint and a prayer!
O brothers, make haste to attend it
Ere comes the grim Reaper to end it.

That ancient and often-told story
Of a prophet despoiled of his glory,
Till, deaf to the praise of vain mortals,
He enters eternity's portals.

JOSEPH JASIN.

As the Stars and the Sands

THE hills and the valleys are flooded with moonlight,
   The radiant stars, how resplendent they gleam!
Before me lies open the dear, olden volume,
   On whose pages I ponder and dream.

I pore o'er its pages so precious and sacred,
   When sudden there whispers a voice unto me:
"I have promised, O Israel, I have sworn to make you
   Like the stars of the heavens, the sands of the sea!"

O Lord of Creation! what mortal dare question
   A single word of Thy Promise of grace?
Every deed Thou hast pledged Thou art mighty to do
   it—
   Each thing in its time, each part in its place.

And one thing e'en now Thou hast surely fulfilled it,
   Mine own eyes behold it, forbidding all doubt;
We have become like the sand that is worthless,
   Trodden and trampled and blown about.

703

Yes, dear Lord, as the sand the pebbles
  Are we scattered and strewn 'neath contemptuous
    feet;
But the stars—how long, O Lord, ere the stars
  The yearning eyes with their glory shall greet?

S. FRUG.

(Translated by Joseph Jasin.)

" . . . Whom You Are to Blame"

(Dedicated to "Mentor.")

ONCE in my secluded chamber
  Late at night I read
Israel's ancient wondrous story;
  How he shone and shed

Light around him, in his homeland
  Thriving free and great . . .
Then my thoughts passed to his later
  Treacherous, cruel fate:

Israel homeless, footsore, captive
  Into exile goes,
And the world has long forgotten
  What to him it owes.

"Gentile world! You have polluted
  Springs from which you drank!"
And in bitter, sad reflections,
  Tired and weak I sank. . . .

.   .   .   .

Stealthily an old man entered
  My secluded room;
On his breast a cross suspended,
  In his eyes—deep gloom.

704

"Fear not," said he, "vain intruder
I am not, you'll find;
You accused me, and I came here,
Came to speak my mind.

"Not defend myself, but tell you
Whom you are to blame"
For your homelessness, your downfall,
For your grief and shame.

"No, not I, but you polluted
Your eternal spring;
Home and faith and pride abandoned,
And to exile cling.

"Kneel and pray to alien altars,
Worship alien gods,
Even like in cast-off garments
Deal in cast-off thoughts.

"Gather crumbs at strangers' tables . . .
No, your pride is gone!
For you glory that you have no
Table of your own. . . .

"Faith, and truth, and pride—all treasures
You have prized of old;
For a lentil-pottage long since
You your birthright sold.

"You no longer feel the horror
Of a slave's disgrace.
Do you want me to respect you,
Honour such a race?

"Once you heroes had and prophets
Noble, great and true;
How much of their daring spirit
Now is left in you?

"Grandsons of the Maccabeans!
 If those heroes came
Saw their servile offsprings—they would
 Die again—of shame!

"Dead is all your pride and valour,
 Silent is your tongue,
Tongue of bards, and kings and prophets—
 You forsook it long.

"And your home that waits deserted
 Do you e'er recall?
Where are all your rich and mighty—
 Mammon's High Priests all?

"Like deserters they are sailing
 Under foreign flags,
Lackeys that their masters' mantles
 Wear—to hide their rags.

"Crumbs of bread, and night of lodging—
 Dare no more expect!
No, a race that lost its self-pride
 No one can respect.

"This is all I came to tell you!
 Now, good-bye . . . I spoke. . . ."

. . . .

"Stay!" I shrieked, "I must reply you,
 Stay"—and I awoke. . . .

P. M. RASKIN.

Side by Side

JEW and Christian, side by side,
 They rest in the cool earth's bosom wide—
Or lying deep where the billows sweep,
In the heart of the great green sea they sleep!
Over them flutters the banner fair,
While a sadness thrills in the Springtide air.

706

Jew and Christian, side by side,
As men they fought, and as men they died!
Like brothers stood fast at the bugle blast,
Until like brothers they sleep at last.
While over them flutters the banner fair,
And a sadness thrills in the Springtide air.

Jew and Christian, side by side,
For their common country they lived and died,
And they vigil keep, in their dreamless sleep,
O'er the brotherhood that is ours to keep.
While over us flutters the banner fair,
Though a sadness thrills in the Springtide air.

ISABELLA R. HESS.

The Young Rabbi

THOU lookest backward reverently. 'Tis well!
    The springs of life and faith are still our shrines,
And, standing strong in living deed, the spell
    Of this day's call thy listening heart divines.

The to-morrow's light is on thy brow, thy step
    Leans forward where the quickening Word abides;
Thy past a pledge that yet that Mystic Roll
    A fuller, holier revelation hides.

Young heritor of ancient faith, thou guide
    Of present need, and seer of faith to be!
The august centuries converge on thee—
    One living God behind, before, beside.

The same Eternal keeps the open door;
Stand forth with Him and sing to-day's Mismor!

E. C. L. BROWNE.

" . . . and Give Thee Peace"

THE Summer glories fade in autumn mists,
  The sombre earth is wrapped in clouds of gloom;
Faint through the storm-filled air a sound is borne,
  A sound of dread—a sound of awful doom.

It is the tread of armed marching hosts,
  The muffled roar of death-dispensing fire,
The cry of anguish, and the piteous groan
  Of brave men dying in the battle mire.

O God! that creatures fashioned in Thy shape
  Should in Thy sight, their brother-creatures slay!
Oh, riddle dire! whose answer we must wait
  Beyond the narrow limit of the day!

Let forth the snow-plumed bird! Speed Thou her
    flight
  Across this world of storm, and stress, and strife,
That where she spreads her magic pinions' shade,
  Joy may awake to sweet and happy life!

FLORENCE WEISBERG.

Twenty-one Years of Rescue Work

SHAMED and degraded you call them—they!
  Flung in the nameless abysses, whose anguish de-
    files,
  Where grief is forbidden to weep, and agony forced
    into smiles.
Shamed and degraded, you say!
  O for a tongue of fire, for words like to scourging
    flame,
  Telling that theirs is the anguish, and ours, ours
    only, the shame.

708

Ours, or we shudder and turn aside,
  Holding our whiteness aloof from the stench and the
    stain,
  While t'wards those pestilent depths there passes a
    pitiful train,
Hunger and evil their guide,
  Innocent, ignorant, starving, thrust forth on the
    fatal track—
  Ours is the shame, for they perish, and we could
    have held them back!

Could—nay, we can, for behold the throng,
  Sad souls ready to perish, still passing the self-same
    way,
  Men and women of Israel, come to their aid this day,
Rise, let your hands be made strong!
  Souls, in God's image created, maimed, prisoned and
    tortured see.
  God do so to us and more also, if we do not set
    them free!

                                        ALICE LUCAS.

A Call to Israel

WHERE is the modern Judah Maccabee?
    He of the dauntless soul in warrior guise,
To lead anew the world's hope of the free,
  While silent nations Israel's claim denies;
Shall tortured hearts by hands tyrannic slain,
Throughout long years bear martyrdom in vain?

Where dwells that silent, kingly soul unknown?
  Predestined champion of illustrious race,—
His portion more than splendors of a throne;
  To bear aloft the Lion standard's grace;
With human voice of God's authority,
To summon all the hosts of Liberty!

709

It may be 'neath compulsion's daily toil,
  Eating the bitter crusts of poverty;
A trembling exile, on a foreign soil,
  Our New Deliverer finds that destiny
Has wrought misfortune for Life's higher aim,
And the world's freedom in God's holy name!

It may be, that by song and music lulled
  Into the selfish life's forgetfulness,
The heart thornless flowers of beauty culled,
  Feels the quick throb of pitying helpfulness;
The wakened conscience, for the needs of Time,
Fashions the hero unto acts sublime.

In Israel's glorious past transcendent shone
  The reverent daring of the Woman-soul;
Fair Esther proved her birthright to a throne;
  Great names adorn eventful centuries' roll,
With trumpet-blast of battle;—silent deed,
Of noblest service to a world in need.

May not the wise, omnipotent decree
  Of the All-Merciful, Eternal One,
Find 'mid the multitude of brave and free,
  Some modern Judith? in ascendance won
For Freedom's holiest cause; to light the way
Unto the Tyrants' overthrow, To-day!

How sweet the peace of blest security!
  As 'gainst all warfare hearts humane declaim;
That is no righteous use of liberty,
  That blends with Freedom's breath a despot's name.
By force and fraud, and cruel wrong assailed,
With sheathed sword, Justice keeps her pure eyes veiled!
And Force and Fraud, hand linked with Bigotry,
Form the Chief Guards of Russia's sovereignty.

Where is the modern Judah Maccabee?
  Welcome the Conqueror in whatever guise!
Life is but living death when liberty
  Beneath Oppression's stifling process dies.

Rise valiant daughters of the prophet line.
Rise, Jewish warriors with the rage divine,
That scorns subjections! better honored graves,
Than longer be the blood-stained Tyrant's slaves.
The world that should espouse your cause is still—
Arise! Arm! Strike! do Freedom's holy will!

CORA WILBURN.

Meditations at Twilight

AH, more and more at evening,
    When twilight edges to its end,
And darkness, eastern caverns leaving,
    Her shadow o'er creation bend;
The lowing moments foster meaning
    Upon the pageant of decay,
As glory into night diffusing
    Brings untoward sadness in her way.

Within that evening calm there comes
    A recollection faint and dim
Of boyhood, of Sabbath hour and homes,
    Of synagogue and temple hymn,
When in abated breath we heard
    The echoes of our spirit-fathers,
In praise and reverential word
    Of prayer. This spirit hovers.

Their hymns re-echo in my dreams,
    They too felt doubt, despondency;
And saw our mistrusts also beam
    In thought. The poet and sages fancy
Gave them hope beyond our mind,
    More truthful to the thought of God,
To attributes that firmly bind
    A God above—yet man to sod.

711

For ages have Thy children sought
   And find Thy mercy hath no end,
Greater, thought and deeds are wrought
   On earth to-day, than in the trend
Of generations turned to dust;
   Still must with love our bosom heave,
With hope and common manful trust,
   The rest—to God we meekly leave.

And lo! upon yon lum'nous ascent,
   There glitters joyously the star
Proclaiming night. Ah, day hath sent
   Her messengers of light afar,
Come spirit of the evening, dwell
   With us, and in our life's increase
Of doubt and the annoying spell,
   Of discontent—to us—bring peace.

JOSEPH LEISER.

The New Jewish Hospital at Hamburg

A HOSPITAL for the poor and weary Jew,
   For sons of man that suffer three-fold ills;
Burdened and baned with three infirmities;
With poverty, disease, and Judaism!

The worst of all has ever been the last,
The Jewish sickness of the centuries,
The plague caught in the Nile stream's slimy vale,
The old unwholesome faith that Egypt knew.

No healing for this sickness! All in vain
The vapor-bath and douch, vain all the tricks
Of surgery, vain all this house may bring
Of simples to its fever-tossing guests.

Will Time perchance, the eternal goddess, blot
This gloomy sorrow that handed down
From sire to son—will some far children know
The perfect happiness of cloudless health?

None can foretell! Yet meantime let us praise
The heart that full of love and wisdom sought
To trickle balm upon the rankling wound,
To give what comfort still is possible.

This loving man has built a shelter here
For suffering that a skillful hand may soothe
Or cure, or haply Death's if others fail.
Beds sets he here and cooling drinks and care.

A man of deeds, he did what one might do
And in the evening of his days he paid
Unto good works the needful due, and dreamed
To rest from labor in kind charity.

Unstinted was his hand—yet richer gifts
Rolled down his cheeks so many a time—the tears,
The precious, generous tears that oft he wept
For his poor brethren's immedicable ill.

HEINRICH HEINE.

The Rose of Sharon

OH! I love to roam in fancy o'er the hills where
   Zion stood,
There to watch the daughter Zion weeping o'er her
   widowhood;
She was like the bride of beauty storied in the Song
   of Songs,
Who was queen of all the maidens, peer among the
   lily throngs.

Sharon's lily, bride of beauty how I love to think of
   thee,
For thy lips were threads of crimson and thy neck
   of ivory,
For thine eyes seemed pools of water, clear as Hesh-
   bon's melted dew,
And thy lips were dripping honey, so I love to think
   of you.

713

Oh! for all the wise king's glory who was Israel's
    paragon,
He was like a stately cedar, cedar of the Lebanon:
I can see his litter lifted by his expert men of war,
As it passed sweet odor drifted, myrrh and spikenard
    through its door.

Israel wedded to its glory, like a garden to its flowers,
When the north wind blew upon it, it was sweet with
    scented showers;
For the bride, the Rose of Sharon, was the land of
    Palestine,
There the fig tree grew and ripened, there the apple
    and the vine.

There sweet cinnamon and saffron and the incense
    bearing trees,
There the calamus and spices perfumed each passing
    breeze;
There grew myrrh and there the aloe, there the nard
    and henna bloom,
There to die on Zion's bosom made of death the
    sweetest doom.
Oh! how I would love to see thee as thou wast when
    in thy prime,
When thy marble pavements echoed with the sandals
    keeping time
To the chorus of the Levites as they climbed the temple
    steep,
Singing psalms and hallelujahs, with their ranks a
    thousand deep.

Yet I would not weep, O daughter, for a better day
    must near,
And I would not back to Zion, for the prophets made
    this clear,
That the world shall be our garden where shall blos-
    som Zion's tree,
This, the "tree of life," the Torah, which shall bloom
    eternally.

Then, away with clouds of ashes and the weeds of
  widowhood,
For the world's a greater temple than the shrine where
  Zion stood;
And I would not back to Zion and I would not back
  again,
For our God has made our mission not for us but for
  all men.   HARRY WEISS.

"The Age of Toleration"

WHAT this "the age of toleration "—Yet
  'Tis well so named for you that wield Earth's state:
  'Tis a vast, bloody show ye tolerate,
Mute mouths, glazed eyes, round Hate's arena set!
Behold your "Christian" robes all dabbled wet,
  With human crimson, stains which to abate
  No throat thrills out—(though soft ye come, too late
With bootless gold and maudlin, vain regret!)
Comes this of Fear, great Nations? Can it be
  None dares the dripping monster's bloodshot eye?
  Not pious Germany, not ransomed Gaul,
Proud Britain, nor— Oh, shame, thy form to see
  With theirs, my country! leaning from thy stall,
  Pale but still mute, while Hell goes glittering by!
                                ARTHUR UPTON.

Intolerance

THOU canst have no other God but mine;
    Of what avail is holy script?
Who is this God thou call'st thine;
    He utters not from heart, but—lip;
Go—get thee hence before ye rue;
    My God, my creed's alone sublime,
Thy creeds, thy laws are all untrue,
    My God, and mine's alone divine.
                          RAY TRUM NATHAN.

715

They Tell Me

THEY tell me, "Give thy nation up;
   The ancient graves resign!
Give us thy soul—then plenty, wealth,
   And greatness shall be thine."

They tell me: "Think not to rebuild
   The City, proud and tall,
Of whose old splendor there is left
   Only a crumbling wall.

"Dream not thy nation to arouse
   Out of its slumber deep;
Behold, it has so many years
   Lain in a marmot's sleep!"

False prophets, hush! Fie, charlatans!
   I swerve not from the goal.
I will not give my honor up,—
   I will not sell my soul.

The path my fathers trod through life
   I follow straight and clear;
Should Death demand me, I will mount
   The scaffold without fear.

My God, my race, I will not change
   For gold or jewels' fires.
More than a stranger's treasure-house
   A grave among my sires.

              EZEKIEL LEAVITT.
(Translation from the Hebrew by Alice Stone
Blackwell.)

Gifts

OH, World-God, give me Wealth!" the Egyptian
    cried.
His prayer was granted. High as heaven, behold
Palace and Pyramid; the brimming tide
    Of lavish Nile washed all his land with gold.
Armies of slaves toiled ant-wise at his feet;
World-circling traffic roared through mart and street;
His priests were gods; his spice-balmed kings enshrined,
    Set death at naught in rock-ribbed charnels deep.
Seek Pharaoh's race to-day, and ye shall find
    Rust and the moth, silence and dusty sleep.

"Oh, World-God, give me Beauty!" cried the Greek.
    His prayer was granted. All the earth became
Plastic and vocal to his sense; each peak,
    Each grove, each stream, quick with Promethean
        flame,
Peopled the world with imaged grace and light.
The lyre was his, and his the breathing might
Of the immortal marble; his the play
    Of diamond-pointed thought and golden tongue
Go seek the sunshine-race, ye find to-day
    A broken column and a lute unstrung.

"Oh, World-God, give me Power!" the Roman cried.
    His prayer was granted. The vast world was
        chained
A captive to the chariot of his pride.
    The blood of myriad provinces was drained
To feed that fierce, insatiable red heart.
Invulnerably bulwarked every part
With serried legions and with close-meshed Code;
    Within, the burrowing worm had gnawed its home;
A roofless ruin stands where once abode
    Th' imperial race of everlasting Rome.

"Oh, Godhead, give me Truth!" the Hebrew cried.
  His prayer was granted. He became the slave
Of the Idea, a pilgrim far and wide,
  Cursed, hated, spurned, and scourged with none to
     save.
The Pharaohs knew him, and when Greece beheld,
His wisdom wore the hoary crown of Eld.
Beauty he hath forsworn, and Wealth and Power.
  Seek him to-day, and find in every land;
No fire consumes him, neither floods devour;
  Immortal through the lamp within his hand.

EMMA LAZARUS.

Hebrew Cradle Song

NIGHT has on the earth descended,
    All around is silence deep,
Sleep, my darling, I am with thee;
    Sleep a calm and peaceful sleep.

I no lullabies shall sing thee;
    Songs are at an end to-night;
Sleep in peace, oh, sleep on sweetly,
    Long as sleep thou canst, my light.

In our native fields aforetime,
    Wondrous songs we used to sing,
Improvising them in gardens
    Turning green with early spring.

Where grew daffodils and myrtles,
    Stately palms upreared their heights,
Cypress trees spread wide their branches,
    Splendid roses blossomed bright.

But those notes are hushed and silenced;
    Ruined now our Zion lies;
Mourning sounds instead of singing;
    Yea, for songs we hear but sighs;

All thou needs must know, my darling,
　Of thy nation's piteous plight,
Thou wilt learn and weep for sorrow,
　As thy mother weeps to-night.

But why now in vain disturb thee?
　Let thy tranquil slumber last,
Until over thee, my dearest,
　The dark day of rain hath passed!

To the school, my son, I'll lead thee
　By the hand; there thou shalt learn
All our Bible and our knowledge.
　Wondrous pearls thou wilt discern—

Pearls of wisdom in our Talmud,
　Gems our sages' lore affords;
Thou shalt taste of prayer's first sweetness
　And the charm of God's great words.

Ne'er forget thou art a Hebrew!
　Little son, remember well,
Even to the grave, the stories
　That thy mother used to tell!

　　　　　　　EZEKIEL LEAVITT.
　　(Translated by Alice Stone Blackwell.)

Jewish Lullaby

MY harp is on the willow-tree,
　　Else would I sing, O love, to thee
　　A song of long ago—
Perchance the song that Miriam sung
Ere yet Judea's heart was wrung
　　By centuries of woe.

I ate my crust in tears today,
As scourged I went upon my way—
    And yet my darling smiled;
Aye, beating at my breast, he laughed—
My anguish curdled not the draught—
    'Twas sweet with love, my child!

The shadow of the centuries lies
Deep in thy dark and mournful eyes;
    But, hush! and close them now,
And in the dreams that thou shalt dream
The light of other days shall seem
    To glorify thy brow!

Our harp is on the willow-tree—
I have no song to sing to thee,
    As shadows round us roll;
But, hush and sleep, and thou shalt hear
Jehovah's voice that speaks to cheer
    Judea's fainting soul!

               EUGENE FIELD.

Patriotism

From the Persian

TO each his country dearer far
    Than the throne of Solomon;
Thorns from home, too, dearer are
    Than myrtle or than cinnamon.
Joseph, in the pride of State,
    Ruling over Egypt's strand
Sighed, and would have changed his fate
    For poverty in Canaan's Land.

      Translated by ROBERT NEEDHAM CUST.

THE MODERN PERIOD

Optimism

THE rose is hid by prickly thorn,
　Behind each night there lurks a morn,
Amidst most threat'ning sombre skies
　The many colored rainbow lies.
No night was e'er so hopeless black
That it at least one star did lack;
　So pleasure lies conceal'd midst pain
　And joy is found in sorrow's train.

I. Z. JOSEPHSON.

To My Lyre

WONDERFUL is my love
　　The love that my songs ye inspire;
My spirit, my flame and my fire,
My trophies, my treasures of old.
My temples, my silver, my gold,
My garden of flowers, my dove,
My comfort, my balm and my lyre
The hopes my years are in ye
More sweet than the world above
　And the sweets of the world to be.

JOSEPH MASSEL.

To Walter Lionel de Rothschild on His Bar-Mitzvah

THINE is the heritage of ancient birth,
　Age upon age hath dawned since first thy race
Was cradled in the empurpled East: the place
Whence seer and king have sprung—the great of earth.
And thine the heritage of higher worth;
　The large-souled Charity, whose pitying grace
　Hath left nor land nor sea without its trace,
And raised a plenteous harvest 'midst the dearth,
But thine a greater heritage than these;

721

The heaven-born Faith, thy sires have taught the
world;
Which lifts thine eyes to God without surcease,
And bid thee guard His banner, wide unfurled.
That deathless Faith make thou thy steadfast star,
Thy heart shall know a peace no pain can mar.

LOUIS B. ABRAHAMS.

Sonnet

Addressed to Sir Moses Montefiore, Dec. 10, 1878.

IF Patriarchal days alone were thine—
　　Though we might well adore the mighty Hand
　Which oft has led thee in the Promised Land
To trace the glories of thine earlier line,
Thou faithful servant of that Lord Divine
　Which tends like Shepherd true the minished band
　Of Israel—though such life in wisdom planned
Might well our hearts to wondering faith incline,
Now wonder yields to high and hallowing thought
　That faith alone could lead thine onward way
And teach our souls with earthly cares distraught
　To follow through the gloom that brightening ray
Which leads thee, now thine earthly work is wrought,
　Leaning on God, to wait the coming day.

CANON JENKINS.

Sir Moses Montefiore

SWEET blue-eyed Charity, devout and calm,
　　Hath been the dear companion of his days,
　How hath he hearken'd to her prayerful lays,
Sad-voic'd and plaintive as an angel's psalm!
She pointed and he hasten'd where the palm
　Sighs faintly in the pitiless Syrian rays,
　Where men sank gasping on the lone highways
And cried aloud for succor and for balm.

The sick he heal'd, the fallen rais'd he up;
Light track'd his footsteps through the darksome land—
And sav'd, men wept and bless'd him in their tears.
Come, friends, lift we on high the loving cup
  And hail with greetings from our distant strand
This hero crested with his hundred years!

E. YANCEY COHEN.

GROUPS of radiant angels soaring
    Upward in the sunshine's gleam;
Watched as through the gates of heaven,
  In their arms a form they bore;
And a thousand angel voices
  Sang the name of Montefiore!

Somewhere I have caught the echo,
  Drifting on till time shall end—
Caught the sound of grief and mourning;
  For the poor have lost their friend!
Silent is the voice that pleaded,
  Motionless the hand that gave,
And the voice that loved and pitied
  Stilled and pulseless in the grave.

Softly rest his soul in slumber!
  He was weary, he was lone;
Long ago his household angel
  Flitted off to heaven's throne.
Weep no tear, nor bow in sorrow,
  Praise the God we all adore,
For He crowned the earth with blessing
  When he gave it Montefiore.

MIRIAM DEL BANCO.

IS life worth living? To the querulous cry
  Let this long record, lately closed, reply!
A century of service to mankind!
Pessimist cold and cynic blandly blind,

'Tis fitter comment on that query stale
Than sneers that pall and arguments that fail.
Long in the land his days, whose heart and hand
All high and human causes could command;
Long in the land his memory will abide
His country's treasure and his people's pride.

PUNCH.

NOT 'mid the clash of arms he won
  An evanescent fame,
Nor in a nation's councils gained
  A statesman's honored name;

But in humanity's great cause
  He nobly did his part,
So shall his loved memory be
  Enshrined in every heart.

With lavish hand, on all alike,
  His charity bestowing,
None sought in vain his kindly heart,
  With generous impulse glowing.

More lasting far than marble shaft,
  Or mausoleum grand,
His mem'ry shall remain, while sounds
  His fame in every land.

LOUIS MEYERHARDT.

I SAW—'twas in a dream, the other night—
  A man whose hair with age was thin and white;
    One hundred years had bettered by his birth,
And still his step was firm, his eye was bright.

Before him and about him pressed a crowd.
Each head in reverence was bared and bowed,
    And Jews and Gentiles in a hundred tongues
Extolled his deeds and spake his fame aloud.

724

THE MODERN PERIOD

I joined the throng, and, pushing forward, cried,
"Montefiore!" with the rest, and vied
    In efforts to caress the hand that ne'er
To want and worth had charity denied.

So closely round him swarmed our shouting clan
He scarce could breathe, and, taking from a pan
    A gleaming coin, he tossed it o'er our heads,
And in a moment was a lonely man!

AMBROSE BIERCE.

Jesse Seligman

HIS was another race than mine
    Another faith, from which mine sprung:
He traced his lineage by another line,
    And gained his manhood in another tongue.

Yet when he sought our common sky,
    And breathed the welcome of its air,
His soul rose up, as eagles fly,
    To the full heights of manhood there.

Oh, Brother ours! whose life has beamed
    With faith in God, with love of man,
Through which thy patriot virtues streamed
    To bless and aid our noble land.

I stand to-day beside thy bier,
    To own thy brotherhood divine,
And proudly claim with many a tear,
    That Israel's God is thine and mine.

NOAH DAVIS.

Benjamin Artom

Chief Rabbi of the Spanish and Portuguese Jews.

WITH mournful pomp they bore him to the grave
  With all the solemn pageantry of woe;
No ancient right or custom would they waive
  Which might their grief and awe-struck reverence
    show;
  With honour and with state they laid him low,
And dignities as if a Prince had died;
  He was a Prince—none nobler rank could know
Than that he bore with such an honest pride—
God's priest! A warrior chief fighting on Heaven's
    side!

He came a stranger from his Southern shore,
  To colder climes, to natures less intense,
He came—and was a stranger then no more,
  For with the music of his eloquence
He won our hearts, and charmed our every sense.
  That music's dead, the earthly bonds are riven,
And he who woke the chords is summoned hence,
  "The Gates of Hope" to which his thoughts were
    given
    Have flung their portals wide and shown the path
      to Heaven!

Patron of learning! Champion of the poor!
  These are the titles that he nobly gained,
These are the honours that will still endure
  And teach mere earthly rank to be disdained.
The empire cannot die for him who reigned
  By sympathy and knowledge; and the host
That will perpetuate a name unstained,
  Poor, seeking wisdom, these shall be our boast,
  He loved them—let them comfort her who mourns
    him most!

                                    RE HENRY.

726

Aaron Levy Green

NOW dimly thro' our tears we see his Face,
  And treasure up his mem'ry in our hearts,
He stood in front a model Priest and Man,
Grand with a righteous energy for good,
Resplendent with a love for all his kind;
But most of all his great love for his Race.
No work too hard—no cause that wanted help,
But he the foremost one in doing good.
Honesty and Manliness and Truth,
A trinity of virtues joined in him.
Too soon for us—but not too soon for him
Has he been taken into Rest and Life.
For that perfection which he sought in us
He now has found in Immortality.
Dry up our tears—our God hath taken him;
He knoweth best. And when we go to rest
May it be found his bright example made
Us worthy of joining him on High.

ANONYMOUS.

Baroness de Rothschild

THOUGH life may fade, love never dies,
  And all but love, is now a dream
To her, who in her long sleep lies
  Enwrapped in flowers, and love supreme.
What, if the solemn shadows stir,
  To sobbing sighs and broken prayer,
Love folds its mantle over her
  And shields her, in its tender care.

Sadly the mystic hours of night
  Flit past, still undisturbed by these,
Or sudden glow of morning light
  Or waking birds, or waving trees.

727

She lies, who heeds not days and hours,·
  The sweet, soft bird song, nor one tear
Beneath her canopy of flowers
  Indifferent now to joy and fear.

Earth's voices touch her not; nor grieve
  Her warm and generous heart with pain,
O sorrowing mourners, we believe
  That God shall raise her up again,
That in some half-guessed, happier sphere,
  Some perfect world, but part confessed
To us poor mortals weeping here,
  "He giveth His beloved rest."

And so Beloved, we part from you,
  We, clothed by you, and housed and fed,
Not hopeless, though the words are true,
  Our blessed Baroness is dead!
The poor, your monument shall raise,
  Statelier than sculptured tomb above
That cherished form, of love and praise
  Who loved her God; whose God is love.

EMILY MARION HARRIS.

Benjamin Disraeli, Earl of Beaconsfield

Born, December 21, 1804. Died, April 19, 1881.

DISRAELI dead! The trappings of late days,
    The Coronet, the Garter, slip aside,
The Peer's emblazonment, the victor's bays,
  The pageantry of pride.

Triumph's mere symbols, badges of success,
  Who weighs, who marks them now when all is said
In simple words, low-breathed in heaviness?—
  Disraeli's dead!

728

So all have known him from that earlier time
 Of meteoric and all-daring youth,
And through the season of his dazzling prime;
 And so to-day, in sooth,

'Tis Benjamin Disraeli all will mourn,
 Nor he the less unfeignedly whose lance
Against that shield and crest full oft had borne
 in combat *à outrance*.

The fearless fighter and the flashing wit
 Swordless and silent! 'Tis a thought to dim
The young Spring sunshine, glancing, as was fit,
 Bright at the last on him.

Who knew no touch of winter in his soul,
 Holding the Greek gift yet in mind and tongue,
And who, though faring past life's common goal,
 Loved of the gods died young.

Like the Enchantress of the Nile, unstaled
 By custom as unchilled by creeping years,
A world-compeller, who not often failed
 In fight with his few peers.

Success incarnate, self-inspired, self-raised
 To that proud height whereat youth's fancy aimed
Whom even those who doubted whilst they praised,
 Admired, e'en whilst they blamed.

No more that fine invective's flow to hear,
 That buoyant wisdom or that biting wit!
To see him and his one sole battle-peer
 Sharp counter hit for hit,

No more to picture that impassive face,
 That unbetraying eye, that fadeless curl,
No more in plot or policy to trace
 The hand of the great Earl!

How strange it seems, and how unwelcome! Rest,
  Not least amidst our greatest! Who would dare
Deny thee place and splendour with the best
  Who breathed our English air?

Peace, lasting Peace that strife no more shall break,
  With Honour none may challenge, crown thee now
Wherever laid, nor Faction's self would shake
  The laurel from thy brow.

And England, who for thy quenched brightness grieves,
  Garlands the sword no more to leave its sheath,
And, turning from thy simple gravestone, leaves
  A tear upon the wreath.   PUNCH.

Peace—and Honor

HUSHED are the sounds of party-strife
  In reverence round the quiet bed,
As all the busy streams of Life
  Seem stayed beside one spirit fled:
And England sends the message on,
To West and East,—a great man gone.

He, but a few short days ago
  Held in a nation's half-mistrust,
Here feared, there followed, lying low,
  Where all may trample on his dust,
Lies safe with laurels round his brow,—
His party's then, his England's now.

Strong loves he conquered on his way,
  Strong as the enmities he woke,
And the loosed passions of the day
  In praise and anger round him broke:
Anger and Enmity's o'erthrown,
Death has for sister, Love alone.

Men called him alien, deemed him set
  On dreams of empire not of ours,
And prone true empire to forget

THE MODERN PERIOD

In the long clash of jarring powers:
But England's 'scutcheon blazons still
The motto of his life,—I will.

In steady purpose, steady toil,
  He followed, and he won, the prize,
Which through the Senate's fierce turmoil
  Lighted, but dazzled not, his eyes:
Nor rank, nor fortune, smoothed the course;
He dared, and conquered, and by force.

As patient as the great should be,
  As watchful as the purposed are,
He marked power's ebbing, flowing sea,
  Now sparkling near, now murmuring far,
Till with strong hand he grasped the helm,
Through storm and shine to steer a realm.

And when, Life's threescore years and ten
  In the long passage overpast,
He yielded up the helm again,
  He stood as steady to the last:
Not Cæsar's robe, when Cæsar died,
Was folded with a calmer pride.

Calmly he gave the reins of State,
  As first he held them, self-possessed;
And undismayed, as unelate,
  Turned to the love once loved the best,
And wooed, from strife of tongues apart,
The Muse of Story to his heart.

So, England's Minister, good-night!
  Nor praise, nor blame, can move thee now;
Safe from the fierce and public light
  Which beat upon thy vessel's prow:
Thy place is with the great alone,
Not one's nor other's—England's own.

                    HERMAN C. MERIVALE.

731

Leopold Zunz

TO thee o'er whose fresh-closed tomb
   The early violets and snowdrops bloom,
With these, for thee, I interweave
This votive wreath of laurel leaf.

Thine was a spirit of an earlier age,
When nobler triumphs graced the stage;
Whereon our country's heroes moved,
Who gloriously their guerdon proved.

And thine it was to flash a clearer light
O'er the tragedy of an age-long night,
And trace, in living words, the story
Of Israel's virile thought and former glory.

Wakening the echoes of a far-off time,
In strains scarce less sublime,
Than those the halls of Zion rang,
When, o'er the land her minstrels sang.

Leaving to Israel a lingering ray,
A promised dawn of a brighter day,
Long o'er thy mem'ry a nation's love will dwell,
Nor soon nor yet will bid a last farewell.

J. F.

Moritz Steinschneider

IF I had known, dear Master, when of late
   I held thy hand within my own to say
   The thousand things I'd thought of on the way,
But sheer forgot for very awe to state;—
If I had known the summons was so near
   And that thy presence never more would grace
   The little room that was the trysting place

Of every scholar, booklover and seer
 That came from North, from South, from East, and
  West
To call himself thy pupil and be blest—
I fain would have besought thee to allow
 My unclean lips to kiss the wizard hand
 That made of learning such a wonderland,
And lost its matchless cunning only now.

GEORGE ALEXANDER KOHUT.

Simeon Singer

"OH, weep not for the dead." Alas! how weak
 The solemn call to dry our tear-dimmed eyes,
Or stay the drops which aching hearts bespeak,
 While hopeless grief in fruitless effort tries
To scan the misty, drear and sombre space,
 Which parts us from the presence that we love,
And from those beaming eyes and saintly face
 And lips that taught the way, to realms above.

Strong, manly mind to gentle heart allied,
 Fit partners of a noble soul that rose
To duty's highest calls, though sorely tried,
 Scorning the urgent temptings of repose;
To him the heart of Childhood bounded forth,
 And feeble Age forgot the weight of years,
And Youth reflected back the genial mirth,
 Which turned to rippling joy their sight and tears.

Say when the bugle call of noble Cause,
 Drew forth the lightning flashes from his eye;
In God's own work he knew not rest nor pause,
 And Faith and Mercy made his pulses fly,
Nor recked he, when a knightly lance he broke
 In chivalrous tilt for Progress and for Good,
Though in the clang of strife he felt the stroke,
 Yet calm and strong and nobly dumb he stood.

733

Too soon, alas! did Time with heavy hand
    Lay on his head his chaste prophetic snow,
And beckon to the far-off promised land,
    The goal to reach with weary steps and slow,
With brave and dauntless heart he nobly strode
    Along the path of duty, cheery, bright,
And uncomplaining bore his heavy load,
    Till summoned out of darkness into light.

Though Earth our gentle Mother in her arms
    Benignly folds thee in thy peaceful sleep,
And in her strong and all-embracing heart
    The mortal fabric of thy frame doth keep,
Freed from the chains that bound thy earthly love,
    Thy spirit joins the Choir of Saints above,
Whose joyous voices calling, welcome thee,
    "An Angel of the Lord of Hosts is he."

                                JOHN CHAPMAN.

My Father's Bible

THERE is one book, far dearer than the rest,
    Upon my treasured shelves: It is not bound
    In costly skin or vellum, yet profound
Is the esteem and rev'rence in my breast,
    As I now lift it from its wonted place,
    To bless it first, and read it for a space:—
It gives me comfort now, though time was when
    Fierce anguish smote my soul, as, all unseen,
    The crumbled leaves I turned, and saw between
The crystal drops of sorrow once again
Which wrung my blessed father's spirit then;—
    But now I read it, ever so serene,
And close the Bible gently, when I've done,
And kiss its covers, too, when I'm alone.

            GEORGE ALEXANDER KOHUT.

David Kaufmann

AMID the murm'ring din and seething strife
    Of all the world's contending victories,
Thou, modest scholar, writing histories
Hast caused Judæa's past to pulse with life;
Hast conjured, with the magic of thy touch,
    Whose quiver had the thrill of the sublime,
    The soul from its clay; and hast rescued time
From its only foe: oblivion's clutch,
Which holds enthralled beneath its aged crust
    The teeming mysteries of throbbing thought
    So many tried to find, yet few have sought
To read aright, and read aright, to trust.
    Great Poet-Thinker, Critic of the Past,
    Thine is a memory to live, to last!

                        GEORGE ALEXANDER KOHUT.

Gustav Gottheil

GOD healed him while he slept,
    And took His shepherd home,
And many thousand tender hands
    Now bear him to the tomb.

His life was crowded with the deeds
    Which crown his calm repose,
Upon his gleaming coat of arms,
    No guilty glory glows.

Dream on, O Prince in Israel, dream,
    In thy celestial home,
While many thousand loyal friends
    Chant Kaddish at the tomb.

                        GEORGE ALEXANDER KOHUT.

735

Flamed the eternal spirit, night and day;
Untouched, unwasted, though the crumbling clay
Lay wrecked and ruined! Ah, is it not so,
Dear poet-comrade, who from sight hast gone;
 Is it not so the spirit hath a life
Death may not conquer? But, O dauntless one!
 Still must we sorrow. Heavy is the strife
And thou not with us; thou of the old race
That with Jehovah parleyed, face to face.

RICHARD WATSON GILDER.

DEAR bard and prophet, that thy rest is deep,
 Thanks be to God! Not now on thy heart falls
Rumor intolerable. Sleep, O sleep!
 See not the blood of Israel that crawls
Warm yet, into the moon and night; that cries
 Even as of old, till all the world stands still,
At rapine that even to Israel's agonies
 Seems strange and monstrous, a mad dream of ill.
Thou sleepest! Yea, but as in grief we said;—
 There is a spiritual life unconquerable.
So, bard of the ancient people, though being dead
 Thou speakest and thy voice we love full well.
Never thy holy memory forsakes us;
Thy spirit is the trumpet that awakes us!

RICHARD WATSON GILDER.

Under No Skies But Ours

EMMA LAZARUS

I

UNDER no skies but ours, her grave be made!
 'Neath blue unblurred and clear stars never
   shamed
'Tis meet that she be laid!
 Just Heaven accorded that sad right we claimed:

738

The soul of Judaism knew;
The Torah was your song and wing,
O'er all the scholars you were king.
Columbus of Ben Sira's book
An X-ray was your every look.
A character unique you were,
The Torah's great interpreter.
A Titan lost the world, a man,
Who was a great American.
Embodiment of wisdom, he
Loved law no less than liberty.
God took a Lincoln mould alit
With gleams of humor and of wit
With light of genius and of art,
And made a scholar with a heart.
And lo, the seer Schechter smiled,
His mind a lion, his heart a child.
O Gaon of our day, your lore.
The testament of truth it bore;
And God, not self, you did adore.
Through life and lore our God you saw;
Your life, the tablet of His law.
In Torah you have left your heart,
An ark of God from us you part.
You found the gems of Torah, we
Will make them our Treasury.
From many a realm some prize you brought,
The jeweled word, the diamond thought,
But oh! a holier land you trod,
You found the manuscript of God.

ALTER ABELSON.

Emma Lazarus

WHEN on thy bed of pain thou layest low
    Daily we saw thy body fade away,
 Nor could the love wherewith we loved thee stay
For one dear hour the flesh borne down by woe;
But as the mortal sank, with what white glow

737

III

This was her home—aye, hers, whose noble pride
Had that dear name denied
To soil whereon her brothers suffered wrong:
    Yet of another country she was free,—
    The golden vales, the fields of Arcady,
The woods that whispered, and the streams of song!
Among the lucent marbles of the Greek
'Twas hers to pass, and charm grand lips to speak,
But as in siren palace reared apart,
    One born to lead his people through the sea,
Saw the Egyptian smite, and felt the smart
Quickening the fire-seed in his Hebrew heart
    To burst in blaze—so she!
Yea, in that bitterest year
    When Russia spurned the Jew,
    She, too, ah, from a lovelier land she, too,
Went forth, and left, for service more austere,
Pure Beauty smiling in the fair white fane
(The strong sweet voice we nevermore shall hear)
Thrilled sword-like through the ear
Of whoso slept, though sleep were dull as death!
    O strange, O holiest hour
    Of rapture and of power,
    When a great soul is girded with a Cause!
    Finding at length, led on by deep hid laws,
That Deed to do, wherefore God lent His breath,
O Awful Hour more strange,
Of chill surprise and change,
Command most stern that bids the doer pause
Ere yet that Deed is done,
The trump be silent, ere the field is won!
    How green, in coming years,
For her the glistening victor-palm had sprung!
Woe for the words unsaid, the song unsung!
    Speech falters into tears
    Tears—but such tears as fed the vital root
Of Hope, and haste the time of bloom and leaf.
None shall forbid high Grief:

But doubt she had forbidden, who deeply know
The vigor of that stem whence life she drew,
  The sure succession, the unfailing fruit!

IV

O faithful Israel, that keep'st aflame
  The Lamp perpetual with remembrance due
Of the undying deed!, Be this her fame:
The source of steadfast purpose, tireless borne.
If, in some dazzling morn
That breaks on e'en the blank eyes, of the blind,
  The flag of Judah shall indeed unfurl,
The hero-Ezra on his arm shall bind
No lordlier hand, no subtler amulet
  Than her linkèd songs of pearl,
And rubies passion-red as with rare life-blood wet!
We, too, we, too, have claim
On this uniting name!
  We of the West may bow where Israel weeps.
Beneath our clear stars, never veiled in shame
  She woke to life, and now, alas, she sleeps,
(Proud May-time heap her painless rest with flowers!)
Under no skies but ours!

HELEN GRAY CONE.

ONCE more a singing soul's most airy vessel
  Hath on its journey sped;
Once more we linger by the shadowy waters,
  Mourning a spirit fled.

Yet, lingering here, we catch the tender vision
  Of Beauty, throned above,
As fondly welcoming a spirit laden
  With beauty and with love;

For she who left us hath with love deep freighted
  Her spirit's ample powers—
She filled her life, her very name with beauty,
  Like a rare urn with flowers.

ALLAN EASTMAN CROSS.

741

A RARE, sweet daughter of a wondrous race
　　She flamed with all the old-time prophet's fire,
And woke again the echoes of that lyre
That from the haunted Saul the clouds could chase,
In her own might the heart of Miriam trace,
　　Or Deborah, aroused to holy ire
　　When her loved people did her soul inspire;
Yet lacked she nothing of a woman's grace.
Would she had lived to right her people's wrongs,
　　To thrill and lift them, with her grand soul's might,
And make them worthy of her noble thought!
But let her Israel still sing her songs,
　　And in her counsels learn to find delight,
And not in vain her suffering soul has wrought.

　　　　　　　　　　　MINOT JUDSON SAVAGE.

FIRE from high, holy heaven down-drawn,
　　By her strong soul and true,
Flashed over Israel, a sudden dawn
　　With star-song wild and new,
A moment silent in her fair, firm hand
　　The harp of David lay,
Then gulfs of hopeless, sorrowing years were spanned
　　When she began to play,
Hers was a woman's song, whose martial force
　　All preludes down-hurled—
Razed every wall that barred its noble course
　　Around the hindering world.
On far blood-hallowed hills the trampled dust
　　Of patriarch sires did glow,
And matchless swords, long buried in their rust,
　　Leaped eager for the blow.
In their lone tombs the Hebrew heroes heard,
　　The prophets felt and knew.
How once again divinest courage stirred
　　The genius of the Jew.

742

A Maccabean influence thrilled the sky,
  And shone from star and sun,
The banner of old days was passing by
  With toph and clarion!

> JAMES MAURICE THOMPSON.

COULDST thou have lived to share with us this
    hour
        Of grateful praise,
When minds of men are turned towards the far
        Columbus days,
Then would thy lyre spell out thy wond'rous thoughts
        In sweetest strain.
Thy soul would sing to us a touching song
        Of fitful Spain;
Of monarchs that thrust forth a helpless band
        Into the night;
Of monarchs that bade speed to him who found
        This land of light.
Ah! now we miss thee. More and more to-day
        We wish thee here,
Thy words are lacking, and the many moods
        That brought us cheer.
Where are the bright inspiring tones of love
        That gave us rest;
And taught us by their ever-charméd lines
        That thou wert blest?

Gone! Gone! 'Tis true, but not without their good
        In lustre shed,
Through hearts whose flames were kindled by the light
        Of one since dead.

> HENRY COHEN.

743

Joseph Joachim

BELOV'D of all to whom the muse is dear,
     Who hid her spirit of rapture from the Greek
Whereby our art excelleth the antique,
Perfecting formal beauty to the ear:
Thou hast been in England many a year
     The interpreter who left us nought to seek,
     Making Beethoven's inmost passion speak,
Bringing the soul of great Sebastian near.
Their music liveth ever and 'tis just
     That thou good Joachim so high thy skill
     Rank (as thou shalt upon the heavenly hill)
Laurel'd with them, for thy ennobling trust
     Remembered when thy loving hand is still
And every ear that heard thee stopt with dust.

ROBERT BRIDGES.

Frederic David Mocatta

OF what avail in low estate to weep,
     To take our harps from off the willow trees?
Will harp or tablet wake him from his sleep?
     Our tears run down—of what avail are these?
For him, the scholar's hope, the poor man's need,
     Who knew the art to benefit unknown,
Who cast at eve and morn the holy seed
     On rugged valleys neither eared nor sown.
Though many a tongue a ready writer's pen,
     Of many kindnesses might tell the tale,
Of what avail these words of many men
     Or dirge, or episode—of what avail?
Be strong and of good courage! freed from ill,
     Fast in life's bundle thy sweet soul is tied,
Sleep! loosed from this low world by God's own will,
     And wake! with God's own likeness, satisfied!

JAMES MEW.

Mrs. Ellis A. Franklin

IT was not granted to her she should lead
  A mighty cause or grace a learned throng,
The humbler task was hers; she lived among
Her children and she taught them to succeed
To her inheritance of faith and deed.
  And what she wrought, unwitting of all wrong,
  Unwitting of her worth, she let belong
To others, and to others left the meed.
The tower to its eminence on high
  Would not have risen at the author's will
Alone; those who builded it may die,
  The name of the designer never will.
So those whose fame and work no records hold
Inspire the deeds that live for time untold.

ANONYMOUS.

Oscar Cohen

OH, that death should lay thee low,
  With thy fame not zenith high!—
Ah, the pity that the foe
  Should have thought thee ripe to die!

Like the greatest one of old—
  Moses, strong of heart and hand—
Thou hast led thy wandering fold
  Onward to the promised land.

Stranger to thy creed and race,
  Alien to the older Word,
Yet I loved thee! On thy face
  Shone the glory of the Lord.

H. B. GAYFER.

745

Leo N. Levi

LET no lament break forth but rather sing
   Hosannas to the Everlasting King;
Let Hallelujahs everywhere resound
And animate the newly hallowed ground
Where lovingly a garland we may place
To symbolize the homage of his race.
No wringing hands, nor shrill-voiced grief shall lift
Our hero from his consecrated crypt;—
If ye would truly honor him, who bore
The ensign of the fathers to the fore,
Then follow on, and raise the battle-flag,
And hasten on each footstep that would lag.
Unfold forsooth the ancient standard, and
Obey our leader's clarion-toned command.

GEORGE ALEXANDER KOHUT.

Esther J. Ruskay

WE meet to-day to call upon thy name,
   With wistful eyes to contemplate and trace
Each feature of thy well-remembered face;
And as we light the faint memorial flame
To hear above the cadence of our prayer
The brush of wings across the tranquil air,
As though thy radiant spirit rustled there;—
To see thee once again, ere yet we go
   Our devious ways, unmindful of the gloom,
   And know that though we robed thee for the tomb
Thou livest yet, transfigured and aglow,
In far-off fields of fragrant asphodel,
Where seraphs and thy starry kindred dwell—
Revered and loved and mourned in Israel.

GEORGE ALEXANDER KOHUT.

THE MODERN PERIOD

Joseph Mayor Asher

DEEP be thy sleep, brave Prophet-Priest of God!
  Thy spirit-wars are waged, and tranquil now—
The laurel of our homage on thy brow—
Thou dreamest; whilst we whisper overawed,
  And name.thee in our hearts, and deep and low
  Say Kaddish o'er thy cerements of snow.
Thine be the peace of God, great, restless heart!
  No more shall wound thee Israel's native woe;
  No more shall strive against thee friend or foe;
Thou art our stern-eyed seer—the counterpart
Of Amos and Elijah, blent in one.
  Our kindred sense perceives thee, and we trace
  The Saintliness of Ages on thy face,
Now that thy work is gloriously done.

GEORGE ALEXANDER KOHUT.

Louis Loeb

THINE was a poet's soul; thine was a heart
  Where love and friendship, truth and right
  abode.
Hebraic rhapsody and Grecian ode
Surged in thy blood. Nature stood not apart;

With gracious smile she wedded thee to Art;
  The seeing eye, the wizard touch bestowed,
  Into thy brain her forms and colors flowed,
Transfixed by Inspiration's flaming dart.
Sweet were the idylls by the genius wooed:

The misty dawn, bright morning, radiant noon,
  The joyous life, the forests' solitude,—
And peaceful reverie. Thine now the boon
  Of bearing a full sheaf, through struggles rude,
Into the twilight's vale,—but all too soon.

LOUIS MARSHALL.

Josef Israels

WHEN the fisher-folk of the Netherland coast
  On perilous cruises sped,
When the howling wind and the swirling foam
  A message of danger read—
There was one to measure the dread of the sea'
  For the helpless women then,
Whose bread was found on the crest of the wave
  By the sturdy fishermen.

There was one to read the cry of the heart
  As it sobbed to the lonely stone,
On the mound of the man who came no more,
  Who left her all alone—
Alone to the wind and the sea and the storm
  That had claimed their murderous fill;
Alone to the break of the taunting deep
  And a cottage void and still.

There was one to sound the plumb of despair
  In the wandering martyr race
That flies with the wind in the fearful round
  Of an everlasting chase;
To note the patient shoulder shrug,
  The pathos of mind and eye,
In the form of the man with the mortal wounds,
  Who yet disdained to die.

Be good to the soul of the master, Lord,
  Who limned with a deathless hand,
The woes of the men whose mettle you try—
  The waifs of the sea and the land.
Be good to his artist soul, O Lord,
  For he ate of the bread of tears
And drank from the bitter cup of those
  Who count the leaden years.
                ELIAS LIEBERMAN.

Phédre

TO SARAH BERNHARDT

HOW vain and dull this common world must seem
To such a One as thou, who should'st have talked
At Florence with Mirandola, or walked
Through the cool olives of the Académe;
Thou should'st have gathered reeds from a green stream
For Goat-foot Pan's shrill piping, and have played
With the white girls in that Phæacian glade
Where grave Odysseus wakened from his dream.
Ah! surely once some urn of Attic clay
Held thy wan dust, and thou hast come again
Back to this common world so dull and vain,
For thou wert weary of the sunless day,
The heavy fields of scentless asphodel,
The loveless lips with which men kiss in Hell.

OSCAR WILDE.

Mayer Sulzberger

THE muse, that first lent grace to gratitude,
Voicing a rhythmic prayer from thankful hearts,
Long since, when passion lisped in accents crude,
Nor knew its handmaid in this art of arts—
Has sounded many a measure through the days,
In stately epic and in roundelays.

The sack of cities, the brave deeds of men;
The doom of Gods, the majesty of Kings;
Strange mysteries beyond our earthly ken,
And gentle fancy's sweet imaginings—
These have the poets woven into rhyme,
To make the past throb in the present time.

But I will weave the laurel of my rhyme
To crown the living with an honor due;
That one, who fearless in the trembling time
Stands forth his people's bulwark, strong and true,

749

May know the muse that graced the ancient days
Has not forgotten how to laud and praise.

If we have grown into such gracious worth,
   And are assembled in this galaxy
To laud the work to which these years gave birth,
   Is it not fitting that our thoughts shall be
Fashioned to form, a grateful aureole
For him whose labor led us to this goal?

Let mine the pride and pleasure be to-night
   To sing his worth, who is our guide and friend;
Who lifts a beacon by whose far-flung light
   We seem to see the lingering anguish end,
Scholar and jurist, need I speak the name
That sheds on all of us its lustrous fame?

How shall I praise him fitly, or begin?—
   Lauding endowments of th' absorbing mind,
Where all things ever known seem gathered in
   To grow into rich blessings for mankind,
We but the medal's silver side behold—
Though fair its sheen, the other side is gold.

For wedded to this rare mentality,
   There beats within his breast a Jewish heart,
That pleads and throbs in ceaseless sympathy
   To right the wrong 'neath which his brethren smart,
The nameless wrong, to which he gave a name—
To prove a Russian envoy's lasting shame.

Small need, in truth, to bring in proud array
   The gracious giving of his bounteous thought.
Wherever Jewish learning lights our way,
   His hand has labored and his genius wrought.
A man of men! 'Twill be our boast we knew
And held in love, our country's foremost Jew!

FELIX N. GERSON.

THE MODERN PERIOD

Isaac M. Wise

HE came into the Camp of Creed,
  The Sword of Strength within his hand,
To scatter forth the bigot breed
  And smite them from the Promised Land;
To hew each hoary falsehood down
  And humble ancient arrogance,
And Error fled before his frown
  While Truth was glad beneath his glance.

He labored where his Duty led—
  Unflinching stood in ev'ry storm
That beat about his fearless head,
  And thundered forth the word "Reform!"
Earth's farthest nations heard his voice
  Unto the utmost purple seas,
And all found reason to rejoice
  From Polar lands to Pyrenees.

From depths of long, nigrescent nights
  We grasp the gospel that he gave,
A message come from starry heights,
  Sent forth to succor and to save.
If Jew or Gentile matters not,
  For rights and righteousness of each,
Alike was wrought his toiling thought,
  And flamed the splendor of his speech.

Our reaching reason gropes along
  His lofty path toward the light,
Consoled and strengthened by the song
  His spirit sends us from his flight.
We pray our searching souls may find
  The higher things for which he stood—
He fought for freedom of the mind
  And for a broader brotherhood.

A modern Moses sent to lead
  His people up to lustrous lands,

751

To free them from the chains of creed
　　And superstition's cruel bands;
To guide uncertain feet from out
　　The darkened paths in which they stray,
Amid the desert sands of doubt
　　Unto the everlasting day.

He told not of God's wrath, but taught
　　The lesson of His love instead,
Till narrow tenets came to naught
　　And fierce fanaticism fled.
Who knew his mental majesty,
　　Or felt his nature's gentle grace,
From pious prejudice was free
　　Nor nursed a senseless hate of race.

Yes, he was great as men are great
　　Who scorn the cramping lines of creed,
Who leave us still our earth's estate
　　Yet fill our nature's inmost need.
And so with each recurring Spring,
　　While roses blow and lilies bloom,
The world will tender tribute bring
　　To lay upon his hallowed tomb.

WALTER HURT.

("God's finger touched him and he slept!")

A BOVE the grief of Israel soars a voice
　　　Rebuking him who weeps;
Bidding the righteous for his sake rejoice,
　　Who, clothed with honor, sleeps.

The victor, bearing home unsullied spoil,
　　The leader, whom God led,
Sleeps 'neath the laurels of completed toil,
　　That crowns his hoary head.

752

THE MODERN PERIOD

As Moses, through the wilderness of old,
  His people led aright,
So he, from worn-out creeds and forms grown cold,
  Led on to warmth and light.

And as old shackles fell from Israel's feet,
  And broader visions rose,
He rested not, until life's task complete
  Had earned Death's sweet repose.

The tired hands upon his breast are crossed,
  The noble heart is stilled!
Yet think not that God's promise shall be lost
  Which he so long fulfilled.

His mantle shall descend, in God's own time,
  Unto some worthy one
Who portions Israel heritage sublime
  From sire to son.

Our leader sleeps; his spirit through the age
  Shall live uncramped and free;
While angels wrote his name upon the page
  Of immortality!   IDA GOLDSMITH MORRIS.

PEACE and remembrance! All the great
  Of Israel's line his brothers are—
Leader and prophet, priest and king;
  Aye, and the bright and morning star!

With force and fire and lofty aim
  He labored, all his crowded years:
Order from chaos, light from gloom
  He brought, and banished narrowing fears.

Nor bronze nor marble rear to him
  Whose fame transcends their poor degree!
His deeds are noblest monument;
  His life is immortality!
             EDNA DEAN PROCTOR.

A FAR the reaches of our land one day,
   Grim tidings, visitants of grief confessed,
As wan the sun full orbed had died away
   In sky-slopes, crimson sheen caressed—
   "Our prince is gone among the blessed."

Entwined the olive branch with cypress bough,
   Alternate tales of peace and woe shall tell
Unlanguaged glory of a man and how
   God's angels kissed him ere he fell,
   And sealed his eyes in slumber's spell.

Though Israel's heart-chords wrung with anguished
      love,
   Now fain his peerless presence would reclaim;
Yet, free from weighing durance here; above
   To high emprise he still doth aim,
   Shrined Nestor dear of sainted name.

In legend heralded a school on high,
   With seraphs' welcome waits our pilgrim guest;
There, world-famed patriarchs his footfall nigh
   Now echoing hear in halls of rest,
   His heart to theirs in love is prest.

Grief's floodgates pour their unstemmed tide amain,
   Our prayers vying throng the stricken skies;
Oh, give us back your sunshine once again!
   Undimmed let flash once more your eyes!
   Our Father hears not, will not rise!

The flowers leagued have taken him away,
   Wee velvet violets and smilax fair;
They called him at the close of shadowed day,
   With amaranths to crown him where
   God's garden greens for e'er and e'er.

Each day the nursling bud shall weep for him,
   Their beaded tears the lucent dew shall be;

754

When sleep-locked world is dawning ashen dim,
  Their fragrance benisons to thee
Shall sweet ascend as off'rings free.

Come, brethren, Master would not have us grieve,
  For sacred joy he loved God's labor due;
His mansion uninvaded let us leave,
  With zeal his mission work anew,
  Disciples, Israel's saving dew!

Nepenthe mingles with the last farewell,
  Oft sunbeams braided are with threads of rain;
The aftermath of grief sweet hope doth tell—
  "We'll meet again, we'll meet again,
  In life that knows no parting pain."

HARRY WEISS.

WHY look ye to the dead? Awake!
  O Israel, be strong—
Be strong to make the truth and right
  Triumphant over wrong;
Know you, O Israel, that he—
He lives and is anear to you;
  And tho' surges roll,
  That the Master Soul
Will guide you safely through.

No need had he for dirges, and
  No need for bells to chime;
For heard ye not the night winds play
  A funeral march sublime—
A requiem on nature's harp,
As he on that April day—
  From the shadow-land
  To the golden strand,
In spirit winged his way.

755

And when the veil was rent and he
    Beheld the Father's face,
He lived, and in Him found his life,
    Saved by His loving grace;
His faith to glorious sight was changed,
As he stood in the presence of Him,
    And of those who trod,
    As the sons of God,
Thro' the shadows dark and dim.

And saw ye not the glory light
    That stole athwart life's sea?
It left the impression on him of
    An immortality;
For when he shed life's robe of clay,
He smiled as his spirit fled—
    And it lit his face
    With a tender grace—
The cold face of the dead.

And nobler far than granite shaft,
    Which storms in time will dim,
The Hebrew Union College stands,
    A monument to him;
While those who knew him—loved him, say
His breast held a lion's heart;
    For the play of life,
    'Mid its din and strife,
He played the better part.

The victor he, though laurel wreath
    Crowned not his aged head;
Still God's reflected glory lit
    His face when he was dead.
And better that than all the crowns,
The world at one's feet might lay—
    As one takes his flight,
    'Mid the shadow-light,
To find eternal day.
               ALBERT FRANK HOFFMANN.

756

THE MODERN PERIOD

Ida Straus

WE wonder at, we praise your life,
    For crowning love with name of wife,
Whose love was young in sunset-time,
As in the blush of morning's prime.
We cry: "Oh, what a miracle she!"
And thus confess how small are we!
Can rose be otherwise than rose?
Can light be less than light? Can those
Who love be less than love? So you
To your angel spirit were but true.
They dreamt she died? O, can it be,
Since love alone's immortality,
And love doth live through such as she?
You live in death. 'Tis we are dead,
In life. For you to love were wed.
Your love was gold and ours dross.
The sea alone can sigh our loss
Of you. The morning stars alone
Can sing your fame to years unflown.
For all we say but tells anew
How small are we; how great are you!

               ALTER ABELSON.

SHE gladly shared his cup of death. She sought
    And chose his stainless shroud of icy sea,
  Her heart was his, to sink with him her plea,
When strained to seek the shore. Her only thought,
To hold his hand and help him die. She caught
  His courage, and felt the rhapsody
  Of joining him in death's wild jubilee
Beneath the roar of sea with soul unwrought.
She was the perfect wife that loved her mate,
Content to crown her life with mutual fate.
She clung to him, her soul of soul, her light;
Without him all were black as starless night.

To-day she sleeps with him in Neptune's grave,
Because she loved him only, and was brave.

BERNARD GRUENSTEIN.

A tribute to the women who went down to death
with their husbands—suggested by Mrs. Isidor Straus's
devotion.

A S side by side they traveled through the years
    Strong in a love that daily grew in power,
So they together faced their final hour
With hearts whose steadfast courage conquered fears;
Eager for life, yet dauntless volunteers
    Among the ranks of death.   So great deeds flower
    From scenes of tragedy.   So great souls tower
Above the grave and bid us dry our tears!

And womanhood throughout the world must thrill
    Before the glory of that sacrifice
To love and loyalty.   The ready will
    That chose to die rather than pay the price
For life; and thus upon its latest breath
Proved to mankind love's triumph over death!

ANNE, P. L. FIELD.

"Loving and Loyal were they in their life—
And in their death, they were not divided."
    David's lament over Saul and Jonathan.

I CANNOT leave thee, husband; in thine arm
Enfolded, I am safe from all alarm.
If God hath willed that we should pass, this night,
Through the dark waters to Eternal Light,
O let us thank Him with our latest breath
For welded life and undivided death.

SOLOMON SOLIS COHEN.

758

PARTING

BELOVED, you must go—ask not to stay,
   You are a mother and your duties call;
  And we, who have so long been all in all,
Must put the human side of life away.
For one brief moment let us stand and pray,
   Sealed in the thought that whatso'er befall
  We, who have known the freedom and the thrall,
Of a great love, in death shall feel its sway—
You, who must live, because of his dear need,
   You are the one to bear the harder part:—
Nay, do not cling—'tis time to say good-by,
   Think of me then but as a spirit freed—
  Flesh of my Flesh, and Heart of my own Heart,
The love we knew has made me strong to die.

TOGETHER

I cannot leave you, ask me not to go,
   Love of my youth and all my older years;
  We, who have met together smiles or tears,
Feeling that each did but make closer grow
The union of our hearts—Ah say not so
   That Death shall find us separate. All my fears
  Are but to lose you. Life itself appears
A trifling thing—But one great truth I know,
When heart to heart has been so closely knit
That Flesh has been one Flesh and Soul one Soul,
Life is not life if they are rent apart —
And death unsevered is more exquisite.
As we, who have known much, shall read the whole
Of Life's great secret on each other's heart!
CORINNE ROOSEVELT ROBINSON.

Julia Richman

COME all who serve the city, all who serve
   The glorious golden city of our dream,
With true heart-service that can never swerve,
   How faint soe'er the strength or far the gleam—

Come sorrow proudly for our comrade passed
  Into the silence: one who served indeed
In all things, even unto the least and last,
  Spending herself to meet the moment's need.
Share memories of that strong, illumined face,
  Keen speech, and courage springing to the test,
And all the fervor of the ancient race
  That finds its longed-for East in this young West.
Be this the sum, the last word best of all:
  She built her life into the city wall.

HELEN GRAY CONE.

Myer Davis

FAREWELL! the word is idle, not in vain
  He lived his righteous life, he must farewell
Who lived for others' good. What man may tell
The rich fruits of his toil, in sun and rain?
What sheaves were garnered from the sacred grain
Sown by his gracious lips, ere on their spell
The lasting silence lingering slowly fell
Down, like a wall between us? Yet again,
Good night! good-bye! There is a time to weep
For us, till the morn break and the shadows fly,
Which long stretched out across the evening creep
Hour after hour until the cock's first cry;
O! holy herald of the day-springs leap
Out of the dying dark, good night, good-bye.

ISAAC LAZAROWICH.

Simon Wolf

THE measure of a worthy man
  Is not the count of days or years,—
That life is noblest, that doth plan
  Assuagement of a people's tears.

His people's tears he did allay—
　O'er rugged steeps his hands were spread
To help his brethren find a way
　From the dark labyrinth of dread.

In the brave heart—the lofty mind—
　The dauntless spirit that outran
The body's strength, the world shall find
　The measure of a worthy man!

FELIX N. GERSON.

To Simon Wolf

DEAR brother, brave and battle-scarred and bold,
　Whose kindling zeal my chastened spirit drew,
And marshals now a myriad retinue
To pave a path of safety for the Jew—
In striving youthful and in service old,
　Alert, unresting, dominant and proud,
　Forgetting not the fealty you vowed
In common with the Fathers, at the Mount,
　Where God revealed His Covenant in flame—
　Yours is a great, imperishable name!
　Who else an equal heritage can claim,
Or render such illustrious account!
　And yet instead of coveting, we plead
　A portion of your spirit for our need.

GEORGE ALEXANDER KOHUT.

To Simon Wolf on His Eightieth Birthday

YOU need no meed of praise in song or prose,
　No thing of bronze or marble to record
How well you served the people and the Lord
Long ere your head was hallowed by the snows
Of four-score years. No respite nor repose
　Your right hand knew which flashed the spirit sword

Of battle for the Maccabean host
   Against the foe that dared with vandal steel
   Profane the shrine. Your Mattathias zeal
   Still sways us by its intimate appeal.
Yours is no wanton pride, no frenzied boast,
But just the picket's password at his post.
   Yours is the right to challenge and repel
   The enemies that trouble Israel.

GEORGE ALEXANDER KOHUT.

VIII

IN LIGHTER VEIN

IN LIGHTER VEIN

The Stamp of Civilization

JAPAN hath Western culture? So you say. O vain
    sophistic thought!
'Tis but the color of its texture that in her life is
    lightly wrought.
Civilization's higher forms belong to Western men
    alone.
As for Japan? Why e'en Anti-Semitism in her land
    is quite unknown.

MAX NORDAU.

(Translated by J. F.)

Confidence

SAID the State to the prelate your pay we will with-
    hold.
Smiled the priest in reply, I scorn your pow'er and
    gold,
You use your godless might with heavy cruel hand,
But back your gifts I fling, nor care for your com-
    mand,
Nor need our Church fear want; aye, money will be
    found.
And free 'twill be given—since rich Jews do here
    abound.

MAX NORDAU.

(Translated by J. F.)

Ein uralter Spruch

MOST prayers of my childhood days
    From memory have fled,
No prayer at meals, at rising,
    Nor when I go to bed,
But one I hold in high esteem,
    And looms in large proportion;

765

My stay it is in happy hours,
  And staff in my misfortune.
And would you know this pray'r of mine,
  Mosaic interwoven?
It is the ancient formula
  Boree Peri Hagofen.   HEINRICH HEINE.

The Vision of His People

ERE yet the morn in glory rose,
  While yet I tuned my harp's sweet string,
A change came over me, alas!
I can but wail—I cannot sing!
For frightful dreams I saw by night,
I saw my people—horrid sight!

LEON GORDON.

Israelite

Juan Alfonso Baena, a converted Jew who flour-
ished in the beginning of the 15th Century, made a
curious collection of the poems of the Trobadores
Espanoles including his own from which Rodrigues
de Castro has given copious extracts. Don Santo, who
flourished about the year 1360, made the following
modest and not inelegant apology for taking his place
among the poets of the land which had given him
birth:

THE rose that twines a thorny sprig
  Will not the less perfume the earth;
Good wine that leaves a creeping twig
  Is not the worse for humble birth.

The hawk may be of noble kind
  That from a soiled eyrie flew,
And precepts are not the less refined
  Because they issue from a Jew.

SANTOB DE CARRION.

766

Between Two Stools

NED will not keep the Jewish Sabbath, not he,
    Because the Church has otherwise ordained;
Nor yet the Christian for he does not see
How alt'ring the day can be maintained;
Thus seeming for to doubt of keeping either
He halts betwixt them both and so keeps neither.

JOHN HEATH.

The Rabbi's Present

A RABBI once, by all admired,
    Received, of high esteem the sign
From those his goodness thus inspired,
    A present of a cask of wine.
But lo! when soon he came to draw,
    A miracle in mode as rapid
But quite unlike what Cana saw,
    Had turned his wine to water vapid.
The Rabbi never knew the cause,
    For miracles are things of mystery;
Though some like this have had their laws
    Explained from facts of private history.
His friends whom love did aptly teach,
    Wished all to share the gracious task,
So planned to bring a bottle each,
    And pour their wine in one great cask.
Now one by chance thought, "None will know,
    And with the wine of all my brothers
One pint of water well may go;"
    And so by chance thought all the others.

ANONYMOUS.

An Epitaph

HERE lies *Nachshon*, man of great renown,
    Who won much glory in his native town;
'Twas hunger that killed him, and they let him die—

They give him statues now, and gaze, and sigh—
While *Nachshon* lived, he badly wanted *bread*,
Now he is gone, he gets a *stone* instead.

BEN JACOB.

(Translated by Joseph Chotzner.)

All Things To All Men

A DAPT thyself to time and circumstance
   So wilt thou be untroubled every way.
Amongst the wise make wise thy countenance
And with the fool the role of dullard play;
Roar, if upon a lion thou shouldst chance;
But if an ass thou meetest simply bray.

BEN JOSEPH PALQUERA.

(Translated by Harry W. Ettelson.)

The Miser

A MISER once dreamed he had given away
   Some bread to a beggar hed'd met in the day.
He woke with a start and solemnly swore
That as long as he lived he would slumber no more.

BEN ZED.

(Translated by Joseph Chotzner.)

The Wife's Treasure

(Midrash Yalkut, Chapter 17)

A T Sidon lived a husband with his wife
   For ten long years, leading a tranquil life,
With but a single grief—they had no child,
And, to his barren lot unreconciled,
The man upon it brooded. Then he bent
His steps to Rabbi Simeon, with intent
To be divorced; and to the woman's tears
He steeled his heart, and said: "Ten happy years

768

In peacefulness with thee, true heart, I spent;
Staunch wert thou ever, nor a word to smart
Escaped thy lips. And now, before we part,
I will accord the treasure thou dost find
In thy old home best suited to thy mind.
Take it; whate'er it be, it shall be thine,
To solace thee when thou no more art mine."
Then said the Rabbi Simeon: "O ye pair!
Before ye separate, a feast prepare,
And pledge each other in the ruddy wine;
Then the feast ended, woman, unto thine
Own father's house do thou repair."
That very night the supper board was spread,
According to the law; one seated at the head,
The other at the bottom. To the brim
The woman filled the bowl and passed it to him,
And then he pledged her, and she filled again,
And he the goblet to his wife did drain
Once more, with many wishes good and fair,
But she the generous liquor did not spare,
Until he fell into a drunken sleep,
With head upon the table, heavy and deep.
And thus concluded the farewell carouse.
So then, she took him up with gentle care
Upon her shoulder, and her husband bare,
Nodding and drowsing, to her father's house,
And laid him on the bed.
        At peep of day
He started up and said: "Woman! I pray,
Tell me, where am I?"
        She to him replied:
"You promised me that nought should be denied
To me of what I valued. I could find,
In all thy house, thee only to my mind,
And I have borne thee hither; now I trow
That thou art mine; I will not let thee go.
When I was thine, thou wouldst be quit of me;
Now thou art mine, and I will treasure thee!"

              SABINE BARING-GOULD.

Water Song

THE Feast's begun
   And the Wine is done,
So my sad tears run
    Like streams of water, streams of water.

Three score and ten were Wine's bold braves,
But a full score more were Water's knaves,
And silent are our watery graves.
   For—whence tuneful note?
   When the minstrel's throat
Tastes naught but Water, Water, Water!

Around the board you see no smile;
Untasted dishes rest in file,
How can I touch these dainties while
   There stands my cup
   To the brim filled up
With hated Water, Water, Water!

Old Moses chid the Red Sea tide,
And Egypt's dusky streams he dried,
Till Pharaoh's fools for Water cried!
   But Moses dear,
   Why dost thou here
Turn all to Water, hated Water?

Can I myself to aught compare?
To the frog who damp in watery lair,
With dismal croakings fills the air.
   So frog and I
   Will sing or cry,
The song of Water, the dirge of Water.

The man whom water can delight
For aught I care may turn Nazirite;
Total abstention shall be his plight!
   And all his days
   To his lips shall raise
Cups of Water, always Water!

The Feast is done,
And Wine there's none;
So my sad tears run
　　Like streams of Water, streams of Water.

　　　　　　　　　SOLOMON IBN GABIROL.
　　　　　　　　(Translated by Israel Abrahams.)

I

FULL sweet of a truth is the sparkle of wine,
　But sorely we miss this blessing divine,
And how can we waken a song or a laugh
When we find that we simply have nothing to quaff
　　　But water, mere water?

II

The banquet has little contentment to bring,
Bears little incitement to joke or to sing,
When the potions we hoped to our future would
Turn out in the end to be nothing at all,
　　　But water, yes water.

III

Good Moses of old caused the waters to flee,
And led all his people dryshod o'er the sea;
But Moses, our host, at the precedent frowns,
And us, his poor guests, he unflinchingly drowns
　　　In water, cold water.

IV

We sit round the table like cold-blooded frogs,
Who live out their lives in the watery bogs;
Well,— if we have fallen on watery days,
Let us, too, like them, croak a pæan in praise
　　　Of water, dear water.

V

Long, long may our host here with main and with
  might
By night and by day for his temperance fight,
And may he and his line find it writ in the law
That their business in life will be ever to draw
    Water, pure water.

                SOLOMON IBN GABIROL.
        (Translated by Joseph Chotzner.)

Wine Song

DEAR friend, beneath this spreading tree
    Where flitting shadows come and go,
With myrtles crowned and roses we
    The joys of wine will freely know.

Drink wisdom in with every draught,
    In wine shalt thou discover here
Thy inner fires, thy mental craft,
    Increasing with each passing year.

The thousand years of this our earth
    To God are but short lasting hours;
A moment's death, a moment's birth,
    To God is one long year of ours.

Ah! would that I might live and laugh
    Through one God-year a thousand fold;
That I, forever young might quaff
    Oceans of wine that e'er grows old.

                JUDAH AL-HARIZI.
            (Translated by I. A.)

The Ballad of Ephron, Prince of Topers

COME listen to a merry song about a merry
    wight—
The sovereign of all topers he, Ephron the Prince
    that hight;
He strict forbade that any lad who aimed to live aright
    Should ever drink a drop—a drop of water!

When with his court he sate at board, they always
    brought him first,
A bowl of twenty flagons for to slake his royal thirst;
Then he'd fall to, and crunch and chew until you
    thought he'd burst—
    But never stop to drink a drop—of water!

Each morn Prince Ephron said his prayers before he
    broke his fast—
"Good Lord!" he'd cry, "My mouth is dry, my tongue
    and lips stick fast;
My throat's on fire, my heart's a pyre, my frame's a
    furnace vast,
    Oh, quench my flames with drink—but not with
    water!

"Make haste, dear friends, for love of God and my
    immortal soul,
And fetch me good old white wine in my lordly silver
    bowl;
Oh, that's the thing to heart a king and make a sick
    man whole—
    But spoil it not, Oh, spoil it not, with water!

"The harm that water does to folk, if that you doubt,"
    says he,
"There's quite a bit in Holy Writ, for everyone to see;
Examples few, I think will do, to make you say with
    me,
    That danger lurks in every drop of water.

"There's Noah's flood—that near made mud of all the
   world then known—
The Nile—wherein by tyrants vile, our baby boys
   were thrown—
And the Red Sea—where Pharaoh's host went down
   like any stone—
   Now what were flood, and Nile, and sea, but water!

"There's Moses—meekest shepherd he, of an unruly
   flock—
Yet lost the Promised Land because, in rage, he
   struck the rock;
If blame to him, no shame to him, for sure 'twas quite
   a shock
   To hear the people grumble so—for water!

"Look ye, how pride," he often cried, "makes for con-
   tracted view;
Your glass-blowers now, from potters well might
   learn—and tinkers too!
This thing they call a wine-glass, pah! 'Twould hold
   a drop of dew—
   But I'm not drinking dew—or any water!"

Prince Ephron kept the sacred days of Israel's faith.
   At least,
If fasts him irked, he never shirked a single holy
   feast;
And on the Days of Penitence, was none, in West or
   East,
   That, more than he, kept gullet-free—from water.

Tebèt would make him whine and fret; through
   Tamuz he would bawl;
And sore he'd moan and fast he'd groan, in Ab for
   Zion's fall,
Till by the ninth too weak he'd grown, to try to fast
   at all;
   Yet still he strict abstained—from drinking water.

Yom Kippurim his eyes went dim, with anguish of
    the soul,
So by the Din it was no sin to call for plate and
    bowl;
But down his cheeks in salty streaks the tears of guile
    would roll,
    And once in every year, he tasted water.

Amends, indeed, he made full meed. Each month he'd
    keep Purim
The four cups he made forty—every night Leil
    Shimurim;
Succòth, Sh'buòth, Kiddùsh and Habdalàh were good
    to him—
    Be sure his cup of blessing wasn't water!

Whene'er it rained or threatened rain, at home would
    Ephron stay;
"If clouds were wine-vats and their showers strong
    drink," he used to say,
"I'd hie me out the storms to flout, and bask in them
    all day—
    "But what's the use of 'ifs,' " he said,—"or water!"

"If 'stead of brine, the waves were wine, of vintage
    fine," quoth he,
"I'd wish to be a Jonah's fish a' swimming in the sea;
None other Eden would I ask to all eternity—
    But for our sins God made the sea of water!

"For had He sent a flood of wine—in Noah's time,
    you know,
Our patriarch had built no ark, to be shut in, below;
In such a tide, Oh, none had died—but all cut up
    Didò—
    And that's why rivers, rains and seas are water!"

* * * * *

Prince Ephron (peace upon his soul!) lies sleeping in
    the dust
Until that day when, sages say, the sinful and the just
Shall rise to meet their due reward. Then, let us
    humbly trust,
    Nor he, nor we, shall crave in vain for water!

IMMANUEL BEN SOLOMON OF ROME.
(Translated by Solomon Solis Cohen.)

INDEXES

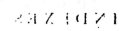

INDEX TO FIRST LINES

INDEX TO FIRST LINES

784

INDEX TO FIRST LINES

INDEX TO FIRST LINES

INDEX TO FIRST LINES

INDEX TO FIRST LINES

INDEX TO FIRST LINES

INDEX TO TITLES

796

INDEX TO TITLES

797

INDEX TO TITLES

INDEX TO TITLES

INDEX TO TITLES

INDEX TO TITLES

INDEX TO AUTHORS

819

INDEX TO TRANSLATORS

CPSIA information can be obtained
at www.ICGtesting.com
Printed in the USA
BVHW040813300721
613246BV00007B/61